The
GEOGRAPHIC BASIS
of
American Economic Life

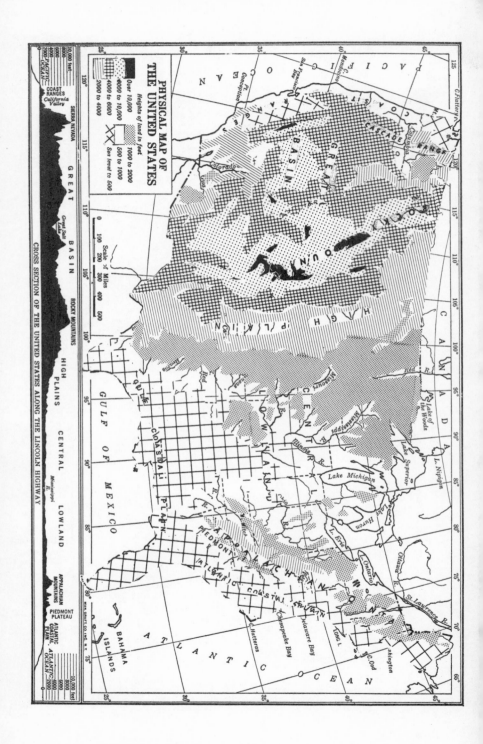

PHYSICAL MAP OF THE UNITED STATES

Heights of land in feet

Over 10,000
6000 to 10,000
4000 to 6000
2000 to 4000
1000 to 2000
500 to 1000
Sea level to 500

Scale of Miles
0   100   200   300   400   500

CROSS SECTION OF THE UNITED STATES ALONG THE LINCOLN HIGHWAY

PACIFIC OCEAN
COAST RANGES
California Valley
SIERRA NEVADA
GREAT BASIN
Great Salt Lake
ROCKY MOUNTAINS
HIGH PLAINS
CENTRAL LOWLAND
Mississippi R.
APPALACHIAN MOUNTAINS
PIEDMONT PLATEAU
ATLANTIC COASTAL PLAIN
ATLANTIC OCEAN

10,000 feet
8000
6000
4000
2000
0

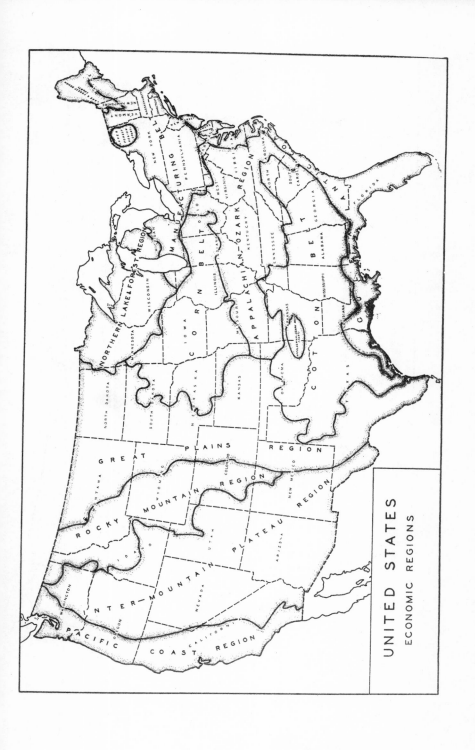

UNITED STATES
ECONOMIC REGIONS

The
GEOGRAPHIC BASIS
of
American Economic Life

by

HAROLD HULL McCARTY, Ph.D.,
University of Iowa

GREENWOOD PRESS, PUBLISHERS
WESTPORT, CONNECTICUT

Copyright 1940 by Harper & Brothers

Reprinted with the permission
of Harper & Row, Publishers, New York

First Greenwood Reprinting 1971

Library of Congress Catalogue Card Number 79-109297

SBN 8371-3840-X

Printed in the United States of America

CONTENTS

vi CONTENTS

FIGURES

PLATES

FOREWORD

HE WHO attacks a problem in economic geography is at once beset with the difficulty of satisfying the criteria of two extremely dynamic social sciences, economics and geography. Because of the wide variation in treatment and point of view employed by writers in both fields, it is almost essential that the author precede his own writings with a statement of his own methods and criteria.

The fundamental purpose of economic geography is to explain the differences in economic development which occur among various areas. Its first task is to classify, measure and delineate the measurable features of economic development; its second is to ascertain the factors which cause different types of development to occupy different areas. Economic geography derives its concepts largely from the field of economics and its method largely from the field of geography.

In determining the types of data which might be considered relevant to economic geography, I have been guided largely by the concepts of economics. In the first place, it quickly became apparent that the analysis must be concerned primarily with production and exchange, and only incidentally with distribution and consumption. The highly significant problems of the geography of consumption must be relegated to another volume.

To the economist, the volume of production is measured as income produced. I have therefore used income data wherever available to measure the quantity of production arising in different areas. Income data were also used to determine the relative importance of various types of economic activity. Where such data were not available, it became necessary to fall back on a cruder measure, the relative numbers of persons gainfully employed in the various occupational groups. In every case, the smallest geographic unit was used for which data could be obtained. In general, these units were the county and city, although finer breakdowns were obtained for certain types of agricultural and population data. The first task was to classify and measure the types and volumes of production in each of these areas.

The classification of production activities follows procedures generally accepted by economists and statisticians. We recognize first of all the creators of *form utility*—agriculture, mining, forestry, fishing and manufacturing; of *place utility*, exemplified by transportation; of *time utility*, by storage and warehousing; of *ownership* and *service utility*, by wholesaling, retailing, banking and the professional and,

xiii

personal services. Finally, we recognize the interlocking and inter-
meshing of all these activities into a complicated mechanism for
production and exchange, an economic system. Soon it becomes apparent that the prime feature of economic life in an area is not the
individual but the institution of which he is a part. We no longer
think of the farmer or miner as *the* producer of food or minerals when
we know the importance of transportation, manufacturing and other
activities in making these raw materials ready for consumption.

In focusing our attention upon the institution, it becomes apparent
that definite patterns of areal association mark the occurrence of
various types of economic activity. Thus we learn that storekeepers,
physicians, transportation agencies, and numerous other types of
productive agents appear in every population center; that a wheat-
growing or coal-mining community inevitably has numerous other
types of workers whose residence in the area is attributable to its
general economic organization.

Eventually it becomes apparent that the first attack upon the location problem is to discover which types of productive activity select
their locations in order to be near other types; and, conversely, to
discover which productive enterprises are located independently of
other types of economic development. The problem becomes one of
explaining the location of the latter group, because their very existence in certain areas largely explains the location of the former types.

Thus the second phase of the problem—the analysis of location
factors—becomes apparent almost before the first phase—classification and measurement—has been completed. Classification and measurement are made both more simple and more realistic by recognizing the institutional nature of economic life. The location problem is
simplified by recognizing the repetitive locational patterns inherent in
the areal association of certain types of productive activity. The
latter principle enables us to focus attention upon a relatively small
number of "key" industries whose locations explain those of nearly
all the remaining types of productive activity. In general, these "key"
industries are those which create form utility, plus those which carry
on exchange. It is fortunate that better data are available for these
types of economic activity than for any of the remainder.

The characteristic types of economic institutions having been determined, the next task is to discover the areas occupied by each type.

Practically, this problem involves little more than the preparation
of maps to show the areal extent of each type. The line marking the
geographic limits of a particular type of economic activity circum-
scribes an area which we may call an economic region. Economic
regions may be large or small. Their size depends upon the degree of
minuteness used in classifying economic institutions. In the present
volume, the institutions have been defined broadly and the regions

are large. Equally acceptable criteria could have been used to define them differently, but the ones employed are felt to be most useful to the general student.

With regions defined to indicate the areal limits of a particular type of economic activity, it is apparent that regional locations and boundaries do not necessarily reflect the locations or limits of any other types of phenomena, whether cultural or physical. The region is delimited solely in terms of the types of productive activity which occupy it. Its boundaries mark the areal limits of that type. Thus the boundaries of the region are not likely to be permanent. They shift with social and economic change.

There remains the problem of accounting for the locations of the "key" industries, of analyzing the factors which have brought about the regional pattern we have discovered. Within this phase of the problem, no type of explanation is barred. Much weight must be given to natural factors such as soil, climate and topography. In nearly all cases one must also consider a great variety of cultural factors. The geographer recognizes the effect of the natural landscape on economic life but he also delves into the history of the people, the technology, the devices of social control and the general aspects of the economic system. Despite the multiplicity of sources of evidence, absolute conclusions are rarely possible. It is felt, however, that the range of accuracy is generally within the limits accepted by scholars in the social sciences.

The present volume attempts to follow these types of analysis. The United States is divided into ten major regions having distinctive types of economic development. The major characteristics of each region are described in terms of the natural and human factors that have been most influential in their development. The emphasis varies greatly from one region to another. In the older and more highly industrialized sections considerable emphasis must be placed upon historical factors, machine technology and the monopolistic nature of large financial and industrial concerns. There we must attach great importance to the inertia of industrial enterprise and the significance of an early start in determining types of economic occupancy. In the farming regions of the mid-continent, business is more highly competitive and we find a greater response to natural factors such as climate, topography and soil. Finally, in the western half of the United States, natural limitations become even more compelling, and the location of economic enterprise can be traced very largely to qualities of the natural environment.

Maps of the distribution of natural resources in the Pacific

Coast region give an excellent clue to the distribution of economic development. The location of valleys, forests, minerals, fishing banks and harbors is likewise the location of agriculture, lumbering, mining, fishing and cities. Because these relationships between natural environment and economic development are easier to comprehend than the historical and cultural relationships which prevail in the eastern areas, the first region to be discussed is the Pacific Coast Region of California, Oregon and Washington. Next in order are the Intermountain and Rocky Mountain regions, each of which is marked by close correlation between the location of natural resources and economic development. In succeeding regions, the importance of physical limitations is lessened and greater emphasis is laid upon cultural factors. The last chapters are reserved for the region marked by the greatest complexity of locational factors, the American Manufacturing Belt.

There is no question that many readers will be disappointed by lack of emphasis in specific areas. The volume of information is so great that the problem of evaluation and elimination quickly becomes acute. It seems certain that despite careful editing and checking there must be many instances of improper emphasis and inaccurate interpretation. It is hoped that the growing interest in research in the economic geography of small areas will continue, so that in the future it will not be necessary to base conclusions almost exclusively on unanalyzed basic data.

The number and variety of sources from which information was drawn is too great to permit individual citations. Practically all the factual information was derived from publications of various departments of the federal and state governments. References to these and other sources of information are contained in the notes at the end of each chapter.

Comments and criticisms have been almost as numerous as printed sources. The author feels indebted to the many students who have used the unpublished materials for classroom work. He also wishes to acknowledge the splendid assistance afforded by Professors W. R. Smith and H. R. Bowen of the University of Iowa; Professor E. W. Zimmermann of the University of North Carolina; Professor Wilhelm Credner of the University of Munich; Ellston Herrald of the University of California at Los Angeles; a capable assistant, George Hartman; and a patient and forbearing wife, Vivian McCarty

HAROLD H. McCARTY

INTRODUCTION

THE problem of the location of economic enterprise resolves itself essentially into answering three questions, "Where?" "What?" and "Why?" We shall want to know where the various types of economic institutions are located and something of their nature and function. In addition, we wish to learn as much as possible concerning why different types of economic development have come to occupy different parts of the nation. The first two questions are relatively easy to answer. We can locate various cities, mines, farms and other types of economic activity on the map and observe their location with reference to other locations and to the nation as a whole. By observation and measurement we can determine the character of economic life in each area. These facts can be placed on maps and catalogued and classified. The result is an areal description, a characterization of economic development in different areas.

But the areal description is little more than a snapshot, a bird's-eye view that gives scant evidence of the forces and movements and trends which underlie the spatial arrangement we have discovered. Economic life is dynamic, and in order to understand it we must view it as a going concern. A moving picture would serve our purposes better than a snapshot, but what we really desire is a working model which will show the action of the various forces that propel the machine. The economic geographer cannot content himself with mere description. He must also inquire into the reasons for the location of economic phenomena.

Factors underlying the areal differentiation of economic development are both numerous and complex. The economic structure of many areas can be explained very largely in terms of natural environmental factors. Among these, the most important are location, topography, soil, climate, minerals, forests and fish. These natural features provide the basic materials and forces with which man must work, and they also set up limits beyond which man's economic development may not go. Yet we also know that much depends upon man himself, and the variations in human capacities and desires. The natural environment becomes economically useful only in his hands. The economic development of an area will be guided and determined by the people who occupy and control it. To understand their behavior, we must know a great deal about their history and culture. We must know the basic features of the economic system under which they live, the most important techniques and machines at their disposal, and the underlying motives and goals of their daily lives as producers and consumers. All these factors must be considered if we are to explain the reasons for the areal differentiation of economic development.

In order to simplify the presentation of these various types of information, a standard outline has been followed in the treatment of each of the regions in the text. The outline begins with natural features: location, surface features and climate. Description of these natural features is followed by a consideration of the types of development most closely associated with natural resources: mining and quarrying, forests and fisheries, and agriculture. These so-called "basic" economic interests are followed in the outline by cities, manufacturing and trade, the more complex types of economic development whose locations generally are less closely associated with natural resources than the "basic" types considered previously. The reader will find it advantageous to keep these major subject headings in mind in connection with the material for each region. They make it easier to remember the text material and to compare one region with another.

The author feels that the need for additional reading is of commanding importance. This need is threefold and arises because (1) much of the text material is highly condensed; (2) economic data become out of date very rapidly; and (3) the student should perform at least a small amount of original research in order to become familiar with geographic method and basic economic data. The following list of references includes the major sources from which material was used in writing this volume. Many of these references will provide the reader with more detailed information to supplement the text. Others will furnish him with current data concerning the major types of economic development.

REFERENCES

A. GENERAL

1. *Economic Geography and Resources:* A number of good text-books on general economic geography are available. L. E. Klimm, O. P. Starkey and N. F. Hall, *Introductory Economic Geography* (Harcourt, Brace, 1937); W. H. Carter, Jr., and R. E. Dodge, *Economic Geography* (Doubleday, Doran, 1939); and C. E. Landon, *Industrial Geography* (Prentice-Hall, 1939), are good introductory texts of recent date. The best statement of natural and human factors is contained in E. W. Zimmermann, *World Resources and Industries* (Harper, 1933).

2. *General Geography* texts generally give greater emphasis to the natural environment. V. C. Finch and G. T. Trewartha, *Elements of Geography* (McGraw-Hill, 1936), is an excellent contribution to the field. E. C. Case and D. R. Bergsmark, *College Geography* (Wiley, 1932), and C. L. White and G. T. Renner, *Geography: An Introduction to Human Ecology* (Appleton-Century, 1936), present different approaches to the general field.

3. *Economic History* is nearly always written from a chronological or topical point of view. Consult H. U. Faulkner, *American Economic History* (Harper, 1938), or F. A. Shannon, *Economic History of the People of the United States* (Macmillan, 1934). Excellent regional historical material is contained in *American Guide Series,* by the Federal Writers' Project, Works Progress Administration. State and city guides are available.

4. *Principles of Economics* textbooks present the clearest statements of the fundamental features of the economic system. P. F. Gemmill and R. H. Blodgett, *Economics: Principles and Problems* (Harper, 1937), is a good reference for the competitive system; and A. M. MacIsaac and J. G. Smith, *Introduction to Economic Analysis* (Little, Brown, 1937), emphasizes monopolistic competition.

B. LOCATION

1. For present purposes, location is defined as *mere* location, or position, and the problem is confined largely to the use and in-

terpretation of maps. All maps in the text are charts, designed
to portray a particular situation graphically. The reader should
have access to a good atlas and should understand the basic
principles of map projections.

2. *Atlases* of the United States are available in a variety of forms
   and at a variety of prices. *Goode's School Atlas* (Rand
   McNally) presents a good combination of physical, political
   and economic information, as do also the various atlases of
   Rand McNally and Company.

3. *Maps* are published by many departments of the federal government, as well as by various state governments, and the geographical societies. Road maps distributed by the various oil
   companies are nearly always reasonably accurate and up to date.

4. *Map Construction and Interpretation* are explained in nearly all
   texts in general geography. A good explanation of air navigation maps is contained in T. C. Lyon, *Practical Air Navigation*
   (U. S. Dept. of Commerce, 1938).

C. SURFACE FEATURES

1. *Topography* and the evolution of present surface features are a
   part of the science of physiography. The author has drawn
   heavily upon the two-volume work in regional physiography by
   N. M. Fenneman, *Physiography of the Western United States*
   and *Physiography of the Eastern United States* (McGraw-Hill,
   1931 and 1938). These books are recommended for additional
   reading on specific areas. A shorter treatment of regional physiography is contained in F. B. Loomis, *Physiography of the
   United States* (Doubleday, Doran, 1937).

2. *Soils.* The standard reference for soils data is *Atlas of American Agriculture* (U. S. Dept. of Agriculture, 1936). This atlas
   contains excellent detail maps and a brief summary of the characteristics of various soils. A better statement of major soil
   classifications is contained in L. A. Wolfanger, *The Major Soil
   Divisions of the United States* (Wiley, 1930).

D. CLIMATE

1. Climate is defined as *average weather*, and an adequate understanding of climate therefore involves some knowledge of
   meteorology.

2. *Weather* in the United States is well treated in T. A. Blair, *Weather Elements* (Prentice-Hall, 1937). An excellent short statement also appears in *Practical Air Navigation* (cited above).

3. *Climate* in the various regions of the United States is adequately described in R. De C. Ward, *Climates of the United States* (Ginn, 1925). Good climatic maps are contained in *Atlas of American Agriculture* (cited above). Nearly all geography textbooks deal with the effect of climate on man; but see especially Ellsworth Huntington, F. E. Williams and S. van Valkenburg, *Economic and Social Geography* (Wiley, 1933).

E. MINERALS AND MINING

1. Perhaps the best discussions of mining are found in the various texts on economic geography. The main difficulty with all publications is that they quickly become obsolete. Good background reading will be found in W. H. Voskuil, *Minerals in Modern Industry* (Wiley, 1930). For more recent trends and statistics consult *Minerals Yearbook*, issued by The Bureau of Mines, United States Department of the Interior, as well as trade publications such as *Mining and Metallurgy* and *Oil and Gas Journal*. Good general discussions may be found in H. Ries, *Economic Geology* (Wiley, 1930).

F. FORESTS AND FISHERIES

1. *Native Vegetation* is mapped and described in *Atlas of American Agriculture*.

2. *Forests and Lumbering* are considered in the general texts in economic geography. A standard source is Raphael Zon and W. N. Sparhawk, *Forest Resources of the World* (McGraw-Hill, 1923). Numerous monographs covering various sections of the United States have been issued by the Forest Service, United States Department of Agriculture. Statistics for the lumber industry are released biennially by the Bureau of the Census.

3. *Fisheries.* Available information for the fishing industry comes largely from the Bureau of Fisheries, United States Department of Commerce. A biennial census is taken and reported in detail in annual reports of the Bureau.

G. Agriculture

1. The areal distribution of various types of agriculture was computed from data taken in connection with the Census of 1930. These findings appear in *Types of Farming in the United States* (U. S. Dept. of Commerce, 1933) and were used very largely to determine the regional boundaries used in the present volume. More detailed type-of-farming studies have also been made by the agricultural experiment stations in many states. An excellent wall map, *Natural Land-Use Areas of the United States*, compiled by C. P. Barnes and F. J. Marschner of the United States Department of Agriculture, represents a consolidation of topographic, soil and climatic features into natural agricultural areas.

2. Agricultural statistics are abundantly available. Recent data (by states) are contained in *Agricultural Statistics*, issued annually by the United States Department of Agriculture. In addition, a census of agriculture is taken every five years. Census publications give detailed data by counties.

3. Recent trends in agriculture are considered in the *Yearbook of Agriculture* (U. S. Dept. of Agriculture), and in a large number of separate bulletins and monographs. A series of ten publications (graphic summaries) presents a large assortment of maps and graphs based on the agricultural census of 1930 and 1935. These bulletins provide excellent supplementary graphic material concerning the areal distribution of all phases of agriculture.

H. Cities, Manufacturing and Trade

1. The material on cities is largely in periodical form. Numerous articles in the *Geographical Review, Fortune,* the *Journal of Geography,* and *Economic Geography* will be found particularly interesting, despite differences in points of view. Many good studies of individual cities are available. See R. S. and H. M. Lynd, *Middletown: A Study in Contemporary American Culture* and *Middletown in Transition: A Study in Cultural Conflicts* (Harcourt, Brace, 1927 and 1937) and G. R. Leighton, *Five Cities* (Harper, 1939). See also R. D. McKenzie, *The Metropolitan Community* (McGraw-Hill, 1933), and Dwight Sanderson, *The Rural Community* (Ginn, 1932).

2. *Manufacturing.* The standard historical treatment is V. S. Clark, *History of Manufactures in the United States, 1607-1914* (Carnegie Inst., 1916-1928). Histories of many of the larger industries and individual corporations are also available. Recent trends must be obtained largely from publications of the Bureau of Foreign and Domestic Commerce (Washington) and from business magazines.

3. *Industrial Location.* The problems of industrial location are argued deductively in *Alfred Weber's Theory of the Location of Industries* (Univ. of Chicago, 1929), and the more practical aspects are considered in W. G. Holmes, *Plant Location* (McGraw-Hill, 1930).

4. *Manufacturing Statistics* are derived from the *Census of Manufactures.* The Bureau of the Census reports data by counties, cities, states and industries from enumerations taken biennially.

5. *Trade.* Statistics of wholesale and retail trade are compiled irregularly by the Bureau of the Census. In addition, excellent statistical handbooks have been prepared by the Bureau of Foreign and Domestic Commerce under titles such as *Market Data Handbook, Consumer Market Data Handbook* and *General Consumer Market Statistics.* These volumes provide the best collections of factual information concerning the volume of business and indexes of consumption in the various counties. The Bureau also publishes atlases of wholesale trading territories which provide much good material for geographic analysis. Many states have published traffic studies showing traffic volumes on highways. These studies give a good clue to the extent of consumer territories reached by various cities.

The

GEOGRAPHIC BASIS

of

American Economic Life

CHAPTER I

GEOGRAPHY AND ECONOMICS

The Need for Geographic Analysis.—If you were a colossus, an all-seeing giant, gazing down on the everyday panorama of human life in the United States, what would you see? Your impressions would depend largely on what kind of colossus you were and the importance you placed on the many types of values which concern our daily lives. If your interests were mainly political, you would be very likely to spend your first few minutes noting the location, scope, and operation of the many legislative assemblies, administrative offices, and judicial centers which comprise a complex governmental organization. Or if you were interested in sociological values, you would spend much time locating focal points for social intercourse and determining the reasons that people associate extensively in these areas. In either case you certainly would be intrigued by the tremendous complexity of the national panorama; and as an inquisitive soul you would want to discover the forces which activate the complicated mechanism that consists of so many thousands of interdependent parts, no two of which are exactly alike.

Or perhaps your major interest would lie in the complex economic mechanism by which mankind makes a living. Perhaps you would have learned that a large share of man's waking hours is spent in obtaining the means to satisfy his wants. You would know that man has an almost endless list of desires, and that he is willing to devote a major portion of his energies to the various processes by which the goods and services to satisfy his desires are created. You would know also that the people of the United States have evolved an economic system based on individual freedom, and private property, in which the accepted motivating force is private profit. From your present vantage point you would be interested in observing the geographic distribution of the hundreds of types of economic activity the system has created. You would be interested in their location and concentration, in the patterns they form on the landscape; and above all you would be interested in the reasons for these locations and patterns, in the forces which have caused different types of economic activity to thrive in some localities and fail to prosper in others.

On many occasions the modern business man wishes he were blessed with the encompassing vision of some such mythical giant as the colossus of old. As businesses become larger and broader in scope, as small local firms are merged into larger national ones, as the economic welfare of one section of the country comes to depend more and more upon business conditions in other sections, the need for an adequate understanding of the basic nature of economic life in the various sections of the nation becomes more apparent. The day is long past when the typical business man may feel adequately prepared for his life work if he is well acquainted only with the basic economic structure of his own community, or even that area with which he can become intimately acquainted through travel and observation. The groceryman stocks his shelves with goods from many states and the manufacturer markets his products over broad areas. A crop failure in Kansas or labor troubles in New York depress the automobile industry in Detroit or the grapefruit business in Florida. When one makes his living in such a complex and interdependent economic system, it is important that he understand its basic features.

The economic development of the various sections of the United States is the complex product of a variety of forces. Some of these forces are historical and lie deep in the traditions and heritages of the people. Others are associated more directly with the prevailing culture, with the desires and ambitions of the inhabitants. Much depends upon the character of the basic natural resources and the capacities of the people to utilize them. These forces combine to influence the economic structure of an area to develop along distinctive lines. Because the forces differ in relative intensity from one area to another, there is a strong tendency for different areas to develop varying types of economic activities. Our task is to discover the nature, extent, and location of these various types of economic development and to relate them to the natural and human factors which encourage their development. Such investigations fall within the realm of economic geography.

Geography has been defined as "a comparative study of the earth's regions."[1] The concept of a region varies greatly from

[1] Vernor C. Finch and Glenn T. Trewartha, *Elements of Geography* (New York: McGraw-Hill Book Company, Inc., 1936), p. 5.

one type of geography to another, but the central idea of all regional treatments is *areal homogeneity*. To the physical geographer a region is an area possessing a substantial similarity of land forms which differ in general characteristics from those of adjacent areas. In economic geography, the prime criteria are human uses of the land.

Economics deals with the general problems and processes of making a living; with the production, exchange, distribution, and consumption of those goods and services that men want and are willing to pay for. Economic geography is concerned with the regional differentiation of economic life over the face of the earth.

Geographic Specialization.—A fundamental concept of economics is the specialization of production by geographic areas. An acre of land in Texas is used to grow cotton, an acre in Iowa grows corn, an acre in Maine grows timber, and one in Manhattan Island holds a skyscraper devoted to trade and finance. Economic geography recognizes this geographic specialization of labor and relates it to the natural and human resources of the area. The economic region is a geographic area having a substantial homogeneity of economic development. It is an area whose economic institutions show a similarity of development and are in contrast with those of adjacent areas.

Economic Institutions.—Economic regions are areas devoted to related types of productive enterprise which in turn differ from the types found in adjacent areas. This does not mean that every person in a region is making his living the same way or that every acre of land is devoted to the same purpose, for our economic system does not operate that way. In a piedmont mill town not every acre is occupied by cotton textile mills, nor does every wage-earner work in them. There must be acres for homes and streets and parks and stores, and there must be grocers and physicians and truck drivers and bankers not only to serve the needs of the textile mill but also to provide the multitude of goods and services demanded by its workers. Fewer than one-third of the town's wage-earners are on the mill payroll, yet no one questions the statement that it is a mill town. Cotton milling is its basic industry, the prime reason for the town's existence. In the same way, not every Corn Belt acre grows corn, and not all Corn Belt residents are farmers, for thousands of urban residents make a living by handling and shipping farm products or by providing the goods and services demanded by neighboring farmers. The Corn Belt economic process begins with the soil, sunshine, and rain, manipulated by the farmer to produce a basic material, corn. This grain is fed to animals which in the plant of the meat-packer become a consumable product, meat. But often the meat is in Illinois and the meat-eater is in New York and between them stand the railroaders and merchants necessary to deliver the much-altered product of the land to its final consumer. These people who handle and process his products are a part of the Corn Belt farmer's economic system just as surely as are the merchants who feed him, the barber who shaves him, and the banker who extends him credit. These commercial and service employees may outnumber the farmers two to one, yet no one contends that the system is not predominantly agricultural.

Nor does an economic region consist of communities or sections whose economic structures are exactly alike. In a world characterized by relativity rather than by identity it would be ridiculous to attempt any such classification. In an assay of economic development one must use a system of classification which permits the inclusion of many slightly dissimilar items under one heading. Practically, the problem is one of choosing between a detailed classification permitting great accuracy but inevitably leading to an unmanageable number of groups, and a broader classification which permits a small number of groups but breeds some inaccuracies because of the broad scope of the classes used. In the geographic analysis of an entire nation, we are confronted with a choice between employing several hundred small regions having marked homogeneity of economic development, and a small number of large regions within which there is considerable diversity. The final decision depends upon the purposes for which the data are intended.

In the present volume, the purpose is to present a simplified working model of the economic system of the United States. We wish to locate and describe the salient features of the system on a national scale. A detailed analysis and classification of every community and section obviously is out of the question. The most that we can hope for is to acquire a generalized pattern upon which more detailed studies of local areas could be based. The criteria selected for establishing regional boundaries have been taken from general economics and business practice rather than from the needs of particular trades and professions. This system of classification has produced a small number of relatively large regions. Within these regions, there are many small areas whose economic life differs considerably from that of the region as a whole. In addition the characteristic economic type which represents a region may be more highly developed in some sections than in others. But despite local inconsistencies and variations in the intensity of development, the criteria used to characterize each region are felt to be those most useful for general economic analysis.

How Regions Are Defined.—The data of economic geography are first of all the evidences of the way the land is being used. Block by block, acre by acre, county by county, the use which is being made of the land is observed and computed. Wheat farm is added to wheat farm, mile after mile, until finally wheat gives way to corn or the forest or the dairy farm, and there lies the boundary of the wheat belt. Within the wheat belt many farms will not grow wheat, but for the section as a whole wheat-growing is the dominant interest. The area is devoted to a type of economic development which contrasts sharply with that of other sections similarly dominated by cotton or ranching or manufacturing.

Regional Differentiation.—In the United States, the typical economic region is marked not only by characteristics which differentiate it from other regions, but also by a marked degree of specialization. It should be remembered, however, that the prime criterion for a region is that its economic development differs from that found in other adjacent areas. In world economic geography we find regions characterized by hunting and fishing, by hoe culture, by machine farming and many other types of exploitation. In these regions, production may be intended primarily for home use, for community use, or for interregional trade. A region may contain practically all of the economic types necessary for the maintenance of its people and thus be nearly independent of the remainder of the world. Or, as in the United States, it may be specialized in the production of a relatively few commodities which it produces for exchange with other regions. Economic geography is a study of regional differentiation. Its regions may be marked by economic specialization or they may not. In the United States, the typical region is one of specialization. In other parts of the world, the region is more likely to be marked simply by regional differentiation.

Specialization Reflects Differences in Resources.—Regional specialization with its complicated and expensive mechanism for exchange and distribution obviously did not arise by chance. Certainly New Yorkers would not pay the freight on California oranges or Wisconsin butter if they could produce them more cheaply at home. New Yorkers buy these products from other regions, essentially because their resources for producing them are inferior to those of other areas. In other words, New Yorkers can earn more money by devoting their energies to other pursuits and exchanging their products for goods produced in other states. We do not mean that Manhattan Island could not grow good grass and raise cows and make excellent butter, for Manhattan did that sort of thing in the hands of the early Dutch colonists with notable success. It is clear, however, that Manhattan has discovered alternative uses for its land which pay much higher rents than might be obtained from keeping cows.

The Natural Environment.—Regional differentiation is primarily the result of man's effort to make the most of his environment. Basic among these resources are the land, with its soil, minerals, and waters, and the climate, with its sunshine, moisture, and wind. Regional specialization could never have developed without transportation, for it is no use for you and your neighbors to grow potatoes exclusively if you cannot get them to a market. Furthermore, transportation must be both inexpensive and fast to permit regional specialization to develop as extensively as we find it in America.

Years ago, when transportation was slow and expensive, nearly everything had to be produced near by, and only small and valuable items could be brought in from a distance. Industries producing perishables were always confined to local areas, and bulky products could not be hauled far. But today modern transportation enables communities to specialize in and produce exchangeable surpluses of bulky or perishable goods, of which wheat, cotton, meat, and butter are prominent examples. In the following chapters, we shall find wheat belts that produce almost nothing else, a cotton belt with hardly another cash crop, a nation with few factories except in a specialized region whose people do little else than operate factories and live in the cities which house them. If the people of an area sell nearly everything they produce and buy nearly everything they consume, the mechanism of exchange and distribution must be highly developed. This, then, is the America of today: a land of territorial specialization in which people, in order to make the most of their resources, have devoted their economic lives to the production of specialized types of goods. This specialization is largely traceable to differences in the natural resources of different parts of the country, but it is also dependent upon the productive capacity of the people.

The Human Element.—The capacity of a people to produce depends not only upon the natural resources at their disposal, but also upon their own abilities and the conditions of demand for their products. It is obvious that a nation cannot count a deposit of iron ore among its resources if there is no known method of extracting or using that ore. The natural environment must always be evaluated in terms of our capacity to convert it into goods and services for which there is a market. Capacity for utilizing the materials and forces of nature is a composite product of inherent ability, education, and technical devices. If we have neither the skill nor machines to convert natural resources into salable items, then these materials and forces are of no positive significance in our environment. Finally, there is no merit in turning out products for which a market does not exist. A region with splendid facilities for turning out cotton hosiery would not employ its facilities to that end if people would not buy that type of hosiery. Consumer demand is affected by changes in style, by modern advertising, by custom, and by many other factors which alter our desires. In addition, there is no demand without purchasing power. Prospective buyers will purchase a product only if they have sufficient money to finance the acquisition.

Thus the economic structure of a community reflects both natural and human forces. An understanding of economic life in the various regions of the United States presupposes a knowledge of (1) the natural environment, (2) the capacities of the inhabitants to utilize that environment for production, and (3) the economic system, or type of economic organization, used in the productive process. In other words, we must know the fundamental aims and purposes of the American economic system before we can evaluate its capacity to produce. Having recognized these goals, we can proceed to an evaluation of the environment in terms of the abilities of the people to utilize it. We turn first to a brief description of the major features of the economic process.

The Economic Process

The economic process arises from the relatively limitless nature of human desires and the relative scarcity of the means of satisfying them. All of us are familiar with the fact that individual wants are practically unlimited. Man is motivated by a constant desire to satisfy individual wants, but just as soon as a given want is satisfied, new ones appear and the effort toward gratification continues. In the realm of economics, man never says, "I'm satisfied."

On the other hand, the means of satisfaction are relatively scarce. Natural resources, machines, and labor are limited in quantity. In this situation men compete with each other for goods and services, a demand which varies from time to time with changing customs and other stimulations to desire. Men go into the market and bid for possession of the limited supply of goods and services. The competition between buyers and sellers sets the prices at which goods are exchanged. These prices in turn constitute the incomes of the various productive agents.

Production.—People make a living by producing goods and rendering services. In the economic world a worker is paid whether his work consists of harnessing the forces of nature on a farm to produce a bushel of wheat, tending a machine which grinds the wheat into flour, hauling the flour to a distant city, baking the flour into bread, or of selling and delivering the loaf of bread to the ultimate consumer.

These types of work are concerned with the creation of goods and with making them more useful. The bushel of wheat that comes from a Kansas farm is in neither the right place nor the right form for consumption. Consequently, we are willing to pay not only the farmer but also the miller, railroad man, baker, and merchant to transform it into consumable goods and bring it to our own dining-rooms. We also are willing to pay for the storage of wheat from the harvest time of plenty to the time of use. We say that these services add form, place, and time utility to the product and are therefore productive. In other words, we are willing to pay for these services because they make the goods more usable in point of form, place, or time. But not all income is derived from handling tangible commodities. Nearly one-third of our workers simply sell services which satisfy human wants directly. In this group are the professional persons, government employees, bankers, barbers, servants, and a long list whose pay is derived not from adding utility to goods, but from rendering services direct to the consumer.

The National Income.—In a recent year (1936) the people of the United States had an estimated income of about sixty-four billion dollars. Of this total, about 14 per cent was derived from the basic commodities, such as farm products (10 per cent), minerals, lumber, and fish. Manufacturing and construction contributed 27 per cent and transportation and trade 23 per cent. In other words, nearly two-thirds of the national income was derived from the production and handling of commodities.

A streamlined description might state that the American people produced nine billion dollars' worth of raw materials, manufactured them into twenty-five billion dollars' worth of consumable goods, and then transported and distributed them to the consumer at a final price of thirty-nine billion dollars. In these processes, nearly two-thirds of the national income was created. The remaining third consisted of the services of government, finance, and many other professional and personal groups not concerned with commodities, but designed to satisfy human wants directly.

Distribution.—The national income is distributed among individuals through the pricing system. We buy and sell the use of land, labor, and capital in the market, and our payments consist of rent, wages, and interest. The hiring of land, labor, and capital is in the hands of the business manager. He is the entrepreneur who pays for the use of these factors of production, who turns out the product or service, and sells it in the market. If his product or service sells for more than his production costs, he makes a profit; if not, he bears the loss. The entrepreneur writes the checks which pay the rent, wages, and interest. In the United States about two-thirds of his payments (or two-thirds of the national income) is for wages and salaries. Another 14 per cent goes for the use of capital (interest and dividends), and rents and royalties require another 3½ per cent. After these expenses are met, about 14 per cent remains for the entrepreneurs, to pay their living expenses as well as rent and interest on their own properties.

The entrepreneurial class includes all independent workers such as farmers, merchants, and professional men, who do not work for a salary or commission. By these routes the national income is distributed among the individuals in the various sections of the economic system. These individuals then proceed to spend it for the very goods and services which the system continuously creates.

Consumption.—Wage-earners, landlords, capitalists, and entrepreneurs spend their incomes in a variety of ways, but an average of about 60 per cent of their pay checks goes for basic necessities to maintain their respective households. Food is the big item which represents nearly one-quarter of the national expenditures. Housing, clothing, and operating expenses require another one-third of the pay check. By the time these bills are paid the average American finds that only about 40 per cent is left for the other items he desires. He spends his remaining money for recreation, for his automobile, health, education, carfare, gifts, direct taxes, and other miscellaneous items. Generally he manages to retain about 10 per cent of his check to spend for savings and insurance. Thus his income goes back to the entrepreneurs who are again in a position to contract for the use of labor, capital, and land, with which to continue the productive process. The entire economic process is circular, because all producers are consumers and all income is expended either for consumption goods or for capital goods such as tools and factories which are to be used for further production.

The Geography of American Economic Life.—If the economic merry-go-round functioned uniformly over the entire breadth of the nation, there would be little use for a national study of economic geography. If individuals or even communities were self-sufficient, about the sole purpose of descriptive economics would be served by explaining the operations of these various independent units. A complete view of business could be obtained by observation within the area of our personal experience. Under those circumstances, economic geography could content itself with analyzing the effect of the environment upon the economic organization of individual communities. Each community would be a complete economic unit, independent of the rest, and making the most of its own resources to fulfill the desires of its people. Transportation and trade would be minimized and every person would live within the limitation of the productivity of the natural and human resources of his own community. Economic life might not be luxurious, but it would be very simple.

Every breakfast-table geographer is familiar with the fact that the American people have advanced far beyond the stage of community self-sufficiency. He reads his metropolitan newspaper over Florida grapefruit, Brazil coffee, Battle Creek cereals, and Corn Belt ham and eggs. His breakfast is a product of basic production *and* transportation and trade. He is eating the product of farms and factories far removed from his own community, and brought to him from regions which are highly specialized in turning out these products. He is enjoying the fruits of an exchange economy, an economy which produces for the market rather than for local use. He is part of an economic system which embraces the entire nation and extends into foreign lands.

This economy consists of communities of wheat-farmers and other communities of coffee-growers or breakfast-food manufacturers. Its economic map is divided into sections devoted to wheat and others devoted to cotton or corn or manufacturing. It is ribboned with arteries of transportation which spider-web the nation and cause commercial cities to appear at their foci. For none of these areas is self-sufficient and all of them must depend upon commerce for most of the goods their people use. The American economy is a gigantic, geographically specialized productive mechanism whose roots are in the soil, but whose manifestation is in the market place.

Geographic Specialization in the United States.—Geographic specialization greets the reader of every table of national production statistics. In agriculture, we learn that the north central states produce two-fifths of the nation's farm products on about one-quarter of the nation's land. Texas produces one-third of the nation's cotton, and Iowa markets one-quarter of its hogs. Mineral production is even more highly concentrated. Two states, Texas and Pennsylvania, account for one-third of the minerals. One-third of the lumber comes from Washington and Oregon. This same areal specialization marks the production of many basic commodities.

Manufacturing is sufficiently localized to warrant the designation of a region as the American Manufacturing Belt. This region, which extends from Portland and Baltimore on the Atlantic Coast westward to Chicago and Milwaukee, manufactures nearly two-thirds of the nation's factory products. Thus the 40 per cent of the economic machine which is devoted to the creation of form utility shows a marked tendency toward regional specialization. This specialization also profoundly affects the location of the other 60 per cent of the economic process whose functions are to provide place, time, and service utility.

Transportation and Trade.—The location of transportation and exchange follows a pattern similar to that of the service groups. Both types of service must be rendered where the goods and people are located. Farm regions must have railroads to haul their goods to distant markets. Factory towns must have their merchants and service agencies. These commercial services are so extensive that Americans spend nearly one-quarter of their incomes for them; but their location depends almost entirely upon the geographic distribution of basic production and manufacturing. The further an area departs from self-sufficiency, the greater is its need for these commercial services and the larger the proportion of its income which will be devoted to paying for them. In recent decades geographic specialization has progressed so rapidly in America that the number of persons engaged in transportation and trade has expanded enormously.

The Service Occupations.—Like transportation and trade, the service occupations are most important where there are the most business and the most people. Government services originate in Washington and the state capitals, but most of the expenditures are outside these cities. Relief costs are heaviest in the most populous states, and other governmental costs vary in the same way. The same generalization applies to banking, finance, and the long list of professional and personal services. Where business is done, where people live, there also must be banks, lawyers, physicians, barbers, beauticians, dry cleaners, and other purveyors of intangible personal services.

The Land-use Region.—An economic region is an area occupied by substantially similar types of economic institutions. In the United States most regions are agricultural simply because about 55 per cent of the national land area is in farms. More square miles are dominated by agriculture than by any other type of economic activity, despite the fact that farming generally contributes only about one-tenth of the national income. Nearly all the land not in farms is in forest, desert, or waste. Its contribution to the national income is very slight. Finally, a minute fraction, less than 2 per cent of the land, is occupied by cities, towns and villages. Yet these built-up areas produce more than three-quarters of the income of the United States.

Economic geography is thus confronted with a twofold analysis. One of these is *qualitative* and consists of determining the types of economic activity in the various areas. The other is *quantitative*, and is concerned with the magnitude of developments in these areas. Economic geography should show not only where the various ways of making a living are prevalent, but also how important they are in the different localities.

The United States has no regions dominated by trade, distribution, or the service occupations. The great transportation network ties all regions together in a national economy, but its importance in any single region is a reflection of the basic industries of that area. Railroads serving the Middle West were long ago known as the "granger roads" because their existence depended upon service to the farms of the area. Railroad men also speak of "coal roads" and "logging roads." These terms signify the dependence of railroads upon the areas they serve. In the same manner, we find no merchandising regions or regions dominated by the service occupations. These activities reflect the basic economic needs of the areas they serve. Where goods are to be moved, there we find the mechanism of transportation and trade. Where people are to be served, there also are the merchant and service groups.

The City.—In 1930, only about one-third of the American people lived in the open country. The remainder lived in incorporated places and pursued occupations involving the use of comparatively little land. Not all of them lived in places large enough to be called "urban," but nearly all made a living in what are known as the "urban occupations." These occupations fall in three major categories which describe the economic functions of the modern city.

A major reason for the rise of urban centers in the modern economy is the need for market places and service centers. Specialization has gone so far, not only among regions but also among individuals, that most Americans go to the market place for nearly all the things they use. The system necessitates the establishment of trading centers where men may buy and sell. Such centers have existed since the dawn of civilization, even in isolated community economies. As regionalism develops, the center acquires transportation facilities. The credit system makes necessary banks and other financial institutions. Professional and personal servants appear because this is the place where people congregate. Eventually the city may erect factories either to process and concentrate local materials for shipment (such as flour mills) or to manufacture frequently needed goods for use in the community (bakeries, etc.). If it occupies a particularly favorable location, it may acquire wholesale and jobbing houses which serve the smaller towns near by. A few will become regional centers, not only for trade and distribution, but also for finance. Regardless of size, this type of city has a definite set of characteristics. It is above all a trading center, a market place, a service center, a town which has grown up to serve the people of its trade territory. We call such centers *commercial* cities.

Quite in contrast with the commercial cities are the other two types whose people make a living by manufacturing or the extractive industries. A factory town exists because it has factories, and its factories are there because of geographic considerations quite different from those which influence the location of commercial centers.

Factories are erected where goods can be manufactured advantageously. The magnet may be local raw materials, location with reference to markets, power, fuel, or other industrial advantage. Mining towns likewise appear because of local mineral deposits, and logging and fishing towns because of local resources for these extractive industries. Because all such occupations require little land, towns and cities develop near the base of operations, be it factory, sawmill or harbor. The factory cities are known as industrial centers, while those dominated by the extractive industries are classed as mining towns, lumber towns, fishing centers, and the like. There is much of the vernacular in these terms, but they have a genuine economic basis. The industrial city differs from the commercial center not only in economic interests but also in appearance. It has a smaller business district and fewer professional persons because it exists for its own people, not for the people of its trade territory. The commercial city is a service center which exists because of its hinterland. The industrial city is a separate economic entity whose existence generally is independent of the economic development of the surrounding area.[2]

The reader will surmise that the United States contains very few cities which could be classed as entirely industrial or commercial. Generally there is some admixture of both types. But in the nation as a whole, nearly all cities lean rather heavily in one direction or another. There are few industrial cities outside the American Manufacturing Belt, and relatively few commercial cities within that region.

All cities essentially are products of location. When compared with other manifestations of economic development, cities are little more than *points* in space occupied by farms and forests and waste land. The location of these points is the resultant of many factors which differ according to the type of city. Some of these factors are historic and technological, but most of them are geographic in that they have made this point a particularly favorable location to carry on certain types of economic activity. We shall examine American cities not only in the light of their early establishment and growth, but also in the light of existing resources and technologies.

Economics and Welfare.—In the United States, the economic system is organized to promote production for the market. To this end, individual areas have become specialized in the types of production for which they are thought to be best suited in the light of their natural resources and human capacities for utilizing them. Thus we are interested primarily in the present economic structure and the way it functions as a productive mechanism.

The key function in the process is exchange. Our inquiry is addressed toward an understanding of the methods by which the productive factors are assembled and made ready for sale and distribution. We are interested in the exchange economy. An equally truthful inquiry might concern itself with a related question, "How well does the American economic system serve the needs of its people?" The problems of exchange economics and welfare eco-

---

[2] The industrial center, in fact, often comes to dominate the economic development of its hinterland. Near-by farms are devoted to supplying the factory town with dairy products and other perishable foods and become utterly dependent upon that city as a market for their produce. In farming regions, the city exists essentially for the surrounding area and reflects its area's economic needs. In industrial regions, the surrounding area exists primarily for the city and its economic machinery is geared to supplying the needs of the people in that center.

nomics often overlap, but because of inevitable differences in point of view and ultimate objectives, it is generally desirable to maintain the emphasis upon one approach or the other. The present volume is confined to an explanation of the geographic phases of exchange economics. Excursions into welfare economics inevitably appear in various chapters, but their extent is restricted to those phases which help explain the productive process. The geographic analysis of problems of economics and the public welfare is the subject of another division of economic investigation.

The Geographic Analysis of Economic Data.—The ultimate aim of the areal analysis of economic data is to discover the part played by each individual in the complex economic life of the nation. Ideally, the analysis would proceed from the individual to the family and from the family to the community. Then, in so far as possible, communities would be combined into areas and areas into regions. Finally the regions would be combined into a national picture.

The minuteness with which economic data should be classified depends upon the purpose for which the analysis is to be used. A retail merchant would be interested in a detailed analysis of the wealth-getting and wealth-consuming capacity of every person and family in his trade territory. He could plan his operations much better if he knew the occupations of his workers, whether their work is seasonal or sporadic, the size and nature of their incomes and the way in which their purchasing power is likely to be affected by changes in economic conditions. The jobber who sells goods to retailers has need for similar information, but in his case the territory is much larger, and use must be made of combinations and averages in order to provide an intelligible picture. Another phase of the problem is encountered by the manufacturer, and falls within the field of market analysis, of which the prime purpose is to provide a better interpretation of the market for particular commodities and services in the sales territory of a business concern.

Economic geography attempts to serve a greater variety of interests than market analysis and does not find it desirable to analyze individual areas or lines of economic activity as intensively as market analysis demands. Economic geography rather attempts to provide generalized information of maximum use by all sectors of the economic system in interpreting the economic life of particular areas. Yet the two fields have much in common. Both recognize the need for an areal interpretation of economic life; and the data and methods of market analysis are very useful in determining the economic characteristics of individual areas. These characteristics, analyzed and classified, are basic criteria for economic geography.

In any type of geographic analysis the investigator is confronted with a lack of pertinent data organized along geographic lines. The reader will have sensed the near impossibility of obtaining data concerning individual consumers needed by the local retailer. Similar difficulties are encountered all along the line. Data are lacking primarily because of the necessity for protecting individuals by not permitting financial details of their lives to become public knowledge. In the United States, it is not considered good policy to require an individual or firm to reveal publicly the amount and source of income or profit, or to release information which would permit competitors to calculate these items. Thus we must remain ignorant of the precise economic importance of a particular John Smith, or the neighborhood movie, or of an individual factory or wholesale house.

The lack of individualized data is relieved appreciably by the practice of consolidating information for concerns of a similar character. Thus the Bureau of the Census publishes combined sales data for three or more firms if that number is found in a given city or county. In addition, there is no hesitation about releasing detailed totals showing the normal occupations of the people of cities and counties in census years. Increased attention has been given in recent years to distributing economic data by cities and counties. Where such data are available, they are much more useful than the conventional state totals which have comprised the bulk of our economic data for many decades.

Income, where it can be obtained in sufficient detail, is the best indicator of both the type and magnitude of economic development in an area. Sources of agricultural income are enumerated for each farm in the decennial census. On the basis of these returns, the Bureau of the Census has classified farms according to their dominant sources of income, and has divided the United States into more than five hundred type-of-farming areas. These areas, combined and generalized, are the basis for most of the boundaries of the agricultural regions used in this text. In the field of manufacturing, income is represented by the figure *value added by manufacture*, which is calculated as the difference between cost of materials and the value of the product. This figure shows the value which was added to the materials by the manufacturing process and is the best measure of the factory's contribution to the social income. A census of manufactures is taken every two years, and totals are released by counties and cities.

Occupations probably provide the most fundamental clue to economic interests in an area. Usual occupations of gainfully employed persons in each of the 3072 counties are enumerated at each decennial census. The geographer uses occupational data to learn which modes of making a living are most important in the various counties, and is thus provided with a crude measure of economic specialization. If a county has more factory workers than farmers or other types of workers, it can be given at least a preliminary classification as an industrial county. This measure obviously is somewhat inexact because it assumes that all workers are equally productive in all occupations and also that they are employed throughout the year. Regardless of these limitations, occupational dominance is considered the best available indicator of prevailing economic types in the various counties and cities.

When the economic analyst is in possession of these data for occupations, agriculture, and manufacture, he is in a position to define the major land-use areas of the United States in the terms of the most important basic industries. For mining, forest, and fishing areas, he consults the annual reports of federal and state departments in these lines. In all cases it is necessary to obtain both qualitative and quantitative measures of the *relative* importance of various economic types. The region thus becomes a framework upon which is built the quantitative and analytical description of the economic life of the nation. It is important to know what areas are dominated by growing cotton, but we also want to know how much cotton they grow, how it is grown, and why it is grown there.

Economic geography is first of all a functional study. It begins by examining the human uses of the land, and continues by relating these uses to the entire economic system. In determining the location of the various phases of economic life, economic geography uses both qualitative and quantitative measures. Areas are established within which particular types of economic activity are dominant. These areas are known as regions and their boundaries are qualitative in that they show the geographic limits of a particular type of economic life. Within the region there are marked differences in the intensity of development. These are measured quantitatively, in terms of income or in bushels, tons, and similar manifestations of the economic contribution of individual areas. When these observations are complete, we have classified and measured the various segments in the economic landscape. The scene is comparatively lifeless, however, until we embark upon the third phase. Here we examine the environment and attempt to discover the factors that have influenced the design of the geographic crazy-quilt we have discovered. These factors lie generally within the realm of natural and human resources and are known collectively as the geographic environment.

Summary.—The purpose of this volume is to present a simplified analysis of the geographic distribution of economic life in the United States. Economic life consists essentially of the production, exchange, distribution, and consumption of the goods and services for which we are willing to pay a price. An adequate appreciation of the parts played by various sections of the country is basic to an understanding of economic life in the United States.

The study of economics arises from a conflict situation—the conflict between the unlimited wants of human beings, on the one hand, and a scarcity of want-satisfying goods on the other. In such a world, there is competition for the possession of productive agents and competition among producers in the market place. Motivated by a desire for profit, producers in various parts of the nation have endeavored to engage in those types of economic activity which bring the greatest return. In doing so, they have attempted to make the best use of their natural resources and the productive capacities of their people. Largely because of differences in these natural and human resources, economic life in the various sections of the country has taken different forms. An examination of the geographic distribution of economic types shows that they tend to become regionalized or concentrated in particular areas. The extent and location of these regions shows a marked relationship to the geographic distribution of natural resources, but it is also related to the prevailing abilities and qualifications of the people. Considerations affecting the importance

and the distribution of these natural and human resources are the
subject matter of Chapter II.

REFERENCES

For a concise statement of the field of geography, read Carl O.
Sauer, "Cultural Geography," in *Encyclopedia of the Social Sciences*,
Vol 6, or Finch and Trewartha, *Elements of Geography*, Ch. 1. Read
the introductory chapters of any standard textbook on the principles
of economics for a definition of the field of economics (see Introduction for general references). The regional idea is well presented in
H. W. Odum and H. E. Moore, *American Regionalism* (Holt, 1938).
For a good statement of methods and problems involved in collecting
and analyzing economic data, consult L. O. Brown, *Market Research
and Analysis* (Ronald, 1937).

QUESTIONS AND PROBLEMS

1. Why should the business man of today concern himself with
   territorial division of labor?
2. Which is the more likely to be true: "The economic development
   of any area varies directly with the environment," or "the economic development of any area depends upon the prevailing culture and capacities of the people"?
3. What is the meaning of the term geography? How does it differ
   from physical geography and economic geography?
4. What is meant by the phrase "economic region"? Would a state
   necessarily be an economic region? a city?
5. What type or types of economic institutions are necessary if
   regional specialization is to become highly developed?
6. What is the significance of unlimited wants to the "economic
   process"? of the scarcity of the factors of production?
7. What is the relationship of form, place, ownership, and time
   to the utility of goods?
8. What is meant by the term distribution? What do we call the
   distributive shares which go to land, labor, capital, and the entrepreneur?
9. How does the economist differentiate between "distribution"
   and "exchange"?
10. Describe the United States in terms of topography. Do the
    boundaries of our economic regions follow topographic lines?
11. What distinguishes a commercial center from an industrial cen-
    ter? Which type is usually found in agricultural areas? Why?
12. Distinguish between an exchange economy and a supply econ-
    omy; between an economic system and an economic region.

CHAPTER II

THE GEOGRAPHIC ENVIRONMENT

It is evident that the economic development of an area is a complex product whose nature reflects the prevailing needs of the economic system and the characteristics of the natural and human resources locally available. The economic system of the United States makes generous use of the specialization of labor which prevails in both industrial and geographic lines. The system is also dominated by production for the market rather than for use. In other words, people engage in those activities which promise greatest profit. In an exchange economy they are free to specialize, to devote their entire productive effort to a single type of economic activity. Competition stimulates every producer to engage in that type of activity best adapted to his own skills and to the natural and man-made resources at his disposal. The entire machine is powered by the changing forces constituting consumer demand which is reflected in the prices that can be obtained in the market. Throughout the nation producers are busy estimating demands for the commodities they might produce and devoting their energies and resources to those activities which promise the greatest returns. In choosing the type of activity which seems most promising, producers are restricted by their own abilities and the character of the natural and human resources at hand. These resources are called the geographic environment. The fact that they vary in quality and quantity from one section of the nation to another gives encouragement to the geographic specialization of labor, the regional distribution of American economic life.

The Physical Environment.—Regardless of a person's occupation, his economic activities are always limited to a greater or less extent by the natural environment in which he works. The older economists credited the "bounteousness of nature" with the fact that some regions are better adapted to human use than others; or they complained of the "niggardliness of nature" in failing to provide all of the resources desired by man in the less productive regions. Throughout its history, however, economics has described the economic process as man working with nature to produce the goods and services desired by people. The older economists called these natural resources "land." Modern students are inclined to examine "land" more minutely and divide this natural factor into categories such as climate, soil, topography, minerals, and location. "Land" also includes the waters of the earth and their fishes as well as the virgin forest and its animal life. It includes all of the native plants and animals, in fact all of the environment not created by man.

Land and Capital.—Economists distinguish sharply between the natural resources, or land, and productive human effort, or labor. They also separate these two factors from the third, which is capital.

Capital is defined as "produced wealth" which has been created by man (and nature) and is used in further production. Thus the fence around a field, or the tile that drains it, or the dams and ditches that irrigate it are capital.

In economic geography, it is not necessary to make such a sharp distinction between the original natural environment and the man-made physical features with which man works. To the economic geographer it makes little difference whether a hydroelectric plant uses a natural waterfall or one created by a dam; and a man-made lake serves as effectively for commerce or recreation as a natural one. Economic geography makes little distinction between the human and non-human features of the environment. In the economic world, man works with the resources of nature and the resources created by man. He uses the sun, rain, and soil to grow crops on fields enriched with manufactured fertilizers, fenced with man-made wire, and served by man-made roads. All of these factors are included in his environment. To the entrepreneur, the problem is one of making the most of the resources at his disposal, of evaluating and combining them in the most profitable manner. Economic geography is concerned with the factors which influence his choice.

Overcoming Natural Handicaps.—The fundamental factors of economic geography are the natural resources such as the climate, soil, topography, minerals, location, and native vegetation and animal life. These features generally set the limits within which man can work. Constantly man endeavors to perfect machines and proceeds to utilize these forces and materials more effectively, but he always works within the limits of the natural environment and his own exploitative ability. If the environment is favorable, he accumulates capital and alters the original landscape to suit his needs. If the climate does not suit him, he shuts himself in an air-conditioned building and manufactures his own weather. But he cannot afford to graze cattle in a building, so cattle are grazed where climate and soil produce good grass. If hills or mountains impede man's progress, he removes them or bores tunnels beneath. But he cannot afford to remove the Sierra Nevada of California in order to give the states of Nevada and Utah more rain. We are greatly impressed with man's mastery over nature when we see a New York skyscraper, a Boulder Dam, or a San Francisco Bay bridge. But a bird's-eye view compels us to admit that over the entire nation, man's improvement on original nature is very slight. Furthermore, man could make these capital expenditures only if his original resources were rich enough to permit the accumulation of surpluses beyond immediate needs. A land so poor by nature that it produces only enough to feed, clothe, and house its people never provides the surpluses necessary to build skyscrapers, dams, and bridges.

Man-made Barriers.—One of man's most remarkable inconsistencies is his feverish effort to overcome natural barriers while at the same time he sets up barriers of his own. Americans spend billions of dollars to encourage trade by deepening rivers and harbors; yet the same legislative bodies calmly pass tariff laws to discourage the movement of goods. The people of the United States have erected around their borders tariff walls which discourage trade more effectively than all the oceans of the world. When viewed realistically, protective tariffs (as well as bounties and subsidies) are simply devices to compel the national economy to assume functions it might not otherwise assume. National policy often demands the development of certain types of industries which are not flourishing because of foreign competition. That policy takes the form of a protective tariff to keep foreign goods out, or a bounty or subsidy to keep home producers in business. All such legislation interferes with the normal flow of trade by erecting artificial barriers or offering artificial stimulations. These barriers and stimulants are intangible, but they are just as effective as the physical barriers and resources of the national landscape. When it becomes more expensive to ship a bushel of wheat across the boundary from Canada to the United States than from the

Canada prairies to Liverpool, economic geography is bound to recognize that boundary as a significant geographic barrier. When a tariff commission devotes its time to fixing rates high enough to "equalize" the costs between relatively inefficient American regions and relatively efficient foreign regions, it is compelling Americans to produce something which they could buy more cheaply from foreign producers.

Economists condemn the erection of tariff barriers because they force home producers into occupations in which they are relatively inefficient. Economic geography must recognize conditions as they exist and must place these artificial acts in the same category with mountains and deserts as barriers in the paths of trade. It is true that the potency of man-made barriers can be altered by a simple legislative act, but in the United States they seem to have become as permanent a part of our economic landscape as the great mountain ranges.

In a similar manner, but to a much lesser extent, state boundary lines may become barriers to trade. States may not levy tariffs, but they do have power to impose a wide variety of taxes, quarantines, and other regulations, most of which tend to restrict trade. By the same token, states may have laws which favor the operation of certain types of business. Mining corporations find it easier to operate in states (such as Montana or Colorado) which have long had important mining interests, than in states whose political history has been dominated by farmers or ranchers. In the aggregate, differences in state laws have had little effect upon the location of economic institutions in the United States, but it is well to remember that in a few types of economic activity the state line is a significant geographic factor. City ordinances, especially zoning regulations, may have a similar effect.

Resources and Barriers.—Economic geography is bound to recognize and describe the limitations within which the economic system functions. Many of these limitations are natural and have to do with items such as climate, distance, topography, and soil. A few are man-made, and foremost among these are the tariffs which turn back commerce at international boundary lines. All of these resources and barriers constitute the many-walled room in which man must make a living. Beyond their boundaries he cannot go. They are the tools and forces with which he must work and the barriers beyond which he may not venture. Within their limits he sets up those systems of economic exploitation which, in consideration of his own productive capacity, promise to yield the greatest returns. The stores and forces of nature are the basic factors in the economic development of a geographic area. These stores and forces are considered collectively as the natural environment.

CLIMATE

Climate and Man.—The most significant and far-reaching natural limitations upon human activity are imposed by climate. Sun, rain, and wind have both direct biological effects upon the human animal and indirect economic effects upon his business of making a living. Man apparently works best in a climate marked by frequent changes in temperature, humidity, cloudiness, and wind, provided there are few extremes in any of these elements. Comparatively, however, man is a tough animal and has succeeded in overcoming many of the climatic handicaps and surviving all of the climates encountered on the face of the earth. He works much better in some than in others, but if the prizes are great enough no climate is too severe to preclude human habitation. The more striking and more important effects of climate are upon the plants, animals, and machines with which man works.

Every newspaper reader is familiar with the destructive effects of the weather elements upon American economic life. Farmers are plagued with droughts, the railroaders fight snow-drifts, and floods devastate valley cities. These catastrophes provide grim reminders of the impotence of man in controlling weather, but they tend to stress the unusual and thereby distort our conceptions of day-by-day weather in the United States.

Weather and Climate.—Climate is defined as *average weather*. The subject of climatology attempts to describe what usually happens in the realm of weather. It deals in averages. Climatology is to be distinguished from meteorology, whose main function is to describe the causes of weather and thereby make forecasting possible.

Precipitation.—In the United States, the principal climatic limitation upon economic development is the unequal distribution of precipitation. The western half of the nation is generally too dry for farming without irrigation, while the eastern half is sufficiently humid to grow crops. Lack of precipitation has done more

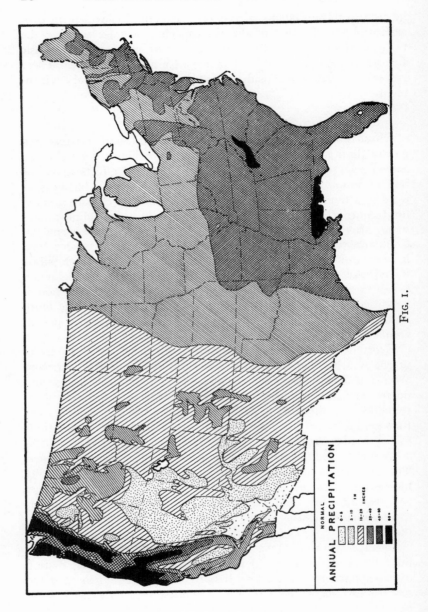

NORMAL
ANNUAL PRECIPITATION

0 - 5
5 - 10   IN
10 - 20   INCHES
20 - 40
40 - 60
60 +

FIG. I.

to limit economic development in the western United States than any other factor. The only western area having plentiful rainfall is a coastal strip extending north from the latitude of San Francisco.

Temperatures in the United States are not unfavorable to economic development except in a few places. Some of the northern states cannot grow corn, and only the South has a growing season long enough for cotton. Temperature limits the growing of certain *crops* to particular regions, but nowhere does temperature alone preclude the growing of all the great agricultural staples such as wheat, corn, cotton, and hay.

The Seasons.—Another important characteristic of American climate is the seasonal variation in both precipitation and temperatures. Like all continental temperate zone countries, the United States is hot in summer and cold in winter. The ocean tempers the climate only along the Pacific coast where westerly winds blowing off the broad Pacific keep winters mild and summers relatively cool. Elsewhere the climate is definitely continental.

Summer Rains.—Summer sunshine warms the land and the land warms the air. Warm air is lighter than cold air, and temperature differences cause air currents which bring in moist breezes from the Gulf of Mexico and the Atlantic Ocean. These masses of warm air collide with colder masses from the polar regions. Where such collisions occur the moist warm air, being lighter, is forced above the heavy polar air. Rising air is cooled and precipitation occurs. Because the land is warmer in summer than in winter, more tropical air is brought in. Thus all of the United States east of the Rocky Mountains receives most of its rain in summer.

The Pacific coast has a different rainfall pattern. The coastal portions of California, Washington, and Oregon receive little or no rain in summer, but their winters are damp. Moist breezes off the Pacific Ocean are cooled when they strike the land in winter and give off much rain in passing over the mountains. In summer, these on-shore breezes are warmed rather than cooled when they reach the land. They give off no rain until they reach the high mountains. Even these mountains receive less rainfall in summer than in winter.

The Pacific coast region is the only part of the United States to receive much rain from the Pacific Ocean. It is also the only region to receive most of its precipitation in winter. East of the Rocky

Mountains nearly all precipitation occurs from tropical air carried in from the Gulf of Mexico and the Atlantic Ocean. These air masses are attracted to the continental interior by low-pressure conditions. Pressures are lower in summer than in winter because the land is warmed more by the summer sun. The eastern two-thirds of the nation receives much more tropical air in summer than in winter. Summer thus becomes the rainy season.

The plateau region which lies between the Sierra-Cascade barrier on the west and the Rocky Mountains on the east receives very little rain. Winds from all directions must pass over high mountains before they reach the plateaus and they come to these lands deprived of nearly all their moisture. The small amounts of rain received may occur in either summer or winter.

Precipitation Depends on Air Movements.—Weather analysis depends upon complex physical forces of which the most fundamental are: (1) the movement of air between the equator and the poles, and (2) the rotation of the earth. Tropical heat makes the equatorial regions areas of continuous low pressure marked by expanding, rising masses of air. At the poles, on the other hand, the air is cold and heavy, and its pressure high. Thus there is a fundamental circulation of cold air from the poles toward the equator. These polar air masses are warmed as they proceed equatorward. As they are warmed they lose pressure and tend to rise. As they rise, these air masses are again cooled and tend to settle back around the poles. The polar-equatorial circulation is a continuous one, with polar air following the surface until it is warmed enough to rise and finally return to the poles by way of the higher altitudes. Weather analysis would be comparatively simple if this circulation were permitted to operate on a stationary globe. As a matter of fact, it is altered enormously by the mechanical forces resulting from the rotation of the earth.

Effect of the Earth's Rotation.—The physical principles involved in the behavior of bodies in motion on a rotating sphere are extremely complicated, especially when they are applied to masses of gas such as the air. For our purposes, it is sufficient to observe that these forces cause air returning from the equator to "pile up" about one-third the way from the equator to the poles. The result is a belt of high pressure which always exists near the outer edges of the tropics. Winds blow outward from these belts in both directions, both equatorward and toward the poles. Those blowing poleward are given an easterly direction by the rotation of the earth. These winds become the prevailing "westerly" winds of temperate-zone countries such as the United States. They consist of masses of tropical air which come to the United States from the south and west.

The Polar Front.—Ultimately this tropical air collides with the colder air coming in from the north and northeast. The line of contact is known as the "front." More specifically the edge of the cold air mass is called the "cold" or "polar" front and the edge of the tropical air mass is known as the "warm" front. The air masses themselves undergo gradual changes as they pass over the land and eventually lose their dominant characteristics of temperature, pressure, and moisture. When these changes occur, the mass is described as "modified" or "neutralized" and additional fronts appear among such areas. A neutralized air mass is comparatively inert and seldom causes weather changes.

In the United States most changes in the weather occur along the polar front. Immense masses of cold heavy air drift slowly down from the north and northeast, commonly thrusting a long tongue into the masses of tropical air from the west and south. The polar air is cold and heavy and clings to the surface. It dams up the eastward progress of the lighter tropical air and forces it upward. When the tropical air rises it is cooled, clouds are formed, and precipitation occurs. The polar mass is pushed slowly eastward by the superior velocity of the westerly winds. Eventually the polar mass loses its characteristics, becomes neutralized and finally passes out over the north Atlantic Ocean.

Seasonal Differences.—This storm zone which marks the line of conflict between polar and tropical air naturally covers more of the continent in summer than in winter. During the winter the land is cold and polar air predominates. But in summer the warm surface warms the air and makes the continent more hospitable to tropical air masses. Tropical air even crosses the boundary into Canada in summer, but relatively little of it reaches the continental interior in winter. Thus the continent imports much less moisture in winter than in summer. Most of the moisture that does come in is precipitated near the coasts of the Gulf of Mexico and the Atlantic Ocean. The mid-continent remains cold and comparatively dry. Between the Rocky Mountains and these two eastern coasts, the climate is marked by cold winters with occasional snow and hot summers with frequent showers. Annual precipitation is heaviest near the coast and decreases to the north and west. The Great Plains have less than one-third as much rain as the Gulf Coast because the tropical air has lost most of its moisture before it reaches them.

Summary.—Weather in the United States can be explained only in terms involving the entire world. Moisture-laden winds from the Tropics meet cold air masses from the poles and precipitation occurs. Winds are the movements of these air masses and their directions reflect differences in pressure and the rotation of the earth. Two great energy sources furnish motive power for the system: the sun and the earth's rotation. Man accepts the results of these forces as he finds them and plans his economic life to take best advantage of the climate of his own locality. With good soil and a favorable climate he engages in agriculture, specializing in the type best suited to his resources. Other occupations are less dependent upon the weather. In some of them he can shut himself in a building and regulate temperature and humidity to his own desires. But in most occupations, man must reckon with the weather and design his life to harmonize with his climatic environment. For the United States as a whole, the greatest single hindrance to economic development is lack of rainfall. This climatic deficiency reduces the number of people which might otherwise be supported in the western half of the nation by at least 70 per cent. No other geographic factor imposes comparable limitations upon the nation's economic development.

TOPOGRAPHY

Mention geography to the average man and he immediately thinks of land forms. For centuries the main concern of geographers was with mountains, oceans, capes, lakes, valleys, and other topographic features. Today the influence of land forms on economic life is so well known that little need be said concerning them. We recognize the configuration of the earth's surface as providing both negative and positive influences in economic development. Among these influences we discover three major types, concerned primarily with climate, agriculture, and transportation.

Topography and Climate.—Surface features affect climate primarily as barriers. Mountain ranges force winds into high altitudes and take away their moisture, leaving dry "rain shadows" on their lee slopes. Because of their elevation, mountains are cooler than surrounding areas and provide good summer-resort sites. The windward sides of mountain ranges capture much rain and provide water for irrigation in the dry valleys below.

Oceans and Lakes Moderate Climate.—Bodies of water affect climate by moderating temperatures and giving moisture to the winds which pass over them. California winters are mild because prevailing westerly winds are kept warm by passing over the Pacific Ocean. Large lakes, such as the Great Lakes, have a similar but less effective influence upon the climates of their eastern shores. The Atlantic Coast, on the other hand, generally experiences off-shore winds and its summers are hot and winters cold. Large bodies of water temper the climate of lands on their lee shores.

Land Forms and Agriculture.—Land forms affect agriculture because of the influence of slope on agricultural land use. Steep land is easily eroded and its soil soon wears out. Again, modern agriculture is highly dependent upon machinery. These machines are not successful on hilly land. During the past quarter-century more American farm land has been abandoned because it was too rough for machine cultivation than for any other reason.

Transportation.—The economic effect of surface features upon transportation is probably of greater importance than in any other type of economic activity. It is difficult to overemphasize the extreme dependence of our modern economy upon transportation and trade. When the products of one region are exchanged for those of other regions, transportation must be employed. Raw materials must be gathered for factories, and markets must be reached for manufactured goods. For this service we depend upon the railway, highway, waterway, and airway.

Water Transport.—Natural waterways provide the cheapest form of transportation known to man, and natural harbors have provided the best locations for commercial cities. Natural inland waterways are effective if they lie somewhere near the natural paths of trade. In the United States, the one great river system, the Mississippi, is a good waterway but it flows in the wrong direction. Most of our commerce moves east and west. In certain instances man has found it profitable to improve waterways to make them more useful. Prime examples of such improvements are the canals connecting the Great Lakes.

Land Transport.—In the United States, most transportation is overland: by railway and highway. These routes follow valleys, seek mountain passes, avoid steep grades, and circumvent lakes, mountains, and similar barriers. Because some transportation routes are better than others some of them are of strategic importance. Atlanta became the railroad center of the South because railroads sought easy grades around the southern end of the Appalachian Highland. Chicago became the leading railroad center of the nation because railroads had to skirt the southern end of Lake Michigan to reach the West and Northwest. Transportation lines follow the best and easiest routes. Where these routes converge or cross, cities arise and commerce and exchange develop. Land forms direct the flow of trade, and the paths of trade become locations for commercial cities.

LOCATION

The location factor is so obvious that it is often overlooked in economic discussion. All of us know that mere distance, divorced from all other factors, is an important frictional disturbance to commerce and trade. Transportation costs money and takes time. Distance from eastern markets keeps the Idaho potato crop small as it is, because other conditions are nearly ideal for potatoes. Distance from raw materials and markets has kept factories out of the West and South. American economic geography has thousands of such examples. In the United States, distance is measured largely in terms of shipping costs. When a manufacturer locates a new factory, he solves a problem in arithmetic. He selects that site at which materials can be obtained, goods manufactured, and products delivered to his markets at the lowest cost. Usually, the freight rates on materials and products are the largest variables in his calculations. Location with reference to markets is important in all types of occupations in which goods or services are offered for sale.

SOILS

Soil is a factor of extreme significance in agricultural geography. The farmer is interested not only in the actual fertility of the soil, but also in its adaptability to various crops. Soils are classified according to parent material, color, texture, structure, and chemical content. All of these factors influence fertility, but a discussion of their relative importance belongs to soil science rather than to economic geography.

Precipitation Affects Fertility.—In the United States there is a close correlation between rainfall and the fertility of the soil. In general, the best soils have been developed where the rainfall is moderate. Soils of arid districts generally are alkaline and although often rich chemically, they are deficient in organic matter. Rainy climates, on the other hand, generally produce acid soils from which most of the needed minerals have been washed away. In addition, rainy lands generally are covered with timber. Falling leaves and branches add some humus to the soil, but usually it is only a thin top layer. Coniferous trees produce poor soils because they do not even shed their leaves.

The Importance of Humus.—To understand soil fertility, we need to look to the needs of growing plants. Vegetation grows by combining hydrogen from water and carbon from the air. The oxygen used in this chemical process is given off by the plant as waste. In addition, all plants need small amounts of certain chemicals such as nitrogen, phosphorus, potassium, and calcium. All of these elements are soluble in water. To be fertile, a soil must have the property of transporting water to the roots of the plants. The rain falls and soaks into the ground. There the water absorbs soluble minerals. Finally, through capillary action, the water reaches the roots of the plants. In order to carry on this function, a soil must contain a generous supply of substances called colloids. Colloids are formed by decayed vegetable matter, and their gelatinous coating around soil particles carries water from one particle to another. Thus the soil which receives the greatest annual accumulation of vegetable matter is likely to have the best colloidal structure. By the same token, it also is a rich soil if its chemical composition is adequate.

Native Vegetation.—The most fertile soils are found on lands whose native vegetation was grass. Tall prairie grass produces enormous tonnages of vegetation every year and it dies down every winter. Here the addition of humus reaches a maximum. Short-grass soils of the drier plains stand next to the prairie soils in productivity. These are followed by the moderately productive soils of the deciduous forest and finally by the poor, thin soils of the coniferous forests and arid districts.

The best American soils are found in the prairies of the upper

Mississippi Valley. Here the humus content is high and the soils are either slightly alkaline or mildly acid. These soils are productive if enough water can be had for crops. Soils of the eastern United States generally are acid and low in humus. They respond splendidly to the application of commercial fertilizers. Proper rotation of crops, including the plowing-under of an occasional hay crop as "green manure," will maintain the humus content of these eastern soils. Thus manipulated they will grow almost any variety of plant suited to the climate of that area.

Soil is a basic natural resource. Proper farm practice will maintain soil fertility indefinitely, but neglect of such practice can ruin the best soils in one or two generations. The United States has a number of areas in which erosion and depletion have removed all topsoil. Fortunately, American agriculture has awakened to the problem and current usages point to better conservation of this basic factor in our economic life.

MINERALS

Rare and useful minerals are always a source of economic stimulation in a community. Like the soil, minerals must be utilized where they are found. Mining towns spring up, and occasional manufacturing cities. Sub-surface minerals are bound to affect the economic life of an area once it is deemed profitable to extract them.

To no small extent, the machine age is an age of minerals. More specifically, it is an age of iron, coal, copper, and petroleum. Iron builds the machines of our factories and transportation systems. Coal and oil provide the power. Copper is the great metal for transmitting electricity. These and the other minerals largely make the exchange economy possible. Mining ranks with agriculture as one of the basic occupations of modern life. In the following chapters we shall find many communities dependent upon mining and many more whose industrial development is partly traceable to location with reference to the source of mined products.

FORESTS AND FISH

Primitive man found forests and fish to be his most important economic resources. From the forest came the game which fed and clothed him, the timber which housed him and the wood which made the fire to keep him warm. Fishing added to his supply of food. As time went on, the forest and fishery became less important as a source of food. Other sources replaced the forest in providing clothing, fuel and shelter. Throughout the ages, however, man has continued to depend upon wood as his chief building material, and the timber has continued to supply fuel and food. Today we value the forest principally as a source of lumber and paper. Fishing is still important along all of our coasts, but fish are not nearly so important as meat in the national diet. These resources are basic to a considerable number of manufacturing industries.

EVALUATING THE ENVIRONMENT

The economic process operates within the limits set up by a variety of natural and human factors. Basic among these are the physical features of the earth's surface. The physical environment includes all of the observable characteristics of the landscape: the winds, rain, and other climatic forces; the land forms, soil minerals, and similar natural features; the element of location; natural vegetation, and plant and animal life *plus* the man-made resources and barriers such as buildings, railroads, machines, and even intangible tariff walls. These properties set the stage for the economic drama.

The drama itself is often described as a conflict between scarce means and unlimited wants. The term "scarce means" refers to the limited nature of both the physical environment and man's capacity to utilize it. We have seen that man's capacity may be defined narrowly to include his ability and skill or more broadly to include the tools and other productive equipment available to him. Either definition implies that man's ability to exploit his environment is limited. The term "unlimited desires" is quickly translated by the economic system into the demand for goods and services. There is no practical limit to man's desires, but his demand is limited by his ability to buy. Demand varies from time to time, and from one commodity to another. The producer is confronted with a problem of anticipating the demand (price) for the various commodities he is able to produce. His ability to produce is stated largely in terms of his physical environment and his own capacity to utilize it. All three elements, environment, ability, and prospective profit, must be represented in his choice of occupation. The working of these factors may be better understood by solving a simplified problem in agricultural land utilization.

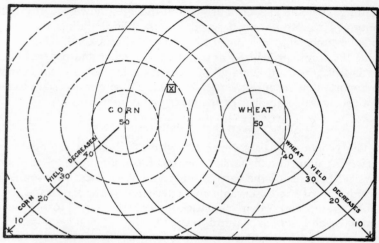

Fig. 2. Will the farmer at point X plant corn or wheat? The problem assumes that the area in the chart can be used only for growing corn or wheat. The best corn land is on the left, the best wheat land on the right. The yield per acre for each grain decreases with distance from the two centers of maximum productivity. Yields per acre are shown by numbers in each of the concentric circles. The problem is to discover which portions of the area will be used to grow wheat and which ones will be planted in corn. The farm at X can be used for either grain, with an expected yield of forty bushels of corn or thirty bushels of wheat. Which crop will be grown? The answer obviously depends upon the prospective return from each crop. As stated in the text, with corn at 50 cents per bushel and wheat at 65 cents per bushel, the farmer will choose wheat. But suppose that the price of wheat dropped to 55 cents. Draw a line to indicate the approximate boundary between wheat-growing and corn-growing under these two sets of prices (corn 50 cents per bushel and wheat 65 cents; corn 50 cents and wheat 55 cents). How would the introduction of cheaper methods of corn-growing affect the problem? Suppose that a new variety of corn were introduced which gave increased yields with no increase in production costs. What effect would a war in Europe have on the situation? What factors affect the rapidity with which the farmer at X will respond to price changes?

A Simplified Problem in Land Utilization.—Assume that the natural environment of an area has been measured and analyzed. When all natural factors—climate, soil, topography, location, etc. —have been evaluated, it is discovered that the area can be used only for the growing of two crops, corn and wheat. Certain sections can grow only corn, others only wheat, but there is a large section that can grow either. The natural productivity for each grain varies. There is a center in which corn grows very well, and another center in which wheat is very successful. Outward from these centers the productivity for each crop decreases until a marginal boundary is reached beyond which that grain cannot be grown. These natural conditions might form a pattern as indicated in Fig. 2.

The farmer at point X anticipates a yield of either forty bushels of corn or thirty bushels of wheat per acre. It will cost him about $4.00 an acre in out-of-pocket expense to grow corn, and $2.00 an acre to grow wheat. (These are operating costs actually necessary to grow a crop. They do not include rent, interest, taxes, or other fixed costs which must be met regardless of what is done with the land, and therefore do not enter the calculation.) His choice between corn and wheat is almost certain to be made on the basis of the relative prospective return per acre. This return depends upon the price to be received at harvest time. He therefore estimates the price that might be expected for each grain.

If he expects corn to be worth 50 cents a bushel and wheat to be worth 65 cents a bushel, his calculations might run as follows:

	Corn	Wheat
Expected yield per acre	40 bu.	30 bu.
Expected price per bushel	$ .50	$ .65
Gross return per acre	$20.00	$19.50
Out-of-pocket cost per acre	4.00	2.00
Net return per acre	$16.00	$17.50

Under these circumstances wheat appears to offer a greater profit. The farmer at X grows wheat and his neighbors make the same choice. The community around point X becomes a wheat-growing community.

But the next year the price situation changes. The price of wheat drops to 55 cents per bushel and the price of corn remains at 50 cents. The farmer at X envisions a net return of only $14.50 per acre from wheat, or $16 per acre from corn. He and his neighbors shift to corn. The boundary of corn-growing shifts to the right into the wheat country and the area of the wheat belt is restricted accordingly. In actual life the boundaries of the American wheat belts may be shifted by such seemingly remote factors as a crop failure in Argentina or a war scare in Europe. Both factors affect the price of wheat and the prospective profit in growing it. The amount of prospective profit is of prime importance in determining whether an individual farmer will grow wheat. Market price assumes an importance commensurate with natural resources in determining the use which will be made of a geographic area.

There is yet another group of factors which influence land utilization where alternative uses are possible. These factors are also expressed in terms of price, but they are related not to the selling price but rather to the cost of production. In the preceding problem it was assumed that production costs remain constant from one year to the next and that a farmer experiences no loss in shifting from one crop to the other. As a matter of fact, production costs are subject to variation and these changes may be sufficient in themselves to affect the choice between two types of economic exploitation. A new machine may lower production costs or a scarcity of labor may raise them. All such changes will affect a producer's expected net income and thereby influence his choice between alternative methods of using his time and equipment.

It is also quite important that producers are not always free to shift from one type of economic activity to another. In choosing between wheat and corn, it was assumed that a shift from one grain to the other could be made without great expense. In practice, the farmer who has grown wheat many years is under strong compulsion to continue doing so even in the face of unfavorable prices. He will do so because he has large sums invested in machinery useful for growing wheat but not corn. To a certain extent, he has built up a specialized plant which can be converted to another type of production only at considerable cost. The change would be even more costly if he were attempting to shift from wheat to meat-animal production or dairy farming. These types of farming require large investments in barns, silos, and other specialized equipment. To acquire them entails heavy expenditures.

If our simplified land-use problem were to be extended into other economic spheres, it would become vastly more complicated, but the principles would remain substantially unchanged. In the United States not two but many types of farming are possible on most of the land. But the owner of farm land chooses among them in much the same manner as the hypothetical farmer at point X decided between corn and wheat. Perhaps the land is fit only for grazing, but there usually is a choice between cattle and sheep. Perhaps the land is so much better adapted to one type of use than to any other that a change from that type is never considered. Certainly there are many areas in Texas where farmers have never considered specializing in any crop other than cotton, and certain acres in Iowa that seem forever destined to grow corn and hogs. But these situations are not typical. One always finds a zone near the borders of the major farm regions in which changes in types of farming occur with marked frequency as first one type and then another seems to promise greater profit.

The process also applies in problems of land use for non-agricultural purposes. Certain areas yield greatest profit if planted in forest. Others are better devoted to highways, mining operations, or the building of cities. In these sectors of the economic system the process is so obvious that we often lose sight of it. Not even the richest farm is likely to be retained if it is possible to build a city on its acres. Urban use yields the highest returns to be obtained from land. Within the city, however, there is abundant evidence of competition among various economic types for use of the available area. Expanding business districts invade and occupy centrally located residential areas. Factories requiring much land are forced into the suburbs. The profitable types of business evict the less profitable types from strategic locations. Banks occupy a financial district and theaters are clustered in an amusement area. A square foot of land in the city is often as important economically as an acre in the country, but its use is determined by competition among a similar group of economic types.

Finally, it should be emphasized that single types of economic development rarely gain *permanent* control over individual areas. Within a single century Americans have seen large areas devoted successively to ranching, extensive farming, intensive farming, and finally manufacturing and city life. One economic type has occupied an area for a time only to be succeeded by a more profitable type for which the first has largely paved the way. Finally, an area approaches a stage of climax or optimum economic use in which each acre and square mile is presumed to be devoted to that type of production for which it is best suited. But in the meantime a new invention, a shift in consumer demand, a government program, or similar force occurs to change the entire process. The stores and forces of nature change but little throughout the years, but the capacities and desires of the people are subject to constant flux. Thus we evaluate the United States as a productive area in terms of the present knowledge concerning its natural and human resources. We seek to learn the basis for the present geographic distribution of economic activity; but we do this with the knowledge that evolution is continuous, and that the structure changes with time.

Economic Regions in the United States.—The geographic environment consists of the resources and barriers encountered by man in his business of making a living. Man's economic life consists very largely of devising means to utilize the resources of nature and overcome her barriers. In exploiting the resources of a continent, the American people have set up a vast nationwide economic machine characterized by the geographic specialization of labor. If an area can grow cotton better than it can engage in any other sort of production, the economic system dictates that that area shall specialize in cotton-growing. If a town serves a copper mine, it concentrates attention on copper-mining and does not waste effort in growing food, manufacturing clothing, or engaging in other activities in which it would be relatively less efficient. By this system the American people strive to make the most of their resources. Economic geography attempts to show the relationships between these environmental influences and the economic development of the various regions.

The purpose of this volume is to explain the manner in which man utilizes the various elements in his geographic environment in the United States. The unit of study is the region, which is defined as an area in which a particular type of environment has encouraged the evolution of a distinctive type of economic life. Discussion begins with the Pacific Coast where climate, topography, and location have encouraged the development of an economy that differs widely from the economy of other regions. The eastern boundary of the Pacific Coast Region is the great wall of the Cascade and Sierra Nevada mountain ranges. These mountains, at once a barrier to climate and transportation, effectively mark the eastern extent of the Pacific Coast type of economy.

East of the Sierra-Cascade barrier we find a new region which stretches eastward to the base of the Rocky Mountains. This region includes the arid inter-mountain plateaus, whose chief drawback to economic development is lack of rainfall. The Rocky Mountains constitute an economic region in themselves, an important study in the effect of mountain topography upon economic life. Boundaries of the three regions which occupy the western third of the United States are mainly topographic, because in this part of the nation we find mountain ranges large enough to affect not only trade and transportation but also climate.

East of the Rocky Mountains there are no significant climatic barriers. Here the use of the land is related more definitely to soil qualities, precipitation, length of the growing season and location with reference to mineral deposits. Immediately east of the Rocky Mountains lie the Great Plains whose chief limitation is lack of rainfall and whose eastern limits are marked by no natural boundary. The Great Plains economy extends eastward to the line where grazing and wheat-growing give way to the corn, cotton, and dairy-farming activities of the more humid eastern half of the nation. The Great Plains Region is a land of rainfall deficiency whose eastern boundary shifts from year to year with the rainfall cycle and the relative prices of the different products which can be grown on its eastern margins. This shifting eastern boundary marks the line which separates the dry-climate agriculture of the western half of the United States from the humid-climate types found in the eastern half of the nation.

East of the Great Plains, regional boundaries generally assume an east-west direction which is most closely related to the length of the growing season. On the north, a forest and lake region is too cool for corn, but finds profit in dairying. Farther south lies the Corn Belt, climatically adapted to the fairly exacting demands of that grain. South of the Corn Belt a broad belt of hills includes the central and southern Appalachian Highland and the Ozark uplift. In this region, topography and soil, rather than climate, are the most important geographic factors. South of the Appalachian-Ozark hill region lies the vast expanse of the Cotton Belt, whose boundaries are definitely related to climate. On the north, the

Cotton Belt stops where the growing season becomes too short, and on the west where the rainfall is too light. Cotton does not reach the coasts of the Atlantic Ocean and Gulf of Mexico because there the rainfall is too heavy. These coastal strips therefore become a separate region. Finally, we discover a region in the northeastern United States which is not dominated by agriculture. This is the American Manufacturing Belt, whose life centers in its cities and whose agriculture is of secondary importance. The Manufacturing Belt region owes its existence primarily to the presence of good transportation and easy access to the raw materials of industry. In this manner the United States is divided into ten regions, each with a distinctive type of economic development.

REFERENCES

Consult Finch and Trewartha, *Elements of Geography,* for a thorough treatment of the geographic environment, also the general references on physiography, climate and soils listed in the Introduction.

The classic statement of *site* as a factor in land utilization is contained in J. H. von Thünen, *Der isolierte Staat,* which presents the problem of differences in rent which arise from varying distances from the market. The theory also appears in condensed form in most textbooks on general economics.

QUESTIONS AND PROBLEMS

1. What is the "geographic environment"? Is there any essential difference between the geographic and the physical environment?
2. Why must the economic geographer consider both human and natural resources?
3. What does the term "climate" usually include? Distinguish between climate and weather, climate and seasons.
4. What is a cyclone? How do high- and low-pressure areas affect precipitation?
5. On which side of the Sierra Nevada is the rain shadow? Why does it occur there?
6. Describe the principal air movements of the earth. Which type prevails over the United States? What is the polar front? How does it differ from the warm front?
7. Compile a list of the influences of topography upon climate, agriculture, and transportation.
8. Do you agree that there is a close relation between precipitation and soil fertility? Why or why not?
9. "Urban use yields the highest returns to be obtained from land." Why is this so? What is meant by "unearned increment"?

CHAPTER III

THE PACIFIC COAST REGION
—NATURAL ENVIRONMENT

THE Pacific states must be recognized as a great economic empire, far removed by mountain and plain from the big three-ring circus of American economic life. But they are no mere sideshow. Since the turn of the present century these states have increased faster in population and industry than any other part of North America. They comprise America's fast-growing Empire of the Pacific Coast.

I have made the Pacific Region include the Cascade and Sierra Nevada ranges, and the territory between these lofty mountains and the coast. It differs greatly from the remainder of North America in topography, climate, and economic life; within its boundaries there is comparatively little variation in any of these factors; its seven million people constitute the only large groups of concentrated population in the western half of the United States. It fulfills admirably the requirements for a region.

Location.—The Pacific Region extends throughout the American section of the Pacific Coast. It is about 1300 miles long and from 50 to 250 miles wide. Because of its length we may expect its climate and consequent economic life to differ somewhat from north to south. The region is from 1600 to 2000 miles removed from the center of American population, and most of that distance is made up of mountains and dry plains of very sparse population. Far removed from the people to whom it would sell its surplus products, it will of necessity be restricted to products which can be sold at a distance for prices which will be sufficient to absorb a high freight charge and at the same time allow a fair price to the producer.

These great distances are apt to be underestimated by the reader, especially if he is accustomed to the compactly grouped cities of the northeastern United States. It is difficult to realize that Los Angeles and San Francisco are farther apart than New York and Pittsburgh, or that a journey from San Diego to Seattle is longer

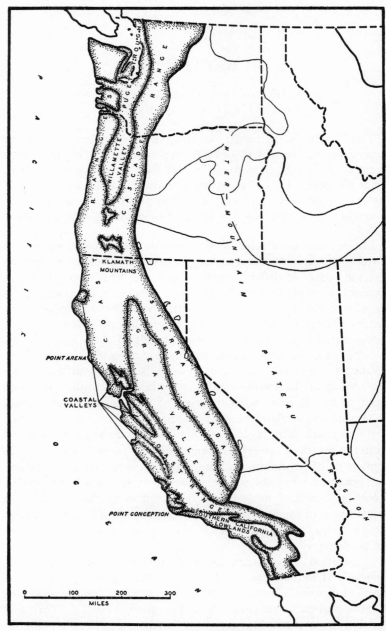

FIG. 3. The Pacific Coast Region.

NATURAL ENVIRONMENT

than one from Boston to Minneapolis.[1] Every map of the Pacific states should contain this warning, "Read the Scale of Miles."

TOPOGRAPHY AND SOIL

The Pacific Coast Region has a greater variety of scenery than any other portion of North America. A day's journey from any point in the region will put you at the seaside, in a fertile valley, high in forest-clad mountains, or on treeless plains. Within the Pacific states are the highest peaks, the lowest valleys, the driest desert, and the rainiest section of the United States. Small wonder that the economic life is also more varied than in any other part of America!

Glance at a relief map (Fig. 4) and you will observe three salient characteristics of Pacific states topography: (1) The coast is paralleled by two long ranges of mountains which extend south from Puget Sound across Washington, Oregon, and the northern three-fourths of California. (2) For a major portion of this distance these mountain ranges are divided by broad, low valleys. Closer examination of the map will also indicate that (3) the mountain ranges join in the vicinity of the Oregon-California boundary and again in the south quarter of California over which they extend in a single, low, irregular mass to the Mexican boundary. Throughout their length the coast ranges rise near the coast, leaving very little level land that could be called a coastal plain. The whole topographic system is appropriately called the *Mountains and Valleys of the Pacific States.*

The Coast Ranges.—The mountains which border the Pacific have varying local names, but commonly they are known as the Coast Ranges.[2] Throughout their length they show similar characteristics.

1. The coastal plain is either very narrow or entirely absent.
2. Although many mountain streams flow down from or across these ranges, their valleys are narrow and ill suited to agri-

[1] A San Franciscan relates that he received a note from a New Yorker stating that a mutual friend would soon be visiting in Los Angeles and suggested that he "run down and see him some evening." Los Angeles is a good day's ride (415 miles) from San Francisco.
[2] Significant exceptions are the Olympic Mountains of northeastern Washington, and a number of smaller ranges such as the Mount Hamilton and Santa Lucia ranges south of San Francisco Bay.

culture as far south as Point Arena (100 miles north of San Francisco).

3. Between Point Arena and Point Conception the coastal mountains are frequently divided into two or more roughly parallel ranges between which are a number of fertile valleys. Several small valleys just north of San Francisco Bay, and two larger ones (the Santa Clara and the Salinas) to the south are the most notable of these tillable intermountain valleys. All of these are important agriculturally. As a group they are known as the *Coastal Valleys of Central California*.

4. South of Point Conception the mountain slopes are generally less steep, the peaks less high. Here are a number of valleys, many of which lead to (geologically) old delta lands which form plains near the coast and make possible the rich farm sections of southern California. Largest and most famous is the plain on which Los Angeles stands. This plain extends about thirty miles along the coast and fifteen or twenty miles inland, but it is connected with interior basins to the east and southeast. The plain also extends (at slightly higher elevation) south to San Diego. Here, however, broken topography leaves only about one-third of the land tillable, and deficiency of moisture limits agriculture to much less than that fraction. The Los Angeles Plain is connected with a small but rich valley and coastal area to the north. These valleys and plains are the *Lowlands of Southern California*.

The Interior Mountains.—The Cascade and Sierra Nevada ranges stretch in a long, high, and relatively narrow chain from Canada south to the vicinity of Los Angeles where they merge with the coastal mountains to form the lower mountains of southern California. Throughout most of this distance these ranges are separated from those of the coast by two great valleys, but for a hundred miles north and south of the Oregon-California boundary they draw slightly nearer the coast and join the coast ranges to form the Klamath Mountains.

The Klamath Mountains are old, geologically, and have the rounded peaks and gentle slopes so common in the mountains of the eastern states. But the Sierras and Cascades are more spectacular. Not only are their peaks higher than those of the other ranges, but their slopes are steeper and they are crossed by few rivers. (But one of these is the mighty Columbia River which has cut a gorge through the 7000-foot Cascade Range at an altitude of less than 500 feet and provides the only low-altitude route from the Pacific coast to the interior.) Streams in these mountains have not had time to wear valleys; they are still in the stage of deep canyons. Consequently, throughout their entire distance the Cascades and Sierras are inhabited chiefly by lumbermen, miners, herdsmen, and a *very few* farmers.

The Great Valleys.—Less picturesque than the mountains but of far greater economic importance are the valleys, of which the Puget Trough and the Great Valley are the largest. These, with the previously described Coastal Valleys and valley-plain areas of southern California, constitute the heart of the Pacific states' economic organization. Here reside the farmers, in fact 95 per cent of the entire population. For here also are the cities, the railroads, the factories, the highways, and most of the wealth of the area.

1. *The Puget Trough and the Willamette Valley.* Topographically, the Puget Trough and the Great Valley have much in common. Both are surprisingly level, too flat for good drainage. Both have floors of rich, brownish alluvial soil washed down from the neighboring mountains. But the portion immediately adjacent to Puget Sound (roughly the northern third of the Puget Trough) must be considered separately. Not only is it low, often marshy in sections, but it is the only valley district showing marked effects of glaciation. The tourist who travels south from Vancouver, in British Columbia, finds little cultivation except on isolated knobs. For the first fifty miles the Puget Trough is glacier-scoured with only occasional patches of good soil. Over the next hundred miles (past Seattle, Tacoma, Olympia), the glacier deposited much gravel from which the soil has since eroded and left little basis for cultivation. Farther south, as one approaches the Columbia River, the gravel ceases with the terminal moraine, and instead rise low hills covered mainly with cut-over and burned-over timber. These low hills continue south of Portland for about twenty miles, but here the landscape flattens out into a plain over which the lazy Willamette (pronounced Willam'met) River meanders hesitatingly over a silt-covered course flowing so slowly

that trees have in many places grown down into the water. Trees and silt so clog the stream that danger from floods increases yearly. But the valley is flat and fertile, one of the richest farm sections of the Pacific Northwest. Only the fact that the level of ground water is frequently near the surface seriously hinders the growing of certain crops.

2. *The Great Valley of California.* Farther south, the Great Valley of California is almost a topographic twin of the valley of the Willamette. It is very flat except near the bordering mountains where streams have brought down silt, gravel, and boulders and deposited them in "alluvial fans" which slope steeply at the mountain base but flatten out rapidly as they extend into the valley floor. These alluvial fans provide some of the most productive farm land in the state of California. Their agricultural advantages are explained in a later section on California agriculture.

Near the south end of the Great Valley of California the alluvial fans from several vigorous mountain streams rising in the highest part of the Sierras have extended entirely across the valley and formed a large area without known external drainage. It is called the Tulare Basin. Perennial streams cascade down from the high Sierras only to become lost in the ever-thirsty alluvial sands of the valley or to form shallow rainy-season (playa) lakes (named Tulare, Buena Vista, and Kern) which almost invariably become dry during the rainless summer. Except for its lack of external drainage the Tulare Basin has topography similar to the remainder of the Great Valley.

The Great Valley has two important rivers, the Sacramento and the San Joaquin, which meet near the center of the valley and flow into San Francisco Bay. Both are of the same lazy, meandering type as the Willamette. Both have deposited so much silt in their beds that their banks are in many places higher than the adjacent plain. In this respect the rivers resemble the lower Mississippi which actually flows along "on top of a hill" for many miles before it empties into the Gulf of Mexico. With banks often ten feet higher than the surrounding country, drainage in the delta lands of the Sacramento and San Joaquin is *away from* rather than toward the rivers, and there are many marshes characteris-

NATURAL ENVIRONMENT

tically covered with a native brush called *tule*. Near Sacramento these swamps have been turned to the production of rice, a crop which thrives best when grown in pools of shallow water. These marshy delta lands cover only a small percentage of the entire great valley. Elsewhere, the lands generally drain well, have rich soil, and are very productive where sufficient water is available.

CLIMATE IN THE PACIFIC REGION

The most unusual and certainly the best-advertised feature of life in the Pacific states is the climate. Everywhere along the coast the prevailing westerly winds sweep in from the mighty Pacific, their temperatures made remarkably uniform by its tempering effect. Tourist circulars dwell chiefly upon the mild winters, but the summers are similarly temperate, cooler than in most other parts of the United States.[3] These westerly winds also yield much rain over the cool northern half of the region, and especially heavy rains and snow in passing over the mountains. The interior valleys, more or less isolated from these breezes by the coast ranges, experience generally cooler winters, warmer summers, and less rainfall than the portions of the coast adjacent to them.

Precipitation.—Three minutes' study of Fig. 4 will give the reader a better notion of precipitation in the Pacific Region than a study of many pages of description. It will be noted that:

1. The rainfall type (dry summer, rainy winter) is the same for all parts of the region, but the total precipitation ranges from *very light* in the south to *very heavy* in the north.
2. Interior valleys generally receive less moisture than neighboring coastal sections. (Compare San Francisco and Sacramento; Astoria and Portland as examples.)

Temperature.—The differences in temperature between the coolest and warmest months may be quickly summarized by reference to the table of normal temperatures. These temperatures are monthly averages. It will be observed that:

1. Winters along the coast are characteristically mild, mildest in southern California. Coast summers are cool, coolest from San Francisco north to the Canadian boundary.

[3] One must seek the higher elevations of New England or the Rocky Mountains to find cooler summers.

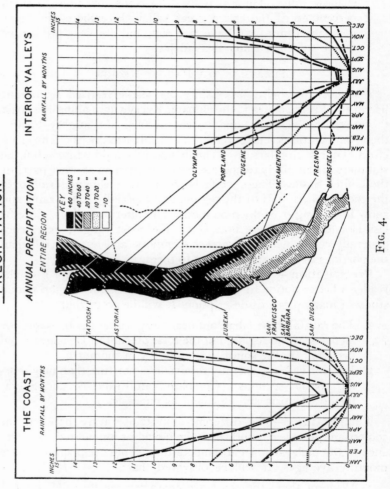

FIG. 4.

2. The interior valleys have slightly cooler winters and considerably hotter summers than the adjacent coastal sections. Both winters and summers are cooler in the north than in the south.

3. When the great length of the region is considered, there is surprisingly little temperature variation from north to south.

NORMAL TEMPERATURES, PACIFIC COAST REGION
Coolest and Warmest Months

(For locations see Fig. 4, Precipitation)

The Coast			The Valleys		
	January	August[a]		January	July[a]
Tatoosh Island....	41.1	55.4	Olympia.........	39.5	63.1
Astoria..........	40.1	61.1	Portland.........	39.4	66.7
Eureka..........	46.9	56.0	Eugene...........	40.0	65.8
San Francisco.....	49.9	59.1	Sacramento	45.8	73.2
Santa Barbara....	53.4	66.7	Fresno...........	46.2	82.1
San Diego........	54.3	68.7	Bakersfield.......	47.4	84.0

[a] August is the warmest month on the coast, July is warmest in the interior.

Other Climatic Factors.—Monthly averages of precipitation and temperature, such as those just presented, are the most useful *single sets* of climatic data that could be presented. But averages of any type generally give an incomplete, and frequently a misleading picture.[4] Additional facts are necessary. Especially important are the variations in temperature between day and night; and the frequency of occurrence of severe winters, or unseasonable frosts, or heat waves, and of very dry or very wet years. Each deserves brief consideration.

1. Nights are almost invariably cool throughout the Pacific Region, despite the fact that interior summer days are frequently very hot. Residents of humid climates find it hard to believe that they will need blankets at night after days on which the thermometer has stood at 100° F. All valleys south of San Francisco are arid or semi-arid. Such dry districts throughout the world experience cool nights.

2. Because of the tempering effect of the Pacific breezes which

[4] The average height of a group of men may be five feet, eight inches, but 95 per cent of them will be shorter or taller. You would not buy the same-sized overcoats for all the men. Neither should a business man plan the same type of marketing program for all districts with the same average temperatures. But many have done so. Fortunes have been lost because of such errors.

blow nearly every day of the year, the coastal districts and those valleys which are open to the sea seldom experience unusual heat waves in summer or cold waves in winter. Temperatures are almost monotonously uniform from day to day.

3. Variations in year-to-year rainfall are smaller in this section than in most parts of the United States. Such variations as do occur have relatively slight effect. The Pacific Northwest receives so much rain even in the drier years that variations produce little or no economic embarrassment. In most sections of California the reverse is true. Even in wet years rainfall is so light that irrigation is necessary, and irrigation makes the farmer independent of local rainfall. Dry years do not trouble him *that same year*. But if the winter snowfall is light in the neighboring mountains, his supply of summer irrigation water may be cut. Happily, such years are infrequent. Except for wide variations between day and night temperatures in certain sections, monthly averages describe the climate of the Pacific Region in a satisfactory manner.

Significance of the Pacific Type of Climate.—If you enjoy throwing snowballs and live in Seattle or Portland, you must work fast, for snow falls infrequently and melts rapidly. In San Francisco you might have to wait several years for enough snow. In sunny Los Angeles your only chance is to share the enjoyment of several truckloads brought down from the mountains each Christmas for the entertainment of the children. But if you lived in the mountains, especially the high ones, you would consider snow one of your worst enemies. All winter it would fall and drift often to the eaves and chimney of your cabin. It would isolate you from civilization. You would spend your summers laying in provisions and fuel for its coming, and you would spend the winters fighting it.

If you like flowers, either to grow or to buy them cheaply, Pacific climate will please you, for in most places flowers bloom abundantly throughout the year. Cities from Portland to Pasadena are famous for rose festivals.

If you dislike fogs, the Pacific coast winters will not appeal to you. Frequently the sun fails to appear for a week at a time from San Diego to Seattle (and north to Nome, Alaska). In Los

Angeles these fogs are damp, in San Francisco very damp, in Seattle downright wet. A Seattle friend writes, "You may fuss a bit at first because the cuffs on your trousers are wet most of the time in winter, but you'll get used to it." Fogs are also common in summer but most of them are "high" fogs, low clouds several hundred feet high, which disappear in mid-forenoon leaving the weather clear and dry until sundown. Interior valleys not open to the sea have few fogs.

The damp climate has made the mountains of the Pacific Northwest and of California as far south as San Francisco the richest timber-growing and lumber-producing section of the United States.

San Francisco has the coolest summers of any large city in the United States. One needs a topcoat almost any mid-summer evening. This coolness extends to the cities across San Francisco Bay, but no farther inland. Well-informed jobbers do not try to sell many straw hats in San Francisco.

Almost invariably the cities of the Southern California Lowlands enjoy cool Pacific breezes during the summer. But on rare occasions the wind veers to the north or east. It is as dry and hot as the desert off which it blows. Residents call it the "Santa Ana" wind. Occasionally it carries a cloud of desert dust. Perhaps once or twice each summer it serves to remind us what the climate of southern California would be without the tempering Pacific breeze.

No other part of the United States experiences such small differences between summer and winter temperatures as this region.

REFERENCES

The treatment of natural resources in this chapter is based largely on Fenneman, *Physiography of the Western United States,* Chs. 9 and 10, and Ward, *Climates of the United States.* Good material also appears in *Commercial Survey of the Pacific Southwest,* U. S. Department of Commerce (1930). The best maps of climate, soil and forests are in *Atlas of American Agriculture.*

QUESTIONS AND PROBLEMS

1. Which city lies farthest west, Portland, San Francisco or Seattle?
2. Why is the California type of climate classified as "Mediterranean"?
3. Why does the Pacific coast have so few good natural harbors?
4. Why do Portland and Seattle have climates similar to those of Paris and London?

5. Why are the climates of Pacific coast cities more moderate than those of Atlantic coast cities?
6. Explain how topography accounts for many of the climatic differences found among various sections of the Pacific Coast Region.
7. How much faster are the airline schedules than the railroad schedules between New York and the Pacific Coast? Of what economic significance are these savings in time?

CHAPTER IV

THE PACIFIC COAST REGION—ECONOMIC LIFE IN CALIFORNIA

THE Klamath Mountains divide the Pacific Region into two sections whose boundary is arbitrarily set as the state line between Oregon and California. Northward are the great ports of the Pacific Northwest, the great sawmills, and the farms of the Willamette Valley devoted to generalized agriculture. Southward is the state of California with its two large metropolitan centers, its oil wells, its tourist trade, and its farms specialized in the growing of fruits and vegetables. Because these two sections differ in nearly every type of economic development they will be considered separately.

CALIFORNIA AGRICULTURE

Californians like to tell easterners that their state can raise any crop that can be grown in any other state and a long list besides. Perhaps that is exaggeration. But the United States Department of Agriculture does list 180 crops for the state, far more than for any other. One hundred eighty crops! But, beware the implication. California *could* grow nearly anything, but it doesn't find every crop profitable. It is notably weak in the production of the three great American staples—corn, cotton, and wheat—growing not enough of any of these to supply the needs of its own people. It must rely upon other sections for most of its beefsteak and bacon. California has nearly 5 per cent of the people of the United States but raises only 1 per cent of the nation's hogs and 4 per cent of its cattle.

It stands higher in the production of sheep with about 6 per cent of the national output. Comparatively, California farmers produce very few field crops and meat animals. They have found greater profit in agricultural specialties such as fruit and vegetables. Not many years ago, few people took California very seriously as a farm state. Californians insisted that their state would soon soar to great agrarian heights; but there is something intangible in the climate or other environment of the state that

55

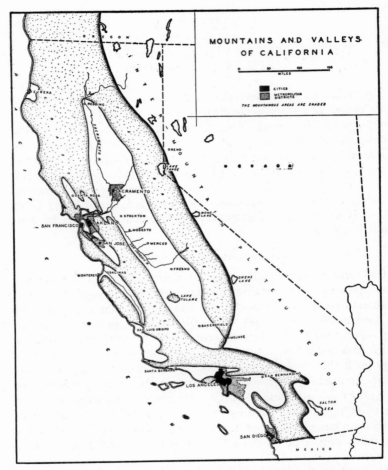

FIG. 5. The major concentrations of population are in the two metropolitan centers, Los Angeles and San Francisco, and the agricultural
areas of the valleys. Secure a road map and railroad map of California
and show how natural features have affected the distribution of transportation facilities. How far is California from the center of population
(near the western border of Indiana)? What effect will improved air
transportation have upon California economic development?

makes each oil well look as if it would be a gusher, every village a metropolis, every peach tree an orchard. Californians are incurable optimists—about California. And here, as in so many cases, they were right. Their farm production increased faster than that of any other state. By 1924, California had joined the élite among farm states, rich Iowa and Illinois, and much larger Texas. By 1929, its gross farm income was 6 per cent of the national total. It had passed Texas which had been second or first in agricultural production for decades. In the early 1930's California achieved first place in agriculture, and it has since been running a close race with Iowa and Texas for national leadership.

The reasons for California's rapid rise in agriculture are not hard to discover. Its farmers were able to sell more products both at home and in other states. The home population increased rapidly. In 1910, the state had 2,378,000 people; in 1920, 3,427,000; and in 1930, 5,677,000—an increase of 139 per cent in twenty years! In the same period the nation's population increased 33 per cent.[1]

Other states also began to demand more California fruits and vegetables. In the first place, American cities had grown rapidly. In 1910, the population of the United States was 45.8 per cent urban; by 1930, it was 56.2 per cent. America had become an urban nation. Many farmers' sons and daughters moved into the more attractive cities. America began to live in apartments, not bungalows. Food came from the grocery store, not the garden. The can opener became the most used article of kitchen equipment. And California sold more fruits and vegetables.

A second change was perhaps even more important in expanding the national demand for her products. This was a change in diet. Almost overnight in the decade of the 1920's America became fruit and vegetable "conscious." Babies have lived on cow's milk since the dawn of history, but the modern infant must also have his daily orange juice, followed later by prune pulp and the detested (but beneficial) spinach—all California products. How the California truck gardener must have smiled when he first beheld the big, brawny man from the Great Plains steak-and-potatoes-for-breakfast belt demanding a salad with each meal! Hollywood told us to stay thin—on California grapefruit and spinach. We became healthier, more sylphlike; and California, which grows

---

[1] Estimates for 1935 place the California population at about six million persons.

more than one-quarter of our vegetables and one-third of our fruit, became a great agricultural state.

There is still another factor which has helped the California farmer market his products. I expect some day to see the state of California erect a monument to the lowly tin can. Without modern canning the Pacific states' fruit and vegetable industry could never have become half so great. Distance makes the shipment of fresh fruits and vegetables to the eastern markets nearly impossible. Canning was practiced in California in Civil War days but the process was not very satisfactory until improved in the 1890's; and canned goods have not been whole-heartedly accepted as substantially equal to fresh products in food and vitamin content until comparatively recent years. California now has more than one-quarter the entire national canning industry, nearly three times that of the second state, New York.[2]

Other Farm Industries.—The reader must not be misled by California's outstanding fruit and truck production into believing that its farms raise nothing else. The state has six million people, nearly three-quarters of whom live in cities and towns. Regardless of Hollywood, these people cannot live on fruits and vegetables alone. It would be especially unprofitable to import such perishables as milk and eggs. Dairy and poultry farms are numerous near the cities. Sheep-raising is important, likewise the raising of field crops in certain sections. In 1935, about one-third of the state farm income was derived from crops. Fruits and vegetables accounted for about two-fifths of the total. Most of the remaining crops and animal products are consumed locally. Dairy products and hay account for about one-quarter of the total. California consumes nearly all its dairy-farm production. *Commercially,* California is known chiefly for its fruits and vegetables.

AGRICULTURAL DISTRICTS

The California agriculturalist tills his land and tends his flocks in a hundred rich, mountain-enclosed valleys. These lowlands, great and small, may be divided into three groups:

1. The Great Valley of Central California, largest and greatest of them all, producer of nearly half the state farm output.

---

[2] More recently, quick-freezing processes have had a similar economic effect. California is also the leading source of frozen fruits and vegetables.

2. The Coastal Valleys of California, small, mountain-separated, their long, narrow floors generally running parallel to the coast. More than a score are large enough to appear on the state agricultural map. The combined farm output of the coastal valleys is about one-fifth of the state total.

3. The Lowlands of Southern California, south of Point Conception and west of the San Bernardino Mountains. These rich valleys, coastal plains and old delta lands produce about one-fourth of the state total of agricultural commodities.

Practically all of the farming of the California section of the Pacific Region is carried on in these lowlands. Indeed, the entire remainder of the state, parts of which are outside this region, has less than one-tenth the state's farming. The California farmer is a valley farmer.

The Great Valley.—The Great Valley is correctly named. It is great not only in size (15,000 square miles) but in farm production as well. Alone it accounts for nearly half the agricultural output of California. The valley has long been great as a farm region. The earliest settlers used it as winter pasture for immense herds of cattle and sheep. A second generation turned it into a vast productive wheat field. In the hands of the present generation it has become still greater as a producer of fruits and vegetables, the products for which California is famous.

It will be recalled that the surface of the Great Valley is almost dead flat, that its soil is generally good, and that it is drained by two sluggish rivers which meet near San Francisco Bay to form a low, marshy delta, much of which has been reclaimed for agriculture by the construction of levees and dikes. It will also be recalled that the rainfall in the northern (Sacramento) portion is heavier than in the southern (San Joaquin) section, and that the adjoining Sierra Nevada receives more winter snow and can provide more water for irrigation in the north than in the south. These factors have an important bearing upon agricultural development, because water is California's great natural deficiency.[3]

---

[3] Easterners are surprised at the prominence given news items concerning snowfall in the Sierra Nevada. The Californian watches these snowfall figures as a broker watches the ticker tape. For this winter's snow is next summer's irrigation water. If the snowfall is light, the farmer must face a short crop, a reduced income. The merchant stocks his shelves less heavily, the jobber anticipates reduced sales to retailers, the banker reduces the credit ratings of his customers. A water shortage affects everyone.

The Water Problem.—The water problem of the Great Valley is confined chiefly to the southern portion of the district, the San Joaquin Valley whose six million arable areas constitute roughly one-third of the California land suitable to agriculture and include half the state's irrigated farm land. Its great problem is the shortage of irrigation water, a deficiency which becomes especially acute near the end of the dry California summer. Conditions are being improved through the construction of dams and reservoirs in the Sierra canyons. These reservoirs store the precious flood waters of winter and spring, most of which formerly rolled down the river in a useless spring deluge, leaving only dry irrigation ditches and thirsty fields in the ensuing fall months. With storage reservoirs, these flood waters are captured and released gradually during the time of need. As each dam is constructed the valley farms below become more certain of their water supply. But even when all are built and every drop of Sierra water is saved, there will not be enough water to irrigate more than half the good land.

If the San Joaquin Valley is to be fully developed, it must import water from some other watershed. Irrigation authorities think this can be done by capturing the excess water of the Sacramento Valley and transporting it to the drier basin of the San Joaquin. The Sacramento basin has less than half as much good land as the San Joaquin. But it has more rain and more water, enough water to irrigate its farms, maintain navigation on the Sacramento River, and care for the San Joaquin deficiency as well. But how can it be transported?

Many schemes have been suggested for bringing water into the southern end of the valley. Canals have been suggested, but the expense is appalling. A more practicable plan apparently is to stop the flow of the San Joaquin River in dry seasons by the construction of a series of low dams. At each dam will be a pumping station for the purpose of lifting water from the lower to the upper level. The idea of reversing the flow of the San Joaquin River is not so fantastic as it may seem. The fall of the river is so slight that the job can be taken care of by lifting the water a total of only 160 feet in 160 miles. This project will cost more than a half-billion dollars, but it will nearly double the irrigated area. A large dam at the northern end of the Great Valley will regularize the flow of the Sacramento River, and another northwest of

Fresno will capture flood waters to irrigate the southern San Joaquin Valley.

Farm Organization.—Great Valley farms represent two very different types of agricultural economy. One of these is the large, unirrigated ranch reminiscent of frontier days; the other is the small, irrigated, intensively cultivated garden plot symbolic of the modern era. As in frontier days the unirrigated farm must be large in order to support a family. Five thousand acres is not an uncommon size. In 1930, roughly two-thirds of the California farm land was in farms of one thousand acres or larger, but less than 4 per cent of the total *number* of farms were of this large size. The large ranch serves as winter pasture for cattle and sheep, and its cultivated sections grow the drought-resistant small grains, barley and wheat. Production per acre is small, and despite the large areas represented, these farms do not contribute greatly to the farm income of the state.

The irrigated farm presents a different picture. It is small, high priced, intensively farmed, and has a large production per acre. Thirty acres is about all that can be managed adequately by one family. In 1930, nearly two-thirds of all California farms had fewer than fifty acres, and one-fifth of them had fewer than ten acres each. Raising fruits and vegetables requires much labor, and the farmer who has five or six acres of grapevines, or spinach, or peach trees, or pecan trees finds his time well occupied. Despite the general adoption of the tractor and other modern forms of farm machinery, the valley farmer can manage only a few acres.

As a consequence of the smallness of the average irrigated farm, these districts can hardly be classed as rural. Rather they are suburban.[4] Homes are close together, so close that a large percentage are cheaply served with electricity, city water, store delivery, and many other conveniences of urban life. The tourist who drives among these orchards and gardens is apt to feel that he is constantly in the suburbs of some city. Yet within a mile he may abruptly lose sight of the deep green of growing fruit trees and garden truck and find his gaze resting upon the dry, yellow stubble of a vast wheat field which stretches endlessly to the mountainous horizon, its monotonous flatness broken only by one or two widely spaced ranch houses.

Products.—The traveler who journeys the 400-mile length of

---

[4] Sociologists employ the term "rurban" to describe such areas.

the Great Valley becomes accustomed to such contrasts. Entering the north end of the valley he first sees many fields of grain, many acres of winter pasture for sheep. Journeying southward he encounters at more and more frequent intervals orchards of prune, peach, and pear trees. North of Sacramento his attention is attracted to the rice fields, swampy river flats reclaimed during the high food prices of the World War at costs as high as $150 an acre. The river bottoms are alkaline, unfit for most crops, but when reclaimed grow a good quality of Japanese rice. Americans care little for this variety of rice however, and three-quarters of the crop is exported, chiefly to Hawaii and Puerto Rico. The tourist finds the rice fields interesting and unique, but after all they grow less than 1 per cent of the world production of this great staple and less than one-sixth of the small American crop. The orchards, vineyards, and vegetable gardens are far more important.

South of Sacramento the tourist enters the rich delta country inland from San Francisco Bay. Here, in the "Holland of America," hundreds of swampy acres have been reclaimed by dikes and levees for the production of trainload after trainload of succulent asparagus, celery, spinach, and a long list of other vegetables. Here too are many dairy and poultry farms which profit by their nearness to the cities of San Francisco Bay. The delta district is the center of the section which produces most of the vegetables and a large portion of the fruits of California. Its cities have many canning factories.

The tourist continues southward. Consulting his map at Stockton or Modesto he discovers that he has seen only about a third of the Central Valley and is now entering the larger and drier San Joaquin Valley. The irrigated orchards and gardens continue, alternating with large areas of flat pastures, green in winter and stocked with sheep or cattle, but dry, brown, and deserted in summer. Approaching Fresno, vineyards become more common, long rows of grapevines between which are trays of grapes being dried into raisins by the rays of the blazing, never-failing California summer sun. Fresno is the raisin center of the world, home of the famous cooperatively marketed Sun-Maid raisins, relished alike by Englishman, American, and Oriental. At Fresno the tourist also encounters his first large orange groves and the new fields of long-staple cotton. This district produces only about 1 per cent of the nation's cotton and its orange crop is much smaller than that of the Southern California Lowland, but the output of each is increasing.

For 400 miles, as far as from New York to Cleveland, the tourist has traveled down a long flat valley. He has never lost sight of mountains, for the valley is seldom more than forty miles wide. He has seen side by side the extremes of farm land utilization, the very large extensively farmed ranch and the small intensively used fruit and vegetable farm. He has seen a truly great valley, largest American producer of vegetables and fruits and creator of nearly 3 per cent of the entire national output of farm products.

The Coastal Valleys.—Instead of touring the Great Valley the California tourist often travels famous "U.S. 101," the much-used highway which skirts the coast from Eureka through San Francisco, San Jose, Santa Barbara and on to Los Angeles and farthest-south San Diego. If so, his impression of California is far different. No long broad valley but a constantly changing panorama of mountains, small valleys, sea cliffs, forests, sandy beaches, and barren hills constitutes his memory of the Sunset State.

The coast ranges have many fertile valleys, more than a score of which are large enough to appear on the agricultural map. All of them are comparatively small and hemmed in by mountains. Some are open to the sea at one end. All have good soil. Their climate is generally more humid than in near-by sections of the Great Valley. They have more fog and more winter rain, so that irrigation is unnecessary north of San Francisco. In most of these valleys summers are comparatively cool, much more pleasant than in the interior. Winters are mild enough to permit the growing of all varieties of temperate-zone fruits, but winter temperatures drop too low for the tender sub-tropical orange, lemon, and grapefruit.

Most productive of these valleys are those which adjoin San Francisco Bay on the north and south. North of the bay, several small river valleys are so close together that they may be considered as one. Their chief agricultural products are fruits, especially wine grapes and dairy and poultry products. Nearness to the Bay cities' million and a quarter people makes these valleys a good location for dairy and poultry farms. One small valley with nine million laying hens calls itself the "World's Egg Basket." The nursery industry is also important. A million apple trees provide a heavy output of that fruit. (But this is less than 2 per cent of the national output. The apple is our most widely produced and most valuable fruit.) Agriculture in this section has grown important partially because of the climate and soil, but chiefly because of nearness to the Pacific Coast's second-ranking center of population. These valleys account for from 6 to 8 per cent of the state's agricultural production.

South of San Francisco Bay the renowned Santa Clara Valley shares the locational advantage of being near a good market for dairy and poultry products, fruit, and cut flowers. These city-supply industries occupy most of the land in the north end of the valley. Other sections appear to the casual observer as one vast irrigated orchard. The Santa Clara Valley produces one-third of the world's dried prunes, as well as many peaches, pears, white cherries, and a heavy tonnage of beans, peas, celery, and other vegetables. Santa Clara County has more canning factories than any other county in California, and San Jose, its chief city, claims title as the canning center of the world. Seldom a week passes in winter that you and I do not eat some product of the Santa Clara Valley. Its farm production accounts for 7 or 8 per cent of the California total.

The remaining coastal valleys are generally smaller and less productive. The far-north section near Eureka is devoted mainly to dairying for local lumber camps. South of the Santa Clara Valley, the drier Monterey Bay-Salinas Valley district is especially noted for lettuce, artichokes, apples, pecans, and sugar beets. Local lettuce fields produce two or three crops a year and enable the district to ship nearly half the lettuce coming from California. Still farther south, just north of Point Conception, several small valleys are devoted to the raising of beef cattle. They also grow a large portion of the nation's flower seeds and several million dollars worth of dry edible beans (chiefly limas). Shortage of irrigation water is a serious problem.

The Lowlands of Southern California.—South of Point Conception and the San Bernardino mountains, the lowlands differ sufficiently in climate and economic activity from the remainder of California to be considered separately. It will be recalled that the climate of this section is very dry and the winters very mild. Irrigation is necessary for all crops and where water is available

the most tender of American tree crops, citrus fruits, are successful. The soil is generally good, highly productive with small applications of fertilizer. Southern California contains considerable
areas capable of more intensive cultivation: the agricultural output
probably could be doubled if more water were available.

Southern California, like the southern portion of the Great
Valley, suffers acutely from lack of water. The district has 20
per cent of the California farm land, and receives only 1 per cent
of its rainfall. At present some water is taken from small streams
which come down from the mountains, but three-quarters of the
farms are irrigated with water pumped from the underground
sands which absorb most of the excess waters from mountain
streams during flood seasons. Unfortunately, the latter source is
being used more rapidly than it accumulates. The water table (level
at which wells reach water) has been falling as rapidly as forty
or fifty feet in three years. Deeper and deeper go the wells, higher
mounts the pumping expense, and sooner or later the entire artesian
basin which underlies much of the Los Angeles plain will be
drained dry. The problem is not simple. Four-fifths of the available water from all sources is now being used and plans are
under way to save the other fifth so that not one drop may reach
the ocean. Los Angeles went first to the Sierra Nevada for water
which it brings in a 225-mile aqueduct across desert and mountain
to the city for domestic use and the irrigation of such farms as
are within its very large city limits. Now the cities of the district
have combined to obtain water for urban use through an aqueduct
from the Colorado River. Urban use is not irrigation, however;
and there is no known way to surmount the legal and economic
obstacles to provide additional irrigation water for the area.

The favored lowlands which can be irrigated produce from 25
to 30 per cent of the California farm output. Citrus fruits are
most important, but there are also orchards of peach and apple
trees, fields of celery, tomatoes and lettuce, and a heavy production
of dairy and poultry products to supply the cities. Los Angeles
County, which occupies the heart of this lowland district, is California's leading county in the production of fruits, and stands
second in the output of vegetables. More than half the county's
farms are smaller than ten acres in size. Intensive cultivation is
nearly universal.

Citrus Fruits.—The citrus groves are thickest (1) along the alluvial fans at the foot of the San Gabriel and San Bernardino mountains, and (2) on the old delta lands of Orange County south and east of Los Angeles; but some are found in the near-by lowland of southern California. Nearly all the American lemons and fully half the oranges come from this district.

The key to the success of the lemon and orange in this region is the mildness of the winter. The lemon tree will stand no frost; and the orange, although somewhat hardier, is easily damaged. Freezing also ruins buds, blossoms, and fruit, and consequently many a grower's fortune. Here, however, science has been able to minimize the danger by (1) providing speedy weather forecasts which flash warnings of cold waves far in advance, and (2) enabling the grower, warned, to protect his grove by lighting oil-burning stoves (smudge-pots) which emit a heavy smoke that hangs over the grove as a blanket, retaining the heat and keeping out the frost and cold from above. California formerly experienced a destructive frost every ten years or so, but with modern equipment frost losses are kept at a low figure. As an added precaution, citrus groves are usually located on the sloping sides of the valleys rather than on their floors. Heavy cold air sinks to the low part of the valley and usually leaves the sloping edges unfrosted. This phenomenon, known as "air drainage," permits citrus fruits to be grown on hillsides as far north as Sacramento in the Great Valley.

In general, other crops have taken second choice after King Orange has selected the most desirable sites. But all of them stand frost better than he. Areas along the coast raise tomatoes, lettuce, celery, and beans (chiefly limas, another California monopoly). Here, too, are many dairy and chicken "ranches."[5] At the eastern edge of the lowland, extending even into the foothills and canyons, are peach and apple orchards and vineyards devoted to the production of wine grapes. Most of the national production of English walnuts comes from groves scattered throughout this district.

The Perris Plain and the San Diego coast share in a small way the agriculture of the remainder of the lowland, but lack of water has limited their farm production to a small fraction (about one-eighth) of the total for the southern California section.

---

[5] A radio comedian observes, "Around Los Angeles, two or more acres of anything constitute a ranch—in fact, two or more chickens make a chicken ranch."

THE MARKETING PROBLEM

No farm district in the world has a more acute marketing problem than the valleys of California, and no group of farmers has battled more valiantly or successfully with the vagaries of nature and economics than the growers of California fruits and vegetables.

Fruits and vegetables are the most difficult to market of all farm products. In the first place, marketing is expensive. These products are perishable and there is frequent spoilage in transit. Furthermore, they are bulky and must be shipped in expensive refrigerator cars. As a consequence of their bulk and perishability, fruits and vegetables travel at high transportation rates. In the second place, the market is easily glutted. Production expands so easily that a small rise in price often results in greatly increased outputs and oversupplied markets. More orderly marketing through storage of surpluses is either impossible or very expensive.

Experiencing these difficulties, maximized by their distance from eastern markets, California fruit and vegetable growers early organized themselves into cooperative societies whose chief purpose is the marketing of their products. The California grower of raisins, or oranges, or walnuts, or peaches, or nearly any other crop, typically holds membership in an organization which literally takes the crop off his trees and carries out all the complicated work necessary to get it to the eastern retailer. It provides laborers at picking time, trucks for hauling, and machinery and men for spraying. It gathers the fruit, grades, packs, sells, and ships it; then advertises its merits in the national press and on the billboard. All of these services it performs at cost. Yet California growers have not always made money. The specter of overproduction constantly lurked in their midst, and in the depression following 1929 it struck hard, turning many a prospective profit into a loss.

The organization which discovers that its production is expanding faster than the markets for its goods has three alternatives open. (1) It can attempt to stimulate the demand by advertising, thus disposing of its surplus to new buyers; (2) it can withhold the surplus from the market until such a time as it will be absorbed without depressing prices; or (3) it can destroy the plant and equipment which created the surplus. Business men are familiar

with all three types of control. Business-wise California cooperative associations have tried all three types. Brilliantly and successfully they heralded the merits of Sun-Kist oranges, Sun-Maid
raisins, even to the point that these brands often commanded
premiums over other products apparently just as good. They
tapped vast new markets, and made possible greatly increased
sales. But that was not enough. Nature was bounteous and Californians were optimistic. Surpluses arose. Discouraged but not
beaten, they took the second course and withheld certain portions
of their produce from the market. In the 1930's, tons of these
products were allowed to wither on the vines or rot on the ground
because prices were too low to pay picking costs.

Even then, prices failed to respond and the California farmers
gloomily went about preparing to destroy parts of their plant and
equipment. Thousands of peach trees became firewood, acres of
grapevines were pulled from the ground, and the loss was appor-
tioned among the cooperating members in order that production
might be reduced to a point where all might make a profit. They
attempted exactly what industrial corporations were doing in that
same era of depression. They did what the more widely scattered
producers of wheat, cotton, and corn have been unable to do—
perfect an organization to dispose of a surplus in such a manner
as to insure a fair price for the balance. Because of their success,
advocates of the cooperative marketing of farm products have
pointed with no little pride to the operations of the California
cooperative organizations.

California Minerals

Gold, yellow gold, glistening in the sands of the tail-race of a
little sawmill in the lonely Sierra was the magnet which first
attracted large groups of settlers to California. They came by
land and water, a heterogeneous group, to found the roaring
mining camps which made California the setting for one of the
most colorful eras in all American history. For half a century after
1849, gold was the major item in California's mineral production,
and gold-miners controlled most of its politics. They staked their
claims in the gold-bearing sands of the central Sierra, and San
Francisco was their metropolis. But neither gold nor gold-miner
was destined to rule the California mineral kingdom after the
close of the century.

Far to the south, Los Angeles in 1900 had just experienced its first boom. It had doubled its population in the previous decade and now boasted 100,000 people. It sighed for new worlds to conquer. The prayer was answered in a smelly flood of crude petroleum that flowed with unexpected and promising fury. Oil had been found in California as early as 1876, but the flow was slight, the prospect disappointing. In 1899, a prospector brought in a different story. He had found oil, immense quantities of it. Another gold rush ensued, not for yellow gold but for the more lucrative black gold, the mineral that has provided the greatest game of chance of the twentieth century.

Los Angeles grew rapidly. Oil derricks sprang up everywhere, in orange groves, in back yards, even off shore in the shallow waters of the beaches. Production sky-rocketed from 4,000,000 barrels in 1900, to 55,000,000 barrels in 1910. New districts were prospected, newer, richer fields brought in. By 1938, production was 250,000,000 barrels, about 20 per cent of the national output. And Los Angeles had become the fourth city in population in the United States.[6]

California's Place in the Mineral Kingdom.—Since 1923, California has regularly been one of the three leading mineral states. In 1937, its mineral production was valued at 477 million dollars, or about 10 per cent of the national total. The annual California mineral product is nearly as valuable as its entire agricultural output.

Products.—Petroleum and natural gas account for more than three-quarters of the state mineral output. The remaining quarter is made up of a number of smaller items. Gold ranks third with about 9 per cent of the state total.

Petroleum and Natural Gas.—Oil and gas frequently occur together. In early days oil prospectors often encountered the unpleasant experience of piercing a pocket of oil under such intense gas pressure that it blew machinery, oil, and occasionally men all over the near-by landscape. Efforts were always made to bring the well under control, but the machinery was inadequate and the "lucky" driller had no choice but to wait until enough oil and gas had escaped to reduce the pressure until it became manageable. In the meantime, thousands of barrels of valuable oil soaked into the arid sands, and millions of cubic feet of natural gas (our

[6] Metropolitan area, 1930. See p. 82.

"most perfect" fuel—high in heat, no ash) escaped into the atmosphere. Fortunately, the technique has been improved and much of the waste stopped. Petroleum geologists study rock formations and are able to judge with fair accuracy the approximate depth at which (if at all) oil will be reached. Forewarned, the driller may insert steel casings and operate his drill through valve-like devices which will hold any normal gas pressure until connections to storage tanks and pipe lines are made. Some wells are drilled for gas alone; in others gas and petroleum rise together. In California today the oil is piped to refineries, ocean tankers, or storage tanks, and the gas is piped to the cities for domestic and industrial use. Fully four-fifths of the city population of California is served by natural gas.

The location of the principal oil fields and the production of oil and other minerals are shown in Fig. 6. In 1938, nearly all the oil was produced in two sections: the Lowlands of Southern California (roughly 51 per cent) and near the south end of the Great Valley (about 38 per cent). Later discoveries in the latter section have increased its output. Most of the production is within the trade territory of Los Angeles, and in no small way responsible for the meteoric rise of southern California in wealth and population.

With practically no coal, the Pacific states are America's greatest users (per capita) of fuel oil, which heats the boilers of their ships, locomotives, and power plants. California gasoline is also in great demand, not only by three million Pacific coast motorists, but also by Easterners because of its superior high-test and anti-knock qualities. It also finds a ready foreign market in England and Chile. In 1938, about 88 per cent of the California crude was refined locally, and about 11 per cent was exported.

Natural Gasoline.—California produces about 15 per cent of the nation's natural gas. In general it is classified as a "wet" gas—it contains much oil in suspension. The oil must be filtered out before the gas can become satisfactory for domestic use. The resultant fluid is a high-test product known to the trade as natural gasoline. Natural gasoline may be added to crude before refining or it may be blended with ordinary gasoline to improve its combustion qualities. In 1938, California led all states in the production of natural gasoline, with more than one-third of the national output.

DISTRIBUTION OF BASIC PRODUCTION

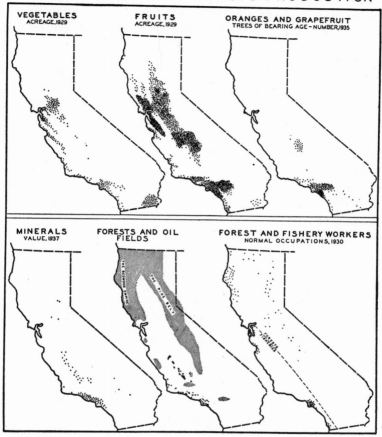

FIG. 6. The mountains of California are not suited to agricultural development, and in the southern half of the state many of the lowlands cannot be farmed because of lack of water. When more irrigation water becomes available in the San Joaquin Valley, what crops are likely to be grown? How would you subdivide California to show the prevalence of different types of agriculture in various sections? Why is the petroleum industry concentrated in the valleys rather than in the mountains? Which city has the more productive hinterland, Los Angeles or San Francisco?

Other Minerals.—Although dwarfed in value by the oil and gas industries, the other minerals of the state have great individual importance. In 1938, California stood first among the states in gold production with about one-quarter of the national total. It also led in the output of borates, chromite, diatomite, mercury, platinum, and several other minerals. California has limited deposits of coal and iron, but mines neither in commercial quantities.

The California Lumber Industry

California is a leading lumber state. In 1935, only Washington and Oregon sawed more lumber. In recent years California has sawed from 6 to 8 per cent of the annual national lumber output. This production was valued at about thirty-seven million dollars in 1935, somewhat less than one-fourteenth the value of the state's agricultural output. Nearly the entire production consists of softwoods. Although ponderosa pine is the leading variety, more eco-

LUMBER PRODUCTION IN CALIFORNIA AND NEVADA,[a] 1935

Variety	Production (Thousands of Board Feet)	Percentage of U. S. Output
Ponderosa pine.........	679,500	50
Redwood..............	328,900	100
Sugar pine............	161,200	83
Douglas fir............	95,500	2
White pine............	61,000	57
All other..............	29,900	..
	1,356,000	6.9

[a] More than 99 per cent from California. The production in Nevada is too small to be reported separately.

nomic significance probably should be attached to redwood and sugar pine, in the production of which California has a virtual national monopoly.

Producing Districts.—Although nearly all the higher California mountains are covered with forest or woodland, lumber production is important in only two sections, both with heavy rainfall: (1) the "Redwood Empire" of the coast ranges north of San Francisco, and (2) the pine belt of the Sierra Nevada and Klamath Mountains. Both are easily located on the forest map of the state (Fig. 6) which also shows the approximate number of persons employed in the sawmills of each section.

Markets.—Despite its imposing sawmill production, California imports much lumber from the neighboring Pacific Northwest. The state is such a large user of wood that its lumber production would satisfy only 60 per cent of its needs even if all California lumber were consumed at home. All California lumber is not used at home; fully one-third of it finds markets outside the state. Citizens of other states are willing to pay a premium for redwood and sugar pine lumber. Redwood is desirable because of its workability. Eastern sash and door factories use much California sugar pine. Within the state most of the lumber goes into buildings,[7] but containers for fruits and vegetables also absorb large quantities.

Future Supplies.—The time is not long past when California, in common with other lumber producers, recklessly cut down her forests without regard for future needs. In recent years, modern methods have generally replaced this wasteful cutting. Encouraged by more favorable tax laws, most California lumber companies now replant their land after the timber is removed. It is calculated that these plantings will produce good lumber in from 40 to 200 years, depending upon the type of lumber desired and the location. Even if the land were stripped completely, the present stand of timber would last at least 140 years at present rates of consumption. Inasmuch as the consumption of wood seems destined to decline rather than increase (because of the substitution of other materials), it appears that with scientific forestry California is fairly assured of an adequate supply of wood for centuries to come.[8]

Other Economic Implications.—To most of us, forests are sources of lumber and little more, but California finds them important for other reasons. The valley farmer benefits because mountain evergreens delay the melting of winter snows, serve to prevent floods, and prolong the flow of irrigation water over a greater part of the dry summer. In addition, the forests have become important summer recreation centers, cool havens of retreat for residents of the sweltering interior valleys. California provides no more beauti-

---

[7] In California 85 per cent of the city houses and 90 per cent of the farm houses are built of wood. For the nation as a whole the percentages are 78 and 90, respectively.

[8] The forest conservation problem is considered in greater detail in connection with the Pacific Northwest.

ful or restful spot than the redwood forests of the "Redwood Empire." Easterner and Westerner alike thrill at the sight of these monarchs of the vegetable kingdom which seem to be all trunk with only a tuft of leaves at the top, far overhead. Many roadside acres have been set aside as state parks where one may pitch one's tent in the cool, moist shade of these giant evergreens.

CALIFORNIA FISHERIES

California is the leading state in value of fishery products. Normally, California accounts for about 15 per cent of the value of the annual catch of fish in the United States. Many of these are consumed locally, but most of the catch goes to canneries. California cans about 45 per cent of the national output of all varieties of canned fish, including two-thirds of the sardines and nearly all the tuna fish. Despite this imposing production, the California fishing industry is small when compared to the other industries of the state. In 1935, California had only six thousand fishermen, whose product was valued at slightly less than fifteen million dollars, about one-thirtieth as much as the state's farm products.

Location.—The fishing industry is important in four sections of the California coast. The number of employees in each location is shown in the map of California fisheries (Fig. 6). Leading fishery centers are:

1. The San Francisco Bay cities, which are the market for about 15 or 20 per cent of the state catch. Most of the fish marketed in that section are fresh fish such as flounders, crabs, and salmon. Few fish are canned.

2. The Monterey Bay district, which is important for pilchard, known commercially as sardines. This district accounts for from 10 to 15 per cent of the state output. Nearly all the fish are canned.

3. San Pedro (Los Angeles Harbor), is the leading fishing port of the state with about 35 per cent of the total catch. The bulk of the catch is made up of pilchard and tuna fish which are canned locally. San Pedro fishermen's wharves and markets are well organized and efficiently operated.

4. San Diego, which with about 25 per cent of the state catch, is essentially a center for the tuna fleets which ply the waters off southern California and near-by Mexico. It profits by

being near the latter fishing waters which provide some three-quarters of the American catch of tuna.

In general, the waters of the northern half of the California coast yield market fish; those of the southern half, cannery fish. Among the latter the most important are tuna and sardines and these constitute more than half the output of the state's fisheries.

Tuna.—Tuna fish, of which there are six varieties, are caught in the open sea off southern California and Lower California (Mexico). The catch is brought to San Pedro and San Diego for canning. With purse seine and hook and line the Japanese are particularly adept at tuna-fishing. The Japanese fishing village perched high upon poles along the shore of San Diego Bay is one of the most picturesque sights in America.

Pilchard (sardines).—On dark fall and winter nights, Italian and Japanese fishermen (in boats flying the American flag) seine the waters off southern California for the tiny pilchard, known commercially as the sardine. Pilchard are surface swimmers and are caught only in the dark of the moon. In port, they are canned, usually in tomato sauce. California sardines are larger than European types: from four to ten fill a one-pound tin. Nearly 50 per cent of the pack is exported.

THE REMAINING FIVE-SIXTHS

The reader should not allow California's greatness in the production of basic commodities to obscure the fact that only one-sixth of her people are engaged in these types of economic activity. The remaining five-sixths are busy operating stores, factories, railroads, ships, motor trucks, hotels, hospitals, theaters, taxicabs —engaging in the type of economic activity found in cities and towns.

California, more than any other western state, is a land of cities and towns. In 1930, nearly three-quarters (73.3 per cent) of its population was classed as urban as compared with 56.2 per cent for the entire nation. Only five states had a larger percentage of their population living in urban places.

In these population centers, however, large (but undetermined) numbers of people are engaged in processing and distributing the state's agricultural, mineral, forest, and fishery products. Additional large numbers are busy importing and distributing to rural areas the goods which the producers of these basic commodities consume. The farmer and the oil man must dispose of their products. Fruits and vegetables must be canned, dried, crated, and packed for shipment. Oil must be refined, lumber sawed, fish dressed and canned. And all of these must be transported to the point of consumption. Again, the oil districts must be supplied with food and clothing, the farms with tractors, automobiles, and gasoline. These processes also require "middlemen," merchants, railroaders, truck drivers. Most California cities and towns, especially the smaller ones, are composed chiefly of people in these occupations.

TRANSPORTATION

The most obvious link between the producer and his market is transportation. In California all valleys are tapped by railroads and the larger lowlands have networks of them. Only a few lines have penetrated the mountains where grades are invariably difficult and population is sparse. The railroad mileage is not large if the size of the state is considered, but it is well designed to carry on the distributing trade previously mentioned. The rail lines converge at the two large cities, Los Angeles and San Francisco, which have become centers for transportation as well as for other types of economic activity.

The highways have in most cases paralleled the rail routes, but in some instances they have penetrated the more inaccessible districts and have added materially to the transportation facilities of the state. California early became a leader in the good-roads movement, both to attract tourists and to provide a more complete marketing mechanism. The automobile is more common than in most parts of the nation. In 1936, California had 8.2 per cent of the nation's motor vehicles, slightly more than one for every three inhabitants, considerably more than the national average of one car for every four and one-half people.

MANUFACTURING

The growth of manufacturing in California in recent years has been no less rapid than other types of economic development. In 1914, California factories produced 2.7 per cent of the nation's manufactured goods. Twenty-three years later, in 1937, they produced 4.3 per cent of the national total. The industrial development of the entire United States was very rapid during these years, but California industries grew even more rapidly. In 1937, California ranked eighth among the states in volume of manufacturing. It must be remembered, however, that California has 4.7 per cent of the nation's population and 5.2 per cent of the national area. In comparison with New York or Pennsylvania, California could not be called an industrial state. Indeed, the state ships in more factory-made goods than it ships out. Nevertheless, manufacturing is the state's leading type of economic activity, nearly one and one-half times as great as agriculture, the second-ranking income producer.

California as a Location for Factories.—Among the causes which ordinarily influence the location of manufacturing establishments, the following in particular apply to California:

1. *Materials and Markets.*
   a. Manufacturers choose California locations chiefly to be near the rich Pacific coast market. Los Angeles bakes and eats more bread than any city west of Chicago. But it also has more mouths to feed. Population centers invariably attract this type of industry whose products are bulky or perishable.
   b. California has many factories which dry, can, pickle, and preserve its fruits and vegetables in order that they may be shipped to distant markets. Food-processing plants are nearly always located in farm states. Petroleum refining, based directly upon a large production of crude oil, is in this same category.
   c. California is relatively near the sparsely settled intermountain country to the east. This area is so thinly settled that factories cannot be scattered over all portions of it. California plants can serve it more cheaply than those in the eastern states because they are nearer to it.
   d. California is advantageously located with regard to the west coast of Mexico, Central and South America. Its factories can obtain raw materials from these sections and can sell goods there without having to pay tolls for use of the Panama Canal. The state is also nearer Hawaii and the Orient than the eastern states. (But Seattle and Portland are even nearer the Orient.)

2. *Fuel and Power.*—California mines practically no coal, but this deficiency is offset by a plentiful supply of petroleum and natural gas. Nearly all factory engines in the state burn oil. Heat is cheaply supplied by natural gas. In addition, California has developed its waterpower resources to the point where it boasts one-seventh the hydroelectric capacity of the nation. Many of these hydroelectric plants have been built in connection with irrigation projects. Once a dam is built to impound water for irrigation, it is a simple matter to place a turbine at its base and capture the power from the water as it flows into the spillway. Dams in the Sierra serve a threefold purpose in providing water for irrigation, water for city use, and electric power which is sent over a network of lines to all parts of the state. About 70 per cent of the state's electricity is generated by water power, most of the remainder by oil-burning steam turbines. California factories are well supplied with power.

3. *Labor.*—During most of its history, California has experienced a shortage of labor. In early decades Chinese were brought in to build railroads, cook meals, and render general domestic service. There was seldom any shortage of jobs. But with the tremendous influx of population after 1920, California began to experience its first labor surplus. Many of these people came from the eastern states. Some of them were skilled laborers, but the greater number consisted of migrant farmers from the Great Plains "dust bowl." The influx of these destitute farm families created an acute surplus labor problem during the 1930's. Wages were forced down, factory costs lowered, and California lost its magic as a place where there is always "plenty of work at good wages."

4. *Climate.*—California sunshine has brought thousands of people to the state but it has been directly responsible for the attraction of few industries. One notable exception stands out: The motion-picture industry has found the California climate better than that of any other section for its purposes. Few other industries have found it a major attraction. Whether the indirect effect, the effect of climate upon labor efficiency, will be detrimental is a matter of great controversy. Certainly California sunshine is delightful, but it is also apt to become monotonous. Climatic monotony lowers

industrial efficiency. California rejects this contention, claims its laborers are as efficient as those anywhere. The opposition replies that if so, they are still using energy accumulated in the bracing air of the eastern sections from which they so recently migrated. Apparently we shall have to wait and examine the efficiency of a second or third generation on which the climate will have had a chance to work its full biological effect.

Products.—The California industrial structure has in fact developed along the lines suggested. The leading industries are printing, petroleum-refining, canning, cinema manufacture, baking, the milling of timber products, and the building of aircraft. Printing and baking are local industries important wherever there are large population groups. Geography has made the cinema a California monopoly. Most of the other leading industries are based directly upon the local production of bulky or perishable commodities: petroleum, fruit and vegetables, and timber. The remainder of the manufacturing industries of the state show similar environmental influences. Before attempting a more thorough evaluation of California's industrial advantages, let us consider the location and development of the principal cities of the state.

CITIES OF SOUTHERN CALIFORNIA

Greater Los Angeles.—With a metropolitan area containing more than two million people, Los Angeles is one of the great cities of the world. In the United States, only three cities—New York, Chicago, and Philadelphia—can claim larger metropolitan populations. Greater Los Angeles is composed of the city of Los Angeles and a cluster of satellite cities of which the largest are Long Beach, Pasadena, and Glendale.

Location.—These cities are located in the Lowlands of Southern California and its bordering foothills. They lie (1) at the base of the San Gabriel and San Bernardino ranges in a long string eastward from the sea, and (2) for forty miles southeast along the coastal plain which stretches back from the sea a distance of fifteen or twenty miles to the Santa Ana Mountains.

Each of these cities has a separate local government, a separate retail-shopping area, frequently a local newspaper, and nearly always a fierce-burning local pride. A man from Pasadena or

Glendale is likely to resent being called a resident of Los Angeles, and vice versa. From the standpoint of the student of economic life, all of these are parts of one city, spokes in a great wheel of which Los Angeles is the hub. All are within shopping and theater-going distance of Los Angeles. They only happened to be divided into separate political units.

Elbowroom and the Transportation Problem.—More than anywhere else in America these cities have spread their residence districts over wide areas. One place is apparently as good as another for home-building, and the "land sharks" saw to it that every possible building site was laid out into city lots. People selected these lots, apparently at random. As a result, one may drive for miles through sections where perhaps every second lot is vacant. Los Angeles looks for all the world like an overgrown country town. It is the most sparsely settled large city in America. There is no shortage of elbowroom.

In the eyes of many people, Los Angeles gains from being so widely scattered. It has fewer apartments, fewer skyscrapers, less traffic noise; its residents have more gardens, more sunshine and a better chance to feel the cooling summer sea breeze than if the town had expanded upward instead of outward. On the other hand, the transportation problem has become difficult. Californians are great walkers, but you cannot walk and "get anywhere" in Los Angeles. Downtown New York has no worse traffic jams during rush hours than those created by a half-million Los Angeles workers all trying to drive their own cars home at the same time. Outside the business district transportation is rapid. These sections were built largely in the motor age. Their streets are wide and straight. In addition, there is a good network of high-speed electric lines.

The freight traffic of these cities travels over the rails of three transcontinental railroad systems and an efficient local electric interurban system. Ocean shipping moves through the ports of Los Angeles and Long Beach, adjacent and interconnected, but under separate jurisdictions. The district also has excellent air facilities.

Ocean Shipping.—The port for Greater Los Angeles is located south of the city. Part of it is in the city of Long Beach, but the major development is within the elongated boundary of the city of Los Angeles. Los Angeles is unique in being the only large Amer-

A Southern California Orange Grove. (*Courtesy Los Angeles Chamber of Commerce.*)

OIL WELLS AT THE EDGE OF THE PACIFIC OCEAN. (Courtesy Los Angeles Chamber of Commerce.)

ican city not originally settled and built upon a navigable waterway. It was not even near a good harbor. Twenty miles south was crescent-shaped San Pedro Bay which afforded some protection from the north and east, but was open to winds from the other directions. Only small boats were safe there. Eventually, the federal government constructed a sea wall from the shore and provided a third side for enclosure.

The town of San Pedro grew up along the shore and became the port for the fast-growing district. But Los Angeles was not satisfied. If it were to become truly great, it needed a good harbor. A good harbor costs much money, and San Pedro was a small town. Los Angeles became courageous, annexed a narrow shoestring of land down to and including the water front from San Pedro to Long Beach (but not Long Beach harbor). There it dug channels, constructed piers and warehouses, leased land to industrial concerns, and literally carved out of the mud one of the best harbors in the United States.

The Port.—Visit Los Angeles harbor any day in the year and you will be impressed with the activity of the place. In the outer harbor (San Pedro Bay) may be riding at anchor a score of war vessels, a like number of private yachts, dozens of tiny fishing vessels, and a few freighters. Except for a few small boats plying between their mother-vessels and the shore, there is little activity. But within the inner harbor (at Wilmington) business is brisk. Tied to a hundred piers and wharves are vessels from all parts of the world. Most of them fly the American flag, but nearly every maritime nation is represented. Each year more than eight thousand vessels enter and leave the harbor, an average of more than twenty for every day in the year.

Most of these ships call at Los Angeles to carry away southern California's great excess of petroleum products. More than half of such shipments go to New York, Baltimore, and Philadelphia, but millions of gallons go to the Orient and Australia. Incoming vessels bring chiefly lumber from the forests of the north coast or iron and steel goods from Baltimore, Philadelphia, and other eastern steel centers. In the decade 1920-29, four-fifths of the tonnage through the port of Los Angeles was outbound. More than 95 per cent of the outbound traffic was petroleum products. The incoming tonnage was 46 per cent logs and lumber, 14 per cent iron and steel goods, and the remainder a long list of mis-

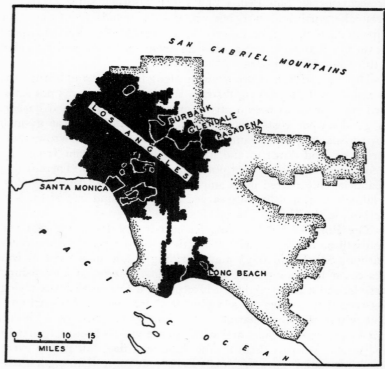

FIG. 7. The "real" Los Angeles includes not only the central city but also a number of adjacent municipalities, the most populous of which are named in this map. The stippled area bordered by a broken line is the Los Angeles Metropolitan District as defined by the Bureau of the Census. Metropolitan districts include "in addition to the central city or cities, all adjacent and contiguous civil divisions having a density of not less than 150 inhabitants per square mile, and also, as a rule, those civil divisions of less density that are *directly* contiguous to the central cities or are entirely or nearly surrounded by minor civil divisions that have the required density," according to the Census of 1930. (See *Metropolitan Districts of the United States*, United States Bureau of the Census.)

Note how the expansion of Los Angeles has completely encircled several independent municipalities. The southern extension of the city limits was made necessary by a desire to improve the harbor.

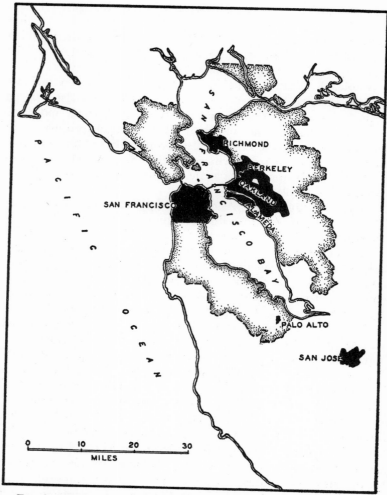

FIG. 8. The San Francisco-Oakland Metropolitan District. Note that this map and the one on the opposite page are drawn to different scales. Los Angeles covers a much larger area than San Francisco-Oakland. Why should the latter cities be so much more compact? Do you expect greater future developments in the Los Angeles area or the San Francisco area? Why? Why has Oakland grown more rapidly than San Francisco in recent years? Why should metropolitan districts such as these be considered as single economic centers?

cellaneous articles, chiefly manufactured goods. Immense oil shipments enable Los Angeles to vie with San Francisco for first position among Pacific ports. In 1936, it moved eighteen million tons, about 6 per cent of the national total, or one-third of the total for the Pacific coast of the United States.

Wholesale Trade.—The Los Angeles trade territory includes not only the rich Southern California Lowland, but also a large portion of southern Nevada and nearly all of Arizona and parts of adjacent Mexico. The volume of wholesale trade originating in this territory has made Los Angeles second only to San Francisco among Pacific coast trade centers. Greater Los Angeles has one-third of the California wholesale business, 2.2 per cent of the nation's total wholesale trade.

Manufacturing.—Los Angeles County produced about two-fifths of the California manufactured products in 1937, or roughly 1.8 per cent of the national total.[9] Greater Los Angeles is the chief manufacturing center of the Pacific coast. Oil-refining, airplane-building, and the production of motion pictures are the outstanding industries. Most of the oil is refined near Los Angeles harbor, while the cinemas come chiefly from world-renowned Hollywood, a section of Los Angeles, and "movie" capital of the world.

Most of the remaining manufacturing industries are concerned with satisfying the wants of the people of the local trade area. Important in the list of their products are bakery goods, machinery, newspapers, and magazines. Los Angeles is a leader in all these industries because it is the largest population center west of Chicago, and such articles are most economically manufactured near the market for them. This district also assembles its own automobiles and manufactures its own tires because such articles cannot be shipped profitably from Detroit and Akron. Los Angeles appears to be on the way to becoming an important regional center for the automotive industries, but the production is still insufficient to satisfy the regional market. Los Angeles manufacturing is still largely in the local and regional stage. It sends few products to national or international markets.

Recreation.—Southern California benefits greatly from its tremendous popularity with vacationists, health-seekers, and those

---

[9] These totals do not include the manufacture of motion pictures. If included, the motion-picture industry would increase the total manufacturing in Los Angeles County by about 30 per cent.

who wish to spend their declining years in the comfort of its delightful climate. There is no denying the lure of southern California. You may go there as a tourist fully convinced that it is the home of the original hundred-per-cent Ananias Club. You may have assured yourself that it could not possibly be as near perfection as the residents advertise. You may arrive with that feeling; but allow yourself a few days of the mellowing influence of the balmy Pacific breezes and you are very apt to capitulate and come away resolving, "Some day I should like to live there."

Climate is one of the great reasons for the district's rapid rise in population. Vacationists and health-seekers came, liked the place, made it their home. They came by the thousands from Iowa, from Utah, from nearly everywhere. Many of them were wealthy and contributed much-needed capital for the building of such a metropolis. More, many more, had accumulated a little money after a life of toil and hoped by living simply to enjoy the remainder of their days in the comfort of frostless winters. Then there were additional thousands of younger men and women, artisans, farmers, and laborers, who heard that here was a job, a position for anyone who would work. So many came that the jobs ran out. But nearly all stayed. They fell in love with the state, "would rather starve comfortably in California than freeze through another winter in Springfield." Each year Los Angeles has its thousands of tourists. They contribute much to the local income and they often become permanent residents. Nearly all Anglo-Saxon, they have made Los Angeles the "only truly American large city in the United States." But many of them had only small fortunes, wanted to live cheaply, would have no part in the promotional ballyhoo so dearly beloved by the up-and-coming native of southern California. Quiet and conservative, many of them added little to the glamour of the district, took little stock in its speculative enterprises.

San Diego.—This is the largest southern-California city outside Greater Los Angeles. Two items loom large on the asset side of its balance sheet: an excellent harbor and a delightful climate. San Diego is the farthest south of American harbors on the Pacific coast, and the only good harbor south of Los Angeles and Long Beach. This harbor, well protected on all sides, is an important base for the United States Navy. It also shelters the boats of tuna fishermen who make their catch off the Mexican coast. The climate is drier than that of any other Pacific coast city, and is cool in summer and mild in winter. Consequently, San Diego has become a mecca for tourists, the home of many retired and wealthy easterners. The city also profits as a tourist center by its nearness to Mexico. San Diego distributes merchandise to near-by valleys and portions of Mexico. Its manufacturing is small, kept purposely so, it is said, by the leaders in its civic affairs who have wished to maintain San Diego as a residential city.

Metropolitan San Francisco

The Great Harbor.—The reader is familiar with the many valleys which lie between the ranges of the coastal mountains of California. At San Francisco Bay nature depressed one of these valleys a little more than the rest and allowed the salt waters of the Pacific to enter a narrow pass in the outer range and cover an area some fifty miles long and from three to thirteen miles wide, at the same time flooding the mouths of the Sacramento and San Joaquin rivers. The entrance to San Francisco Bay, the world-renowned Golden Gate, is less than a mile wide, merely a break in the chain of mountains which fringe the coast and form a rugged location for San Francisco and the smaller towns of the two peninsulas. The bay itself is deep. It is large enough to float the navies of the world and it is amply protected in time of storms. These qualities have earned for San Francisco Bay the title of "one of the three best natural harbors in the world." (The others: Rio de Janeiro and Sydney, Australia.)

The military and commercial attractiveness of its site has been a potent influence in the history of San Francisco and its neighboring cities. Nature gave San Francisco a superior harbor and fitted it to become a great seaport. The city has always had its ships and sailors, its many flags and tongues, its cosmopolitan atmosphere. Since the days of its Spanish birth it has been America's "romantic Mecca of the Pacific."

Chiefly because of its cosmopolitan atmosphere, San Francisco is said by authors to be one of three great "story cities" of America, sharing the distinction with New York and New Orleans. Tourists revel in the curiosity shops of its (greatest American) Chinatown. Fiction readers delight in visiting old Barbary Coast, silent reminder of the roaring days when it was the haunt of pleasure-bound sailors, the scene of many a nautical orgy. Culinary connoisseurs tell us one can procure a meal "in any language" in the many foreign restaurants of the city. Lovers of art praise the art galleries, and musicians the symphony orchestra. Yet all of these nationalities are mere segments in the life of the city. San Francisco is not nearly so "foreign" as the cities of the Atlantic seaboard. It is nearly as "truly American" as Los Angeles. Distinctive elements do serve, however, to make San Francisco sufficiently unique that it has become dear to the heart of many a tourist.

Topography.—The western peninsulas (the "gateposts" of the Golden Gate) have little level land, but the eastern shore is more fortunate. The low peaks of the treeless San Juan Range rise steeply within five miles of the water's edge, but between mountain and shore is a gently sloping plain. San Francisco is one of the hilliest cities in America, but its sister-cities across the bay are built on smoother ground.

Land Transportation.—San Francisco wears its sea-going clothes well, but it is hardly a fashion plate for those municipalities which exist solely upon the land. It berths ships well but moves its people and goods in and out of town with considerably less efficiency. Located at the tip of a long peninsula and separated from its neighbors by its big harbor, long considered too wide and deep to be bridged, sea-faring San Francisco has forced its incoming goods and visitors to "go to sea" before they could enter its portals. Even today, only one railroad has a direct all-rail entrance and that is from the south. Railroads from the east and north maintain termini on the opposite sides of the bay and transport both freight and passengers the remainder of the distance on ferry boats, trucks, or buses. Passengers must detrain, cars of freight continue on car-ferries. The peace and quiet of San Francisco is seldom disturbed by locomotive whistles.

A City of Hills.—The backbone of hills which comprises the San Francisco peninsula would hardly have been chosen as an easy place to build a great city. Level land is relatively scarce and much that exists has been made by filling former marshes on the eastern edge of the peninsula. But here beside the great inland sea the Spaniards built their little trading post, and here grew up as if by magic the boom town of the days of the gold rush. San Francisco was never a small town; first it was a trading post, then, almost overnight, a city. Of course it was poorly laid out, with narrow, crooked streets and winding trails into the hills.

The earthquake and fire of 1906 helped the situation by so completely destroying the business section that it was possible to replat the area with a wide diagonal street as its "main stem." This thoroughfare, 120-foot-wide Market Street, is one of the famous business streets of the world. Practically, it solved the traffic problem. San Francisco has little traffic congestion. Some of its streets are so steep that ordinary street cars are useless and cars are propelled by underground cables. There are also two (competing) electric street-car systems, one of which has bored a tunnel 12,000 feet long under the mountainous backbone in order to reach residential sections on the west side of the peninsula.

The East Bay Cities.—It was only natural that satellite cities should spring up at the rail termini on the east shore of San Francisco Bay. There topography is smoother, transportation easier, access to the interior better, and access to the great harbor nearly as good. With a natural environment superior in many ways to that of San Francisco, the cities of Oakland, Berkeley, and Alameda sprang up, grew rapidly, and soon became lusty children of the mother-city. By 1930, the string of cities which occupies the eastern shore of the bay had a combined population as great as that of San Francisco. These cities are new, modern, and ambitious. Their streets are wide and straight, their business districts spacious, their foothill residential sections models of beauty. Originally residential in character, the East Bay cities have recently come to share the industry and commerce of San Francisco. Oakland manufactures electrical goods, assembles automobiles, and cans foods. Its harbor is busy, its distributing trade large. Berkeley, best known as the location of the University of California, boasts fine homes and a large retail trade with residents of the "up-bay" cities. Most notable of the latter cities is Richmond, famous for its oil refineries and heavy shipments of oil.

Bridging the Bay.—The student must envision metropolitan San Francisco as a large metropolitan center split in half by from five to ten miles of deep salt water. On the west, two hilly peninsulas, on the east a smooth coastal plain. On the west, San Francisco, cosmopolitan business and financial center of the Pacific coast, and amusement and shopping center for the metropolitan area; on the east, the young and ambitious East Bay cities with rapidly rising institutions of finance and trade. One city, in two parts. Recently these parts have been united. San Francisco had long hoped for a bridge across the bay. But generation after generation of engineers had drawn plans, taken soundings, estimated the cost, and shaken their heads. Finally a plan was drawn to bridge not only San Francisco Bay but the Golden Gate as well. These bridges were completed in 1936 and 1937. The larger bridge spans the bay from San Francisco to Oakland by way of a small island midway between.[10]

These bridges are still so new that it is impossible to judge their effect upon commerce and economic development in the bay area. They definitely unite the two halves of metropolitan San Francisco, and remove for all time the older city's greatest geographic handicap, difficulty of access from the interior. These bridges tie the city more closely to its rich trade territory and render unnecessary the forty-minute trolley and ferry ride formerly made by the hundred thousand people who cross the bay each day.

Commerce and Industry.—With more than one and one-quarter million people, metropolitan San Francisco ranks eighth in size among the large population centers of the United States, second only to Greater Los Angeles on the Pacific coast, and almost exactly as large as metropolitan St. Louis. San Francisco is essentially a commercial city, a center for the transfer of goods and the transactions of business. As in all western cities, its manufacturing industries are only moderately developed. San Francisco's greatness lies essentially in its wholesale trade, its banks, and its shipping. In 1937, the San Francisco industrial area accounted for 1.4 per cent of the nation's manufactures. Printing, petroleum-refining, and canning are the leading industries.

Wholesale Trade.—The market area tributary to San Francisco is richer than that served by any city west of St. Louis. Loading docks at Oakland and San Francisco are piled high with a vast array of manufactured goods: machinery for the valley farmer, jackets for redwood lumberjacks, and bacon for Nevada miners and ranchers. Incoming trains and trucks bring canned foods, dried fruits, wool, and grains from the same districts. San Francisco wholesalers serve the northern two-thirds of California (including nearly all of the Great Valley) and parts of Nevada,

---

[10] This island, Yerba Buena, is a small mountain peak rising from the depths of the bay. It provides a good anchorage for the spans to either shore, but is so steep that the roadway across it must be carried through a tunnel. The San Francisco Bay Bridge thus consists of two bridges connected by a tunnel.

Oregon, and Idaho. Interior centers such as Sacramento, Stockton, San Jose, and Fresno serve portions of this territory, but more than 80 per cent of the business originates in San Francisco and Oakland. Metropolitan San Francisco handles nearly 3 per cent of the nation's wholesale trade, nearly half the California total, and more than any other Pacific coast center.

Ocean Shipping.—The shipping facilities of San Francisco Bay have been designed to care for the great variety of commodities handled there. It is said that no American port is better equipped for handling miscellaneous cargoes. Incoming products consist largely of miscellaneous manufactures from eastern cities and petroleum from the oil fields of southern California. Outgoing ships are loaded mainly with food products from near-by California valleys. The tonnage handled is greater than that of any other Pacific port.

Railroads and Highways.—San Francisco wholesalers reach their trade territory over the lines of four railroads and an excellent system of paved highways. Both rail and highway lines cover the productive valleys, avoid the difficult mountains and converge at their natural outlet on San Francisco Bay. A railroad map shows how the railroads have avoided the mountains to gain access to this harbor.

Finance.—San Francisco rightly calls itself the financial center of the West. Only four American cities (New York, Chicago, Philadelphia, Boston) regularly have a larger volume of bank transactions.[11] Here also is located the Federal Reserve Bank of the Twelfth District which includes all of the Pacific states, as well as Idaho, Nevada, Utah, and most of Arizona.

OTHER CITIES

Cities of the Coastal Valleys.—San Jose is the most notable city of the coastal valleys. In the heart of the rich Santa Clara Valley, San Jose claims to be the greatest canning center for fruit and vegetables in the United States. Because its climate is more favorable for canning operations than that of the Great Valley, San Jose packs many trainloads of vegetables and fruits from that section (especially the near-by delta district) each year.

The remaining cities of the coastal section are important chiefly as seaports or seaside resorts. Eureka mills and ships lumber,

---

[11] As indicated by debits to individual accounts.

Manufacturing Airplanes in the Los Angeles Area. (*Courtesy Los Angeles Chamber of Commerce.*)

prides itself that it has the best harbor and is the largest city between San Francisco and Portland. Monterey cans fish and is the center for a noted resort section. San Luis Obispo is an important port for the shipment of petroleum from the southern end of the Great Valley.

Cities of the Great Valley.—Great Valley factories are generally busy canning fruit and vegetables, drying fruit, manufacturing tin cans and packing boxes. Shipping agencies are busy loading and routing hundreds of carloads of these foods to markets in all parts of the United States and many foreign countries. They also ship wool, and, in the northern portion, lumber and wheat. Stores are filled with stocks of goods for sale to both farmers and urban residents. Gasoline pumps and garages are much in evidence. Great Valley cities generally fill the role of department store, service station, and shipping agency for the people in their surrounding territories.

The largest of these Great Valley cities is Sacramento, the state capital and an important distributing point for the northern half of the valley. In the heart of a rich fruit and truck section, Sacramento cans fruit and vegetables, manufactures tin cans, shells almonds. Centrally located, it is an important railroad center. Except for its stores, Sacramento's railroads are its greatest employers of labor.

Sacramento is at the head of deep-water navigation on the Sacramento River. Some forty miles south, the city of Stockton is also reached by ocean steamers on the San Joaquin River. The tonnage shipped from either port is not large, and consists mainly of local food products such as potatoes, rice, and canned goods. Stockton gives more business to its six railroads. Its industries are similar to those of Sacramento.

Fresno is the chief city and distributing center of the southern end of the Great Valley. Fresno is proud to be the "raisin capital of the world." In the south end of the valley, Bakersfield has grown large chiefly through the heavy production of oil within its trade territory.

More than three-quarters of the manufacturing output of the state of California originates in the Los Angeles and San Francisco-Oakland industrial areas. Outside these centers, most of the cities are essentially commercial, concerned mainly with trade and distribution rather than manufacturing.

SUMMARY—THE INTERPRETATION OF LOCATION FACTORS

A review of the economic development of California recalls the fact that Nature has not lavished her gifts uniformly over the length and breadth of the United States. Nature bequeathed California a mild climate with damp winters and rainless summers. The heritage also included rich pools of petroleum and a strategic location on the rim of the Pacific Ocean. There are long chains of high mountains and a variety of large and small valleys. Fish are plentiful off the coast and there are good forests in the northern mountains. Yet the rainfall is generally too small for ordinary agriculture, and the combination of rough topography and deficient rainfall conspires to limit the amount of land that can be farmed to about one-fifth the total area of the state.

Within the limitations of these natural resources, the people of California have developed an economic system with unusual characteristics. Many of their problems have been in the field of marketing. With respect to the major concentration of the American population, California's location is definitely peripheral. California and the remainder of the Pacific Region constitute the most remote American source of materials for the people of the United States. Pacific coast products require longer shipments to reach national markets than those from any other region of the United States. Isolation has been a strong limiting factor in California's economic development.

The problem is made still more difficult by the nature of the goods California can produce most advantageously. Foremost in the list are fruits and vegetables, both of which are perishable and expensive to ship. California farm lands formerly were devoted to relatively non-perishable products such as wheat and wool, plus such fruits and vegetables as could be sold locally or would stand long shipment. Before 1900, California farmers entered national markets mainly with wheat, wool, and citrus fruits. But in the ensuing years a series of developments enabled them to turn to more profitable crops. Canning and preserving processes converted perishables into non-perishables. The Panama Canal brought cheaper freight rates to eastern markets after 1914. Refrigeration processes were improved, and both railway and highway brought faster and more widespread transportation service. During the same period, the American diet underwent a decided change, aided and abetted by effective advertising by California producers. Fruits and vegetables became more firmly established as essential items in housewives' grocery lists from coast to coast. Within a generation, technology had made possible a more profitable adaptation to the natural environment. The population grew rapidly and California became one of the three leading states in farm production.

Agriculture obviously is only one sector in the California economy. Other sectors have expanded similarly since the turn of the century. Dwindling eastern forests neared the end of their heavy production around 1900, and the nation soon turned to the Pacific coast for lumber. The discovery of petroleum and rapid popularization of the automobile brought California into a leading position among mineral-producing states. Finally, the California climate proved attractive to certain types of manufacturing industries employing outdoor operations. Among these, moving pictures and airplanes are prominent examples. In the meantime, the climate continued to attract an increasingly mobile nation. Thus California evolved from a sparsely populated mining and ranching state into an urbanized producer of specialized commodities for national markets.

At this point it seems desirable to reexamine the objectives of geographic analysis in the light of our experience with the California section of the Pacific Coast Region. Our purpose is to describe the geographic distribution of economic life in the United States in relation to existing natural and human resources. Realizing the danger of obscuring the functional pattern by too much recitation of detail, we seek to characterize the economic life of each area rather than describe it minutely. At best, we can hope to trace only the overall pattern of American economic life. This result is best attained by fastening our attention on what appear to be the key industries, the driving forces in the various geographic segments in the national economy. These basic economic activities may employ only a minor fraction of the local population, but they constitute the economic mainspring of the community and dictate to a large extent the structure of the remainder of its economic pattern. We speak of them as "dominant" economic interests, not because they dominate in any physical or moral sense, but rather because they have the greatest bearing upon the economic welfare of the community. They are the industries which one would examine first in any attempt to appraise local economic conditions.

In the California section of the Pacific Coast Region, the dominant features on the economic landscape are the fruit and vegetable industries, the oil wells and other mining operations, sawmills, fisheries, and a few manufacturing industries. It is quite true that the combined income of all these basic industries is only a minor fraction of the total for the section. A very large income is derived from wholesale and retail trade, from transportation, from banking, and the service occupations. There is a large output of manufactured goods beyond that of the few national industries just described as "basic." But these latter activities may be viewed as strictly consequent to developments in the basic groups. Transportation agencies are highly developed only because there are goods and people to be transported; and the same reasoning applies to merchandising, banking, many types of manufacturing, and certain types of agricultural development.

California manufacturing enterprises are generally of the consequent type. In other words, they are of the types we would expect to find in a section having a population of six million persons and basic economic interests such as those which prevail in California. Most California manufacturers turn out goods for localized markets. Their plants are of the types familiar in every populous section of the nation: bakeries, ice-cream factories, printing establishments, and many more whose products are in almost universal demand and whose production processes are fairly simple. Such industries are subject to decentralization and will be found wherever considerable population clusters appear. We call them local industries.

In the field of manufacturing, a local industry is one most profitably located near the general consumer market. Its products are generally classified as convenience items: they are purchased regularly by large segments of the population. Its raw materials are readily obtainable; if not locally so, they can be imported more cheaply than the finished products. Its manufacturing processes are of such a nature that they can be carried on efficiently by relatively small factory units. In other words, if a product is commonly and regularly used, if the materials can be shipped in more cheaply than the finished products, and if it is adapted to production by small-scale plants, the industry which manufactures it is subject to decentralization, and its factories will be found scattered among cities and towns throughout the country. Most common of the local industries are those whose products are perishable and therefore cannot be imported successfully from outside areas. Bakery goods, ice cream, confectionery, and the quickly obsolete daily newspaper are important perishable items whose manufacture is decentralized. These items loom large in the total industrial output for the California section. We say that their location is consequent to the concentration within the section of some six million customers.

A second type of manufacturing industry derives its location from a nearly opposite set of manufacturing conditions. It is concerned with products which can profitably be concentrated or otherwise processed before being shipped to distant markets. This group includes smelters which reduce ore to metal in order to lower marketing costs. It also includes a large number of food-processing industries which reduce either the weight or the perishability of farm products. Important members of this group are the canning and preserving industries, butter- and cheese-making, meat-packing, and similar processing industries whose function is to prepare products for shipment to markets removed from the center of basic production.

In characterizing the economic development of different sections of the United States, it is desirable to maintain a clear distinction between these consequent types of manufacturing industries and those whose locations are largely independent of local materials and markets. The location of consequent types of manufactures is subject to fairly definite generalization and prediction, once one knows the location of basic material centers and the distribution of consumers. It is not inaccurate to consider, on one hand, the smelting and refining of minerals and the canning and packing of foodstuffs as the final stage in the local production process necessary to prepare the products of local land, labor, and capital for sale in distant markets. On the other hand, it is convenient to consider the manufacture of items such as ice cream, newspapers, confectionery, and bakery goods along with the manufacture of gas and the laundry and dry cleaning industries as essential features of every concentration of population. Future changes in technology may alter the attractiveness of these factors, but for the present we had best recognize the fact that in a considerable group of manufacturing industries the manufacturers have little or no choice of location; and, conversely, these manufacturing industries arise as a consequence of the remaining local economic development rather than acting as a major cause for it. Manufacturing industries of these types cannot be considered as "key industries."

Let us now apply this type of analysis to the data for manufacturing in the state of California. In 1937, the total value added by manufacture for the state was about 1092 million dollars.[12] This total credits California with about 4 1/3 per cent of the nation's manufacturing and gives California a ranking of eighth among the states in industrial output. But should we consider California as an industrial state? Let us examine the data for individual industries. The accompanying table gives the figures for the ten leading industries, whose combined output is about 40 per cent of the state total.

LEADING MANUFACTURING INDUSTRIES OF CALIFORNIA, 1937

(Value Added by Manufacture)

	Millions of Dollars	Percentage of U. S. Total
1. Canned fruits and vegetables..............	76.2	29.7
2. Petroleum-refining......................	75.5	15.7
3. Printing—newspapers and periodicals.......	61.2	6.1
4. Bakery products........................	43.8	6.3
5. Lumber and timber products..............	41.1	8.1
6. Aircraft and parts......................	30.4	44.7
7. Machinery, miscellaneous.................	29.2	5.0
8. Printing—book, music, and job............	24.7	4.9
9. Chemicals, miscellaneous.................	21.0	4.4
10. Steel works and rolling mill products........	20.5	1.4

Further perusal of the list (which includes 213 classifications)

---

[12] Not including the motion-picture industry. The Bureau of the Census does not include figures for this industry because it is impossible to ascertain the value of its products for any given year immediately after its close. The difference between cost of materials and total production costs for the California motion-picture industry in 1937 was 141 million dollars. This figure is roughly analogous to "value added" but obviously does not include profits or losses since actual sales of a film may be spread over a period of several years. These and other data for manufacturing are taken from the Census of Manufactures for 1937.

would indicate that these leaders are fairly representative. California regularly manufactures a relatively high percentage of the national output in four of these ten industries: canning, petroleum-refining, lumber, and aircraft. It is significant that the first three of these process local raw materials. Such industries would ordinarily be located in any state producing types of basic materials which are profitably concentrated or processed before being sent to market. Among the remainder, we recognize three which always appear in population centers: bakery products and the two publishing industries. The machinery and chemical groups are so heterogeneous that classification is impossible without a more detailed breakdown of the data. (Such a breakdown seems to indicate that these industries should be included very largely in one or the other of the two groups just mentioned.) Aircraft and steel classify differently. There is no apparent, compelling reason why California should manufacture airplanes and steel rather than buy these products from other regions. The national aircraft industry is relatively young and probably has not reached that stage of maturity in which competition forces the scientific location of factories. But the California production of aircraft has grown very rapidly in recent years, and we are led to believe that the state has superior conditions for manufacturing these products. The California steel industry is likewise very young and represents no radical departure from the tendency of the steel industry to remain concentrated in the eastern states. Yet California mines neither coal nor iron ore, and we must recognize California steel as an evidence of industrialization. The aircraft and steel industries represent (so far as this list is concerned) California's claim for consideration as an industrial state.

In summary, we might say that under present manufacturing conditions, four of the ten leading California industries have grown large because of the state's partial natural monopoly in producing their raw materials. Four more have prospered because of the large concentration of individual consumers, most of whom came to California for pursuits other than manufacturing. This group may be thought of as having a monopoly on the California market for these types of goods, inasmuch as they are protected from outside competition by technological factors involving expensive transportation or deterioration in transit. But in the other

THE PACIFIC COAST REGION

two industries, aircraft and steel, California factories are in a strictly competitive sphere, for they are operating in an industry the location of whose plants is dictated by neither raw materials nor markets. In so far as a state is able to develop national industries whose locations are tied to neither local raw materials nor local markets, it may claim distinction as an industrial state.

The import of the foregoing discussion is simply to classify manufacturing industries according to dominant locational factors. A certain group of industries is almost inevitably attracted to the source of a single raw material because outside markets are served more advantageously if the goods are processed before shipment. Since these types of industries tend to occur wherever their materials are produced, we associate them with the basic form of production with which they are connected. Another large group of industries finds it possible to reach its customers more advantageously by locating plants near them. Industries of this type resemble service establishments and can therefore be considered as a nearly inevitable concomitant of the agglomeration of population. They follow the people. By distinguishing these two types of industries we are enabled to simplify the discussion of manufacturing in the chapters which follow. Most of the manufacturing enterprises of the western two-thirds of the United States are of one or the other of these consequent types.[13]

REFERENCES

Consult the list of general references for additional information concerning California's economic development. Special bulletins published by the University of California describe various phases of agricultural and business development. Reports of the state mineralogist cover recent developments in the minerals field. *Commercial Survey of the Pacific Southwest* (see Ch. 3) gives good information but it is somewhat out of date (1930). The fruit industry is described in *Fortune* for July, 1936. *The Migratory-Casual Worker,* published by the Works Progress Administration (Research Monograph VII), gives an illuminating account of the California labor problem. See also Carey McWilliams, *Factories in the Field* (Little, Brown, 1939), for a discussion of the general problems of the agricultural wage-earner.

---

[13] This discussion falls far short of exhausting the subject of industrial location. The problem is considered in greater detail in the chapters on the American Manufacturing Belt.

QUESTIONS AND PROBLEMS

1. Trace the historical development of agriculture in California.
2. Describe the agriculture of California, giving emphasis to the kinds of crops grown and the agricultural districts.
3. Discuss the water problem of metropolitan Los Angeles.
4. In what way is the Great Valley dependent upon the Sierra Nevada?
5. Describe in detail the two major types of farm organization in the Great Valley.
6. Describe the agriculture of the coastal valleys; of the Lowlands of Southern California.
7. What problems arise in the marketing of fruits and vegetables? What can be done about them? How have Californians attempted to solve these problems?
8. Name the principal minerals of California. Where are they found?
9. Name the different varieties of lumber produced in California. What is being done to replace the trees that are cut?
10. Of what importance is fishing to California? Where are the principal fisheries? What varieties of fish are caught?
11. What role do the cities and towns play in California's agricultural, mineral, forest, and fishery development?
12. Why is California a good place for the location of manufacturing? Why not?
13. What are the principal manufacturing industries of Los Angeles? How important are manufacturing and the wholesale trade to the city? What does Los Angeles offer the tourist?
14. Outline the economic activities of San Diego.
15. Where is San Francisco located with respect to Los Angeles and San Diego? What are its advantages or disadvantages when compared with these cities? What are the names and locations of its satellite cities? What important roles do they play?
16. What is the capital of California and of what economic importance is it?
17. Name and describe the "consequent" types of manufacturing. How do they figure in the California development? What grounds does California have for calling itself an industrial state?
18. Certain areas in the Central Valley of California can grow wheat better than any other part of North America, but they are devoted to other crops. Why?
19. Write a brief comparison of the probable futures of Los Angeles and San Francisco in terms of their economic resources.

CHAPTER V

THE PACIFIC COAST REGION—WASHINGTON-OREGON SECTION

The Oregon Country.—The early history of California was made by miners and ranchers, but that of the Pacific Northwest is written in terms of furs, forests, and farms. Fur trade provided the first stimulus for settlement in the early decades of the nineteenth century. The second wave of settlers consisted of farmers from the eastern states. Hard on their heels came the lumbermen to fell trees and export lumber from the "best forests on the face of the earth."

The fur-traders were few and their régime came to an end with the subjugation of the Indian and the advance of the farmer. Forest districts still yield furs but their importance is far surpassed by the output of farm and timber products.

The fertile grasslands of the Willamette Valley had achieved fame as early as 1845. Eastern church societies had sent small groups of colonists into the valley and these had found the growing of wheat, peas, potatoes, and fruit highly successful. Rainfall was abundant, winters mild, and the soil rich. Nature was bounteous, but the district suffered from lack of markets. Ships seldom entered the Columbia River and the colonists had no means of disposing of their surplus crops. The communities languished, rich in foodstuffs, but poor in clothing, tools, and machinery. Prosperity awaited the development of a market.

That discovery came in 1848, with the electrifying news that gold had been found in California. Hundreds of the colonists abandoned their fields and joined the gold rush of 1849, but most of them remained and found their first prosperity in sending fruits and grain to the San Francisco market.[1] Ships appeared in the Columbia River and the village of Portland quickly established itself as the outlet for Willamette Valley products. With markets established and prosperity assured, the valley population

---

[1] In 1852, four bushels of Oregon apples sold in San Francisco for $500; in 1853, forty bushels brought $2500. Shipments thereafter were larger, prices less fantastic, but still highly profitable.

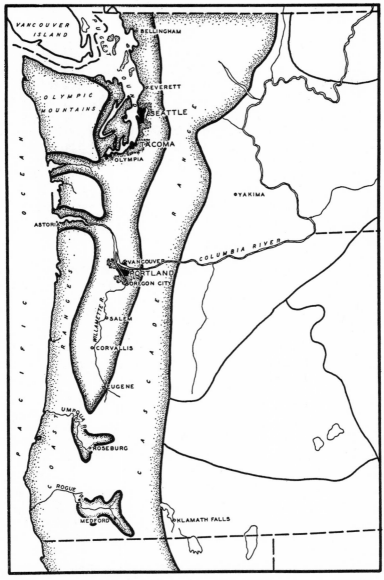

FIG. 9. The Washington-Oregon Section of the Pacific Coast Region. Like California, the Pacific Northwest has two major seaport cities and two north-south mountain chains separated by a valley. But the cities are smaller and the valley less productive. Why?

grew rapidly, spreading northward up the Cowlitz Valley to the shores of Puget Sound. Seattle was founded in 1852.

In the meantime, residents had begun to exploit their third and greatest natural resource, the forest. California demanded lumber and ships as well as food, and the Oregon country began to furnish them. Forestry became the leading occupation almost from the beginning along Puget Sound, and soon the ring of the axe was almost drowning out the hum of the reaper from Canada to California. With the coming of the railroads, Washington lumber began to appear in the eastern states whose forests were being rapidly depleted by the construction demands of the youthful nation. By 1925, the Pacific Northwest was furnishing one-third of the American lumber. Today the leading occupation in nearly every county of western Washington is lumbering or one of its allied industries. Near-by farms are devoted largely to supplying these lumber towns with butter, eggs, milk, vegetables, fruits, and other perishable food products.

The lumberjack has not attained such complete domination over the economic life of the Willamette Valley. Here natural conditions favor farming and the timbered mountains are not so productive of lumber, with the result that farmers outnumber lumbermen in most sections. But the economic life of the entire district rests in no small part upon a wooden foundation, a foundation composed of one-third of the national production of lumber.

AGRICULTURE

The agriculture of the Washington-Oregon section of the Pacific Region is carried on in (1) the Puget Trough and Willamette Valley, (2) two mountain valley districts of southern Oregon, and (3) a half-dozen small, scattered lowlands along the coast.

In 1930, about 100,000 farm-owners and operators occupied these lands. Of these, about 82 per cent lived in the Puget Trough and Willamette Valley, 8 per cent in the two mountain valleys, and 10 per cent along the coast. These percentages measure roughly the relative agricultural importance of the three principal agricultural districts. Their combined farm output is approximately 1½ per cent of the national total, about one-fourth as great as that of the state of California.

The Puget Trough.—Physiographers call the broad valley which lies between the Cascade and Coast ranges and extends from west central Oregon northward until it becomes drowned in the waters of Puget Sound, the Puget Trough. The reader will recall that it has three sections, a northern third comprising the gravelly shores of Puget Sound, a middle third which has low hills, and a southern third, the flat fertile valley of the Willamette River. The climate is similar to that of the Great Valley of California except that it is cooler both summer and winter, and much more humid. Too much rain rather than too little is the chief problem. Very few acres are irrigated, but the area in drainage projects is relatively large.[2] Summers are cool, too cool for corn, but excellent for most other crops. Winters are moderate. Frosts occur and even light snows, but temperatures almost never drop low enough to endanger fruit trees. Nearly all the precipitation falls in winter; clear summer days bring only light showers. Grass remains green throughout the winter. Pastures are excellent.

Such is the "Oregon Country," and such were the conditions of nature met by the pioneer who traveled the famous Oregon Trail. Here, after weeks on the desert, he saw again the green trees and grass of the eastern farm he had left behind. When he found the soil fertile, the winters mild, and the rainfall abundant, there is little wonder that he fell in love with the country. He planted, reaped abundantly, and prospered. Indeed, he found only one mid-western crop that would not thrive—corn. Thus, the Willamette Valley and the lands to the north early became the home of the general farm, the diversified farm with its fields of clover and small grains, and its small herds of cattle and sheep. Even today, except for the absence of corn, the average Willamette Valley farm resembles the farm of Iowa or Illinois. But the trend toward specialization which characterizes the agriculture of California has also appeared in these valleys. The Willamette Valley has found success in the growing of prunes, pears, and strawberries. To the north, the Washington farmer has frequently specialized in poultry and dairy products or the growing of berries. In consequence of this specialization, farms have become smaller, cultivation more intensive, and population more dense. With the

---

[2] The only important irrigated district is in the Rogue River Valley. Plans have been projected for additional works in the Willamette Valley to supply water during the dry summer.

passing years these trends have become more pronounced, so that today the geographer feels quite safe in classifying most portions of the Washington-Oregon section as areas of specialized agriculture, not yet so highly specialized as that of California, but sufficiently similar to have like problems of farm marketing and management.

Agricultural Products: *The Puget Sound Valley.*—The traveler who skirts the east shore of Puget Sound from Olympia northward through Tacoma, Seattle, Everett, Bellingham, and on to near-by Vancouver in Canada is impressed by the great lumber mills, the many tidal bays and drowned rivers, the great highway bridges with wooden floors, the thousands of acres of cut-over and burned-over forest, and the dense stands of Douglas fir in the state parks and national forests; but he is almost certain not to remember the district as a farm country. Many acres are not devoted to agriculture. Large areas are in swamp, others have poor soil, and the huge stumps are so expensive to remove from cut-over forest land that only the richest acres can be cleared with profit.[3] Yet the shores of Puget Sound show a large production of dairy and poultry products, enough to satisfy the large urban demand and provide a surplus for shipment to eastern markets.[4] Most of these farms are small. Dairy barns and chicken houses are much in evidence. Farms nearest the cities often specialize in vegetables or small fruits, especially strawberries and raspberries. The entire agricultural development of the Puget Sound Valley is based directly upon and remains subsidiary to the needs of the cities.

The Tacoma-Portland Area.—The hilly middle third of the Puget Trough, extending roughly from the south end of Puget Sound to the falls of the Willamette River at Oregon City (just south of Portland) is even less a farm district than the northern third. The valleys of the upper Chehalis and Cowlitz rivers provide pasture for dairy cattle, and many farms raise poultry, but neither

[3] For nearly half a century the marshes near the mouth of the Skagit River have been devoted to the growing of cranberries. This district produces about 4 per cent of the national output.

[4] Among the earliest farmers in this district were a group of Hollanders who diked the tidal lands at the mouths of the streams and reclaimed the rich flats. With a climatic environment strikingly similar to that of their native country these Dutch farmers have built up in the "Holland of America" a large production of dairy products and tulip bulbs.

of these agricultural pursuits is so highly developed as in the northern section. Near Portland, the growing of fruits and truck crops is of major importance. Just north of the city is an important prune-growing section, and immediately southward is Oregon's leading vegetable-growing area. The prunes are the Italian variety, not sweet enough for drying but excellent for canning or marketing fresh. Nearly all the vegetables are sold in the Portland markets.

The Willamette Valley.—South of Oregon City the north-flowing Willamette River meanders across a flat valley famed for nearly a century for its richness. Nearly all the valley is farmed. Willamette Valley farmers raise dairy cattle, a few hogs, sheep, and chickens. They grow the small grains, a little corn for forage, half the nation's hops, and nearly all its flax for fiber. But the valley is most famous for its fruit, especially its prunes, pears, and strawberries. The Willamette Valley is one of the nation's leading sources of sour prunes (for canning or marketing fresh) and late strawberries. Fruit-growing is a major farm industry in many sections of the valley, but nowhere is it dominant. Specialization is far less than in many of the valleys of California. The Willamette Valley is best classified as an area of mixed farming, with dairy products, fruits, poultry products, and wheat as the major sources of income.

The Valleys of the Umpqua and Rogue Rivers.—These valleys in southern Oregon are small and isolated, but of sufficient agricultural importance to warrant separate consideration. The Umpqua Valley is especially famous for its prunes, the Rogue River Valley for its pears. The pasturing of beef cattle is important in both sections. Irrigation is generally unnecessary in the high valley of the Umpqua, but is almost universal on the crop lands of the lower and drier valley of the Rogue River.

The Coastal Lowlands.—Those portions of the coastal lowlands which are devoted to agriculture consist principally of the land near the mouths of the many rivers which reach the Pacific from the rainy coast range. Many of these areas suffer because of inadequate transportation and distance from large urban markets. Consequently, the raising of dairy cattle is the major agricultural interest. The long rainy growing season produces good pasture and has encouraged the development of dairying. Too far from urban markets to deliver fluid milk, the Oregon coast has become specialized in the manufacture of cheese. Farther north, the urban population is larger and most of the product is sold as fluid milk or butter. The farmed portion of the coastal lowlands consists of a narrow strip of land, seldom extending more than five miles back from the seacoast.

In review, the agricultural development of the Washington-Oregon section of the Pacific Coast Region reveals definite responses to the natural environment. The long growing season and abundant rainfall make the section a good pasture area. Except in the Willamette, Rogue, and Umpqua valleys, soils are of such a nature that crops are not generally profitable. Where local urban markets are available, the most advantageous use of agricultural land is in dairying and poultry. Along Puget Sound, these markets are provided by the numerous seaports and saw-mill centers. The agriculture of the Puget Sound Valley and the Tacoma-Portland section of the Puget Trough is specialized in these city-supply types of agriculture. Along the Oregon coast, dairying is also important, but in this section the main product is cheese rather than fluid milk.

The valleys of the Willamette, Rogue, and Umpqua rivers are drier, warmer, smoother, and richer than other portions of the section. Grain farming is successful and many farmers grow fruit for market. Willamette Valley farmers receive their incomes from the sale of dairy products, fruit, poultry products, and grain, and thus classify the district as a mixed-farming area. The Umpqua and Rogue River valleys are more highly specialized in fruit-raising. Most of the farms north of Portland are specialized in providing dairy and poultry products for near-by cities, while those south of Portland produce for regional or national markets.

FORESTS

The northern half of the Pacific Region is a land of big trees. Giant Douglas firs, giant cedars, and giant redwoods originally crowded the moist mountain slopes and the floors of all but a few valleys[5] from Canada to San Francisco Bay. Favored by nature with abundant moisture, these forests have the densest stands

---

[5] Notably the Willamette, Umpqua, and Rogue River valleys of Oregon, none of which was originally in forest.

and largest trees to be found in North America.[6] Located near the ocean and on ground generally not too rough for easy transportation, they constitute the richest and most accessible source of lumber on the continent, if not in the world.

Types of Trees.—The mighty Douglas fir is preeminent throughout the territory west of the summit of the Cascade Range. East of the summit are thinner stands of ponderosa pine. The higher lands near the summits have valuable stands of spruce and true fir. Southern Oregon has a considerable area in sugar pine and (near the coast) a few redwoods and the valued Port Orford cedar.

All of these woods are classified as softwoods, the product of coniferous trees. The heavy production of Douglas fir lumber goes largely into the building trade. Carpenters find it fairly hard, strong, durable, inexpensive, and rather difficult to work, but excellent for heavy construction. The softer, lighter and finer spruce is used for interiors and in the making of boxes. Ponderosa and sugar pines resemble spruce, are light, easily worked, and valued for interior construction and box manufacture.

The durable, close-grained Port Orford cedar is a specialty among woods, highly desired by manufacturers of boats and woodenware. A considerable production of western red cedar is made into shingles, telephone poles, and fenceposts. Redwood is used for interiors as well as for wood pipe, silos, and other products where decay-resistant wood is desirable.

History and Location.—Although the Pacific forests were early recognized as a rich potential source of lumber, distance from the eastern markets retarded their exploitation until nearer sources were exhausted. For nearly three centuries after the founding of the American colonies, the excellent forests of the

---

[6] Big trees have long been a source of controversy. If bigness means bulk, the redwood is preeminent. A single California redwood has yielded 360,000 board feet of lumber, enough to build twenty-two average five-room houses. In height, however, the redwood must yield to the thinner-trunked Douglas fir. Redwoods will grow to a height of 360 feet, but Douglas fir trees twenty feet higher have been measured, and foresters claim to have cut one specimen measuring 417 feet. Apparently these are the world's tallest trees, about as tall as a forty-story building. Redwood forests generally have the thickest stands, with Douglas fir in second position. Yields of 250,000 board feet per acre are common in redwood forests, 40,000 board feet per acre in Douglas fir districts. Maximum yields per acre for the former are well over a million board feet; for the latter, 150,000 board feet.

northeastern part of the country proved adequate to supply the building needs of the growing nation. Those forests were rich, accessible, but not inexhaustible. Near the end of the past century their end was in sight and production began to shift to the southern states and the Far West. It was not long until the populous East was not cutting enough lumber to satisfy the needs. Along the west coast production was first centered in the Puget Sound district. Washington became the leading state in lumber production in 1905, and except in one year (1914) Washington has held this distinction ever since. California and Oregon rose more slowly.

Two factors account for Washington's leadership in lumbering: an abundance of excellent timber and accessibility. Not only were her forests unexcelled in area, density of stand, and quality of product, but they were also easily reached by water and land transportation. More than half the original forest area (the richer half) was within fifty miles of the manifold channels of deep Puget Sound and the remainder was located chiefly in broad valleys or on low hills. Nearly all the large lumber mills of Washington have been built on tide-water with easy access both to forests and to ocean steamers.

Oregon, with nearly as large areas of good timber as Washington, lacked its splendid accessibility and consequently developed its lumber industry more slowly. With many Washington areas already cut over, Oregon now has the largest timber reserves of any American state, is already in second position in lumber production, and promises continued advancement.

Lumbering.—Regardless of species, lumbering operations are similar throughout the territory. These operations consist of cutting, hauling to the mill, sawing, processing, and milling.

1. A tree is felled by first cutting a notch with an axe, then finishing the cut with a two-man crosscut saw. Mechanical sawing is not common, but portable sawing machines are being introduced.

2. "Donkey" engines are used to skid the logs to near-by temporary railroads which take them to tide-water sawmills where they are kept in log ponds until needed.

3. The modern mill is a marvel of mechanization. First the logs are elevated to the second floor, then fed through a

variety of sawing machines which remove the bark, saw the log into lumber, and cut off the ends in even lengths. Over all these machines stands the sawyer, an expert judge of timber. From his platform the sawyer plays constantly upon a maze of levers and foot pedals, directing the machine which whisks the log back and forth until it finally emerges cut into a variety of sizes of lumber as planned by the sawyer from his first examination of the log.

4. Processing is essentially seasoning, done usually in steam-heated kilns from which the lumber emerges ready for the planing mill or market, depending upon its prospective use.

5. The planing mill may only serve to dress lumber by smoothing off the rough saw marks, or it may be a complete factory from which emerge doors, window frames, and other mill-work.

Shipping.—Although much lumber is consumed in the Pacific states, most of the product is shipped to the Atlantic seaboard by rail or boat. Forest products have long held an important position in the east-bound traffic of the northern transcontinental railroads. Large quantities of lumber also reach the eastern states over the longer but cheaper water route through the Panama Canal. Considerable quantities are exported. Lumber is the leading article of export from every port in the Pacific Northwest.

The Future.—With its greatest resource constantly being cut down and hauled away and little or no attempt being made to build up new supplies, the Pacific Northwest long ago began to ask itself, "What will happen when the forests are gone?" The problem has two phases: conservation (wise use) of existing timber, and the building up (through forestry) of new supplies. Both phases have received strong support from national and state governments. Conservation is concerned with the elimination of waste and the encouragement of efficient and economical use of existing timber. Forestry contemplates the replanting and reestablishment of denuded forest lands.

The conservation movement is scientific management applied to a great social resource. "Wise use" is its motto and it contemplates every segment of the lumber industry from tree to consumer. Its worthiness is undenied. Each year since colonial days more forests have been cut than were grown; and today the end of the forest is in sight. Remaining resources must be used wisely to avert a timber famine.

Conservation begins in the forest. It demands that only good, full-sized lumber trees be cut and that they be removed with a minimum of damage to the smaller adjacent trees. It demands that forest fires, our "most wasteful and devastating agency," be prevented through constant vigilance. National and state governments have done much to lessen the fire hazard.

At the mill, conservation recommends the use of as much of the tree as is feasible. Typically, only 55 per cent of the volume of a log comes out as useful lumber. The remainder consists of bark, slabs, sawdust, edging, trimming, and other odds and ends used in most mills as fuel. Many of these by-products have had little value, but modern lumber producers are finding many ways to turn them into valuable goods such as short-length lumber, lath, and pulp for paper and insulating board.

Heavy waste also occurs in wood utilization. Most wood is too valuable to use as fuel, but nearly as much timber is consumed as fuel as for lumber. With rising wood prices, this use is decreasing and other fuels are being substituted with consequent savings in timber. Additional savings have been made through the substitution of metal and fiber in the manufacture of boxes, furniture, and other articles formerly made of wood. Concrete, brick, steel, and stone have continued to form an increasingly large percentage of the materials used by the construction industry. Indeed, the substitution of other materials has of late become so widespread that the lumber industry, seriously cramped by declining markets, has found it desirable to advertise the good properties of wood in order to persuade people to use more of it.

The general substitution of other materials has reduced the rate of consumption materially in recent years, but it has not solved the problem. In 1930, the Washington-Oregon section had nearly half the remaining saw timber of the United States, but forestry experts said that trees were being cut ten times as fast as new ones were growing, and predicted exhaustion within a generation. Modern civilization has discovered many ways in which other materials can be substituted for wood, but there remain dozens of uses for which no substitutes are available. And even if we could get along entirely without wood, there would still be a great need for trees to prevent erosion, provide recreational facilities, reduce flood hazards by delaying the melting of snow, and for other indirect uses.

Economic Importance of the Forest.—It is difficult to over-emphasize the importance of the forest in the economic life of Washington and Oregon. Approximately three-fifths of these states' factory workers are employed in industries using forest products as raw materials. Forest products fill two out of every three freight cars leaving the states, and provide two-thirds of the tonnage of water-borne commerce bound for the Atlantic sea-board. Local residents have become very active in recent years in promoting forestry and conservation. Theirs is a battle to conserve a resource which in some years provides almost half the total income of the Washington-Oregon section of the Pacific Region.

Recognition of the seriousness of the forest problem has led to action by both federal and state governments. Early in the present century, Congress began to set aside large areas of forests in all parts of the country in which lumbering was to be carried on systematically and scientific forestry practiced. Practical scientific forestry contemplates the planting of new trees as fast as the old ones are removed, and the selective cutting of old trees to insure a constant, unending supply of new timber. It considers timber not as a *mine* to be worked, destroyed and abandoned, but as a *crop* to be cared for and kept in continuous production.

Conservation and Forestry in the Pacific Northwest.—All of these methods have been applied to the forest problem in Washington and Oregon. The generally moist climate makes the forests somewhat less susceptible to fire than are those in the drier sections of the country, but the hazard nevertheless is great and practically all sections are patrolled by rangers. National forests have been established over large areas. Lumber companies, some of which are huge corporations with millions of acres of forest land, have done much to reduce waste in logging and in manufacture. Tax laws have been modernized but still bear entirely too heavily on forest land.[7] Progress along all these lines has been

---

[7] The tax problem is acute in every forest state. Under the general property tax, forest lands are assessed *each year*, regardless of whether timber is cut. Tax economists agree upon the unsoundness of such a tax, advocate instead a *severance* tax to be levied only upon the timber at the time of cutting.

As an illustration of the unfairness of the general property tax, assume that the timber is valued at $100 per acre, the tax one-tenth of one per cent. Under

encouraging, but there is no indication that the problem has been solved. Apparently it is only a question of time until a great many of the big mills, largest industrial employers in the Pacific Northwest, will be forced to close down. The future is still darkened with the smoke of dozens of annual forest fires, and the landscape is blackened with the gaunt, ruined trunks of burned-over forests. A future generation, confronted with high lumber prices, will replant these forests, perhaps extend the national forests to include all potential timber land, and restore to this district its supremacy as a timber-growing region. But in the meantime, the thoughtful resident still wonders, "What will happen when the timber is gone?"

FISHERIES

The names of North Pacific cities have long appeared prominently on the labels of the various sizes, shapes and grades of canned salmon which find an important place on every American grocery shelf. Pacific coast salmon have been considered a delicacy since the days of the Indian, and shipments of dried, canned, or frozen salmon have left the ports of Washington and Oregon for nearly a century.

A peculiar habit of the salmon makes it unusually easy to catch. These fish, born in the cold headwaters of mountain streams, early swim down to the ocean to spend their years of growth (from two to six years) in salt water. Finally, the salmon again ascend the river of their birth to spawn. At this season huge schools of them crowd the river mouths and these "cattle of the sea" ascend the streams almost in a body. The "run" may last a few days. It occurs every year, but at different times in different streams. Certain species, such as the Chinook, king of the salmon, can be counted upon for a "big run" only once in three years. The pink varieties run more frequently. The fisherman is skilled in the knowledge of all these movements, knows with remarkable accuracy the best time to fish in certain streams. But the job is all

---

the best management it takes fifty years to mature a "crop" of timber. At the end of fifty years an annual tax of only ten cents per acre with interest at 6 per cent compounded annually will amount to $29.03—nearly 30 per cent of the value of the timber—a tax so high that it encourages early cutting and abandonment, for the land frequently is worth little or nothing for agriculture. It is encouraging to note that these states have recently reduced the tax on reforested areas to a minimum rate.

too certain, too easily overdone. Salmon fishing *was* overdone in Oregon and Washington. Too many fish were caught, not enough left to lay eggs. Eventually the federal government set up regulations designed to limit the catch and prevent the complete exhaustion of this valuable resource. In the meantime, however, the productivity of these waters was greatly reduced, and the world now depends for the major portion of its salmon not upon Washington and Oregon, but upon Alaska and British Columbia. Salmon still constitute half the local fishery output, and the Washington-Oregon coast was able, in 1935, to report 10 per cent of the national fishery output. Other varieties of fish come chiefly from Puget Sound, whose halibut and small but delicious Olympia oysters add to the variety of seafoods on the tables of near-by cities. The Oregon fishery output consists mainly (75 per cent) of Columbia River salmon.

The salmon fisherman utilizes a variety of equipment. About one-quarter of the fish are caught by old-fashioned hook and line equipment, but most of the catch is taken in nets, half in gill nets, most of the remainder in haul seines so heavy that horses are generally used to pull them to shore. His catch landed, the salmon fisherman turns his motor boat toward one of a dozen cities along Puget Sound or the Columbia River where salmon canneries form an important (but seasonal) element in the local industrial structure. At the cannery, the salmon are fed into the "iron chink," an almost human machine which cleans fish at the rate of sixty a minute, then along moving belts to workers who cut them up, seal them in cans, and cook them. The process is rapid and almost completely mechanized. In 1935, the Washington-Oregon fishing industry employed 14,000 fishermen, 1300 cannery operatives.

Cities

Cities Along Puget Sound.—The heavy production of lumber, farm, and fishery products of the Pacific Northwest was certain to lead to the growth of urban centers interested primarily in processing these products and forwarding them to distant markets. Certainly also it might have been foretold that many of these centers would develop along the shores of Puget Sound. The deep salt waters of this arm of the sea extend far into the district of most accessible timber. Its shores were early dotted with sawmills which formed the nucleus of many a frontier village that later achieved greatness as a seaport and commercial center. Additional advantage accrued from the fact that these seaports are nearer the Orient and Alaska than other Pacific cities—nearer by two or three days than San Francisco and Los Angeles. Finally, these cities had along the shores of Puget Sound spacious and deep harbors unequaled in natural advantage at any point north of San Francisco Bay. With a productive hinterland, a strategic location in foreign trade, and excellent harbor facilities, the Puget Sound cities were well equipped by nature to assume a position of commanding importance in the Pacific Northwest.

The commercial development along Puget Sound was destined to be concentrated not in one city, but in a long string of ports which stretch from Vancouver, in British Columbia, to Olympia at the southern tip of the Sound. Nature was lavish in giving the district many rivers whose mouths provided numerous harbors, each without great natural advantage over the others, and each the location of one or more pioneer sawmills which chose these locations because they were the focal points for logs floated down from the mountain forests. Seattle, at the mouth of the Duwamish River, was the first sawmill village to rise to importance. Its supremacy was challenged by Bellingham and Everett to the north and by Tacoma to the south. Tacoma became the terminus of the first transcontinental railroad, the Northern Pacific, in 1887.[8] Seattle had already become renowned as a shopping and recreational center among local lumberjacks, and it continued to attract the largest trade from the interior. Seattle quickly established a rail connection to Tacoma, shortly acquired other transcontinental facilities, and continued to maintain its position as the commercial, financial, and shipping center of the Puget Sound district. The other cities grew rapidly, but with no such diversity of economic interests. Everett and Bellingham have come to be important lumber-shipping ports, while ambitious Tacoma calls itself the "lumber capital of America."

---

[8] Tacoma was selected as the terminus of the Northern Pacific railroad in 1887. At that time the town boasted 200 persons. The railroad sold adjacent land (granted to it as government aid) to its own land company which laid out the city, including notably wide streets, and sold lots to the rapidly incoming settlers.

Seattle.—The casual observer might adjudge the site of Seattle to be an ideal place to locate a city. Situated between a spacious bay on Puget Sound and Lake Washington, the city can offer ocean steamers the choice of a salt-water or fresh-water harbor. There are hills, but the land at least is not swampy—an important consideration in a rainy climate. But Seattle has found difficulties in its location, chiefly because it has outgrown its site. Cramped between salt water and the lake, the city has found it possible to expand only to the north and south. Traffic between the sections has had to filter through the narrow business district like sand through an hourglass. Crowding has resulted, and Seattle, Manhattanlike, has expanded upward with many a lofty office building, and many an apartment. The crowding has had no noticeable ill effect. Apparently it has quickened the business life rather than strangled it and has made the crowded business district even more attractive to shoppers. Expansion to the north and south has become marked. Industries have been attracted to the flat lands to the south, and the hills of North Seattle contain some of the nation's finest residential sections. Cable-drawn street cars have conquered the steep hills, and one hill that proved particularly annoying was scooped up, hauled away, and dumped into Puget Sound.

To understand Seattle, it must be remembered that although lumber and fish have always played an important part in its economic life, these industries never have been of such all-absorbing importance to Seattle as to other cities along the Sound. Seattle showed an early interest in trade and distribution. While other villages were busy exploiting the forests and building great lumber mills, the little settlement on Elliott Bay was devoting the major portion of its attention to establishing a reputation as a trading center for neighboring lumbermen, fishermen, and miners. It prospered in the Fraser River gold rush of 1857, but did not gain prominence as a port until 1897 with the arrival of the first gold ship from Alaska. On that day Seattle established itself as the base of operations for Alaskan trade; and Seattle today remains for practical purposes the commercial and financial center, the extraterritorial economic capital of Alaska. But Alaskan commerce was only the beginning of Seattle's excursion into ocean shipping. Beyond Alaska lay the Orient, of growing importance in American foreign commerce. Nearer the Orient than any other major United States port, Seattle early assumed importance in this trade. The Panama Canal lessened this advantage, especially for the importation of heavy commodities (such as rubber and tin) destined for the Atlantic seaboard. But costlier items such as silk are too valuable for such long shipment, and Seattle remains the leading American port (challenged only by Portland, Oregon) in the importation of silk and similar valuable commodities from the Orient.

In its commercial development, Seattle has made good use of its natural advantages. The deep waters of Elliott Bay have been lined with docks, piers, and other shipping facilities. The mouth of the meandering Duwamish River has been straightened, deepened, and equipped with docks and piers. The entrance (or outlet) to Lake Washington has been widened, deepened, and provided with locks through which all but the largest ocean vessels may gain access to this fresh-water harbor. At present the city has found it unnecessary to develop shipping facilities along the lake, but there is abundant room for future expansion.

In foreign trade, Seattle regularly ranks third (in tonnage) among Pacific ports of the United States. Los Angeles and San Francisco handle a larger sea-borne commerce. In diversity of products handled, in number of steamship lines, in variety of flags flying in its harbor, Seattle is exceeded by none. Seattle ships much lumber and grain to the Orient and to Europe, receives many cargoes of silk and a long list of other Oriental products. It also receives much oil from Los Angeles, and manufactured goods from the Atlantic coast. It ships much lumber to timber-lacking Los Angeles, to South American cities and to the cities of the Atlantic seaboard. Typical of young and resource-rich districts, the Puget Sound district exports more than it imports.

A large and diversified foreign trade is dependent to a large extent upon well-developed internal commerce. The Seattle trade territory includes not only the forest and farm lands of the Puget Sound Valley but also a vast productive area in eastern Washington and adjacent Idaho and Montana. To these lands Seattle acts as a gatherer and distributor. From this territory Seattle railroads gather wheat, fruit, flour, and animal and mineral products; to it they distribute manufactured goods and other articles for home consumption. Leadership in commercial development is almost invariably accompanied by leadership in finance. Seattle is banker not only to its own shipping interests, its lumbermen and fish merchants, but to Alaska and portions of interior Washington.

Because Washington and Seattle are still young and because they have found the greatest profit in exploiting their natural resources, manufacturing industries have been developed chiefly (1) to supply staple articles to the local population, or (2) to process locally-produced raw materials such as timber, fish, and agricultural produce. The leading manufacturing industries of Seattle are lumber mills, printing establishments, machine shops, and bakeries, all characteristic of cities which have not yet attained maturity as industrial centers. With its excellent climate highly productive of human energy, ocean-cooled summers and winters mild enough to permit year-round outdoor work, Seattle expects continued expansion of its manufacturing industries. Markets are expected to include not only the near-by territory but also distant Alaska and the Orient.

Despite dreams of future greatness along industrial lines, the Seattle of today must be described as a commercial city favored by nature with a good harbor, a strategic location, and a productive hinterland made accessible by far-flung railroads and highways. As in the past, Seattle's wealth lies in its foreign and domestic trade, enriched by local shipments of products from near-by forests, fisheries, and farms.

Tacoma.—Scarcely an hour's motor trip south of Seattle, but located on an arm of Puget Sound which is even nearer the best remaining stands of saw timber, Tacoma calls itself the "Lumber Capital of the World." The visitor finds the sobriquet well earned. Everywhere he is assailed by the fragrant aroma of newly sawed fir lumber and the incessant whir of circular and band saws as they plow through millions of board feet of Washington's greatest natural heritage, and transform it into lumber for the great cities from Tokyo to Liverpool. Out of the mills it streams, in all lengths and sizes, down to the loading platforms of the railroads or to the huge docks at the head of Commencement Bay. In 1930, the woodworking industries employed more than 5800 persons, one-eighth of all Tacoma workers. Only the stores, wholesale and retail, employed more. Tacoma is the West's leading lumber-manufacturing city, deserving of its title of the nation's lumber capital.

But Tacoma is not a one-industry town. Commencement Bay receives many shiploads of copper ore from Chile, Alaska, and Canada for Tacoma's large copper refinery. Railroads bring in thousands of bushels of western wheat for its flour mills. The copper refinery utilizes cheap Tacoma electric power for its electrolytic process. Lumber, flour, and copper and brass products are the chief exports from the port of Tacoma and these are likewise the most important products of Tacoma factories. These industries, together with large railroad shops, machine shops, and miscellaneous woodworking establishments give Tacoma an industrial appearance unusual in the West. With hardly one-third of the population of Seattle, Tacoma has an industrial output half as large and a foreign commerce almost as great. On the other hand, Tacoma's wholesale trade, banking, and other commercial interests are overshadowed by developments in its sister-metropolis to the north.

Other Cities.—The smaller cities of western Washington are almost without exception located on tidewater and their economic developments are closely connected with the processing and shipment of timber products. Economic activity centers in the huge tidewater sawmills and at the lumber docks. Here lumber is indeed king. This description holds for Everett and Bellingham, Puget Sound ports north of Seattle, for Hoquiam and Aberdeen, twin seaports of Gray's Harbor, and for a dozen others of less importance. As supplies of timber have lessened, these cities have sought other economic interests with partial success. Bellingham has become an important base for Alaska salmon fleets and its canneries hum at the end of the fishing season. Everett, still one of three important lumber centers of the state, has found diversification in acting as a distributing center for expanding local farming interests. The ports on Gray's Harbor, already the world's greatest lumber-shipping center, feel assured of future prominence because their trade areas still contain some forty billion feet of good saw timber, the largest remaining stand of virgin timber in the United States. With good harbors, a large export trade, and good railroad facilities, all of these cities have long been eager to supplement their lumber and fishing industries and achieve the economic diversification which marks the Seattle-Tacoma district. Thus far the ambition is largely ungratified. The momentum of an early start, coupled with the early establishment and growth of commercial, financial, and industrial institutions, has given the larger centers a long lead in the race for economic supremacy. The future will likely bring increased diversification and perhaps greater prominence to some of these smaller centers, but it appears that their great salvation lies in fostering the conservation and wise exploitation of the great forests of this region which some day will become one of the timber-*growing* districts of the United States.

Portland and the Other Columbia River Cities.—The frontier village of Portland first rose to prominence as the gateway to the rich Willamette Valley. It is apparent that the New Englanders who founded the village foresaw the development of an important commercial center on these terraced lands opposite the point where the Willamette ceases to be navigable. It is not so apparent, however, that these pioneers appreciated the fact that the mouth of the Willamette is also the head of practical navigation on the Columbia River, and that the deep gorge which that river has cut through the Cascade Range is by all odds the premier low-altitude route from the great "Inland Empire" to the East. The Columbia Gorge (elevation 100 feet) is Portland's great heritage, and the two railroads which cling to either bank of the river deliver inland freight to this city with less expense than to any other point on the Pacific coast. Portland had the double advantage of being at the crossroads of two natural highways, and at the same time of being located at the head of navigation on the second largest river in the United States. Portland could hardly have avoided becoming an important commercial city. Nor was the site undesirable. At this point nearly level terraces rise from the Willamette and the Columbia. The lowest terrace, originally the town site, is now occupied by the business district. Truly, the opposite bank of the Willamette is very hilly, and the south bank of the Columbia is bordered by swamp. But Portland has found ample room for expansion in the other directions and its growth will not be hindered by lack of good building sites.

The traveler finds Portland somewhat unique among western cities. The city apparently has never forgotten its New England traditions. Substantial, conservative, almost sedate, Portland seems far removed from the pioneer exuberance which still crops out in most western cities. Its climate, strikingly similar to that of Paris, seems to have imparted an interest in the esthetic as well as the practical. But Portland *is* practical, and it is progressive. Its trade territory is less rich than that of Seattle and its general economic importance is somewhat less.

Portland is older than Seattle, but Seattle has grown faster, especially since the Alaska gold rush which established it as the commercial center of the North Pacific coast. In late years, however, Portland has experienced expansion along several lines of economic activity, in many of which it has recently been able to challenge the supremacy of its northern neighbor. Many, indeed, are willing to predict that Portland is destined to become the leader in the business life of the section. Without commenting upon the soundness of this prediction, we may compare with interest the importance of the four major Pacific coast cities in various types of economic activity.

PACIFIC COAST CITIES—COMPARATIVE ECONOMIC DATA

(All Data in Thousands)

	Portland	Seattle	San Francisco	Los Angeles
Population of city (1930).....	302	366	634	1,238
Metropolitan district........	379	421	1,290	2,318
Retail sales (1935)...........	$147,413	$163,185	$ 298,371	$593,902
Wholesale sales (1935).......	$266,779	$329,668	$1,149,864	$939,461
Manufacturing (1937)[a].......	$ 59,280	$ 78,582	$ 356,821	$466,080
Water-borne commerce (1935)[b]	4,657T	5,432T	18,065T	13,850T
Foreign commerce (1935)[b]....	1,647T	774T	3,303T	4,847T
Bank debits (1936)..........	1,954	2,316	10,638	10,216

[a] County totals, except for San Francisco whose total includes Oakland and the other East Bay cities.
[b] Cargo tons.

It will be observed that in most lines the economic development of Seattle and Portland is very similar except that the Portland development is about four-fifths as great as its northern rival. Certain differences appear, however, and these should provide a key to variations in the economic life of the two centers.

Wholesale Trade.—Both Seattle and Portland are predominantly commercial cities, but the Seattle wholesale trade is about 20 per cent greater than that of Portland. This difference results almost entirely from the fact that Seattle's trading area is more populous. Seattle serves not only the populous Puget Sound district, but much of western Washington and far-off Alaska, with a combined population of about 1,300,000 persons. Portland dominates nearly the entire state of Oregon and sections of southern Washington—a vast area, but for the most part sparsely populated. The Portland trade territory has only slightly more than one million persons. Furthermore, Seattle customers include many lumbermen and other wage-earners. Most Oregonians are farmers who produce part of their own foodstuffs and buy correspondingly small quantities of goods.

Manufacturing.—The types of manufacturing found in these two cities are strikingly similar. In both cities the majority of products are destined for local markets, or represent the processing of local raw materials such as timber and fish. Woodworking industries are of greater importance in Portland than in Seattle. Of these, perhaps the most promising is furniture. Portland already claims importance as the leading furniture-manufacturing city of the Pacific Northwest. Portland-milled flour, ground from Columbia Plateau wheat, is the chief locally manufactured article to enter national and international markets. Its output of textiles (mainly woolens) is also increasing in importance. As in Seattle, many eastern industrial concerns have lately established manufacturing branches.

Shipping.—The rise of Portland to a position of major importance in ocean shipping has been very rapid. As late as 1914, Portland was a second-rate Pacific port, far behind San Francisco and Seattle, then the leaders in Pacific shipping. Stimulated by the World War and the opening of the Panama Canal, Portland began a period of expansion which has become more marked throughout recent years. The port of Portland is located on the Willamette River 13 miles from its mouth and 113 miles from the ocean. Throughout this distance a channel 300 feet wide and 35 feet deep is maintained. This channel, well marked and free of ice throughout the year, has made the fresh-water port of Portland easily available to ocean steamers. Lumber, of course, is the leading item of shipment, followed by wheat and flour. Because of its natural advantage in the low-level Columbia River route to the interior, Portland receives a lower freight rate on wheat from the "Inland Empire" than the Puget Sound ports. Much of the wheat and flour and large amounts of lumber are destined for foreign markets. Portland ordinarily handles about as much foreign commerce as Seattle. On the other hand, Seattle has almost a monopoly of the Alaskan trade, and exceeds Portland in the commerce with Hawaii as well as with the Atlantic seaboard. Seattle is somewhat nearer the Orient, but this advantage is of small consequence.

Against these trump cards, Portland is able to match the Columbia River Gorge and cheaper transportation by motor and rail from the interior. This advantage has already made it the nation's chief wheat-exporting port and second primary wool market. In the future, water transportation probably will be added to the list, for work is in progress on a huge project to construct dams and make the Columbia River navigable for river boats far into the interior, to provide water for the further irrigation of Portland's hinterland, and to supply cheap hydroelectric power for future Portland industries. The project is expensive, perhaps impractical, but its completion might well supply a mighty impetus to the city's commerce and industry. It may to a large extent offset Seattle's present marked advantage in these lines. In the event of such a development, Portland may be depended upon to build slowly but solidly. Conservative Portland, whose citizens love their homes and their roses, whose night life is noticeable by its absence, whose ideals are still strikingly those of New England, can hardly be expected to stage a "boom" in the well-known Los Angeles manner.

Other Cities of the Lower Columbia.—Unlike Puget Sound, the lower Columbia River has not produced a number of large and medium-sized cities in addition to the major metropolis. Perhaps the reason is in the geography. It will be recalled that the deep waters of Puget Sound penetrate a large area and provide it with numerous good harbors—a decentralizing factor favoring the growth of many port-cities. This setting is in marked contrast to Portland's crossroads location at the head of navigation on the Columbia River. Nature marked the site of Portland as clearly the best city location on the lower Columbia and in consequence Portland dominates the economic activity of the territory much more completely than Seattle has been able to dominate the trade of the shores of Puget Sound.

Other centers have arisen along the lower Columbia, however, and a few of these claim considerable importance as lumber ports, fishing ports, and minor distribution centers. Near the mouth of the river, Astoria, oldest city of the Pacific Northwest (1811), ships lumber, markets fish, and is the distribution point for a growing resort section on the Pacific beaches south of the city. Farther up-stream the new town of Longview is justly famous for having been plotted according to modern specifications by a large lumber company which selected the site and built the town as a lumber center and port on the Washington bank of the Columbia River fifty miles below Portland. Longview soon boasted the world's two largest lumber mills and docks for the export of this commodity. The lumber industry is likewise dominant in Vancouver, opposite Portland on the Washington bank of the Columbia River. Vancouver is a suburb of Portland and shares some of the economic development of the larger city.

Cities of the Willamette Valley.—The small cities of the Willamette Valley are chiefly distributing centers for the farms of that area and the more distant and less important lumber camps in the mountains. Salem, largest of these, is a center for the marketing of locally grown hops and flax for linen. Salem's small industrial development is based largely upon local needs and the processing of agricultural products.

Farther south, Eugene, Corvallis, Roseburg, and Medford have achieved an importance in merchandising greater than their populations would indicate. Along the Pacific coast of Oregon the communities are small, devoted largely to a relatively small production of lumber and fishery products. Throughout its entire trade territory, Portland has seen no city arise to contest, even faintly, its position of extreme dominance in economic affairs.

The Future.—For the future, the North Pacific coast has long been pointed out as an important potential location for cities. Those who foresee such a development base their hypothesis on these facts:

1. *Climate.*—Temperatures in the Puget Trough are lower and more energizing than those of California, but the winters are mild enough to permit outside work and reduce expenditures for heating considerably below those of eastern cities. Industrial concerns are promised low production costs and high productivity per worker.

2. *Power.*—Abundant rainfall and strong stream gradients combine to give the Pacific states the lion's share of the nation's potential water-power resources. Engineers estimate that Washington, Oregon, and California have approximately two-fifths of the water-power resources of the United States (based upon amounts that would be available 90 per cent of the time). Washington ranks first among the states of the Union with about 20 per cent of all the nation's available water power. California and Oregon rank second and third with about 10 per cent apiece. No section of equal size in the United States has water-power resources as great as those of Washington and Oregon.

Nor have these potentialities gone unused. In 1937, California was the leading state in water-power development (14 per cent of the national total). Washington ranked third (7 per cent). Oregon was further down the list (eighteenth) but, like its sister-states, was developing elaborate plans for the development of hydroelectric projects. In Washington and Oregon, the main plan calls for a combination of navigation, irrigation, and power on the Columbia River system. Two large dams (Grand Coulee and Bonneville) on the Columbia and a series of smaller developments in the Cascade Mountains are to be tied together into a super-power distribution system to serve Seattle, Portland, Tacoma, Spokane, and the other cities of the Pacific Northwest. Completion of these facilities will give North Pacific cities an abundance of cheap power.

Whether cheap power can serve as a magnet to attract manufacturing industries is a moot question. In the past, few large power-users have sought locations far from the Appalachian coal fields and the hydroelectric plants of that same region. There is no question that for a few industries power is the major item of production cost. Notable among these are the industries using electric furnace processes for reducing minerals. Refineries for many types of non-ferrous metals are commonly located near hydroelectric power sites. Just now, the Pacific Northwest is busy examining the list of industries in which power is the principal location factor. The future may witness the migration of such industries to this area. Unfortunately, the list is not very long, and there are the additional handicaps of distance from eastern markets and a lack of many of the more important types of raw materials for such industries. But in the chemical industries technological change is very rapid and there is a possibility that almost any day may see developments which will make Seattle and Portland industrial sites more attractive.

3. *Markets.*—Nearness to large groups of consumers is often the chief factor in industrial location. Markets for the cities of the Pacific Northwest are of two types: (a) the "home" market, including the coastal areas and the interior districts which extend eastward to the Rocky Mountains; and (b) foreign markets, especially in Asia, Alaska, and Oceania. From these districts Portland and Seattle and the neighboring cities receive large quantities of raw materials and to them they distribute manufactured goods. From the hinterland these cities obtain lumber, wheat, and other farm produce, most of which are processed locally and shipped to all parts of the world. From the Orient come tin, silk, and a growing list of other materials. To all of these sections Portland and Seattle ship lumber, flour, and manufactured goods. The prediction that these cities will grow in economic importance is based upon the thesis that (a) the productive and consumptive power of both the hinterland and the Orient may be expected to show continued growth, and (b) as these cities become more mature they will advance in importance in manufacturing and trade in response to the economic expansion of their market areas. New irrigation projects are expected to increase the productivity of the "Inland Empire" to the west. Trade with the Orient is expected to grow because it is based upon a difference in resources—the United States has no tin and grows no silk or rubber in commercial quantities. Pacific coast chambers of commerce point to the increasing importance of Asiatic trade in the foreign commerce of the United States—that it advanced from 12 per cent in 1913, to 27 per cent in 1936. They show further that Portland and Seattle are two or more days' sailing distance nearer the Orient than any other major United States port. If the anticipated increase in Oriental trade occurs,

Portland, Seattle, and the neighboring cities are in a position to profit by it.

There are others, less optimistic, who find it easy to shoot holes in this prediction. They point out that Washington and Oregon lack good coal for power purposes; but of course there is oil from California, coal from British Columbia and, more important, a tremendous reserve of "white coal," hydroelectric power. They show that the present importance of these ports is based very largely upon lumber, that the lumber resources are being depleted, that no new resources have been developed to replace them. In addition, they say that it is easy to overstress climatic advantages, that modern factories "manufacture" their own climate. Finally, it is asserted that the Panama Canal has so cheapened the transportation charge from the Orient to the eastern Manufacturing Belt that fewer and fewer steamers will tie up at Puget Sound ports and Portland, that only expensive commodities such as silk can be expected to absorb the high rail rates across the continent. By this reasoning they argue that the economic importance of these cities will dwindle with the declining natural resources of their local trade territories.

The reader may choose between these extreme views. His choice should depend very largely upon his evaluation of the available resources of the district and his estimate of the extent to which these people may be expected to utilize them. The average American business man is an ingenious person, and the people of this district may be expected to permit no opportunity to pass for the business development of their territory. But in all respects they are limited by the tools with which they must work—the resources, natural and human, of their own trade territories.

Summary

The Washington-Oregon section of the Pacific Coast Region has developed an economic structure based primarily upon forest products and secondarily upon agriculture, fisheries, and trade. In the past, the forest industries have regularly contributed nearly a half of the income of the region. They are the basis for the leading manufacturing industries of Washington and Oregon. Three industries, lumber, pulp, and paper, accounted for more than half the industrial output of these two states in 1937. Lumber also constitutes the chief tonnage of shipments by both rail and water. Much depends upon a wise administration of the remaining stands of saw timber, which constitute about half the lumber reserves of the United States. Beyond its excellent forest resources the Washington-Oregon section has good facilities for farming. At present, the less productive soils of the northern districts are devoted largely to providing dairy and poultry products for near-by cities. The Oregon section has generally richer soils and grows a variety of crops for sale in other regions. A heavy fruit production has been important in placing the canning industry second (after lumber) among Oregon manufacturing industries.

The section's third major resource lies in its location with respect to both a productive hinterland and trade routes to Alaska and Asia. Seattle and Portland are the seaports for the increasingly productive Columbia Plateau whose wheat for export regularly fills many a vessel in these harbors. These ports also profit by nearness to the Orient and to Alaska. They handle most of the American imports of silk as well as the large salmon catch of the North Pacific coast. These fishery resources should also appear on the asset side of the balance sheet.

The area produces few minerals. Its coal deposits are expensive to exploit and the best power resources apparently lie in the enormous amounts of electricity now being made available by hydroelectric developments. The extent to which cheap power will prove attractive to manufacturing industries is impossible to predict, but it seems likely to effect at least a measure of industrial stimulation. Certainly the climate is such that a high degree of efficiency may be expected from laborers, especially those in industries requiring outside work.

REFERENCES

The agricultural colleges of Washington and Oregon have published good studies of agricultural problems in those states. Studies of water-borne commerce and trans-Pacific relations made at the University of Washington throw much light on foreign commercial interests in Pacific Northwest cities. The Pacific Northwest Regional Planning Board has issued a series of bulletins concerning the resources of this area. A U. S. Department of Commerce study, *Commercial Survey of the Pacific Northwest* (1932), contains good information. Seattle is considered in Leighton, *Five Cities*. Several bulletins of the U. S. Forest Service describe the forest industries of the area.

1. How does the early history of the Pacific Northwest differ from that of California?

2. Where are the main agricultural sections in the Washington-Oregon section? What types of agriculture prevail in them? How does climate play an important role in determining what these farmers can grow? topography? soil? markets?

3. Where are the principal forest resources of the Pacific Northwest? What kinds of trees are found? How is the lumber prepared for market? Where are the principal markets? What measures would you recommend to assure this section a permanent logging industry?

4. What kinds of fish are caught in this section? What are the problems connected with this type of business?

5. How important are the agricultural, mining, fishing, and forest resources of this section to the business life of its cities?

6. In your opinion what does the future hold in store for this part of North America?

7. Which Pacific Coast Region city would you choose as a location for a branch house to distribute oil-well machinery? tin cans? salmon-fishing equipment? clothing for lumberjacks? Justify your selections.

8. Prepare an imaginary history of the first hundred years of the English colonies in America based on the assumption that they were located on the Pacific coast rather than the Atlantic coast.

CHAPTER VI

THE INTERMOUNTAIN PLATEAUS—
ENVIRONMENT AND AGRICULTURE

AREA AND EXTENT

BETWEEN the Sierra-Cascade ranges and the Rocky Mountains is a vast plateau country larger in area than all the United States north of the Ohio and east of the Mississippi rivers. These plateaus constitute a distinctive, mountain-rimmed natural region which extends from near the Canada-United States border southward to the Mexican border and far south into Mexico to the latitude of the city of Mexico where the bordering mountains converge and complete the encirclement of a vast, parched plateau area. Bordering mountain ranges have proved effective barriers not only to transportation, but also to rain-bearing winds which deposit their moisture on the borders of the region but leave the lower intervening plateaus deficient in moisture—arid districts with scant native vegetation, adapted to farming in only a few favored spots. In consequence the Intermountain Plateau Region is a district of small population, its people clustered about irrigated oases or centers for mining operations, or widely scattered over scantily grassed hills in the region's most prevalent occupation—the grazing industry. The geographic distribution of these three leading types of economic activity can best be understood by an examination of the region's two great natural limiting forces. They are topography and climate.

TOPOGRAPHY

The topography of this region is a mixture of land forms so intricate that generalized description is nearly impossible. The plateau type predominates, but there are high plateaus and low plateaus in all stages of dissection; and there are isolated ranges of low mountains as well as basins and river and lake plains. Soils likewise are found in great variety, although all are alkaline and light in color and texture. In short, both the topography and soil of the intermountain plateaus are subject to great local variations. These variations are so great that the physiographer has found

129

FIG. 10. Major Hydroelectric Plants and Transmission Lines of the Western States. There are many economic connections between the Pacific Coast region and the Intermountain Plateau region. Important among these economic ties are the hydroelectric developments which supply Pacific Coast cities with power. Many of these power developments have been built by the federal government and provide irrigation or navigation improvements as well as power. The principal federal power projects are named on the map. Note the heavy concentration of plants in the Sierra Nevada of California. Power is the major product of the Sierra Nevada. To what extent will cheap power offset the Pacific Coast region's lack of coal for industrial purposes?

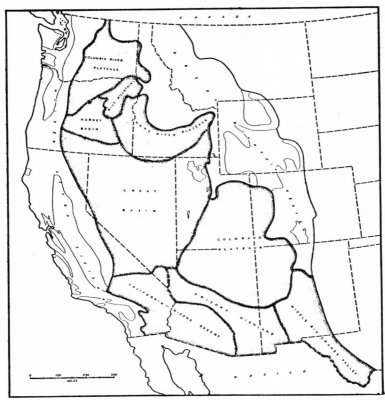

FIG. 11. The Intermountain Plateau Region. The major divisions of the intermountain region are traced to physiographic and climatic factors. A more detailed analysis would require splitting these sections into dozens of smaller ones, because the region has hundreds of small sections, each of which differs in some respect from the rest. Most of the people live near the margins of the region. The central sections are generally very sparsely populated. How do you account for such a distribution of the population? The Blue Mountain section is often included in the Rocky Mountain region because it has more rainfall, occasional forests, and good summer pasture.

it necessary to divide the region into a number of sections and sub-sections, a procedure which the geographer is also obliged to follow if a clear and reasonably adequate picture of this phase of the natural environment is to be obtained.

Division into Sections.—It is nearly impossible to acquire a systematic knowledge of environmental factors in the Inter-mountain Region without dividing it into at least six sections. These sections, closely linked to the principal drainage systems of the region, are roughly defined as follows:

1. *The Columbia-Snake River Plateaus,* comprising the drainage basin of this river system, excepting those portions which are in the Rocky Mountains; and including a small area in central Oregon (the Harney Basin) without external drainage but having other characteristics similar to those of the remainder of the section.

2. *The Great Basin* of Nevada, western Utah, and a small portion of southeastern Idaho, a large area without external drainage.

3. *The Arizona-California Desert,* which includes the desert lands of southeastern California, southern Arizona, and a small portion of adjacent Nevada. The district has insufficient rainfall for a drainage system, but it lies adjacent to the Gila and lower Colorado rivers.

4. *The Colorado Plateaus,* a section of high elevation embracing all the non-mountainous portions of the basin of the Colorado River above the Grand Canyon.

5. *The Arizona Highland,* a foothill-like belt of mountains which lies between the Colorado Plateau and the Arizona Desert. It is drained by the Gila River.

6. *The Middle Rio Grande Valley* of central New Mexico and extreme western Texas.

In nearly all cases the boundaries of these sections are fixed in a somewhat arbitrary fashion, but they provide a satisfactory and reasonably accurate basis for describing the environmental factors and economic life of the various portions of the region. These divisions correspond generally to those designated by physiographers and they also mark the approximate limits of the chief types of climate found in this region. Both climate and topography have been considered in determining sectional boundaries within the region.

The Columbia-Snake River Plateaus.—The outstanding surface feature of the lands drained by the Columbia and Snake rivers is the presence of ancient extensive lava flows of varying geologic ages which cover nearly all of the section as here defined and have exerted a pronounced influence upon both the topography and soil of the district. Geologists believe that these lava sheets generally originated in fissures rather than volcanoes. From these fissures the hot rock oozed and flowed, cooling and hardening as it extended, filling old valleys, covering low mountains and leaving its slate-gray ash in nearly horizontal sheets. Not one but dozens of these flows occurred, filling mile-deep valleys, covering mile-high mountains in some sections, gradually obliterating the old landscape and superimposing the nearly level terrain characteristic of many parts of the section today.

In a later epoch, the Cascade Mountains were uplifted and gave the new lava plain its basin-like character. More recently the entire Columbia Basin was depressed while the Snake River Plain, including the older Blue Mountain section of northeast Oregon, was raised. Rivers were rudely forced from their old channels by these geologic changes, the Columbia finally choosing a long, roundabout course at the foot of the Cascades, while the Snake, driven from its old course by the Blue Mountain uplift, began cutting a deep gorge through the high lava deposit which separates those mountains from the Rockies. Canyon-cutting was easy in those soft lava rocks, especially after the melting northern glaciers began to add volume to the streams. Today a large area in west-central Washington is cut into deep canyons (called coulees) and nearly worthless scablands, former courses of the Columbia, but now without flowing water. The Snake River flows in a deep, steep-walled canyon, locally several hundred feet below the flat lava plain, throughout most of its course from eastern Idaho to its confluence with the Columbia in southwestern Washington.[1] The Deschutes River which hugs the eastern base of the

---

[1] Opposite the Blue Mountains, the Snake River, which here forms the boundary between Idaho and Washington and Oregon, traverses a mile-deep gorge as deep, precipitous, and highly sculptured as the Grand Canyon of the Colorado. It lacks only the color of the famous canyon to be regarded as its equal. The lava walls of the Grand Canyon of the Snake are dull gray in color. The canyon marks the boundary between the plateau region and the Rocky Mountains.

Cascade Range in Oregon likewise traverses a deep canyon throughout most of its course. Such canyons, with their strong gradients, steep sides, and occasional falls or cascades are common along the courses of major streams, but they occupy only a small percentage of the area and they are not characteristic of the general landscape, which is composed largely of nearly level or rolling plains, with occasional beds of old lakes and, in a few favored spots, river valleys broad and level enough to permit the growing of crops. In some sections isolated buttes or low mountains appear above the sea of lava—relics of an older geologic age which were not engulfed in the lava flows. Most significant of these mountain masses is the Blue Mountain group of northeast Oregon, whose ranges rise some three thousand feet above the general level of the surrounding plain.

In central Oregon a large district is without external drainage. This district, which centers in the Harney Basin, retains most of the features of the remainder of the plateau. It has more lakes and old lake beds, fewer canyons, and a somewhat rougher topography; but most of its soil is decomposed lava and its relief features are relatively simple. Despite its canyons and isolated mountains, the Columbia-Snake plateau has the least relief of any major section of the Intermountain Region.

Altitude.—The altitude of the Columbia-Snake River Section ranges from less than 200 feet at the entrance to the Columbia River Gorge (at The Dalles) to 6000 feet at the headwaters of the Snake in eastern Idaho. Occasional mountains reach higher levels. The bulk of the Columbia plateau lies between 1000 and 2000 feet elevation; of the Snake plateau between 3000 and 5000 feet; of the Harney Basin between 4000 and 5000 feet. The whole district, although lower than the Great Basin to the south, may be characterized as one of medium elevation, too low to receive sufficient rainfall for agriculture as ordinarily practiced in humid regions.

Soil.—When basaltic lava becomes sufficiently weathered and decayed it forms good soil. In consequence, most of the soil of these sections is fertile. The best of these are the comparatively limited areas of alluvial plain along the rivers; but elsewhere the soils generally prove highly productive where sufficient moisture can be obtained. "Old-timers" in the West say that if land will grow good sagebrush the soil is rich. In the Columbia-Snake plateaus their claims are borne out. In few places does sagebrush grow more luxuriantly—and few sections are more productive when irrigated.

Not all sections of the district have soils suitable to crops. The outer margins of the Snake River plateau and certain central portions nearer the river have patches of lava still in the rock stage with only a thin mantle of soil on the surface. The western portion of the Harney Basin, too, has a large area of sand and gravel, known locally as the Great Sandy Desert. Rainfall there is deficient but the "desert" is more the result of porous soil than small rainfall. In Washington the district of coulees and scablands is likewise unfavorable for farming, in both topography and soil. Other sections are generally productive where water can be obtained, a productivity which will be more fully explained in connection with the agriculture of the district.

The Great Basin.—Long familiar in the literature of geography, the term "great basin" is in fact a misnomer. This large area is substantially without external drainage, but the implication that it could be filled to the rim before overflowing is grossly inaccurate. Large areas near the center of the Great Basin are above 6000 feet, while the southern "rim" is below 2000 feet. Nevertheless, the term "basin" is apropos, for this district is beyond question a basin country, not one basin, however, but approximately a hundred. Characteristically these basins are elongated and lie between nearly parallel ranges of low saw-toothed mountains which run nearly north and south. Many of them are "bolsons"—basins filled, often deeply, with desert detritus. Roughly half the total area is in basin, half in mountain. Near the mountainous boundaries of the section, some of the basins are watered by mountain streams which provide water for irrigation and occasionally form lakes, the most notable of which is Great Salt Lake. Central basins are characteristically dry, and occasionally form playa lakes, some of which are salt-encrusted and are called salinas. Even the high sections of eastern Nevada, containing large areas above 6000 feet elevation, give rise to only one perennial stream, the Humboldt River, which runs westward some 200 miles only to be lost in desert lakes, but not without first providing water for the irrigation of a number of farms along its banks.

Altitude.—The Great Basin section varies in altitude from 2000 to 10,000 feet, but regardless of this divergence it is not a section of strong relief. There are no canyons of importance, no cliffs or escarpments of prominence. Long, gradual slopes and slightly concave basins are the characteristic topographic features. Topography, indeed, has done little to hinder directly the economic development of this arid section. Transportation is comparatively easy and good soil is much more prevalent than the water with which to irrigate it. Only a minute fraction of the district will ever be farmed, but the limiting factor is not topography or soil, but lack of rainfall and streams for irrigation.

The Arizona-California Desert.—In southern Nevada the Great Basin descends gradually into lower altitudes until it reaches the "basement" of North America in two small areas below sea level—the Death Valley and the Imperial Valley of southeastern California. These areas and the surrounding country are absolute desert, relieved only by four irrigated oases: (1) in the Imperial Valley, where the waters of the Colorado River have been diverted to provide water for one of the most important irrigation projects in the United States; (2 and 3) two districts along the Lower Colorado River at the California-Arizona boundary; and (4) in the Antelope Valley, some fifty miles northeast of Los Angeles, where artesian water is used. This section also includes the valley of the Lower Colorado River below Black Canyon (near the point in southeastern Nevada where the river first runs south). At the mouth of Black Canyon, the great river emerges from its hundreds of miles of canyons and enters a valley over which it flows placidly southward toward the Gulf of California. A few small canyons are found in this lower section of the river, but it usually occupies a broad flood plain which contains some 375,000 acres of irrigable land. This land is too high above the river to permit local gravity irrigation, but the whole district promises to become agriculturally important with water provided by the great Boulder Dam. Water from this reservoir will be diverted through canals to irrigate a large section of the river plain, chiefly the portion south of the Williams River in Arizona. These irrigation enterprises constitute the California Desert's only hope for future agricultural importance. Tillable land with good soil is relatively abundant—less than 20 per cent of the area is mountainous. Climate is excellent from the standpoint of growing certain subtropical specialties. Only moisture is lacking, and that moisture must come from the Colorado River and its tributaries.

The Arizona Desert.—The Arizona portion of the California-Arizona Desert district differs little in topography from the California section. Its elevation is higher, however, and it has external drainage. All of the Arizona desert is drained by, or at least slopes toward, the Gila River. Frequent basins and low mountains are characteristic, some of the mountains rising three or four thousand feet above their adjacent basins. The area in basin far exceeds that in mountain, however, and as a result railroad-building has been relatively easy. Considerable areas of good soil exist, especially in the flood plains of the rivers. Where water for irrigation is available (as in the vicinity of Phoenix) these lands have proved remarkably productive.

The Colorado Plateaus.—The waters which fill the great reservoir behind Boulder Dam are gathered by the Colorado River from a drainage basin more than twice as large as the New England states. The headwaters of the Colorado are in the Rocky Mountains, but most of the drainage basin consists of a high plateau country. On three sides the boundaries are clear: on the north and east rise the Rocky Mountains, and on the west (in Utah) the plateau overlooks the Great Basin from a high escarpment, often considered a southern extension of the Wasatch Mountains. The southern boundary is less distinct, but in most places it is likewise an escarpment overlooking the Arizona Highland to the south.

Topographically the Colorado Plateaus are a land of sharp angles and marked local contrasts in elevation. Steep escarpments and deep, labyrinthine canyons are the most spectacular features of the landscape. The Colorado River and its tributaries occupy deep canyons throughout nearly their entire courses, culminating in the colorful and awe-inspiring Grand Canyon of Arizona—justly the world's most famous canyon. The district also contains smaller but equally impressive canyon lands, most noted of which are the Zion and Bryce canyons of southern Utah. Brilliant colors—fiery reds, gaudy yellows, chocolate browns, even shades of purple—make these fantastically sculptured canyon lands first-ranking points of interest for the tourist. But not all the plateau is in canyon and cliff. Certain portions, especially in Arizona, are only partially dissected, and where elevation is sufficient these areas are covered with cool open forest, occasionally favored with lakes and trout streams. Other lower sections are in places occupied by basins or valleys wide enough to permit farming where water is available for irrigation. These basins and valleys are the most productive parts of the plateau country. Their locations and importance will be indicated in the pages on agricultural development.

The chief effect of the remarkable roughness of the Colorado Plateau has been to place a severe handicap upon transportation. Few railroads penetrate the plateau and only two cross it. Railroad construction has been extremely expensive with resulting financial difficulties to the lines which operate here. Highway building has been somewhat more successful, but most of this plateau country will long find it unprofitable to transport agricultural products to outside markets. Most roads are mere dry-weather trails, with steep grades that are both hazardous and expensive from the point of view of truck transport. Little wonder, therefore, that this is the least-known section of the United States, that its natural bridges, deep canyons, prehistoric cliff dwellings and sand-strewn deserts are just beginning to receive their deserved reputation as points of interest to the tourist. Until very recently, these rarities were available only to the explorer with his pack train. Thanks to state and federal interest in road-building, they are now accessible to the less hardy tourist and his automobile.

Elevation.—The Colorado Plateaus are the highest section of the Intermountain Plateau Region. Most of the area is above 5000 feet, and many sections reach 10,000 feet above sea level. But for their inaccessibility many of these higher sections might become important for certain types of farming and forestry. The latter industry has made some progress in portions of Arizona, but the production is a small fraction of the national output. The lower sections are located chiefly near the Colorado River and its branches. These lower (but drier) districts have good soil in numerous places and, where water for irrigation is available, small farming industries have appeared.

The Arizona Highland.—The belt of foothill-like mountains which separates the Arizona Desert from the Colorado Plateaus and extends eastward into New Mexico is known as the Arizona Highland, the American portion of a physiographic province which extends far south into Mexico. It is a section of rough topography, a transition zone between the basin country and the plateaus. Physiographically, it partakes of the nature of both.

Valleys and small basins are present but they are small and isolated. The frequent mountain ranges have no definite pattern.
Generally too low for good timber, they nevertheless provide good
winter pasture. Transportation is more difficult than in either the
desert or plateau sections and such railroads as have been attracted
to the Arizona Highland by its large copper-mining development
have come in as spurs, branch lines from main-line tracks to the
north and south. A few valleys are extensive enough for irrigation farming, but most of the wealth of the district comes from its
mines and cattle ranches.

The Middle Rio Grande Valley.—Although the lands drained
by the Middle Rio Grande in New Mexico and western Texas
differ but little in topography from the Arizona foothills they have
been placed in a separate section because of their different climate
and economic development. The outstanding topographic features
of the section are three or more roughly parallel north-south mountain ranges (or plateaus) interspersed with numerous desert-like
basins. The chief economic effect of these mountains, which are
sometimes considered a southern extension of the Colorado
Rockies, is to isolate the intervening basins from rain-bearing
winds. Their rainfall is very light, and farming is practiced only
where the land can be irrigated. As a result, both farming and
population in central New Mexico and western Texas are concentrated along one important stream, the Rio Grande, which
traverses a series of basins after it emerges from the Colorado
Rockies in northern New Mexico. Its waters have been diverted
in several places and the narrow valley of the Middle Rio Grande
may well be considered the heart of the section, a long narrow
streak on the map of irrigation districts, culminating in a considerable area of irrigation farming in one of the larger basins north
of El Paso, Texas. The mountains have also had the effect of discouraging east-west transportation and of making El Paso the
natural focus for trade in the Middle Rio Grande section. Although the higher sections of the neighboring plateaus are forested and provide good summer pasture, these sections have little
other economic importance.

CLIMATE IN THE INTERMOUNTAIN PLATEAUS

General Characteristics.—Previous paragraphs have indicated
that the chief handicap to economic development in the inter-

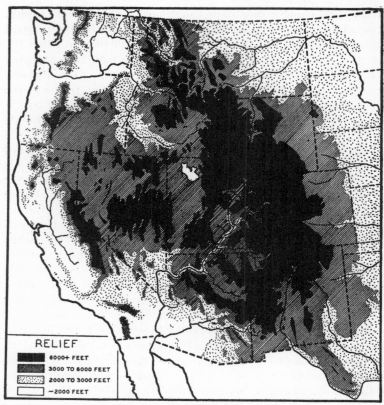

RELIEF

■ 6000+ FEET
▨ 3000 TO 6000 FEET
▦ 2000 TO 3000 FEET
□ −2000 FEET

FIG. 12. Relief in the Western United States. These two charts (Figs. 12 and 13) are designed to show the extent of correlation between relief and rainfall in the western states. They are worthy of several minutes' study. Note that broad generalizations are difficult but that definite relationships between topography and climate exist in individual areas. Note how the Intermountain Region is bordered on three sides (west, north and east) by high mountains. Prevailing winds blow from the west, giving the coast ranges and the higher Sierra Nevada and Cascade ranges moderate to heavy precipitation. The Rocky Mountains (on the east) receive less rainfall but are well watered in the higher elevations. The Colorado Plateaus are high, but not high enough to receive much rain. Many sections of the Great Basin have high altitudes, but the rainfall is also light in this section.

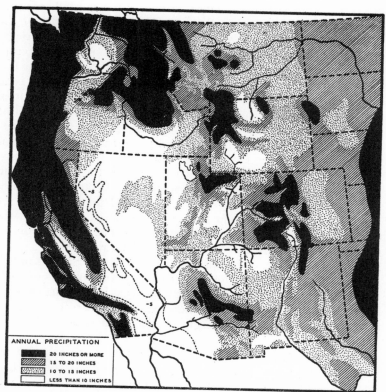

FIG. 13. Average Annual Precipitation. It appears that the distribution of precipitation is as much affected by latitude as by altitude. Northern sections are cooler than southern sections and therefore produce more condensation. Cyclonic storms are also more frequent in the north. In general, areas having less than five inches of precipitation are absolute desert and those having less than ten inches produce little vegetation. Twenty inches of precipitation is about the minimum for crops, but much depends upon the seasonal distribution of rainfall, the capacity of the soil to retain moisture, and the rate of evaporation. In certain portions of the northern sections, a combination of frequent light showers, a moisture-retentive soil and low evaporation rates makes wheat-growing successful in areas having less than twenty inches of rain.

mountain region is lack of rainfall. Nowhere in this vast region except in the districts of greatest altitude is the rainfall sufficient for farming as practiced in the more humid eastern half of the United States. Inasmuch as these favored sections of high elevation almost universally lack soil or accessibility suitable for crop-raising, all crops must be grown either by irrigation or, in a few districts, by dry farming. In every section the thundershower is an important topic of conversation, a leading news item in local newspapers. Rainfall in far-away Colorado or New Mexico is of great importance to down-stream irrigation farmers in the "American Egypt" of southern Arizona and California, for those rains provide water for the next year's crops.

To this first generalization, that rainfall in the region is universally too light for ordinary farming, may be added a second: that rainfall varies directly with altitude and inversely with the height of near-by mountain barriers. In general, the greater the elevation the heavier the rainfall. The lowest districts of all in the California Desert are also the driest. In a general way, also, those lands lying just east of the highest portions of the Sierra-Cascade barrier are drier than sections adjacent to lower portions of these ranges. The high Sierra Nevada of California is the most effective climatic barrier in North America, because of its great height and continuity. At its eastern margin lie the driest deserts of North America.

With these influences in mind, it is profitable to examine the maps of topography and rainfall (Figs. 12 and 13). From these maps the reader will be able to verify both generalizations. It will be noted that (1) for like elevations, rainfall is generally heavier in the northern portions of the region, where the mountain barrier is less effective than farther south, and cyclonic storms are more frequent; (2) the true deserts, districts with less than five inches annual rain, occur generally in the "rain shadow" just east of the Sierra-Cascade Mountains; (3) in the north, elevations of 4000 feet ordinarily have fifteen inches of rain, lower elevations less, while in the south elevations of 6000 feet are necessary for fifteen inches of rainfall and lower elevations descend into absolute desert. The correlation between elevation and rainfall is at once the most striking and the most easily remembered generalization concerning intermountain climate.

Hardly less obvious is the correlation between elevation and temperatures. Northern temperatures, of course, are generally 10° or 20° lower summer and winter than those in the south, but the effect of elevation is even more striking. Normal temperatures for January and July, for two towns in southeastern Utah illustrate this point. At Bluff, Utah, altitude 4200 feet, the January normal is 28.4°F., the July normal, 78.9° ; at Monticello, only thirty miles distant, but at an elevation of 7000 feet, the January normal is 23°, and the July normal 66.3°. By way of comparison, Spokane, near the Canadian border, has a July normal of 68.2°, while Nogales near the Mexican border has a July normal of 79.1°. Summer-resort climate in the intermountain plateaus is almost literally "in your own back yard" but you may have to do some mountain-climbing to get there. Temperatures are related much more closely to elevation than to latitude.

Characteristic of arid climates, the Intermountain Region experiences wide differences in day and night temperatures. Daytime temperatures approaching 100°F. are not uncommon in most of the lower parts of the region. In the south, readings are often much higher. But nights are almost invariably cool, even after days in the desert when the thermometer passes 110°F. But the humidity is low and one does not "feel" the extremes of heat or cold. They cause nowhere near the same discomfort that attends equally high or low temperatures in the eastern states.

Seasonal Distribution of Rainfall.—Having established the two most important characteristics of intermountain climate, (1) aridity and (2) the effect of elevation upon precipitation and temperatures, the reader is ready to attack the third major feature, the seasonal distribution of rainfall. It is apparent that the kind of climate in these sections is a combination of the Pacific type and the type found in the eastern two-thirds of the United States. Ignoring differences in topography, seasonal variations in temperature are greater than those of the Pacific Region but not so great as in sections farther east. The seasonal distribution of precipitation is likewise a combination of the two climatic types. Certain sections show a distinct winter maximum with heavy snows in the mountains; others have the decided summer maximum characteristic of the central states; still others record a combination of the two, with maxima in both summer and winter. Inasmuch as these seasonal variations in rainfall have a pronounced effect upon agriculture, they have been given due consideration, together with topography, in determining sectional boundaries within the region. A brief description of the precipitation in each section will be of material aid in understanding the economic development of each.

Rainfall in the Columbia-Snake River Plateaus.—Despite their comparatively low elevation, the northern plateau sections suffer less from lack of precipitation than other sections of the Intermountain Region. Four factors account for this advantage: (1) the precipitation in general is somewhat heavier than in other sections of similar altitude both because the western mountain barrier is less effective and because cyclonic storms are more common in these northern latitudes; (2) summer sunshine is less intense than in more southerly districts and in consequence evaporation is less—an inch of rainfall "lasts longer" here; (3) the porous lava soil, almost a sponge for water, is exceedingly retentive of moisture. There is little run-off. Tilling the soil properly and keeping down weeds enable the farmer to conserve the moisture for a long period, so that dry farming (the growing of one crop in two years) is successful in areas having as little as thirteen inches annual rainfall. A map of wheat production shows the approximate extent of these dry-farming areas. Unfortunately, they occupy only a small percentage of the district. Elsewhere irrigation is necessary for the growing of crops. (4) Precipitation is distributed with remarkable regularity throughout the growing season. Rains are most common in winter and spring, while July and August are generally the dry months. This combination of a moist growing season and a dry harvest is excellent for wheat which has long been the district's chief farm product. Cloudburst and torrential rains are uncommon. In short, the farmer of the rainier portions of the northern plateaus is seriously restricted by lack of precipitation, but receives it when he is most in need and is able to conserve it through dry farming to the best possible advantage. It is probable, indeed, that an inch of rainfall is more thoroughly utilized in these lava-soil districts than anywhere else in the United States. Little rain falls but nearly all of it can be used.

Outside the dry-farming areas and a few high valleys in the Blue Mountains, rainfall is too light for crops, and farming is practiced only where water is available for irrigation. Elsewhere, grazing is the chief industry, most highly developed, of course, in the higher districts where heavier rainfall produces better pasture. Certain sections, such as the coulee district of Washington and the western portion of the Harney Basin are almost absolute desert, but this aridity is as much the result of abnormal soil and surface conditions as of lack of rainfall.

Residents of the Columbia-Snake River Plateaus are often quite as enthusiastic (although perhaps not so vocal) over their climate as the people of the southern portions of the Pacific coast are over theirs. They are quick to inform you, especially in the Columbia Plateau and the western half of the Snake River Plateau, that their winters are mild and fogless, mild enough to grow all types of temperate-zone fruits. Summer days are occasionally hot, but the air is dry and the heat is not oppressive. Rainfall is deficient in many districts but there are still thousands of acres of irrigable land. Winters are not cold enough nor summers hot enough to discourage human activity. Climatic changes are frequent enough to prevent monotony and decreased efficiency.

Rainfall in the Great Basin.—Most of the Great Basin has less than ten inches annual rainfall, and nearly all of it has less than fifteen inches. A considerable portion of western Nevada just east of the Sierra barrier has less than five inches. The entire district has arid or desert conditions. The effectiveness of the Sierra Nevada as a climatic barrier is shown by the fact that even the high sections of eastern Nevada, most of which are above 6000 feet, receive less than fifteen inches of rain, in contrast to the northern plateau district where elevations such as these ordinarily bring twenty or more inches of rain. Furthermore, the soil is not favorable to the retention of moisture, and no portion of the district is well adapted to dry farming.

The seasonal distribution of rainfall is similar to that in the northern section except that the maximum occurs usually in spring. Summer months have the least rainfall.[2] Temperatures are somewhat higher both summer and winter than in the northern plateau section, but the seasonal distribution of temperatures is much the same. In all sections irrigation is necessary for farming, and grazing is the most widespread occupation.

The California Desert.—The California Desert, driest portion of North America, differs little in type of climate from the Great

---

[2] A small portion of the western tip of Nevada is included in the Pacific Region, and is not a part of the Intermountain Region. Rainfall in that area is of the Pacific type, heavy in winter, light in summer.

Basin. Its annual rainfall is less and its temperatures are higher, but the seasonal distribution of both is similar to that in Nevada and western Utah. Few sections average five inches annual rainfall and some portions have less than three inches. A true desert, practically without vegetation except for scattered forms of cactus, its diurnal temperature range is enormous: scorching summer days are followed by nights so cool one needs a light blanket. So rare is a genuine shower that the residents find them distasteful. In the Imperial Valley a recent shower, the first of consequence in many months, worked genuine damage. House roofs leaked, side-hill irrigation ditches were washed out, and sewers were clogged with mud. A good shower in the desert country apparently is as damaging as a prolonged drought in other regions. Devoid of pasture, this section is entirely dependent upon irrigation for its agricultural production.

Nearly useless by ordinary standards, the climate of the California desert, as well as of adjacent desert portions of Arizona, has been utilized for profit in unique ways. The desert sets many climatic records. It is the place of highest summer temperatures, lowest humidity, least cloudiness, and highest rate of evaporation to be found on the entire continent. Nearly constant sunshine and low humidity have made it a haven for sufferers from respiratory disorders. Its high summer temperatures provide relief for those suffering from arthritis. It is a winter playground not only for the ailing but for numerous others who find its mild, dry winters the equivalent of joyous springtime in other parts of the country. Increasing numbers of persons from the Pacific coast migrate to the desert to escape winter fogs and high humidity. The climate is also adapted to the production of Egyptian cotton as well as dates, figs, olives, and other tree crops of desert lands. Climate, long considered a hopeless handicap, bids fair to become the most important resource of the district.

Not far east of the Colorado River the desert climate has a markedly different type of rainfall: a type which is in evidence not only in the Arizona Desert but also, with some variations, in the Arizona Highland and most portions of the Colorado Plateaus. These similarities in rainfall make it possible to consider the climate of these three sections in a single statement.

Arizona and the Colorado Plateaus.—Because of their wide variations in altitude, these districts may be expected to have varying climates. Such variations exist, but they are differences in degree rather than in kind. The high and rugged Colorado Plateaus have ten to twenty inches annual rainfall, hot summers and cold winters, varying, of course, with the elevation. In the lower Arizona foothills, rainfall is less and temperatures are higher. The Arizona Desert has annual climatic characteristics similar to those of the California Desert.

One climatic characteristic, however, distinguishes the Arizona Desert and foothills from all other portions of the region. The seasonal distribution of rainfall in these areas is unique, so different from that of other portions of the United States that it has been called the "Arizona type." Its salient characteristic is an extreme summer maximum. A dry June, the driest month of the year, is followed by a "cloudburst" season in July and August. Torrential rains in those two months bring from one-third to one-half of the entire annual rainfall. October and November are again dry followed by a slightly increased precipitation in mid-winter which tapers off into an extremely dry early summer— April, May and June. These heavy summer "cloudbursts" have an important bearing upon economic life in Arizona. In the first place, they come too late for growing crops and therefore are useful to agriculture only if held in reservoirs for irrigation during the next growing season. In addition, these downpours, occurring in an arid country, often rush down hillsides in terrific torrents bringing great loss of property and life. Many a tenderfoot tourist has been caught in a "wall of water" which rushed down a dry canyon and flooded his trail. The extent of damage to lands below can well be imagined. Emerging from the canyon the "wall of water" spreads in all directions, becoming a "sheet flood" and spreading its heavy load of sand and gravel over the flat country below the canyon mouth. In a few hours the water is gone, but its load of detritus remains, perhaps completely covering rich fields of farm land. Such "dry-washes" of torrent-borne gravel are a common surface feature in these districts. The destructive effects of such "cloudbursts" upon railways and highways is obvious. Obvious also is the fact that Arizona needs many dams to hold these waters for irrigation purposes and to prevent their destructive floods.

The Arizona type of rainfall is found with slight modification in the Colorado Plateaus to the north. It differs chiefly in that the late summer maximum is less pronounced and that there is also a secondary winter maximum of almost equal importance. June is invariably the driest month. The rainfall type is almost a perfect combination of the Arizona and Pacific types, with a double maximum, one in late summer, and the other in late winter. In other climatic characteristics these districts differ little from those previously described. Precipitation and temperature vary more with differences in elevation than with differences in location.

The Middle Rio Grande Valley.—Not to be outdone by Arizona, New Mexico also has a distinctive type of rainfall. Strikingly continental in character with a distinct summer maximum and winter minimum, it is known as the "New Mexican" type. On a rainfall chart its trend is simple, exhibiting a gradual increase from a late winter minimum to a midsummer maximum which in turn merges into a fall and early winter of decreasing rainfall. The Middle Rio Grande Valley is the only section in the Intermountain Region which shows no resemblance to the Pacific type of rainfall. Its type is eminently continental, and for that reason it is recognized as a separate section of the region.

In other respects, the climate of the district resembles that of the remainder of the region. Its higher elevations receive fifteen or more inches of rain and its basins are arid or nearly desert. Irrigation is necessary for farming, and grazing is the leading agricultural pursuit. Diurnal variations in temperature are large. Winters are cool, and summers are hot. As in the remainder of the Intermountain Region, the chief handicap to economic expansion is lack of rainfall.

AGRICULTURE

Lack of rainfall, universal in the arable portions of the Intermountain Region, has limited agricultural activity to three types: (1) grazing, (2) dry farming, and (3) irrigation farming. Natural features have restricted the last two types of farming to a few localities, and as a result the grazing industry is at once the most widespread and the most important economic activity in the region.

The Grazing Industry.—A rainfall too light for crops may produce good pasture; not the highest grade, for the best pasture requires as much rainfall as corn, but pasture of sufficient quality to support a profitable livestock-growing industry. Except in the desert sections, all portions of the Intermountain Region provide

grass of some sort, varying from the short-lived desert-like vegetation of the Great Basin to the bunch grass of the plateaus and
the alpine pastures of the higher mountains.[3] Most of the livestock
is found on ranches adjacent to the mountains or higher plateaus,
for these locations are accessible to both summer and winter
pastures.

The herding of sheep and cattle retains much of the nomadic
nature that this occupation has had since antiquity. In winter, the
Utah herdsman tends his sheep on the "desert" south of Great Salt
Lake. These pastures provide grass in winter months, but as
summer approaches and the gray-green landscape begins to turn
yellow and brown, the herdsman drives his sheep toward the
mountains and plateaus to the east where melting snows provide
the precious moisture for summer pastures. Higher and higher
the sheep are driven until by late summer they have reached the
open forest near the mountain tops. As the fall approaches they
begin the descent and Christmas finds them back on the "desert,"
a migration involving perhaps eight thousand feet in elevation. In
the meantime, many of the animals have matured and are ready
for feeding and the final preparation for market. Irrigated lands
on the home ranch provide alfalfa and small grains for these feeding operations.

With a few exceptions the grazing industry in the Intermountain Region follows this general pattern. Cattle are more
important than sheep in a few sections, but in the region as a whole
the sheep is the dominant farm animal, chiefly because of its
ability to graze on poorer and rougher pastures, its ability to
withstand longer periods without water, and its relative freedom
from injurious disease in this dry climate.[4] Sheep do not thrive in
the heat of the Arizona foothills and the "big bend" country of
western Texas; these sections are devoted almost exclusively to
the raising of cattle. Elsewhere the two animals exist almost side
by side, with sheep in the ascendancy in the sections of rougher
topography. The California-Arizona Desert has almost no grass,
therefore no grazing industry. Cattle assume considerable impor-

[3] All non-desert portions have some pasture, excepting, of course, the widely
scattered areas of barren rock. These rocky areas are not characteristic of any
section, but they are present in all of them.
[4] Freedom from disease is important. These diseases are common and very
destructive in the more humid sections of the country. Farmers say a sick sheep
nearly always dies.

tance in the irrigated sections of central Washington, the Snake River Plateau, western Colorado, the Imperial Valley, and the Phoenix section of Arizona. In all of these irrigated sections dairy cattle swell the numbers of cattle on farms. The Snake River Plateau is especially noted as a cattle-feeding district, utilizing the pulp from locally grown sugar beets to fatten the cattle. To a limited extent, the same situation is found in the Colorado and Utah districts.

With these few exceptions the entire Intermountain Region is a sheep country. Normally, the region has about one-quarter of the nation's sheep, and produces a like fraction of its wool. It also has about 6 per cent of its cattle and calves. Livestock constitutes a major source of income for the three million people who live there.

Dry Farming—the "Inland Empire."—Few portions of the world are adapted to dry farming, but one of these, probably the most noted, is in the Columbia Plateau of Washington. There the porous lava soil not only soaks up all rainfall, but if properly cultivated, retains that moisture for long periods. By dry farming this rich soil has been made to produce wheat with such success that a great undulating wheat field now stretches from the base of the Idaho Rockies westward and southward into the plateau country to the very limit of wheat culture—ten or twelve inches annual rainfall. This productive section, centering in the 'Palouse Hills" of southeastern Washington, normally produces about 8 per cent of the nation's wheat and its people have coined for it the name "Inland Empire." Spokane is its economic capital but most of its wheat goes down to Portland through the Columbia River Gorge and out to sea for the markets of the world.

People in other sections have tried dry farming, especially in the near-by Snake River Plateau where soil conditions approximate those of the Inland Empire, but the rainfall is less. Success here as elsewhere in the region has not been marked, and as a result both dry farming and the production of wheat are confined almost exclusively to the west and south portions of the Columbia Plateau.

Other drought-resistant plants such as barley and rye are grown in a few of the less arid sections, but their production is extremely small, their importance negligible. Where dry farming fails, only one resource is available to those who would grow crops—irrigation.

Irrigation—Crop Specialties.—Farming by irrigation is often considered the most spectacular type of agriculture. Irrigation appeals to the city dweller. Its engineering works fill the eye and the ability to "turn on the rain" at will fills the imagination with thoughts of scientific crop-raising. But the spectacular is frequently overemphasized. Perhaps this fact accounts for the willingness of a Congress to appropriate millions of dollars for irrigation works in a country already cursed with farm surpluses! If all the irrigated land in the United States were in one plot it would cover an area approximately the size of the state of South Carolina. Of this total, about one-half is in the Intermountain Region.

Despite this tendency to magnify the national economic importance of irrigation, there is no denying the importance of irrigation in the economic life of this region. No traveler can fail to be impressed with the way in which irrigation has transformed sunparched deserts into productive oases. And no person can deny the high quality of Arizona cotton or Washington apples or the dietary desirability of midwinter fruits and vegetables from the "American Desert." In short, these lands, like sub-tropical California, have been able, through irrigation, to supplement existing American agriculture by the production of specialties for which other sections of the country are ill suited.

Irrigation Districts.—The map of the Intermountain Region is rather thoroughly splattered with irrigation districts which range in size from a few acres to areas as large as the state of Delaware. Of these hundreds of separate irrigation areas, several stand out as being of particular importance. These may be identified either on an irrigation map or on a map of farm population.

It is evident that the irrigation districts are also the centers of rural population. In arid countries mankind seeks the oases. Just where to draw the line between major and minor irrigation projects is a difficult matter at best. Mere size is not an adequate measure, because hundreds of acres of irrigated land are in pasture and in no way comparable in economic importance to the intensively farmed truck gardens of other projects. Nor would any classification be permanent, for new projects are almost constantly in preparation and old ones are being enlarged or consolidated. For practical purposes, however, some such classification is necessary, and in a somewhat arbitrary manner we have selected eight irrigation areas as being of major importance. To this list is being

FIG. 14. Principal Irrigation Districts of the Intermountain Plateau Region. Only the most important districts are shown on this chart because there are hundreds of smaller areas too small to map. The Intermountain Plateau region depends very largely upon the Rocky Mountains for irrigation water. Lee slopes of the Sierra Nevada and Cascade Range are dry because they are in a "rain shadow." Water from the Sierra Nevada irrigates the Central Valley of California. In the development of irrigation, small streams were utilized first, because of the smaller expense of development. Many of the smaller projects were developed by private capital. Larger streams have generally been developed by the federal government. Federal irrigation projects account for the largest areas on the map. Additional areas are being developed, notably at Grand Coulee Dam, which will irrigate a large section in the central portion of the Columbia Plateau, and at Boulder Dam, whose waters will be used largely in western Arizona.

added another, the Boulder Dam project, and yet another in the Grand Coulee project of Washington. We turn our attention, however; to the eight projects already established and of a national importance.

The Apple Valleys of the Western Columbia Plateau.—No state is better known for any product than is Washington for its apples. From these irrigated orchards at the eastern edge of the Cascades come the smart forty-eight-pound boxes of carefully selected and wrapped apples which enter the grocery stores in every state in the Union. Fully 25 per cent of the nation's commercial crop of apples comes from Washington. Most of the boxes are marked with the names of two cities—Yakima or Wenatchee. The Yakima district has about two million trees, the Wenatchee about one and one-half million. Farther north the irrigated Okanagan Valley boasts nearly half a million trees, and southward just across the Columbia River in Oregon, the Hood River Valley has nearly the same number. These four valleys produce the major portion of the famous western apple crop. Their rise to leadership in the apple industry is based partially upon the excellence of their product, but even more upon their remarkable organizations for growing, packing, advertising, and marketing. Rigid inspection takes care that no blemished, worm-eaten, or unmarketable apples are shipped. Upon that basis, growers have been able to assure us that a Washington apple is always a "good apple." National advertising has done the rest.

Despite the importance of apples in these valleys, none of them are one-crop districts. Soft fruits are important, especially pears and plums. Washington grows nearly one-fifth of the nation's commercial crop of pears and nearly all of these come from the apple valleys. The Yakima Valley alone grows nearly three-fourths of the state output. Dairying, poultry-raising, potato-growing and other types of intensive farming are also increasing in importance as these valleys gradually accept the principle of diversification in agriculture.

The Lower Snake River Plateau.—The lower (western) portion of the Snake River Plateau shares a considerable portion of the western apple production. Especially near the Idaho-Oregon boundary the traveler is impressed with the large orchards and numerous fruit cellars—low, earth-covered structures capable of storing a carload or more of apples through the winter. The district is chiefly famous for its alfalfa, however, which supports an important sheep and cattle industry and makes the Lower Snake River Plateau one of the most important livestock centers of the West. Dairying has also increased in importance in recent years.

The Middle and Upper Snake River Plateaus.—Farmers to the west may pick their incomes from trees, but those who till the land in the irrigated sections of the Middle and Upper Snake River Plateau literally dig theirs from the soil. Potatoes and sugar beets are their chief cash crops. The rich, loose lava soil and the dry but cool climate of these high altitudes favor both crops. Idaho is especially proud of its potatoes, said to be the nation's best for baking purposes. It is unfortunate that high freight rates seriously restrict the sale of these potatoes in the eastern markets. But despite this handicap, Idaho regularly produces about 10 per cent of the commercial crop of potatoes, ranking second only to Maine which normally ships about twice that many. In addition to its potatoes and sugar beets, the middle plateau has also specialized to a certain extent in the growing of beans and peas, partially dried and marketed as such but also grown for seed. Idaho seed peas and beans are sent to all parts of the United States.

Utah.—Far back in 1847, the Mormons, seeking an isolated location in which to live and carry on their somewhat unconventional religious and social affairs, crossed the high Wasatch Range and descended into the valley of Great Salt Lake, there to introduce to western America the irrigation ditch and a type of agriculture destined to change the entire economic and social organization of the western half of the United States.[5] Irrigation farming proved profitable for the Mormons, especially after the opening of the West in the California gold rush. Settlement was pushed both north and south of Salt Lake City. Within a few years a long string of settlements extended along the base of the Wasatch Range from southern Idaho southward into the Salt Lake Valley and along the western edge of the Colorado Plateau into southern Utah. Today, one may travel through this district, almost the entire length of Utah, and seldom be out of sight of irrigated land. As in Idaho, the grazing industry (sheep) predominates, but the agriculture is nevertheless highly diversified. Dairying

[5] The Mormons were not first historically, but they began the modern irrigation era. Indians had practiced irrigation in Arizona centuries before, and the Spanish *padres* had also practiced it in the early days of the Spanish conquest of California and the Southwest.

and the growing of sugar beets are important north of Salt Lake City and Ogden. Vegetables, especially peas for canning, vie with the sugar beet and the dairy cow as the leading farm interest of the Cache Valley of northeast Utah. The Salt Lake Valley is the home of the well-known Utah peach, and also grows many vegetables for city markets in that area.

Southward, in the valleys of Utah Lake and the Sevier and San Pitch Rivers (the latter two in the Colorado Plateau section), alfalfa for livestock, and the many small grains and root crops which characterize diversified irrigation farming, occupy the bulk of the land. The same generalization holds for the lesser irrigated sections in southern Utah. "Dixie," as the natives know this section, is favored with a mild winter and promises to develop a fruit industry of some importance if water for irrigation can be obtained. In general, this irrigated belt, long known as the "granary of Utah," is the home of diversified irrigation agriculture. The major emphasis is upon livestock, but there is an increasing tendency toward the growing of crop specialties, especially in the cooler and more densely populated northern portions of the section.

The Imperial Valley.—Far back in the geologic past, the Lower Colorado River evidently flowed somewhat west of its present course and the Gulf of California reached inland into what is now southeastern California. Later the river shifted its course and began pouring its muddy waters east and south of the old mouth. Eventually the delta reached south and west until it clogged the outlet of the old basin and transformed it into a lake. Geological changes caused the basin to settle and the arid climate caused the lake to recede until it (the Salton Sea) occupied only a small fraction of the basin, its waters more than 200 feet below sea level. The explorers found the Salton Sink a desolate land, devoid of all except desert vegetation, a place of terrific summer heat—a place to avoid!

Perhaps it might have remained so had not someone conceived the idea of diverting a portion of the waters of the Colorado River by way of an old river bed across the Mexican portion of the depression and into the American portion. Apparently the valley needed only water to establish its position as a leading producer of winter fruits and vegetables. Water and real-estate promoters transformed the desolate Salton Sink into the thriving

Imperial Valley of California. As soon as water was made available, the growing of cotton, vegetables, and fruit began to become important. Between 1919 and 1929 the acreage in vegetables in the Imperial Valley increased fivefold. In the latter year, two crops, cantaloupes and lettuce, occupied four-fifths of the 72,000 acres of truck gardens. Cotton held third position with 22,000 acres, and grapefruit ranked fourth in land use with 8000 acres. The Imperial Valley grows practically all of the nation's early (winter) cantaloupes and two-thirds of its early lettuce. These come into eastern markets at Thanksgiving time or earlier, and make the Imperial Valley a highly significant name in the winter vegetable trade. In addition, the valley has developed an important dairy industry with the populous metropolitan areas of Los Angeles and San Diego as its markets. Upon these four products, winter vegetables, cotton, grapefruit, and dairy products, the economic life of the Imperial Valley largely rests.

The Salt River Valley.—Strikingly similar to the Imperial Valley of California in climate and economic development is the equally famous Salt River Valley of central Arizona. Here the federal government in 1910 built the Roosevelt Dam some seventy-five miles above Phoenix on the Salt River, a tributary of the Gila. And here emerged an oasis which is now responsible for growing nearly the entire American crop of long-staple Egyptian cotton (but less than 1 per cent of the national production of cotton of all types). Winter vegetables are likewise of prime importance. The Salt River Valley regularly grows about one-seventh of the nation's commercial crop of lettuce and a similar fraction of the nation's cantaloupes. Local farms also grow much alfalfa for the pasturing of sheep and cattle. In general, however, the agriculture of the district is devoted to specialties such as winter vegetables, sub-tropical fruits, and long-staple cotton.

The Salt River Project, with Phoenix as its economic focus, has been pointed out as the most successful (perhaps the only financially successful) irrigation project financed by the federal government. Attracted by the mild winter climate and the possibility of growing sub-tropical crops in the "American Egypt," settlers flocked to the project and Phoenix developed from a desert hamlet into a city of 48,000 people, a favorite winter resort and commercial center for Arizona and a large section of the Southwest.

Cultivating Sugar Beets. (*Courtesy John Deere.*)

The "Western Slope" of Colorado.—Two neighboring irrigation projects in the valleys of the Upper Colorado River and its chief branch, the Gunnison River, have brought western Colorado to a position of importance in irrigation agriculture. The type of farming does not differ greatly from that in Utah and Idaho. Alfalfa for sheep and cattle is the mainstay, but there is also an impressive production of vegetables (chiefly onions and tomatoes), temperate-zone fruits (apples, peaches, pears), and sugar beets.

The Middle Rio Grande Valley.—The narrow valley (or, more strictly, series of basins) through which the Rio Grande flows from the southern tip of the Rocky Mountains southward to the Mexican border at El Paso is irrigated for nearly four-fifths of its length. Most notable of these projects is that at Elephant Butte Dam, some seventy miles above El Paso, where water is stored to irrigate a strip of land which extends down the Rio Grande Valley for 125 miles. Farmers in this section grow cotton and a small acreage of vegetables and fruit, but farther north alfalfa is supreme and the feeding of huge flocks of sheep and herds of cattle is the principal occupation.[6] El Paso is the natural outlet for products from this area.

This list of irrigated sections could be continued. Completed it would fill the volume, but enough have been described to furnish the reader with an outline of irrigation agriculture as carried on in the Intermountain Region. Everywhere it has two dominant interests—alfalfa for the sheep and cattle which roam the near-by hills, and agricultural specialties: apples, potatoes, and sugar beets in the north; cotton, winter vegetables, and sub-tropical fruits in the south. In part, irrigation farming has supplemented the previously established grazing industry; in part also, it has provided America with specialties not easily produced in other sections of the country.

In summarizing the agriculture of this region it is well to point out that despite its large area, the Intermountain Region regularly accounts for only about 5 per cent of the agricultural production of the United States. Its greatest importance is in the grazing of sheep. Roughly one-fourth of the nation's sheep are pastured in the region, chiefly along its mountainous borders where both

[6] The Estancia Valley, a small area southeast of Albuquerque, is highly specialized in the growing of dry edible beans. Dry-farming methods are used.

summer and winter pasture are available. Except for wheat in the Columbia Plateau, practically all other farm enterprises are concentrated in the irrigated sections. These irrigated farms have become famous for the crop specialties mentioned in the preceding paragraphs.

FORESTRY

The lumber interests of the Intermountain Region can be described in a brief paragraph. Because of the arid climate, trees are rare throughout the region. Forests are found only on the highest elevations, and even in these places inaccessibility, thin stands, and inferior types of trees have ordinarily discouraged the sawmill industry. The region as a whole imports nearly all its lumber from the forested portions of the Pacific Region or the Rocky Mountains. Occasionally a small sawmill will be found on the plateaus of Arizona, New Mexico, or Utah, but in no section is the industry of more than local importance. Cities near the timbered borders of the region occasionally have sawmills using mountain-grown timber, but most of these are local institutions, interested primarily in providing their own treeless communities with building materials.

REFERENCES

The reader will find profit in reading Chs. 6-8 of Fenneman, *Physiography of the Western United States,* for a description of natural features in the Intermountain Region. The Bureau of Reclamation, United States Department of the Interior, has issued bulletins describing each of the federal irrigation projects. *The Western Range, a Great but Neglected Natural Resource* (U. S. Forest Service, 1936) describes the problems of the livestock industry.

QUESTIONS AND PROBLEMS

1. Procure a relief map of the United States. Locate the Intermountain Plateau Region. How closely do the boundaries follow physiographic lines? What effects do the topographic features of the regions to the east and west have on the climate of this region? On transportation to and from this region?
2. Break the region down into the indicated sections and describe the topography, soil, and climate of each.
3. What significant differences in soil types are found between the northern and southern sections of the Intermountain Region?

4. Why is the Middle Rio Grande Valley placed in a separate section?
5. Geologically speaking, why is the Plateau Region not like the surrounding mountains? How much has man altered the natural landscape of this region? Will this situation continue?
6. Why do temperature and rainfall vary with the elevation? What are the three most important characteristics of intermountain climate?
7. Why is the grazing industry most highly developed near the boundaries of the region? Why is the typical sheep-herder's home a wagon rather than a building?
8. Why is the sheep the dominant farm animal in this region? How important is the region in the nation's sheep industry?
9. Locate the dry-farming areas. What is grown there? Why do other crops not do well?
10. Locate the irrigated spots for this region. What kinds of crops are grown there? Are these areas larger or smaller in total acreage than the dry-farming areas? Why is it true that rural population is heaviest in these areas?
11. Describe the importance of forest products in this region.

CHAPTER VII

THE INTERMOUNTAIN PLATEAUS—
MINING AND CITIES

MINING

MINERAL production in the Plateau Region consists primarily of five metals, copper, gold, silver, lead, and zinc, to which can be added an important output of coal and a long list of minor products, both metals and non-metals. As in California, most of the early settlers were prospectors and miners who tramped these arid wastes from the Gila River to the Columbia in search of the elusive gold. Gold had lured the Spaniards into this country a half-century before the English had settled Jamestown or Plymouth, but the Spaniards had found little to encourage settlement. When the feverish gold rush to California began in 1849, the prospectors found the sun-parched intermountain country very much as the Spaniards had found it three centuries before, nearly devoid of civilization, an inhospitable land. It must be admitted that the Plateau Region was seldom a goal. More often it was a highway, a barrier to be passed by prospectors, trappers, traders, and farmers, whose goals were the more attractive sections along the Pacific coast. The Mormons settled the Salt Lake Valley in 1847, but their settlement was unique. Except for a few score of fur-traders, few white men had seen the vast intermountain country before the California gold rush of 1849.

In following the slow ox-team across these lands the traveler had ample time to observe the country, perhaps to prospect for minerals. Out of these reconnaissances came the first settlements and the first gold discoveries. In 1859, the famous Comstock lode (silver) was discovered in western Nevada and prospectors came not only to Nevada, but to other sections to reenact the colorful days of the California gold rush. Nevada became a leading producer of silver and gold, and prospectors began scouring the rock-strewn wastes of what is now Utah, Arizona, and New Mexico. As in California, gold held the center of the stage for one or two generations, but today it is far exceeded in importance by other minerals.

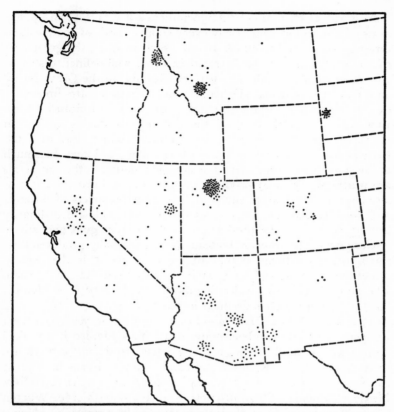

Fig. 15. Production of Gold, Silver, Copper, Lead and Zinc in the Western States, 1937. The major concentrations of mining activity in the Intermountain Region are found in the copper districts. In 1936, the value of mineral products in the four principal intermountain states was:

| | (In Thousands of Dollars) | | | |
	Arizona	Nevada	New Mexico	Utah
Gold...............	$11,287	$10,023	$ 1,156	$ 7,820
Silver..............	6,495	3,926	901	7,743
Copper.............	38,874	13,008	583	23,224
Lead...............	983	986	610	6,430
Zinc................	359	1,348	2,067	3,619
Coal...............	.....	.....	4,325	6,619
Other minerals.......	2,314	3,402	36,216[a]	5,649
Total value........	$60,312	$32,693	$45,858	$61,104

[a] Mainly petroleum and natural gas from the Great Plains Region.

Mineral Districts.—Although minerals are present in all sections of the region, and nearly every county south of the Nevada-Oregon boundary has mines of some sort or other, the great bulk of the production is concentrated in three well-defined districts: (1) north-central Utah, (2) eastern Nevada, in the Great Basin, and (3) the Arizona Highland. Other districts are important in the output of certain products, but their significance in no way compares with that of these major producing areas. In all three districts copper is the leading product, but in Utah there is also a heavy production of lead, silver, and zinc. Inasmuch as most of these ores are of a complex nature, other minerals are nearly always a by-product. Copper and lead centers are usually important for silver and gold. The copper districts of Arizona and Nevada and the copper-lead district of Utah are ordinarily leading centers in the production of by-product gold and silver.

Copper.—The Interior Plateau Region normally produces two-thirds of the national output of copper. Copper is the leading mineral in Arizona and Utah, and generally ranks first in Nevada. For many years it was the leading metallic mineral of New Mexico, but this production has declined in recent years.

Arizona and New Mexico.—For a number of years, Arizona has been the leading copper state, while New Mexico has ranked from sixth to ninth. The most important producing centers are scattered along the Arizona Highland south and east in a great arc from Jerome to the Mexican border near the Arizona-New Mexico boundary. These districts, known as the Verde, Warren Globe-Miami, and Pioneer, embrace the leading copper-producing area of America. In fact, the Arizona Highland may well be characterized as a copper-mining section. Outside the Highland, the leading Arizona copper center is at Ajo, located about one hundred miles southwest of Phoenix in the low mountains of the Arizona Desert.

Utah and Nevada.—The Utah-Nevada copper country has its greatest producing area in the vicinity of Bingham just south of Great Salt Lake. Bingham vies with Butte, Montana, for the title of America's leading copper-mining center. Nevada copper is mined principally at Ely, some 150 miles west of Bingham. Either Utah or Montana regularly ranks second among copper-mining states. Nevada holds fourth position. The Utah-Nevada output is about one-third of the national total. The Arizona Highland

and Utah-Nevada districts supply about four-fifths of the copper output of the region, or slightly more than half the copper mined in the United States.

The copper-mining industry of the interior plateaus has become important through relatively recent developments in the science of metallurgy. Vast deposits of readily available ores were known to exist in these sections, but their copper content was so low, generally less than 4 per cent, that operations were not profitable. So long as the copper industry followed methods used in iron manufacture the industry could not profit by using low-grade ores. The older method was to crush the ore and separate the metal from the waste materials by melting the ore in blast furnaces and drawing off the heavier copper from the lighter gangue (waste). This process was not successful with Utah and Nevada ores because the copper was so thoroughly disseminated in small veins and fissures that crushing failed to break apart the copper from the rock. In consequence, the operator must either smelt almost the entire ore output (at an extremely high fuel cost) or discard enough of the lower-grade ore to make the whole mining process unprofitable. Moderately high-grade ores had been discovered in Montana and Arizona, but the biggest reserves consisted of large blankets of low-grade ore. Thus the western copper industry languished and the United States depended upon the high-grade deposits of Michigan for its copper until about 1886.

In that decade improvements in recovery methods began to remake the world map of copper production. Basic among these improvements were the processes for grinding the ore into finer particles before it is separated from the gangue. Finer grinding brought a greater recovery of metal from low-grade ores, but it also sent much unrecovered metal to the scrap pile. Leaching processes were perfected by means of which copper could be dissolved from certain types of ores by treating them with sulfuric acid. The leaching process helped the western copper industry but little, since most of its ores are sulfides and cannot be separated by leaching.[1] The definite emancipation of western copper did not occur until about the time of the World War with the invention of the flotation process.

---

[1] It is possible to convert sulfide ores into carbonate by soaking them with lime water and permitting them to weather. This process has been effective in treating ores from a stock pile, but cannot be used in reducing newly mined ores.

In the flotation process the ore is first reduced to a powder and then placed in a mixture of oil and water to which is added a small amount of sulfuric acid. The copper adheres to the oil and rises to the surface while the waste materials sink to the bottom of the tank. Removed from the surface, the copper is freed from the oil by heating. The remaining copper sulfide is then roasted to burn out the sulfur and reduced to "blister copper" in a Bessemer furnace. Blister copper is about 99 per cent pure, but the remaining impurities must be taken out for most industrial uses. Further refining is necessary to produce pure copper. This is done usually by an electrolytic process. Because it made possible recovery of more than 95 per cent of the copper from the ore, the flotation process enabled copper companies to utilize ores running (in some cases) as low as 1 per cent copper. In addition, the electrolytic process made possible the separation of other metals in the final refining process. Previous (furnace) refining methods did not remove other metals such as gold, silver, and lead; their success depended not only upon pure ores, but on high-grade ores as well.

These two processes, flotation and electrolytic refining, were well adapted to intermountain ores which, though plentiful, were not only of low grade, but usually complex in nature. The industry began to grow. Steam shovels began to eat away whole mountains of ore at Bingham and in Arizona. Underground operations were also stimulated. Arizona passed both Michigan and Montana, and became the leading copper state, while Utah rose to third position. Complex ores containing mixtures of copper, lead, zinc, silver, and gold were utilized for the first time, and the copper camps became leading producers of all of these metals, valuable by-products of the major industry. Low-grade complex ores which a prior generation had considered worthless quickly became these communities' most valuable resource. Utah and Arizona may thank the gods for their vast ore deposits, but they must also thank science for making them useful.

Lead and Zinc.—It has been indicated that the story of copper in this region is also very largely the story of lead and zinc, the production of these latter metals depending largely upon the types of ore available. Production is centered in central Utah where the working of complex ores has been made practicable in recent years by the selective flotation process. The Bingham copper-mining district is the leading producer, but the true lead districts (where lead is the primary product and copper the by-product) are found at Tintic, Park City, and Rush Valley. Utah regularly ranks third among the states in lead production (Missouri, Idaho), and produces from 10 to 20 per cent of the national output. The Intermountain Region mines about one-quarter of the nation's lead and one-eighth of its zinc.

Gold and Silver.—Nearly half the United States' silver production regularly comes from the Intermountain Region and most of this silver is taken from the lead and copper mines of northern Utah. The copper section of Arizona is the second-ranking producer, and the remaining production comes largely from independent silver mines in Nevada. Silver is thus largely a by-product of mines handling the baser metals.

To a certain extent gold occupies the same by-product position as silver, but the region produces only about 20 per cent of the national output, divided roughly as follows: Arizona 7 per cent (chiefly Bisbee and Jerome), Nevada 7 per cent (scattered), and Utah 5 per cent (mainly Bingham). More than half the region's gold production is of a by-product nature, derived mainly from copper ores.

Coal and Iron.—The small coal production of the region is found in east-central (Carbon County) Utah, central (Kittitas County) Washington, and northwestern New Mexico (near Gallup). Of this total more than half is from the Utah field. The regional production is less than 1 per cent of the national output. Its economic importance is not great, but one must not lose sight of the deficiency of coal not only in other portions of this region, but also on the near-by Pacific coast. The day will doubtless come when Pacific cities must stop burning fuel oil and wood and in that day coal must come either by water from distant mines or from these sections of the Plateau Region. Utah coal is of good quality and high in heat value, occurs in generally horizontal seams, and is easily mined. Some of it is made into coke for use in a budding Utah steel industry which utilizes iron ore from the southwestern portion of the state. Utah is not yet an important steel state, but it bids fair to assume growing importance in this industry in supplying intermountain markets.

Other Minerals.—Only confusion would result from further perusal of the region's mineral production. Oregon's large production of mercury (25 per cent of United States production),

Arizona's asbestos (the leading state, but production is very small—nearly all our asbestos is imported from Canada), Nevada's tungsten, Colorado's vanadium, Washington's magnesite: all these are important locally, but have a very slight bearing upon the general economic structure of the region.

In general, the mineral industries vie with agriculture for leading position among the economic interests of the intermountain plateaus. South of the Nevada-Idaho boundary minerals generally outrank agriculture in economic importance. In these southern sections the miner takes a place alongside the rancher and irrigation farmer in the gallery of representative citizenry.

CITIES, TRANSPORTATION, AND TRADE

The trade of the Intermountain Region consists essentially of (1) assembling and shipping to outside markets the excess production of agricultural and mineral products, and (2) shipping in and distributing manufactured goods to the farms, ranches, and mining centers of the area. Except in a few districts, the tonnages to be moved are not heavy; and this fact, coupled with the difficult topography, has held railway mileage at a low figure. Except for the seven transcontinental railroads which cross the northern, central, and southern sections of the region, the only important railway developments have come in those sections devoted to dry farming (wheat) or mineral production. Rail networks appear in the wheat belt of western Washington and the copper districts of Arizona and Utah. Elsewhere the railroad map consists of long lines whose special function is the carrying of goods and passengers to and from the Pacific coast. Here and there a lonely looking branch stretches out to tap an isolated irrigation project or mining property, but the general effect is that so often felt by the traveler in these lands—goods and men often go through the region but seldom to or from it. Nevertheless, the observer must agree with the historian that the development of this region is the result of advances in the technique of transportation, that it never was and probably never can be a self-sufficing area. Take away the railroads and the trucks and buses and this region must revert to its original status—a sun-parched waste, a barrier to the conquest of a continent.

Our interest, however, is not in such speculation. The intermountain country is an experiment in geographic specialization based upon transportation; but the Corn Belt, the Cotton Belt, the Manufacturing Belt, and all other such areas of specialized economic life come in the same category. The final difference is in degree, not in kind. The intermountain country will continue to produce for distant markets in which it will exchange its surpluses for manufactured articles which it cannot economically produce in its own area.

Trading Centers.—This exchange of commodities between East and West made inevitable the growth of important distributing centers at the three transportation foci which railroads have created in their desire to utilize three important breaks in the Rocky Mountain barrier. Geography has been important in the economic development of Spokane, Salt Lake City, and El Paso as the leading cities of the intermountain country. All three of these cities have locations opposite favorable passes. Near the passes, where the railroads first begin to radiate their branches, there is need for railroad yards and shops, for warehouses, for wholesalers, and, presently, for banks, exchanges, and all the offices which comprise a transfer center. A city arises, devoted primarily to the collection and concentration of east-bound shipments and the receipt and distribution of west-bound shipments— a funnel for out-going products, a spray-nozzle for incoming goods. Such is the nature of the economic life of the three principal cities of the Intermountain Region, Spokane, Salt Lake City, and El Paso. Theirs is a development based upon railroad shops and offices, the wholesale and jobbing trades, bus and truck headquarters, banking and brokerage establishments. Primarily they are market places. Factories are present, either to process certain local products for shipment or to manufacture certain goods for local markets, but these cities as well as dozens of smaller centers in the region must be classified as commercial rather than industrial cities.

Trade Territories.—The Intermountain Region may be divided into a few large major trading areas tributary to the more important centers, and subdivided into smaller areas which are served by cities of less magnitude. Each of the major centers, Spokane, Salt Lake City, and El Paso, is located at the extreme eastern edge of the region, and their trade territories thus include large areas to the east of our regional boundary in addition to their respective sections of the plateau country. In addition, it will

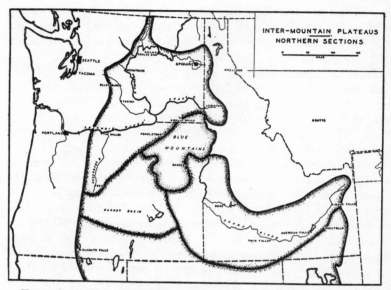

Fig. 16. Northern Sections of the Intermountain Plateau Region. The basins of the Columbia and Snake rivers consist of plateaus having relatively smooth surfaces. Both areas are floored with productive soil which was formed from volcanic ash. These sections are separated by the Blue Mountain uplift, a mountainous area not covered with lava. The Snake River traverses a deep canyon west of the Blue Mountain section. This canyon separates the section from the Rocky Mountain region. A fourth section, the Harney Basin, is marked by porous soils, aridity, and a relatively smooth surface broken by occasional low mountains.

Trade of the northern plateaus is shared by Spokane, Portland, Seattle, and Salt Lake City, as major centers, and several smaller cities. Most important of the smaller centers are Yakima, Wenatchee, and Boise. The completion of Grand Coulee Dam will bring an abundance of cheap power to the Columbia Basin and will also increase its agricultural capacity. Why is Spokane strategically located to serve the Columbia Basin?

be recalled that the Pacific coast cities, especially Los Angeles, San Francisco, Portland, and Seattle, include in their respective market territories large areas in the western portions of the region. The trading territory map therefore shows the trade of the Intermountain Region divided among the three regional centers— Spokane, Salt Lake City, and El Paso—and four outside centers —Portland, San Francisco, Los Angeles, and Denver.

Spokane and the "Inland Empire."—Previous to 1918, the trade of the Columbia Plateau went largely to Seattle, Tacoma, and Portland, whose dominance was maintained by railroad-rate structures which effectively discouraged interior jobbing centers. In 1918, however, Spokane was able to have the rate structure revised and since that time it has grown rapidly as a distribution center. Spokane now claims as its trade territory a large area it calls the "Inland Empire," which embraces not only all of central and western Washington, but also the "Panhandle" of Idaho, sections of northwestern Montana and northeastern Oregon. It is a vast territory, more than half of which is outside the Intermountain Region, but its most productive sections are the wheat and fruit districts of the Columbia Plateau.

To these districts Spokane sells farm machinery, clothing, automobiles, and other manufactured goods, produced largely in eastern markets. For them it sells wheat, lumber, fruit, and other farm, forest and mine products. With a branch of the Federal Reserve Bank (of San Francisco) and numerous other financial institutions, governmental and private, it is the financial center of the Inland Empire. A junction for five transcontinental railroads and twelve branch lines, it is likewise the transportation center for the area. Railroads are its largest employers of labor. Industrial development is not great, but Spokane has flour mills, meat-packing plants, and saw and planing mills as well as a considerable array of purely local industries such as bakeries and ice plants.

Even Spokane must admit that its claims to some of the outer margins of the Inland Empire are somewhat doubtful. To the west, especially in the apple valleys of central Washington, both Seattle and Portland normally have a portion of the wholesale trade, and in addition these valleys themselves boast growing trade centers at Yakima and Wenatchee. Each of these cities has economic importance far beyond what would be indicated by population figures. Both are located in irrigated sections where small farms prevail and where semi-urban conditions are found far beyond the corporate limits of the city. Both Yakima and Wenatchee have become important through the shipments of apples and other fruits as well as lumber from the adjacent Cascade Mountains. Local residents boast that "every fourth apple and every fifth pear comes from the state of Washington," and that nearly all of these come from the trade territories of these two cities. In recent years, an average annual total of fifty thousand carloads of fruit and vegetables has been shipped from these districts. Handling these shipments is the major interest of both cities.

Just as the names Wenatchee and Yakima have become synonymous with apples, so that of Walla Walla has become identified with wheat. Walla Walla and near-by Lewiston, Idaho, are markets for the famed Palouse country. Wheat is the dominant crop and the commercial activities of these cities are thoroughly tied to the wheat farm. Lewiston, nearer the Idaho Rockies, also has a growing trade with the expanding lumber industry of that section.

Central and western Oregon as well as the Lower Snake River Valley of Idaho normally look to Portland for large purchases, but within the area are important centers, notably Boise and Klamath Falls. Boise merchants serve the rich fruit district of southwestern Idaho as well as the important livestock industry of the Lower Snake River Valley. Klamath Falls, blossoming as a transportation center since the completion of its third railroad southward into California, is the trade center for its own adjacent irrigated area and for ranches of southern Oregon and lumber camps in the near-by Cascade Range. The city has risen to prominence in recent years as a center for the processing and shipment of pine lumber.

Salt Lake City.—Railroads which enter the plateau region at the Salt Lake City-Ogden gateway have spread their branches in three directions: (1) northward into the Snake River Valley and thence westward toward Portland and Seattle, (2) westward into Nevada with San Francisco Bay as the terminus, and (3) southward along the base of the Colorado Plateaus and across the desert to Los Angeles. Situated at the focus of these lines, Salt Lake City early became the trading center for an area which embraces the middle and upper Snake River Valley of Idaho, the copper district of eastern Nevada, and the entire state of Utah.

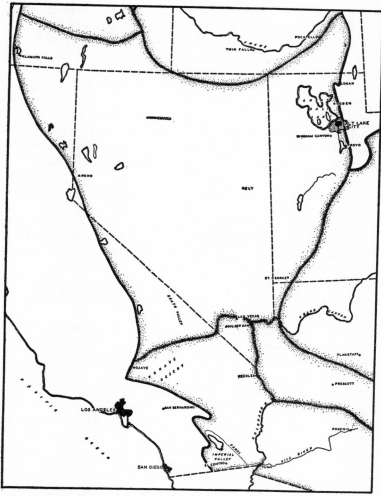

FIG. 17. The Great Basin and Adjacent Areas. The numerous basins and ranges which occupy the Great Basin section receive little rainfall and are used almost entirely for grazing. Most of the people live near the eastern borders of the section, where water for irrigation is available. The map also includes the California Desert section, the driest part of the United States. Why does this section receive so little rainfall? What is the basis for the development of Ely, near the center of the Great Basin?

The broad streets of Salt Lake City are lined with shops which outfit miners, ranchers, and farmers. Potato and sugar beet farmers from Idaho finance their operations in Salt Lake City banks. The great copper- and lead-mining companies have their offices there. In like manner Salt Lake City ranks high as a primary wool market. Its business men are as much interested in the price of copper, wool, and sugar as are those of Spokane in the price of wheat, for these prices are their business barometers. Wages in the mines are commonly raised or lowered with the price of metal, and purchasing power is thus readily determined by watching market quotations. Salt Lake City smelts lead and refines sugar and a little salt from the lake; but its factories play a relatively minor role in its economic life, which is thoroughly tied up with its commercial institutions.

Smaller centers have risen to claim a part of the Salt Lake City trade territory. Most important of these is Ogden, some forty miles to the north. Ogden has become very important as a transportation center and its wholesale houses serve much of northern Utah and southern Idaho. In the Snake River Valley, Pocatello, a leading railroad center, has come to considerable importance as a jobbing center for southeastern Idaho.

Looking southward, Salt Lake City finds its richest trade territory in the Utah mining camps, all within seventy-five miles of the city. In that direction, too, is the city of Provo, located in the valley of Utah Lake, the richest valley in Utah. Provo's trade is largely agricultural, its markets chiefly the irrigated valleys of central Utah.

Western Nevada.—Salt Lake City wholesalers have extended their trade territory westward to include the Ely copper district and the eastern portion of Nevada, but beyond the central portion of the state of Nevada they encounter active competition from San Francisco and Oakland. These cities rightfully claim western Nevada as a part of their trade territory. Locally, Reno is the most important jobbing center for those western Nevada farming and mining districts which lie at the eastern base of the Sierra Nevada. Roughly half of the people (91,000) of Nevada live within sixty miles of Reno.

El Paso and the Pacific Southwest.—The trade of New Mexico, Arizona, and the Imperial Valley is divided among El Paso and Los Angeles, as major centers, and several smaller

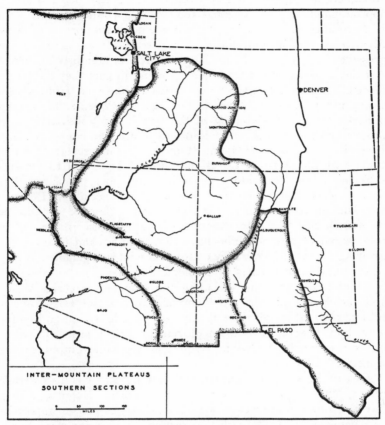

FIG. 18. The Southern Intermountain Plateaus. The nearly circular
Colorado Plateaus are high, deeply canyoned and arid in most sections,
but the remainder of the southern portions of the intermountain region
is lower and more accessible. The Arizona Highland is lower than the
Colorado Plateaus but receives more rain. Why? This section also has
many copper mines. The Arizona Desert resembles the adjacent California Desert in surface and climate. Important irrigation districts are
found in both areas, as well as in the Middle Rio Grande Valley section.

centers of which the most important are Phoenix, Tucson, and Albuquerque. The division between Los Angeles and El Paso is approximately at the Arizona-New Mexico boundary line, with El Paso in control of all but the extreme northern portion of New Mexico as well as extreme western (trans-Pecos) Texas. Aggressive Los Angeles firms have labored assiduously to make Arizona a part of their trade territory and in part they have succeeded. They have met strong competition, however, from wholesalers and jobbers in Phoenix. The city of Phoenix has grown remarkably since the opening of the Salt River Valley irrigation project and the rise of Arizona to first position in copper-mining. In addition, Phoenix has gained fame as a winter resort. The dry climate of the Arizona Desert has proved beneficial to persons suffering from respiratory disorders and this popularity has brought a considerable increase in population, especially in Phoenix and Tucson. In consequence of these trends, Phoenix has become the fourth city of the Intermountain Region, both in size and in commercial importance. Phoenix collects, ships, and finances the growing of Salt River Valley cotton and winter vegetables. It also serves the copper districts to the north and east.

Other desert sections, including the irrigated Imperial Valley and the Yuma district, are definitely within the Los Angeles trading area, although there is a growing trade by rail and motor with San Diego. Several small centers (El Centro, Brawley, Calexico) handle the winter fruit and vegetable output of the Imperial Valley.

East of Phoenix and Tucson each mining center is also a trade center, but none of these serve large territories. Nogales, with a direct rail line to the west coast of Mexico, has grown important as a gateway for trade with that section. (Cedar for cigar boxes is a leading import item.)

El Paso might be called the economic capital of the state of New Mexico. Much of the trade of the Rio Grande Valley passes through the city. El Paso also serves the New Mexico copper area and is one of the important copper-refining centers of the United States. As the largest city along the Mexican border, El Paso carries on extensive trade with the grazing and mining sections of northern Mexico. El Paso has gained much trade from irrigation projects on the Middle Rio Grande and expects to gain more as additional projects are completed.

In the Middle Rio Grande Valley, Albuquerque is the leading center for the local distribution trade. Railroad shops, lumber, and farm products from near-by irrigated sections are important in its economic development.

Western Colorado.—Although Salt Lake City firms occasionally find customers in western Colorado, the district lies well within the trade territory of Denver, some 300 (railroad) miles to the east. Denver is the logical center through which this district markets its beet sugar, minerals, and livestock.

Locally, the leading trade center is Grand Junction, important first as a railroad town, later as a jobbing center. Near-by irrigated districts and mines (coal, silver, copper, vanadium) provide Grand Junction merchants with their best customers.

In all of these trade territories the reader must not lose sight of the large areas that are involved. Each of the major trade areas mentioned is considerably larger than the New England states, yet the population of the entire region is less than two-thirds that of the state of Massachusetts. Most of these trade areas are empires in size but their populations are smaller than any one of a half-dozen large eastern cities.

Manufacturing.—The Intermountain Region supplies less than 1 per cent of the nation's manufactured goods. Previous paragraphs have indicated the nature of these manufacturing enterprises. Manufacturing is not highly developed, or even moderately developed in any section of the region. Most of the manufactured goods are brought in from other regions. The region's few manufacturing industries are concerned almost entirely with processing local materials for shipment or turning out frequently demanded articles for local markets.

The smelting and refining of metals is the leading manufacturing industry of Arizona, Utah, and Nevada. Smelters are usually located near the mines, but refining is more likely to be carried on at more remote points where cheap electric power, good transportation, and a stable labor supply are available. Much copper is refined on the Atlantic seaboard, but recent years have brought a marked tendency to locate refineries nearer the western mining centers.

Summary.—Economic life in the Intermountain Region is represented almost entirely by scattered agricultural, mining, and commercial interests. Economic development is still closely connected with the soil. Whether the region acquires more manufacturing industries in future years is largely dependent upon its ability to attract a larger population to its farms, ranches, mines, and resorts.

The tourist "industry" should not be overlooked as an important source of income in many sections of the region. The desert sections of the "Sunshine State" of Arizona have already become famous as winter resorts. The Grand Canyon and its smaller brothers and sisters of the plateau country are important magnets for tourists. In a similar manner, other less-famous sections are certain to prove more attractive in the future, especially for the summer tourist who desires the invigorating effect of the dry air in this land of magnificent distances.

Despite the limited nature of their natural resources, the people of the plateau region have generally made a good living. Per capita wealth and income are definitely above the national average. Relief loads have been low during depression years, and incomes have been high during years of prosperity. The Intermountain Region is not overpopulated. It has as little poverty as any region of the United States.

The Future.—Economic life in the Intermountain Region promises to continue to rely very largely upon the three industries which are most important today: mining, grazing, and irrigation farming. The mining industries will thrive for many years, because there are good reserves of non-ferrous metals. Cattle and sheep will occupy most of the land, for the rainfall is too light for crops. Irrigation will continue to expand until eventually the rivers of the region will carry very little water down to the sea. Waters from behind Boulder Dam will be used to irrigate a large section in southwestern Arizona. Irrigation officials estimate that by 1993, the Grand Coulee project will be supplying water for twenty-five thousand farms in south-central Washington. These projects and the many less-noted ones will enable this arid region to support perhaps a million more people. Less than half of them will be on farms, but many others will be required to operate the exchange economy of these areas. Cheap power is a by-product of irrigation enterprises. This factor may attract certain types of manufacturing industries, but distance from the large centers of population is a potent hindrance to industrial development. Except for its mining camps and irrigated valleys, the Intermountain Region seems destined to remain an area of sparse population.

REFERENCES

Mining operations in each of the intermountain states are described in *Minerals Yearbook*. Problems of power and manufacturing have been reviewed by the Pacific Northwest Regional Planning Board for the northern portions of the region. Business studies by the University of Arizona describe economic conditions in that portion of the region. A good account of the relationships between power and industry is contained in *Power Requirements in Electro-Chemical, Electro-Metallurgical and Allied Industries* (Federal Power Commission, 1938).

QUESTIONS AND PROBLEMS

1. Why did the "forty-niners" and later pioneers dread passing through this region? What later discoveries made this country more populous?
2. Where are the present-day mining districts of the Intermountain Region? Why are several minerals usually mined together? Compare the importance of mining and agriculture in the various sections of the region.
3. Describe the location of the copper districts. What process made these deposits more valuable?
4. What is the importance of railroads to this region? Do the railroads consider that the area carries its fair share of their expenses?
5. Are the cities of this region commercial or industrial centers? What are their functions?
6. Locate and describe the wholesale trade territories of the three major cities.
7. What types of manufacturing are found in this region? Is the region more or less self-sufficing with respect to manufactured goods than the Pacific Coast Region? Why?
8. Write a paragraph on the future of the Intermountain Plateaus.

CHAPTER VIII

THE ROCKY MOUNTAINS

THE significance of the Rocky Mountains in American economic life need hardly be emphasized. Their importance both as a barrier and as a goal fills the pages of our history. As a barrier they did much to hinder the early westward expansion of the American people, but their mineral wealth later proved a powerful magnet to that same westward migration. A modern generation finds them still playing this dual role—a barrier which not only makes transportation to western points difficult, but also acts as a climatic factor in shutting off all the eastern two-thirds of the continent from the mild Pacific winds. As a goal the Rockies have grown increasingly important with tourists who find their scenery and high-altitude climate unequaled in sheer grandeur and exhilarating effect.

TOPOGRAPHY

The Rocky Mountain system forms the eastern boundary of the Interior Plateau Region from the Canadian border as far south as central New Mexico. In most places the boundary line is clear, for the mountains rise distinctly above the adjacent plateau.

At this point the reader may well be ready to ask, "What is the basis for distinguishing between these two topographic types, plateaus and mountains?" There is doubtless a great deal of reason for this confusion. The intermountain plateaus are in some places much higher than some sections of the Rocky Mountains, so the distinction is not to be made solely on the basis of altitude. Nor can it be said that there are no mountains in the plateau region, for there are thousands of square miles of them, steep mountains, domed mountains, saw-tooth mountains, and mountains of nearly all shapes and sizes. But there is a difference, and that difference is largely a matter of spacing. The Rockies are a series of almost continuous mountains. In Colorado and Wyoming these are chiefly ranges, chains of mountains which may run in almost any direction but almost invariably join with some other chains, either end-to-end or at the flanks. Intervening valleys may

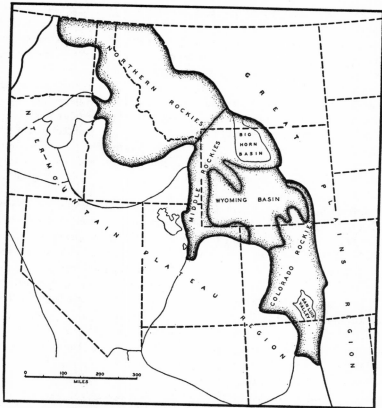

Fig. 19. The Rocky Mountain Region. This region includes three rugged sections of mountainous topography and a large intermountain basin known as the Wyoming Basin. Smaller basins and high valleys are found in the mountainous sections but none of them is large. The Colorado Rockies are very sheer and include the highest ranges of the region. The northern Rockies are lower and have more valleys. Precipitation is heaviest in the northern section and lightest in the mountain-rimmed valleys of the Colorado Rockies. The Wyoming Basin has light rainfall and little agriculture except for the grazing industry. Some geographers include the Wyoming Basin with the Great Plains region because of its similarity of economic development. Most areas of the Rocky Mountain Region are highly mineralized. Mining has always been the leading economic interest in the Rocky Mountain states. Why are mountainous regions so often mineralized?

appear, and the area of these is relatively large, but one cannot cross the region without climbing mountains. In Montana and Idaho there are fewer linear ranges and the mountains occur mainly in patches with small intervening valleys. But here again, the mountains are so closely spaced that mountain-climbing must be resorted to in getting from one valley to another. In other words, valleys or basins in the plateau country are generally open and the mountain masses are isolated, but in the Rockies the valleys are generally closed and the mountains are connected into a system. Once this distinction is made, it is easier to understand how the Rocky Mountains contain a considerable area of relatively smooth land, and yet constitute the most formidable geographic barrier in the United States.

Division into Sections.—It is customary to divide the Rocky Mountains into four topographic sections, of which three are distinctly mountainous and the fourth is a large mountain-rimmed basin. These divisions arise because the system is nearly severed by lower passes in two places. The conspicuous breaks in the system are in (1) northeastern Utah and (2) northwestern Wyoming. In northeastern Utah a relatively smooth area of low altitude connects the Wyoming Basin with the Colorado Plateaus, effectively cutting off the Colorado Rockies from their northern sisters. The mountainous terrain is resumed in the Uinta and Wasatch ranges of Utah and extends at high elevations to the vicinity of Yellowstone National Park, where a high, dissected plateau joins the Great Plains with the Snake River Plateau and effectively separates the Middle Rockies from the Northern Rockies which stretch northward into Canada. The Rocky Mountain Region is thus divided into four topographic sections: (1) the Colorado (or southern) Rockies, (2) the Wyoming Basin, (3) the Middle Rockies, and (4) the Northern Rockies. Because of the importance of topography in the economic development of the region, each of these sections merits separate consideration.

1. *The Colorado Rockies.*—The Colorado Rockies may well be thought of as consisting of two main north-south series of ranges, connected at intervals by spurs which enclose four important intermountain valleys and a number of smaller ones. The ranges themselves are nearly all linear: long chains of high peaks cut here and there by gorges of streams escaping from the

mountain-enclosed valleys. Elevations of 13,000 to 14,000 feet are common, but no peaks reach 14,500 feet. Railroads cross the ranges by following the narrow canyons, of which the most famous is the Royal Gorge, the scenic canyon cut by the Arkansas River through the granite of the front ranges. The Royal Gorge is followed by the Denver and Rio Grande Western Railroad, the only east-west line to cross the Colorado Rockies.

These mountains are probably most impressive when approached from the Great Plains. Here the "front ranges" rise a mile or more above the plain in a distance of fifteen or twenty miles, a rise that is most extreme at Pikes Peak, which stands more than 5000 feet above the nearly level plain below. West of the front ranges, mountains of all types appear, either rising above near-by plains or having been cut from them. Most of the rock is granite, but in southwestern Colorado the San Juan Mountains are of volcanic origin.

The valleys are of greater economic importance than the ranges, because most of them have considerable areas of good soil and have developed various types of agriculture. In Colorado these high enclosed valleys, if relatively free of forest growth, are called "parks." Hence, we find North Park, Middle Park, and South Park, and farther south, the San Luis Valley, all of which lie between the front ranges and the ranges to the west. Each of these valleys is enclosed by mountains, the drainage being by streams through deep canyons. The western ranges, largest of which are the Park Range, Sawatch Range and San Juan Mountains, ordinarily equal in height the front ranges to the east, but they are less spectacular because their elevation above the surrounding country is less. Both the Colorado Plateau to the west and the mountain parks to the east have high elevations ranging from 7500 to 11,000 feet, whereas the normal altitude at the Great Plains base of the front ranges is from 5000 to 6000 feet. Topography in these western mountains is similar to that in the front ranges. Transportation routes generally follow the deep canyons of the streams which drain the area. The San Juan Mountains are also noted for their landslides, a result of their volcanic origin. In this district whole mountains are said to be in motion, and streams of gravel, analogous to glaciers, will be found creeping down numerous canyons. This tendency to landslides has presented a severe handicap to both transportation and mining in the vicinity of Durango.

2. *The Wyoming Basin.*—The level of the Colorado Rockies recedes in southern Wyoming and only a few spurs extend into the state. These spurs shortly descend to lower altitudes and are finally lost beneath the sedimentary floor of the Wyoming Basin. The section is in reality a series of basins, generally 6500 to 7500 feet above sea level and separated by low mountains some of which are mere swells on which the relief is hardly apparent. The west-bound motorist is amazed to cross the highest point on the Lincoln Highway (8832 feet elevation, just west of Cheyenne) in high gear, and truly astounded some 200 miles beyond to find himself on top of the continental divide, apparently a perfectly flat plain with not a mountain in sight!

Nearly 250 miles in diameter and 40,000 square miles in area, the Wyoming Basin not only effectively separates the Colorado Rockies from those of western Wyoming, but it also provides an excellent transportation route across the highland. Selected as the site for the first transcontinental railroad, the basin has been important as a highway ever since.

Most of the small basins which compose this section have fair or good soil, especially in the flood plains of the rivers which rise in the neighboring mountains and traverse these basins on their way to form the Missouri and Colorado rivers. Rainfall is scanty and irrigation is necessary for crops, but where irrigation is possible the soil is usually found to be highly productive.

3. *The Middle Rockies.*—Extending northward from the Uinta and Wasatch mountains of Utah to the vicinity of Yellowstone National Park, the Middle Rockies show characteristics similar to the ranges of the Colorado Rockies. The Uinta Mountains are a great rounded mass, much dissected in many places, but with few crags or peaks. The Wasatch Range, on the other hand, rises precipitously above the Salt Lake Valley, forming a wall similar to that of the Colorado front range, but facing west instead of east. Transportation routes across the Wasatch Range invariably follow the canyons which lead to the drainage system of Great Salt Lake. Most noted of these is Ogden Canyon which carries the Union Pacific Railroad and a transcontinental highway by easy grades from the crest of the range to the level of Great Salt Lake. Other canyons emerge opposite Salt Lake City and Provo.

Companion ranges extend northward along the Wyoming-Idaho boundary. These partake of the nature of the Wasatch Range, but ordinarily are less precipitous although they culminate in the high and sharply sculptured Teton Range, acclaimed by many as the most spectacular mountains in America.

Mountain parks and valleys are found in the Middle Rockies, but they are not so large as those of Colorado. Most noted of these are Jackson's Hole and the Upper Snake River Valley (both drained by the Snake River and located near the middle Wyoming-Idaho boundary), the Bear River Valley of southwestern Idaho, and a few smaller parks in the Wasatch Range in Utah.

4. *The Northern Rockies.*—Some disappointment is frequently registered by tourists who enter Yellowstone Park from the west or south. For the park is a plateau, monotonously unimpressing over its southwestern half. The wonders of Yellowstone Park are really carved from this plateau whose altitude is from 7500 to 8500 feet. The scenic appeal of Yellowstone Park is threefold: (1) its lakes, notably Yellowstone Lake with an area of 150 square miles and an elevation of 7741 feet; (2) its stream gorges, especially Yellowstone Canyon, whose colorful walls are a thousand feet deep and which has two waterfalls with a total fall of 422 feet; and (3) its hot-water phenomena, consisting of some four thousand hot springs and one hundred geysers. The park includes the greatest geyser region of the world. Despite its rugged character, the Yellowstone district is largely a plateau which joins the Great Plains and the Snake River Plateau and separates the Middle Rockies from the Northern Rockies of Idaho and Montana.

The Northern Rockies differ from those farther south chiefly in their lesser altitude and the small number of linear ranges. In a few small districts, such as Bitterroot Range which forms a part of the Idaho-Montana boundary, linear characteristics are present, but in general the mountains such as the Salmon River, Clearwater, and Coeur d'Alene mountains of Idaho are huge jumbles without definite spatial characteristics.

In Idaho these mountains are generally closely spaced and without large intermountain valleys, but several such valleys are found near the southern portion of the section where the mountains meet the lava of the Snake River Plateau. In Montana, wider spacing is prevalent and there numerous valleys of fair size embrace perhaps 15 or 20 per cent of the area. These valleys are known by the geologist as "tertiary lake basins" because of the large amount of sediments from the tertiary period which cover their floors. These sediments, which usually occur in gently sloping terraces, often provide good soil for agricultural purposes.

Valleys are found in nearly all portions of the Montana Rockies, as well as in extreme northern Idaho and northwestern Washington. In northern Montana and Idaho they are so common that the range is practically severed and railroads are able to cross into the Columbia Plateau at a low altitude by way of the "Spokane Gateway."

Near the Canadian boundary the Northern Rocky Mountain section is occupied by a jumble of mountains cut by numerous small valleys, trenches, and canyons, most of which have a north-south trend. As a result, the district is divided into a dozen groups of mountains, each with its own local name and no one of which is of commanding importance. The most westerly of these depressions, the broad valley of the lower Okanagan River separates the Northern Rockies from the Cascade Mountains of the Pacific Coast Region. With these numerous breaks, the international boundary traverses a mountainous and little-used district from Puget Sound eastward to the Great Plains. The trenches of the Northern Rockies provide splendid natural transportation routes through an area of otherwise difficult terrain, but they are little used because their direction is counter to the usual course of trade, which generally takes an east-west direction.

The Rocky Mountain system is geologically young and presents the angular characteristics generally associated with recent formations. The region is a land of steep slopes, marked local contrasts in elevation, numerous canyons, and a scarcity of low passes. The very height of the system makes it a potent barrier to climate and the rugged topography makes transportation difficult.

THE ROCKY MOUNTAINS AND TRANSPORTATION

The Transcontinental Railroads.—The Rocky Mountain barrier has had a marked influence on the location of transportation routes in the western United States. Rough topography and a scarcity of low passes have contributed much to restricting the seven transcontinental railroads to three widely spaced locations.

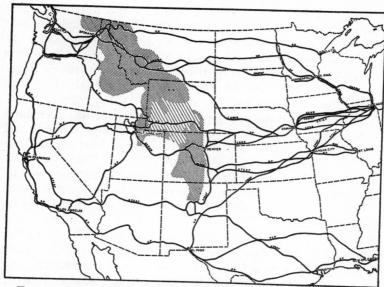

Fig. 20. Transcontinental Railroads and Major Connecting Lines. Railroads play an important part in the economic geography of the western United States. Most of them were built before the country was settled, and their routes became the sites for the major cities of the western regions. The map shows the location of the seven major lines which connect the Middle West with the Pacific Coast. It also shows the location of important connecting lines, but does not show branch lines. Shading indicates the location of the Rocky Mountain region, with the Wyoming Basin shaded more lightly than the remaining sections. Notice how these railroads converge on the three principal intermountain cities, Spokane, Salt Lake City and El Paso, and on the four principal Pacific seaports. Why did the northern transcontinental lines go so far north to cross the Rocky Mountains? Make a list of the principal freight-originating areas of the western states from your knowledge of economic development in these regions. Then see if you can determine which railroads are likely to carry this freight eastward. If possible, check your estimates against the annual reports of the railroads as published in one of the investment guides such as *Poor's Manual*. Why must investment analysts know something about economic geography?

In the field of transportation,[1] the term "transcontinental" is used to describe the railroads which extend from the Middle West (usually Chicago) to the Pacific coast. Seven lines fulfill this requirement, but only two of them (the Santa Fe and the Milwaukee) are under one management all the way from Chicago to the Pacific coast. Railroad geography divides these lines into three groups, known as the northern, central, and southern transcontinental railroads whose Pacific coast termini are Portland-Seattle, San Francisco, and Los Angeles.

The northern transcontinental group consists of three lines which compete for business in the territory between Chicago and the Pacific Northwest. Two of these, the Great Northern and the Northern Pacific, terminate in Minneapolis-St. Paul, but reach Chicago over the rails of the Burlington which they own jointly. The third northern transcontinental road is the Milwaukee which serves much the same territory as its neighbors all the way to Seattle and Portland.

The central transcontinental lines extend from Chicago to San Francisco. Both of these lines are divided among three or more companies. The Union Pacific, pioneer transcontinental.line, extends from Omaha to Ogden. Its Omaha traffic reaches Chicago over the lines of several companies. West of Ogden, its traffic is carried by the Southern Pacific (the Union Pacific also has its own lines into Los Angeles, Portland, and Seattle, and thus competes with both the northern and southern roads). The second central transcontinental line runs through Denver and Salt Lake City. Several roads operate between Chicago and Denver, but between Denver and Salt Lake City there is just one, the Denver and Rio Grande Western. West of Salt Lake City, the line follows the

---

[1] Railroad names used in this section are the "short names" commonly employed by the public and the railroads themselves. The full names of these railroads are:

Santa Fe—Atchison, Topeka, and Santa Fe Railway
Milwaukee—Chicago, St. Paul, Milwaukee, and Pacific Railroad
Great Northern—Great Northern Railway
Northern Pacific—Northern Pacific Railway
Burlington—Chicago, Burlington, and Quincy Railroad
Union Pacific—Union Pacific Railroad
Southern Pacific—Southern Pacific Company
Denver and Rio Grande Western—The Denver and Rio Grande Western Railroad Company
Western Pacific—Western Pacific Railroad
Rock Island—The Chicago, Rock Island, and Pacific Railway Company

rails of the Western Pacific, whose western terminus is San Francisco. Omaha, Denver, and Salt Lake City are important intermediate points between Chicago and San Francisco on both the central transcontinental lines.

The two southern lines avoid the Rocky Mountains in reaching Los Angeles. The Santa Fe runs from Chicago to Kansas City and skirts the southern end of the Rocky Mountain system at Albuquerque. West of Albuquerque, the Santa Fe takes a course nearly due west across the Colorado Plateau and Mojave Desert to Los Angeles. Los Angeles traffic also reaches Chicago over the rails of the Southern Pacific and Rock Island lines. This route runs from Chicago to Kansas City, but west of Kansas City it takes a more southerly route than the Santa Fe, passing through southern New Mexico and Arizona on its way to Los Angeles. The southern transcontinental lines generally compete for traffic throughout the entire distance from Chicago to Los Angeles. There are also north-south lines along the Pacific coast and the eastern edge of the Rocky Mountains which interconnect all of the transcontinental lines. It is significant, however, that the seven transcontinental lines are grouped geographically into three widely spaced routes whose location was strongly influenced by breaks in the Rocky Mountain barrier.

Railroads Across the Rocky Mountains.—Railroad-building in the Rocky Mountains has been restricted to relatively few lines and these are found only where the lowest passes are available or where a large tonnage of minerals provides an important revenue tonnage. Lowest and easiest routes across the barrier are found just south of the Canadian border. The three northern transcontinental lines pursue their winding paths from one Montana valley to another and finally pass over low passes (5211, 6317, and 6374 feet) into northern Idaho to enter the Columbia Plateau by way of the "Spokane Gateway." Each of the three penetrates the Butte copper country, and a fourth (Union Pacific) reaches Butte from the Snake River Plateau to the south.

Railroad-building was comparatively easy in the Wyoming Basin, but the traffic density is small and the only railroad which crosses it is the Union Pacific. The Union Pacific divides in western Wyoming, one branch extending into the Snake River Plateau, the other crossing the Wasatch Range into Ogden and

Salt Lake City. Two other lines enter the Wyoming Basin, but neither crosses the continental divide.

The higher and steeper Colorado Rockies have been crossed by only one railroad, the Denver and Rio Grande Western, which winds through the deep Royal Gorge, crosses the continental divide at a height of 10,000 feet and reaches Salt Lake City after a difficult ascent of the Wasatch Range in east-central Utah. Other railroads have penetrated the Colorado Rockies, but none have crossed them.

Highways.—In general, highway construction has been similarly curtailed, although mountain roads are surprisingly good when one considers the difficulty of construction and the sparseness of the tax-paying population. Per capita expenditures for highway construction are above the national average and the tourist is assured all-weather roads (usually gravel) over a considerable number of interstate highways. These roads have done much to open many mountain sections to outside markets and have made many a mining camp or mountain valley a better place to live.

CLIMATE

As in all districts of marked irregularities in topography, the climate of the Rocky Mountains varies greatly with altitude. If allowance is made for the greater elevation the climate is similar to that of the plateau region to the west. Precipitation is generally heavier in the north, the Idaho Rockies receiving from fifteen to forty inches annually. Higher sections of the Middle and Colorado Rockies receive thirty inches annually, but the total diminishes rapidly as lower altitudes are reached. The San Luis Valley of southern Colorado records less than ten inches, as does the western (rainshadow) portion of the Wyoming Basin. Montana valleys receive fifteen to twenty inches a year. Most of the tillable sections are thus near the lower limit of rainfall for agriculture, and irrigation is generally resorted to. Streams from near-by mountains provide abundant water except in the Wyoming Basin where the area of cultivable land exceeds by far the acreage for which water is available. The seasonal distribution of precipitation varies with location. Eastern portions receive most of their moisture in summer, while western portions have the spring and fall maxima of the plateau region.

Temperatures likewise vary with altitude. Winters are apt to be cold and long except in the lower valleys, and summers are mild. The crisp summer air is one of the region's chief reasons for popularity with tourists. With a growing season seldom longer than three months, mountain agriculture is restricted to quick-maturing crops. Corn does not thrive, but the small grains and hay crops are successful in all sections. Winter temperatures are generally above those of the Great Plains, but somewhat lower than those of the plateau region. Heavy winter snows in the Wasatch Mountains and the Montana and Idaho Rockies have compelled railroads to build many miles of snow sheds and provide themselves with many snow plows and other types of special snow-fighting equipment. Higher highway passes in the Colorado Rockies are clogged with snow until mid-June each year.

In winter, most valley communities receive from time to time "chinook winds." The chinook is a wind which blows down the mountain, becoming drier and warmer as it descends. When it comes, it melts the snow, occasionally drying snow banks so completely that the ground is not even left muddy. In its wake comes the inevitable cold wave characteristic of mid-continental winters.

Climate in itself is not a severe limitation to economic development in most sections of the Rocky Mountain Region; but the combination of climatic and topographic handicaps has kept agricultural production low. The higher portions of the region generally receive ample rainfall, but these portions contain little land fit for cultivation. Lower areas, on the other hand, are generally too dry to grow crops. Rainfall deficiency marks the climate of the Wyoming Basin, Big Horn Basin, San Luis Valley, and most of the valleys of the Montana Rockies. These relatively smooth areas contain nearly all the potential farm land of the region. Where water is available, these basins have become productive through irrigation; but lack of water restricts this type of agriculture to a small percentage of the total area.

AGRICULTURE

The Rocky Mountain Region normally contributes slightly more than 1 per cent of the national output of farm products. But agriculture is nevertheless the leading occupation in most sections and its importance in the general economic development of the region cannot be denied.

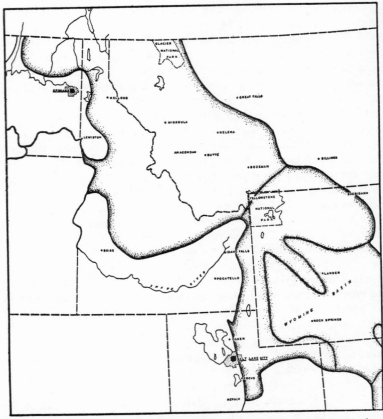

FIG. 21. The Northern Rocky Mountains. Principal urban developments in the northern Rocky Mountains have occurred in the mining and irrigation-farming areas. Butte, Montana, is the largest center, and its interests center mainly in the copper mines. Several small cities are found in the silver-lead district of northern Idaho. The Idaho Rockies have little economic development, but in Montana there are many irrigated valleys, nearly all of which have spawned small cities. The Middle Rockies are high and rugged, the least-used section of the Rocky Mountain system. The Yellowstone-Grand Teton section is an important summer vacation area. Many of the wholesale interests of the Northern Rockies are served by Spokane, and Salt Lake City performs similar functions for the Middle Rocky Mountain section.

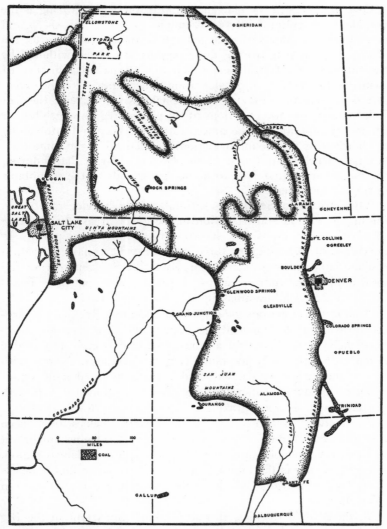

FIG. 22. The Southern Rocky Mountains and the Wyoming Basin.
The southern Rocky Mountains lie largely in the state of Colorado and
are often known as the Colorado Rockies.

Grazing.—As in the plateau region to the west, grazing is the dominant agricultural interest. Summer pastures for sheep and cattle bring thousands of these animals to the mountains after the pastures of the neighboring drier regions have been withered by the summer sun. It will be recalled that the seasonal nature of pastures is an important consideration in accounting for the extensive development of grazing in the Snake River Plateau, the Salt Lake Valley, and other portions of the plateau region which border the Rocky Mountains. The concentration of sheep and cattle along the borders of the mountain region is explained in the same way. Animals which are pastured on the plateaus or Great Plains during the winter are transferred to higher grasslands in the mountains during the summer.

The Northern Sections.—Stimulated by heavier rainfall in the higher valleys and irrigation in the lower areas, the growing of short-season crops has shown considerable development. In northeastern Washington, three or four valleys have developed a small dairy industry catering largely to the Spokane market and local mining and lumber camps. A similar development is found in the Wasatch Mountains opposite Salt Lake City.

Among the numerous valleys of the Montana Rockies the largest agricultural development has been in the Bitterroot and Flathead valleys which extend as one structural trough almost due north and south nearly 300 miles. General farming is the rule with special emphasis upon dairying and a small output of fruit. Other Montana mountain valleys have a similar development, but with greater emphasis upon grazing.

Agricultural developments in the Idaho Rockies have been meager. Only around the lower margins is farming important and there it resembles agriculture in the adjoining plateau region. Wheat-growing is the major interest and it is most highly developed on the margins of the Palouse country of southeastern Washington.

In the Middle Rockies, farming is most important in the Big Horn Basin which raises sugar beets and dry beans and pastures a large number of sheep. Dairying and general farming are most important in the Wasatch-Bear River Range District.

The Wyoming Basin is devoted almost exclusively to grazing. Rainfall is light and crops are grown only in the irrigated areas.

Population is sparse, farms are large and the tending of sheep is the leading farm occupation.

Colorado.—Grazing is also important in the higher portions of the Colorado Rockies, especially in the western ranges. In the parks and valleys, however, crop specialties are of greater importance. Lettuce, green peas, and other vegetables are important in North, Middle, and South Parks. The flat San Luis Valley shows similar specialization, with areas devoted to lettuce, peas, potatoes, dry beans, cauliflower, and celery. Colorado regularly grows from 3 to 5 per cent of the nation's lettuce, and nearly all of it is mountain grown. Between 1 and 2 per cent of the nation's commercial crop of potatoes and nearly 4 per cent of its dry beans are grown in the irrigated sections of the dry San Luis Valley. Farming in the northern portions of the Colorado Front Range from Denver northward to Wyoming partakes of the nature of that in the adjacent Great Plains Region and probably should be assigned to it. Sugar beets are the leading crop.

MINERALS

To most of us, the Rocky Mountains stand for mineral development. Historically, this relationship is true, for no section of the entire Rocky Mountain system has been without its prospectors, its miners, its roaring frontier camps, its fevers of prosperity and chills of depression. Here, more than in any part of the United States, history has been written by the miner with his pack and pan who followed each mountain brook to its source in alpine snows and combed the entire area for gold. And the gold was there, so plentifully that the federal government early established a mint at Denver to care for this production, just as it established one at San Francisco in response to the California output. Gold is still there, and so is the miner with his pan. Mining still is the leading occupation in the entire region, but modern history is not being written by the gold-miner. Rather, it is written in terms of copper, lead, zinc, coal, and silver, and the chief characters in its drama are the large corporations whose services are made necessary by the heavy expenditures required for mining these less-valuable minerals.

Mining Districts.—It is hardly an exaggeration to state that except for the numerous basins and valleys where agriculture prevails, the Rocky Mountain Region is a mining community.

Mines of some sort are found in nearly every county from New Mexico to the Canadian border (and beyond), but from these lists one quickly selects two centers of major importance and a half-dozen of lesser magnitude. The remainder are so numerous and diverse that they defy generalization and classification.

Montana.—The one leading mineral product of the Rocky Mountain Region is copper, and the one leading mining camp is in the Butte Mining District of Montana. Highly concentrated in Silver Bow County, the Butte Mining District is recognized as the leading copper camp of the world. From it has come nearly one-fourth of the nation's copper, and from it, almost alone, comes the copper which normally places Montana in second or third position among copper-producing states. The Butte mines regularly produce from 15 to 18 per cent of the national output of copper.

Unlike the majority of workings in Utah, Arizona, and Nevada, the copper ores of the Butte area are found at great depths. Here relatively high-grade ores are mined at levels from 2000 to 5000 feet below the surface in the heated atmosphere characteristic of deep rock formations in these sections. Huge financial outlays have been necessary and as a result the mining industry is almost entirely in the hands of one large corporation (Anaconda) which not only mines the ore, but also operates its own smelter (at Anaconda) and refinery (at Great Falls), and likewise has far-flung holdings of a similar nature in many parts of the world.

The Montana copper industry is thus a chain with three distinct links. Ore is hoisted from (1) the Butte mines and sent by the trainload to (2) the smelter at Anaconda, some twenty-five miles distant. From Anaconda the blister copper moves to (3) an electrolytic refinery at Great Falls, where cheap hydroelectric power is utilized to turn out pure commercial copper for American and foreign markets. As a result of this copper development, Butte has become Montana's chief city and Great Falls its chief manufacturing center. Silver, zinc, and gold are the most important by-products of these operations.

Most Montana ores are complex, and the Butte district is also important for other non-ferrous metals. Scattered gold, silver, lead, and zinc mines are found throughout the Montana Rockies, but the most important outlying producers are within a radius of sixty miles of Butte. In 1937, the Montana Rockies produced 17 per cent of the nation's silver, 4 per cent of its gold, 4 per cent of its lead, and 6 per cent of its zinc. Together with copper, these four metallic minerals account for about two-thirds of the Montana mineral output. The Montana Rockies are also an important source of high-grade manganese ore.

Non-metallic minerals of Montana are mainly petroleum, natural gas, and coal, all found near the west margin of the Great Plains, just beyond the eastern boundaries of the Rocky Mountain Region.

Idaho.—The other major mining area of the Rocky Mountain Region is the Coeur d'Alene district of northern Idaho which i the leading lead-producing district of the West. Idaho is surpassed only by Missouri in lead production, and the Coeur d'Alene district normally produces about 25 per cent of the national output. Lead and zinc are closely associated in the ore bodies, and because of this complexity the district has become important only with the perfection of the selective flotation process (see Chapter VII). Silver has lately become important and is derived not only from the lead and lead-zinc ores, but also from ores containing mainly silver. The Coeur d'Alene district had the nation's largest silver mine in 1938, and for several years Idaho has been the leading silver state, with nearly one-quarter of the national output. Nearly all the lead is smelted and desilverized locally (at Bradley, Idaho) or at East Helena, Montana. Zinc, derived mainly from lead-zinc ores, is refined chiefly in the electrolytic plants at Kellogg, Idaho, and at Anaconda and Great Falls in Montana.

The Coeur d'Alene district produces more than 90 per cent of the Idaho mineral output. Other production is scattered and of minor importance. In recent years a small quantity of phosphate rock has been mined near the southeast corner of Idaho. In northeastern Washington mining is general, but not of economic prominence. A small output of lead, zinc, gold, and molybdenum is reported.

Wyoming.—In Wyoming the chief minerals are fuels—coal and oil. Good coal is well distributed around the outer portions of the Wyoming Basin, and the output of the state's five scattered producing districts is sufficient to give Wyoming second position among the states in the western half of the United States in coal production. Only Colorado reports a larger output. The Wyoming production is about 1 per cent of the national total, while that of Colorado is about 2 per cent. The largest mining development is at Rock Springs. Smaller operations are found at Kemmerer, Sheridan, Hanna, and Gebo. Railroads traversing the Wyoming Basin have found these coal deposits extremely valuable, located at almost exactly the points where they are most needed.

Wyoming petroleum comes largely from the Salt Creek District near Casper, just beyond the regional boundary in the Great Plains Region. Wyoming refines much of its crude oil for local consumption, but the fields are connected by pipe line to eastern and midwestern refineries.

Other Wyoming minerals have small importance when compared to coal and oil. Metallic ores are found in few places, notably iron ore (about 1 per cent of the national output) from the southeastern portion of the state, near the town of Sunrise. A small output of phosphate is also reported from southwestern Wyoming (Cokeville).

Colorado.—The Colorado mining industry is characterized by a variety of products the output of which is widely scattered. Historically, Colorado has had several important mining centers (such as Cripple Creek and Leadville), but the present mineral industry is not dominated by any particular section of the state. Coal is usually the leading mineral, its production divided among several fields, the largest of which is at the edge of the Great Plains at the Colorado-New Mexico boundary. Trinidad (Colorado) and Raton (New Mexico) are its mining centers.

Central Colorado.—In central Colorado the mountains which rim South Park yield gold (Cripple Creek is the center), lead and zinc (Leadville), silver, molybdenum, and a small amount of copper. Molybdenum has been Colorado's most phenomenal mining industry in recent years. The mine at Climax (near Leadville) is the largest in the world and produces 90 per cent of the national output. In recent years molybdenum has become one of the principal mineral products of the state. The metal is used as an alloy in the manufacture of high-speed steels.

Other Sections.—In the southwest, the San Juan District (Silverton and Eureka) produces a similar variety of metals from equally complex ores. Northern Colorado has coal fields, the most important of which are near Steamboat Springs and Boulder. A small production of petroleum, iron ore, and fluorspar is also reported from scattered sections of the state. The Colorado mineral industry is thus unlike that of any state in the West in that it is not dominated by a single mineral and has no dominant center.

Other States.—Mineral production in that portion of the region which lies in Utah (i.e., the Park City silver-lead district) was described in connection with the plateau region (Chapter VII). Topographically, the Wasatch Mountains are a part of the Rocky Mountain system, but their mineral development, like their agriculture, is thoroughly tied to the Salt Lake Valley economic structure. The portion of the Rocky Mountain Region which lies in New Mexico is small in area and its mineral output is of minor importance. Practically the entire New Mexico mineral production is found in other regions.

The Rocky Mountain Region produces about 4 per cent (by value) of the nation's minerals. The foregoing description probably places too great emphasis upon mineral development in the region, but in doing so, it follows the precedent of history and of the people who live in those districts today. Minerals have always been the most talked-of feature of Rocky Mountain economic development despite the fact that in many sections other industries are of greater importance.

FORESTS

Nearly all the mountainous portions of the Rocky Mountain Region are forested, and small sawmills which cater to local demands for mine props or rough lumber are found in almost all sections. Inaccessibility, inferior quality, and thin stands have restricted the lumber industry of the Middle and Southern Rockies, and the only major sawmill development is found in northern Idaho and adjacent portions of Montana and northern Washington. Here the rainfall is heavier and transportation is less difficult than in sections farther south. Not only is the rainfall heavy enough to have produced fine stands of large trees, but topography has not greatly hindered cutting, milling, and marketing the lumber.

The Rocky Mountains regularly produce 4 or 5 per cent of the United States lumber output, and of the regional total fully two-thirds comes from Idaho. White pine, marketed as Idaho white pine, is the chief type of tree. The wood, remarkably soft and easily worked, is especially valued for sashes, doors, and wooden matches. A large portion of the lumber for the American wooden-match industry is Idaho white pine. Inasmuch as Idaho has the largest remaining stands of white pine in America, its importance in lumbering seems destined to continue. Across the Bitterroot Mountains in Montana the chief types of trees are ponderosa pine, larch, and Douglas fir. Ponderosa pine is their chief type of lumber, but Montana is the leading state in the production of larch, while Idaho leads the nation in the output of white pine. Ponderosa pine is also important in northern Idaho and adjacent portions of northern Washington.

THE RECREATION INDUSTRY

The Rocky Mountains offer the summer tourist vacation facilities which are unsurpassed on the continent of North America. The Rockies have every conceivable variety of mountain scenery from sheer crags and deep canyons to alpine meadows, dense forests, and glaciers. Swimming and boating are available on numerous small lakes and the streams are famed for trout. Above all, mountain summers are cool, twenty degrees cooler than those of the farm and factory belts to the east. Recreational opportunities are manifold, from well-upholstered resort hotels to free tent sites in the national parks, and from the dude ranches of Wyoming and Colorado to trail-end shelters miles from civilization.

More than half the area of the Rocky Mountains is owned by the national government, as national forests or national parks. All such districts are designated as recreational areas, and are being made accessible by good roads and trails. The outstanding recreational centers of the region are the three national parks: Yellowstone, Glacier, and Rocky Mountain. Little need be said about the attractiveness of these parks, for their features are well known to every American who reads the vacation advertisements. These parks contain unusual concentrations of scenic attractions, but they are only representative of the recreational resources which fill the region from Santa Fe to the Canadian boundary and beyond.

The people of Colorado recognize the vacation industry as one of their major sources of income. Estimates of annual expenditures by out-of-state tourists vary from thirty million dollars a year upward, but certainly rank the vacation business among the leading industries of the state. The Colorado Rockies receive more tourists than other sections of the region because they are nearer the national centers of population; but the vacation industry is of major economic importance in every part of the Rocky Mountains. Gateway cities such as Denver, Santa Fe and Colorado Springs profit considerably by handling the summer tourist business.

CITIES

Geographers have long observed that mountainous regions of the temperate zone do not produce great cities. In the tropics, where the task of avoiding the ill effects of lowland climates is a major problem, most of the large cities have grown up in the more healthful climate of higher altitudes; but in the temperate zones such measures are unnecessary, and man has built his cities in the easier topography of adjacent lowlands. Except for a few summer resorts, such population centers as have arisen in our mountainous areas have usually remained small, unless they have grown in response to a large local production of minerals or some other raw material requiring the services of many people.

The Rocky Mountain System of America is no exception to this generalization. The previous chapter has indicated that the major cities of the Intermountain Region are located near the eastern margin of the region. Salt Lake City is so near the towering Wasatch Range that the visitor feels he can almost "reach out and touch the mountains." Spokane is farther from the base of the Northern Rockies, but its position is similar. At the eastern base of the Rockies the situation is much the same. Denver, the chief city, is located on the edge of the Great Plains, a very few miles from the foot of the Colorado Front Range. Minor centers follow the same pattern. Pueblo and Colorado Springs, second and third cities of Colorado, have locations similar to that of Denver. From Great Falls on the north to Albuquerque on the south, the major trading centers of the Rocky Mountain Region are located just beyond its borders. The reader will recall a similar distribution of population centers in the Intermountain Plateau Region.

Denver is the capital city of the Colorado Rockies, and its development reflects both the mining and vacation-industry aspects of their economic life. In addition to serving the mountains,

Denver is the commercial center for the rich irrigated districts of the Colorado Great Plains. Denver grew into a city as a supply base for the silver and gold miners of the mountains. Later it became the terminus for railroads from Chicago and the eastern cities. North-south railroads skirting the Front Range made it their headquarters. Eventually, Denver acquired far-flung commercial interests, and became the wholesale, financial, and shopping center for both the Colorado Rockies and the adjacent Great Plains.

Today, Denver is the leading commercial and banking center between the Missouri River and the Pacific coast. It is an important livestock market and has several meat-packing plants. Denver manufactures clay products and mining machinery and assembles automobiles. It has large railroad shops and sugar refineries. All of these manufacturing industries are definitely local or sectional in scope. Denver processes the products of its hinterland and manufactures a portion of the equipment and supplies used there. Essentially, however, it is a commercial center, a focal point for trade, distribution, and finance.

South of Denver, the cities of Colorado Springs, Pueblo, Santa Fe, and Albuquerque likewise occupy sites at the border of the region. Colorado Springs is best known as a summer resort, the central attraction being Pikes Peak. Pueblo claims distinction as the largest steel center between Chicago and the Pacific coast. At Pueblo, iron ore from Colorado, New Mexico, and Wyoming is combined with local coking coal to manufacture iron and steel from the Rocky Mountain states. Pueblo is the second city of Colorado in population, manufacturing, and wholesale trade.

Santa Fe and Albuquerque, in New Mexico, are distribution centers for the northern portions of that state. The quaint pueblo architecture of Santa Fe is a never-failing attraction for tourists. Albuquerque has a small lumber industry.

Northward from Denver, the Rocky Mountains have no important urban centers except in the mining districts of Montana, where Butte is the ranking commercial center, as well as principal headquarters for the mining interests. Trade of the Wyoming Basin is shared by Denver, Salt Lake City, Casper, and Cheyenne, all located outside the region. Major center for the Idaho white pine district is Lewiston, located at the eastern margin of the Columbia Plateau section of the Intermountain Plateau Region.

Spokane is the trading center for the Idaho Panhandle and its mining interests.

Summary.—Difficult topography and lack of good soil have prevented the Rocky Mountains from acquiring a large population based upon agricultural or commercial interests. There is some farming throughout the region, but generally the most important sources of income are mining and forestry. Most of the cities have grown up at the margins of the region where city-building has been easier and access to transportation better. These cities are dominated by commercial interests. One (Pueblo) is a steel center and another (Butte) is a mining city. All of the other major centers of the Rocky Mountain Region are interested primarily in trade and distribution.

PRODUCER-CONSUMER RELATIONSHIPS IN THE WESTERN STATES

We pause now for a brief evaluation of the part played by the western states in the drama of American economic life. The term "western states" has no authoritative definition, but for present purposes it includes those eleven members of the American commonwealth which contain the Rocky Mountains, Interior Plateaus, and the Pacific Coast Region. It includes two groups of states in the standard American classification: the Pacific group, including California, Oregon, and Washington; and the mountain group, embracing Idaho, Montana, Nevada, Utah, Wyoming, Colorado, Oregon, and New Mexico. These states occupy slightly less than two-fifths of the area of the continental United States and hold a little less than one-tenth of the national population.

The change in attack from a regional approach to one involving states as units is made deliberately. The reader should be familiar by this time with the location of economic regions in the western United States. He should know that a typical western state includes several segments from economic areas whose boundaries are entirely unrelated to state lines. He is familiar with the fact that the state is not a good unit for the presentation of economic data because of this geographic diversity, but he must also face the fact that for most types of economic data the unit is the state. Up-to-date information for smaller units is not ordinarily available. One of the fundamental purposes of this volume is to provide the reader with a framework for relating such generalized data to the particular areas in which they are likely to be most important. When, in the future, the reader comes across annual statistics for apple production in Washington or copper production in Montana, let us hope that he will not conceive these activities as being spread uniformly over the entire state! Yet for most types of current economic information we are likely to be compelled to work with state data for years to come. The preceding chapters should provide a framework for localizing such data in that 40 per cent of the continental United States which we find listed in statistical tables under the headings "Pacific States" and "Mountain States."

Characteristic Products of the Western States.—To the corner grocer and the housewife, the western states are important as a source of many types of fruits, vegetables, and fish. To Wall Street, these states stand for mining corporations, railroad interests, lumber companies, oil wells, the movies, aircraft factories and a sizable list of lesser industries engaged principally in producing or transporting raw materials or semi-manufactures. To the eastern manufacturer, the West is a vast, scattered market which buys a wide variety of manufactured goods and manufactures few products locally. To the national economy, the western states contribute mainly food and industrial raw materials, of which the most important are fruit, vegetables, fish, wool, meat animals, lumber, copper, lead, and silver. These are the products which the western states send to national markets to be exchanged largely for manufactured goods. But we are neglecting a very important phase of economic life. What do the western states mean to their own people? How do the people of these eleven states share in the income produced within their borders? What are the amounts and sources of the income of the residents of the Pacific and mountain groups of states? Do they receive all of the income derived by local economic institutions? Is not a considerably larger portion of their incomes derived from intraregional trade than from the interregional trade so often emphasized? Answers to these questions can be found only by analysis of the incomes of the people. We turn the spotlight from the problems of the creation of income to a consideration of the distribution of income among the residents of the western states.

The Distribution of Income.—It is fairly obvious that income created in a community may not be paid out in the same community. An example will clarify this point. Let us assume that a western mining center turns out each year a quantity of copper ore valued at one million dollars at the mine. This is new wealth. A million dollars in income has been created. Who receives the proceeds from the sale? A portion of it goes to local employees for wages and salaries and represents a definite contribution to the income of the community. But the mines use much machinery which is constantly being replaced, and this is bought elsewhere. There is no local power source, so coal and electricity are imported from the outside. The mine is owned by outside capital. Dividends and interest payments, partially to amortize the original investment, are made to outsiders. In the final analysis, about the only contribution of the mine to this community consists of wages, salaries, and fees paid to persons on its local payroll. In mining communities these local payments often represent as little as one-tenth of the income realized from the mines. Thus it becomes very dangerous to assume that all of the income appearing in a community is actually attributable to it. A large portion of the receipts may go to pay for parts of the productive process which are performed elsewhere.

The portion of locally produced income which remains in a community varies greatly from one industry to another. At one extreme is the small owner-operated farm which uses little machinery and whose debt-free operator retains practically the entire proceeds from the sale of his produce. At the other stands a hydroelectric plant generating thousands of dollars' worth of electricity, but employing only a few persons. Most of its expense is incurred outside the community. Income from the hydroelectric plant is distributed largely to investors who may live in all sections of the country. The major task of this volume is to identify the location of productive activities. But we must not lose sight of an equally important phase of economics, the location of purchasing power. In the final analysis, every portion of the economic process is performing some function designed to supply goods and services to the consumer. Ability to consume is dependent very largely upon the possession of income. Thus the geographic distribution of income receipts becomes an important part of economic analysis.

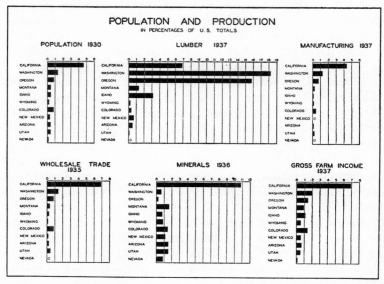

Fig. 23. Population and Production in the Western States. The function of Figs. 23 and 24 is (1) to provide a review of the relative national importance of the western states in various types of production, and (2) to give some idea of the differences which arise between income produced and income received. All charts show each state as a percentage of the national total. Fig. 23 shows the position of the western states in representative types of productive activity. For purposes of comparison, the population of each state is also shown graphically. Note that these states hold relatively high national positions in lumber and mining, but that their share of the national total of manufacturing is relatively small. The charts also show how far California leads other western states in most types of economic activity. The data shown for various types of production were derived from government publications listed in the Introduction. The figures are not strictly comparable, because different government agencies use different classifications. For example, the mining figures include a certain amount of manufacturing and transportation. There are no trustworthy estimates of income produced in individual states, but the figures cited above give a fair clue to income produced by certain types of industries.

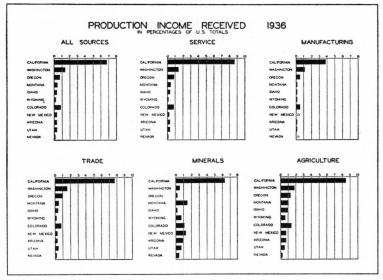

FIG. 24. Production Income Received in the Western United States, 1936. Data for these charts are taken from the annual estimates compiled by the National Industrial Conference Board. These estimates are designed to show income *received* rather than income *produced* ·in the various states. These figures obviously differ materially from those used in Fig. 23. All of the income produced in a state may not be received by the people of that state for a number of reasons, as explained in the text. In the western states, the disparity between income produced and income received is especially notable in the mining industries. Mining corporations typically buy large quantities of machinery and supplies in other states. Most of them are national concerns owned by stockholders residing in many states. Thus the mining operation that extracts a million dollars' worth of ore in a community is not at all likely to create a million dollars' worth of income in that community. Much of the proceeds is spent elsewhere. In the final analysis, about the only portion of the income which is made available in the community is the expenditures for labor and other personal services. The problems of absentee ownership are beyond the scope of this volume, but comparisons between income produced and income received provide a clue to the intensity of the problem.

A fair evaluation of the outstanding features of economic development in the western states can be obtained from Figs. 23
and 24. These charts should be studied together in order to obtain
comparisons between income produced and income received, and
also to facilitate comparisons among the various states. Data of
this type become available annually and should be brought up to
date by consulting the sources indicated.

Income Produced.—The purpose of Fig. 23 is to provide
a recapitulation of the production data given in the preceding
chapters. These charts show the relative importance of the western
states in various types of productive activity and indicate in a
rough way the importance of each state in these sectors of the
national economy. They do not show the relative importance of
these activities within each state, because trustworthy estimates
of income produced are not available.

Income Received.—The analysis of income received sheds
additional light on the fundamental nature of the economic process and indicates more clearly the problems of geographic analysis.
Typically, the production of a commodity begins in a very small
way with the exploitation of natural resources. At the point of
production the product of the land is likely to be in neither the
right place nor the right form for final consumption. Transportation becomes necessary as well as manufacturing, each of which
adds to the value of the material. Finally the product reaches
the consumer through the manifold avenues of trade. By this
time the value of the commodity has been increased, perhaps several fold, by the additional productive effort expended upon it.
These additions to its value have been paid for all along the
line and form the incomes of the people making them.[2]

The Location Problem.—In studying the location of economic
activities it soon becomes apparent that certain types tend to
group themselves about the centers of primary production. The
processing types of manufacturing industries are prominent in
seeking such locations. Other economic activities are nearly always located near the market for their products. The retail
trade and the service occupations are important examples of productive activity best carried on wherever population is clustered.

---

[2] In addition to commodities, producers also sell intangible services which
satisfy human wants directly. These service groups normally create nearly one-
third of the national income (see Chapter I).

Thus the key factors in economic location are associated with either the location of raw-material production or the location of population. The relative attractiveness of these two types of location varies with technological change, but at any given time the result of these forces is reasonably predictable. In the western states, the dominant attractive force has generally been raw materials, the products of the farm, mine, forest, and fishery. Only around the metropolitan seaport centers of Los Angeles, San Francisco, Seattle, and Portland do we find large groups of producers whose location is associated primarily with the concentration of population.

In the western states, the major concentrations of productive activity are found in areas possessing unusual natural advantages. Again we are reminded that agriculture can be practiced only in those locations whose natural resources are favorable to it; that mining, forestry, and fishing are possible only in areas containing the resources for these industries; that the types of manufacturing concerned with processing goods for shipment generally find greatest profit in locating plants near the sources of their raw materials; that the facilities of transportation, trade, and finance demanded by these exchange economies must likewise be located near the producers they serve. In this way the essential features of the economic structure of the western states are traced to the natural resources of the areas they occupy. These resources largely dictate the location of a major group of their economic institutions. They limit the location of basic economic activities to certain specific areas, and account very largely for the clusters of farmers, miners, lumbermen, and fishermen which appear on the economic map. These producers of basic commodities are in the minority throughout the area, but their very location is the most important factor in determining the residence of many other persons whose economic functions are of an allied character. Location near the point of basic production is almost essential for a large group of persons engaged in transportation, trade, and the processing types of manufacturing industries. Their function is to prepare the products of the farm, mine, forest, and fishery for shipment to outside markets and to perform the exchange and transportation functions necessary to effect their delivery to these markets. Thus the very act of basic production also involves the local services of many persons not directly engaged in these types of economic activity.

We also recall that all producers are also consumers who do not ordinarily produce the things they consume but must obtain them by exchange. Goods for their consumption must frequently be brought in from outside areas, and many services must be provided. A large portion of these exchange and service functions must be performed locally. In this way, the local occupational pyramid appears. At its base are the natural resources, exploited by a minor fraction of the whole population whose location in this area is dictated very largely by the nature of the resources and their own abilities to exploit them. Associated with these producers of basic commodities, both geographically and economically, are large numbers of additional workers whose functions are associated with exchange. These producers are needed to carry on exchange among local producers as well as between the local area and outside areas. The same community also has numerous workers whose functions are of a service nature, designed to satisfy local wants directly. Adding these groups together, we find the essential features of the typical community in the western states. Competition has directed primary production into certain locations and these locations have consequently become attractive for large groups of additional producers whose functions are associated with exchange and personal services.

The close relationship between natural resources and economic development in the western states has prompted a comparatively detailed treatment of natural environment in the preceding chapters. In the remaining regions of the United States, the natural environment has less diversity and its effect upon the location of economic activities has not been so precise as in the western regions. In many of these eastern regions the reasons for the geographic distribution of economic life are to be found as much in history and economics as in the natural environment. The chapters which follow are therefore marked by a lesser emphasis upon the natural environment and a correspondingly greater emphasis upon the history and culture of the people.

REFERENCES

The geological surveys of Montana and Colorado have issued numerous bulletins concerning both surface features and minerals. Fenneman's treatment of the Rocky Mountains in *Physiography of the Western United States* provides an excellent basis for understanding local economic developments. Bulletins of the National Park Service, United States Department of the Interior, describe the various national parks and analyze their patronage.

QUESTIONS AND PROBLEMS

1. Why have the Rocky Mountains been made into a separate region?

2. How do the four sections of the Rocky Mountains differ in topography and soil? Which is steeper, the east or west slope of the Rocky Mountains?

3. Characterize in a sentence the topography of this region. Would a noticeable difference be found if the topography of the Plateau Region were characterized in a similar manner?

4. Locate the main "transcontinental" railroads on a map. Why do they fall into three major groups, the north, middle, and south?

5. What is the main characteristic of climate in this region? Present a brief summary of the major climatic features. What is a chinook wind?

6. Agriculture is difficult in the Rocky Mountain Region. Why is it still the most important occupation in many districts? What agricultural interest is most important? How does the agriculture of the Rocky Mountain Region differ from that of the Central Valley of California? Why?

7. Where are the leading mineral districts of the Rocky Mountains? What minerals are most important? Anaconda became a city because the site provided good water for smelting copper. Why did Butte become a city?

8. The Coeur d'Alene district is included in this region. It is serviced by Spokane, but Spokane is not included in this region. Why? Why are the boundaries of economic regions not based on trade areas?

9. Why is the Rocky Mountain lumber industry centered in Idaho?

10. Why is the recreation industry important to the people of this region? Why is the region so popular with summer tourists?

11. Locate the main cities of the region. Why did cities grow up on these sites? What functions do they perform? How do they differ from eastern cities such as Pittsburgh and Detroit?

12. Carefully outline the section on "Producer-Consumer Relationships in the Western States."

13. Why has natural environment received so much attention in these first chapters? Will it continue to be of such importance in the next chapters on the remainder of the continental United States? Why or why not?

14. How do you account for the location of the major cities which serve the Rocky Mountain Region? Why do the boundaries between economic regions often prove advantageous sites for cities?

CHAPTER IX

THE GREAT PLAINS GRAZING AND WHEAT REGION

NATURAL ENVIRONMENT

Physiographic History.—Before we drop down out of the Rocky Mountains and start our inspection trip across the less spectacular but more productive lands which comprise the eastern two-thirds of the United States, it might be well to pause for a moment and undertake a brief survey of the country we are entering. You can see a long way from these lofty peaks of the front ranges; and when you turn your face to the east and contemplate the flat featureless landscape that sweeps eastward to vanish in the purplish haze of the level horizon, you are bound to feel yourself on the threshold of a different world. Behind you stand the rugged peaks and forested slopes of a spectacular but difficult mountain country; but your face is turned toward the smooth lands which here begin their eastward sweep across half the continent. At the eastern edge of the Rockies you are standing on the rim of the great interior basin that comprises geographically and economically the heart of the North American continent.

Perhaps you are familiar with the differences in geologic history which account for the contrast between the mountainous topography of the western states and the smoother relief features of the central and eastern states. If so, you have a good background for appreciating contrasts in economic development between these areas. You will know that the recent geologic history of the central and eastern regions has been comparatively quiescent, that their present features relate more to the leveling action of water than to recent cleavages in the earth's crust. You know that the mountains of the central and eastern regions were already old when the mighty uplifts which created the Rockies were revolutionizing the topography of the western half of the continent, and that the present rounded slopes of the Appalachian and Ozark highlands show the results of millions of years of erosion not yet experienced by the younger mountains of the West.

Geologic History.—In a very early period, the continent of North America was marked by a massive upland occupying much of what is now the eastern portion of the continent. Another elevated area occupied what is now the western margin. Between these areas lay a vast shallow basin which at various times was below sea level. Both highlands were made nearly level by later erosion, but eventually a new warp appeared to form the ancestors of the present Appalachian and Ozark highlands. West and north of this uplift there was little crustal change and the sea continued to deposit limestone, sand, and shale, interspersed with occasional deposits of coal and petroleum. Later periods brought the Rocky Mountain uplift, an intrusion of molten granite which raised the old sedimentary rocks more than a mile above the adjacent plains. Erosion began and sediments from the Rockies were deposited around their bases. Streams cascading down the eastern slopes of the uplift spread their sediments on the floor below. Thus began the formation of the Great Plains by the same processes that ages before had built a piedmont-alluvial plain around the base of the older Appalachian Highland. Consideration of these eastern physiographic changes can well be postponed to a later chapter. Our immediate interest is in the Great Plains.

Formation of the High Plains.—It is clear that the present surface of the Great Plains consists almost exclusively of materials eroded from the Rocky Mountains. In this history, two stages should be distinguished. First came the original Rocky Mountain uplift which was followed by a long period of erosion that lowered the mountains materially and deposited a thick mantle of sediment over a broad belt to the east. This formation was well established when, in a later period, both the mountains and the western portions of the plains were uplifted (without notable crustal fracture) and a new era of erosion began. This later period rejuvenated the rivers, which began to attack the soft sediments of the older plains. The effects of this last stage are apparent today. In eastern Colorado, Wyoming, and Montana, much of the older plain has been removed, and the surface has been left rolling by stream action. But in western Kansas and Texas much of the old plain remains, higher and flatter than the more recently eroded low plains near them. These older plains are known to physiographers as the High Plains, and include the Staked Plains of New Mexico and Texas. Similar topography is found on the Edwards Plateau of Texas, but in this section the surface is the result of resistant rock strata rather than the deposition of sediments.

The Low Plains.—Erosion also removed much of the old-plains surface from the lands farther east, and left a low, broadly undulating surface which today characterizes the landscape of the central portions of Nebraska, Kansas, Oklahoma, and Texas, making these areas resemble the northern parts of the region. Topographically, the plains merge almost imperceptibly into the prairies in the eastern portions of the Dakotas, Nebraska, Kansas, and Oklahoma. The prairies differ from the low plains essentially in having shorter slopes and heavier soil. Their native vegetation was tall grass, whereas the original cover of most of the plains was the short grass characteristic of semi-arid lands.

Physiographic Sections.—In descending from the Rocky Mountains, one enters a relatively smooth and treeless country which dips gently toward the east. From Nebraska northward, these plains are comparatively low and the surface is rolling, with occasional rough areas. South of Nebraska, three distinct physiographic belts are noted. Near the base of the mountains one crosses a belt of piedmont hills which lead to a slightly higher table land to the eastward known as the High Plains. The High Plains terminate on the east, usually as an east-facing escarpment or narrow belt of rough country. East of this break lie the low plains whose broadly undulating landscape extends eastward to merge almost imperceptibly into the rolling topography of the more humid prairies. The High Plains are the geologic remnant of an older plain which was elevated during the last uplift of the Rocky Mountains. Where this surface has been removed through erosion, we have the low plains which occupy the central portions of Texas, Oklahoma, and Kansas, and nearly all of the states farther north. The physical characteristics of these plains are traceable partly to their alluvial origin, and partly to their climatic history.

Climate and Native Vegetation.—The Great Plains Region marks the western limit of the continental type of climate which prevails over the eastern two-thirds of the United States. This climatic type derives its most important characteristics from the fact that the western mountain barriers remove the moisture from the prevailing westerly winds.

The area east of the Rocky Mountains is in a rain shadow and must depend for its moisture upon tropical air brought in from the Gulf of Mexico and the Atlantic Ocean. These sources generally provide ample moisture for the eastern portions of the

United States, but precipitation gradually decreases toward the west, leaving sections west of the one hundredth meridian with rainfall generally inadequate for crops. Throughout all of these eastern regions most of the precipitation occurs in the summer months, the months of highest temperatures during which tropical air masses find the continent most accessible. An important feature of continental climates is a summer maximum in precipitation. Another characteristic is the marked seasonal variation in temperatures. Far removed from the moderating effect of the oceans, mid-continental areas become hot in summer and cold in winter. The continental type of climate is one of marked seasonal change.

In the Great Plains, the continental climate achieves an extreme form. Here the precipitation is light and the summer maximum is pronounced. Winters are cold and summers are hot. Greatest seasonal variations in temperature are found in the northern sections which include the geographic center of the North American continent. These climatic features have been the most important limiting factor to economic development in the plains country. Their effect is well illustrated by the history of the farming industry.

AGRICULTURE

The Farmer on the Great Plains.—The Great Plains have long been an important factor in American economic life. The pioneer found this broad belt of semi-arid, short-grass country alive with buffalo and populated with scattered bands of nomadic Indians. The short grass provided a scanty pasture when compared with the tall grass of the more humid prairies farther east, but cattle and sheep could be grazed successfully if sufficient space could be provided. The Great Plains offered space a-plenty. From the Rio Grande northward to the Canadian border and far beyond into the Peace River country of western Canada, millions of undulating, treeless acres became the home of vast herds of cattle and sheep. In the first and second decades following the close of the Civil War, the Great Plains consisted of open range, government land, free to be grazed by any herdsman who drove his flocks across them.

Government Land Policy and Barbed Wire.—The Great Plains might have remained an open range, common grazing land without individual ownership, but for two factors. First came a greatly liberalized government land policy, inaugurated during the Civil War, under which it became very easy to acquire land, even in large tracts. But the lands thus acquired could not have been held by the owner without the coming of the second factor— the invention of barbed wire. The vast ranches necessary for grazing purposes simply were not worth fencing by old-fashioned methods. Barbed wire greatly reduced the cost and increased the ease of fencing. Soon thousands of miles of barbed wire enclosed the newly acquired ranches, and by the end of the century the open range had practically disappeared from the Great Plains.

We have been taught that in the growth and development of a new country, the pioneer grazing industries are inevitably followed by the introduction of farming in all cases where soil and climate are favorable. The Great Plains proved no exception to the rule. Farmer followed herdsman across the prairies of the Mississippi Valley, pushing the cattle and sheepmen westward across Iowa, Missouri, Minnesota, Kansas, Nebraska, and the Dakotas, sinking the plow into the dry, fertile plains, ever westward, even to the base of the Rocky Mountains. Central Kansas and the eastern portions of North and South Dakota became vast wheat fields, and Nebraska divided its interests between wheat and corn. Cotton became important in Oklahoma and Texas.

This westward migration of the plow and reaper which had continued for more than a century was destined to meet a reversal on the Great Plains. Time after time, the loose gray soil was plowed and planted, only to produce promising young shoots of corn and wheat which were blasted, withered, and dried in the hot searing winds of a dry summer. Thus the advance legions of the plow and reaper were thrown back, defeated, and often broken. By the end of the first decade of the present century the western limit of profitable farming seemed to have been reached at about the middle of the United States, which is about the one hundredth meridian, and also near the line marking twenty inches average annual precipitation. At the beginning of the World War, in 1914, it seemed fairly certain that there would remain between the great farm belts and the Rocky Mountains a broad strip of semi-arid country which would forever be devoted to grazing. A few favored valleys near the base of the Rockies had been opened to irrigation, but elsewhere we were quite willing to predict that very little of the land between the one hundredth meridian and the mountains would ever be devoted to crops.

The World War.—Then came the World War with its terrific demand for wheat to feed war-engrossed Europe. Farm prices rose enormously. High-priced wheat and hogs pushed the wheat and corn belts far into the short-grass country where, under normal conditions, farming never would have been attempted. Grasslands were plowed up far west of the one hundredth meridian, in areas whose annual average rainfall was fifteen inches or less.

The World War ended, and in 1920 came a post-war depression which brought disastrously low farm prices. The expected abandonment of these semi-arid areas began in the manner which had been anticipated. It was forecast that within a very few years after the collapse of the war boom the newly plowed areas would again be in grass, and the old boundaries reestablished. That forecast proved to be erroneous.

When the agricultural census of 1925 was taken, it showed that, despite five years of low prices, wheat, corn, and cotton were still being grown on the farms which had been placed in cultivation during the World War. Instead of the expected abandonment, actual expansion of these crop areas had taken place.

Farm prices had improved somewhat by 1930, the year of the next census, but this improvement was not sufficient to explain the additional expansion of crop areas in the Great Plains. Millions of acres had been placed in cultivation in this semi-arid belt at the same time that other millions of acres were being abandoned in the more humid but less fertile areas of the hilly eastern states. Thousands of square miles had been added, permanently, it appeared, to the western portions of the wheat, corn, and cotton belts.

Power Farming.—The reasons behind this farm-belt expansion relate primarily to the introduction of power farming. Tractors and harvester-threshers had been in use in the wheat belts for many years, but these machines had been heavy, unwieldly, and costly to own and operate. During and after the World War, however, rapid progress was made in the development of light oil-powered tractors which were fast and economical to operate. At the same time the combination harvester-thresher, universally known as the "combine," had been made smaller, lighter, and more efficient. Farm machinery manufacturers introduced multiple-row planters and cultivators in the Corn Belt, so that not one or two but three, five, or as many as fifteen rows of corn could be planted or cultivated by one man at a speed two or three times as great as was formerly made with horse-drawn, single-row equipment. In the southern sections, the new equipment included a "sled" which is driven over ripe cotton plants and does an inefficient but very economical job of picking the cotton. All of this new equipment required relatively smooth land, free from stones and boulders, and available in large plots at low prices. Such land was to be had only in the Great Plains. Improved machinery thus made possible the extension of farming into vast areas formerly considered suitable only for pasture. By 1930, the Great Plains grazing areas had shrunk to less than two-thirds of their pre-war size, and large areas had been added to the farm belts.

Drought, Dust, Depression, and Defeat in the 1930's.— There was one important weakness in this expansion. A half-century before, pioneer farmers had met defeat in their battle with the plains climate. One of two good years of better-than-average rainfall had encouraged settlement, but these were followed by many years of complete drought, utterly without the possibility of crops. The 1920's again brought a few such years of abnormal rainfall, but the following decade was less kind. Terrific droughts scourged the plains states in the summers of 1932 to 1936, and again there was much abandonment of the land.

Worse, indeed, than the loss of crops was the loss of topsoil. Successive years of deficient rainfall had left the cultivated surfaces a mass of dust. The loose soil was driven aloft by summer winds until dust storms darkened the sky as far east as Illinois and Kentucky. Many inches of precious topsoil were removed from this newly plowed land, leaving a surface inevitably less fertile and less capable of producing even the grass for which these districts are undeniably best suited.

Conservation and the Future.—Wind erosion in the Great Plains has thus become a conservation problem of national significance, comparable in gravity with the water-erosion problems of the South and East. Strangely enough, the methods of treatment are quite similar. Where topography is unfavorable for farming, trees, shrubs, and grass are planted. On the farmed slopes, contour farming is resorted to. Rows of trees are planted at intervals to break up the air currents and prevent the winds from attaining such destructive surface velocities. By following these principles,

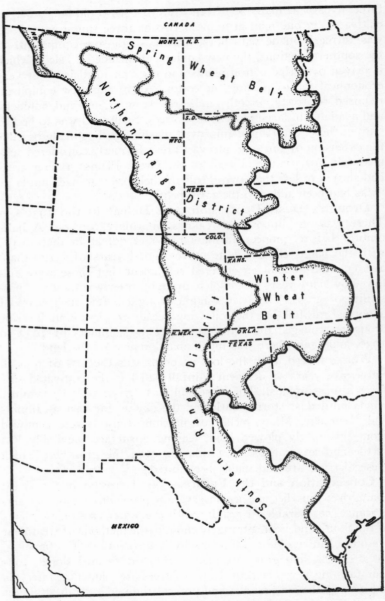

FIG. 25. The Great Plains Region.

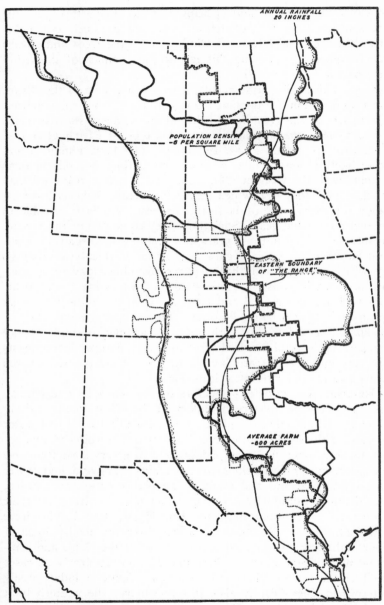

FIG. 26. Possible Eastern Boundaries of the Great Plains Region.

much of the cropped land is being returned to pasture, and the areas which are still cultivated are protected as much as possible from the erosional effects of wind. If only the trees and shrubs can be made to live—and this is uncertain—much of this wind erosion can be prevented.

Despite these discouragements, it seems that most of the wheat, corn, and cotton farmers will not withdraw from these newer, drier parts of the great farm belts. Many farmers, short of capital or temperamentally unsuited to this type of life, have moved back to more humid areas. But many more have remained and seem likely to stay. Today they are calculating the odds in their gamble with the weather. "One good crop in five years will pull us through," they say, which means four years of heart-breaking labor for every year of bountiful harvest. Nor is it possible to predict these good years. Sometimes they come two or three years in succession, and in those years new buildings and roads are built and salesmen are active. Again, as many as thirteen years may go by with no crops. This life requires the philosophy of a gold-prospector, who toils on fruitlessly always expecting a rich strike. But with enough capital and tenacity, farmers of the plains say grain-farming can be made to pay. The land, of course, must be cheap and taxes low. But with modern machinery a single farmer can care for several hundred acres of wheat, and production costs are very low. The Great Plains farmer must always be prepared to withstand a long series of lean years.

Regional Boundaries.—Factors of physiography and climate unite to make the western boundary of the Great Plains entirely obvious. Geologically, the plains were formed by wind and water erosion of the Rocky Mountains. The crystalline rocks of this uplift apparently reached great heights and rose very abruptly above the sedimentary formations of the plains. As wind and water eroded the highland and mantled the plains with their burden, the mountains gradually lost height, but never entirely lost their sheerness. Throughout most of their length, the Rockies have few foothills, but rise almost as a wall from the plains. Some of their highest peaks are within a few miles of the plains and command magnificent views of the range country. In nearly all cases the break is quite evident and the physiographic boundary easily determined. Significantly also, this line marks the western limit of the Eastern Climatic Province. Small wonder, therefore, that land-use boundaries coincide with these natural ones. The line between the Great Plains and the Rocky Mountains is a definite physical and economic boundary. Unfortunately for the student, the eastern border of the Great Plains is not so definitely established.

Economic Change and the Eastern Boundary.—Agricultural history indicates that the Great Plains have been the scene of a rapidly shifting drama of American agricultural development. Land utilization on the plains has varied enormously from year to year and from decade to decade. Most of the region has always been in grass and probably always will be, for even the most optimistic farmer would not attempt to grow grain in those dry sections nearest the mountains. But in the more humid eastern sections a new invention or a change in the price of grain may alter the agricultural landscape almost overnight. The eastern boundary of the Great Plains thus cannot be defined either accurately or permanently in terms of land use.

Absence of Clear-cut Natural Boundaries.—It is likewise impossible to locate an eastern Great Plains boundary in terms of climate, topography, soils, or native vegetation. In central Nebraska the plains merge with the prairies so imperceptibly that no line can be drawn. To the north and south it is possible to follow a series of escarpments and belts of hills along a line which generally separates the higher plains from the somewhat lower prairies to the east. Using these structural differences as a basis, the physiographer has established an eastern boundary which in most places has genuine physiographic significance. This boundary has had little or no effect upon economic development, however, and it is confusing if used in designating the limits of the economic region.

Climatic boundaries likewise have little significance beyond determining the zone within which these oscillations of grain-farming and ranching occur. There is, for example, a western limit, a rainfall line beyond which wheat will not conceivably grow; and an eastern line indicating an average rainfall adequate to make wheat almost certain to be grown. The eastern limit of the area originally in tall grass has been used as the boundary, but here again we find little correlation with present land-use policies. Several of these possible dividing lines are shown in Fig. 26. All of these factors are significant, but no one of them determines land use.

Yet there is a Great Plains Region, despite the impossibility of establishing a permanent eastern boundary for it. This mid-continental area receives separate treatment in practically every study of natural or social development in the United States. In our reading we encounter the plains type of topography, soil, climate, and vegetation; and we have come to distinguish the plains Indian, the plains community, and the plains economic organization as human features associated with this region. We have come to associate the Great Plains economic structure with an agricultural development involving large farms and a specialization along lines best adapted to a dry climate with great seasonal extremes in temperature and marked annual fluctuations in precipitation. More recently, we have also recognized the smooth topography as conducive to the development of power farming.

In general, the greatest competition between types of farming for occupancy of the Great Plains has been between grazing and wheat. We have already indicated that the line of battle is never clearly marked and that it moves backward and forward as price and technology favor one opponent or the other. In view of these frequent changes, it seems desirable to distinguish three types of farm areas in the Great Plains country. First is the area dominated by grazing, in which little or no wheat is grown. Second are the old wheat belts, one-crop areas long dominated by wheat and having little grazing. Between the grazing areas and the old wheat belts lie broad zones of mixed farming in which both types are intermingled. These are the "new" wheat belts, products very largely of recent technological change, the newest additions to the grain belts of the nation. Because they are newer, less productive, more sparsely settled, and less specialized in wheat-farming than the old wheat belts, these newer wheat sections are classed separately as the third major type of land-use area in the non-irrigated portions of the Great Plains Region.

Because wheat has been the most commonly farmed crop of the non-irrigated portions of the plains, it has seemed desirable to include both types of wheat areas within the boundaries of the region.[1] Those portions of the Corn and Cotton belts which might

---

[1] At the same time we must recognize the fact that wheat-farming and ranching are very different types of farming. It happens that wheat has been the foremost invader of the grazing area, mainly because it has been better adapted to the dry climate than any other agricultural staple.

be included are, on the other hand, relatively small, and these have been excluded. The Great Plains Region, as here described, therefore consists of three distinct types of agricultural land-use areas:

1. *The Grazing Sections,* devoted primarily to range livestock, and occupying the more westerly and more arid portions of the region.
2. *The Wheat Belts,* occupying the more humid sections of the region, and including the older and newer wheat-growing areas. Geographically, the wheat belts consist of:
   a. A southern section which grows winter wheat.
   b. A northern section which grows the spring-sown varieties.
3. *The Irrigated Sections,* agricultural specialty areas occupying certain river valleys generally adjacent to the mountains.

We turn first to the grazing sections.

The Southern Grazing Section

The Old West, with its cowboys, coyotes, and large ranches, has been less disturbed in the southern Great Plains than in any other section of the old range country of the West. Here is a long belt extending from the vicinity of Denver southward across eastern New Mexico and into south-central and southern Texas, where herdsmen still reign supreme. Except in a few irrigated valleys, practically all of the land is in pasture. A family-sized farm contains from one thousand to ten thousand acres and practically the entire income is from the sale of cattle or sheep.

These conditions are maximized in the famed Edwards Plateau District of south-central Texas. The Edwards Plateau occupies an area nearly as large as the state of Pennsylvania and is devoted almost exclusively to the raising of cattle, sheep, and a considerable number of Angora goats. The plateau rises abruptly from the low coastal plain and Texas prairies, its southern and southeastern borders clearly marked by the Balcones Escarpment. Much of the surface of the Edwards Plateau is remarkably level, although a belt of rugged hills marks the eastern border. The limestone soil produces good grass, but precipitation is too light for farming. Large ranches occupy the plateau. In several counties the average farm contains five thousand acres or more, and individual holdings occasionally exceed one hundred thousand acres.

The Cattle Industry.—The organization of a hundred thousand acres of stock ranch is something to delight the most ardent advocate of scientific industrial management. Here, indeed, is a far-flung empire. Its main office is the ranch house where live the foreman and most of the cow hands. Private roads lead many miles to all parts of the ranch. Here and there shelters are erected, usually with telephone connections to headquarters. Then there are miles of fences to be maintained, inasmuch as each ranch is divided into a number of large and small tracts. (A small tract may contain only five thousand acres!) Actual handling of the stock is still done on horseback, but each ranch has a number of small passenger automobiles for traveling from one part of the ranch to another, as well as large and small trucks for hauling supplies. Thus the ranch is a well-organized business establishment, a factory for turning out beef and mutton on the hoof.

But even the ranch is only a link in a chain. Animals ordinarily come off the short grass well developed and healthy, but too thin for market. As yearlings or two-year-olds, the cattle are commonly sent to Kansas City or some near-by market to be sold as stockers and feeders to Corn Belt farmers who will fatten them for packing-house markets. Sheep usually follow the same marketing channels. Just as in many other lines of business, a tendency toward integration has been evident. Many large ranchers have made arrangements for intermediate grass-fattening stations in the Flint Hills section of eastern Kansas, or the neighboring Ozark area of Missouri. Final feed-lot finishing is often carried on by additional arrangements with farmers in the cash-grain section of Illinois near the Chicago market. There has also developed near the borders of the range country a considerable amount of feeding and fattening in which the principal feed is cottonseed cake. Despite these tendencies, however, the Edwards Plateau is still primarily a cattle-raising area which does comparatively little feeding or breeding. Many of its calves come in from the winter pastures of the Gulf Prairies of the Texas coast. They spend a season or two on the plateau and are then ready for richer pastures, or feeding operations which cattlemen call "finishing off" for market.

The Edwards Plateau thus exhibits a nearly pure type of agriculture devoted almost exclusively to range livestock. This same type of farm dominates the economic development of the remainder of the southern range section, but nowhere else does it completely exclude other types of agriculture. South of the plateau, on the Rio Grande Plains, a hilly, semi-arid portion of the coastal plain, one finds scattered fields of winter vegetables grown under irrigation. Even here, however, livestock contributes three-quarters of the gross farm income.

Eastern New Mexico is also dominantly a range livestock country. More than 90 per cent of its farm land is in pasture, and from 75 to 80 per cent of the farm income is derived from the sale of livestock. Here, and on the Rio Grande Plains, there are relatively few sheep, and ranches show a marked specialization in the grazing of beef cattle.

The high plains of eastern New Mexico are continued northward into Colorado where they merge with the Colorado Piedmont. This latter district is drained by the upper Arkansas and South Platte rivers, which have made it somewhat hillier than other portions of the section. Here, also, there is more diversification. These streams provide water for two important irrigation districts devoted primarily to crop specialties. In addition, the western extension of the Winter Wheat Belt has brought much wheat into the eastern portions of this district. The stock ranch, however, is still the dominant economic institution of the area. Cattle are pastured on these grasslands and many of them are fed beet pulp from the irrigated sections, or corn from the western portions of the Corn Belt.

In summary, the Southern Great Plains Grazing Section is a semi-arid country, a land of short-grass pastures and few crops. Although marked by generally high elevations and numbers of hilly areas, the surface is mostly undulating and there are no significant barriers to transportation. Lack of rainfall has been the primary reason for keeping nearly all of these lands in grass. A few districts are too hilly for machine farming and in a few others the soil is not sufficiently productive for crops. Over most of the district, however, the sod has not been broken because rainfall is considered insufficient for wheat or cotton. The section promises long to remain a stock-raising area.

The Northern Grazing Section

The Southern Great Plains Grazing Section gradually merges into the Winter Wheat Belt in northeast Colorado. Wheat dominates the area between the South Platte and North Platte rivers, but just north of the latter the traveler again finds himself in a livestock country.

The North Platte River forms the southern boundary of the northern grazing area in western Nebraska. South of the river, wheat fields dominate the horizon; but north of it lies a large oval-shaped area of thinner soil—the Sand Hills of Nebraska. This district derives its name primarily from the fact that its light soil has in past ages been blown into hundreds of low dunes. Today these dunes are carpeted with grass and the lowlands between them contain many lakes. The grass holds the dunes in place, but once this grass is plowed under, drifting again starts. There is little land in cultivation and pasturing livestock is the dominant occupation. Cattle from the Sand Hills are fed low-priced western Nebraska corn, and generally can be marketed in Omaha at a good profit. The area has slightly heavier rainfall than other grazing districts of the Great Plains and its pastures are correspondingly better.

The northwest border of the Sand Hills adjoins a narrow belt of heavier and richer soil. This belt lies in northwest Nebraska and southern South Dakota, and is known as the Rosebud Plains. Much of this strip is in Indian reservation. The area grows both wheat and corn, but produces neither in sufficient volume to warrant inclusion in the Corn or Wheat belts. Even here, ranching vies with farming as a source of income.

North and west of the Rosebud Plains, the ranch country spreads across western South Dakota, northeast Wyoming, southeast Montana, and finally reaches the Canadian border in a detached section of foothills known as the Blackfoot Piedmont. Climate, topography, and soil combine to make this a pasture country. Everywhere except in the eastern portions, the rainfall is too light for wheat. In addition, much of the soil is not retentive of moisture and dry farming is impracticable. Finally, large areas of "bad lands" are to be found in all the states of the section. These erosion-carved areas are unfit for machine farming, and public policy demands that they be left in grass, wherever grass will grow. Today from 80 to 95 per cent of the farm land of the northern grazing section is in pasture, and there is little indication that much of it will ever be plowed. Ranches, although not so large as those of the Edwards Plateau, often include from 2000 to 2500 acres. Cattle are the dominant livestock, but there are many flocks of sheep, especially near the western margins.

The bench lands along certain small valleys near the base of the Montana Rockies also grow considerable quantities of wheat. Cash grain is of particular importance in the upper Yellowstone, Big Horn, and Tongue River valleys of Montana and northern Wyoming. Even here, however, ranching is of generally greater importance than farming.

One other exception must be noted to the otherwise undulating landscape—the Black Hills of South Dakota and adjacent Wyoming. The "hills" are really mountains, a great uplift geologically associated with the Rockies. They are "black" because of their forest covering. Their higher elevation brings heavier rainfall, but there are few areas smooth enough for farming. The Black Hills are therefore included with the range livestock country because their chief use is as pasture for cattle and sheep.

In comparing the northern and southern Great Plains grazing areas there are more points of likeness than of contrast. Both sections are devoted to grazing rather than crops primarily because of deficient precipitation. Given ample rainfall, these sections would be as productive as Ohio or Indiana, for the soil is generally fertile. With annual precipitation averaging fifteen inches or less, they grow only short grass and are best used for pasture. Topographic differences between the two sections are significant, but not of major economic importance. The northern section contains a slightly higher percentage of rough waste land and its elevation is generally less than that of the southern section. But long gentle slopes dominate the topography of both areas. Climatically, there are, of course, the differences in latitude, which give the northern districts longer and colder winters. Shorter northern summers cause less evaporation, which means that better grass will grow with the same amount of rainfall. These differences in evaporation are important. It is significant that good wheat is being grown near the Canadian border with an annual rainfall which produces only mediocre pasture in southern Texas. In both sections most of the precipitation occurs in the summer, but intense summer sunshine usually turns pastures brown in early August. Climate has been of primary importance in limiting these sections to the production of range livestock.

THE WINTER WHEAT BELT

The reader will recall that wheat-growing on the Great Plains fluctuates considerably from year to year under the influence of price changes and technological improvements. The eastern borders of the wheat belts, where they touch the dairy, corn, general-farming, and cotton belts, are comparatively stable, being marked by zones or belts which contain mixtures of the two dominant farm types. These zones migrate little from year to year, and it is possible to predict their locations for several years in advance.

This comparative permanency of the boundary is not found in the western margins of the wheat belts where they merge into the grazing sections. Here the boundary is much more mobile and is highly responsive to changes in prices. Plains states residents say that it is possible to predict with fair accuracy in some localities just how far out into the dry country wheat-farming will extend simply from noting the prevailing price of the grain at sowing time. The western boundaries of these sections are given as they appeared in 1930; more recent trends have not changed them materially.

The Old and New Winter Wheat Belt.—At the beginning of the World War winter wheat production was well centered in central Kansas. Its eastern boundary was definitely set at the eastern edge of the Flint Hills pasture section. To the west, it included the central third of Kansas and it extended a short distance northward into Nebraska. Its southern boundary was in the vicinity of Oklahoma City. West of this belt, from west-central Kansas to the Rocky Mountains, was a ranch country with little or no thought of wheat or tractors or combines.

Then came war prices and improved machinery, and wheat moved west-southwest across the Oklahoma and Texas panhandles, and northwest across northern Colorado to the base of the Rockies. Thus in the course of a little more than a decade, the area dominated by cash-grain farming was nearly doubled.

The new wheat-growing area is not quite like the old. As a matter of fact, there are many points of difference. In the first place, the western advance of wheat was not along a solid front. Back in central Kansas, whole counties are devoted almost entirely to wheat and it is nearly impossible to look any direction and see anything else in the fields. Farther west, on the other hand, the wheat fields are farther apart. There is much pasture, especially in the hillier sections. In actual area occupied, wheat is much less important than grass, but the cash income from wheat is normally greater. Again, the new western wheat farms are much larger than those farther east. From three hundred to four hundred acres is a normal undertaking in central Kansas, but single operators often plant a thousand acres or more farther west. Many times they do this by "absentee" methods, loading a few plows, seeders, and tractors on trucks in the fall, traveling perhaps a hundred miles to the farm, plowing and sowing the grain in a week or ten days, and returning home to remain until harvest time the following summer. When the grain is ripe (if there is a crop), combines are hauled to the fields, night and day shifts are operated, and the grain is loaded and sold within ten days or two weeks. Small wonder that the new wheat belts present a deserted appearance! Farmhouses are almost as far apart as in a ranch country, although the towns generally appear more important and closer together. There is also the fact that much of the land, especially in those sections far from a railroad, is still in grass and will long remain so.

Thus it seems desirable to differentiate between the old and new Winter Wheat Belts. The old Winter Wheat Belt lies well to the east. It is on the prairies, not the plains. It receives twenty inches or more of rain rather than fifteen inches or less, and it matures at least a fair crop almost every year. Its farms are medium-sized and the owners live on them. The old wheat belt grows wheat to the almost complete exclusion of other types of agriculture. It shows very prominently on the map of wheat production.

The new Winter Wheat Belt, the recent western extension, is an area of mixed farming, a combination of range livestock and cash grain. Its farms are large, running into thousands of acres. They do not grow a crop every year, perhaps only once in five years, and their operators often pursue their roulette-wheel agriculture from a near-by village or a distant city. In contrast to the old wheat belts, comparatively small percentages of the farm land are under cultivation. The rest is devoted to range livestock, usually cattle.

The Spring Wheat Belt

These generally stated facts apply equally to the other great wheat-growing district—the Spring Wheat Belt. In the north, the western boundary of the spring wheat section formerly followed the Missouri River across middle South Dakota and diagonally northwest across North Dakota to the western North Dakota-Canadian border. Recent maps place all of North Dakota as well as large sections of eastern, northern, and central Montana in the Spring Wheat Belt. The western half of South Dakota is still a range livestock country. The "new" wheat belt of the north is thus in southwestern North Dakota and Montana. Here, as in Colorado, wheat production has become dominant in a belt which extends to the base of the Rocky Mountains.

The westward migration of spring wheat came a little earlier and somewhat more gradually than in the case of the winter wheat. Several decades ago, land had been plowed in the fertile Triangle Plains of northern Montana, and a succession of good years had brought the area a great land boom. Dry years followed the good ones, however, and it was not until the World War period that wheat-farming really became dominant. It was the World War and power machinery which lifted spring wheat off the Dakota Black Prairies and onto the higher plateaus of the northern Great Plains. Here, as in Kansas, however, the new wheat belt is unlike the old. Its farms are larger and its production per square mile much less. The new wheat belt also contains many more acres of pasture than wheat. It is an area of mixed farming, with wheat dominating and range livestock in second place.

Other Crops.—The agricultural system of the Spring Wheat Belt shows greater diversity than that of the Winter Wheat Belt. The older winter wheat sections grow a small amount of corn and the drier southern and western areas produce large quantities of the grain sorghums (for feed). But the Winter Wheat Belt as a whole is highly dependent upon the proceeds from its major crop or (in the newer western portions) from wheat and livestock. The Spring Wheat Belt grows a greater variety of crops. This section is the leading American center for the production of flax (for linseed oil), barley, and rye. In addition, dairying has been of increasing importance in recent years in the more humid eastern parts of the section. This combination of other grains and animal industries makes the Spring Wheat Belt less dependent upon its major crop than the Winter Wheat Belt.

THE IRRIGATED SECTIONS

Not enough water comes down the west slope of the Rocky Mountains to irrigate more than a minute percentage of the arid lands below. Only a few favored valleys, tiny splotches of green in a sea of brown grass, have been located so fortunately as to have water for irrigation. These small districts are intensively farmed, however, and together they constitute a very important segment of Great Plains agriculture. Wherever a great river spills out of the Rockies onto some flat plain, wherever a tiny perennial stream crosses a mountain-edge farm, there one will find waters being diverted to supply moisture for crops.

The Great Plains Region is crossed by a number of large rivers, the most important of which are the Missouri, Platte, Arkansas, and Rio Grande. Each of these has spawned one or more major irrigation projects. In Montana, the tributaries of the Missouri show as long thin lines on the irrigation map, each stream irrigating a ribbon of land across the plains. Farther south, the North and South Platte rivers have been diverted to water large areas in the Scottsbluff Basin of western Nebraska, and the Denver-Greeley-Ft. Collins district of Colorado. Near Pueblo, the Arkansas River leaves the Royal Gorge to irrigate a long belt of valley land extending eastward into Kansas. In the extreme south, the Rio Grande has given birth to several small projects in southern Texas, as well as the large fruit and vegetable area in the extreme southern tip of the state. To these major projects should be added literally thousands of smaller ones, varying in size from a few to several hundred acres. Water for these smaller projects may be diverted from the smaller streams, or obtained by sinking wells into the deep sands which are fed by the melting snows of the Rockies.

In a certain sense, the irrigated districts do not belong to the Great Plains. They violate the immense quiet of the place, and offer a rude contrast to the broad, sweeping, treeless slopes. For the irrigated farm is small, and it is farmed intensively. Farmhouses are closely spaced, there are many trees, and there is water along the side of the road. There are paved highways, telephones, and electric lights, and these are not of the Great Plains. They do violence to the landscape. But all of this is mere whimsy. The irrigated sections have become so thoroughly integrated with the remainder of the Great Plains economic life that it is difficult to see how one could prosper without the other.

To the livestock industry, the great contributions of irrigation agriculture have been alfalfa and sugar-beet pulp. Not many years ago, it was absolutely necessary to ship range cattle to the Corn Belt in order to fatten them for market—for the Corn Belt had good grass and feed, and the plains had neither. With alfalfa growing in the irrigated valleys and beet pulp pouring as a by-product from sugar refineries, the situation soon changed. Colorado now slaughters steers which were born, raised, and fattened in her own piedmont area. Other plains sections are doing the same thing. Most western cattle and sheep still follow the familiar trail through the Corn Belt to Chicago and other packing centers, but there is a definite trend toward feeding and finishing these animals in the irrigated sections of the Great Plains.

Not all irrigated land, of course, is devoted to alfalfa and sugar beets, although these are the major crops in Colorado and the states to the north. The Billings-Red Lodge District grows large tonnages of dry edible beans, and the Arkansas Valley is famous for its cantaloupes. Potatoes are grown in nearly all these northern irrigated sections, and there is a long list of miscellaneous vegetables and fruits.

In the southern part of Texas, two irrigated areas have become definitely specialized. Along the upper Neuces River and the adjacent Rio Grande, near the towns of Uvalde, Eagle Pass, and Laredo, is the famous "Winter Garden" section which ships large quantities of winter vegetables to northern markets fulfilling for the Middle West a function similar to that of Florida in supplying winter vegetables to the eastern states. Farther south, at the extreme south tip of Texas, is the Lower Rio Grande Valley, which likewise grows many winter vegetables, but is perhaps most famous for its fruits, especially the well-known Texas grapefruit. The Lower Rio Grande Valley grows approximately one-third cf the national output of grapefruit. It is also an important source of early cabbage and Bermuda onions.

Together these irrigated areas provide a distinct contribution to Great Plains agriculture. With their heavy tonnages of sugar, fruits, vegetables, and other specialties, these districts supply an important element in the present-day threefold agriculture of the region, which has been described as an area of cash grain, range livestock, and crop specialties.

MINERALS OF THE GREAT PLAINS

The one great mineral of the Great Plains has been petroleum, and the major producing fields have been south of the southern boundary of Nebraska. Here lie the great mid-continent oil fields, a number of which are in the grazing and wheat sections, but most of which are in the Cotton Belt. Because of its importance as the leading mineral-producing area of the United States, this entire province has been considered separately in a later chapter. (See "Oil Fields of the Southern Mid-continent" in Chapter XV.) In the present chapter, we may confine ourselves to a statement that no consideration of economic life in the southern half of the Great Plains can possibly ignore the most potent stimulant the region has ever received, "black gold."

Oil has been found in many scattered locations in the Winter Wheat Belt, and in the southern grazing section. The Edwards Plateau has not produced oil, but productive wells have been sunk along its east and south margins. Western Texas and southeastern New Mexico have been heavy producers and there have been enormous outputs of both oil and gas in the Texas Panhandle and western Kansas. Central Kansas and northern Oklahoma have been oil centers for many years.

A few successful wells have been brought in near the eastern base of the Rocky Mountains, the most productive of which are in central Montana. Montana produces about one-half of one per cent of the nation's petroleum.

The heavy production of oil and gas in the southern half of the plains region makes all other minerals seem insignificant. Locally, however, other minerals are of great economic importance. Foremost of these is gold, taken largely from the famous Homestake Mine in the Black Hills of South Dakota. This mine (at Lead) regularly produces approximately one-seventh of the United States' gold output, and is considered the largest gold mine in the nation. South Dakota ranks next to California in gold production.

With the exception of oil, gas, and gold, Great Plains minerals are mostly in the realm of potential reserves rather than income-

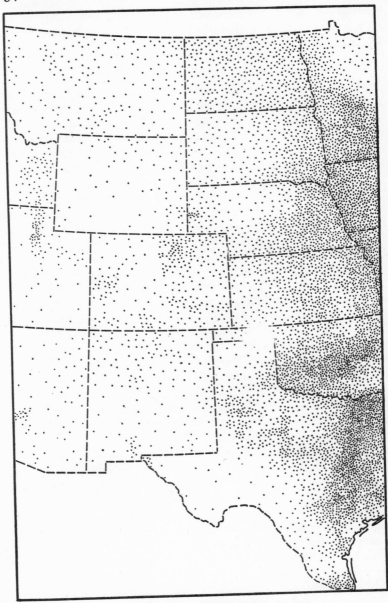

Fig. 27. Rural-farm Population, 1930.

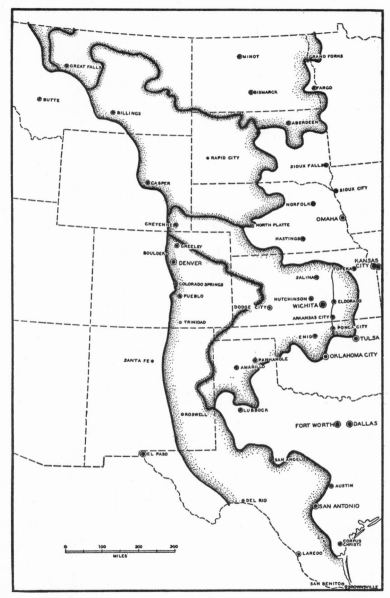

Fig. 28. Cities of the Great Plains and Adjacent Sections.

producers. Much of North Dakota and Montana are underlain with lignite, and there are several small mines serving local areas, but the total production is not heavy. Better grades of coal are found near the base of the Rocky Mountains in Montana (east and north of Billings), and at the foot of the Front Range near the Colorado-New Mexico border (Trinidad and Raton). Similarly located mines between Denver and Cheyenne are also important. It appears that good qualities of coal are available at the foot of the Front Range across the entire state of Colorado. The Great Plains Region produces about 3 per cent of the nation's coal, mainly from mines located near the western margin of the region.

Many sections of the Great Plains have good limestone and shale, and there are a few cement plants. Salt is mined in central Kansas (near Hutchinson), and the production is sufficient to give the state fifth position among salt-producing states, with about 8 per cent of the national production. Southeast New Mexico is the nation's leading area in the mining of potassium salts. These deposits, located near the famed Carlsbad Caverns, are being carefully exploited because of the United States' great lack of this strategic chemical. Most of the world's potash normally comes from Germany.

The oil towns of the southern sections, the Black Hills gold camp, and the half-dozen coal-mining towns of the western margin of the region are the only communities in the Great Plains that are dominated by minerals. Elsewhere, one has to go a long way to find a man who makes a living from what is dug out of the earth.

CITIES OF THE GREAT PLAINS

The broad undulating lands of the Great Plains Region have produced no great cities. Their topography has no natural transportation routes, hence there are no natural gateways or transportation foci. More important negative influences are the low productivity per square mile and the relatively sparse population. Most of the region's products do not require local processing to make them ready for market and there is need for few factories of this type. The local population is too sparse to support many industries of the types that manufacture for local markets. Hence there is very little manufacturing, and most of the urban population is engaged in trade, transportation, and the service occupations.

Cities and towns are widely spaced, since their frequency necessarily varies with the density of the open-country population. The wholesale and shopping facilities of the region are provided largely by cities located near its eastern and western margins, either near the base of the Rocky Mountains or in the more productive sections of the wheat belts. Population distribution favors both the eastern and western locations. Better rainfall supports a larger agricultural population and consequently larger cities on the eastern margin; and irrigation agriculture serves a similar function at the base of the Rocky Mountains. In addition, several of the cities of the western margin occupy strategic sites opposite some of the better transportation routes across the Rocky Mountain barrier. The distant horizon of the great open spaces is seldom interrupted by the spires and smokestacks of cities.

Influence of the Railroad.—The typical plains city started as a livestock shipping center, perhaps attaining first importance in the days of the open range when it was the temporary terminus for a railroad. Fiction recounts the story of rail-end towns such as Abilene and Dodge City, with cattlemen, rustlers, and gamblers as important characters. Later the railroad pushed westward, order was established, and the communities solidified into trade centers. Often the railroad continued to maintain shops there and perhaps one or two other lines reached the town. In such cases the plains community usually developed into a center of local prominence. In the beginning its location was determined by the railroad, and in later years its growth and rising commercial importance were contributed largely by this same factor. Today we find these cities scattered from one end of the region to the other. In the wheat belts, grain elevators have generally replaced cowpens as the visible insignia of the city's major function, but elsewhere the livestock business is much in evidence. Cities of the irrigation districts, newest of all, greet the traveler with long loading-sheds for potatoes and refineries for sugar beets. On the main street one finds a great variety of retail stores and service establishments, mostly with goods for farm markets displayed in their windows. The railroad yards are filled with outgoing farm products during marketing seasons and the freight depots are busy unloading manufactured goods throughout the year. The motor truck is much in evidence, unloading livestock or grain from these surrounding counties, or loading goods for distribution to retail establishments in outlying villages. The traveler is impressed by the fact that everyone in town seems to be either buying or selling something and has used his dusty automobile or mud-splattered truck to bring him there. The radius served by such centers is amazingly large, perhaps eight or ten times as great as that of an eastern city of the same size. Transportation is an important item of cost to producers in the Great Plains Region.

Cities of the plains grew up at strategic points along the early railroads. They rose to importance as collection-distribution centers and have retained that essential characteristic to this day. The geographer must place the railroad high in the list of factors influencing the location of urban centers in this region.

Cities of the Western Margin.—The string of cities which marks the boundary between the Rocky Mountains and the Great Plains Region clearly belongs to both regions, and any assignment of an individual city to one region or the other necessarily must be arbitrary. All of these cities were described in connection with the Rocky Mountain Region, and in the present chapter only enough additional information is given to indicate their importance to the western portions of the Great Plains (see Chapter VIII).

Denver is by all odds the queen city of both the plains and the mountains. Her trading territory includes all of the irrigated sugar-beet section of northeast Colorado as well as southeast Wyoming and western Nebraska. Denver's sugar refineries handle some of this sugar and her packing plants kill many of the meat animals fattened in these districts. North of Denver, the cities of Greeley, Boulder, and Fort Collins also have sugar refineries, but their main interests are in trade and distribution. Coal is also mined in this section. Cheyenne, just north of the Colorado boundary, is essentially a transportation center, with extensive railroad shops and a large staff assigned to the principal operating base and repair shops of the United Air Lines' transcontinental air route.

North of Cheyenne the cities are farther apart, but their functions resemble those of the cities between Denver and Cheyenne. Casper serves both the Wyoming Basin and eastern Wyoming, and its trade is enriched by ranching, irrigation farming, and petroleum. In Montana, the major western border cities are Billings and Great Falls. Billings has railroad shops, sugar refineries and flour mills, while Great Falls has the largest factory output north of Denver, chiefly caused by its electrolytic refineries for copper and zinc from the northern Rocky Mountains. Wholesalers of these cities serve the southeast and northeast sections, respectively, of the state of Montana.

South of Denver, several cities lie at the edge of the Rocky Mountain Region. Most important of these is Pueblo, noted for the largest steel mill west of Chicago. This plant is complete from blast furnace to rolling mill and turns out a wide variety of products, mostly of the heavier types. Pueblo wholesalers serve the southern third of Colorado, including the irrigated strip along the Arkansas River in the Colorado Piedmont. Colorado Springs is best known as a resort center. Farther south, Trinidad mines coal. The Rocky Mountains reach their southern extremity near Santa Fe, but this same string of cities is continued by Roswell, New Mexico, center for the irrigated cotton and oil sections of the Pecos River Valley. The western group of cities ends at the Rio Grande, where Del Rio is a distribution center for the Edwards Plateau sheep and goat country.

Cities of the Eastern Margin.—Cities of the eastern Great Plains are found principally in the older eastern portions of the spring and winter wheat belts. In North Dakota, four small cities, Fargo, Grand Forks, Minot, and Bismarck share the trade of the wheat country. Fargo lies at the western edge of the Dairy Region, but its commercial interests, like those of other North Dakota cities, lie well to the west, and are thoroughly tied up with wheat. Railroad shops and a few small flour mills are almost the only evidences of manufacturing. Aberdeen, South Dakota, has a similar development.

The Black Hills mining-ranching-irrigation-lumber areas have small towns, most important of which is Rapid City. Near-by Deadwood and Lead are mining centers. The Nebraska Sand Hills have given rise to no city, but on their southern margin North Platte is the principal trading center, most important as a railroad division point.

Western Kansas has little urban population and the trade of the area is handled largely by a number of cities in the central part of the state. Wichita, second city of Kansas, is the economic capital of the Winter Wheat Belt. This city packs meat, mills flour, and refines petroleum, but the dominant interests are commercial. Wichita stands second only to Denver among Great Plains cities in the wholesale trade. Adjacent cities have similar interests in trade, petroleum, and flour. Hutchinson has large wholesale interests and is the center of the Kansas salt industry. Salina is a commercial city; and El Dorado, Arkansas City, and neighboring Ponca City, in Oklahoma, have oil refineries.

Enid is the major center for the Oklahoma wheat country, and in the Texas Panhandle the chief city is Amarillo. Amarillo has important interests in oil and gas, and is the distribution center for the Texas Panhandle. Near-by Pampa manufactures carbon black from natural gas. South of Amarillo, the cities of Lubbock, San Angelo, and Abilene are commercial centers for both the range country and the western Cotton Belt. Austin and San Antonio are located at the western edge of the Cotton Belt but obtain much trade from the Edwards Plateau grazing section.

The Lower Rio Grande Valley has four small cities, all specialized along commercial lines. Laredo and Brownsville carry on much trade with Mexico and are the principal centers. Harlingen and San Benito pack and ship truck and citrus fruits from near-by irrigated farms.

Despite this imposing array of small and medium-sized cities, we have not exhausted the list of cities which serve the Great Plains Region. Considerable trade is handled by larger centers lying farther east. In the north, Minneapolis handles much Dakota and Montana wheat and Sioux City receives much South Dakota livestock. Omaha, St. Joseph, and Kansas City are the major markets for stocker and feeder cattle from the central plains, and Fort Worth functions similarly farther south. These regional centers also distribute many lines of goods over their respective territories.

Summary.—The position of the Great Plains Region in the national economy rests very largely upon its production of approximately half the nation's wheat and one-tenth of its animal products. Within the region, the production of these agricultural staples is definitely sectionalized into two wheat belts and two grazing sections. Boundaries between the wheat and grazing areas are not clearly defined. The true grazing areas are separated from the true wheat areas by a broad zone in which both types of farming are practiced, and within which their relative importance varies from year to year. In most years the regional income from farm animals exceeds the income from wheat. Beyond these two major sources of revenue, the most important basic industries are the extraction of oil and gas, and irrigation farming. There is very little manufacturing because most of these raw materials need not be processed adjacent to production centers. The region's wheat is milled, its animals slaughtered, and oil refined in cities which generally lie east of the production centers and beyond the boundaries of the region.

Like other regions in the western half of the United States, the Great Plains look eastward for both markets and consumer goods. The Great Plains Region produces only a small fraction of the goods it consumes and likewise consumes only a small share of its production. Its economic life exists largely by interregional trade. Its cities have been developed as commercial centers whose leading interests are the buying of grain and livestock and the selling of goods for consumption in their trade territories. In these ways it has become possible to develop income-producing activities within the relatively narrow range of the region's natural resources.

References

The Great Plains have been analyzed from many angles, and there is a wealth of information concerning them. W. P. Webb, *The Great Plains* (Ginn, 1931), is a well-written overall treatment. Range problems have been considered by the United States Department of Agriculture and by the Great Plains Committee. A series of reports by the Works Progress Administration (Special Reports, Division of Social Research) describes the social effects of the drought of 1932-36. Read particularly *Farming Hazards in the Drought Area* from this series (1938).

Questions and Problems

1. How do geologists explain the origin of the Great Plains?
2. Describe the topography and soil of the region. How have the boundaries been determined? Are they permanent? Why or why not?
3. What type of climate prevails in the Great Plains Region? When does most of the precipitation occur? Why?
4. What was the original vegetation here, and how does it differ from that of regions to the east?
5. How were the Great Plains settled?
6. Describe the history of Great Plains agriculture, paying particular attention to the effects of the World War, power

machinery, and droughts. Why have parts of this region been called the "dust bowl"?

7. What are the reasons behind the westward extension of the farm belts?

8. What suggestions have been made regarding the future use of this region?

9. What is meant by "economic change and the eastern boundary"? Why is the amount of prospective profit of prime importance in determining whether or not individual farmers will grow wheat?

10. Locate the two wheat areas of the Great Plains Region. Why is there a difference in the type of wheat grown?

11. What is meant by a "cattle drive"? Where did these drives normally start and end? Describe the cattle industry, giving particular attention to where the cattle are fattened for market. How has irrigation affected the location of cattle feeding?

12. In what respects does the northern grazing section differ from the southern grazing section?

13. How were the Black Hills formed? Why have they been included in this region?

14. What differentiates the agricultural system of the Winter Wheat Belt from that of the Spring Wheat Belt?

15. Locate the irrigated sections. What is grown there?

16. What is the main mineral of this region? Name and locate a few others. What is meant when "mineral reserve" is mentioned?

17. What are the functions of the cities in this region? Do these functions differ from those of the cities farther west?

18. What effect did the railroads have upon the location of cities in this region?

19. Southern Texas is not a part of the Great Plains physiographic province. Why is it included in the region?

20. The Great Plains have long been the scene of political unrest. Can you discover any reasons for this?

CHAPTER X

THE NORTHERN FOREST AND LAKE REGION— FOREST AND MINING SECTIONS

THE preceding chapters have been concerned largely with those regions in the western half of the United States in which deficiency of precipitation is a major cause for lack of fuller economic development. We are now prepared to consider the more humid and more densely populated regions of the eastern half of the country. In these eastern areas, the major limitations to economic development are more often associated with factors of location and surface features than with climatic deficiencies. The eastern half of the United States has sections as sparsely populated as many areas in the arid sections of the western states; but the lack of economic opportunity which is reflected in the smallness of the population is more directly traceable to lack of soil resources than to any other natural factor. It seems logical to begin the consideration of the humid eastern regions with the one in which paucity of agricultural resources has held population densities at the lowest figure.

The Northern Forest and Lake Region includes those sections of the United States from which the great continental glaciers removed the surface and left a terrain consisting of exposed crystalline rocks. It also includes other areas surfaced similarly with poor soil-building materials, as well as a considerable belt of moderately productive territory which represents a transition zone between the poor soils of the glacier-scoured areas and the richer lands of the Corn Belt.

In the northeastern United States, the relatively fertile soils of the Corn Belt and Manufacturing Belt gradually give way to poorer soils and rougher terrain as the northern boundaries of these regions are approached. These northern soils are inferior to their southern neighbors, first, because the original glacial deposits were poor soil-building materials, and second, because the native vegetation was coniferous forest which adds little humus to the soil

Glacial History.—Nearly all of the United States north of the Missouri and Ohio rivers, including New York and the New England states, has been glaciated at least once in comparatively recent geologic history. These huge ice sheets originated in central and eastern Canada and their slow, grinding southward journey completely altered the surface of the lands they covered. Passing over relatively soft rocks and soil, they planed off the surface and carried their scrapings along with them. In other places, rocks were more resistant and scouring was less pronounced. In many localities, especially near their southern termini, the glaciers deposited this reworked material as they melted and retreated to the north. Several times the ice advanced and retreated, with long intervening interglacial epochs during which surface materials were weathered into soil.

In the middle and eastern Corn Belt the final result of glaciation was to leave a relatively smooth topography, and a soil rich in lime, favorable to the growth of tall grass but hostile to the growth of trees. Tall grass contributed a maximum tonnage of humus to the soil, and completed the process of giving the Corn Belt the richest soils in the United States. North of the Corn Belt boundary, the glaciers were less kind. The last glacier (known as the Wisconsin) completely denuded thousands of square miles in east-central Canada, and scooped out the great depression for Lake Superior. The scouring process was continued into the United States, but was less effective. Tops of the old Superior uplift (or northern Minnesota, Wisconsin, and Michigan) had been removed, but the most obvious result was the deposition of much loose stone and gravel, and the formation of numerous lakes.

Farther east, the glacier ran roughshod over the highlands of New England and the Adirondack Highland of northern New York. Here the underlying rocks were unusually resistant, and when the glacier melted the topography was still rough, despite the fact that many valleys had been floored with sand and gravel and many lakes created by dams of glacial débris.

In all areas, the remaining rocks were generally crystalline and not of the types which readily disintegrate into good soil. Soils which did develop were acid and eventually the entire area was covered with forest. Most of the trees were coniferous (soft-woods) and capable of adding little humus to the thin soil. De-

ciduous trees and open forest occupied the southwestern sections
of the region, and here the soils are better, not only because the
original glacial till contained more limestone and was more thoroughly pulverized, but also because falling leaves and dying
grasses added more humus to the soil. Finally, in the middle Corn
Belt, trees were almost entirely absent, the entire area was in
grass, and optimum soil-building conditions obtained.

Boundaries.—The southern boundary of the Northern Forest
and Lake Region is a land-use boundary, but its location is a
definite reflection of the natural environment. Most sections of
Minnesota, Wisconsin, and Michigan, as well as the northern
parts of New York and the New England states, do not grow
corn successfully. Corn is not profitable, partially because the
growing season is occasionally too short, but more because soils
are not adapted to the crop. In western Minnesota, the same soil
deficiency limits the eastern boundary of wheat-growing. From
western Minnesota to northern Illinois, the regional boundary
follows a line where wheat or corn first becomes the dominant
farm interest. Within the region, corn, wheat, and meat animals
give way to grass, root crops, and dairying as the major types of
agricultural land use. Along this boundary, farmers would say
that corn requires better land than dairy farming and root crops.

East of Chicago and Milwaukee, dairying continues to be the
dominant agricultural interest in a long wedge-shaped area whose
boundaries reach the Atlantic coast near Baltimore and Portland,
Maine. In this region, however, the economic structure is dominated by manufacturing and city life, and the region is known
as the American Manufacturing Belt. Boundaries of the Manufacturing Belt are drawn to include all agricultural districts devoted to serving the individual cities of that region with perishable farm produce. The southern boundary of the Northern
Forest and Lake Region is located along the line where these city-
supply farms first become more important than the lumber-mining-
subsistence farming economy of the northeastern region. East of
Lake Michigan, the region becomes an area of cut-over timber
land, forest, and very limited agricultural development. Most of
the land of these sections is not devoted to agriculture. West of
Lake Michigan, two types of land use are discovered: (1) a
northern cut-over area which resembles the sections farther east,
except that it has important iron and copper mines; and (2) a

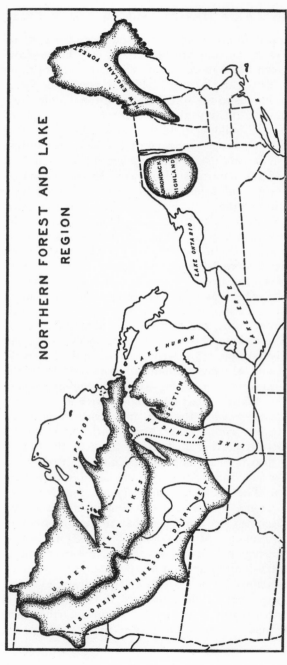

Fig. 29. Northern Forest and Lake Region. This region consists of four sections. The western portion is composed of a northern cut-over section which has very little farming, and a southern dairy belt whose economic life is dominantly agricultural. The boundary between these western sections is not sharply defined. On the east, the region includes the Adirondack Highland and the New England forest section. These forested eastern areas are separated from each other and from the western sections by farming sections of the Manufacturing Belt.

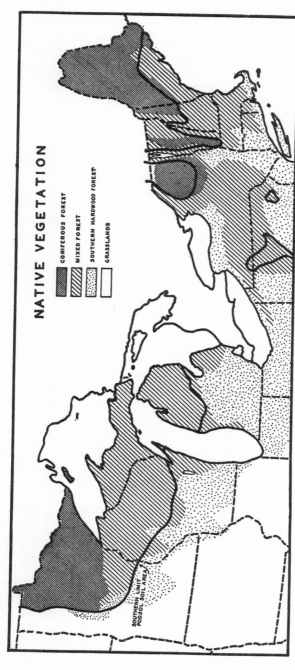

FIG. 30. Native Vegetation and Soils in the Northeastern United States. Both the nature of the forest cover and the character of the soils have had a bearing on the configuration of the Northern Forest and Lake Region. The podsol soils are light in texture and generally infertile. Their native vegetation was usually northern coniferous forest or northern mixed forest (hardwoods and softwoods). These forests and soils occupied large areas in the northeastern United States.

broad southwestern marginal belt which has better soil and is devoted to intensive dairy farming.

In relating this lack of agricultural development to natural environmental factors, the most pronounced negative influence is found in the soil. Good soil bounds the region on the west and good soil isolates the Adirondack Highland and New England Forest section from the western portions of the region. In New England, the regional boundary generally follows the southern limit of the forest, and here again soil is the most important limiting factor.

Sections.—Similarities in natural environment and land use prompt the inclusion of four separate sections in the Northern Forest and Lake Region. These are: (1) the Northern Great Lakes section of northern Michigan and Wisconsin; (2) the New England Forest, of Maine and New Hampshire; (3) the Adirondack Highland of northern New York; and (4) the Wisconsin-Minnesota Dairy Belt, a section of richer soil which borders the Northern Great Lakes section on the south and west, and is devoted to dairy farming. All of these sections were originally in forest, and the first three are largely forested today. The fourth, the Wisconsin-Minnesota Dairy Belt, was long ago cleared for agriculture which has remained its most important type of land use. In the other three sections the landscape is filled with growing trees and cut-over timber. Throughout the region, the persistence of the lumber, paper, and vacation industries reveals the importance of forest and lake in local economic development. Scattered mining interests attest the mineralized nature of the rocks uncovered by the ancient glaciers. Economic development in the region is closely related to its basic material resources.

THE NORTHERN GREAT LAKES SECTION

Forests and History.—When the pioneer settlers pushed north and west from the Ohio River country into the lands which border the western Great Lakes, they found themselves in a region of dense forest. Early agriculturists found little of promise in these north woods and the stream of settlement was directed elsewhere, mainly to the prairies of Indiana and Illinois where timber was less common, soil was richer, and grass for pasture more plentiful. But the new West grew rapidly and its building created a demand for lumber which sent lumbermen into the great forests of

Michigan, Wisconsin, and Minnesota. There they set up lumber camps, some of which were to develop into cities, where they began to cut the most extensive and densest white pine forests of the United States. First by water and later by rail, lake states lumber was sent south and east to build the rapidly growing cities of the Middle West and the Atlantic seaboard.

The forest was the first resource to be exploited in the lake states area. Northern white pine was the most highly prized and most common variety of tree, but there were also large areas of northern hardwoods—beach, birch, maple, and hemlock. Most of the white pine was found on the lighter soils, and the best of these forests were in (1) the northern portion of the lower peninsula of Michigan, (2) northeastern Wisconsin and upper Michigan, and (3) central and northern Minnesota. The white pine belt occupied most of the northern portion of the lake states. South of the pine belt soils are of heavier texture, and these sections were largely covered with hardwoods.

Furiously the lumbermen cut into these forests as the lake states strove to supply the seemingly limitless demands of a growing nation for lumber. By 1870, Michigan was the leading lumber state, a position it retained for a quarter-century before yielding first place to Wisconsin. At the end of the century, Wisconsin, Michigan, and Minnesota were the three leading lumber states and were supplying one-quarter of the national lumber output. But the end was in sight. One by one the last remaining stands of virgin timber in each state were opened. First Michigan, then Wisconsin, and finally Minnesota reached the practical end of their forest resources. By 1910, these states were not supplying their own needs for lumber. Thus the first exploitation came to an end with the establishment of a few fortunes, the abandonment of many towns and railroads, and the desolation of cut-over forest land. Abandonment gave free rein to destructive forest fires which not only killed most of the remaining small trees of "second growth" timber, but often burned the soil so that it would no longer grow the same high-grade lumber species it grew before. Many sections, indeed, were left entirely barren, the soil so poor that even inferior types of trees would not restock it. Over most of the area, however, a scrubby second growth has appeared where the land has not been devoted to agriculture.

Coming of the Farmer.—Once the land was cleared, agriculture began to develop. This development was slow because of the expense of clearing the land of stumps and because the short growing season and thin soil of the northern portions of all three states confined agriculture to the growing of a relatively few short-season crops. Wheat grew rather well over most of the area, but after a few years of wheat-farming the thin soil was exhausted and large areas were abandoned. That abandonment became well-nigh permanent in most of the old pine belt where short summers and poor soils have kept the farm population small to this day. But it was not permanent on the heavier soils farther south. The agricultural revival began in Wisconsin in the last days of wheat-farming, and it was based primarily upon two types of agriculture: (1) dairying, and (2) agricultural specialties such as potatoes, sugar beets, vegetables, and fruit. Climate and soil were adapted to both types of agricultural activity.

Topography and Soils in the Lake States.—It has been indicated that differences in economic development in the Mississippi-Great Lakes Basin are more directly related to soil and climate than to topography. Lake-states topography has not been hostile to economic development. Much of the terrain consists of low hills, although a few places such as the west and south shores of Lake Superior have hills high and steep enough to be known locally as mountains. Certain larger streams also have narrow belts of bluffs and other rough land along their courses. But these are exceptions. The typical lake-states topography is a rolling plain with numerous low hills and frequent basins which hold small fresh-water lakes. These glacier-scoured basins with their numerous lakes of clear water, often frequented by fishermen, hunters, and vacationists, are undoubtedly the most famous topographic features of the area.

Variations in soil have been of greater economic importance. It has been indicated that the northern portions of these three states have light-textured soils low in fertility. These northern soils are known as podsols, the outstanding features of which are (1) a light-textured surface soil upon which is (2) a layer of partially decomposed vegetable matter, such as leaves, sticks, and moss. This upper layer may be as much as a foot thick. It is rich in vegetable matter but not in a form which makes it available as plant food. The lower layer (the true soil) is of very low fertility and of such a porous nature that the mineral salts have been very largely leached from it and carried into the subsoil below. As a consequence, the soil has small agricultural value. Trees whose roots penetrate the subsoil grow very well, but no manner of deep plowing can bring the plant food within the reach of annual crops. Because these lands were originally forested, relatively little humus was added to the soil each year. Such leaves and other tree growth as have accumulated remain on the surface, largely undecomposed and unavailable for plants. Small wonder, therefore, that agriculture has found little success. Such farming as is done in these areas is largely of a subsistence nature. Commercial farming exists only around the mining or lumber camps or near the commercial cities along the lakes. Apparently the current movement toward reforesting the old pine belt is thoroughly in keeping with its limited possibilities for agricultural development.

Southward of the old pine belt, the soils gradually become heavier in texture and richer in plant foods, culminating in the black prairies (old grasslands) of Iowa and Illinois. This transition zone of gray-brown soils shares some of the characteristics of both the podsols and the prairie soils. Originally covered with aspen forest, these soils are not so rich as the grassland soils farther west. Furthermore, the rainfall has been sufficient to have deprived them of most of their lime. But on the other hand, their texture is comparatively heavy, the plant food has not been deposited in the subsoil (as in the podsols), they are only mildly acid, drainage is generally good, and they are therefore generally classed as moderately fertile and well suited to cultivation. A shortage of plant food can be corrected by the application of fertilizer, for these soils are easily fertilized and loss through leaching is very small. The gray-brown soils are adapted to a wide variety of crops.

Intermingled with these major soil types are considerable areas of sandy soil (central Wisconsin and Michigan), barren rock (northern Minnesota), and alluvial plains (along the rivers and in old lake beds). The first two types have been generally hostile to agricultural development, while the alluvium has stimulated farming in those richer areas.

Climate.—Except for the shortness of the growing season in their northern portions, climate has not been a serious handicap to agriculture in the lakes states. The northern sections have a growing season averaging slightly longer than ninety days, but even this short season is long enough to mature wheat and the other small grains. The central portions of these states have growing seasons of from 120 to 150 days, while in southern Wisconsin and Michigan the average is greater than 150 days, or enough to mature corn. Thus the shortness of the growing season, while it does preclude the growing of certain crops, does not restrict agricultural development. Farming has been restricted more by soil than by the temperature factor.

Precipitation is adequate throughout these states. All sections receive more than twenty inches annual precipitation and all except extreme northwestern Minnesota receive more than twenty-five inches. Lack of moisture is not a handicap except in occasional dry years which are infrequent in Middle America. Where soil for grass is adequate, good pasture is available throughout the summer—an important factor in the success of the dairy industry.

A special climatic effect has been responsible for the development of a fruit-growing area on the eastern shore of Lake Michigan. There the prevailing westerly winds are tempered by the waters of the lake so that spring is retarded one or two weeks. This delay is long enough to postpone the budding of fruit trees until the danger of late spring frosts is practically over. The effect of the lake upon the climate of western Michigan has made it an important center for fruit-growing, an industry which is hazardous elsewhere in the Middle West because of the menace of late spring frosts.

Gradation Boundaries.—Since both soil and climate become increasingly favorable as one progresses southward from the Canadian boundary, agriculture increases in importance in the same manner. In the northern portions of the lake states, farms are indeed few and far between. Most of the area is in cut-over timber and farms appear generally as clearings in the forest. This statement is especially true of the "Arrowhead" country of northeastern Minnesota, but it is also true in lesser degree of northern Wisconsin and all of the upper peninsula of Michigan. The summer tourist finds these lands excellent for vacationing if he wants to free himself from the hectic life of a crowded city. Here he finds "ten thousand" lakes well stocked with fish, mile after mile of timber and underbrush alive with game, and very few evidences of human habitation. Cultivated fields are the exception in this landscape, not the rule. But as he travels southward farms become more common. Timbered areas are fewer and smaller. The land is fenced. Farm buildings are larger and there are many silos. Green pastures dominate the landscape, and there are increasingly frequent fields of oats, barley, and corn. Colorful herds of dairy cattle indicate the chief agricultural interest. Every small town has its creamery, cheese factory, or condensery. Near the cities, scores of milk trucks dispute his right of way.

Finally the corn fields become more common and the pastures are smaller. Farms have fewer silos, villages fewer butter factories and more loading-pens for livestock. Dairying is no longer the dominant occupation. By this time the tourist has witnessed a cross section of the greatest dairy district in America. Whether his route lay across eastern Minnesota, Wisconsin, or Michigan his panorama has been much the same. Minnesota would have had more creameries, Wisconsin more cheese factories, and Michigan more truckloads of fresh milk, but in each state the dairy cow is the undeniable mistress of farm life. And in each case the shift from dairying to livestock would have become noticeable approximately at the southern boundary of the state. We return to the Northern Great Lakes section.

Agriculture.—Delineation of the Northern Lakes section is made relatively easy by soil differences. This section contained the old pine forests which occupied the light soil. The southern boundary of the podsol soil belt is the approximate northern boundary of intensive dairy farming. In terms of agricultural development it is roughly the line north of which less than 40 per cent of the land is in farms. North of this line there are fewer than thirty milk cows per square mile of farm land, while south of it the number per square mile ranges from thirty to seventy. As thus delimited the Northern Great Lakes district is one of inferior soil, few farms, and relatively small development on each farm. It is, however, primarily a dairy section in its agricultural interests. Dairy products are the leading source of farm income in nearly all localities. Cattle are pastured on the cut-over forest lands, primarily to supply dairy products to the mining towns, lumber camps, and lake ports of the section. But not all of these farmers tend dairy cows and not all of them sell their products in local mining and commercial centers. Short-season crops have been tried, and of these the most successful is the potato. Potato production, which is highly developed in the dairy belt farther south, has also been successful in a few portions of the Northern Great Lakes section.

Other crops of the Northern Great Lakes section are largely incidental. Vegetables are grown near the urban centers and there is much part-time farming in which the farmer supplements his income by work in the mines and forests during the operating season in those industries. Many of the farms (15 to 20 per cent in 1929) are classed as self-sufficing, with few farm products offered for sale. Farm life is frequently on a pioneer basis, with hunting and fishing (and, in some sections, acting as guides for summer tourists) major sources of livelihood.

Farming has never been of major importance in the Northern Lakes section and for the past several decades it has shown a declining tendency. Except for the mining centers and lake ports, the section is a frontier, sparsely populated and economically undeveloped. In fact, it is a receding frontier, for in the modern era of agricultural intensification people are moving out of the area rather than into it. After all, many portions of America offer greater promise to the farmer.

Lumber.—The importance of the lumber industry of the lake states is largely historic. The excellent forests which early made this area the leading source of American lumber remain in only a few areas and occupy less than one-sixth of the timber land. Largely because of lack of care, the second growth has been disappointing both in type and in quality. A few lumber camps are still in existence but their product is not nearly large enough to supply the needs of these states. Building in the lake states as well as elsewhere in America is dependent very largely upon lumber from western and southern forests. In recent years, Wisconsin has cut about 3 per cent of the national lumber output, and Michigan and Minnesota have each cut about 2 per cent of the total. Most of this production comes from the northern peninsula of Michigan and from the northern portions of Wisconsin and Minnesota.

For the future it is apparent that the social interest will be best served by returning the northern portions of the lake states to forest. The land is not adapted to agriculture. Replanting the area has long been considered desirable by both the states and the federal government. Both agencies have been attempting it for a number of years. But these programs have encountered difficulties. In 1925, 95 per cent of the forest land was privately owned, 2 per cent was under federal control and 3 per cent under state control. Little forestry work had been carried out by the governments and practically none by the private owners. This situation might have been prolonged indefinitely had it not been for the business depression which began a few years later. This depression had two pronounced effects: (1) large areas of forest land reverted to the county and state governments because of unpaid taxes, and (2) federal reconstruction and reemployment measures were directed partially toward reforestation. In 1930, Congress provided increased funds for tree-planting and thereby made possible reforestation of the national forests in thirty or forty years. (Under the former appropriation it would have taken 120 years.) Government reemployment measures of later years (notably the Civilian Conservation Corps) also speeded this program in both state and national forests. Sooner or later most of the Northern Lake states will be returned to that type of land use to which they are best suited. Through selective forestry they should become an important source of lumber for future generations in the eastern United States.

The Lake Superior Iron Mines.—The Northern Great Lakes section is primarily a mineral-producing area, whose major product is iron ore. Vast deposits of these ores were laid down in past geologic ages to form several distinct beds or "ranges," of which six are of importance in production. These ranges have a common characteristic in that they have a generally elongated shape with a nearly east-west axis. Beyond this the similarity ceases. The ore is classed as hematite, but there is a wide variation in quality. Some of the beds are found at depths of several hundred feet and are mined by ordinary underground methods utilizing a shaft through which the ore is elevated to the surface. Other beds, and these are the most famous and most productive, lie near enough the surface to be mined by open-pit methods. Where such methods are possible, the surface overburden (soil and other worthless débris) is removed with power shovels and piled near by, preferably in some neighboring swamp. Once exposed, the ore is dug by power shovels which load it directly into strong gondola railroad cars run into the pit on full-sized temporary railroad tracks. Once a trainload is ready, it is hauled to docks at near-by lake

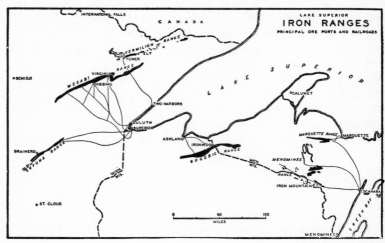

FIG. 31. The Lake Superior Iron Ranges. About the first comment to be made concerning the iron "ranges" is that they are not mountains but beds of iron ore which generally lie near the surface. Their geological history is associated with mountain-building forces, but erosion has long since removed the mountains and today the iron range country is nearly level. The principal ore-carrying railroads and lake ports are shown on the map. Train loads of ore are made up at the pits and sent down to the long ore docks at the lake ports. Ore boats tie up along the docks and are soon loaded and on their way to steel centers along the southern Great Lakes.

The mining operation is highly mechanized. Working in the deep pits, power shovels scoop enormous tonnages from the ore beds. Most of the ore is loaded directly into railroad cars, but in some of the mines endless belts carry it up an incline to waiting ore cars or stock piles near the edge of the pits. Some of the mines are too deep for open-pit mining and underground methods are used. Underground mining is more expensive than open-pit mining. The largest tonnages are taken from open-pit operations on the Mesabi Range. This range also contains the largest reserves of ore.

ports, there to be dumped into specially constructed ore boats which take it to the blast furnaces along the southern shores of the Great Lakes. The extent of mechanization and the speed in handling these huge tonnages are almost unbelievable. At Hibbing, scene of greatest activity on the Mesabi Range, the visitor who reaches the edge of the pit and first views the operation is amazed to learn that the toylike locomotives and cars he sees below him are full sized, and that the power shovels are large enough to accommodate a low-priced automobile. So large is the undertaking and so deep is the excavation that from his vantage point they resemble toys! It is all but impossible to read the foot-high numbers on the cabs of the locomotives working below. Trains of brownish-red ore are being assembled and dispatched to Duluth and Superior over railroads which carry some of the heaviest tonnages in the United States. At the lake ports the trains are run out on long docks which stretch out into the lake and beside which ore steamers tie up for loading. The ore cars are equipped with hopper bottoms and the train is hardly stopped before workmen open these hoppers and send the ore down into the storage bins below the tracks. These bins are high enough so that the ore is transferred by gravity through chutes to the ore boats. The boats, in turn, are designed for fast loading.

The transportation of ore from the other ranges follows a substantially similar routine. On the Cuyana and Vermilion ranges, because of the depth and steepness of the deposits, mining must be carried on by underground methods. On the Gogebic, Marquette, and Menominee ranges of upper Michigan and adjacent Wisconsin, underground operations are also necessary. Most of the Minnesota ore is shipped through Duluth and Superior, while Michigan ore reaches the lake boats at Marquette, Escanaba, and several other lake ports.

Underground mining employs methods similar to those used in coal mines except that greater mechanization is usually possible because the ore generally occurs as a loose gravel and needs little breaking up for hoisting. In some mines, by a process known as caving, it is possible to operate mine cars on a level below the ore workings and push the ore through short chutes to the cars below.

Because of the accessibility and richness of these ores, Minnesota and Michigan have become the leading iron-ore states and the Lake Superior district is one of the two leading iron-mining areas of the world. The Mesabi Range alone supplies roughly 60 per cent of the annual iron ore production of the United States, and the Marquette and Menominee ranges about 10 per cent each. In 1937, the Lake Superior region supplied five-sixths of the United States production. In no other part of the world can iron ore of comparable quality be obtained so easily.

Steel men say that the problems which beset the lake states iron-mining industry are chiefly technical, based primarily upon the gradual lowering of quality as mining progresses. In a competitive system the richest resources are ordinarily utilized first. Steel concerns (most of the iron is mined by steel companies or their affiliates) which opened mines some years ago to extract ore running 60 to 70 per cent iron, are now using 50 per cent ore and finding it difficult to obtain. Hauling so much worthless rock for a thousand miles adds much to production costs, even with the low costs of lake transport. Methods of "beneficiating," or concentrating the ore, are being tried and apparently will be utilized when the richer ores are exhausted. But such processes are expensive and probably will not come into general use for several years. Again, there is the question of the reserves. Sooner or later the big shovels are going to "scrape bottom" in these great pits. How soon, no man will predict, because the problem is one not only of measuring existing reserves, but also of estimating future demands for steel. New discoveries often upset the first calculation, and unforeseen developments in the use of scrap, the competition of other metals, and the general tempo of mechanization invalidate the latter. In 1938, it was estimated that the Lake Superior district had about 1.4 billion tons of ore reserves of all grades, enough to last 28 years at existing rates of consumption. Of these reserves, 80 per cent were in the Mesabi Range.

Other Minerals.—Although iron-mining dominates the economic life of the Northern Lakes district, iron was not historically the first mineral to command attention. The first of the iron ranges was not opened until Civil War days, but Michigan had become established as the leading copper state as early as 1847, and remained the leader for forty years thereafter, or until western copper deposits were opened. Despite the rise of Montana, Arizona, Utah, and Nevada, each of which has passed Michigan in production, Michigan is still the fifth state in copper output with from 5 to 10 per cent of the annual national production.

The copper-mining district of Michigan is confined to the Keweenaw Peninsula which juts out into Lake Huron. The ores are unique in being composed of native (metallic) copper rather than the sulfides, oxides, carbonates, and silicates which form the reserves of most of the rest of the world. Years of continued production have carried these mines nearly a mile below the surface, and, although this great depth has increased mining costs, there is no indication of exhaustion of the ore body. Smelters and refineries for these ores are located at near-by Hubbell and Houghton.

Other mineral production is of less importance. Large stone quarries in the vicinity of Alpena supply fluxing limestone for the steel industry of the Manufacturing Belt, and there are occasional smaller quarries and gravel pits scattered over the region. None of these is comparable in economic importance to either iron or copper.

Transportation on the Great Lakes.—Nowhere in the world has nature provided so fine a fresh-water inland waterway as the Great Lakes. No other continuous body of fresh water extends so far into such productive territory. And no comparable inland waterway could be made fit for heavy shipping at so little cost. Except for locks at Sault Ste Marie and the deepening of the river at Detroit, all of the Great Lakes are naturally navigable for large steamers from Duluth and Chicago in the west to Buffalo in the east. Lying in the direct path of east-west commerce, these lakes must of necessity have become important highways, a powerful magnet for the location of great commercial and industrial interests.

Yet the reader must not be deceived into believing that the Great Lakes have actually become an important highway except for the transportation of certain bulky commodities such as ore, wheat, and coal. The tonnage of these heavy commodities is very large, large enough to make the Great Lakes carry more tons of freight than any other inland waterway; but in value it represents only a small fraction of the traffic interchange between the agricultural West and the industrial East, most of which is carried by the railroads which traverse the states south of the lakes. The reasons for this preponderance of rail traffic are historic and

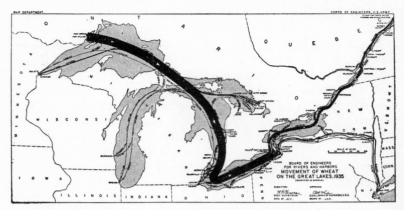

FIG. 32. Movement of Wheat on the Great Lakes.

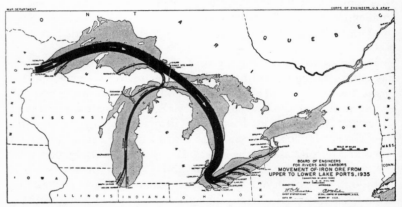

FIG. 33. Movement of Iron Ore on the Great Lakes. The origin, volume, and destinations of the principal commodities hauled on the Great Lakes are shown in the four maps on these pages. These maps are reproduced from *Transportation on the Great Lakes*, by the Corps of Engineers, United States Army. Historically, the wheat traffic has been very important in Great Lakes transportation. The waterway serves the spring wheat belts of the United States and Canada, generally considered the foremost wheat-exporting territory in the world. In 1935, the year of this report, a severe drought had cut wheat production and the lake movement was correspondingly curtailed. Much Canadian wheat has also been diverted to the Pacific coast at Vancouver in recent years. Ore exceeds wheat in tonnage. The year 1935 was not one of great activity in iron and steel but the ore movement was nearer normal than the wheat movement.

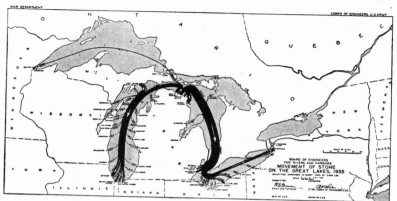

FIG. 34. Movement of Stone on the Great Lakes.

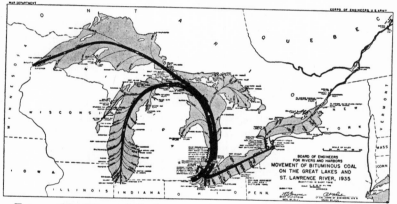

FIG. 35. Movement of Coal on the Great Lakes. Stone and coal movements show a different pattern from ore and wheat movements. Most of the stone is fluxing limestone which originates at quarries near Alpena, Michigan, and is sent to blast furnaces in the Chicago, Lake Erie, and Detroit areas. The coal movement originates largely along Lake Erie, where Toledo is the major shipping center. This coal comes largely from southern West Virginia and eastern Kentucky. The main stream of coal traffic goes northwest through Lake Huron, then splits, part going to the southern Lake Michigan ports and the remainder to Lake Superior. Many ore boats use coal as return cargo. Duluth-Superior distributes lake cargo coal over Minnesota and North and South Dakota. A considerable portion of the receipts of the Chicago area consist of coking coal for eventual use in Chicago and Gary blast furnaces.

economic, as well as geographic. (1) Most significant of the natural limitations is the freezing weather which clogs upper lake harbors with ice for a third of the year. (2) From Chicago, where the lakes penetrate most deeply into the farm country, the waterway is at best a circuitous route to the east. For perishable commodities this added distance is a genuine handicap. (3) No large navigable streams enter the Great Lakes which might act as "feeders" to the "main line." A rail or highway haul is necessary to get the traffic to the lakes, and once the goods are loaded on a train or truck it is expensive to transship them to a boat. (4) Historically, the railroads, always contending that their greatest profit lay in the "long haul," have maintained attractive rates and service on lines through this territory. Potential lake competition has tended to keep rail rates reduced to the great benefit of the Great Lakes cities, but to the detriment of lake shipping. In other words, nature placed certain handicaps such as frozen harbors, circuitous routes, and lack of branches upon Great Lakes shipping and these have been supplemented and augmented by railroad-rate policies which have been designed to divert all but the heaviest traffic to their own overland routes.

In 1935, the Great Lakes waterway carried about 18 per cent as many ton-miles of freight as all the railways of the United States, and ranked among the major traffic arteries of the world. The Great Lakes have become "great" in a transportation sense primarily because they provide an economical and fairly direct route between the iron mines of the Lake Superior district and the blast furnaces of the Manufacturing Belt. Special steamers handle ore cargoes with great efficiency. On their return trips these freighters are loaded with coal. In 1935, nearly two-thirds of the commerce of the Great Lakes consisted of iron and coal, the remainder largely of stone, grain, and package freight. As a transportation medium, Great Lakes shipping is highly specialized in the carrying of bulk freight.

The Waterway.—The Great Lakes are a nearly natural inland waterway, extending from Montreal, the head of deep-draft ocean navigation on the St. Lawrence River, far into the interior of the North American continent: 1340 miles to Duluth and 1260 miles to Chicago. There are about a thousand miles of open lakes in either route, and the remainder consists of rivers and canals. Twin canals and locks carry ore boats over the 21½-foot fall between Lakes Superior and Huron, and the fall of eight and one-half feet to Lake Erie is taken care of by the canalized St. Clair and Detroit rivers. The 327-foot fall of the Niagara Escarpment is handled by eight locks of Canada's Welland Canal, which carries vessels between Lake Erie and Lake Ontario. Boats drawing not more than twenty-four feet of water can be operated from Duluth or Chicago eastward to the head of the St. Lawrence River at Galop Island. Below that point the river has numerous rapids, and existing canals are only fourteen feet deep. Eventually, Canada and the United States will perfect a long-pending agreement to canalize the St. Lawrence, generate much electric power, and make the Great Lakes accessible to good-sized ocean vessels.

The Bulk Freighter.—The typical Great Lakes freighter is a nautical oddity whose design reflects the desire for speed in loading and unloading. Essentially, the bulk freighter is little more than a 200-yard-long ore bin with a power plant in one end (aft) and the quarters in the other (forward). Between power plant and quarters is an unobstructed cargo hold, consisting of twelve to thirty hatches with partitions twelve feet apart to match the spacing at the ore piers. These bulk freighters will carry an 11,000-ton cargo at twelve miles per hour. At the ore docks all hatches are opened and loaded simultaneously with marvelous efficiency. The ore-loading record was made at Two Harbors, Minnesota, in 1921, when 12,500 tons were loaded in sixteen and one-half minutes. Quickly on its way, the freighter heads for unloading docks at the southern lake ports. Unloading takes longer, but generally can be accomplished in about three hours. The return cargo is usually coal and can be loaded in about four hours. A cargo of coal can be unloaded in Duluth in six or seven hours. Shipowners measure the efficiency of their crews in terms of the time spent in port. In 1936, the average stay in port for each round trip was nineteen hours. Time is precious because the season is short. No freighter has ever made more than twenty-four round trips in a season.

Traffic.—The Great Lakes waterway is a vital link between mine and factory. In 1935, upper lakes iron mines provided 28 per cent of its total traffic, and the Appalachian coal fields furnished 36 per cent of the total. Stone was the third-ranking commodity with 9 per cent of the total. Nearly all the stone originated on the northern shore of the lower peninsula of Michigan. Package freight ranked fourth with 4 per cent, and grains fifth with 3 per cent of the total lake tonnage. Most of the package freight originated in Buffalo and Detroit for distribution on Lake Erie. Nearly all the grain was wheat, shipped mainly from the great Canadian wheat-shipping lake ports, Fort William and Port Arthur. The relative importance of various types of traffic varies from year to year, depending much on industrial activity in the steel centers and the size of the wheat crop in the spring wheat belts of the United States and adjacent Canada.

Railroads and Canals.—Inasmuch as the great traffic-originating centers are not located on the shores of the lakes, railroads play an important part in serving as "feeders" for the Great Lakes transportation system. Railroads haul the iron ore from the Lake Superior ranges to upper lake ports, and the same railroads distribute local coal receipts throughout the hinterland. At the Lake Erie ports, railroads transship nearly three-quarters of the ore receipts to furnaces located outside these cities, mainly in the Pittsburgh and Mahoning Valley steel districts. Into these lake ports roar sixty-car coal trains to provide bulk freighters with return cargoes. In addition, the New York State Barge Canal (twelve feet deep to Albany) distributes some grain and coal eastward from the Buffalo lake terminus.

Lake Ports.—The location of the principal ports of the Great Lakes is indicated in Figs. 32 to 35. Iron-ore shipments make Duluth-Superior the leading port on the Great Lakes. Second position is held by Toledo, which is the leading coal-shipping port. Buffalo generally ranks third because of its receipts of grain and ore, while Chicago and Cleveland rank fourth and fifth. Chicago receives both ore and coal, and Cleveland receives ore and ships coal. These five ports handled four-fifths of the Great Lakes traffic in the decade 1926-1935. The remainder was distributed among more than a hundred smaller ports, largest of which are ore-receiving Conneaut and coal-shipping Sandusky in Ohio, stone-shipping Calcite in northern Michigan, and coal-receiving Milwaukee in Wisconsin.

Position of the Northern Great Lakes District in Great Lakes Shipping.—By originating all of the iron ore and stone and most of the grain, the ports of the Northern Great Lakes district account for about two-fifths of Great Lakes freight shipments.

The Hull-Rust Open Pit Iron Mine at Hibbing, Minnesota. (*Courtesy Duluth Chamber of Commerce.*)

Nearly all of these shipments consist of ore and stone which originate within the district. The Great Lakes, in turn, provide the link between this great mining area and the Manufacturing Belt to the south. Without this waterway the industrial geography of the United States would have been greatly altered, because no other mode of transportation could deliver these tonnages so cheaply and permit the concentration of steel manufacture so near good coal and the center of population.

These northern ports are less prominent as freight receivers, but they do unload nearly half the coal shipped on the Great Lakes waterway. Here the waterway serves to bring coal-poor Minnesota and Wisconsin much nearer (in dollars) to the Appalachian coal fields. When miscellaneous traffic is added to these major commodities, the ports of the Northern Great Lakes section are found to handle nearly three-fifths of the Great Lakes traffic.

Cities.—The resources and trade of the Northern Great Lakes district have fostered the development of two types of cities: (1) lake ports, most of which ship iron ore, stone, and wheat and act as distribution centers for their adjacent areas, and (2) mining centers of the iron and copper ranges. Largest and most prominent of the lake ports are Duluth and Superior, twin cities at the western end of Lake Superior.

Duluth and Superior.—Located at the extreme head of Great Lakes navigation, adjacent to the world's most productive ore fields, and nearest of all lake ports to the greatest wheat-shipping region in the world, it was only natural that the twin cities of Duluth and Superior should develop into an important shipping center. In 1930, metropolitan Duluth had a population of 155,300, of whom approximately two-thirds lived in Duluth and the remainder in Superior, Wisconsin, just across the drowned mouth of the small St. Louis River which forms the Duluth-Superior harbor. The cities in fact constitute an economic unit made more thorough by modern transportation between them. Duluth, whose long shoestring business district hugs a narrow bench of land below a high bluff which overlooks the lake, is the major business center, but Superior has its own retail shopping district and well-developed commercial interests. Shipping is the all-absorbing interest in those seven or eight summer months when the harbor is free from ice. Heavy trains of ore creep down almost by gravity from the iron ranges of the interior. Long narrow ore boats nose into the harbor and tie up alongside the huge ore docks only to be loaded with ore and on their way in a few hours to the blast furnaces of the southern lake ports. Returning boats bring much coal for distribution throughout the northwest. Ore is the leading commodity handled, but there are also many cargoes of Dakota and Montana wheat bound for Buffalo or for export. Duluth ranks third among the primary wheat markets of the country. Such huge tonnages have given the Duluth-Superior harbor the distinction of "second port in tonnage in the United States." Only New York handles greater tonnages. In value, of course, the story is different. Iron ore is not a valuable cargo.

Other economic activity is generally subordinate to shipping. Duluth and Superior have jobbing houses which serve the mining districts and the sparsely populated hinterland, chiefly with food products. Manufacturing is not highly developed. Duluth has a steel mill which uses local ore and lake-cargo coal, but its production is not large, chiefly because the market area is not populous. Lake-borne commerce and the outfitting of mining communities are the major economic interests, interests which promise to remain dominant because of the small opportunity for agricultural development in the northern lakes country.

Minor Lake Ports.—Scattered along the shores of Lakes Superior, Michigan, and Huron are a large number of small cities which are important chiefly as lake ports. Those which are adjacent to the iron mines ship much ore in the manner of Duluth-Superior. Others engage in a general distribution trade, and ship lumber, copper, fruit, and other farm products. Each important center is served by one or more railroads which facilitate the development of a small local wholesale trade. Manufacturing is only slightly developed and largely local in nature.

Along Lake Superior the largest of these minor lake ports are Ashland in Wisconsin, and Marquette and Sault Ste Marie in Michigan. Although it ships less than one-sixth as much ore as Duluth-Superior, Ashland frequently stands second or third among lake ports in iron-ore shipments. Marquette also ships ore from the mines of Upper Michigan, but most of this production passes through Escanaba and other ports on Lake Michigan. Sault Ste Marie, located on the canal, has a considerable distribution trade in Upper Michigan.

On Lake Michigan the ports are generally larger, less dependent upon lake shipping and more highly industrialized. Escanaba ships iron ore from the Marquette Range, but lake traffic at the other ports is relatively light.

The eastern shore of Lake Michigan has fewer cities, largely because the hinterland is not so productive. Traverse City, the largest of these, has interests in lumber and fruit, while Manistee, some fifty miles south, is an important salt-refining center. On the opposite side of the peninsula, Alpena manufactures cement and quarries much limestone for shipment to the steel mills of the Detroit industrial area. Other important lake cities of Michigan lie well to the southward and will be considered in connection with the Manufacturing Belt.

Mining Centers.—Although all the mineral-producing areas of the Northern Great Lakes section have given rise to urban centers, the largest of these are the cities of Hibbing and Virginia, both located on the Mesabi iron range of northern Minnesota. These cities are genuine "mining towns" in the accepted sense, but they have numerous characteristics which differentiate them from the mining centers of other parts of the country. In the first place, much of the mining is done by machines in open pits and calls for a generally higher type of workman than that employed in underground working. But perhaps even more startling to the visitor is the lavishness with which local governments spend money for public improvements. The public high school at Hibbing is world-famous for the excellence of its equipment, most of which rivals in both quantity and quality that of first-rate universities. In like manner, concrete highways have been extended through mile after mile of almost unpopulated forest. To understand these seeming extravagances one need only remember that most miners are voters but not taxpayers. The big steel corporations own almost everything and pay nearly all the taxes. It must be said, however, that these corporations generally have been liberal toward such public improvements, especially in the field of education. Most of their leaders have long insisted that an educated man makes a better employee. Hibbing and Virginia, as examples of iron-mining towns, are thus free from much of the grime and sordidness of other mining centers. On the other hand, their economic interests are confined almost entirely to this industry. Neither the wholesale trade nor manufacturing is highly developed.

The iron ranges of Upper Michigan have likewise developed

urban centers, the largest of which are Ironwood and Iron Mountain. These cities have somewhat more diverse economic structures than Hibbing and Virginia, chiefly because their lumber interests are more highly developed. The Copper Range of the Keweenaw Peninsula has developed several small cities, the largest of which is Calumet. The smelting of copper is important in these cities.

In the future, there is little reason to expect marked change in the economic organization of the Northern Lake cities. Iron and copper will be mined for decades to come and the larger mining towns are now located strategically with reference to known ore deposits. Lumbering may suffer a gradual decline, but present programs of reforestation should offset this tendency. The recreation industry, recently subject to marked growth in most localities within the district, will doubtless continue to expand. Heavy movements of lake-borne wheat, iron, and coal should continue to make Duluth-Superior one of the great harbors of the world. In the not too distant future the mines will of course become exhausted. Two generations hence, or three—it is hazardous to predict—the great shovels will strike bottom and the corporations and their miners will move out. With them will go the business and professional people and most of the farmers who now sell them milk, eggs, and vegetables. When that day comes the area will again be producing lumber if present programs continue. The forest with its lakes and recreation and lumber should provide the basis for a modest but permanent economic program.

The New England Forest Section

The early colonists found the hills of New England covered with excellent timber. The timber was first cut down to clear the land for farming, but before many decades the lumber industry had become important in New England economic life. Hardwoods were cut for firewood and occasionally for lumber, but the prize trees were the softwoods: white pine, spruce, and fir. New England built its homes of white pine, and made this wood the basis for a large colonial ship-building industry. Gradually the pressure for more farm land and the demand for lumber pushed the timber frontier back into the interior mountains and northward into Maine. Farming was attempted nearly everywhere south, east, and west of the White Mountains.

In a later era, many of these farm lands were abandoned and

became pasture and woodlot. Today, more than half the area of the New England states is in timber, but nearly all the remaining forest is in the state of Maine and northern New Hampshire. Once-cleared areas to the south are still in farms and are dominated by dairying, with forest products as an important subsidiary source of income. Our regional boundary is drawn to include only those areas dominated by lumbering and the forest. The dairy sections are included in the American Manufacturing Belt.

The New England Forest section consists of three districts with differing economic interest. Largest of these is (1) the Maine Woods, a rough area dominated by forest industries. North and east of the forested area is a basin drained by the St. John and Aroostook rivers, and known as (2) the Aroostook Valley, nationally famous for its potatoes. In northern New Hampshire, the section includes (3) the White Mountains, nearly all forested, but deriving most of its income from the summer-vacation industry.

Forests.—Lumbering began in New England in colonial days and reached its peak about 1840. By 1870, practically all the virgin pine had been cut. Attention then shifted to spruce and fir, first for lumber and then for paper. The pulpwood industry reached a peak about 1910. Today, New England imports nearly two-thirds of its lumber from other regions. Remaining stands represent about 4 per cent of the total for the United States, and consist mainly of spruce and fir. In 1935, the Maine Woods accounted for about 3 per cent of the national cut of lumber and about one-sixth of the production of wood pulp. More than three-quarters of the original forest area has been cut over. Cutting proceeds at about twice the rate of annual growth. In recent years, increased attention has been paid to reforestation, and New England confidently predicts that within a few years its forest resources will again be on the upgrade for the first time in three centuries.

Potatoes.—The flat lands of the Aroostook Valley of northern Maine contain one of the most important crop-specialty farming areas of the United States. Here a light, fertile soil and cool climate are combined to produce nearly one-quarter of the national crop of potatoes. From the 150,000 acres of Aroostook Valley potato land, potatoes come by the trainload down the coast to industrial New England and the cities of the Atlantic seaboard. Fertility is well maintained, and yields are the highest obtained in any part of the United States. The alluvial soils of the Aroo-

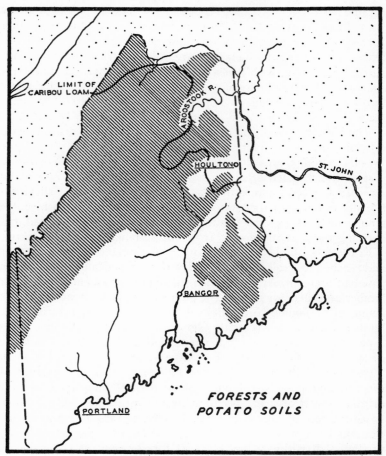

FIG. 36. Forests and Potato Soils of Northern Maine. The potato district of northern Maine occupies several valley areas near the northeast margin of the state. These valleys are drained by branches of the St. John River, most important of which is the Aroostook River. In these valleys the surface is nearly level. A combination of smooth topography, light-textured soils, abundant rainfall, and a cool growing season makes the district almost ideal for growing potatoes. The best potato soil is the Caribou loam. The outer limits of this soil area are shown on the map. Approximate limits of the forested area are indicated by shading. Potatoes are grown in all the non-forested areas within the Caribou soil belt. Note that there is an abundance of additional potato land that could be made available by clearing additional forest areas.

stook Valley support the only significant agricultural development of the New England Forest section. Elsewhere the topography is rougher and the soils are not productive.

Cities.—The Maine Woods and woods-encircled Aroostook Valley have produced few cities and towns. Bangor, railroad terminus and trade center for the section, is located just beyond its southern border, in the Manufacturing Belt. This city has the advantage of being located in a narrow trench which is the natural transportation outlet for the valley of the St. John and Aroostook rivers.

Within the section urban centers are small. There are almost no towns in the forested areas. Maine lumber is still cut during the fall and winter and floated down to the mill on the spring freshets. The mill towns generally are located near the southern border of the region.

Recreation.—The White Mountains of New Hampshire have long been a cool summer playground noted for its mountain scenery. Many a resident from the sweltering seaboard journeys into these higher altitudes every summer for a cool vacation, a little mountain-climbing, or occasional fishing and swimming. The center of this White Mountain vacation area is at Mt. Washington, highest peak of New England, nearly one and one-fifth miles above sea level.

The Adirondack Highland

The nearly circular Adirondack uplift is almost blank on most maps of economic development in the United States. The whole section is rough and the eastern half is definitely mountainous. New York lists sixteen peaks in this area with elevations above four thousand feet. Nestled among these mountains are numerous lakes, most famous of which are Saranac Lake and Lake George. This scenic combination of mountains and lakes is nearly unique in North America. Adirondack resorts are most popular in summer, but there is a growing interest in winter sports. There is little agriculture, and the best lumber was removed years ago. About the best the Adirondacks have to offer is scenery, but the scenery is superb.

Summary

The three cut-over sections of the Northern Forest and Lake Region are tied together by factors influencing the use of the land.

Soils have not generally responded favorably to the growing of grains. All of the region was originally in forest and in the future forestry should again become the leading occupation. Cool summers and ample rainfall produce good pastures where soils are fertile, and this resource has made dairying the most common type of agriculture. The dairy industry is most highly developed in the Wisconsin-Minnesota Dairy Belt, a fourth section of the region which is made the subject of Chapter XI.

Mining is the leading source of income of that portion of the Northern Great Lakes section which lies west of Lake Michigan. Iron ore is the major product, followed by copper. Forest industries have played a leading role in the history of the region but are of less importance today. Reforestation and the practice of scientific forestry will restore some of the former importance of this industry. Lumber and pulp still rank high among the region's products, but their contribution to the national income is not great.

Recreation is being rapidly recognized as a major economic interest in all parts of the region. Best known of the recreational areas are the Adirondack Mountains, the White Mountains, the "Ten Thousand Lakes" of northern Minnesota, and the northern portion of the lower peninsula of Michigan. Summers are cool in these areas, and the scenery generally combines timber, lakes, and mountains. These are the favorite inland resorts for vacationists from the populous Manufacturing Belt to the south.

REFERENCES

A review of glacial history will provide valuable background for the study of this region. See Loomis, *Physiography of the United States,* or Fenneman, *Physiography of the Eastern United States.* The podsol soil belt is well described in Wolfanger, *The Major Soil Divisions of the United States,* and mapped in the *Atlas of American Agriculture.* See studies from the University of Minnesota concerning the Lake Superior iron mines. *Transportation on the Great Lakes,* Corps of Engineers, U. S. Army (1937), presents a complete analysis of Great Lakes shipping. Material from this publication was used extensively in writing this chapter.

QUESTIONS AND PROBLEMS

1. Why is a knowledge of the surface and soil important to an understanding of economic life in the Northern Forest and Lake Region?

2. Why is this area not a cash-grain region? a meat-animal region?
3. Why has dairying generally proved more profitable than wheat-farming in this region?
4. What is a podsol soil? For what uses are these soils best suited?
5. Why is the southern boundary of the region a "gradation boundary"? What factors might cause it to shift?
6. Why do potatoes, sugar beets, and peas do well in this region?
7. Describe the topography of the iron ranges of Minnesota. Consult a dictionary for definitions of the word "range." How many of the definitions listed are applicable to geography?
8. Many of the early settlers of the Northern Great Lakes section came from northern Europe. Why did the people of Sweden, Norway, Finland, and Denmark feel at home in the natural environment of this section?
9. How would business activity in the Northern Great Lakes section be affected by an expansion of shipbuilding? a war? a decline in automobile production?
10. Why do the Great Lakes carry greater tonnages than any other inland waterway? Why do they not carry even larger tonnages?

CHAPTER XI

THE NORTHERN FOREST AND LAKE REGION— WISCONSIN-MINNESOTA DAIRY BELT

Growth of Dairy Farming in the Northeastern United States.—The belt of specialized farming which stretches from central Minnesota across Wisconsin and Michigan and continues across Pennsylvania and New York to the Atlantic seaboard is one of the great agricultural belts of the United States. Its present development is relatively new, largely a creature of the twentieth century. Small areas of dairy farming were in existence in the eastern states in 1900, and a few dairy farms were clustered about the mid-western cities, but most of the lake state areas were still vainly trying to grow wheat or fatten livestock. The dairy industry was destined for marked growth, however, and these states were geographically situated to receive the benefit from it.

Several factors influenced this expansion, but four of these are especially noteworthy. (1) The popularity of dairy products in the diet increased greatly in the first quarter of the present century. We began eating more butter and cheese and drinking more milk, not only because they taste good but also because we are assured of their importance in the diet. Dairy products became popular along with fruits and vegetables, and Wisconsin prospered simultaneously with California and Florida in this change of diet. (2) Refrigeration and rapid transportation made long-distance shipments possible. This factor was important in developing such far-away areas as Wisconsin and Minnesota whose butter could never reach the eastern seaboard in prime condition without the refrigerator car. (3) The continued trend toward farm specialization tended to reduce the production of farm butter. Pioneer farmers were nearly self-sufficing and such products as they sold were of necessity valuable in proportion to their bulk. Every farm had a few cows and the surplus cream was churned into butter to be sold at the village store, much as eggs are sold today. Unfortunately, however, butter was more perishable than eggs, and by the time it was collected and sent

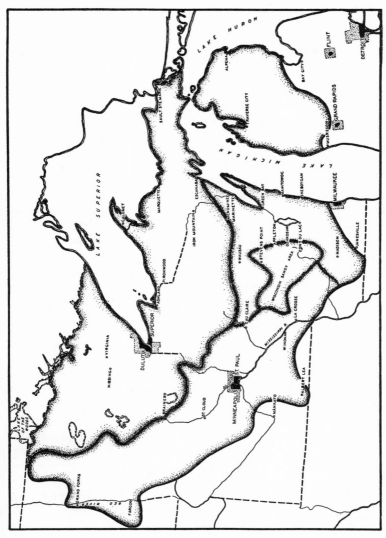

Fig. 37. Western Sections of the Northern Forest and Lake Region.

to city markets it was often in inferior condition. Renovating plants were set up to sweeten stale butter by removing the butyric acid. But the butter-renovating industry had a short life. A butter factory with proper control over sanitary conditions and churning processes could make better butter and make it very cheaply. Creamery butter began to command a premium in the market. At the same time other forces were acting to decrease the number of cows on farms in many areas. Milking cows is hard work and much of it must be done by lamplight in early morning and late evening. Add these hours to a long day in the corn, wheat, or cotton fields and you have made the task unreasonable. In a choice of occupations the Corn Belt farmer chose to concentrate his attentions upon corn and meat animals, and the southern farmer upon cotton. If he kept cows he sold cream, but he began buying butter instead of churning it at home. In some sections, especially the Cotton Belt, this trend toward specialization was pronounced. Specialization in other types of agriculture in different sections of the country fostered specialization in dairying in Wisconsin and Minnesota. (4) Stronger than any of these forces was the urbanization of the country which went on very rapidly in these decades. The growth of cities necessarily stimulated dairying, for the average American in his city apartment is far removed from the dairy cow by both distance and experience.

Growth of a Specialized Dairy Area.—Most of the reasons for the development of the lake states into a specialized dairy section have already been mentioned. Some of these reasons are negative: the short growing season and frequently inferior soil which make corn-growing and animal-feeding unprofitable, but which still allow for good pasture and the growing of forage crops. These influences were paramount in making dairying the most profitable type of agriculture in Wisconsin and eastern Minnesota. In Michigan and northeast Illinois, however, another factor appeared in the growth of manufacturing and cities—the westward extension of the American Manufacturing Belt. We are familiar with the fact that dairy farming is important in the vicinity of every large city for the obvious reason that fresh milk is too bulky and perishable to ship long distances. As cities grow and become more numerous in the course of the industrial development of an area, these local dairy areas expand until finally they are contiguous. The whole industrial belt becomes a dairy belt whose farmers are engaged primarily in supplying market milk to neighboring urban centers. The rise of dairying in Michigan is largely attributable to the rise of Detroit and the other Michigan industrial centers; and northeast Illinois is a dairy district almost entirely because it is near the Chicago metropolitan area.

From this discussion it is readily seen that dairy-product districts are of two types: (1) market-milk areas, and (2) those which produce butter, cheese, and condensed milk for distant markets. In line with this division, the dairy-farming area may be divided into two sections. (1) Largest of these is an eastern market-milk area which begins at Milwaukee and extends eastward to the seaboard. This area is a separate region, the American Manufacturing Belt (Chapters XX-XXIX). (2) A western butter-and-cheese district occupies much of Wisconsin and Minnesota, and is here assigned as a separate section of the Northern Forest and Lake Region. This latter area is the most highly specialized dairy section in the United States. It may be further divided into (a) a cheese area in southern and eastern Wisconsin, and (b) a butter area in Minnesota and western Wisconsin.

Emphasis is necessary at this point upon the fact that dairy farming does not terminate with the southern boundary of the Dairy Belt. Dairy farms are numerous in the Corn Belt, especially in the northern portions. In fact, the state of Iowa has more dairy cattle per square mile than Michigan or that portion of the Dairy Belt which lies in western Minnesota. Iowa stands second only to Minnesota in butter production. Wisconsin regularly ranks third and the Corn Belt states of Nebraska, Ohio, and Missouri are next in line. It only happens that dairying dominates the agricultural development of the area we have marked off as the Wisconsin-Minnesota Dairy section, while meat-animal production is of greater relative importance on the richer soils of the Corn Belt.

Dairy-Farm Organization.—Some differences in farm organization are noticeable between the butter, cheese, and market-milk areas, but the general pattern in dairy farming is much the same whether practiced in California, Wisconsin, or New York. These characteristics arise primarily from (1) the nature and habits of the productive machine, the dairy cow, and (2) the peculiarly perishable nature of the product.

As a milk-producing animal, the dairy cow requires a bulky ration. Her feed consists largely of grass in summer and hay in winter. Cows will stay alive indefinitely upon such a diet but their milk will be of poor quality, so that for rich milk and cream more concentrated feeds must be added to this roughage. Small grains are fed and, where available, corn. Prepared feeds, especially bran and shorts (flour mill by-products), are always included. In the winter, hay is supplemented with silage which is made by cutting green corn stalks (immature ears and all) and preserving them in a silo, a cylindrical structure usually about thirty-five feet high and ten to fifteen feet in diameter. These feed requirements practically dictate the use of land on the dairy farm. Pastures ordinarily occupy the hillier portions of the farm. On the crop land, hay has the greatest acreage followed by corn, oats, or wheat, depending upon local climatic and soil conditions. In general, corn is most important in the southern sections which lie near the Corn Belt. Corn will ordinarily ripen in these areas.

Farther north, corn is still important, but the shortness of the growing season often prevents it from ripening, and nearly all the crop is converted into silage. Oats are grown throughout the section. Wisconsin and Minnesota dairy farmers also grow much barley, while those of Michigan grow a considerable acreage of wheat. In this manner, the use to which farm land is put is adapted to the dietary demands of the dairy cow: pasture, hay, and silage for bulk; corn, oats, and other small grains for concentrated feeds.

In the western portions of the Dairy Belt, the presence of cheap corn, either grown locally or shipped from the adjacent Corn Belt, has brought a specialization in butter. Corn-fed dairy cows produce a rich milk high in fat content and therefore well adapted to butter-making. Thus the typical dairy farmer in Minnesota, western Wisconsin, or adjacent Iowa (in the Corn Belt) obtains the major portion of his income from the sale of cream to the neighborhood creamery. His interest in obtaining a high yield of butter-fat has prompted the breeding of cows which have become famous not for the number of gallons of milk they produce but rather for the pounds of butter-fat they are capable of returning for a given amount of feed. Milk, skim milk from which the cream has been separated, is nearly worthless in this community. Farms are too far from the large cities to reach their markets.

But the milk is not wasted. Always there are growing calves, of which the females, if potential milk-producers, will be retained and added to the dairy herd.

The calves will not consume all the milk, however, and the remainder is fed to hogs, the universal scavengers without which no dairy farm is successful. Hogs consume the extra milk and follow the cattle over the pasture and in the feed lot, picking up a good living from the scraps left behind by the less efficient and more particular bovine. Milk and barley never make these hogs very fat, but they produce good lean bacon and for that reason dairy-farm hogs find a ready market. From 10 to 20 per cent of farm income in the dairy belt is derived from the sale of hogs and calves. Such feeding operations are most important, of course, in those areas adjoining the Corn Belt.

In eastern and southwestern Wisconsin, where dairying is more highly developed than in any other large area in the United States, the emphasis has been placed more upon cheese than upon butter-fat. Cheese is a whole-milk product, hence the cheese cow is selected for her ability to produce a large amount not only of cream but also of the other solids contained in milk. *Gallonage* is more important here, and there is less emphasis upon the richness of milk than in the butter belt. Lack of corn for grain lessens the butter-fat content and in this way the Wisconsin cheese industry represents a nice adaptation to the geographic environment. Without a heavy corn ration, the cows failed to give rich milk, but the best cheese is made from milk only moderately rich. Hence Wisconsin turned from butter to cheese and now produces more than two-thirds of the national output. Most of the product is American cheese, but there are also factories specializing in Limburger, Roquefort, Swiss, and all the other fancy cheeses formerly imported from Europe.

The principal area in the production of these "foreign" cheeses is in southwestern Wisconsin. There you may duplicate in taste and appearance the famous cheese specialties of all parts of the world. Wisconsin boasts that regardless of whether you like your cheese mild or "nippy," foreign or domestic, your appetite can be satisfied with one of the dozens of local varieties which Wisconsin ships to all parts of the country.[1]

---

[1] Monroe, Wisconsin, calls itself the "Swiss cheese capital of the United States." Dodge County is famous for its brick and Limburger cheeses.

In the butter-and-cheese areas the cooperative creamery and cheese factory are very much in evidence. National concerns have many factories scattered over the area, and there are also numerous independent, privately owned plants. In most communities, however, the producer-owned creamery or cheese factory predominates, and the farmer who hauls his cans of cream or milk to market knows that he is selling his product to an organization of which he is a part-owner. Profits at the end of the year are prorated to producers on the basis of the quantities they have sold.

Creameries market their butter in all parts of the United States but their best markets are in the industrial areas. Historically, nearly all butter has been sent to market in wooden tubs, but recent years have brought a marked increase in the sale of packaged butter, both because it remains in good condition longer and because the carton makes a good advertising medium through which definite markets for particular brands of butter may be built up. Summer pastures bring a heavier butter production and this surplus is placed in warehouses at below-freezing temperatures and withdrawn the following winter. If properly cared for, butter can be stored for many months without deterioration.

Because it is less perishable, cheese is marketed in a somewhat more leisurely manner than butter. All the cheese must be aged, and each cheese factory has a storage room, frequently a basement, in which the curing process is carried on at temperatures somewhat above freezing. Fancy varieties require different manufacturing processes and different methods of curing. Many special brands are also reworked and blended before being placed on sale.

On the dairy farm itself life is often considered monotonous and extremely confining. No factory laborer ever punched a time clock with greater regularity than that with which the dairyman milks the cows morning and night, seven days a week, with never a vacation unless someone is hired to come in and do the work. During the winter both the morning and evening milking must be done by lamplight. Caring for the milk, separating the cream, feeding the cows, and caring for the crops as well as the hogs and chickens keep the dairy farmer well occupied in the interval between milkings. Routine work ties him more closely to his farm than it does in any other type of agriculture.

But there are compensations, and not the least of these has been the steadiness of dairy-farm income. Throughout years of farm depression the demand for these products has been relatively constant. There are no crop failures to wipe out an entire year's income. Foreign markets do not matter, for we sell almost no butter and cheese abroad. Protective tariffs prevent the intrusion of low-priced foreign dairy products. Week after week the cream check comes in and the farmer can count on its coming. Prices are depressed many times, but they go through no such wild fluctuations as the prices of grains or cotton. The dairy farmer is held very closely to his farm and he has little chance of extreme prosperity, but his income is remarkably steady. There is little of the gambler's chance in dairy farming. He who enters it loses much liberty but gains much security.

Other Farm Activities.—Not every farm in the Dairy Belt is a dairy farm and not every dairy farm depends exclusively upon milk and cream for its income. Cash crops are grown in nearly all parts of the section and four of these are of particular importance: (1) potatoes, (2) fruit, (3) tobacco, and (4) vegetables.

Potatoes.—The loose soil and cool summers of the lake states are well adapted to white potatoes. Potato-growing is common, either on crop-specialty farms or on dairy farms, in all sections of these states, but a map of potato acreage shows three areas of particular importance: (1) the Red River Valley of northwestern Minnesota and adjacent North Dakota, (2) the Twin Cities area near Minneapolis and St. Paul, and (3) the Central Wisconsin sandy area. It will be noted that all of these areas are near the northern border of the Dairy Belt and that they are located on loose sandy or alluvial soils. Minnesota regularly produces about 8 per cent of our potato crop, while Wisconsin produces about 7 per cent. These states are thus responsible for nearly one-sixth of the national potato output and they supply most of the potatoes used in the Middle West. Except in the Red River Valley, dairying is more important than potato-growing in all of these areas, and most of the potatoes are grown on farms classed as dairy farms.

Fruit.—A small but highly specialized fruit-growing area is found in northeastern Wisconsin on the pointed peninsula east of Green Bay. Here the famous Door County cherry orchards occupy a considerable portion of the land. The cherries are of the red (sour) variety and in recent years much of the production has been canned.

Tobacco.—The growing of tobacco has become important in

two small sections of Wisconsin: (1) in Vernon County, near the Iowa-Minnesota boundary, and (2) in Dane County, in the vicinity of Madison. The production consists of a type known as "cigar binder," the leaf which is wrapped around the inner "filler" of the cigar to hold it together, and over which is wrapped the tough tissue-thin "wrapper," the outer covering. The Wisconsin production, which is evenly divided between these two localities, is only about 3 per cent of the national output of tobacco of all kinds, but it constitutes nearly two-thirds of the total production of binder tobacco.

Vegetables.—The relatively light soil and cool summers of the Dairy Belt have made it a desirable place to grow certain types of vegetables. It is far superior to the Corn Belt, for example, in growing beans and peas. These vegetables tend to become dry and tough in the hotter summers of sections farther south. The short growing season is also desirable for growing sweet corn for canning, inasmuch as the cool weather of an early fall prevents the corn from ripening. Sweet corn grows well and can be produced very cheaply in the Corn Belt farther south, but often a period of hot, dry weather in the canning season will cause standing corn to become so dry and tough as to make it unmarketable. In Minnesota, this type of weather is less probable. The canning season is prolonged and the probability of obtaining uniformly high quality is correspondingly increased. Vegetables such as these, which are most successful in districts having short, cool growing seasons, have become important in many areas in the Dairy Belt. Minnesota is most famous for its canned corn, regularly ranking among the three leading states in this product. Wisconsin grows roughly half the national output of green peas, most of which are produced and canned in the east-central portion of the state. Wisconsin is also a leading state in the growing of late cabbage, much of which is made into sauerkraut.

From these sources is derived the farm income of the Dairy Belt. Except in a few small areas, dairying is the leading occupation and the great majority of farmers receive the bulk of their incomes from the sale of dairy products. It is equally true, however, that no large number depend exclusively upon this source of income. Specialization has not gone that far. Most farmers also sell a few meat animals and many of them have a few acres of vegetables, potatoes, or tobacco from which to supplement their income from the sale of cream or milk. Nearly all farms are family-sized, averaging from 120 to 160 acres. A few large-scale establishments are found, but they are exceptional. Most dairy farmers milk from ten to twenty cows. Many of them have milking machines and nearly all of them use mechanical separators to separate the cream from the milk where cream is to be sold. In some sections, farmers haul their cream or milk to the creamery or railway station, while in others regularly scheduled trains or trucks pick up these products. Rural conditions prevail. The Dairy Belt is an important stronghold of rural democracy.

Forests.—Inasmuch as practically the entire Wisconsin-Minnesota dairy area was long ago cleared of forests and transformed into a farming area, lumbering is no longer of economic importance. An occasional portable sawmill may still be found working over a small timbered area, but its products are for local consumption and of little commercial significance.

Minerals.—Except for a small output of granite in central Minnesota (near St. Cloud), this area is singularly devoid of mining activity. Local gravel pits supply materials for an excellent system of farm-to-market roads, but practically no mineral products from this district enter the channels of commerce.

CITIES OF THE DAIRY BELT

The reader will recall that it has seemed desirable to separate the Dairy Belt from the Manufacturing Belt, whose farmers, although primarily interested in dairying, obtain most of their income from the sale of fluid milk. The Wisconsin-Minnesota Dairy Belt is predominantly an agricultural area. Its cities are commercial centers and the manufacturing which has developed in them is largely (1) local or regional in character, or (2) closely related to the agricultural development. Manufacturing is most important in those cities which lie near the Manufacturing Belt. These cities (of east-central Wisconsin) form a part of a "pioneer fringe," a frontier industrial area at the edge of the Manufacturing Belt. This fringe of cities also appears in the Corn Belt. In the future they and their environs may be added to the manufacturing area, but at present agricultural and commercial pursuits are of greater economic importance than manufacturing and they are appropriately assigned to the Dairy and Corn belts. It must be emphasized, however, that cities in this frontier zone, even in their state of industrial immaturity, are more highly industrialized than any other group of American cities outside the Manufacturing Belt.

Beyond this fringe of commercial-industrial centers, cities of the Dairy Belt partake more truly of the nature of commercial cities. Commercial agencies, wholesale and retail establishments, railroads, banks, and similar establishments are their leading business institutions, the leading employers of labor. Next in importance come those institutions which serve the city's trade territory either as processors of farm products or as manufacturers of goods for the specific regional market. Butter and cheese factories are the most common industrial establishments. Then there are canning factories and meat-packing establishments to convert other farm products into less perishable and more concentrated forms. Each city may also be expected to have its local factories, such as machine shops, ice plants, gas plants, and bakeries, which supply near-by markets, and perhaps those which turn out farm machinery and equipment for the larger regional market. The whole economic life is closely associated with the region and not the nation. Essentially, therefore, these cities, like those of the many sections previously described, are commercial centers—foci for the trade of a particular territory, the size of which varies, of course, from one city to another.

It must also be recognized that, as in the Corn Belt, a large percentage of the trade of the district is concentrated in the cities of the adjacent industrial belt. Chicago and Milwaukee have a large distribution trade in the Dairy Belt as well as in the Corn Belt. As the "economic capital of Wisconsin," Milwaukee wellnigh dominates the larger commercial activities of all but the northwestern portion of the state. In like manner, Chicago, which fairly justifies its reputation as the "market place of the Middle West," also has extensive commercial interests throughout much of the Dairy Belt.

Within the designated boundaries of the Dairy Belt and its mineralized sister-section to the north, the major center is Minneapolis-St. Paul, the twin cities of Minnesota and the commercial focus of an area which extends westward to the Rocky Mountains.

The Twin Cities.—Adjacent municipalities which call themselves "twin cities" are fairly common in America. Frequently the accident of a state boundary line, or a once-potent but now unimportant river barrier, has caused cities to develop as two or more separate municipalities, divided only by imaginary political boundary lines or by much-bridged rivers. Economically, such an agglomeration is one city, with a major business section, amusement area, banking center, and other characteristics of a trading center. Perhaps one of these "twins" specializes in industry, the other in commerce. But in nearly all cases they are one metropolitan economic area. If they are twins, they are Siamese twins, each thoroughly dependent upon the other.

In Minneapolis and St. Paul, however, the twins have long been physically separate entities. Neither is a satellite of the other and each is a complete city in itself. Their economic development has progressed along strikingly similar lines. So complete is their independence that were one to be blotted out entirely, the other could function the next day with very little inconvenience. That two pioneer settlements, originally ten miles apart, but now grown together in the motor age, should have developed as independent economic units is partially explained in the historical importance of the geography of the area.

In a general way the establishment and early growth of Minneapolis and St. Paul may be said to reflect the relative importance which business interests placed upon water power and river transportation. Even before pioneer days the government had built a fort at the mouth of the Minnesota River which was also the head of navigation for small craft on the Mississippi. Early settlers chose a site a short distance down-stream and founded St. Paul at the head of "practical" navigation. The village grew to importance in the ensuing lumber development, became the terminus for river steamboats in pre-railroad days, and was soon firmly established as the commercial center for a large area to the north and west. Naturally it was chosen as the site for the state capital. Minneapolis developed more slowly. Ten miles to the west of St. Paul a village had arisen on the west bank of the river opposite the falls of St. Anthony, the best power site on the Mississippi. Soldiers had used power from the falls to saw lumber for the building of Fort Snelling. Other mills were set up and the settlement grew. But it was not to become important until the arrival of the railroads which soon turned the Red River Valley and later the Dakota prairies into a vast wheat field. Wheat naturally came to Minneapolis to be milled. Grinding stones (and later steel rollers) replaced saws in the mills and Minneapolis shortly became the flour-milling center of the state. Thus St. Paul's early interests were commercial, while those of Minneapolis were industrial.[2]

This distinction was not destined to remain. Minneapolis, not satisfied with buying western wheat, soon began to sell goods to the wheat-farmers. Its banks began to act as correspondents for country banks in the Wheat Belt. Before long, Minneapolis became the commercial and financial center for a far-flung mid-continental area stretching westward to the Rocky Mountains. Today, Minneapolis is definitely a commercial city: banker, broker, and wholesaler for western Minnesota, North and South Dakota, and Montana. The trade of these states is funneled into Minneapolis by the three northern transcontinental railroads, all of which converge upon the Twin Cities and two of which terminate there. The Dairy Belt has now extended far beyond Minneapolis, but her interests are still largely in the wheat country. St. Paul, on the other hand, has not remained entirely commercial. Numerous manufacturers have been attracted to this position at the head of Mississippi River navigation. In late years, several factories have been built in the formerly undeveloped "Midway" area between the two cities but within the limits of the city of St. Paul. In the meantime, St. Paul's commercial interests have continued to grow, but her trade territory is largely the same as in the early days when Indians still roamed western Minnesota. Northern and western Wisconsin and southeastern Minnesota still comprise her trading area. To these districts St. Paul is both a wholesale and a jobbing center. Butter and meat animals rather than wheat and range livestock are her chief agricultural interests.

Thus have arisen the twin cities of the north, not Siamese twins and not identical twins, but fulfilling the latter qualification more nearly than any other pair of large American cities. Today the student of economic life is anxious to discover what indications,

---

[2] Considerable importance also attaches to the fact that early railroads found no suitable terminal sites between Minneapolis and St. Paul from which both cities could be served. Each center was of such importance that all railroads found it advantageous to seek terminal sites in both of them.

if any, point to specialization, interdependence, and the development of a typical metropolitan center.[3]

Analysis of the individual items in the wholesale trade discloses a striking similarity of development with three notable exceptions: (1) the assembling of grain accounts for more than one-third of the total wholesale activity of Minneapolis, and is negligible in St. Paul; (2) St. Paul has nearly three times as large sales of dry goods as Minneapolis; (3) the St. Paul wholesale grocery trade is nearly as large as that of Minneapolis. In all other types of goods, Minneapolis leads St. Paul by a wide margin. These data indicate that Minneapolis commercial interests are far-flung and regional while those of St. Paul are more highly localized. St. Paul has a smaller trade territory and serves it more thoroughly.

Apparently Minneapolis has become a regional center with a widespread territory for which she is banker and wholesaler. It is not possible, however, for her wholesalers to cover this vast territory thoroughly with such commonly demanded articles as dry goods and groceries. That function is carried on by smaller jobbing centers within the trade area. Minneapolis is first of all a transaction center, a location for bankers' banks and for branch offices of commercial firms.

Such specialization as has arisen in manufacturing is traceable to the nature of the trade territory. In Minneapolis, flour is the leading product, followed by machine-shop products, printing, and bakery goods. The most important industrial developments in the St. Paul area are the breweries and the meat-packing industry of South St. Paul. In the city itself, printing, railroad car repairs, and the manufacture of advertising novelties are leading factory industries. With the possible exception of advertising novelties, in which St. Paul is a leading mid-western center, all of these industries are either local or closely related to the agricultural development of the trade territory. Minneapolis, although somewhat troubled lest the cheap lake transportation of wheat transfer the

---

[3] Delving into such economic data as are available, he discovers the following indicators:

ECONOMIC DEVELOPMENT OF THE TWIN CITIES

	Minneapolis	St. Paul
Population, 1930	464,356	271,606
Wholesale trade: Net sales, all wholesale establishments (1935)	$ 626,009,000	$ 162,486,000
Value added by manufacture (1937)	$ 112,838,000	$ 74,523,000
Bank clearing (1936)	$4,170,000,000	$1,993,000,000

crown of "Nation's Leading Flour Miller" to Buffalo, regularly stands first or second among United States flour-milling centers. South St. Paul, drawing largely from the milk- and corn-fed hogs of southern Minnesota, has become a leading livestock market and meat-packing center. Other major industries of the area are local in character. In 1937 the Twin Cities produced nearly 1 per cent of the nation's manufactured goods. About four-sevenths of this production came from Minneapolis factories.

From this brief sketch it is apparent that although some economic specialization has appeared, there is scant basis for belief that the Twin Cities are being welded into an economic center of interdependent, non-competing parts. It is indeed possible that such a coalescence will occur in the future; but for the present Minneapolis and St. Paul remain twins, more nearly identical twins than any other well-known type. With a metropolitan population which places them thirteenth among metropolitan centers of the United States, the Twin Cities have become one of the leading focal points in American economic life.

Cities of Eastern Wisconsin.—Perhaps the reader might have obtained a clearer picture of the cities of eastern Wisconsin if they had been described as satellites of Wisconsin's great industrial center, Milwaukee. Unfortunately, however, such a treatment would lack strict accuracy. These cities have grown up independently of Milwaukee and have shared with it the growth of manufacturing industries, but they are in no sense offshoots from the major center. They belong rather to that zone of semi-industrial cities which is found so generally on the outer margins of the Manufacturing Belt. In Wisconsin, three of these semi-industrial cities are of sufficient importance to command our attention. These are: (1) Appleton (with its suburbs, Menasha and Neena), (2) Oshkosh, and (3) Fond du Lac, on the shores of Lake Winnebago. These cities have rich trading areas in the fertile Fox River Valley (partially occupied by Lake Winnebago), which is justly famous for its dairy-farm production. In addition, an extensive paper-manufacturing industry, based upon northern timber and an abundance of clear water, has developed in the Appleton district at the north end of the lake. Midway down the lake, at the mouth of the Fox River, Oshkosh has large sash-and-door factories as well as plants manufacturing furniture and automobile bodies and parts. Fond du Lac at the "head of the lake" also has woodworking industries as well as an important leather production. All of these products are of more than local importance and make the Fox River Valley a significant industrial area. In all these towns, however, the wholesale and retail trades are of equal or greater importance than manufacturing; hence the classification as semi-industrial cities.

Menominee and Marinette, twin cities at the mouth of the Menominee River, are distributing centers for the growing dairy interests of the area. In addition, these cities have experienced a considerable industrial development, most of which is concerned with converting the local production of forest products into lumber and paper.

The Green Bay area is dominated by the city of Green Bay whose trade territory includes not only the rich peninsula but also the equally productive mainland to the north. An important center for paper manufacture, Green Bay also has machine shops and other local industries.

South of Green Bay, the cities of Manitowoc and Sheboygan fall within the classification of semi-industrial cities. Manitowoc, smaller but more highly industrialized than its southern neighbor, is a center for the manufacture of aluminum articles, ships for use on the Great Lakes, and cement. Its trade territory runs inland to Lake Winnebago. The economic development of Sheboygan is more diversified. In the center of an intensive dairy development (cheese), Sheboygan merchants have a rich and concentrated market. Her factories turn out furniture (especially chairs), enameled ware, and a long list of other products designed for a more localized market.

Other Cities of the Dairy Belt.—Those remaining cities of the Dairy Belt which lie west of the semi-industrial zone generally have an economic development similar to that of Minneapolis and St. Paul. All of them are essentially commercial, with smaller manufacturing interests characterized either as local or based upon the products of near-by farms. Creameries and meat-packing plants are fairly numerous and several cities produce farm machinery and other types of agricultural equipment. Almost invariably, however, the real business center is the main street with its retail stores and service establishments. Transportation interests are important and local railroad shops contribute heavily to the industrial payrolls. These cities are true distribution centers.

In Wisconsin, the largest city of this class is Madison, state capital, educational center, and market place for a rich dairy district of southern Wisconsin. Located between two lakes, Madison occupies one of the most picturesque urban sites in America. Its factories turn out machinery, farm equipment, and a long list of miscellaneous items. North of Madison, beyond the sandy plains, Stevens Point and Wausau are local distributing centers. The latter city also has extensive paper and lumber industries. In western Wisconsin, Eau Claire and La Crosse serve the butter area as jobbing centers. Their manufactured products are of a diverse nature and commercial interests are of generally greater importance.

Minnesota cities resemble those of Wisconsin except that their industrial development is less. Winona, Rochester, Austin, Albert Lea, and Faribault all serve the intensively developed dairy and meat-animal interests of near-by farm areas. Winona and Faribault have several local manufacturing industries, while Rochester is noted chiefly as a medical center. Austin, at the edge of the Corn Belt, has a thriving meat-packing industry. Albert Lea also packs meat, but its major interests lie in the distribution field. Northwest of the Twin Cities the chief centers are St. Cloud and Brainerd. St. Cloud is important for the quarrying and manufacture of building stone (granite), and Brainerd is a shopping center for the Cuyuna iron range and an important center for summer tourists visiting the popular "Ten Thousand Lakes of Northern Minnesota."

Extension of the Dairy Belt to include the potato and sugar-beet section of the Red River Valley also includes Fargo and Grand Forks, first and second cities, respectively, of North Dakota. Both cities have a large wholesale and jobbing trade. Their trade territories include not only the productive Red River Valley, but also a large portion of the wheat-growing sections of the central portion of North Dakota.

SUMMARY

Dairying and Industrialization.—In the Wisconsin-Minnesota Dairy Belt we again encounter an intensive type of farming last observed in the irrigated valleys of the western states. It is perhaps confusing to include the Dairy Belt in the Northern Forest and Lake Region, because it differs notably from other sections of the region in adaptability to human use. Yet there are important similarities among the sections in that all of them experience relatively cool summers and have relatively poor soils for grain production. In these respects, the Dairy Belt stands in marked contrast to the warmer and more fertile Corn Belt which adjoins it on the south. The Dairy Belt cannot compete with the Corn and Wheat Belts in growing grain, but its succulent pastures make it an excellent location for the dairy cow. Refrigeration, transportation, and the rise of urban markets have enabled the section to specialize in the production of butter, cheese, and condensed milk, the products from which it derives greatest profit in national markets.

Dairy farming has been described as one of the most confining types of agriculture. Because production is continuous and the product perishable, every day is both work day and market day on the dairy farm. The typical dairy farm operates by the clock. In addition, it must be stocked with a considerable amount of specialized equipment. Such heavy investments in specialized capital make it difficult for dairy farmers to shift to other types of production on short notice. For that reason, the boundaries of the Dairy Belt remain relatively stable from one year to another.

On the southeast, the Dairy Belt borders the industrialized region known as the American Manufacturing Belt. Farming in the manufacturing region is also dominated by dairying, but its main product is fluid milk for city use rather than butter and cheese. The manufacturing region has pushed westward with the years. As one section after another has witnessed the growth of industry and the rise of cities it has also witnessed a change in farm types in its hinterland. Dairying and the growing of fresh fruits and vegetables for local city markets have become more profitable than the older types of farming, and gradually these agricultural interests have come to characterize the rural economy of the area.

At the present time the Wisconsin-Minnesota Dairy Belt is beyond the industrial frontier which marks the western limit of the manufacturing region. Its farmers are still producing dairy products for a generalized national market and not for a particular city. Yet the margins of the American Manufacturing Belt are nowhere clearly defined. Around its borders are the familiar zones of mixed economic development which mark the margins of all regions in the eastern United States. In southeastern Wisconsin a considerable group of small cities has a greater degree of industrialization than we have encountered thus far in this volume. These semi-industrial cities may constitute an imminent addition to the American Manufacturing Belt, but at present we are not justified in attaching them to that region. If this addition should take place, we may also expect a change in farm type from butter and cheese to market milk. It also would probably bring a further migration of intensive dairy farming into the more westerly portions of the section. If southern Wisconsin becomes a bit more highly industrialized, the butter and cheese center of the United States will likely shift westward into Minnesota and northeastern Iowa. Such a transformation would carry southern Wisconsin through a virtually complete series of economic successions. For Wisconsin was exploited first for furs and timber, later for soil-robbing wheat production, and still later for the production of dairy products for national markets. Industrialization would bring the final stage in so far as modern agriculture is concerned: the growing of perishable foods for near-by city markets. In the meantime, however, the Wisconsin-Minnesota Dairy Belt remains the leading source of the nation's butter and cheese, the nation's only large area devoted to the production of dairy products for inter-regional trade.

REFERENCES

The dairy industry has been the subject of many reports by the United States Department of Agriculture and by the University of Wisconsin. The state planning boards of Minnesota and Wisconsin have issued many studies of natural resources and economic development in those states. Rural community studies from the University of Wisconsin are noteworthy, as are the employment studies from the University of Minnesota.

QUESTIONS AND PROBLEMS

1. Why were Wisconsin and Minnesota good states in which to develop a dairy industry capable of serving national markets?
2. Describe the land-use pattern and the physical appearance of the farmstead of a typical dairy farm. How do these landscape features reflect the nature of dairy-farm organization?
3. Many of the early settlers of Wisconsin came from western and northern Europe. Of what importance are these origins in explaining the development of the Wisconsin dairy industry?

4. Discuss the relative importance of cultural and natural factors in the location and growth of Minneapolis and St. Paul as twin cities.

5. Why are the cities of eastern Wisconsin more highly industrialized than other cities of the Dairy District? Contrast the industrial development of these two groups of cities.

6. How does dairy farming in the Wisconsin-Minnesota Dairy Belt differ from dairy farming in the American Manufacturing Belt? What are the advantages and disadvantages of each type of farming?

7. Why is a portion of the valley of the Red River of the North included in the Northern Forest and Lake Region?

8. What factors have contributed to the position of Wisconsin as a "stronghold of rural democracy"?

9. Assume that the urbanization of the United States is to continue. How might such a trend affect the boundaries of the Dairy Belt? Would an increased demand for dairy products be met by areal expansion or greater intensification? What would happen to the fluid-milk areas? Would portions of the Corn Belt be added to the Dairy Belt? What factors other than the demand for dairy products must be considered?

10. If you were a dairy farmer, would you prefer to produce milk for market or milk and cream for industrial use (butter, cheese, etc.)? Why?

CHAPTER XII

CORN BELT AGRICULTURE

Boundaries of the Corn Belt.—In the interior lowland of the United States, boundaries of the different farm belts are determined by the relative advantage of engaging in various types of farming. Regional boundaries nowhere remain permanent because there are no clear-cut natural divisions, topographic, climatic, or pedologic, within the area. In consequence, regional boundaries tend to broaden out into zones within which two types of farming are so thoroughly intermixed as to defy classification. Furthermore, the relative advantage of two types of agriculture varies remarkably from year to year with changes in the prices of farm products, so that such boundaries as can be defined have a distressing habit of shifting back and forth with these price changes.

Thus there exist on the outer edges of the Corn Belt extensive "zones of indifference" in which it matters little over a period of years whether farmers engage primarily in corn production or in the type of farming practiced in the neighboring farm belt. Those near the western boundaries shift rapidly from corn to wheat when wheat prices advance more than corn prices, and they shift back again when corn appears more profitable than wheat. Along the southern boundary of the Corn Belt farmers are constantly changing from specialized corn-belt farming to the more diversified corn-wheat-crop-specialty system of the Ohio Valley, and next year perhaps reversing their stand because corn appears more profitable than diversified cropping. Adjacent to the Dairy Belt, such changes are less marked because the dairy farm requires large amounts of specialized capital and fluctuations in dairy-product prices are less marked than are those in grains and meat animals; but here also there is a broad zone of slowly oscillating predominance of one system or the other.

The Corn Belt thus has a core and periphery, a periphery that is as difficult to delimit as the exact extent of a shower of rain. At the core, corn, oats, and the small grains are grown year after year and meat animals are always in the pasture. But as one approaches the outer limits of the Corn Belt, farm life partakes increasingly of the nature of that in adjacent regions. Wheat, dairy, and general farms exist side by side with corn farms, and each farmer tends to shift from one type to the other with the changing profitableness of each type.

It is important that the reader keep well in mind these "zones of indifference" which separate our specialized farm belts. It must be apparent, for example, that any effort to solve the "wheat problem" or "hog problem" cannot be confined to the Wheat or Corn Belts. A program to reduce wheat acreages in Kansas might very well be offset by increased sowings in Illinois and Nebraska; or the benefit of a restriction on hog marketings in Iowa might be nullified by a larger pork output in the Dairy Belt of Minnesota. What was once a "side line" in those marginal zones is quickly converted into a major interest when it appears profitable. On the maps it has seemed desirable to draw the limits of the Corn Belt as definite lines, because any other treatment is confusing to the reader. As conditions existed in 1929, these lines are accurate, and they are approximately correct today; but in reading these maps the reader should think of these boundaries as falling near the middle of zones of mixed farming rather than as the absolute limit within which all is corn and beyond which corn is never a major interest. It is unfortunate that the boundaries for the farm belts cannot be located more definitely, but such definition does not exist in fact, and the accuracy of our picture would be seriously impaired if such spuriously exact limits were created.

Division into Sections

1. **The Inner Corn Belt.**—We have indicated that the Corn Belt consists of at least two types of areas which differ chiefly in the extent of their specialization in corn production. The "heart" of the Corn Belt occupies a strip of rich prairie averaging some 200 miles wide extending from eastern Nebraska and South Dakota across Iowa and central Illinois to Indiana and Ohio. This area shows a greater concentration of corn-growing and meat-animal production than any other portion of the United States. Beyond its margins are the districts which comprise the "outer" Corn Belt, in which corn and meat-animal production still exceed other types of farm activity, but where farming also partakes of the nature of the adjacent wheat, dairy, and general farming belts. Farm organization in these outer sections closely resembles that of the inner

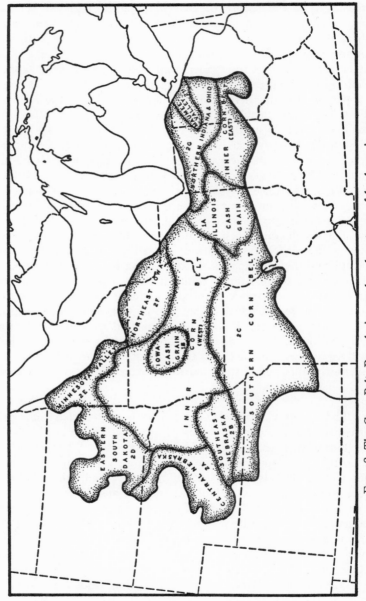

FIG. 38. The Corn Belt. Boundaries are based on types of land use in 1930.

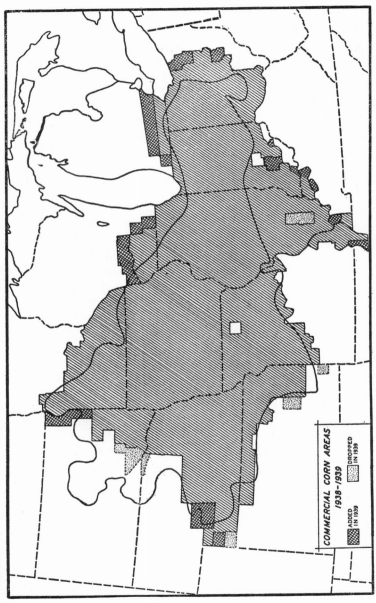

FIG. 39. Counties Designated as Commercial Corn Areas in 1938-1939. Has the corn belt shrunk or expanded since 1930? Why are all the counties which grow corn commercially not necessarily included in the corn belt region?

COMMERCIAL CORN AREAS
1938-1939

ADDED IN 1939

DROPPED IN 1939

Corn Belt, but specialization in corn and meat-animals is less common and less highly developed. We turn first to an examination of agricultural development in the inner Corn Belt.

Physical Features.—Agriculturalists tell us that the world affords no larger belt of rich land than the section we have called the inner Corn Belt. Ancient glaciers deposited these soils in a thick mantle of fine, rich materials, some of which were reworked by wind and water but all of which, except in a few narrow belts of hills along the major streams, remained exceedingly fertile. In the ensuing ages most of the area was in grass, tall grass, waist-deep to the pioneers, which each year added new humus to the soil and enhanced fertility. The pioneers, once they had broken the thick prairie sod, found the area very productive of wheat, but even better adapted to corn. More exacting than wheat in its climatic requirements, corn proved well adapted to the hot summers of these prairies. Corn thrives in a hot summer with frequent showers and it produces best where nights as well as days are hot. The plant needs frequent showers in June and July during which months it frequently grows one or two inches in a twenty-four-hour period. All of these conditions were realized in this area, and it was only a few years after their settlement that these prairies were recognized as the premier corn-producing area of the world.

Corn itself has little merit as a commercial product. Except in the southern states, very little is used for food and the grain is too bulky to be shipped far. Both of these difficulties are remedied by feeding the corn to livestock. Meat animals are the Corn Belt farmers' vehicle for converting bulky corn into more valuable meat products. So general is this practice that approximately one-half the farm income of the inner Corn Belt is derived from the sale of meat animals—a relatively high degree of specialization. Except in two important areas, nearly all the corn is fed on the farm on which it is grown. In these two sections, however, the sale of corn rivals meat animals as a source of farm income and these areas will be given special consideration as "cash-grain areas." First, however, let us examine the organization of a typical Corn Belt farm.

Farm Organization: the "Meat Belt."—Perhaps a more descriptive name for the inner Corn Belt would be "meat belt," because the entire business organization of the typical Corn Belt farm is geared to the production of meat animals, chiefly hogs and cattle. The average farm has about 160 acres, those of the eastern sections being somewhat smaller than this average, and those of the western areas somewhat larger. Practically all farms are family-sized and individually operated. Approximately half the farms are operated by tenants, and tenancy has been increasing steadily, especially in the richer areas. Additional hired labor was formerly necessary in certain seasons but with the advent of the tractor, the multiple-row cultivator, the corn-picker, and the automobile, the "hired hand" has very generally disappeared from farm life, creating at the same time a rural group of "technologically unemployed" analogous to the group of urban factory workers whose unemployment arises from similar technological changes.

The selection of crops is made with a view to economizing both the farmer's time and the fertility of his soil. Maintenance of soil fertility demands the rotation of crops. A field is planted one or two years in corn, then one year in small grain (oats or wheat), and finally one or two years in hay (usually clover and timothy) to complete the rotation. A leguminous hay crop such as clover restores to the soil the precious nitrogen so necessary for good corn. Oats or wheat provide a good "nurse crop" if sown with the hay, for their quick growth shields the young hay plants from the hot summer sun and the grain is cut early enough to allow their root systems to become sufficiently developed to withstand the succeeding winter.

The choice between oats and wheat as a secondary grain crop is governed largely by climatic factors, tempered by the relative prices of the two grains. Wheat *can* be grown in all portions of the Corn Belt, but oat yields are much better; and unless wheat prices are unusually high farmers usually sow the coarser grain. In the northern portions of the region the winters are generally too severe for winter wheat. In addition, this grain is not adapted to the frequent June and July showers so important for successful corn culture. Farmers say that one shower on the "wrong day" (when the plant is in flower and pollination takes place) will ruin the wheat yield. Oats withstand these showers more successfully and a good corn climate is generally satisfactory for oats. The greatest density of oat-raising is in the northwestern portion of the inner Corn Belt. Other more southerly sections often find winter wheat successful and some wheat is grown from southern Iowa to central Indiana. The inner Corn Belt, however, does not grow enough wheat for its own use.

Economy of time also dictates the growing of grains other than corn. Oats or wheat are planted earlier than corn, require no care in growing, and mature before the corn is ripe. Growing these grains keeps the farmer busy throughout most of the summer: first, he sows the oats (April or May), then plants the corn (May or June), then cultivates the corn until it is "knee high" (which it *should be* by the Fourth of July). By this time the oats are nearly ripe, and July or early August finds them cut and threshed. Corn-gathering usually begins in the crisp mornings of October or November and is generally completed by Thanksgiving Day. In the meantime, however, there are two or three crops of hay to be cut and stacked or placed in the barns, and by fall the young pigs must be farrowed and ready to begin concentrating the corn into a salable product—meat. Or perhaps beef steers are the major interest, and in that case the farmer either will have purchased yearling steers (perhaps grass-fed steers from Texas in the Kansas City market) or will have bred his own stock. Farmers having much rough land which must be left in pasture usually prefer cattle to hogs because they utilize the pasture more effectively. Those occupying smoother land naturally prefer hogs whose pasture requirements are small.

All cattle-feeders also keep hogs which serve as effective scavengers if allowed to run with the cattle. Midwinter and spring bring the heaviest marketings of these meat animals, practically all of which are slaughtered at the numerous meat-packing plants scattered over the Corn Belt or near its margins. The time-honored practice of butchering hogs on the farm and curing and smoking the pork for home use has nearly disappeared from the Corn Belt. The practice has been replaced to a certain extent by freezing processes. Nearly every medium-sized Corn Belt town now has a cold-storage plant which rents locker space. Farmers are finding sub-zero storage much more satisfactory than the older curing and preserving methods. But the growth of cold storage for home use is hardly more than a minor variation in the general trend away from self-sufficiency. The Corn Belt farmer continues to become a better customer of the village store. In 1929, only 10 per cent of his farm production was devoted to family use. The farm automobile has done much to foster this departure from self-sufficiency. Factory-baked bread, factory-canned foods, and factory-slaughtered meats have become nearly as common on Corn Belt dining tables as on those of the city-dweller. Fresh summer vegetables from the farm garden and milk from the farm cows are the chief home-produced items in the modern rural Corn Belt diet.

This concept of the Corn Belt farm as a highly specialized commercial establishment should not be allowed to obliterate the fact that in addition to the main product, meat, there are also important by-products. Most important of these are poultry and dairy products, generally of about equal value and normally representing a combined contribution of 15 or 20 per cent of the gross farm income.

Feed is cheap in the Corn Belt and most of the nation's poultry is found in or near the margins of this area. Chickens are allowed the "run of the farm" and usually are cared for by the farmer's wife. The sale of eggs and poultry has long provided a small but important income to Corn Belt farm families. Milk cows also constitute a similar type of productive equipment. Where pasture is available, a few cows can be kept very cheaply. Corn Belt farmers steadfastly refuse to embark upon dairying as a major interest, but they almost invariably keep three or four cows— enough to provide a steady income from the sale of cream, but not enough to make milking a drudgery.

Other sources of farm income are minor and local in nature. Northwestern Corn Belt farmers feed many sheep, but their interest is in mutton more than wool. Other sections grow vegetables. Central Indiana is famous for tomatoes, northern Iowa and central Illinois for sweet corn, the Mississippi River bottoms for onions and other vegetables, and there are scattered orchards producing apples and other fruit. Every city has its own trucking and dairy areas which are devoted to furnishing fluid milk and fresh vegetables to its urban dwellers. These developments, however, are local in nature and do not alter materially the agricultural structure of the entire area.

The Cash-grain Areas of the Inner Corn Belt.—Certainly a part of the inner Corn Belt because of their heavy corn production, but not part of the "meat belt" because of their greater dependence upon the sale of corn, the cash-grain areas require separate consideration on account of their different type of farm organization.

The Corn Belt has many cash-grain farmers, especially in the western portions and in the rich bottom lands of the larger rivers. Two areas, however, are large and important enough to merit being shown separately.[1] (1A) Most highly specialized of these is the eastern Illinois cash-grain area where roughly two-thirds of the farm income is derived from the sale of corn. (1B) The other cash-corn area, in central Iowa, derives roughly one-third of its income from corn and about 40 per cent from meat animals. Inasmuch as the Corn Belt as a whole derives less than 15 per cent of its farm income from the sale of grain, it is readily observed that these two areas should be regarded as differing from the remainder of the section. Farmers in these districts sell from two to five times as much corn as typical farmers in other portions of the inner Corn Belt. In Illinois, especially, they are essentially grain farmers, not feeders. Despite the truth of these statements, however, this distinction is more apparent than real. The central Iowa cash-grain belt has as many hogs per square mile as adjacent sections of the inner Corn Belt; and although the hog population is more sparse in eastern Illinois, that district also compares favorably with adjacent areas in meat-animal production. In these areas, in fact, a large cash-grain interest has been superimposed upon an already important animal-specialty type of farming.

Both areas are located at the headwaters of numerous streams and their lands are nearly level. Their topography differs somewhat from that of the remainder of the Corn Belt where small streams and shallow gullies have given nearly every farm a small plot of "natural" pasture unsuited to machine cultivation. Where all the land is nearly level and suited to machine cultivation there is strong temptation to devote nearly all of it to crops. Less than half as much land is in pasture as is the case in adjacent areas. Beef production is thus made unprofitable and the feeding of hogs is somewhat curtailed. As one farmer said, "It seems a waste of money to let good crop land stay in grass." Much corn is thus grown for sale, to be purchased by farmers occupying rougher lands. The Illinois area also profits by its nearness to the Chicago market where corn prices are from five to ten cents higher than on the farms west of the Mississippi River. Again, there is the matter of custom. Once a community is organized for handling

---

[1] Numbers and letters in parentheses refer to Fig. 38.

grain, with elevators, dealers, and the attendant economic set-up, it is difficult to persuade farmers to change, especially when a change to meat-animal production would involve the construction of additional barns, feed lots, and cribs, as well as the prospect of many long hours of additional labor during the winter months which grain farmers have long considered their vacation period. Except for these differences, the cash-grain sections have farm systems similar to those in the remainder of the inner Corn Belt. Oats and hay occupy most of the remaining land. Occasionally the traveler discovers a farm devoted to intensive feeding on a feed-lot basis. Such farms are small and their operators buy feed from near-by grain farmers rather than grow it on their own acres. In any case, grain-area farming is more highly specialized, more dependent upon the sale of one or two products than farming elsewhere in the Corn Belt.

2. **The Outer Corn Belt.**—Outer margins of the Corn Belt are occupied by farm systems which for one reason or another differ from those of the inner Corn Belt. These differences are chiefly: (1) a smaller dependence upon corn as the leading crop, which here occupies only from 15 to 30 per cent of the farm land as contrasted with 30 to 50 per cent in the inner Corn Belt; (2) a tendency toward mixed farming in which the Corn Belt type is increasingly intermixed with the types found in the adjacent sections as the boundaries of the Corn Belt are approached; (3) larger percentages of the farms in pasture; and (4) the concentration of meat animals considerably less than in the inner Corn Belt. Specialization in meat-animal production ordinarily is not so great as in the "meat belt" and there is a corresponding tendency to devote larger acreages to wheat and the other small grains.

These differences in the development of the inner and outer portions of the Corn Belt are traceable largely to differences in topography, soil, and climate. None of the outer areas happens to have the same productive combination of these natural factors as is found in the inner Corn Belt. These differences vary so much for the different outer sections that it seems desirable to consider each of them separately.

a. *The Feeding-grazing Area of Central Nebraska.*—Central Nebraska has the rich soil and nearly level surface of the Great Plains and except for a smaller precipitation it has most of the climatic characteristics of the inner Corn Belt. Wheat does not thrive, for this area is in the non-wheat-growing zone which separates the Spring and Winter Wheat belts. But there is excellent soil, both in the river valleys and on the plains. In the years when summer rains are sufficient, central Nebraska produces a heavy corn crop—a crop which can be grown very cheaply by the use of power machinery. Unfortunately, however, dry seasons occur so frequently that central Nebraska farmers have found it unwise to place complete dependence upon corn. Many farmers have been content to allow most of their (relatively large) farms to remain in pasture. Half the central Nebraska farm land is in pasture. Corn occupies from 20 to 25 per cent of the land and the remainder is largely in alfalfa hay. Central Nebraska is thus a livestock country, or, to be more exact, it is a cattle country. Cattle are bred and raised there and when the corn crop is good they are fattened there. In bad years either corn is shipped in or the cattle are sold as feeders. Fifty-five or 60 per cent of the farm income is derived from the sale of meat animals and an additional 10 per cent from the sale of dairy products, the latter a normal by-product of the cattle industry. Other sources of income are of minor importance. Central Nebraska has come to place its chief dependence upon cattle—cattle-raising, and cattle-feeding when corn is available.

b. *The Cash-grain Section of Southeastern Nebraska.*—That portion of eastern Nebraska which lies south of the Platte River has developed a specialization in cash-grain farming which is similar to that of the cash-corn section of central Iowa. Here, however, the entire dependence is not upon corn but upon both corn and wheat. This section might almost be considered as a detached portion of the Winter Wheat Belt, because it shows prominently on wheat maps. Closer examination reveals that the acreage in corn is normally 50 per cent greater than that in wheat. Both grains are grown largely for sale, and account for from 40 to 55 per cent of the section's farm income. But, like central Iowa, this area also feeds many cattle and hogs. Meat animals follow closely upon cash grain in the farm income, with from 35 to 40 per cent of the total. Southeastern Nebraska has thus developed an agricultural system based upon these twin sources of income, the relative importance of which fluctuates greatly with the relative prospective profit in the two types of farm activity.

A Light Tractor Is Often Used to Cultivate Corn. (*Courtesy John Deere.*)

Cattle and Hogs in a Corn Belt Feedlot. (*Courtesy John Deere.*)

c. *The Southern Sections.*—The long strip of territory which separates the inner Corn Belt from the general farming areas of the Appalachian-Ozark Region, and stretches from northern Kansas eastward to southern Illinois, supports a farm organization characterized by (1) a major dependence upon corn grown for feeding to hogs and cattle, and (2) a relatively large area in pasture, which occupies about 35 per cent of the farm land of the section. The agricultural development of the area differs from that of the inner Corn Belt chiefly in its smaller productivity. Much of the land is hilly, and although the slopes are ordinarily gentle, there are large areas of "natural pasture" which wise farmers do not attempt to cultivate because of the danger of erosion. The soil is generally classed as "good," but not so rich as the black prairies of the inner Corn Belt or of central Nebraska. Climate, on the other hand, is excellent for corn and will grow good winter wheat, which in some areas (notably northern Kansas, the bottom lands along the Missouri and Mississippi rivers, and southwestern Illinois) provides from 10 to 20 per cent of the farm income. The chief dependence, however, is upon the feeding of cattle and hogs. Most areas also feed a considerable number of sheep which help utilize the rougher pasture lands. Returns from the sale of meat animals constitute half the income for the average farm. Dairying is not highly developed except in one or two localities such as the valleys of the Missouri and Kansas rivers in the Kansas City-St. Joseph territory. This small but fertile area also grows fruit, potatoes, and vegetables, and thus represents a more diversified type of farming than does the remainder of the section. Dairying has also assumed an importance second only to livestock-feeding in the coal-mining territory near Pittsburg, Kansas, and in the Mississippi bottoms north of St. Louis. In these three sections, income from the sale of dairy products comprises one-fifth or more of the farm income, but elsewhere it accounts for less than one-tenth—or about the average for the entire Corn Belt. As in other sections, poultry is raised on nearly every farm and the sale of poultry products ordinarily provides an income about equal to that derived from cream and milk.

The southern Corn Belt section differs from the inner Corn Belt chiefly in the smaller productivity of its land. Maps of corn production show somewhat less density in this section and the density of hog and cattle populations is likewise less. But *quali-*

tatively the general pattern of farm life is much the same. The specialization in meat production is as great as in the "meat belt," with secondary sources of income from dairy products, cash grain, and poultry assuming a similar importance. These farmers have substantially the same interests and problems as those who live in the richer and smoother areas farther north, but factors of topography and soil have held their productivity at a lower level.

d. *The Corn and Wheat Section of Eastern South Dakota.*—The length of the growing season is largely responsible for dividing the eastern half of the state of South Dakota into three farm zones. The northern portion is too cool for corn and falls within the Spring Wheat Belt, while the southern portion is devoted to intensive corn-growing and the feeding of livestock and is a part of the inner Corn Belt. Between these areas is a corn and wheat section, with wheat assuming increasing importance toward the north as the southern boundary of the Wheat Belt is approached. Farm organizations in the eastern South Dakota section of the Corn Belt are a result of this combination of crops. Corn is everywhere the leading grain, followed by wheat, barley, and oats. Approximately one-third of the farm land is in pasture.

Upon this pattern of land utilization farmers of eastern South Dakota have developed farming systems with two major interests: meat animals and cash grain. Nearly all the corn is fed to cattle, hogs, and sheep. The relative importance of these animals varies from one locality to another. Cattle assume a major importance along the western boundary of the section, but in localities farther east both hogs and sheep are found in greater numbers. For the section as a whole, income from the sale of animals accounts for from one-third to one-half the farm income. The second major interest is cash grain. Eastern South Dakota grows much wheat, barley, oats, and flaxseed. Nearly all the oats and much of the barley are likely to be fed, but the wheat and flaxseed are cash crops. From 25 to 30 per cent of the farm income is derived from the sale of grain. In this way, eastern South Dakota agriculture has become specialized along two lines—the growing and feeding of livestock, and the growing of wheat, flaxseed, and barley for sale. Dairying and poultry-raising have an importance comparable to that in other Corn Belt areas. Less than 10 per cent of the farm production is consumed by the farm family. As in other Corn Belt sections, the eastern South Dakota farm is a highly commercial venture.

e. *The Minnesota River Valley and Northeastern Iowa.*—The strip of territory which separates the inner Corn Belt from the Wisconsin-Minnesota Dairy Belt reflects the characteristics of both areas not only in economic organization but also in natural features. Its western portion (2E) is a basin and lake country cut through by the broad valley of the lazy Minnesota River. Its soil is relatively rich. Northeastern Iowa and adjacent portions of Minnesota and Wisconsin (2F) bear signs of relatively recent glaciation. Lakes are few but occasional glacial boulders are found on the gently rolling landscape. Near the Mississippi River the tourist encounters picturesque bluffs, and signs of glaciation are absent. Soils are less fertile than in the adjacent inner Corn Belt but they are highly productive, far above the national average.

The relative importance of dairying and corn and wheat production varies from west to east. Minnesota Valley farmers derive about one-third of their farm income from meat animals, 15 to 20 per cent from dairy products, and from 20 to 30 per cent from cash grain (wheat, barley, flax). Less than one-fifth of their farm land is in pasture. The Minnesota Valley is a mixed farming area, with a threefold development consisting of meat animals, cash grain, and dairying. Both cattle and hogs are fattened, but the major emphasis is upon the latter. The recent rapid increase of hog-raising in this area has been important in the rise of South St. Paul as a meat-packing center. The agricultural development of northeastern Iowa resembles that of the Minnesota Valley except that very little grain is grown for sale and there is a correspondingly greater dependence upon dairying and meat production.

With one-quarter of its farm income arising from the sale of dairy products, this area has frequently been included in the Dairy Belt. Such an inclusion seems unwarranted, however, in view of the fact that 44 per cent of the farm income (in 1929) was derived from the sale of meat animals. Both hogs and cattle are fed in large numbers throughout the area. Land utilization in northeast Iowa follows a fairly simple pattern. About one-third of the farm land is in pasture and one-quarter is in corn. Oats occupy an additional 17 per cent and hay 14 per cent of the average farm. Northeast Iowa thus represents a true specialization in the two great animal industries, meat production and dairying.

Although there is some tendency for individual farmers to specialize in one type of farming or the other, most farmers spread their activities to include both.

f. *Northern Indiana and Ohio.*—The agricultural development which has been established on the rolling lands of northern Indiana and Ohio resembles that of southwestern Minnesota in many respects. Pastures are somewhat larger in this district, aggregating 30 per cent of the farm land, but the leading crops are corn, oats, and wheat. The feeding of livestock is everywhere the major interest, but receipts from this source aggregate only about one-third of the farm income, and in all communities there are at least two other major income sources. Usually there are three others: dairy products, poultry products, and cash grain (corn and wheat). Except in the Maumee Valley (2H), which is a cash-grain area with one-quarter of its farm income derived from the sale of corn, none of these other income sources is nearly so important as the feeding of livestock. The Maumee Valley has less specialization in cash grain than other cash-grain sections of the Corn Belt, but much of the valley is sufficiently level and fertile (it is an old lake plain) to encourage this type of farming. The sale of grain (corn, wheat, and oats) provides more than one-third of the farm income of this area. Outside this valley topography is less smooth and soils are generally less productive. Larger areas are in pasture and the feeding of cattle and sheep is the major agricultural interest. Hogs are raised with the cattle but their importance is less. Nearness to urban markets has made poultry-raising in this area more important than elsewhere in the Corn Belt. Income from poultry products normally constitutes 15 per cent of the total. Similar factors have encouraged dairying, which returns slightly more than poultry-raising for the section as a whole. This area, in short, is the home of the general farm with diverse sources of income, but with a definite specialization in meat-animal production.

The Corn Belt Landscape.—Perhaps the best way to study the Corn Belt agricultural pattern is to view it from the air, because the areal distribution of crops, buildings, highways, and villages traces the economic pattern with remarkable clarity. From the air, the midsummer Corn Belt landscape is a checkerboard of dark green corn fields, lighter green hay fields, and yellow fields of ripening small grain. Fields and farms are rectangular and country roads gridiron the landscape like lines on a sheet of cross-section paper. The fields of dark green generally predominate, for the area in corn is nearly as great as the combined acreage of hay and small grain. Farmsteads scatter along the rural roads at the rate of about two per mile, for the average square mile of farm land includes four farms of 160 acres. From the air the farmstead is a cluster of buildings, the largest of which we recognize as hay barns and the farmhouse. Near by stand the smaller buildings which house the poultry, the family automobile, the all-important hogs, and some of the farm machinery. Barns are more numerous in the hay and cattle areas, less noticeable in the areas which specialize in hog production. There is much bright-red machinery in evidence, and if we fly low we can recognize corn-planters, cultivators, light tractors, corn-pickers, harvesters, small combines, and numerous other types of farm machines either in the fields or stored near the barns.

The landscape is cut at frequent intervals by gray-white ribbons of surfaced highways which seem inevitably to focus on scattered villages. Approaching one of these villages, we also notice the angling slash of a strip of darker gray which is the railroad. The village itself is a one-street town with an imposing brick building that must be the school. The main street has many parked cars and a few in motion. Down by the railroad tracks we find a grain elevator and loading-pens for livestock. There are no prominent factory buildings, no rows of identical houses, only scattered white homes nearly hidden among the trees. Here is a rural agricultural village, base of supplies for the surrounding farming area, and market place for a major portion of its products. Such villages are the tentacles of a complicated economic circulatory system whose functions will be described in the next chapter. For the present, let us consider them as the points of contact between the Corn Belt farmer and the outside world, with whom he exchanges his meat animals, grain, poultry, and dairy products for articles such as manufactured goods which he consumes but does not produce.

The airplane view reveals the agricultural pattern, a pattern in which the land is used to grow grain and hay which is fed to livestock. The entire process is definitely capitalistic, requiring heavy investments in land and machinery. When the grain, hay, and grass are converted into animal products they are sold in near-by markets for prices which reflect supply and demand conditions over many regions. The Corn Belt farmer's prosperity depends

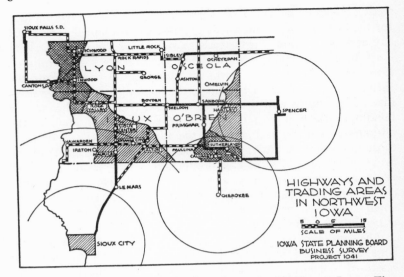

FIG. 40. Highways and Trading Areas in Northwest Iowa. The charts on these two pages are taken from studies made by the Iowa State Planning Board in 1934. These studies were designed to show the nature and functions of towns and villages in dominantly agricultural areas. This area lies in the western corn belt where the average farm has about 160 acres (¼ square mile) and the density of farm population is about eighteen persons per square mile. The major portion of the farm income is derived from the sale of meat animals, and corn is the principal crop. Only about 10 per cent of the farm production is retained for home use. The remainder is sold for cash. Farmers sell nearly everything they produce and buy nearly everything they consume. Where do these exchanges take place? Farmers in this area are located within easy trucking distance of a major livestock market, Sioux City. Nearly all the meat animals are sold in that market, delivered by truck and converted into cash.

A portion of this income is spent in Sioux City, but most of it is spent in the smaller towns near by. In the four-county area there are three towns (with populations of about 2500) which offer fairly complete shopping facilities. In addition, the area has about fifty smaller towns and villages where one can buy groceries, gasoline, and similar types of convenience goods. Nearly every farm family owns an automobile and most farms are located on all-weather roads, so that a considerable number of trading centers can be reached within a relatively short time. With money in the bank and a wide choice of trading centers available, how will the farmer distribute his purchases? Or, conversely, what is the economic function of the villages and towns of a purely agricultural area such as this one?

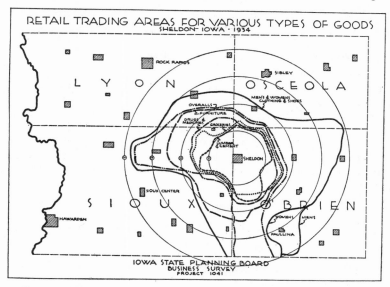

RETAIL TRADING AREAS FOR VARIOUS TYPES OF GOODS
SHELDON- IOWA · 1934

IOWA STATE PLANNING BOARD
BUSINESS SURVEY
PROJECT 1041

FIG. 41. Retail Trading Areas for Various Types of Goods. The town of Sheldon exists almost entirely as a trading center. It is not a county seat and its industrial development is practically negligible. The incomes of its people are derived almost entirely from trade—the handling of commodities and the rendering of services. Sheldon's main street is the heart of its economic life. There one finds a variety of general stores, drug stores, restaurants, movies, dry cleaning establishments, beauty parlors, doctors' and dentists' offices, banks, gasoline stations, farm implement dealers, building materials dealers, and other types of retailers whose functions are to provide goods and services to consumers in the Sheldon trading area. Approximately half the retail sales made in Sheldon go to residents of the town itself. The remainder go to farm families of the surrounding community. The size of these trading areas varies for different types of goods. The Sheldon retail grocery territory is comparatively small, because groceries are purchased frequently and grades and qualities are well standardized. The typical farm family is likely to buy groceries and other convenience goods in a near-by village, just as the city family is likely to buy these same types of commodities in neighborhood stores. But for larger purchases of style goods (especially clothing) the city resident goes to a down-town store; the town resident does likewise. Instead of a fifteen-minute trip to the crossroads grocery store, he makes an hour's trip to a larger center. Thus the Sheldon area for women's apparel is larger than its area for groceries. The farm resident makes contact with different trading centers for different types of goods, and still other centers to market his products.

not only upon the magnitude of his crop, but also upon prices which reflect business conditions over the entire nation.

REFERENCES

Corn-growing and meat-animal raising have been the subjects of many studies by the colleges of agriculture in the Corn Belt states. Read the *Agricultural Emergency in Iowa* (Iowa State College, 1933) for a statement of the major agricultural problems. State planning boards in all of these states have been active in analyzing and mapping their resources. The meat-animal industry is well described in Zimmermann, *World Resources and Industries*. Typical farm organizations are described in *Types of Farming in the United States* (see Introduction).

QUESTIONS AND PROBLEMS

1. Why are the boundaries of economic regions in the Mississippi-Great Lakes basin zones rather than lines? What is the nature of farming in these zones?
2. Which regional boundaries are apt to shift more slowly and why: those between the wheat and corn belts, the corn and dairy belts, the dairy and manufacturing belts?
3. The Corn Belt farm grows many kinds of crops, but it is not classified as a "general" farm. Why not?
4. How does the Inner Corn Belt differ from the various sections of the Outer Corn Belt?
5. Why is so little corn sold in the market?
6. Alcohol for motor fuel can be made from corn, but the product is more expensive than gasoline. How might the Corn Belt economy be affected by the exhaustion of our petroleum supplies? Where would you expect alcohol factories to be located? Why?
7. Why has the growing of corn for sale become important in eastern Illinois and north-central Iowa?
8. How does the farm organization of central Nebraska differ from that of eastern Nebraska? Why?
9. In the late 1930's a new variety of corn was introduced in the Corn Belt. Assume that this variety of corn is capable of increasing the yield of any corn land by 20 per cent without materially increasing production costs. How would its widespread adoption affect the location of the boundaries of the region? What other assumptions are necessary before one can attack this problem?
10. Draft a report to a manufacturer of farm machinery who wants to know how such a change would affect his sales territories in the region.
11. What is the function of the village in the Corn Belt economy?

CHAPTER XIII

THE CORN BELT—NON-AGRICULTURAL INTERESTS

ALL sections of the Corn Belt are dominated by commercial agriculture. But, as in other farming regions, the mechanism of exchange demands the services of many non-agricultural workers. Farm products must be processed and transported to distant markets. Large numbers of workers are also required to import and distribute the many types of goods used on the farm. All of these services are non-agricultural and most of them are logically performed in towns and cities. In addition, the Corn Belt has a small production of forest and timber products and a few communities devoted to mining. In the eastern sections, manufacturing is important. These commercial and industrial occupations round out the economic structure of the Corn Belt.

MINERALS

Although large areas of the Corn Belt are underlain with coal and there are several important localized deposits of other minerals, the mining industries have not become highly developed. Only a few localities can be designated as mining communities and nearly all of these are coal-mining towns.

Coal.—Coal deposits which underlie the Corn Belt are generally of poorer quality than those of the hillier region to the south. Most of it has a higher ash content which makes it objectionable for domestic use. Its thermal value is nearly as high as that of eastern coals, however, and properly designed industrial power plants have been able to use it successfully. The heaviest Corn Belt coal production is in central Illinois. These mines supply local areas and compete rather ineffectively in the Chicago industrial area with higher quality coals from southern Illinois and Indiana. A similar but less important coal-mining area is found in southern Iowa. These mines serve the local area. Outside these districts, little coal is mined in the Corn Belt, and the vast bulk of the coal consumed within the region is imported from other mining areas.

Other Minerals.—Deposits of other Corn Belt minerals are highly localized. Northeastern Illinois (in the vicinity of La Salle and Ottawa) has a large production of silica sand, used in both

313

local and eastern glass factories. North-central Iowa (Ft. Dodge) mines gypsum and manufactures it into wall plaster for mid-western markets. Practically the entire section is underlain with limestone. This limestone is the major raw material for numerous cement plants within the area. With the two major raw materials, limestone and clay, so generally available, cement plants have been located wherever a sufficient market exists. Each plant serves a territory with a radius of from 100 to 200 miles. Much limestone is also fed to crushers to provide the aggregate for use in highway and other concrete construction. Some of it is also used as a flux in the furnaces which turn out steel for the numerous machinery factories of the eastern half of the Corn Belt. Historically, limestone was an important building material, but the advent of cheap lumber and concrete has made this use practically obsolete. Nevertheless, it is the most widely distributed and most commonly mined mineral of the Corn Belt. Limestone quarries are found throughout the region.

Petroleum.—Scattered pools of petroleum in Indiana and adjacent sections of Illinois and Ohio have given the eastern portions of the Corn Belt a small oil and gas industry. The production has never been large but it has been fairly constant over the past quarter of a century. These fields were important in establishing the Cleveland, Toledo, and Chicago districts as early refining centers. Refineries near those cities are supplied today almost entirely with oil piped from Oklahoma and Texas, but their founding is closely related to the early importance of these midwestern oil fields.

It is thus apparent that the Corn Belt contains very few communities dependent upon minerals. Coal, limestone, and petroleum are the most important products, but they are generally of local interest only. Gypsum, silica sand, and a considerable list of lesser minerals have attained importance in a few small areas, but these developments are not large. Minerals constitute an extremely small fraction of the wealth and income of this great agricultural area.

FORESTS AND FISHERIES

Except for narrow belts of timber along the larger streams, only that portion of the Corn Belt east of the Illinois-Indiana state line was originally forested; and even the Indiana and Ohio portions originally contained large areas of grassland. Most of the timber was quickly removed to clear the land for cultivation, and the Corn Belt has been a lumber importer since these pioneer days. Except for an occasional portable sawmill engaged primarily in sawing wood for fuel or cutting scattered walnut trees for shipment to furniture centers, the Corn Belt has no forest output. The western portions, in fact, have few trees except those which have been put in for shade or for the protection of farm buildings against winter winds.

Fishery products are likewise of very small economic importance. The Upper Mississippi River (near Muscatine, Iowa) yields a large production of clamshells and this area accounts for about one-third of the national output of pearl buttons. Elsewhere, fishing has a purely recreational value and even that phase is entirely local, for fishermen greatly prefer the waters farther north.

CITIES OF THE CORN BELT

The Corn Belt is notable for having developed a large number of small and medium-sized cities, and it is equally notable for having produced no large metropolitan centers. Large cities have arisen in the Middle West, but the most important of these—Chicago, St. Louis, Detroit, Cleveland, Minneapolis-St. Paul, and Cincinnati—are located beyond the margins of the Corn Belt. All of them have grown up in strategic locations, either along the Great Lakes or on the banks of the Mississippi or Ohio rivers. Perhaps the most important reason for the comparative absence of large cities on the Corn Belt prairies is the lack of such strategic locations. On the rolling prairies of Illinois and Iowa one urban location is about as good as another.

Early settlers unloaded their household goods from pioneer wagons, took up farms almost at random, and founded villages wherever a convenient trading post was desirable. The earliest settlements were made along the streams, and some of these grew to importance in pre-railroad days when the surplus production of wheat and pork was floated down to St. Louis and New Orleans for sale to southern planters and eastern merchants. In those days frontier villages along the Ohio and Upper Mississippi rivers enjoyed a profitable business based upon the exchange of farm products for household and farm necessities. But the railroad came and very early upset this triangular trade between the West, South, and East. River ports were only from ten to twenty-five years old when railroads reached their pork houses and flour mills and their trade was diverted to the east-west all-rail routes. Except for Cincinnati and a few sister-cities on the Upper Ohio River, none of these river ports had become large or powerful enough to remain an important regional distribution center. Railroads were quickly extended into almost every interior settlement, and from that day the crossroads community on the prairie had about the same chance for development as its older sister-city along the river. Very generally, too, it made the most of these opportunities. Railroad-building was easy on the prairie and the whole Corn Belt was soon covered with a close network. Wherever two or more railroads intersected, there grew up a village, and there often were located small factories aided by the low freight rates resulting from the competition of rival railroads.

These settlements grew, all at about the same rate, and by the turn of the century nearly every county could boast at least one village of more than one thousand inhabitants. Most of them had towns of four thousand population or larger. Scattered here and there at intervals of perhaps fifty or seventy-five miles were centers with populations of twenty thousand or more—these latter frequently division points or important junctions for railroads. But even as late as 1900 the Corn Belt could boast only a half-dozen towns with populations larger than one hundred thousand.

The next generation bought automobiles and paved its highways. Nearly every farmer purchased a car and found it useful not only for pleasure but for hauling cream, eggs, and other perishable farm produce to market. Horizons expanded with the automobile and the farmer became a more frequent patron of the county-seat department store. Most of the small villages languished. Towns of less than one thousand population found they could no longer support furniture and clothing stores and a long list of similar establishments selling "shopping goods." Many of them even lost a considerable portion of their grocery trade as farmer patrons sought bargains in county-seat chain stores. Even the filling stations and garages moved to the village edge in order to be on the paved highway. Inevitably the villages lost population and what they lost in both population and trade went to the county-seat towns. But the migration has not been concluded with this shift from village to county-seat town. Already the city has become attractive as a trading center. After all, it is probably not more than a two-hour journey and to visit it consumes less time than a trip to the neighboring village in horse and buggy days. Thus the small and medium-sized city has tended to become the final benefactor in the change in consumer trading habits. These cities have grown in population and in trade and many of them have acquired important manufacturing interests. The trend toward industrialization is especially noticeable in the eastern Corn Belt where numerous cities have become important industrial centers. The semi-industrial cities of central Indiana and Ohio have received an important overflow from the recent wave of industrial development which has swept the Detroit, Chicago, and Cleveland areas in the Manufacturing Belt to the north. Industrial development becomes gradually less as one progresses westward. Central Illinois cities have numerous factories but most of these centers are dominantly commercial. In the Iowa, Missouri, and Minnesota sections there is less manufacturing, and in Nebraska, Kansas, and South Dakota still less. In all of these areas, however, industrial production has shown a tendency to expand and it appears that all of the Corn Belt may expect the expansion to continue.

Urban development in the Corn Belt consists of three types of centers: (1) small towns and villages whose primary interest is in providing groceries and other convenience goods for a small local area. These towns also are shipping points for a considerable amount of grain and livestock. (2) Larger towns (frequently county seats) have become increasingly important with the development of the automobile, but their function is very similar to that of the village except that their business is conducted on a larger scale. These centers are likewise losing a portion of their shopping trade to (3) the small and medium-sized cities of twenty thousand population or larger. The larger communities usually have department stores, banking establishments, and manufacturing plants of more than local importance. In them will be found meat-packing plants, corn-products plants and, in the eastern portions of the Corn Belt, a considerable number of furniture factories as well as heavy industries using iron and steel with an apparent specialization in the manufacture of automobile parts. This threefold classification embraces the urban development of the Corn Belt. The first and second types are almost entirely commercial, while the third type is almost always more commercial than industrial.

Cities of the Western Corn Belt.—A line drawn southward from Minneapolis through the approximate center of Iowa and Missouri separates in a rough way the commercial cities of the western Corn Belt from the semi-industrial cities of the eastern half of the area. Largest and most prominent of these western Corn Belt cities are Kansas City, Omaha, Des Moines, Sioux City, St. Joseph, and Lincoln. The reader will observe that four of these six cities are located on the Missouri River. He should not conclude, however, that this river has ever been an important highway. On the other hand, railroads have long made a practice of basing rates on the Missouri River crossings, so that all four of these river cities pay approximately the same freight rates to the east and all receive lower rates than cities west of them. All of the Missouri River cities are commercial centers whose trade territories extend westward almost to the Rocky Mountains. All of them have likewise become important in a single industry, meat packing. Cattle and hogs are marketed in these four cities from the western Corn Belt, and here have been erected large meatpacking plants which kill and dress meats for eastern markets.

Kansas City.—The city of Kansas City happens to lie on both sides of the Kansas-Missouri state line. There is no barrier, natural or otherwise, between the two municipalities and they are, in fact, one urban center. Only the accident of a political boundary line has made necessary the separate incorporation of the two municipalities. With a metropolitan population of 600,000, of whom approximately three-fourths live in Missouri, Kansas City is one of the major economic centers of the Middle West. Its trade territory includes the Winter Wheat Belt as well as the rich oil-producing territory of Oklahoma. Kansas City firms have even penetrated into western Texas and eastern New Mexico. As the seat of one of the federal reserve banks, Kansas City has become an important financial center for the wheat and oil districts as well as the southwestern Corn Belt. Industrial development is confined very largely to the milling of wheat from the Winter Wheat Belt and to the preparation of meat products. Kansas City regularly ranks second only to Chicago as a livestock market and meatpacking center. The city has profited greatly by the recent rapid growth of the wheat and oil industries and its distribution trade

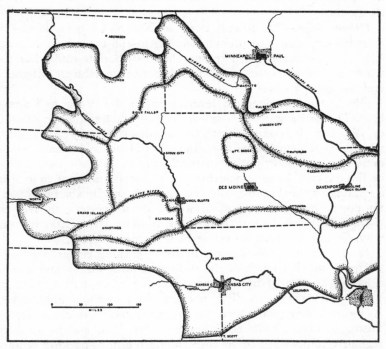

FIG. 42. Cities of the Western Corn Belt. Urban development in the western Corn Belt is closely associated with the basic economic interests of the area. Wholesale and retail trade, transportation, service, and the processing industries are the principal urban economic interests. The leading manufacturing industry is meat packing. Meat-packing plants are found throughout the area, but the Missouri River cities are the most important national centers outside Chicago. Railroad shops and other transportation agencies are large employers, but the largest payrolls are found in the retail and wholesale lines.

The eastern Corn Belt (See Fig. 43) is more highly industrialized. The east-bound traveler first encounters evidences of industrialization near the middle of the region, in the vicinity of the Mississippi River. Farm machinery is the leading factory product of the Middle Corn Belt. Farther east, the pattern changes. In Indiana we find a greater emphasis on automobile bodies and parts, and in Ohio, on heavy machinery. The eastern Corn Belt includes many industrial cities, but its urban development generally is more commercial than industrial.

in the southwest has come to rival its older and larger sister-city, St. Louis.

Other Cities.—St. Joseph, north of Kansas City, is likewise a meat-packing center of prominence. St. Joseph is too near Kansas City to have developed a comparable distribution trade, but its wholesale houses serve a considerable area in northwest Missouri and northeast Kansas.

Omaha has experienced a development similar to that of Kansas City. The entire state of Nebraska is its trade territory, contested only by Lincoln, sixty miles to the southwest, and by Sioux City, which serves a small area in northeastern Nebraska. Omaha, however, is more important commercially and industrially than either of these rivals. Its meat-packing production is sufficient to give it a ranking of third in this industry. In 1930, the Omaha metropolitan population was 274,000, of whom about one-seventh lived in Council Bluffs on the Iowa side of the Missouri River. Like Kansas City, Omaha is a railroad center of major importance.

Sioux City is a distribution and meat-packing center. Its trade territory includes much of the state of South Dakota and a considerable portion of northwestern Iowa. Sioux City's population (79,000 in 1930) is hardly a measure of its economic importance. Its meat-packing plants serve the productive hog, cattle, and sheep-raising sections of the northwestern Corn Belt, and Sioux City regularly ranks sixth or seventh among the meat-packing centers of the country.

Des Moines is primarily a distribution center. Its wholesale houses serve central Iowa and its farm journals have a national circulation. Des Moines also takes pride in its reputation as the insurance center of the Middle West. The development of manufacturing in Des Moines has been diverse and of far smaller importance than the commercial interests.

Cities of the Eastern Corn Belt.—Although the urban development of the eastern half of the Corn Belt follows a pattern very similar to that of the western half, certain differences are evident which make desirable a separate treatment of the cities and towns of these eastern sections. Greatest of these differences are: (1) a larger number of small and medium-sized cities, and (2) a larger degree of industrialization within these cities. Towns with populations of three thousand or less are similar in economic development to those in the western sections. These towns serve

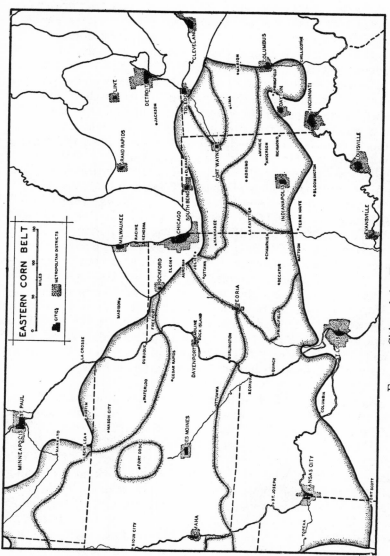

FIG. 43. Cities of the Eastern Corn Belt.

primarily as centers for the purchase of convenience goods by the farm population of the small surrounding local territories. The general store, grain elevator, a small bank, filling stations, garages, and livestock markets are the principal business institutions. As in other sections, a considerable portion of the retail shopping trade has gravitated to the larger cities.

These larger cities, which are considerably more numerous than in the western sections, generally have a considerable measure of industrial development. In eastern Iowa the dominant industry is meat packing and there are also large cereal plants, farm-machinery factories and corn-products refineries. Along the Mississippi River, a series of small cities from Dubuque southward to Quincy has developed three types of manufacturing industries. (1) The northern group (Dubuque, Clinton and Muscatine) has woodworking industries which specialize in doors, windows, and other fabricated building materials. (2) The Tri-Cities area (Davenport, Moline, and Rock Island) is an important center for the manufacture of farm machinery. These cities also have other machinery industries and constitute a distribution center for eastern Iowa and western Illinois. (3) South of the Tri-Cities, the industrial development shows greater diversity. Farm machinery, shoes, and pearl buttons are important manufactured products. The reasons for the development of these cities are similar to those which gave rise to the Missouri River cities to the west. Railroad rates "break" at the Mississippi River in such a way as to give these cities advantages in transportation rates over centers farther west.

East of the Mississippi River, in central and northern Illinois, the cities have shown a marked specialization in the manufacture of farm machinery. This development, which may be considered an overflow from the machinery industry of the Chicago area, includes practically all kinds of implements used by Corn Belt farmers. Peoria, while it is one of the nation's largest distilling centers, is probably more famous for its production of tractors. Decatur takes pride in its large corn-products plant. Other Illinois cities have a smaller industrial development, but the general pattern is much the same. In the Upper Illinois River Valley a cluster of cities, notably LaSalle, Ottawa, and Peru, show prominently on the industrial map. Their products consist largely of glass (based on local deposits of silica sand), clocks and watches, zinc, and cement. Butter and condensed milk are produced in the northern portions of Illinois, and the canning industry (especially corn) is widely distributed over the entire area.

Industrialization increases toward the east. Those cities of northern Indiana and Ohio which lie within the Corn Belt have shown a marked tendency to specialize in automobile parts and furniture. Most important of these are Indianapolis, Fort Wayne, and a group of intervening cities in eastern Indiana. This district deserves special consideration.

The Indianapolis-Fort Wayne District.—The state of Indiana contains two well-defined industrial areas. First of these is the highly industrialized Gary-South Bend district which is included in the American Manufacturing Belt. Second, but hardly less important in factory production, is a cluster of semi-industrial cities in the northeast quarter of the state. This cluster extends from Indianapolis to Fort Wayne and includes the intermediate cities of Anderson, Muncie, Kokomo, and Marion.

The Indianapolis-Fort Wayne district represents the intrusion of important manufacturing interests into productive agricultural territory. Here are some of the finest farms of the Middle West, and here also are flourishing factories which have arisen to challenge the dominance of farming in these counties. That battle is not over, as is indicated by the continuance of the Corn Belt type of farming. This section has not yet been added to the Dairy Belt as a supplier of milk to cities. Trade and distribution are still important activities in the cities and much evidence of the importance of farming is found in the stores, banks, and other commercial institutions.

Industry, nevertheless, has come along very rapidly, especially with the rise of the automotive industries. Factory workers outnumber farmers throughout the district. Here, indeed, is an important segment of the "outer ring" of rising industrial cities which has grown up around the Chicago industrial center. This "ring" of cities, largely specialized in various types of machinery, has a radius of from 100 to 150 miles and lies almost entirely within dominantly agricultural territory. Just why it should have arisen is a matter for additional research, but the cause probably lies more in the historical development of railroad rates than in any other single factor.

The Indianapolis-Fort Wayne district is therefore not so highly industrialized as most sections of the Manufacturing Belt. Its great center, Indianapolis, may in fact be designated as a commercial city. Wholesaler, jobber, and banker for two-thirds the state of Indiana, Indianapolis is in many ways unique. Located on a nearly level plain, it is the largest American city not situated on a navigable waterway. The city developed early as an important crossroads for land transportation. Trunk-line railroads connecting Pittsburgh and Buffalo with St. Louis and Chicago passed through it. Other lines connecting Chicago with the "southern gateways," Cincinnati and Louisville, also passed through it. Today, railroads and highways radiate from Indianapolis like spokes in a wheel. Indianapolis indeed looks impressive on a transportation map of the Middle West. Thus the city developed as a commercial center. Located near the center of population, Indianapolis is national headquarters for many organizations. It carries on more than half the wholesale trade of the state of Indiana, and its financial institutions are of similar importance.

Indianapolis also proved attractive to many types of manufacturing industries, especially those requiring quick transportation to near-by markets. Today this Indiana metropolis packs pork and bakes bread in the fashion of most Corn Belt cities, but its greatest factory payrolls go to workers in its machinery, hosiery, and automobile parts plants. Indianapolis factory products are of extremely diverse character, but the list contains many types of automobile parts, the dominant industry of this section.

North of Indianapolis, smaller cities show greater industrialization and more specialization in certain types of products. Anderson has large factories for the manufacture of electrical goods (starters, generators, coils, etc.) for automobiles; Muncie is a national center for the making of fruit jars and other glass products; Kokomo has glass works and wire mills; and Marion makes motor trucks and oil-well machinery. Local supplies of natural gas were important in the original location of the glass industries. Fort Wayne, metropolis of northeast Indiana, has a greater commercial development than the smaller cities just named. It stands as the second-ranking commercial center of Indiana but has less than one-eighth of the wholesale trade of Indianapolis. Fort Wayne factories turn out electrical goods, gasoline pumps, hosiery, and a long list of automobile parts.

The Indianapolis-Fort Wayne district has about 1.2 per cent

of the nation's manufacturing, or about one-third of the total for the state of Indiana. Of this output, about one-half comes from the city of Indianapolis, which is also the accepted economic center of the state. In summary, the factory output is relatively diverse. Automobile bodies and parts are the leading products. Indianapolis, because of its commercial importance, has a large number of industries which could be classified as local and regional.

Western Ohio.—Only a small portion of the state of Ohio lies within the Corn Belt, and the cities of these areas have smaller factory developments than those of other portions of the state. Trade of the area is divided between Columbus and Dayton, both of which occupy the margin of the region and are described in the chapters on the Appalachian-Ozark Region. Most important of the smaller centers are Lima and Marion, both of which are classified as semi-industrial cities. Lima refines oil, but the principal factory products of both cities are various types of machinery. Lima manufactures locomotives, motors, and other metal products, while Marion is well known for excavating and farm machinery.

Summary.—The eastern half of the Corn Belt has shown a distinct trend toward industrialization in recent years. In eastern Iowa and Illinois the principal manufacturing industries are meat packing and the manufacture of farm machinery, both reflecting the agricultural nature of these areas. Farther east, Indiana has received an important share of the overflow of the automobile industries from the Detroit center. Indiana assembles few cars but manufactures many automobile parts. Eastern Ohio industries show the influence of the Pittsburgh-Cleveland steel industry in their specialization along lines of heavy machinery and other iron and steel products. Many students believe that within a decade or two much of western Ohio and eastern Indiana will have been added to the American Manufacturing Belt. At the present time, however, these sections are more agricultural than industrial.

Features of the Corn Belt Economy.—The Corn Belt economy follows a familiar pattern involving regional specialization of production, and marketing through interregional trade. The Corn Belt farm is a strictly commercial venture in that its product is destined almost entirely for the market. Little of the farm production is retained for home use. The Corn Belt farmer sells nearly everything he produces and buys nearly everything he consumes. He markets his produce in a near-by village or city. Most of these products are destined for markets in other regions. To facilitate their marketing, animals are butchered, poultry dressed, and butter churned in factories located within the region. This processing type of manufacturing is important in all parts of the region, but it is the leading type in the western half of the Corn Belt.

The typical Corn Belt farmer sells his produce for cash and is proverbially independent in his choice of a purchasing center. The motor age finds him buying convenience goods such as groceries and gasoline at a near-by village, but depending more and more for shopping goods such as clothing and furniture upon trips to the department stores of more distant cities. His social and cultural contacts have much the same diversity. He may attend the village church and send his children to the village high school, but he goes to the city for the movies and many other types of entertainment. The mid-western farmer of a generation ago was a definite member of a community which centered in his neighboring village. There he sold most of his produce and bought most of his supplies. The community provided most of his social contacts, recreation, and amusement. His son, occupying the same farm, has contacts which are much more diverse. He buys a few items locally and participates in certain neighborhood activities. But he also spends much of his income in distant department stores and movies, and much of his leisure outside the community. The result has been a general decline of certain village functions, a decrease in the importance of the community in the lives of its inhabitants, and the development of a more cosmopolitan attitude in the people of the rural Corn Belt. Many factors have influenced this change but most students place greatest emphasis upon the automobile and the radio. The increased speed of both transportation and communication has placed the farmer in more frequent contact with metropolitan goods and ideas, and drawn him bodily into the swirling current of everyday economic life. When the hogs are ready for market, he determines the time and place of marketing by listening to radio market reports. Having chosen a time and place, he sells them by telephone or delivers them to market next morning by truck. He selects his purchases with the combined aid of the mail-order catalog, the radio, the daily newspaper, and national magazines. Little wonder that he considers himself one of the world's freest individuals.

MECHANIZED AGRICULTURE REQUIRES MECHANICAL PRECISION IN THE FIELD. THE
LONG STRAIGHT ROWS ARE SIGNIFICANT. (*Courtesy John Deere.*)

Mechanization Is Quite Possible in All Stages of Cotton Farming Except the Picking. (*Courtesy John Deere.*)

On the consumption side, the Corn Belt is preeminently an importer of consumer goods. The region manufactures a large share of its farm machinery, bulky items best produced near the market. The Corn Belt, like other regions, also bakes its own bread, prints most of its own newspapers, and engages in similar manufacturing activities of a local nature. But most of its automobiles, radios, lumber, clothing, shoes, furniture, coal, electrical appliances, and the remaining goods it consumes come from other regions. It is hardly an exaggeration to characterize the Corn Belt economy as a regionally specialized productive mechanism which produces food products and exchanges them for manufactured goods. This exchange process obviously necessitates the services of thousands of persons who handle, transport, process, and transfer the goods entering the exchange transaction. Nor should we overlook the additional thousands who render personal service to a people who are unable or unwilling to perform these services for themselves. In the aggregate, these transporters, handlers, merchants, and service people are even more numerous than the farmers themselves. But at the foundation of the structure stands the Corn Belt farmer, the producer who starts the long chain of exchange processes which serve as the spark plug for the entire economic mechanism.

REFERENCES

For a study of a typical eastern Corn Belt city read *Middletown*, and for a western city of the region, read the section on Omaha in *Five Cities*. The meat-packing industry is described in H. H. McCarty and C. W. Thompson in *Meat Packing in Iowa* (University of Iowa, 1933). State planning boards in the various states have made numerous surveys of mineral and industrial resources.

QUESTIONS AND PROBLEMS

1. What is the meaning of "commercial agriculture" as used in the first sentence of this chapter? Are there other types of agriculture? What are they? How do they differ from this type? Why are they not predominant in this region?
2. In what ways has technological change threatened the Corn Belt village? Do you expect the village to disappear? Why or why not?
3. What factors favor the Corn Belt as a location for the meat-packing industry? for farm machinery factories? Why is it not also a center for the manufacture of textiles? for iron and steel?

4. Select an important city of the western Corn Belt such as Kansas City, Omaha, or Des Moines, and compare its economic function with some eastern Corn Belt city such as Indianapolis or Fort Wayne. How do you account for the differences?

5. Why did the mail-order houses decide to establish retail stores in the larger Corn Belt cities? Should grocery firms follow their example?

6. Write a brief criticism of the statement that for purposes of economic and social analysis the Corn Belt farmer may be considered as a member of a community whose center is the neighboring village. Why have the patterns of economic and social contact of rural residents come to resemble those of city residents in recent years?

7. Select a commodity of common household use and devise an advertising campaign for selling it to rural Corn Belt families. What advertising media would you use? Why?

8. What factors should be considered in accounting for the location of cities in the Corn Belt?

CHAPTER XIV

THE COTTON BELT—THE COTTON ECONOMY

History and Economics.—Every grade-school child knows that the Cotton Belt includes that section of the United States whose economic life is dominated by the growing and marketing of cotton. We learn very early that cotton is the second-ranking crop of the United States, exceeded in annual value only by corn; that it is the nation's leading cash crop; that the American Cotton Belt is certainly the most important and probably the best region in the world for growing cotton; that half the people of the southern states normally make their living from growing or handling cotton; that cotton is the leading agricultural export of the United States; and that with half its crop normally sold in foreign countries, the South never could see any sense in a protective tariff and once felt so strongly on such matters that it was willing to secede from the Union and set up a government whose policies would better suit the needs of a great crop-exporting region. What we ordinarily do not learn is that the Cotton Belt is not a homogeneous region either naturally, socially, or economically except in so far as cotton happens to dominate its agricultural economy from one end of the region to the other. We discover, in the Cotton Belt of today, sections of worn-out soil, declining agriculture, and rural poverty, and other sections of rich soil and profitable agriculture. And we find many other sections which fall somewhere between these extremes. But before we examine these various sections, it will be profitable to discuss a few of the more important considerations affecting the cotton-growing industry. Later we shall consider variations among the sections into which the region must be divided if an adequate appraisal of its economic development is to be attained.

Early Specialization.—Historically, the Cotton Belt was the first of the major specialized farming regions to appear in the economic evolution of the United States. Long before the Civil War, plantation owners on the Mississippi bottoms were devoting their major energies to growing cotton and a little corn, importing much of their meat, flour, and potatoes from up-river sections and their manufactured goods from the Atlantic seaboard. The entire belt of farm country which stretched from Richmond to the Texas frontier was similarly specialized in the production of this single international commodity. There were very few factories or mines. The South was getting most of its pay checks from the cotton brokers in Liverpool, with New England purchasers providing a growing but still secondary market. The great British cotton-textile industry was founded on American cotton.

Cotton and the Tariff.—After the Civil War there was comparatively little change in the southern economy. Tariff-protected manufacturing industries multiplied rapidly north of the Ohio River, but the South remained the realm of King Cotton. The Cotton Belt still buys most of its manufactures and much of its food from other regions. Since the World War, a tariff-mad world has made it increasingly difficult for American cotton to enter foreign markets. Wages have been low and there has been widespread unemployment. Exports have dwindled and menacing surpluses have kept prices low. There has been much talk of diversification along both agricultural and industrial lines. New crops and a greater emphasis upon farm animals have appeared, and many new factories have been built. Thus far, however, these trends have made no significant impression upon the economy of the region. Cotton is still the most profitable crop and occupies the best crop land. The remainder is largely in corn which is grown for both food and feed. Business in the South is good or bad according to whether the price of cotton is high or low. A future generation may see greater diversification, but the present economy of the South is a cotton economy.

Specialization and Protection.—This dependence upon cotton is a familiar theme to anyone who reads the current magazines. It is not always made clear, however, that the Cotton Belt is no more dependent upon a single source of income than the other cash-farming regions of the United States. The Mississippi farmer is no more dependent upon the sale of cotton than is the Kansas farmer on wheat, the Iowa farmer on meat animals, the Wisconsin farmer upon milk, the Wyoming farmer upon range livestock, or the California farmer upon fruits and vegetables. Only in the Appalachian-Ozark general farming region is there greater agricultural diversification, and even in that region the most productive sections are effectively dominated by tobacco or other specialties. Too many magazine writers appear to assume that the great curse of the South is one-product agriculture. It should be remembered that one-product agriculture occupies the richest and most prosperous farm regions of the United States, and there is ample reason to believe they are more prosperous because of that specialization, which permits the best use of their agricultural resources.

On the other hand, there is much significance over considerable periods of years in the type of product in which an area specializes. The situation of a Wisconsin butter farmer, producing for a domestic market effectively protected by a high tariff wall, is far different from that of a Texas cotton farmer who cannot possibly sell more than two-thirds of his crop in the United States at a remunerative price and must therefore allow the whole price level to sink to the figure he can get in Liverpool in competition with cotton producers of fifty other nations. Agricultural economists tell us that no other large area in the world can lay down cotton in Liverpool and Yokohama as cheaply as the American Cotton Belt. By nature, it is the premier cotton-growing region of the world. But nations can buy only from those who are willing to buy from them. So long as Americans persist in preventing the sale of foreign goods in this country, the South will have difficulty making the most of its natural advantage as a cotton producer. In short, the major economic problem of the South is one not of production, but of international politics.

Natural Factors.—The American Cotton Belt is able to produce half the cotton of the world primarily because of its natural resources, principally its climate and soil. The cotton plant is fairly exacting in its climatic and soil requirements and is adapted to relatively few regions on the face of the earth. A humid subtropical climate, with a dry fall and long growing season, is seldom found in connection with calcareous soils having a good humus content and good under-drainage. Yet these are the fairly exacting needs of the plant from which most of the world's clothing is made, and these are the natural conditions which prevail over a large area in the southern United States.

CLIMATE

The boundaries of the Cotton Belt are closely related to climatic factors. The northern boundary is a frost boundary, adhering closely to the line marking an average growing season of 200 frostless days. On the west the boundary is one of drought. Most varieties of cotton require at least twenty-three inches annual rainfall, but recently developed drought-resistant varieties have reduced this minimum to about twenty inches, with the result that the western boundary of the region has been pushed westward into the semi-arid High Plains of northwest Texas. Little cotton is grown west of the line marking twenty inches annual rainfall. On the south and east, we find a rain boundary. The Gulf and Atlantic coasts are too rainy for cotton, especially during the fall ripening period. Here the boundary follows rather closely the line marking ten inches average precipitation during the three fall months, September, October, and November.

Precipitation and Cloudiness.—The cotton plant is of tropical origin and by nature a perennial, but it was early adapted to sub-tropical conditions. Present varieties bear abundantly only in regions having a long growing season followed by a cool autumn, but the woody stalks and long bearing season indicate the plant's origin as a tropical perennial. To produce high quality fiber, the cotton plant needs an abundance of sunshine. The world's highest grades of cotton are grown in the nearly cloudless deserts of Egypt and Arizona, where irrigation provides the needed moisture. In the more humid sections such as the Cotton Belt the best form of precipitation is the thundershower. Thundershowers form quickly, are soon gone, and precipitation is attended by a minimum of cloudiness. Leaden skies produce a cotton which is off-color and often has short fibers. Cloudiness also encourages the growth of fungi. Cloudiness and excessive rain are most damaging during the fall season. During these months the plant blossoms, the bolls form and open, and the cotton is picked. If the open boll does not receive sufficient sunshine the fiber is tinged with color and is hence an inferior product. Cotton bolls do not ripen all at one time. Typically sub-tropical, the plant bears blossoms, unripe bolls, and mature fiber ready for picking, all at the same time. A pro-longed bearing season makes it necessary to pick several crops each fall. If the fall season is a cloudy one, the crop is not likely to be successful. Hence the line marking ten inches average precipitation during the fall months is a significant boundary for the Cotton Belt.

Temperature and Rainfall.—The climate of the Cotton Belt is usually classified as humid sub-tropical. The annual rainfall varies from twenty to sixty inches, but most of the region has between thirty and fifty inches of rain per year. This precipitation is well distributed throughout the year, but the summer rainfall is somewhat greater than that of other seasons. The fall months, especially October and November, are drier than the rest, but even these months have occasional showers. Temperatures, both day and night, are normally high. Average summer temperatures at the northern boundary are about 77°F., and near the southern boundary they average from 80°F. to 85°F.

Thermometer readings occasionally creep up to 100°F., but are not ordinarily higher than in the Middle West. The humidity, on the other hand, is invariably high, and temperatures above 90°F. produce discomfort. The hillier piedmont areas are fairly comfortable in summer, but elsewhere the climate is often enervating and is generally considered less productive of human energy than that of the regions lying farther north.

The growing season ranges from 200 days at the north boundary to nearly nine months in the southern sections. Winters are short, and although crisp winds often bring low temperatures from the north, severe cold waves are short-lived and relatively rare. All of the region has frost and most of it experiences some snow every winter. Nearly every section has seen the thermometer dip to zero at least once during its history; but pastures stay green throughout the year and barns and sheds are not necessary for the protection of cattle.

Climate and Living Costs.—Cotton Belt climate makes for cheap rural living. Food crops are cheaply grown and the grocery bill can be kept low. Heavy winter clothing is not needed and the cost of housing is kept down by the absence of central heating plants and insulating materials. A subsistence can be obtained more cheaply than in the other regions because the climate is favorable. Wages, on the other hand, are correspondingly low, so that the worker's real income shows no gain because of these savings.

TOPOGRAPHY AND SOILS

Cotton Soils.—Although the margins of the Cotton Belt are determined very largely by climatic factors, the major concentrations of cotton-growing are definitely related to the soil. The cot-

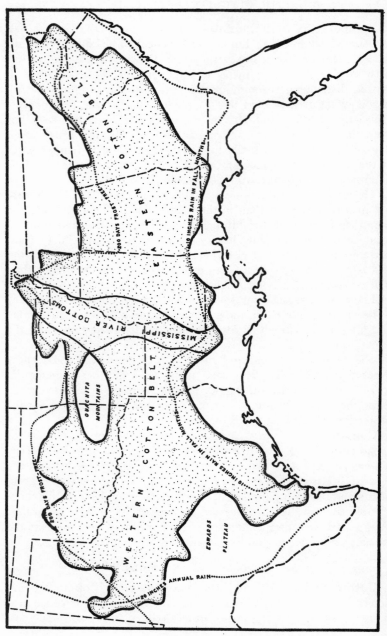

FIG. 44. The Cotton Belt.

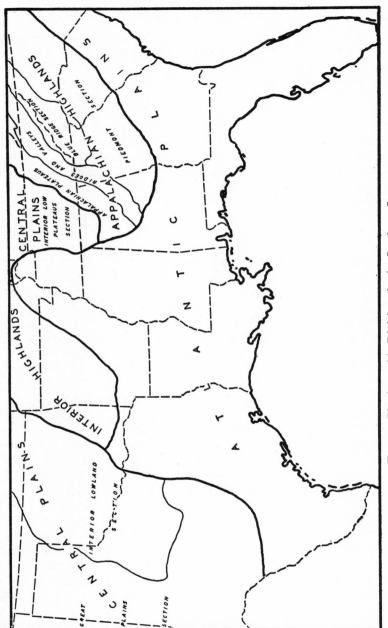

FIG. 45. Physiographic Divisions in the Southern States.

ton plant will tolerate a great variety of soils, and fair crops can be grown on almost any soil if the under-drainage is good. The best yields are obtained, however, where the soil is rich in calcium and contains considerable amounts of humus. For these reasons, nearly one-third of the crop is grown on the Cotton Belt's three relatively small areas of black prairie soil: the Black Prairie of Texas, the Black Belt of Alabama and the Mississippi River Bottoms. The first two belts are local limestone soils formed in much the same manner as those of the Upper Mississippi Valley, while the river bottom soils consist largely of alluvium brought down from the northern prairies by that river. These three districts appear prominently on every map of cotton production.

Physiographic History.—Limestone prairies occupy less than one-tenth of the surface of the Cotton Belt. King Cotton, in fact, has extended his domain to include parts of four major physiographic divisions. His flag flies over nearly all of (1) the Atlantic Plain between North Carolina and southern Texas. He likewise dominates the southern portions of (2) the Appalachian Highlands. Farther west, cotton occupies the warmer slopes of (3) the Interior Highlands, and sections of (4) the Interior Plains, including a small portion of the Great Plains. Cotton occupies some of the oldest as well as the youngest geological formations in the country. This diversity of geologic heritage has caused the Cotton Belt to have a wide variety of topography and soils. Physiographic factors are so important in influencing the development of southern agriculture that it is difficult to understand the resources of the area without some knowledge of these factors.

The Coastal Plain.—Geologists tell us that at one time the seacoast was much farther seaward than we find it today. In a later period either the land sank or the level of the sea rose until it lapped at the feet of the Appalachian and Ozark uplifts. Tracing this later coast line today, we find it running southeast from New York City, through Philadelphia, Baltimore, Richmond, and on south through Augusta and Columbus in Georgia. The present Lower Mississippi Valley was an arm of the sea. The Mississippi River emptied near Cape Girardeau, Missouri, and the mouth of the Ohio River was near Cairo, Illinois. On the west shore of this Mississippi embayment, the present site of Little Rock was at the seacoast, which extended westward to the vicinity of Ardmore, Oklahoma, and then south around the east and south margins of the Edwards Plateau to the Rio Grande. All of the present states of Florida, Louisiana, and Mississippi were submerged under a shallow sea whose waves smoothed the original topography by planing off the high places and filling the low ones.

During this smoothing process, the submerged beach received much marine sediment, largely fine sand, but also considerable amounts of clay. Finally the sea subsided and left the present coastal plain. It is apparent, however, that this evacuation was not completed during any short period, but rather took the form of a series of withdrawals, or probably a long series of retreats and advances. At the present time most of the coast seems still to be rising.

Along the Atlantic portion of the coastal plain these various stages in the ocean's withdrawal are rather plainly marked by a series of roughly parallel terraces, each of which at one time constituted a beach. These terraces are generally distinguished by differences in soils and elevation. Their margins have become difficult to distinguish because of erosion, but enough remains of the original surface to characterize the coastal plain from New York to northern Florida as a *belted plain*. The old seacoast, the line marking the maximum intrusion of the sea, is generally marked by a narrow belt of hills. This belt marks the boundary between the older piedmont and the younger coastal plain and is known as the Fall Line Hills.

West of the Florida peninsula the coastal plain is also belted, but here the belting is traced to the underlying rocks rather than to terraces. The story of these physiographic belts which dominate both soil and topography from Florida to the Mississippi Bottoms starts with the great Appalachian uplift. Originally, the Appalachians were much higher than at present and the uplift covered a territory much larger than the present boundaries of the mountains and plateau. Erosion planed off the upper portions of the uplift and in doing so exposed the various rock strata which underlay it. Later, the outer portions of the uplift were submerged, and the sea continued the leveling process, finally depositing the sediments that form the terraces of the Atlantic coast portion of the coastal plain.

For some reason, sedimentation was much less pronounced along the Gulf than along the Atlantic slope. In the Gulf section the soils are therefore closely related to the exposed rocks and little of their origin can be traced to marine sedimentation. This section is also belted, but here the belting is related to the varying characteristics of the exposed rock strata. Some of these rocks have produced good soil, while others are poor. Weathering has left some belts nearly level, others rolling or hilly. The belted characteristic remains, however, and continues westward to the great alluvial deposits which form the Mississippi River Bottoms.

The Mississippi River Bottoms.—The marvelously rich soil of the Mississippi River Bottoms consists almost entirely of fluvial deposits brought down from the northern prairies. The Mississippi always has carried a heavy load and each flood has added its thin layer of good soil. The river is very sluggish and its flood plain is flat. Sedimentation is greatest near the banks of the normal channel, with the result that the land generally slopes away from rather than toward the river. Several small rivers, notably the Yazoo, St. Francis, White, and Ouachita, paralleled the main stream for long distances before emptying into it. These streams often have tributaries which rise on the very banks of the Mississippi and flow away from it toward the lower, smaller streams at the margin of the flood plain. Because much of the bottoms area is subject to flood it has not been a desirable location for railroads or cities.

The eastern border of the Mississippi Bottoms is clearly marked by a line of bluffs. These are composed of wind-blown soil eroded into a narrow belt of remarkably rough topography. Cities have appeared where these bluffs reach the river, as at Memphis, Vicksburg, Natchez, and Baton Rouge.

Soils of the Western Sections.—West of the Mississippi River Bottoms, the soils are again closely related to the underlying rocks. Again the belted characteristic appears, the belts having a generally northeast by southwest direction. Numerous rivers, all with considerable flood plains, cross this section. In Texas, long ranges of low hills generally separate the various belts. One of these soil belts, the Black Prairie, has the largest area of good soil to be found in the Cotton Belt. Here the parent material is marl and the resulting soil is high (above 25 per cent) in calcium carbonate. Such soils discourage trees and encourage grasses. Hence the Black Prairie was originally a grassland and its soils are high in humus.

Black-soil Areas.—Alabama and Mississippi have a similar belt of black prairie soil in the Black Belt. It had the same origin and is nearly as fertile as the Black Prairie of Texas. Three black-soil areas, the Black Prairie, Black Belt, and Mississippi Bottoms, have the best cotton soils of the South. Elsewhere, coastal plain soils are generally red or brown and their fertility varies with the structure of the parent material. All of them lack the calcium which makes the black-soil belts so productive.

Coastal Plain Topography.—The topography of the entire coastal plain could be described generally as rolling. The seaward margins are generally low and flat and are not a part of the Cotton Belt. Back from these flats the land generally becomes more hilly as one approaches the higher land of the interior provinces. The river bottom areas are flat and the Black Prairie and Black Belt are gently rolling. Outside the black-soil areas, the portion of the coastal plain occupied by cotton is generally described as rolling to hilly. Hills often mark the boundaries between different belts and some of these are surprisingly rugged. In general, however, there are no significant barriers to transportation outside the Mississippi Bottoms. Railroads and highways run from city to city in nearly straight lines. Relief is generally sufficient to make erosion a serious problem, but not to produce barriers to transportation.

The Southern Piedmont.—Cotton dominates the agricultural economy of that portion of the piedmont south of central North Carolina. Piedmont soils are generally reddish-brown clays, formed by long erosion of the underlying crystalline rocks. Piedmont clays are moderately productive and, like most soils in the eastern half of the United States, respond well to the application of chemical fertilizers. But fertility has declined from continuous cropping, and erosion has carried away much of the topsoil. The southern piedmont is the most heavily fertilized section of the Cotton Belt. The topography is generally described as rolling to hilly. Railroads find little difficulty traversing the area.

The Appalachian Valley and Cumberland Plateau extend into the Cotton Belt in northern Georgia and Alabama. As in the region farther north, the Appalachian Valley has good soil and a nearly level topography interspersed with numerous ridges. The limestone soil of this section is excellent for cotton. The Cumberland Plateau, which borders the Appalachian Valley on the west, is generally hilly and its soils, derived from crystalline rocks, are not highly productive. Railroads crossing the plateau have generally followed the river valleys.

The Interior Lowland becomes a part of the Cotton Belt in western Oklahoma and northern Texas. Topography in this section is generally undulating or rolling, and the reddish soils are fertile. Western Oklahoma is one of the newest and most productive sections of the Cotton Belt.

The Ozark-Ouachita physiographic province is represented in several small foothill sections in Arkansas and Oklahoma and the ridged valley of the Arkansas River which flows between these two rugged areas. Cotton-growing in these areas is generally a hillside proposition.

The Great Plains have been invaded by cotton in a small area in west-central Texas. Here cotton is grown on the sandy high plains which normally receive only twenty inches annual rainfall. High plains soils are generally considered fertile and the plains topography is smooth enough to encourage large-scale farming. This section has the largest cotton farms of the South.

Soils of the Southern Boundary.—The southern and eastern boundaries of the Cotton Belt are more definitely related to climate than to soil, but it is also true that the wet soils of the coastal belt generally are too poorly drained to permit the growing of cotton. The Cotton Belt reaches the coast only in the Corpus Christi area of Texas, whose rainfall is comparatively light and whose coastal prairie soils are comparable in character with those of the Black Prairie. Elsewhere the coastal belt is occupied generally by forest and swamp grasses, and its economic exploitation is confined to products other than cotton. This coastal belt is therefore considered as a separate region.

AGRICULTURE

Specialization.—The great majority of farms in the Cotton Belt are devoted primarily to the production of this major cash crop. Cotton is grown on the best land or the land which receives the commercial fertilizer. After cotton, the main crop is corn, grown for roasting ears, for grinding into meal, and for feeding the farm animals. The average acreage in corn about equals the acreage in cotton, but corn is a supply crop and receives comparatively little attention. In the dry western sections, the second crop is likely to be kaffir corn, which is grown mainly for forage. The third crop usually is a forage crop, often a legume. Velvet beans, cow peas, and peanuts are important from the Black Prairie of Texas eastward. The Black Prairie and the sections north and west of it grow oats or wheat as the third crop. In 1930, cotton occupied about one-third of the crop land of the entire region, but in the more fertile districts such as the Mississippi Bottoms more than 70 per cent of the cultivated land was in cotton.

Drawbacks to Diversification.—Despite long agitation, the typical southern farmer does not find it profitable to diversify his crops. Typically, he grows cotton on the same land year after year, and when it shows signs of depletion he applies commercial fertilizers. Under normal conditions, cotton-growing is by all odds the most profitable type of farm activity. Other regions can grow corn and fatten meat animals more cheaply, and distance from industrial markets makes it difficult to compete in the poultry and dairy-products markets. Other regions have better grass and cheaper feed. But none of these other regions can grow cotton. Cotton is a cash crop, a relatively sure crop in most parts of the South, and one which consumes most of the farmer's time through-out the year. Ordinarily, there is not only little incentive but also little opportunity for diversification. March and April are occupied with preparing the soil and planting the crop. Cultivation continues through July; picking ordinarily starts in late August and is not likely to be completed before Thanksgiving Day. From Thanksgiving to Christmas the South takes a well-earned holiday, but even in this season there is much clearing away of old plants and cultivating of the soil for the new crop of cotton or corn. Corn-growing helps the farmer's schedule hardly at all, for it is planted and cultivated at about the same time as cotton, and is "snapped" in about the middle of the cotton-picking season. Where machine farming is possible, and in the northern sections where the growing season is shorter, more time is available, but a com-bination of inertia, habit, and lack of prospective profit has been sufficient even in these areas to keep diversification at a minimum.

Most Cotton Farms Are Small.—A number of factors have contributed to keep the cotton farm small. In the first place, the crop is still picked by hand and in most sections operations are limited to the number of acres that can be picked by the grower and his family. Casual labor is not abundant in the southern states, and only near the larger cities can workers be hired for the picking season. In the second place, operations are not ordinarily adapted to machine cultivation. Usually there are many weeds which can be cut only with the hoe. Again, many of the fields are rolling and cannot be cultivated with anything larger than a one-mule plow. Two-mule and four-mule equipment is successful on the smoother western prairies, and is in general use where extra help can be obtained at picking time. The situation will be changed radically with the successful introduction of a mechanical cotton-picker. When picking machines come into general use, we may expect to find an even greater emphasis upon level land and a further decline of the hilly piedmont areas in cotton production. In the meantime, however, the typical cotton farm from the Black Prairie eastward is a small, one-mule farm seldom exceeding forty acres in size and usually farmed by a tenant or cropper.

The Plantation.—In addition to the small farm, the plantation also persists throughout the Cotton Belt. Plantations are less important in acreage and production than small farms, but they exert an enormous social influence, especially from the Mississippi Bottoms eastward to the piedmont. The Cotton Belt contains between 30,000 and 40,000 plantations.[1] The average plantation is a carefully organized productive mechanism specialized in the production for market of a single crop. From the labor standpoint it consists of a manager (nearly always the owner) and an indefinite number of resident tenant families. In size, it will vary from 260 acres up well into the thousands, but nearly all plantations contain fewer than a thousand acres. Somewhat less than half the land is ordinarily in crops, divided about equally between cotton and corn. Land not in crops is in woodland or pasture. A small portion is usually in fallow (idle), and as on most southern farms, there is likely to be some waste land along the streams.

Tenants and Croppers.—Plantation organization is designed strictly to promote the growing of cotton. The laborers are tenants who own no part of the establishment and are paid according to the crop they produce. Three methods of renting are in use, the most common of which is known as share-cropping. These renters, known as croppers, furnish practically nothing except their labor.

---

[1] A plantation is defined for statistical purposes as a farm having 260 or more acres and five or more resident families. There are, of course, thousands of smaller farms which have two, three, or four families.

The landlord provides the land, cabin, fuel, tools, seed, and the work animals plus their feed. The cropper receives half the crop grown on his section of the plantation. A second system is known as share-renting. Share tenants provide their own animals, feed, seed, and tools, and receive two-thirds or three-quarters of their crop. Finally, there is the relatively rare cash tenant who contracts for use of the land and buildings for a fixed sum and receives all of the crop less the amount of his rental contract. In all classes, fertilizer is paid for pro rata according to the division of the crop: the cropper bears half the cost, the share tenant two-thirds or three-quarters, and the cash tenant all the cost.

On the typical plantation, the crop land is parceled out among the tenants, each of whom lives near his plot. Each tenant receives about twenty-five acres which he farms in accordance with instructions from the owner. Possibly five-sixths of these plantation tenants are Negroes, but the number of white tenants has been increasing in recent years.

The Plantation, a Large-Scale Enterprise.—As a business and social organization, the plantation is much more than a parcel of land subdivided into smaller plots. The owner is not only the business manager but also the social arbiter and general guiding spirit of his plantation-bounded community. As manager, he makes all plans, buys all farm supplies and frequently operates a commissary to sell household supplies to his workers. Often he hires additional workers such as bookkeepers, blacksmiths, and mechanics to assist in the non-farming phases of his business. Inevitably he becomes the creditor for his tenants, whose cash is low at planting time and whose store accounts must be guaranteed until the crop is marketed. Always the manager must be interested in personnel problems, which may vary from getting workers out of jail to aiding churches and contracting for medical services. The welfare of the tenant family on the plantation is his definite responsibility during the cotton season. Inevitably, also, the planter is in a position to become a man of prominence in local community affairs. In an agricultural society whose best evidence of wealth is the ownership of land, he is the "head boss" of all that is economic and nearly all that is social.

Tenancy on the Smaller Farms.—The smaller farms are generally managed like the plantations. Tenancy is very common, exceeding 70 per cent in many of the areas. In general, the smaller farm is less productive than the plantation because it is operated less efficiently. Absentee management, relatively rare in plantations, is more common in small farms. Thus the tenants generally receive less of the much-needed advice on farm management.

On the small farms, as on the plantations, tenants commonly start the season by arranging credit through the landlord at the local store. Landlords universally find it desirable to restrict these purchases to items of food and a very few articles of clothing. Practically all clothing and the more expensive purchases must be postponed until the crop is sold. Cotton Belt retailers are most active during the month of December.

Problems of the Cotton Economy

For the better part of a century, the literature of economics and sociology has recurrently described the Cotton Belt as a problem area. Monograph after monograph and report after report have been devoted to the ills of the cotton economy, have pointed out the need for reform, and indicated a drab future if reforms are not instigated. The fact remains that the South has lived through those hundred years, has preserved and increased its scale of living, and has found the cotton economy better adapted to its resources than any of the thousand-and-one experiments designed to substitute some other type of economic life in the South. Economic life in the South today retains many of the characteristics of a hundred years ago, when the wave of exploitation that followed the discovery of the profit in cotton had just about reached its zenith. Today there are a few more factories and considerably more erosion, a few more farm machines and a somewhat greater specialization along lines of a one-crop agriculture. But the fundamental pattern—the planter with his large holdings, the poor-white tenant on his forty acres, the impoverished farm worker, the utter dependence upon a single cash crop, and the lack of opportunity for investment or employment in other types of industry—remains essentially the same. The problems of the cotton economy are of long standing. It is significant that they have persisted so long and have survived so many years of discussion, recognition, planning, and experimentation. They can be read as well from histories as from current literature.

Two Types of Problems.—In all of these discussions two types of problems are recognized: the first group revolves around the problems of price, and is definitely economic or socio-economic; the second type is distinctly physical and is concerned with the problems of production, of the best and wisest use of the land and of maximum production. While each of these groups of problems is thoroughly interwoven with the other, the criteria are so different that they must first be considered separately.

Cotton Economics.—The year-to-year problems of the Cotton Belt are essentially those arising from fluctuations in the price of cotton, while the long-run problems are definitely social and are associated with economic maladjustment or the conservation of the region's resources. A prime distinguishing feature of the cotton economy was described in a previous section as the dependence upon foreign markets. When a region is primarily dependent upon the sale of a single product, and when half that product is normally sold in foreign markets, the welfare of that region is thoroughly bound up with international economics. It is also a matter of international politics, which since the World War has shown distinctly nationalistic tendencies. Commercial nations, for one reason or another, have placed increasingly large barriers in the paths of international trade. The consequence of such commercial policies has been a marked decline in trade between nations and the creation of acute economic conditions in those regions and nations whose economies had been geared to production for international markets.

Cotton has been less subject to the imposition of trade restrictions than many other commodities, but the loss of foreign markets has been sufficient to cause a severe depression in cotton prices and a corresponding decline in the income of the American Cotton Belt. Instead of selling eight or nine million bales abroad, the Cotton Belt is finding it difficult to dispose of five or six million bales, and these at reduced prices. The natural result of such a decline in markets is idle land and idle workers with correspondingly depressed rents and wages.

Wages never have been as high in the Cotton Belt as in other sections of the country. Low wages can be explained in part by lower living costs, but they are more directly attributable to the necessity for competition with other low-wage areas in international markets and the lack of alternative sources of employment. In the South there have been very few ways to make a living except from the land, and the product which the land produces most abundantly is cotton.

Cotton Surpluses and the Boll Weevil.—There is also reason to believe that the Cotton Belt was approaching disastrously low prices from too rapid expansion of its production. This expansion generally is associated with the boll weevil, an insect which first began to wreak havoc with the cotton crop of Texas and Louisiana in about 1905. The pest nearly destroyed crops in that area and began its steady march eastward. Cotton had not yet become important in those western areas and it was not difficult to offset the reduction in yield by larger acreages and increased plantings beyond the western margin of infestation. Within a few years production trends were again increasing in the western Cotton Belt. In the meantime, the eastern areas noted the steady eastward migration of the pest, the area of infestation advancing upon them at a rate of about 100 miles a year. The Mississippi Bottoms began to suffer severe losses about 1910. Ten years later the piedmont was similarly attacked.

In all of these areas, the immediate reaction was larger plantings. Texas and Oklahoma doubled their acreages between 1910 and 1930, and now have half the cotton land of the country. Other individual states suffered temporary relapses but there was never a reduction in the national output. Higher prices, based on predicted crop shortages, failed to materialize. Thus when the depression years of the 1930's came along, it was patently clear that the Cotton Belt was plagued with a too-common American malady—excessive productive capacity. Such a situation can be made profitable only by a development of additional markets. International commercial policies blocked this path of escape.

The Cotton Economy Runs on Credit.—Low wages are the starting point of many serious social problems. One of the oldest of these is tenancy. Few cotton farmers have ever been able to accumulate enough capital to buy even a small farm, and most of them receive just about enough from a year's crop to pay accumulated bills at the local store. That is the southern system. You start out the season flat broke. Your landlord furnishes the land and the mule and plow and you assign him a share of the crop you are going to grow. You buy food and clothing at the store and give the storekeeper a lien on your share of the crop. When the crop is picked, you haul it to the gin, and the ginner takes his pay in seed. You sell the cotton, usually to the store-keeper, and he pays your landlord and credits your share on your store bill. If the crop is good, and the price is favorable, and the bill not too large, you may have some money for a Thanksgiving feast, some new clothes or a few Christmas presents. Usually, however, you handle very little cash. Cash-and-carry stores do not thrive in the rural South because the cotton economy runs on credit.

Social Problems.—It is only natural that such a system should operate inefficiently and leave the way open for many abuses. Interest rates are high, for the risk of making a loan on a growing crop is great. Investigators find many instances of unjustifiably high interest rates and carrying charges, but in justice to the southern landowner it must be said that few of them get rich, and that many of them accept the philosophy that proprietors "take care" of their people, tiding them over bad years of pestilence, flood, drought and illness. There are very few evictions and correspondingly few cases of deliberate defalcation on the part of tenants and croppers. By the same token, the South has had relatively few rural families on relief.

Low incomes also contribute to low educational standards for the mass of the people, inadequate housing, questionable sanitation, unbalanced diets, and a host of similar deficiencies which unquestionably lower the productivity of the population. Southern houses do not need to be of heavy construction, for the winters are not severe; but the up-and-down siding with strips to cover the cracks, a plasterless interior and an open fireplace for heat are not adequate protection against piedmont weather which freezes over the small creeks every winter.

Remedies.—The southern wage problem is one that eventually will adjust itself through migration and the introduction of new industries. A heavy movement of southern Negroes to industrial cities of the North took place during the World War and there has been a constant trickle of both Negroes and whites from these areas ever since. More important, perhaps, is the renewed interest by industrialists in plant locations in the South. Low wage scales are always an important magnet to industry and many economists predict a pronounced southern migration by American industry within the next few decades. In addition, there is reason to believe that a saner world will eventually reduce tariff barriers sufficiently to promote a freer exchange of commodities in international trade, and all such agreements between the United States and industrial Europe will tend to restore the foreign market for cotton.

Such adjustments seem painfully slow to many a Southerner. Natives find it difficult to migrate because most of them are not qualified to accept the types of work offered in other regions. Industries change locations only after long hesitation. Agreements to lower tariffs by reciprocal action take much longer to perfect than the simple erection of a tariff wall. And looming on the horizon is the greatest specter of them all in the ungainly automaton of the cotton-picking machine. That the machine will come eventually no one seems to doubt, for it works experimentally. The revolution which it will bring to southern agriculture is almost unpredictable in its ramifications. Certainly it will place an additional premium on level land, and certainly the number of laborers that will be displaced will run into the millions. It seems likely also to bring increased competition from countries such as Argentina and Brazil which can grow good cotton but lack the labor for it. To many a Southerner it looks as if the slow working-out of economic law would never keep pace with the disemployment of his people by technological change.

Physical Factors.—An entirely different set of problems has arisen in connection with the actual management of the Cotton Belt farm. Southern climate, with its long growing season and plentiful rainfall, is a great boon to vegetation, but it has also brought two problems common to the humid sub-tropics. These are erosion and insect pests.

Soil Conservation.—From the long-run point of view the most serious problem of the Cotton Belt is the depletion and erosion of its soil. Cotton is a clean-tilled crop which returns little or no humus to the soil and subjects every sloping field to erosion. The frequent showers, so favorable to cotton, quickly cut rivulets which grow into gulleys, which in turn eventually can ruin an entire field. Erosion is most severe in the piedmont, and is nonexistent on the flat Mississippi Bottoms. The Black Prairie has little, but Oklahoma is badly gullied. In a few sections the land has been ruined beyond reclamation, and more than one-third of the Cotton Belt has lost most of its topsoil. The traveler who first visits the piedmont is impressed with the vivid red gashes in the green landscape. These are eroded belts where the red, unproductive subsoil has been exposed.

Depletion of soil fertility is a less serious problem because the South has long met soil deficiencies with the application of commercial fertilizers; nitrates, phosphates, potash, and calcium. Fortunately, most southern soils respond well to the application of the mineral salts removed by cotton cultivation. It must be remembered, however, that fertilizers cost money and the necessity for such expenditures places the depleted areas in an inferior competitive position with respect to the more fortunate areas at home and abroad which do not require such rejuvenation. Erosion is a more difficult problem, and one which calls for careful planning. Small dams must be built and provision made for contour farming, strip cropping, and planting the steeper slopes to perpetual grass or timber. The task is a huge one and will not be completed in time to save millions of acres of land that were once productive, but are destined to become gulley-washed waste.

Insect Pests.—Among insect pests which survive in this climate because of the mild winter, the most destructive has been the boll weevil. This insect, whose unpredicted stimulation of cotton-growing was described in a previous section, infests the entire Cotton Belt and does its damage by eating the germ, or growing portion, from the inside of the unripe cotton boll. Once attacked, the bolls wither and fail to develop. The insect is difficult to combat because it works unseen inside the boll, and to destroy the insect is also to destroy the cotton crop. Preventive measures are confined largely to spraying, dusting poison from airplanes, and keeping fields clean to destroy breeding grounds and expose the eggs to the freezing temperatures of winter. The boll weevil has been called "the bug with a billion-dollar appetite" because it probably destroys one-third of the potential cotton crop each year. Economists remind us, however, that if all the insects were somehow destroyed and the South harvested 50 per cent more than its normal crop, the price probably would drop so low that the average grower would be little better off than before. Such statements drive home the point that the demand for cotton is relatively inelastic. Every increase in supply is accompanied by a corresponding decrease in the price per pound.

Localized Problems: Flood and Wind.—The other major physical problems of Cotton Belt agriculture are more definitely localized. The Mississippi Bottoms have a distressing and much-publicized flood problem, while western Texas and Oklahoma experience occasional drought and wind erosion. At this point we are reminded that the Cotton Belt covers an area of great diversity in topography, soil, climate, and agricultural development. Problems which are urgent in the Georgia piedmont do not exist on the Black Prairie; and the Mississippi Bottoms cotton-grower faces a different set of enemies from those which attack his fellow worker on the Atlantic slope. Such considerations make it desirable to subdivide the Cotton Belt into several sections, each of which differs from the rest by reason of natural environment or type of development.

REFERENCES

The data for climate, soils, and other natural features in this chapter were taken largely from *Atlas of American Agriculture* and *Physiography of the Eastern United States*. A. E. Parkins, *The South* (Wiley, 1938), is an excellent volume. An exhaustive consideration of regional differentiation is found in H. W. Odum, *Southern Regions of the United States*. This volume also contains a good statement of methodology. Research monographs of the Works Progress Administration carry good material, especially *Landlord and Tenant on the Cotton Plantation* and *Part-Time Farming in the Southeast*.

QUESTIONS AND PROBLEMS

1. Why is a knowledge of international commercial policies essential to a consideration of the economic geography of the American Cotton Belt?
2. If only one-third of the American cotton crop is sold in foreign markets, why is the domestic price determined by prices prevailing abroad?
3. In the 1930's the federal government attempted to meet the problem of declining markets for cotton by persuading every grower to reduce his acreage by one-third. Comment on the soundness of such a plan as a long-run policy.
4. Show how climate influences the location of regional limits in the Cotton Belt.
5. Of what significance are soil areas in determining the boundaries of the Cotton Belt? in determining the location of the major concentrations of cotton production within the region?
6. The South has about as many acres in corn as in cotton. Why is it not included in the Corn Belt?

7. Describe the appearance of a typical cotton farm. Would your description fit the eastern sections as well as the western sections? How does the plantation fit into the picture?

8. Why do many cotton farmers continue to specialize in cotton-growing despite the prospect of low returns?

9. Why does the author not define an oil and gas region? Would it be correct to speak of an area which derives most of its income from oil and gas as a region?

10. Why were the petroleum pools exploited long before the natural gas deposits in the Mid-Continent area?

11. What factors appear to be most important in determining the location of petroleum refineries?

12. How has the utilization of minerals altered the economy of certain sections of the Cotton Belt? Do you expect this change to continue? Why or why not?

CHAPTER XV

AGRICULTURAL SECTIONS OF THE COTTON BELT

Division into Sections.—Nearly all economic and social criteria divide the Cotton Belt rather sharply into two sections, with the division falling near the Mississippi River. If state lines are taken as boundaries, the river itself may be used as the dividing line, but a more accurate division is made by designating the Mississippi River Bottoms as a separate section and making them the boundary between the eastern and western divisions. The Mississippi Bottoms are a distinctive sub-region naturally, economically, and socially, and they do not share many of the more acute problems of the other two sections. In addition, there are numerous differences, recognized by all students of the Cotton Belt, between the older eastern section and the newer western section. The Mississippi River Bottoms are a small but distinctive and fairly homogeneous area. Within the eastern and western sections, on the other hand, there are numerous local differences which make it necessary to subdivide these sections into smaller districts.

AGRICULTURE IN THE EASTERN COTTON BELT

Cotton states lying east of the Mississippi River have been variously designated as the "Old South," the "Deep South," and the "Cotton Southeast." Regardless of designation, this section has had the longest cotton-growing history and its present-day existence is marked by economic and social problems differing materially from those of the Mississippi Bottoms and the western Cotton Belt. Here, for example, the farms are smaller and the land less fertile than in the other two sections. Here we find the greatest erosion problems, the smallest farms, the lowest farm incomes, the highest percentages of illiteracy, the most impoverished local governments, and the poorest housing facilities of any major farm area in the nation. Here, on the other hand, we find dependable rainfall, nearness to eastern markets, an introduction of manufacturing, and numerous other factors which tend to favor this section over the more westerly cotton areas.

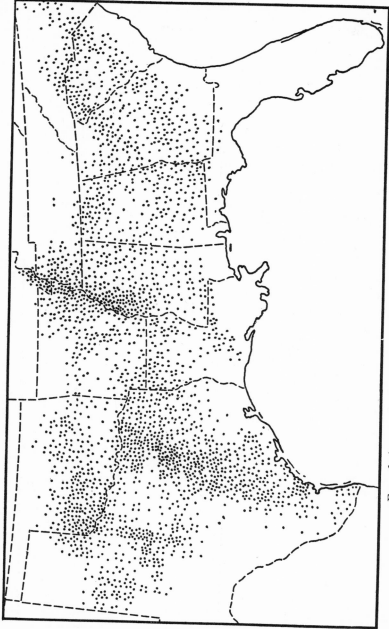

Fig. 46. Acreage in Cotton, 1935. Each dot represents 10 thousand acres.

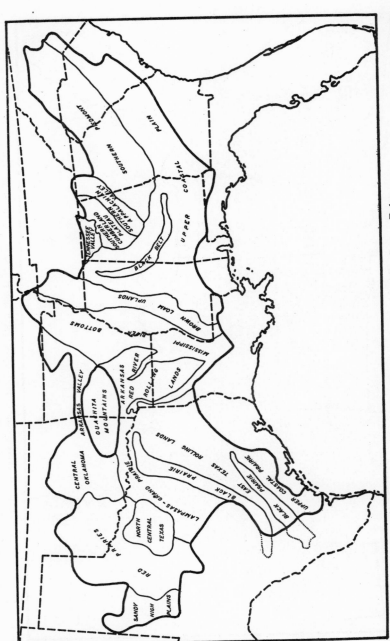

FIG. 47. Agricultural Sections of the Cotton Belt.

Natural Factors.—It will be recalled that the eastern Cotton Belt occupies portions of six natural areas. Largest of these is (1) the coastal plain, an undulating-to-rolling area, whose soils and topography form well-defined belts extending from central Mississippi east and north to the boundary of the region. In central Mississippi the coastal plain merges with (2) a north-south strip of loess-mantled hills whose western edge is a series of bluffs which overlook the low bottom lands and mark the western edge of the eastern Cotton Belt section. Northeast Alabama and northwest Georgia are occupied by the southern members of the Appalachian Highland, here represented by (3) the rugged, unproductive Cumberland Plateau, which is flanked on either side by a smoother, richer limestone plain: on the west by (4) the Middle Tennessee Valley, and on the east by the southern extremity of (5) the Appalachian Valley. Finally, the eastern Cotton Belt occupies a large area of (6) the southern piedmont, whose red hills stretch northeast from central Alabama to the northeast boundary of the region.

The Agricultural Pattern.—Throughout the eastern Cotton Belt the agricultural pattern differs little from the generalized descriptions given in the preceding pages. In 1930, no area in the section had fewer than half its farms classified as "cotton farms" and in the section as a whole, nearly three-quarters of the farms were devoted primarily to cotton. Greatest specialization is in the Tennessee Valley and the Loess Hills of Mississippi and western Tennessee, where nearly 90 per cent of the farms were specialized in cotton production at the time of the 1930 census. The extent of non-agricultural land varies considerably, but in most areas from 50 to 60 per cent of the land is in farms. In 1929, slightly more than half the gross farm production was represented by cotton, and about one-fifth of the production consisted of food consumed by farm families. The remaining 30 per cent was represented largely by feed crops consumed by the farm work stock. Dairying is not developed to commercial proportions except near the larger cities. Specialties are rarely grown, but in a few sections they stand second to cotton as a source of income.

Specialties.—All of the eastern Cotton Belt can grow fruits and vegetables and there are numerous farm orchards. The commercial production of these specialties is very small, however, and is important in only a few areas. Most popular and most universal of the southern specialty crops is the watermelon, which is grown in nearly every community and enters extensively into local trade. Georgia grows nearly one-third of the national commercial crop of watermelons. In addition, nearly every farm is likely to grow sweet potatoes or yams, generally for family use but occasionally for sale in local trade. Sweet potatoes and yams generally rank third in value among the farm products of the eastern Cotton Belt. Their farm value is regularly exceeded by cotton and corn. Yams and grits (from corn) are the great energy foods of the South.

A few localities have developed crop specialties to a point of commercial importance. In several counties of central Georgia (south of Macon) peaches are a major crop, outranked only by cotton as a source of farm income. Georgia regularly stands second only to California in peach production, with about one-quarter of the national commercial crop. Peaches are also grown commercially along the sand-hill border of the piedmont in Georgia, South Carolina, and North Carolina.

Peanuts are an important secondary crop in a belt which begins in southern Alabama and forms the southeast boundary of the region about half the distance across Georgia. Georgia and Alabama regularly account for about half the national production of peanuts. Most of the production consists of the small Spanish varieties. About one-third of the crop is fed to hogs which harvest their own feed from the fields.

In southwest Mississippi, Copiah County has become highly specialized in the production of tomatoes. Its production regularly provides from 5 to 10 per cent of the national carlot shipments.

The eastern Cotton Belt has a considerable number of cattle and hogs but produces excesses of neither meat nor dairy products for shipment to other regions. The typical Cotton Belt hog is a semiwild razorback which spends most of its life in the piny woods and lives mainly on mast. Cattle are likewise turned loose to obtain a living from the native grasses. A little corn attracts these animals to a farm enclosure a short while before time to butcher them.

The whole agricultural landscape of the eastern Cotton Belt is dominated by one-crop agriculture. Most of the farm land not in cotton is devoted to food and feed crops or left in timber and pasture. There are relatively few fields devoted to crop specialties; these products achieve commercial importance in only a few areas along the southern and eastern margins of the region. Progressively toward the interior, one encounters more and more specialization in cotton.

The Mississippi River Bottoms

A Distinctive Area.—The low, flat, and occasionally swampy Mississippi River Bottoms have achieved a specialization in cotton which sets them off from the remainder of the Cotton Belt. The rich alluvial soil has resisted depletion from continuous cropping better than the soils of any other area. Erosion has not been a problem because the topography is almost dead flat. Consequently, the Mississippi River Bottoms have been the home of the specialized cotton farm for more than a century.

The bottom lands of the Mississippi River differ little in most respects from the bottoms of the other rivers which cross the coastal plain, especially in the western section. They are flat belts of alluvial soil which cut directly across the various soil belts of the coastal plain. Nearly all have rich soil, a level surface, considerable areas in swamp, and a flood problem. The main reason for treating the Mississippi flood plain as a separate section is that it is much larger than the rest, and therefore multiplies both the advantages and disadvantages of this type of area.

Topography and Soils.—Physically, the Mississippi River Bottoms consist of the basins of several tributaries of the great river. Largest of these rivers are the Yazoo on the east and the Arkansas, Ouachita, and Red rivers on the west. The Mississippi itself has practically no drainage area below the mouth of the Ohio, because it flows between levees almost the entire distance. Its tributary streams tend to run parallel to it for considerable distances before they empty. Much of the water of the Red River does not flow into the Mississippi at all, but reaches the Gulf through the Atchafalaya River, the latter a minor mouth of the Mississippi. These descriptions emphasize the flatness of the section and lead one to expect large areas of swamp. The bottoms are as famous for mud and mosquitoes as for their excellent cotton.

Specialization.—Land utilization is largely a reflection of the prevalence of swamp in the various basins. Nearly two-thirds of the land in the Yazoo and St. Francis basins is in farms, and here 97 per cent of the farms were classed as cotton farms in 1930.

Elsewhere, conditions are less favorable, and considerably less than half the land is in farms. Swamps, lakes, and rivers occupy the remainder. This means that there is less good cotton land and correspondingly less specialization. Even in these less-favored sections, however, cotton furnishes nearly four-fifths of the gross farm income. Cotton occupies from one-third to two-thirds of the farm land throughout the section, and less than 10 per cent of the farm production is devoted to family living. There are few cattle, hogs, or chickens. This high degree of specialization is not matched in any other portion of the Cotton Belt. Most of the farms are of the very small, "one-mule" size, but there are some large plantations. Tenancy is almost universal.

Problems of the Bottom Lands.—Problems of the bottom lands are centered around the physical difficulties of drainage, sanitation, and floods, as well as the socio-economic consequences of one-product agriculture, tenancy, and low incomes. Drainage is difficult because the land is so low and there is no place to send the water. Water tables are often too high for the cotton plant. Sanitation involves elimination of malaria and control of the mosquito. Progress has been encouraging along both these lines. Much land has been reclaimed through drainage, and the toll of malaria has been reduced appreciably. The flood problem, most spectacular of all, also seems about to be conquered.

Floods.—No one who reads the newspapers misses the accounts of destruction brought by floods on the Lower Mississippi. When spring freshets bring the run-off from the million square miles drained by the river down into the narrow channel below Cairo, that channel is simply unable to care for the discharge. Levees break, good farm lands are flooded, buildings and people are carried away. At New Orleans the capacity of the river is about one and one-half million cubic feet per second. During the great floods the volume is more than twice that capacity. It is obvious that higher levees cannot solve the problem. Army engineers decided that some place must be found for the water to go. Their plan, finally put into effect, designates certain areas which will be allowed to overflow in case of flood. These areas are protected by low levees and may not be touched in minor floods. But when the river reaches a certain stage and other areas are endangered, these "fuse-plug" levees are dynamited to relieve the pressure elsewhere. In addition, New Orleans is protected by spillways—alternate mouths for the river whose gates may be opened to carry flood waters to lake Pontchartrain and the Gulf by other routes. By these means, all of the cities and fully two-thirds of the open-country area are kept safe from flood. The entire section contains about 35,000 square miles, of which 30,000 are subject to flood. Engineers estimate that by leaving 10,000 square miles subject to overflow, the remainder can be kept safe from any conceivable flood of the future. Inasmuch as most of the land left to overflow never was in farms, the plan has not seriously disrupted the agricultural pattern of the section. Those who remain in these areas are cognizant of the fact that if the flood comes, it is their move.

Continuous Cropping and Soil Depletion.—Inevitably these bottom-land soils have suffered depletion, and each year brings greater need for fertilizers. Thus far, however, the bottoms have needed much less fertilizer than the piedmont and coastal plain areas farther east. Cotton from the area usually is above the average in length of staple and commands a premium in the market. But the whole economy is strictly at the mercy of the price of cotton, and is prosperous or depressed according to the price at picking time.

The Arkansas Rice District.—The supreme dominance of cotton in the Mississippi Bottoms section is broken in only one small section, the Grand Prairie of southeast Arkansas. Here conditions of subsoil and water supply have encouraged the growing of rice. This small area grows about 20 per cent of the national crop. Methods are similar to those used along the Gulf coast (see Chap. XIX).

AGRICULTURE IN THE WESTERN COTTON BELT

West of the bottoms of the Mississippi River the Cotton Belt occupies a great variety of land. The coastal plain itself is traversed by numerous rivers, each with its flood plain similar to that of the Mississippi and generally almost as productive. Higher areas between these rivers have generally poorer and heavier soil much of which has poor under-drainage. This factor excludes a large area of the "piney woods" section of southeast Texas from the Cotton Belt and makes it a part of the Gulf Coast Region. Poor drainage and heavy rainfall keep cotton away from the Gulf coast as far west as Corpus Christi, where for a short distance the Cotton

Belt reaches tidewater on the rich and relatively dry Corpus Christi Prairie.

Back from the coast, cotton-growing becomes increasingly more successful as one approaches the northern and western limits of the coastal plain. In east-central Texas the acme of all American cotton lands is found in the Black Prairie, whose rich black soil gives cotton-growers fewer problems than the soil of any other southern area. The Texas Black Prairie ranks with the Mississippi Bottoms as one of the two major cotton-growing districts of the nation.

West of the Black Prairie the country is less well adapted to cotton, and livestock (cattle) is the major interest on many of the farms. This belt, which includes the Grand Prairie and Western Cross Timbers, is unfavorable to cotton because of its hilly topography and only moderately productive soil. Beyond this belt, however, lie the famous Red Prairies of northern Texas and western Oklahoma. These reddish and brownish chernozem soils grow good cotton and the rolling topography favors tillage. The Texas-Oklahoma Red Prairies appear prominently on maps of cotton production.

West of the Red Prairies, cotton has climbed onto the dry High Plains of west-central Texas to establish the western boundary of the Cotton Belt. Here, with an average annual rainfall of only twenty inches, cotton has braved the danger of drought and become the chief farm interest in eight counties which not many years ago were dominated by ranching. West of these counties, cotton is not successful unless irrigated. Drought plagues the existence of these High Plains cotton farmers as it does the lives of wheat farmers in the dry areas north of them. When rainfall is sufficient, they make a "killing," but the too-frequent droughts leave them with no crop worth harvesting. Dry years, incidentally, are equally destructive to the boll weevil, so that this section has few of these pests.

The Cotton Belt of eastern Oklahoma and northern Arkansas generally lies in the hills. The rugged Ouachita Mountains grow little cotton and are excluded from the region, but the ridged valley of the Arkansas River which separates the Ouachitas from the Ozarks is a cotton area. Cotton also dominates Ozark foothill areas in northeast Arkansas and eastern Oklahoma. In all of the hilly areas, cotton-growing vies with general farming for agricultural supremacy. The rougher areas are in pasture, and corn is raised to feed the cattle. Many farmers also grow oats and wheat. In most years, however, the majority of the farm income is derived from cotton even though comparatively small areas are devoted to it.

In summary, it is well to observe that the cotton map of the western Cotton Belt is definitely "spotty." The great center is the Texas Black Prairie with its southern extension to the Gulf at Corpus Christi. There is also a heavy production just east of this belt, in northeast Texas and adjacent portions of Louisiana and Arkansas. West and north of the Black Prairie, cotton is not very important over a belt nearly 200 miles wide. Then we encounter the great concentration of western Oklahoma and northwest Texas, which centers on the Red Prairies. Elsewhere, there are no important concentrations.

The western Cotton Belt normally grows nearly half the American crop of cotton. The state of Texas, partly because of its size, but more because it has the Black Prairie, produces about one-third of the national crop. The western Cotton Belt, especially from the Black Prairie westward, generally has larger farms and uses more machinery than other parts of the region. Some single-family farms in the newer areas grow as much as 200 acres of cotton. It is there that people most expectantly await the coming of a mechanical picker. Drought is their great menace, but over a long period of years these farmers are making money. The economy of the country is benefited by the greater diversity which arises from more cattle and the presence of oil and gas. Three sources of income, not one, characterize these western sections, and have kept their per-capita incomes well above those of the eastern sections of the region.

FORESTS

With the exception of the Black Belt of Alabama, the Black Prairie of Texas, and the Red Prairies and the High Plains of the west, all of the Cotton Belt was originally in forest. Pines covered the coastal plain and met the hardwood forests in the foothills of the north. Cypress and tupelo were found in the swamps. Excellent forests they were, too, with long straight trees that yielded a high quality of lumber and grew more rapidly than those of any other forest area in the country.

The southern forest remains today the largest and most productive forest area in the country. The South (including roughly the Cotton Belt and the Gulf-Atlantic Coast Region south of Chesapeake Bay) normally provides from one-third to one-half the annual lumber cut of the United States. Good trees, a smooth topography, and an eager market have combined to make lumbering profitable; so profitable, in fact, that the original stand is sadly depleted. In 1930, it was estimated that the South had about one-eighth of the remaining saw timber of the United States, less than one-fifth as much as the Pacific forest, and enough to last only ten or fifteen years at existing rates of cutting. Later years have brought a slackening rate of cut, but it is obvious that the original forests of the South are nearly exhausted. This does not mean that the South will furnish no more lumber. Rather, it indicates the need for a now-recognized change in emphasis.

As a timber-*growing* area, the South stands preeminent. Ample rainfall and abundant sunshine cause trees to grow faster here than elsewhere in the country. Foresters estimate that nearly three-fifths of the annual national growth of new lumber occurs in the South. A pine tree will grow to a size suitable for lumber in thirty or forty years, and it will make good pulpwood in less than half that time. All of which means that the South is now engaged in growing lumber as a crop rather than mining it as one would an ore. The thousands of farm wood lots are being cleaned up and pointed toward lumber production. Federal and state departments are teaching farmers the rudiments of forestry. Large areas of cut-over land are being reclaimed and made to produce straight, high-grade trees by judicious planting and thinning. Large paper mills are practicing forestry in their own extensive forests and teaching wood-growers to do likewise. These trends indicate that the South will consider the forest an important source of income in years to come; but they should not hide the fact that these states are still cutting lumber much faster than they are growing it.[1]

Lumber production is rather evenly distributed among the states of the South. Mississippi, Louisiana, and Alabama generally lead in production, but every southern state is important in the

---

[1] More accurately, the South is not cutting timber faster than it is growing it, but cutting plus the destruction by fire, storms, pests, etc., exceeds the annual growth. The net result is depletion of the timber resources.

national list. Even Texas regularly produces about 4 per cent of the nation's annual cut. Production centers have generally shifted toward the seacoast as the more accessible lands of the interior have been cut over. The southern lumber industry of today belongs as much to the coastal region as to the Cotton Belt, but the future should see this emphasis shift back to the interior as more attention is paid to forestry. The naval stores and paper industries are most important in the coastal region and are considered in connection with the chapter for that area (Chap. XIX).

The great trees of the South are the pines, and the original forests were largely of this coniferous species. In the flatter sandy areas one finds the long-leafed yellow pine and the slash pine, so often tapped for turpentine. Hillier areas grow the shorter-leafed varieties. These in turn merge with the deciduous hardwoods in the foothills. Memphis is an important market for oak, hickory, red gum, and numerous other hardwoods. From the swamps comes the famous cypress, a tree which grows in water and is often cut by lumbermen standing in boats. These species constitute the bulk of the present-day cut, and they are the ones which these states will grow in the future.

MINERALS OF THE COTTON BELT

The Cotton Belt has two dominant minerals and a long list of minor ones. West of the Mississippi River, the Cotton Belt includes the larger portion of the great Mid-continental Oil Province, largest and most productive oil-producing area in the world. Associated with this oil, and occurring in the same general fields is the world's foremost supply of natural gas. These two minerals overshadow all other mine products of the Cotton Belt, and without them no southern state would be outstanding in mineral production. These oil and gas fields are not confined to a single geographic region, but because of their outstanding economic importance and relative geographic concentration they are considered independently in the following paragraphs.

OIL AND GAS IN THE SOUTHERN MID-CONTINENT

The Mid-continental and Gulf Coast Oil Provinces.—The many oil fields which occupy a roughly triangular area whose base stretches from western Texas to eastern Louisiana and whose apex is near the middle of the Kansas-Nebraska boundary were long ago grouped together by geologists as the Mid-continent Province. The first wells were in the Kansas-Oklahoma area, and in that day the term mid-continent was fairly descriptive. Later discoveries carried the operations west and south, until today the Mid-continent Province is separated from the Gulf Coast Province by a purely arbitrary line. At the present time, operations are centered considerably south of the middle of the continent, in that group of states often called the "Gulf Southwest." Petroleum provinces are not subject to strict delineation, but the mid-continent area may be said to include all of the territory east of the Rocky Mountains, south of Nebraska, west of the Mississippi River, and north of the Gulf Coast Province. The latter province occupies a belt about 100 miles wide which borders the Gulf coast in Louisiana and Texas. The productive area has been much smaller, as is indicated in Fig. 48.

Black Gold in the Gulf Southwest.—The Mid-continent Province has been the world's premier producer of petroleum for more than half a century. It has brought to the western Cotton Belt, the southern Great Plains, and adjacent portions of the Corn and Winter Wheat belts an additional source of income which has altered their economic structure. Oil has made it possible for Texas to vie with coal-producing Pennsylvania for first place among the states in mineral production, just as it has caused California and Oklahoma to climb to third and fourth positions, respectively, in the list. For the nation as a whole, petroleum is the most valuable mineral, exceeding in "mine value" the combined output of bituminous and anthracite coal. Texas is generally the leading state in farm income, but in most years the value of her oil and gas output nearly equals the gross value of her farm production. In Oklahoma, oil and gas surpass agriculture as an income-producer. These mineral industries are a potent factor in the prosperity of the states of the western Cotton Belt. In 1936, the Mid-continent Province produced about 60 per cent of the nation's petroleum and the adjacent Gulf Coast Province an additional 13 per cent. Here, therefore, is the primary center of the American petroleum industry. The only other area of comparable importance is California, with about one-fifth of the annual national output.

Petroleum Statistics.—The old saying that "statistics are always a matter of history" is never more true than in the oil and gas industries. All of us have followed the stories of the fugitive "black gold" and the even more elusive natural gas. A new field is brought in, a new pool discovered, competitive drilling begins, and production soars to dizzy heights. In a month, or a year, or a few years the pressure decreases, production slackens and finally stops. Oil crews and their drills and derricks pull out of the field and leave the cotton and wheat farmers to return to their crops and resume the more prosaic business of agriculture. Mining for oil is a migrating industry, and the statistics of last year are not very descriptive of operations today. Talk to an oil man and you find he has lived in many places. Look at this year's dot maps of production and you find that they too have migrated from county to county and from state to state. But for this migrating characteristic, it would be proper to designate a subregion which might be the oil and gas belt. Such an oil-dominated area could be delimited at any given time, but its boundaries would probably be changed before the ink was dry on the page, and certainly would be inaccurate a few years hence. The following descriptions are purposely kept general with the hope that they may not become hopelessly obsolete before they reach the reader.

Districts.—Oil-producing districts have been minutely defined by the industry, but for present purposes it seems desirable to use states as units except in two cases: Texas, whose size and importance warrant further subdivision, and Louisiana, whose Gulf coast district is logically separated from the northern fields of the state. Thus divided, the major sections and some of their more important producing areas are shown in Fig. 48. The legend for that chart also lists representative production figures. These should be supplemented by reference to the most recent production statistics.

Production.—The techniques of exploration and drilling for oil are beyond the subject matter of the present volume. Most readers are familiar with the general scheme of exploitation. Geologists explore the field and select a likely location. A test hole is dug and drill cores are carefully inspected by geologists as new formations are reached. Petroleum accumulates in the upward folds of certain rock formations, and the oil-bearing sands are recognized by geologists. After considerable depths have been reached, geophysicists may be called to lower sensitive electrical devices into the hole and test the underlying formations for elec-

FIG. 48. Oil Fields of the Gulf Southwest. The area mapped includes the most productive petroleum and natural gas fields in the world. The most productive fields are shaded on the map. In 1937, the various states and districts produced the following percentages of the national output of petroleum: Texas, 39.9% (Gulf, 8.8%; East Texas, 16.4%; North Texas, 3.0%; Panhandle, 2.2%; South Texas, 3.5%; West Texas, 6.0%); Louisiana, 7.1% (Gulf, 4.8%; Northern, 2.3%); Oklahoma, 17.9%; Kansas, 5.5%; Arkansas, 0.9%; New Mexico, 3.1%.

The percentages of the national output of natural gas in 1937 were: Texas, 35.5%; Louisiana, 13.1%; Oklahoma, 12.3%; Kansas, 3.5%; Arkansas, 0.4%; New Mexico, 1.9%.

trical conductivity and reflection. The well may go down a mile or more and drilling requires precise calculations. Finally, if oil is struck it *should* rise to the surface through pressure. If it does not, perhaps gas from another well is introduced to lighten the physical structure of the oil. In some areas wells are flooded with water to float the oil. In the mid-continent and Gulf coast fields, however, the well usually flows, at least for a time, from its own pressure.

Refining and Transportation.—From the well the oil is piped to a refinery. Today the Texas Gulf coast is the refinery center of the world, with about one-quarter of the United States (or one-eighth of the world) refinery output. Texas refines about 60 per cent of its oil output, and ships most of the remainder to the Atlantic coast (mainly the Philadelphia area) by tanker. Oklahoma, on the other hand, refines only about one-third of its crude and sends the rest by pipe line, mostly to refineries along the southern Great Lakes. Nearly two-thirds of the Kansas crude is refined in the state, while the Louisiana output is divided between home refineries and those on the Texas Gulf coast, with smaller quantities going by tanker to the Atlantic seaboard. Recent years have witnessed a pronounced trend toward locating refineries in the producing states. Not many years ago nearly all the crude was piped or barged to eastern refineries, but today most of the new plants are being built in the mid-continent and Gulf coast areas. In 1938, the Texas Gulf coast refineries produced 25 per cent of the nation's gasoline, while interior Texas produced 8 per cent. The Louisiana coast produced 3 per cent and inland Louisiana 2 per cent. The combined Oklahoma, Kansas, and near-by Missouri output amounted to 10 per cent. Thus the mid-continent and western Gulf states accounted for nearly half the nation's gasoline output. The modern trend apparently is to utilize the tanker and pipe line for gasoline rather than crude oil. In 1938, about 17 per cent of all gasoline shipments was made by pipe line.

Natural Gas.—Almost from the first, oil drillers discovered that natural gas generally accompanies petroleum in underground formations. In many drillings, both minerals are found under terrific pressure and all too often the drill has gone through the cap rock and turned loose a stream of oil and gas which blew oil and equipment over considerable areas of the surrounding country. Heart-breaking accidents of this sort were gradually eliminated by the introduction of better drilling techniques, and only rarely today does a well run wild as a gusher for any considerable period. Most of these techniques provide for valving off the excess gas so that it is permitted to escape into the air or is piped a safe distance from the well and ignited.

Natural gas has long been considered the "perfect fuel" because it has a high heat value and leaves no ash. Industries, public utilities, and domestic users are eager to substitute gas for other fuels. Pipes were run from the Appalachian gas fields to Pittsburgh and the cities of the Lower Great Lakes many years ago, and numerous wells were sunk solely for the extraction of natural gas.

The High-pressure Pipe Line.—Years ago the mid-continent and Gulf coast fields were known to have gas in unheard-of quantities, but there was no way to transport it to the eastern markets. Northern Louisiana developed a carbon-black industry which used local gas, but elsewhere there were few local uses. Thus for many years gas was a worthless by-product of southwestern oil wells, one which was not only unmarketable but highly dangerous if not properly disposed of. Thousands of gas-burning torches punctuated the darkness of the oil fields and made them resemble hundreds of border-lighted airports. The southwest disposed of trillions of cubic feet of the "perfect fuel" by burning it or permitting it to escape into the air, while hundreds of cities in other districts found it necessary to manufacture gas from coal.

The end of this colossal waste was forecast with the development, in the late 1920's, of a satisfactory method of welding gas pipe in the field. High-pressure pipe lines soon connected the mid-continent with the Middle West, and for the first time Oklahoma, Kansas, Texas, and Louisiana had a market for their gas. Feeder lines connect wells with the trunk lines and there compressors start the fuel on its high-pressure journey to the Manufacturing Belt.

Processing for Use.—The natural-gas industry involves something more than the mere collection and distribution of gas. Some gases are "dry," nearly odorless, and fit for use as they occur. Many others are "wet" or "sour." A wet gas is one which has considerable quantities of petroleum. Such gases must be processed to take out the oil. The resulting by-product is a high-grade gasoline known as natural gasoline. Natural gasoline is highly volatile and much in demand for blending with lower-grade gasolines. This same affinity of gas for oil has been utilized to rejuvenate many old oil wells which could no longer be pumped (or are too deep for pumping). Where gas is abundant it is often piped into these old wells and permitted to "soak up" the remaining oil. Then the gas is withdrawn and the natural gasoline extracted. "Sour" gas contains chemicals which cause it to burn with a disagreeable odor. Prices of gas have been so low that sweetening this gas does not pay. Most of it is disposed of locally.

Gas for Its Own Sake.—Finally, the industry has responded to newly developed markets by exploring the reserves and drilling wells solely for the production of gas. As in the Appalachian fields, the best gas resources are not located in the major oil-producing areas. In Texas, the greatest production comes from the Panhandle, which probably has the largest reserves in the country. Most of the Louisiana production comes from the northern part of the state. Fully three-quarters of the Texas production and nearly all of the Louisiana production come from gas wells. In Oklahoma, on the other hand, nearly two-thirds of the gas comes from oil wells. These states produced about two-thirds of the nation's natural gas in 1938. Texas alone accounted for about 40 per cent of the national output.

Local Uses. Natural Gasoline and Carbon Black.—The production of natural gasoline and carbon black is concentrated near the gas wells. In 1938, Texas and Oklahoma produced more than half the nation's natural gasoline, the major centers being the Texas Panhandle, East Texas and the Oklahoma City fields. The Oklahoma production reflects extensive use of the "gas lift" to restore oil production from old oil wells. Three-quarters of the nation's carbon black is manufactured in the Texas Panhandle, and most of the remainder in northern Louisiana (Monroe is the center). Carbon black is made by burning gas in a closed shed. The "lampblack" is collected and sold primarily to the manufacturers of automobile tires. Smaller amounts go into printer's ink and paint.

Economic Significance of the Oil and Gas Industries.—With nearly three-quarters of the nation's oil production and two-thirds of its gas production, the states of Texas, Oklahoma, Louisiana, and Kansas constitute the richest mineral-producing area in the world. In 1937, the wealth which flowed from the oil and gas wells of these states exceeded the value of the nation's entire cotton crop by nearly two hundred million dollars.

This ever-shifting oil and gas production is not confined to the Cotton Belt, but also occupies adjacent portions of the Great Plains, Winter Wheat Belt, Appalachian-Ozark Region, and the Gulf Coast Region. For many years, however, the major producing centers have been within the boundaries of the western Cotton Belt; and so long as the fabulous East Texas fields continue to lead in oil production, the center seems destined to remain in this region.

Previous paragraphs have shown many points of difference between the eastern and western Cotton Belt sections. One of the major points of difference arises from the presence in the western section of a half-billion-dollar oil and gas industry. A half-billion-dollar hypodermic is bound to speed up the economic activity of *any* section of the country.

OTHER MINERALS OF THE COTTON BELT

After petroleum and natural gas, the most important mineral of the Cotton Belt is coal. The leading center is in northern Alabama, but there is also a considerable production near the base of the Ouachita Mountains in western Arkansas and eastern Oklahoma. Texas has widespread deposits of lignite which is mined mainly in the northeast portion of the state. The Cotton Belt regularly mines between 3 and 4 per cent of the nation's coal, and of this amount more than two-thirds comes from northern Alabama. This section is also noted for its output of iron ore and limestone and, except for the oil and gas fields, is the most important mining district of the Cotton Belt.

The Northern Alabama Coal and Iron District.—The great Appalachian Coal Province (see Chap. XVIII) terminates with the Cumberland Plateau and Appalachian Valley in the Birmingham district of northern Alabama. These coals, together with local deposits of iron ore and limestone, have made Birmingham an important iron-manufacturing center. Alabama mines are also the chief source of coal for power and heat in the eastern states of the Cotton Belt. In 1936, about 40 per cent of the production was made into coke for use by the local iron and steel industries. Almost the entire production is recovered by deep-mining methods and there is little machine mining. Marketability is improved by cleaning, and the coal is widely used throughout the South.

Iron-mining operations of the Birmingham district produce about one-third as much income as the coal mines. Alabama produces between 8 and 10 per cent of the nation's iron ore, generally ranking third after Minnesota and Michigan. The largest operations are the underground workings in Red Mountain, near Bessemer. One of these mines is rated as fourth largest in the nation. Most of the product is hematite and the major portion goes to the Birmingham blast furnaces. Red Mountain hematite generally contains enough limestone to make it self-fluxing and hence needs only the addition of coke before charging into the blast furnaces. Smaller operations using open-pit methods are found near Gadsden. There is also a small production of brown ore.

Stone and blast-furnace slag are used for making cement. Alabama produces from 2 to 3 per cent of the national output. The extent and importance of these manufacturing industries in northern Alabama are indicated in a later section, "The Birmingham Coal and Iron District." (See Chap. XVI.)

Clay and Stone.—Clay and stone are mined in several sections of the Cotton Belt, especially the piedmont, the foothills of the Ozarks, and south-central Texas. Georgia produces nearly two-thirds of the nation's kaolin, or "china clay," and South Carolina an additional 20 per cent. Most of the kaolin is used for filler in the manufacture of paper. These same areas also quarry considerable quantities of stone ranging in quality from Georgia marble to low-grade road materials. Georgia ranks third among the states in the production of building and monumental marble and granite. Texas has several plants manufacturing cement and wall plaster from local stone and gypsum. Austin is an important center.

Mineral Districts.—The only important mining districts of the Cotton Belt are the ever-shifting oil and gas areas west of the Mississippi River and the Birmingham coal and iron district of northern Alabama. In these areas minerals are the principal source of income and dominate the economic structure. Elsewhere, one encounters occasional small mining communities but nowhere are these large enough to be comparable in importance with agriculture and trade. Industrially, Cotton Belt minerals have been the basis for two important types of manufacturing, the oil refineries of the western Cotton Belt and the iron industry of the Birmingham district.

REFERENCES

Land-use sections used in this chapter were derived mainly from *Types of Farming in the United States*. Several southern state universities have published valuable studies which pertain to the geography of southern agriculture, notably the University of North Carolina and the University of Texas. The latter university's *The Natural Regions of Texas* is particularly good. See also R. M. Harper, *The Natural Resources of Georgia* (University of Georgia, 1930). Nearly all the sources cited in Chapter XIV also apply to this chapter, since most of the studies are of a social and economic nature.

QUESTIONS AND PROBLEMS

1. If the United States were to lose its foreign markets for cotton, what portions of the Cotton Belt would most likely be abandoned? Why? Suppose, on the other hand, that the demand for cotton expands. Where would the new cotton fields be most likely to appear? Why?
2. Why are the problems of the Mississippi River Bottoms unlike those of other sections of the Cotton Belt?
3. Why has the Western Cotton Belt often been more prosperous than the Eastern Cotton Belt?
4. What differences would you expect to find in the physical appearance (land, buildings, and equipment) of cotton farms in (a) the Piedmont, (b) the Black Prairie, and (c) the High Plains? How would these differences reflect differences in farming practices?
5. In what districts of the region is cotton of least importance as a source of farm income? Why?
6. Why are insects a greater menace in the Cotton Belt than in the Corn Belt?
7. What is a pine tree? How many kinds are there? In what regions have we found pine forests? Are there differences among them in appearance, type of lumber, and climatic requirements? Carpenters often refer to southern pine as hard pine; lumbermen advertise "southern soft pine." Are these the same? Could both be right?
8. How good are the prospects for the South becoming a timber-growing region? What sections and varieties of trees are most promising?

CHAPTER XVI

COTTON BELT CITIES

IN GENERAL, the southern states have just about enough cities to care for the commercial needs of their agricultural economy. Manufacturing is not highly developed except in the southern piedmont. Mining communities are important only in the Birmingham coal and iron area and in a few of the oil fields of the western Cotton Belt. Lumber, like oil, has been a fleeting industry and has contributed to the development of few urban centers. In short, all of the large cities and nearly all of the·small cities of the South are commercial centers which exist primarily to assemble and ship the products of their surrounding areas, and to import and distribute goods for consumption by the people in those areas. Some of the largest of these commercial foci have grown up along the Atlantic and Gulf coasts, and these cities are considered in connection with that region. Other cities of the southern states are located in non-cotton-growing regions to the north and west. The reader should bear in mind the fact that many of these cities serve the Cotton Belt, despite the fact that, geographically, they fall outside the limits of the region.

Distribution and Trade.—A one-product economy maximizes the importance of exchange. In highly specialized farming regions such as the Wheat, Corn, and Cotton belts, a vast amount of attention must be given to interregional trade. The mere handling of the region's chief product and the multitude of articles which it must import from other regions often requires the services of nearly as many persons as are actually engaged in primary production on the land. A complete hierarchy of crossroads villages, county-seat towns, and larger cities develops to house these middlemen and their associated services and industries. In the Wheat Belts, the terminal tentacles of this collection-distribution systen are the grain elevator and the country general store. The Corn Belt has its country stockyards which start its raw materials to market, and the Cotton Belt has its cotton gins.

High-boarded wagons and trucks carry the loose cotton from the fields to the neighborhood gin. There the seed is removed and the fiber baled and made ready for storage or shipment. Every small Cotton Belt village has one or more gins, just as it has a general store, filling station, and other service institutions universal among agricultural villages the country over. Cotton is too bulky to be hauled very far unbaled, and inasmuch as the ginning machinery is not very complicated, there is ample economic justification for placing a gin in every cotton-growing community. Larger towns, frequently the county seats, serve as cotton markets. They may have compresses for reducing bales to smaller sizes for shipment. Many of them have mills for extracting the oil from cottonseed. They generally have warehouses for storing the crop. As service centers, they have the physicians, dentists, druggists, attorneys, bankers, and similar professional and service classifications generally associated with medium-sized towns. Some of them are jobbing centers. Their railroad and trucking interests are highly developed. Here also are a few local manufacturing industries such as bakeries, ice plants, and printing establishments.

The large city caps the pyramid of commercial development. Here we find department stores, terminal warehouses, a wide variety of professional services, amusements, educational institutions, railroad offices, brokerage firms, wholesale houses, and a considerable array of manufacturing establishments of the regional type. These larger cities are the nerve centers of the cotton economy, the commercial, financial, and industrial centers of the South. About half of them are located within the boundaries of the Cotton Belt and the other half are equally divided between the Gulf-Atlantic and the Appalachian-Ozark regions which border it.

The Southern Piedmont Industrial District

Consideration of the cities of the Cotton Belt logically begins with the industrial-agricultural district of the southern piedmont. These red hills of the Carolinas, Georgia, and Alabama have some of the oldest cities of the present Cotton Belt as well as some of the newest industrial villages of the United States. The piedmont is the most highly industrialized section of the South. Atlanta and numerous lesser cities of the Old South are located in the southern piedmont, and this section produces more than three-fifths of the national annual output of cotton textiles. The southern piedmont is also recognized as one of the fastest-growing industrial districts of the United States.

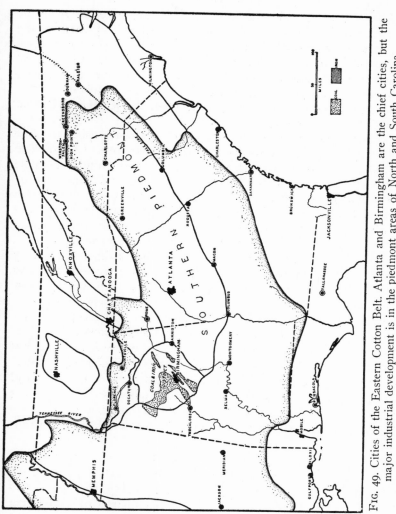

FIG. 49. Cities of the Eastern Cotton Belt. Atlanta and Birmingham are the chief cities, but the major industrial development is in the piedmont areas of North and South Carolina.

The traveler who journeys southwest from Washington and Richmond first encounters signs of industrialization in the cigarette factory towns of northern North Carolina. The cities of Winston-Salem and Durham obtain their raw materials from the bright-leaf tobacco district and are considered as part of the Appalachian-Ozark Region. Their industry springs from the tobacco fields rather than the cotton fields, and the visitor is more impressed by the aroma of tobacco than by the hum of spinners and the clicking of looms. Both cities have important textile interests, however, which help make them the leading industrial cities of North Carolina.

Winston-Salem and Durham, located on a nearly east-west line and only about seventy-five miles apart, constitute a formidable portal to the southern piedmont. Between and around them lie cotton-mill towns and south of them the industrial landscape of the piedmont is dominated by the cotton mill to its terminus in central Georgia and Alabama. Save for Atlanta, these cities are not large. The vast majority have but one mill and many an entire town is owned by the company which operates the mill.

The cotton-textiles industry came to the piedmont primarily because of cheap labor, abundant power, cheap cotton, and low taxes. The latter attraction has largely disappeared, but nearness to the cotton fields and national markets has kept down non-manufacturing costs, while an abundance of off-the-farm labor has served to keep wages low.[1] Detecting these advantages, cotton-millers began a serious consideration of piedmont sites several years before the World War. The first mills were erected to manufacture only the coarser products such as denims, muslins, and toweling. Gradually, however, piedmont labor was found quite capable of manning the looms for shirtings and the finer weaves. New England began to lose its historic supremacy in the manufacture of cotton textiles. In 1914, New England was manufacturing about 55 per cent of the nation's cotton goods, and was only mildly disturbed over the 30 per cent which was coming from the southern states. Twenty-three years later (1937), the figures had been more than reversed, with less than one-quarter of the product coming from New England and about 60 per cent from the

---

[1] In general, it costs no more (frequently less) to ship raw cotton than cotton textiles; but a piedmont mill can reach most national markets more cheaply than a New England mill because it has a shorter haul for its products.

South. New England was prepared to accept the loss of all but the highest quality items in her once-imposing list of cotton textiles. This shift in location of the cotton-goods industry from the cities of New England to the mill towns of the piedmont is the most important migration ever experienced by a major branch of American manufacturing industry.[2]

In general, the new industrialization seems to have had a favorable effect upon both the economy of the piedmont and the economics of the textile industry. Thousands of jobs have appeared in a section whose population was rapidly becoming excessive. Low wages, of course, cannot last indefinitely, except as they are based upon lower living costs. Unions will appear, higher living scales will be desired, and wages will rise. Always, however, there remain cheaper housing and food, and a cost of living for factory workers sometimes estimated to be at least 10 per cent lower than in New England. Granted reasonable freight rates, the piedmont miller should be able to buy cotton more cheaply than his New England competitor, because he is nearer the source of raw materials. In addition, he is nearer national markets. The piedmont has good water power and easy access to south Appalachian coal. These latter advantages are genuine, and appear to be permanent.

Because the piedmont had no cities of consequence, and because all locations were about equally desirable, the incoming cotton-miller usually started a town of his own. There you find them today, strung along the principal railroad lines. Some of them are strikingly well planned, with ample recreational space, neat well-built houses, and well-landscaped mill yards. Others, of course, are helter-skelter and grimy, with workers' shacks that would be habitable only in a mild climate. These mill towns are utterly dependent upon their single industry, but depressions bring less misery than might be. expected because most families still have relatives on farms in the near-by hills. There is added security in the fact that over a considerable period of years the demand for cotton textiles is relatively inelastic. The American family cannot

---

[2] The term "migration," when used to describe the relocation of manufacturing industries, applies to the general process involving the decline of an industry in one area and a simultaneous rise of the same industry in another area. Such shifts do not necessarily involve the physical movement of manufacturing facilities, but are more often associated with a shift in the location of investment capital.

go long without buying new clothing, even in periods of depression.

The importance of the piedmont in cotton-milling should not obscure the fact that the district is not outstanding among industrial sections in aggregate industrial output. The southern piedmont district regularly accounts for from 2 to 2½ per cent of the United States factory output. Addition of the tobacco towns of the northern border (Winston-Salem and Durham) would bring this figure to something over 3 per cent, but even this total is small when compared with the various districts of the Manufacturing Belt.

Other Piedmont Manufactures.—The industrial structure of the piedmont is dominated by the cotton-goods and allied textile industries. This industrial family includes not only gray-goods mills but also dyeing and finishing plants. There is also a growing output of hosiery and other knit goods using both silk and rayon. The North Carolina district is most important for these related lines. In addition to the textiles-clothing group, the North Carolina piedmont also has an important furniture industry. This area is the national center for the manufacture of medium-priced bedroom and dining-room furniture. High Point and Winston-Salem are important furniture centers, but the industry is also found in many smaller towns.

Atlanta is the outstanding city of the southern piedmont, and one of the major economic centers of the South. Located near the southern end of the Blue Ridge mountain chain, it occupies a strategic position with regard to transportation. Railroads from east and west of the Appalachian barrier meet at Atlanta and make it the leading railroad center of the South. Such facilities make the city an excellent location for wholesale houses and financial institutions. Atlanta ranks with Dallas, New Orleans, Memphis, and Houston as one of the major commercial cities of the South. Its wholesale trading area includes nearly all the Georgia piedmont, and its banking interests serve a much wider territory. For more than a century, Atlanta has been the economic and social center of the Old South. Today, it remains a commercial city. Its manufacturing, as befits a city of a quarter-million population, is developed to considerable local and regional importance. Atlanta is the most important manufacturing city between New Orleans and Winston-Salem, but it is not an industrial city. Atlanta has textile mills, and manufactures cotton-oil products, fertilizers, and soft drinks. Its largest manufacturing interests, however, are its bakeries, railroad shops, and similar local establishments characteristic of commercial cities. Outside Atlanta, the major piedmont commercial centers are Charlotte and Greenville, both of which have large wholesale territories and similar evidences of commercial importance. At the northern margin of the section, Greensboro, Winston-Salem, and Raleigh serve the commercial interests of both the cotton-textiles and tobacco districts.

On the outer border of the piedmont, a string of cities at the fall line have become important commercial centers. Largest of these are Raleigh (N. C.), Columbia (S. C.), Augusta (Ga.), Macon (Ga.), Columbus (Ga.), and Montgomery (Ala.). All of these cities have textile mills, but they are most important as distribution centers. The genuinely industrial centers of the southern piedmont are the "mill towns" of the interior margins of the section.

CITIES OF THE SOUTH APPALACHIAN BORDER

The Southern Appalachian Valley.—The Appalachian Valley section of northwest Georgia and northeast Alabama has experienced an industrial development resembling that of the southern piedmont. Cotton textiles are manufactured in numerous small mill towns. Rome (Ga.) is the most important center, but the wholesale trade of the section is dominated by Atlanta and Chattanooga. This section has about 5 per cent as much manufacturing as the southern piedmont.

The Middle Tennessee Valley.—This same type of industrial development extends westward into the Tennessee Valley of northern Alabama, but in this area there are fewer mills and a smaller degree of industrialization. Decatur, Huntsville, and Florence are small commercial cities which anticipate industrial growth because of cheap hydroelectric power from the government dams on the Tennessee River. The oldest and most famous of these dams is the power and navigation dam at Muscle Shoals, near Florence. This dam was started during the World War to provide power for manufacturing nitrates to be used in munitions. Later developments brought forth an ambitious plan which combines navigation, flood control, soil conservation, and cheap power to attract industry under the supervision of the government's Tennessee Valley Authority. A series of dams has been built to the very headwaters of the river. Industry has been slow to respond to the double attraction of cheap power and low wages, but local residents confidently expect a wave of industrialization to sweep the valley from Knoxville to Florence. The section apparently has the same industrial advantages as the southern piedmont. Better farm practices employing soil conservation, and better economic balance based upon a mixture of manufacturing with agriculture, are the cardinal aims of the Tennessee Valley plan.

THE BIRMINGHAM COAL AND IRON SECTION

Alabama people like to tell you that the site of the present city of Birmingham was a cotton field in 1870, and that today it is one of the leading cities of the South. It is true that as late as 1897 there was little in the Birmingham district to cause a concentration of population. Coal was being mined in the Warrior River field, and neighboring Red Mountain was known to contain iron ore. In addition, there were good supplies of limestone and dolomite for fluxing. A small iron industry had been started but it lacked capital and was making little headway.

This close geographic grouping of the three major materials for iron-making persuaded outside capital to begin developing these resources in the year 1897. The venture was taken over by the United States Steel Corporation in 1907, and rapid expansion followed. Their subsidiary, the Tennessee Coal, Iron and Railroad Company, operates mines, quarries, furnaces, railroads, and barges, and is the dominant industrial concern of the district. There are, however, a large number of coal-mining companies, a few engaged only in mining ore, and several smaller producers of pig iron or steel. Birmingham is the location for most of these mills, but the industry is also represented at Alabama City and Anniston. In 1935, the Birmingham district had about 6 per cent of the nation's blast furnaces and 3 per cent of its steel-making capacity. The district is a national center for cast-iron pipe and has an extensive output of railroad rails and galvanized sheets. Within the industry, Birmingham is known as an iron rather than a steel center.

The Alabama steel industry is not larger primarily because of lack of markets. The South is not highly industrialized and uses comparatively little steel. Birmingham has been unable to compete with other steel centers for markets outside the South because of transportation costs. In addition, the ore is of low grade (about 37 per cent) when compared to Lake Superior ore (50 per cent or higher), and most of it is mined by underground methods. These disadvantages are partially offset by the availability of coal and limestone in the immediate neighborhood. The Birmingham district is said to have sufficient ore reserves to last 300 years at existing rates of production.

Although the Birmingham district is dominated by coal and iron, and Birmingham stands as the most highly industrialized large city of the South, there are also important commercial interests. As a wholesale center, Birmingham ranks with Charlotte, Oklahoma City, and Fort Worth, and is about one-third as important as Atlanta. Birmingham commercial interests serve the northern half of Alabama.

Outside Birmingham, Bessemer is noted for iron-ore mining, Alabama City and Gadsden for iron and coal, and Anniston for cast-iron pipe. Tuscaloosa has near-by coal mines and a small iron industry. The Birmingham district has about one-half of one per cent of the manufacturing of the United States, or about 10 per cent of the total for the Cotton Belt.

CITIES OF THE INTERIOR COASTAL PLAIN

Few important cities have arisen between the fall line and the Atlantic coast in the Carolinas and Georgia. Here the topography is relatively smooth and there are no locations which could be termed strategic. Hot, humid summers have discouraged factory work. Occasional sawmills and turpentine stills are the only important evidences of manufacturing. Trade of the area is divided among the fall line cities and seaports of the adjacent Atlantic coast.

West of central Georgia, the Gulf section of the coastal plain has been more productive of urban development. The fall line ceases to be important in this section, but this same line of commercial centers continues westward through Montgomery, Selma, Meridian, and Jackson to Vicksburg on the Mississippi River. This line of commercial cities, all located about 150 miles from the coast and stretching from Raleigh to Vicksburg, is one of the most striking features of urban geography in the Cotton Belt. None of these cities are very large and none of them have extensive trade territories; but their intermediate positions between the coast and the major interior centers have made them good locations for commercial establishments. Manufacturing is not highly developed and is concerned primarily with lumber and timber products. Railroad shops and similar local industries are the leading employers of factory labor. There are a few cotton-textile mills. These cities are dominantly commercial.

Memphis and the Mississippi River Bottoms

The city of Memphis occupies a strategic position with reference to the productive and densely populated Mississippi River bottoms. Here, and nowhere else between Cairo and Vicksburg, the bluffs reach the river and provide a flood-free site where railroads can reach the river shore. This unique location and the marvelous richness of its hinterland have gone far to make Memphis the most important river city between St. Louis and New Orleans, and one of the half-dozen major commercial centers of the South.

In 1935, Memphis stood third among the cities of the South in wholesale trade and was only slightly below the two leaders, New Orleans and Dallas, in volume of sales. The Memphis trade territory includes the western third of Tennessee, the northern half of Mississippi, the Mississippi River bottoms of northeast Arkansas and the southern tip, or "panhandle," of Missouri. This area has a population of about two and one-half million people.

Major Memphis interests are its wholesale and retail firms, its banks and insurance companies, its railroads and their shops, and its cotton carnival, so symbolic of the city's wealth. Memphis is a major cotton market and one of the leading hardwood markets of the country. Its manufactures are almost exclusively local or sectional in nature.

Below Memphis, several smaller cities share the jobbing trade of the river bottoms section. Greenwood (Miss.) serves the Yazoo delta, and Vicksburg and Natchez are important river crossings.

Cities of the Western Cotton Belt

The western Cotton Belt has its full quota of large and small cities, noted mainly for their new and clean appearance, their

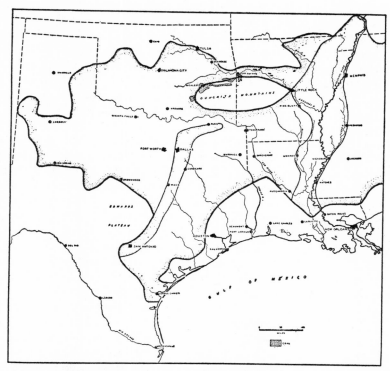

FIG. 50. Cities of the Western Cotton Belt and Mississippi River Bottoms. The cities of Texas and Oklahoma are new and most of them are growing rapidly. Oil, gas, cotton, and beef cattle are the basic economic interests, and these activities are reflected in the economic character of the cities. Western Cotton Belt cities are commercial centers whose interests lie largely in trade and transportation. Industrial development is not extensive. The processing industries, such as petroleum refining, cottonseed oil extracting, and meat packing are important, but most of the industries are purely local in type. In the Mississippi River Bottoms section the largest city is Memphis, important as a cotton market and wholesale center for an extensive area in the northern Cotton Belt. There are few river cities in the Mississippi River Bottoms section because nearly all river-bank sites are subject to flood.

highly developed commercial interests, and their relative lack of national types of manufacturing. Good soil and an expanding cotton industry have made these cities grow commercially. Natural gas for heat and power has kept them clean, and the oil and gas industries have brought them sudden wealth. To the traveler, these cities appear busy and prosperous with their new buildings, wide streets, cotton gins, and oil refineries. The Gulf Southwest has grown remarkably in recent years because of the western extension of cotton-growing and the phenomenal output of mid-continent oil. Its cities show the effect of this recent growth.

Largest and most important of the cities of the western Cotton Belt are Dallas, Fort Worth, San Antonio, Oklahoma City, Little Rock, and Shreveport. In addition, much of the section is served by the two major cities of the Gulf coast: New Orleans and Houston. With the exception of Dallas and Fort Worth, all of these cities are located near the margins of the Cotton Belt Region, and all of them have interests other than cotton. The list of genuine cotton cities includes a large number of scattered smaller centers. All of them, large and small, are definitely commercial. Above all, they are trading and financial centers, cotton, wheat, and cattle markets. Their manufacturing industries are either local in nature or concerned with processing the products of neighboring farms, mines, and forests. National types of manufacturing have not been developed. The manufacturing output of the entire western Cotton Belt is only about 1¼ per cent of the national total. Petroleum refining, woodworking and meat packing are the leading industries, all of which process local raw materials for national distribution. In addition, there are hundreds of local machine shops, bakeries, printing establishments, and similar institutions catering to the needs of the local population. The wealth of the cities of the Gulf Southwest is derived almost entirely from commerce.

Cities of the Northern Hills.—The strip of foothills which surrounds the Ouachita Mountains and extends westward into central Oklahoma has produced five medium-sized and small cities whose interests reflect the diversity of their trade territories. Oklahoma City, the largest of these, is a commercial center whose activities are divided among cotton, wheat, and petroleum. Oklahoma City occupies a crossroads position in American agriculture. To the north and west lie the nation's greatest wheat fields, and to the south and west its greatest cotton fields. To the east lie the Ouachita Mountains and associated hills from which come a variety of minerals and whose slopes are grazed by cattle or occupied by a diversity of crops. At Oklahoma City the one-mule cotton plow meets the labor-displacing wheat combine, and the steer from the western ranch competes with the razorback hog of the subsistence farmer from the Ouachitas. To complete the confusion, Oklahoma City sits on one of the most productive gas and oil deposits of the country.

As a result of this diversity of interests, Oklahoma City shops carry a wide variety of merchandise, and her streets throng with many types of people. Most important of her interests, however, is cotton, for the Oklahoma City trade territory includes the rich red prairies of the southwest portion of the state. Bustling Tulsa has much of the oil trade and serves as headquarters for many refining companies. One of the newest and most attractive cities of the Southwest, Tulsa is growing in importance as a commercial center for eastern Oklahoma. Enid and Wichita serve near-by portions of the Wheat Belt. To the east, a number of small cities serve the hill country. But in the Oklahoma cotton belt, Oklahoma City reigns supreme.

East of Oklahoma City, Muskogee and Forth Smith (Ark.) share the trade of the Arkansas Valley. Both are essentially trading centers. Furniture and glass are manufactured in Fort Smith. Farther down the Arkansas River, Little Rock and Pine Bluff are commercial centers for the central and southern parts of the state of Arkansas. Little Rock occupies a strategic site at the eastern end of the Arkansas Valley which traverses the Ozark-Ouachita highland. Railroads following the southeast edge of the highland cross the east-west routes at this point and make Little Rock an important railroad center. Railroad shops, cottonseed oil mills, and woodworking plants are the most important manufacturing establishments.

Texarkana and the North Louisiana Cities.—Lumber, gas, and oil are the principal non-agricultural interests of the cities which lie between the Ouachita Mountains and the Gulf coast. The most important center is Shreveport, second city of Louisiana and trading center for the northwest portion of the state. Shreveport manufactures oil-well machinery, glass, and lumber products, but its largest employers are its commercial establishments. North of Shreveport, Texarkana has similar economic interests, and to the south, Alexandria falls in the same classification. Monroe is important for the manufacture of carbon black (from natural gas) and also has pulp and saw mills.

Cities of the Texas Cotton Belt.—The most important cities of the Texas cotton belt are located on or near the famous Black Prairie. Beginning near the northern boundary of the state, this row of cities starts with Dallas and Fort Worth and is extended south by Waco, Austin, and San Antonio. The same general soil type also surrounds Corpus Christi, where the Cotton Belt reaches the Gulf of Mexico. East and west of the Black Prairie, the cities are smaller. Abilene and Lubbock serve the newer cotton area of west-central Texas, and Wichita Falls is a center for the cotton and range-livestock area of the northwest. Northeast Texas is served by several small cities, most important of which is Tyler.

The simultaneous growth of Dallas and Fort Worth, situated only forty miles apart and in an area where large cities are relatively rare, has been a source of considerable dismay to students of economic geography. Dallas has grown larger and is more important both commercially and industrially than Fort Worth, but it has by no means become the dominant city. Dallas is the home of the Federal Reserve Bank of the southwest region and is the most important banking center of the South. In wholesale trade, Dallas vies with New Orleans for first place among southern cities. Its trade territory includes a large section of the cotton and oil country of northeast Texas. Dallas stands as one of the major commercial cities of the United States. Its department stores take pride in high-quality merchandise and the latest styles in women's apparel. Fort Worth has developed similarly, but in that city the traveler somehow feels more of the flavor of the West. Dallas has been a favorite location for national firms desiring to locate branch houses and branch manufacturing plants in the Southwest. These plants turn out many varieties of foods, as well as automobiles and miscellaneous machinery. Dallas ranks second to Houston among Texas cities in manufacturing.

South of Dallas and Fort Worth, the city of Waco serves the central Black Prairie. Like its sisters to the north, Waco is not highly industrialized, but is supported by its commercial institutions. Austin, state capital and trading center, has important limestone workings.

San Antonio has long been the center for the sheep and cattle industry of the Edwards Plateau, and many of these interests maintain headquarters there. The city is also important as an army air base and aviation training school and is popular as a winter resort. San Antonio has extensive trade relationships across the international boundary in Mexico. The tourist finds the city intriguing from the historic Alamo to the modern air-conditioned business houses.

The remaining Cotton Belt cities of Texas are of this same commercial type. There are numerous cotton gins, frequent cotton-seed oil mills and occasional oil refineries. Lumber becomes more important toward the eastern border of the state and in this section economic development resembles that of adjacent Louisiana and Arkansas. National manufactures have barely penetrated the area; there are few metal-using, textile, or clothing industries. Productive soils and rich mineral resources are the basic factors in the prosperity of the cities of the western Cotton Belt.

SUMMARY

Industrialization and the South.—In summary, the Cotton Belt, although not an industrial region, has two sections in which manufacturing has achieved greater than local importance. These are (1) the southern piedmont, now the home of nearly two-thirds of the nation's cotton-textile industry, and (2) the Birmingham Coal and Iron District, with about 4 per cent of the national production of iron and steel. These specialized sections account for about 50 per cent and 10 per cent, respectively, of the manufacturing output of the region. Large southern cities in the Cotton Belt or the Coastal Region are not industrial centers. Even Birmingham is not so highly industrialized as the average city of its size in the Manufacturing Belt. Atlanta, Memphis, Dallas, San Antonio, and the other large cities of the region are almost entirely commercial in nature.

For the future, there seems to be strong reason to anticipate further industrialization for the South. The textile industries have shown the way, and textile-using industries such as clothing and automobile tires may follow. The South offers an abundance of cheap labor and relatively low living costs, and is eager for industrialization. In addition to cotton, the South has large resources of growing timber recently attractive to the pulp and paper industries. Possibilities for the expansion of timber-using industries are discussed in connection with the Gulf-Atlantic Coast Region, whose timber resources exceed those of the Cotton Belt. In all discussions of industrial migration, it must be remembered, however, that southern summers are long, hot, and humid, and that the climate has never been considered as productive of human energy as that of the colder regions farther north. When and if industry comes to the South it is likely to look with greatest favor upon those higher, hillier, and cooler sections of the northern margins of the Cotton Belt and adjacent Appalachian-Ozark Region.

REFERENCES

The best statements of general economic geography for the southern states are contained in Parkins, *The South;* in Odum, *Southern Regions;* and the WPA series. Read "Industrial South," in *Fortune* for November, 1938, for a good review of southern industrial development. Consult *Minerals Yearbook* for recent statistics of mineral production. Read C. L. Hodge, *The Tennessee Valley Authority* (American University Press, 1938), and various reports of the Tennessee Valley Authority for information concerning that development.

QUESTIONS AND PROBLEMS

1. What are the major functions of most southern cities? Why are many of the most important ones located outside the Cotton Belt?
2. Describe the stages followed in taking cotton from the field to the textile mill. How many times is it handled? What business institutions have arisen to care for each of these stages? Where are they most likely to be located?
3. What types of business enterprises not concerned directly with the handling of cotton are important in southern cities? Why are they important?
4. Why did the textile industries grow to importance in the piedmont? Do you expect this section to remain the national center for the cotton-textiles industry? Why or why not?
5. Why does the piedmont have many small cities, but few large ones?
6. How does the typical piedmont city differ in appearance from cities of similar size in other sections of the Cotton Belt? Why?
7. Why did Atlanta become an important city?

8. What are the prospects for the further development of manufacturing in the Middle Tennessee Valley?

9. What circumstances led to the development of Birmingham as an important city? Do you expect it to become greater? Why or why not?

10. Why are there so few cities along the Mississippi River south of the mouth of the Ohio River? Do these factors help explain the importance of Memphis as a regional commercial center? What other factors must also be considered?

11. Why do many Texas cities appear "new and clean"?

12. "Three important income sources, not one, distinguish the Western Cotton Belt from the eastern sections." How does this broader economic base affect the functions of the cities of the western section?

13. What functional differences appear between Dallas and Fort Worth? between Oklahoma City and Tulsa? In what ways do these differences reflect variations in environment and history?

14. What are the advantages and disadvantages of the Cotton Belt as a location for manufacturing industries? How do these factors vary from one section of the region to another?

CHAPTER XVII

THE APPALACHIAN-OZARK REGION—AGRICULTURE

Geographic and Economic Diversity.—The broad area of hills which rises from the Atlantic coastal plain on the east as the Appalachian Highland and stretches westward to terminate in the Ozark and Ouachita mountains of Missouri and Arkansas is the most highly diversified geographic region in America. This diversity is both physical and economic, for the section contains all forms of topography from river flats and open plains to rocky peaks and forested plateaus. Its economic life varies from that of the self-sufficing mountaineer farmer at the remote end of a rocky trail to that of the industrial worker at his machine in some of the largest cities of middle America, or the coal-miner busy at his work of furnishing a great industrial nation with fuel. Yet through all this diversity runs a distinct thread of continuity. These people, after all, dwell in the hills. Their hills are green with the verdure of spring and ablaze with its autumn colors. Chasms and canyons are indeed rare, but valleys there are by the score, and if ever a part of America has developed a hill and valley culture, it is in this region. Few stretches of broad prairie encourage transportation and the development of regionalism. Commerce rather is restricted to the valleys and is made sufficiently difficult to discourage long journeys. Such an environment tends to keep trading areas small and encourages the development of agriculture on a self-sufficing basis. On the river plains and the occasional patches of limestone prairie, transportation is easier and these areas have developed a true commercial agriculture, definitely specialized in cash crops such as tobacco, fruits, and vegetables. But the section as a whole is aptly described as one of general farming with larger and larger percentages of the farm production devoted to family living as one penetrates the more remote and rugged sections of the Ozark and Appalachian highlands.

Topography and Soils.—The region as a whole contains four general types of topography. (1) Smallest in area but first in commercial importance are the narrow flood plains of the rivers.

These bottom lands contain some of the best soil and have given rise to the largest cities. River plains are nowhere very extensive, however, and generally constitute only narrow ribbons through a sea of low hills. (2) A second distinctive type of soil and topography occurs in the small detached areas of limestone soils of which the most notable are the Blue Grass district of Kentucky and the Central Basin of Tennessee. In both these areas the topography is relatively smooth and the soil is productive—approaching in fertility the prairies of the Corn Belt to the north. Surrounded by clay hills of much lower fertility, these areas appear to the traveler as garden spots in a land whose soil generally requires the best human efforts to make it return a living. (3) Outside these relatively productive but areally restricted areas of river plain and limestone prairie, the hill and valley topography predominates. The hills vary in steepness and fertility. (4) The intervening valleys have floors which may cover thousands of square miles as in the Appalachian valleys of Tennessee and Virginia or, more typically, a few acres as in the thousands of small valleys which mark the region from one end to the other. The soil of these valley floors ordinarily is alluvial and in many instances highly productive. Railroads crossing the region have penetrated a few of the valleys and as a result most of the commercial agriculture and nearly all of the larger towns of the hill country are located in them. Modern highway development has followed a similar pattern.

The Hill and Valley Civilization.—The hills, dominant feature of the area, are far from being unoccupied. Their soil is heavy, often stony, and usually of low fertility. But ordinarily the rainfall is adequate and the land will grow corn and a wide variety of other crops. Production is not heavy and the marketing of bulky farm products is all but impossible. But here is a living, even though it consists chiefly of corn bread and side pork; and a very large percentage of these hills is in farms. Amazingly steep farms, some of them, with the use of wheeled tools quite out of the question. One farmer told me that they always plant potatoes with rows running down the hills. "Planting them is a little hard," he told me, "but in the fall when potatoes are ripe, all we have to do is open the lower end of the row and the potatoes just roll out." Erosion, of course, is terrific and most of these hills have long since lost their topsoil where cultivation has been attempted.

But a living is still there, even if it is a scanty one. Furthermore, the "mountaineer" loves this country even if he hates its land. It is nearly impossible to persuade him to move out. The Appalachian-Ozark region promises long to remain one of the "problem areas" of America. A national policy of land conservation demands that most of the hills be retired from cultivation and returned to grass and trees, but a mountaineer civilization, deeply rooted in these clay knobs, is reluctant to abandon the land.

Land Utilization.—The great diversity which marks the surface features and soil of this section of the United States has made it impossible to prepare anything more than a generalized map of land-use areas. These areas, defined by the United States Department of Agriculture, are based upon conditions of topography and soil, and were designed to show recommended practices in the use of land for agricultural purposes. These data have been made the basis for Fig. 52, which shows the three principal types of areas of the region: (1) the fertile limestone prairies, notably (a) the Blue Grass district of Kentucky, (b) the Highland Rim of Indiana and Kentucky, and (c) the Nashville Basin. These are areas of "proved agricultural merit," with good soil and generally smooth topography. (2) The hills and mountains comprise a second group which is in sharp contrast to the first. Much of the land is too steep for ordinary agriculture and the heavy soil is generally of low fertility. These are the areas of subsistence farming, the districts in which much land should be returned to forest and pasture. These statements apply to (a) the southern Appalachian Highland and (b) the Carolina Mountains on the east, (c) the Ozark-Ouachita uplift on the west and to most of the intervening hill lands. (3) The third group occupies an intermediate classification. (a) In the north it consists of a large area of rolling or hilly land, a zone of general farming which marks the shifting southern boundary of the Corn Belt. Soils are of moderate fertility in these sections of southwest Missouri and southern Illinois, Indiana, and Ohio. (b) In the same classification is the outer Blue Grass, a hilly rim around the rich inner area. It also includes (c) the Appalachian valleys of eastern Tennessee and western Virginia, and (d) the Virginia-Carolina piedmont. These moderately productive areas are generally suited to commercial agriculture but problems of erosion and soil fertility make farming less profitable than in the grain belts farther north and west.

It is upon these types of land that the resident of the Appalachian-Ozark region lives. Considered minutely, county by county or valley by valley, it is a region of continuous contrast, a rapidly shifting panorama to the tourist who lays his route through these hills. Yet they clearly dominate the life of the region from one end to the other. Their deteriorating soil has depressed farm production and their steep slopes have restricted transportation and prevented the general use of farm machinery. But to the natives these hills are not hostile. Certainly no large group of Americans loves the land as fervently as do these "mountaineers." A sentimental attachment, born of the fact that the hills mothered him and his parents and grandparents, dominates the attitude of the native. The hills have always been friendly to him. In their own poverty-stricken way they have shared what wealth they possess. In their forests he has found game and wild fruits and nuts, as well as fuel and building materials. And he has never gone hungry, for there is almost never a crop failure. Yet the crops are always small and there is never a large excess for sale. The house is often poorly furnished, the farm poorly equipped, the people poorly dressed, and the children poorly educated, for it takes money to provide all these things.

Through it all, however, is a sort of security that must not be underestimated. No fickle friends are the hills. So long as you cooperate, you are fairly certain to go on living much as you always have, and you do not worry much about fluctuations in markets, or about mortgages or freight rates, or depressions, or bank failures. Your friends the hills, eternally poor as you yourself, promise freedom from many of the ills which bedevil the lives of farmers in the great rich farm belts of surrounding regions. Those who would move these "underprivileged" hill-residents off the poor land and out onto the fertile flats must bear in mind that they are also thrusting them into one of the most hazardous businesses in modern America—commercial farming.

Agricultural Land Use.—In the Appalachian-Ozark section, the "typical" farm is thus located in the hills, with a wide variety of crops and livestock, and a large percentage of farm production devoted to the living of the family. Thousand of farms, of course, are not "typical." Where soils are better and cheap transportation

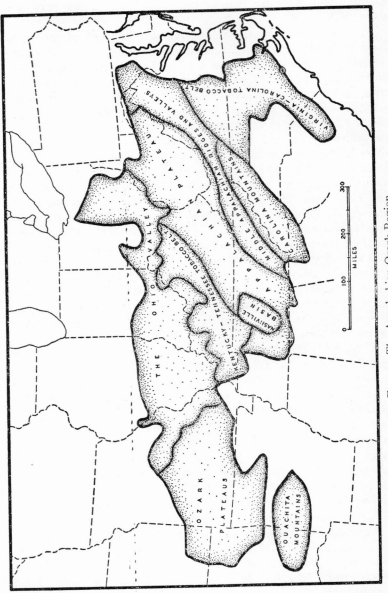

Fig. 51. The Appalachian-Ozark Region.

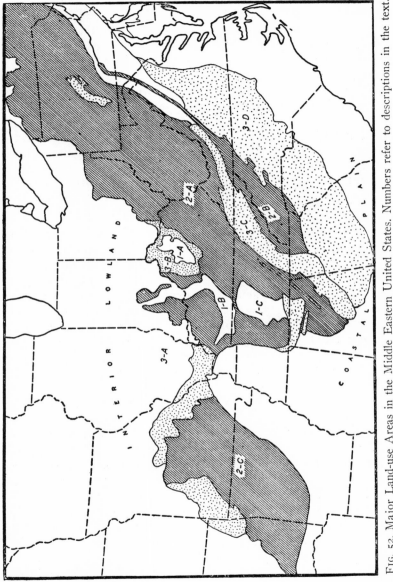

FIG. 52. Major Land-use Areas in the Middle Eastern United States. Numbers refer to descriptions in the text.

is available, or where near-by mining centers or commercial cities are to be served, specialized farming on a commercial basis has become common. These farms often specialize in the growing of tobacco, fruits, or vegetables, and if near the cities they have turned to dairying or truck gardening. These areas of specialized commercial agriculture are of great importance to the economic development of the region, and worthy of separate treatment in any study of its economic geography—for these are the areas of high cash incomes among farmers.

Division into Sections.—The Appalachian-Ozark Region consists of seven major sections, whose boundaries are determined principally by factors influencing land utilization. As in most agricultural regions, these factors represent differences mainly in topography and soils, and their influences are felt largely in the types of farming which have been undertaken. The sections are:

1. *The Ohio Valley Hill Section* of Illinois, Indiana, and Ohio, and adjacent sections of Kentucky. This section borders the eastern Corn Belt and is distinguished from it by less productive soils and a lesser specialization in corn and livestock. It is a section of general farming.

2. *The Ozark Section,* embracing (a) the Ozark Plateau, and (b) the Ouachita Mountains. This section has much rough land and is the home of the general farm with a major dependence upon livestock and hill pasture. Self-sufficing farms occupy the rougher districts.

3. *The Kentucky-Tennessee Tobacco Belt,* which has much good soil and a highly developed crop-specialty type of agriculture.

4. *The Appalachian Plateau,* an area of rough topography, hillside farms of the self-sufficing type, and a great wealth of coal in the middle Appalachian coal fields. This division also includes the fertile Nashville Basin of Tennessee and the less productive "Highland Rim" which surrounds it.

5. *The Carolina Mountains,* eastern wall of the Appalachian Highland, generally rough and unproductive, and the home of a subsistence type of agriculture.

6. *The Middle Appalachian Valleys,* a series of long, narrow structural folds which are the central portion of the long structural valley that splits the Appalachian Highland from

the Hudson River to Birmingham. Here relatively fertile soils and good transportation have encouraged commercial farming along diversified lines.

7. *The Colonial-Virginia Tobacco Belt,* which occupies much of the piedmont and a portion of the adjacent coastal plain in Virginia and North and South Carolina. This district is dominated by bright flue-cured tobacco, and is classed as a crop-specialty area.

Each of these sections could also be split into a number of subsections, each with its own peculiar set of criteria. In regions of such diverse topography, it would be necessary literally to study each small valley separately to obtain an accurate picture of economic development. Such minute consideration is obviously impossible in a general discussion. The sections as here delineated should provide the reader with at least an introduction to economic life in the most highly diversified region in the United States. In combination, these sections form a vast region which includes nearly one-third of the eastern half of the United States. It is a region of diversity, surrounded by regions of specialization. On the north, west, and south, its boundaries are the great commercial-farming areas of America, the Corn, Wheat, and Cotton belts, while on the east it forms the boundaries of the Manufacturing Belt and the Gulf-Atlantic crop-specialty area. The region as a whole is the most nearly self-sufficing major area in the United States, yet it contributes much to the nation's economic life, providing nearly all the tobacco, half the coal and an important share of the manufacturing output of the nation. The complexity of this economic pattern can be understood only by considering separately the agricultural development in each section.

THE OHIO VALLEY SECTION

Adjoining the Corn Belt on the south and east, in southern Illinois, Indiana, and Ohio, lies a belt of hills drained very largely by the northern tributaries of the Ohio River, and known as the Ohio Valley. Practically all of its land is in farms and most of these farm lands are above the national average in productivity. Yet nature was less kind than in the grain belts to the north and west. The last great glacial sheet left no mantle of smooth fertile soil for it did not extend southward into these sections.

Terminal moraines lie somewhere near the line which separates this section from the Corn Belt.[1] Thus these lands are older geologically, and more highly dissected. Their original vegetation was timber which added little to the fertility of the topsoil. Erosion has been more widespread and more destructive than in the smoother and colder grain belts. For this is a land of hills—old plateau remnants in eastern Ohio, worn-down plains in southern Illinois and Indiana. Its clay soils are only moderately productive, and only a few favored silt-covered river bottoms are capable of growing "bumper" crops. Yet, with a long growing season and ample rainfall, farming can be carried on almost everywhere with a fair measure of success. A wonderful variety of crops can be produced and there are many attempts to introduce specialty farming in the form of fruit, vegetables, tobacco, poultry, and dairying.

Meat Production.—Much of the Ohio Valley is natural pasture, too steep to cultivate because of the danger of erosion. As a consequence, the growing of meat animals is the chief occupation on farms from one end of the section to the other. Many sheep are raised in eastern Ohio, an area which has long been famous for its wool-producing Merinos. For many years, Ohio has grown more sheep than any other state east of the Mississippi River, and about half of these have been pastured on the eastern Ohio hills of this section.

Sheep have also become increasingly important in the neighboring Blue Grass area of Kentucky in recent years (see section on Kentucky-Tennessee Tobacco Belt). These areas (the eastern Ohio hills and Blue Grass) are the leading eastern centers in sheep production, each area marketing 3 or 4 per cent of the national total. Farmers in the Ohio hills cling to wool-producing Merinos, and regularly market 5 per cent of the nation's clip of wool. Kentucky raises dual-purpose animals marketed chiefly for their mutton. Sheep are less important in the western two-thirds of this section, but here there are large numbers of cattle and hogs.

Although the Ohio Valley has fewer hogs per square mile than the Corn Belt, the density of its cattle population is nearly as great. The most important beef and pork area is in the lower Wabash River Valley, whose flats grow excellent corn for feed. Sale of

---

[1] The boundary between the Ohio Valley section and the Corn Belt follows approximately the southern and eastern limit of the last glacier (Wisconsin) across Ohio, Indiana, and most of Illinois.

these meat animals constitutes the chief source of farm income; but nowhere in the Ohio Valley does meat production dominate farming as it does in the neighboring Corn Belt. The interests of Ohio Valley farmers are more diverse. Other sources of farm income have greater relative importance.

Cash Grain.—Although there are no significant cash-grain areas in this section, much wheat is grown and it often constitutes the second-ranking source of cash farm income. Yields are good, but fields are small and there is little chance to use power machines. Nearly every farmer, however, is likely to have a few acres of wheat. When grain prices are high, this section turns rapidly to wheat and adds materially to the national production. Ordinarily it will grow more wheat per acre than the Great Plains states, but lower production costs favor the wheat belts. Practically the entire output consists of winter wheat. The heaviest production is in southern Illinois.

Other important sources of farm income are poultry, dairy products, potatoes, fruits, and vegetables. All of these items are of greater relative importance than in the Corn Belt. Cheap feed and comparatively mild winters favor poultry production, and nearness to eastern markets means higher prices for the products. Specialized poultry farms are found throughout the section, but most of the output comes from the ever-present non-specialized general farm.

Dairying.—Good pastures and feed resources, and the presence of a number of large cities have stimulated dairy farming. Near the cities, especially Cincinnati, Columbus, and Louisville, farmers sell market milk, and the usual local dairy areas have developed in these localities. Farmers living at greater distances sell butter fat to near-by creameries. Nearly every farmer (or his wife) milks a few cows.

Specialties.—Fruit and vegetable production calls for more highly specialized establishments and in such lines the general farm is less in evidence. Fruit farms and truck or vegetable farms provide the bulk of these products for the section. In addition, the production of perishables has tended to become concentrated in definite areas because of the necessity for local packing houses and canneries. Apples are the most important fruit particularly in three areas in southern Illinois whose production normally aggregates about 3 per cent of the national commercial crop.

Among the vegetables, tomatoes are the most popular. Central Indiana is the most important location, the production being split about equally between the Corn Belt and the Ohio Valley section. Indiana normally is the leading state in the production of tomatoes for canning.

In the Miami Valley of southwest Ohio, the growing of cigar leaf tobacco has long been important. Recent years have brought a marked decline in production, however, and tobacco no longer is a dominant source of farm income. Much tobacco is also grown in one or two areas adjacent to the Ohio River in southern Ohio and Indiana. These have been included in the Kentucky-Tennessee Tobacco Belt.

In summary, the reader will not go far astray in picturing the typical Ohio Valley farm as a veritable department store of farm production; not a very great or prosperous department store, but a truly non-specialized institution nevertheless. He should picture this farm as composed of several types of land—grassy hills, rich "second bottom," sandy "first bottom" which often overflows, stony patches, timbered patches, and all combinations of these. He should picture a barnyard with dairy cows, beef cattle, sheep, a few hogs, mules or horses (or both), and a flock of chickens; and a field of corn, a smaller patch of wheat, a field of clover or of timothy hay, and perhaps one or two other crops. Then he should picture the farmer turning as many of these products as possible into cash, and canning, preserving, or storing the remainder. Here, then, is a non-specialized general farm, whose manager, if successful, is a jack-of-all-trades or a wizard. But he eats well, his risks are well distributed, and he is as likely to miss the depths of an economic depression as to fail to reap the fortunes of prosperity.

Spread these farms thickly among the hills from one end of the Ohio Valley to the other. Here and there add a specialized establishment, a farm devoted to poultry, dairying, vegetables, fruit, or tobacco, and you have a fairly accurate picture of the agricultural development of the Ohio Valley.

THE OZARK SECTION

The belt of hills which constitutes the Ohio Valley section extends westward beyond the Mississippi River to terminate in the Ozark Highlands of southern Missouri. Differences in land utilization, rather than differences in topography or soil, dictate the separation of these two sections at the Mississippi River. Physically, they have much in common.

The Ozark section consists of (1) The Ozark plateaus, a large area of maturely dissected plateaus which cover most of those portions of the state of Missouri lying south of the Missouri River, and additional plateau-like areas in adjacent Kansas and Arkansas. The surface of these plateaus ranges from nearly level to rough, but there are few areas of strong relief. In southern Missouri, the plateaus merge with and become (2) the Ozark Highland, a mountainous area which strongly resembles the Blue Ridge and occupies a small section in northern Arkansas. Here there are many steep slopes and much waste land. Separated from the Ozarks by the narrow cotton-growing valley of the Arkansas River, (3) the Ouachita Mountains belong both physically and economically to the Ozark group. Ouachita (from the same Indian word as Wichita) landscapes are dominated by steep parallel ridges and narrow intervening valleys having a dominantly east-west direction. Here also there is much waste land and transportation facilities are poorly developed.

Soil qualities throughout these areas vary enormously, although the section as defined contains practically no soils of the highest grade. In general, the soil becomes poorer as the topography becomes steeper. Most of the waste land is found in the two mountainous districts and in a half-dozen stone-strewn counties of southeast Missouri known as the "Ozark Center." In these areas less than 40 per cent of the land is in farms, the remainder being largely in national forest.

Outside these poorer areas, more than three-quarters of the land is in farms. This percentage is about the same as in the Ohio Valley section. Outer Ozark soils are apt to be moderately productive except on the steeper slopes where erosion has long since taken its toll. In general, the best soils are in the northern and western parts of the Ozark plateaus—those districts nearest the Corn and Wheat belts.

Climatically, the Ozark-Ouachita section resembles the Ohio Valley, except that it is somewhat warmer. Rainfall ordinarily is ample, and the winters are mild enough to permit the growing of a variety of fruits. The growing season is generally too short for cotton.

This plateau section differs from the Ohio Valley not so much in natural environment as in economic development. The difference is expressed chiefly in the smaller number of important agricultural products and the correspondingly stronger emphasis upon meat-animal production. In most portions of the Ohio Valley section, 20 per cent or less of the farm income is derived from the sale of meat animals and wool. In Missouri, on the other hand, approximately one-third of the farm income comes from these sources. This statement applies to all portions of the section except the three rugged areas in which most of the farming is of the self-sufficing type. The Ozark plateaus pasture many cattle, and many districts grow enough corn to fatten them for market. Grass-fed Ozark cattle go to the Kansas City market as stockers and feeders; corn-fed Ozark steers go directly to packing-house markets, chiefly in Kansas City, East St. Louis, and Chicago. Hogs are common, but of less relative importance than cattle. Sheep are found occasionally on the rougher pastures, but are seldom a major farm interest. Approximately half the farm land is in pasture. Corn is the leading crop throughout the section and ordinarily occupies more land than all other field crops combined. Wheat is grown extensively along the western margins of the district (in Oklahoma and Kansas). Occasional cotton fields are found in some of the lower valleys of the Ouachitas and southeastern Ozarks.

Other sources of farm income are of lesser importance than meat animals. Fruit is grown throughout the section but it is important in only one small district in the northwest corner of Arkansas. Here apple orchards occupy much of the land, roadside stands serve cider to tourists, and vinegar factories are found in the towns. Less than 1 per cent of the nation's apples are raised in this district, but they provide about one-sixth of the local farm income. The Ozarks also grow potatoes (but not enough to supply the state of Missouri) and a few miscellaneous vegetables. Dairy products and poultry are important sources of farm income, regularly ranking next to meat animals in importance. Except near St. Louis and Springfield, however, no areas have yet become specialized in dairy farming. Poultry-raising is widespread, but is usually carried on in connection with other farm activities. Fried chicken is a standard item in local menus. Restaurant keepers apologize if they are unable to serve it.

The Ozark farm is truly of the general type, but its income is derived from three major sources, meat animals, dairy products, and poultry. In the more productive and accessible districts, 20 or 25 per cent of the farm production is devoted to family living— about twice the percentage found in the Corn Belt. Meat animals account for an additional 30 or 35 per cent, and two additional items, dairy and poultry products, each average from 10 to 15 per cent of the total. Grain, fruits, and vegetables contribute the remainder. In the more rugged sections, self-sufficing farms predominate, and from one-third to one-half of the farm output is consumed by the family. But here also meat animals are the principal source of the cash income. The hilly general farm characterizes the agriculture of the Ozark-Ouachita section.

The Kentucky-Tennessee Tobacco Belt

Tobacco Soils.—A belt of limestone soils extends from southern Ohio southwestward across Kentucky and into northwest Tennessee. These soils vary in fertility but all of them are at least moderately productive and all originated from limestone. The belt includes the famous Kentucky Blue Grass section, a rich and nearly level area in north-central Kentucky famed for excellent pastures and fast horses, but also a leading center for the production of Burley tobacco. Less famous but of comparable fertility are the rolling lime sink lands of the Highland Rim, a narrow belt which extends southward from the Indiana prairies into west-central Kentucky and southwestward to the tobacco-farmed areas near Hopkinsville, in Kentucky, and Clarksville, in Tennessee. (Fig. 53.) The limestone soil areas constitute the backbone of the Kentucky-Tennessee Tobacco Belt which produces annually from 35 to 40 per cent of the national tobacco crop. In addition to this backbone of limestone soil, the Tobacco Belt also includes adjacent areas such as the fertile outer Blue Grass, additional cherty lands of the Highland Rim, and a portion of the moderately hilly Mississippi Silt Loam Uplands, which lie between the Mississippi and Tennessee rivers in extreme western Kentucky and adjacent Tennessee. There is also an outlying tobacco district near Owensboro, Kentucky, on the Ohio River. With the exception of the Mississippi Silt Loam Uplands, all of these districts have considerable areas of limestone soils, and it is on such soils that tobacco is generally grown.

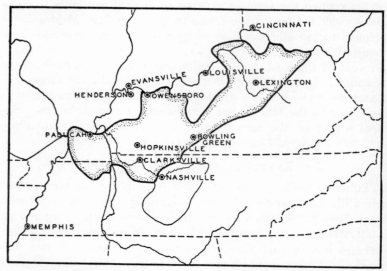

FIG. 53. Kentucky-Tennessee Tobacco Belt. Nearly all the American crop of tobacco is grown in the Appalachian-Ozark region. Tobacco is grown in nearly every section, but the major centers are in the piedmont areas of the Carolinas and Virginia, and the limestone plains of Kentucky and Tennessee. The Kentucky-Tennessee Tobacco Belt occupies some of the richest soils of the Appalachian-Ozark region. The Blue Grass district of Kentucky is the major center, but production is also important along a narrow belt which extends southwest into western Kentucky and Tennessee. This section also includes the western Kentucky coal area, in which most farms are of the general or self-sufficing types, and relatively little tobacco is grown.

The configuration of the Kentucky-Tennessee Tobacco Belt shows marked response to the location of limestone soil areas as mapped in Fig. 52. The cities of Lexington, Bowling Green, Hopkinsville and Clarksville are well located to serve these limestone soil areas which produce most of the tobacco of the Kentucky-Tennessee section. The coastal plain soils of the area south of Paducah have also been used successfully for the growing of tobacco. In what ways has this section been specialized in the growing of different types of tobacco? Where are these types grown? (See pp. 405-407).

Tobacco Types.—From the economic standpoint, tobacco cannot be viewed as a single commodity because of the wide variety of qualities required for use in various tobacco products. In the first place, cigar tobacco differs from all others. Cigar leaf should be thin, and all cigar tobacco should be only mildly aromatic. Cigarette tobaccos, on the other hand, should be highly aromatic, quick-burning, and not heavy. Smoking tobacco is somewhat heavier but is sold in almost every conceivable color and flavor. To complicate matters, practically all tobacco products are blends of different tobaccos, and each manufacturer has his own secret blend and his own system of grading.

It also happens that no two areas grow tobaccos exactly alike. Different fields on the same farm often produce surprisingly varying qualities from the same seed. Then, of course, there is a long list of varieties each of which is supposed to have special merit if grown in a particular locality. These differences are obviously traceable largely to differences in soils. The physical and chemical composition of not only the surface soil but also the subsoil is important. Some tobaccos attain highest development on relatively poor soils, while others demand high fertility; some mature best in sandy soils that drain well, while others need a soil which has good under-drainage but holds moisture well in the topsoil.

Burley and the Blue Grass District.—In the Kentucky-Tennessee Tobacco Belt three leading types are grown. Most important of these is Burley (with several sub-varieties), a light aromatic tobacco developed originally (1864) for use in plug chewing tobacco, but now in general use in the manufacture of cigarettes and smoking tobacco. Between 25 and 30 per cent of the American tobacco crop is Burley and nearly all of this is grown in Kentucky. The phosphatic limestone soils of the Blue Grass section seem ideal for its growth. Burley dominates the northern half of the Tobacco Belt.

In curing, Burley tobacco is ordinarily hung in sheds to be cured only by the drying effects of the air passing among the "hands" or bundles into which leaves are tied at the time for harvest. Hence Burley is designated in the tobacco trade as an "air-cured" tobacco.

Western Fire-cured District.—Other methods of curing are often used on other varieties and in other sections. In the southern portions of the Tobacco Belt, the Clarksville-Hopkinsville and Paducah areas, the leaves are cured by the use of open fires and smoke in a process which differs little in the fundamentals from that taught by the Indians at Jamestown in the early colonial history of Virginia. Fire-cured tobaccos are much heavier than Burley and are grown largely for export. Most of them are grown on the heavier soils. In normal years, four-fifths of this crop is exported. Kentucky-Tennessee fire-cured tobacco goes largely to France, Spain, Holland, Belgium, and Germany. England, formerly a good customer, now prefers the lighter and more aromatic air-cured and flue-cured tobaccos. The fire-cured tobacco sections of the Kentucky-Tennessee Belt normally produce 8 or 9 per cent of the United States tobacco crop.

Central Dark-air-cured District.—Between the Burley and fire-cured districts is an area specializing in dark-air-cured tobacco, which goes largely into the manufacture of chewing tobaccos and snuff. Both the Bowling Green and Owensboro areas grow these varieties, known commercially as one-sucker and Green River. The output aggregates about 2 per cent of the national tobacco production and has declined markedly in recent years because of decreased demands for these types.

Other Land Uses.—Despite specialization, less than 5 per cent of the farm land of the Tobacco Belt is in this crop. Tobacco demands extravagant expenditures of labor, and a family-sized field is seldom larger than four or five acres. The work is done almost entirely by hand, although machines are in use for setting out plants and for between-row cultivation in the early stages of growth. There is much weeding with the hoe, however, and, in addition, all of the topping, suckering, spraying, harvesting, curing, and stripping must be done by hand. The average yield is about 800 pounds per acre and from 350 to 400 man-hours are required to produce it.

With less than 5 per cent of the farm land in tobacco, and enough tobacco planted to utilize nearly all the farmer's time, the remaining acres usually are in easily tended pasture and feedgrains. Pasture predominates except in the very richest areas such as the inner Blue Grass, where farms are smaller and more cropping is done. On the pastures, the favorite animals may be cattle or sheep (as well as horses and mules), depending upon the price ratios for these animals. In recent years, the trend has been strongly toward sheep-raising, and the Blue Grass stands out prominently in recent figures as a sheep-producing area. There are a few hogs, but sheep and cattle are much more common. The animals are sold to packers in near-by cities. Their feed consists largely of corn, grown universally throughout the section.

Here and there one also finds flocks of poultry and herds of dairy cows as well as occasional orchards and vegetable fields. These are not common in the Tobacco Belt, however, and show an average development below that for the nation at large. In the poorer sections (notably the coal country of western Kentucky, near Owensboro, Hopkinsville, and Bowling Green) less tobacco is grown and most of the farms are the self-sufficing type found in the mountainous sections of the eastern portions of the state. Coal-mining dominates the economic life of several communities in this district. Elsewhere, farming is largely on a commercial basis, with tobacco the chief source of income and meat animals an important secondary source.

The Central Appalachian Plateaus and Central Tennessee

This series of hills and mountains includes all of those portions of the Appalachian Highland which lie west of the Appalachian Valley and south of the Manufacturing Belt, as well as a non-plateau hill area with a similar economic development in central Tennessee. Essentially it is a section of steep slopes, poor soil, and self-sufficient farms. It includes only one large area of relatively smooth topography and moderately fertile soil, the Nashville Basin of central Tennessee.

Three Topographic Districts.—Topographically, there is (1) a central backbone of rugged mountain-like country which runs the length of the section, across central West Virginia and western Kentucky and Tennessee. This same backbone extends northeast across the Manufacturing Belt in Pennsylvania and south into the Cotton Belt in Alabama. It is the central feature of the Appalachian Highland, and in these West Virginia, Kentucky, and Tennessee areas it is the home of the most thoroughly self-sufficing agriculture to be found in the United States.

Associated with this rugged central plateau area is a series of less rugged and somewhat more accessible districts which lie roughly parallel to the main plateau and border it on either side. (2) To the west of this belt is a jumbled mass of hills extending southwest from near Pittsburgh, in Pennsylvania, to central Tennessee, where the hills encircle (2a) the Nashville Basin and are known as the Highland Rim. These hills, too, are the location of self-sufficient farms, but they are not so self-sufficient as are those in the higher plateau to the east. (3) On the eastern side the central plateau is bordered by a relatively narrow belt of ridges and valleys which lie between the plateau and the Appalachian Valley. Here the valleys contain substantial areas of good land, and, although subsistence farming prevails, larger percentages of the farm production are grown for market than in the central plateau area.

Thus the Appalachian Plateau section may be characterized as an area of subsistence agriculture, of remote farms and poor transportation. But to this generalization we must quickly add several exceptions: (1) that the degree of self-sufficiency is smallest near the margins of the section and becomes progressively greater as one approaches the central plateau; (2) that in the Nashville Basin and a few other less notable districts agriculture is definitely commercial and may be classified as general farming. (3) To these exceptions must also be added the usual reservations that occasional areas of dairy farming are to be found near the population centers; and that truck gardening, fruit-raising, and crop-specialty farming are important in a few small and scattered farms and valleys.

It is evident that all portions of this section are not devoted to subsistence agriculture primarily because of local differences in topography and soil. Another element has entered, however, and this factor is transportation. In northern West Virginia for example, one is amazed to discover a considerable livestock industry in a country so rough that one would expect to find only self-sufficient farms. The reason is, primarily, the railroad. Railroads came to West Virginia to tap the rich deposits of coal which underlie the state. With rail transport at hand, farmers could abandon hoe culture and turn to producing for the market. Unable to compete with more fertile areas in crop production, West Virginia farmers could still capitalize on their excellent grass. Cattle and sheep are pastured there to be fed on grains from the Corn Belt. A thriving stock-ranching industry, reminiscent of the western cattle country, has been developed. Cattle and sheep are found wherever good transportation is available in this section.

The Nashville Basin appears prominently on maps showing the number of sheep, cattle, and even hogs. The adjacent Highland Rim also has many of these animals. Meat animals are also well distributed throughout the eastern belt of ridges and valleys. In the central plateau, however, they are relatively rare. Nevertheless, they constitute the principal source of cash income throughout the section. After meat animals, the second and third-ranking sources of cash farm income are dairy and poultry products. Very little grain is grown even in the Nashville Basin, which has a larger percentage of cultivable land than any other district in this section.

The reader will discover the striking similarities in the agricultural development of this section and the Ozark-Ouachita upland. In both sections unfavorable topography has led to depleted soils and difficult transportation; but rainfall and temperatures have been favorable to agriculture. Each section has developed a farming system dependent upon a variety of sources of income. The more remote areas in each have become the location of self-sufficing farms from which few products are sent to market; but the more accessible portions have come to sell more farm products and their farms are of the general type. Production of food is not a serious problem; families eat regularly and well. The opportunities for enhanced scales of living, however, are extremely limited.

THE CAROLINA MOUNTAINS

The eastern margin of the Appalachian Valley is marked throughout its length by a nearly continuous ridge of mountains. It can be traced from northern New Jersey southwestward through Pennsylvania and Virginia and into the Carolinas, and is known in all these states as the Blue Ridge. Throughout this entire distance the Blue Ridge is seldom more than ten miles wide and is broken by numerous gaps so that it has become neither a barrier to transportation nor a factor of more than local importance in land utilization.

In the Carolinas and adjacent Tennessee, the Blue Ridge becomes wider, higher, and more rugged, with an average width of more than fifty miles and genuinely mountainous topography. Numerous ridges and individual mountain masses carry various local names, best known of which are the Great Smoky and Unaka mountains of the North Carolina-Tennessee border. In Georgia, the highland again bears the name Blue Ridge. Because of their ruggedness, the southern portions of the Blue Ridge highland have been a significant barrier to transportation. Their area is large enough to have made most of these districts inaccessible to modern transportation, and the soils and topography have further discouraged the growth of commercial agriculture. The Carolina Mountains stand out on any map of land utilization as a section of self-sufficing farms. Their isolation is somewhat less than that of the Appalachian plateau, chiefly because their area is smaller. But the environment is much the same: steep eroded hills, narrow silted valleys, poor roads, much forest, and a climate favorable to agriculture and human habitation.

The Blue Ridge farm resembles that of the Kentucky and Tennessee districts of the Appalachian plateaus. Outside the Great Smoky Mountains National Park, which is not farmed, approximately 70 per cent of all the land is in farms, and on these farms from one-third to one-half the land is in pasture. Cattle and sheep are raised for markets. But there are evidences of specialization. In the basin which holds the city of Asheville, a popular inter-season resort, dairy farming has become important. Northward of this basin, in the valley of the French Broad River, tobacco is grown on many of the farms. Elsewhere meat animals and poultry products are the chief sources of cash income. Little grain is grown for market, although there are many small steep fields of corn used for both food and feed. It is too cool for cotton. Despite such variations from true self-sufficiency, however, the typical Carolina mountain farm is of that type, with from one-third to two-thirds of its output converted into food for the farm family. Economically and socially, therefore, the Carolina mountains are strikingly similar to the Appalachian plateaus, from which they are separated only by the forty-mile ribbon of limestone soil which is the Appalachian Valley.

THE MIDDLE APPALACHIAN VALLEYS

The most striking physical feature of the great geologic uplift which forms the Appalachian Highland is the long structural valley which splits the great highland from one end to the other and separates the Blue Ridge from the Appalachian plateau. This valley can be traced from the vicinity of Birmingham, Alabama, north and east through Virginia and Pennsylvania until it becomes the valley of the Hudson River and Lake Champlain and finally joins the St. Lawrence River Valley near Montreal. Physiographers include its entire length in a single region, but a geographic analysis based upon land utilization must separate the middle sections from the northern and southern extremities. South of Chattanooga the valley grows cotton. North of the Potomac River it is devoted to dairying, and is included in the Manufacturing Belt. In its central portions, the Appalachian Valley, as well as several other adjacent parallel valleys which are included with it in this section, is the home of the general farm, similar in nature to the general farms of the Ohio Valley, the Nashville Basin, and the distant Ozarks.

Topographically, the Appalachian Valley section is marked by (1) a long central valley which stretches throughout the length of the section, and (2) a number of smaller valleys, parallel to the larger one and interspersed with sharp intervening ridges. Most of these smaller valleys are found in the northern half of the section. They are not without local names, most of them famous in American history. In Tennessee, the Tennessee Valley becomes the twin valleys of the Clinch and Holston rivers. Northward, in Virginia, we are in the Civil War-famed Valley of Virginia, which in the northern part of the state becomes the Shenandoah Valley. These valleys merge one with another almost imperceptibly.

Appalachian Valley soils are generally described as moderately to highly productive. They are best in the northern districts, but the entire section is underlaid with limestone, and limestone generally produces good soils in humid climates. Occasional limestone outcrops, especially prominent in the ridges, make scattered areas unfit for cultivation. A great majority of the land is tillable, however, and nearly all of it is in farms. Even the stony areas grow good grass.

The Appalachian valleys have long been a major highway between the Northeast and the Southwest. Pre-Revolutionary War days saw the first of the western pioneers following the valley southward to Cumberland Gap and across the plateau country into "Boone's Wilderness" in Kentucky. Post-Revolutionary pioneers followed this same route by the thousands. In Civil War days the valley was fought over from one end to the other, from Gettysburg in the North to Chattanooga and Lookout Mountain in the South. And today if you travel from New York or Philadelphia to Atlanta or New Orleans, your Pullman or automobile is most likely to follow this route—because it is short, scenic, and without heavy grades.

This very accessibility and the presence of better than average soil have lifted valley farms above the subsistence level and placed them on a commercial basis. But they are generally not specialized. They have the great variety of crops and farm animals to be found in other general farming sections. In the fields are corn, wheat, rye, barley, vegetables, and (occasionally) tobacco. Nibbling on the rich pastures are cattle, sheep, hogs, horses, and mules. There are many chickens and not a few dairy cows—for this section has a number of cities of its own as well as being accessible to the large metropolitan centers of the seaboard.

Such specialization as exists is largely in fruits. The Shenandoah and adjacent valleys of northern Virginia are famous for apples, producing about 8 per cent of the national commercial crop of this fruit. The annual apple festival in Winchester, Virginia, is known throughout the eastern states.

THE CAROLINA-VIRGINIA TOBACCO BELT

The average American now smokes more than one thousand cigarettes each year and his cigarette appetite has been increasing steadily and rapidly for many years. In 1919, he smoked barely half that many, and before the World War he smoked very few indeed. This rapid rise in cigarette consumption has placed new demands on tobacco-growers, and among other things has created from parts of the old cotton and general farming areas of the Carolinas and Virginia a new section specialized in the growing of cigarette tobacco.

Tobacco has been grown on the red hills of the Virginia-North Carolina piedmont for many years, but it did not come to dominate the agriculture of any large section until after the World War. Increased demands extended the area of production until today not only a large strip of the piedmont but also a newer coastal plain area to the southeast is dominated by the crop. South Carolina joined North Carolina, Kentucky, Virginia, and Tennessee as a leading tobacco-producing state. These piedmont and coastal plain areas form a single land-use section, popularly known as the "Bright Tobacco Belt." Their specialty is the bright flue-cured tobacco which goes into cigarettes. The Carolina-Virginia Tobacco Belt grows more than half the nation's quarter-billion-dollar crop of tobacco. North Carolina alone raises more than two-fifths of the national crop.

Distribution of Production.—Within the bright tobacco belt, production is rather evenly divided between the older piedmont of North Carolina and Virginia and the newer upper coastal plain of North and South Carolina. The tobaccos are essentially similar in grade and command about the same prices in the market. Farm specialization is somewhat less in the coastal plain district, because cotton is successful in most of these counties.

In this section the typical tobacco farm is small and usually has not more than ten acres in tobacco. Both cotton and corn occupy larger acreages but their values are considerably below that of the tobacco crop. From 15 to 20 per cent of the farm production is devoted to family living. Prosperity depends essentially upon the price of tobacco, and when there is a large crop declining prices force many of these people on to the relief rolls. No part of the section ever has been extremely prosperous, and living conditions frequently have been undesirable. Increased opportunities for factory work through the coming of textile mills and cigarette factories to the piedmont have helped this situation materially. The section has come to depend more and more on commercial fertilizers. Erosion is a serious problem and many of the most productive farms of past years are now worthless. The most encouraging factor is the continued rise in the national consumption of cigarettes.

SUMMARY—AGRICULTURE IN THE APPALACHIAN-OZARK REGION

The dominant characteristic of Appalachian-Ozark agriculture is lack of specialization. The two tobacco belts are exceptions to this generalization, but they are favored with good soil and relatively smooth topography. Outside these belts, topography discourages machine farming of the grain-belt types and the growing season is not long enough for the other great American crop, cotton. Inferior soils and distance from major population centers have discouraged the growing of vegetables and fruits, as well as the introduction of dairying. But the rainfall is ample and the growing season is long enough for a great variety of crops. Most farms include a variety of land, and to make the most of his plant and equipment the farmer produces a corresponding variety of products. He grows corn and the small grains on the smoother plots and pastures meat animals on the rougher pastures. He sells wheat, poultry, cream, wool, and tobacco to secure cash for his farm operations. If he lives far back in the hills and cannot get these products to market, they are devoted to family living. Thus the self-sufficing farm of the Ozark Highland or the Appalachian Plateau is a blood brother of the commercial farm of the Ohio Valley or Appalachian Valley. They grow about the same crops, and are organized in about the same manner. Only the mountain farm produces for family use rather than for the market. The tobacco belts are the only large areas in which farmers depend extensively upon a single crop.

FORESTS

The Appalachian-Ozark Region was originally entirely in forest. Southern hardwoods covered the higher elevations and in the lower valleys there were good stands of southern coniferous forest. Much of the original forest cover is gone, but the Appalachian-Ozark Region is still the source of nearly one-third of the nation's hardwood lumber. Oak is the leading variety, followed by yellow poplar and red gum. Oak is taken from all sections, but the greatest sawmill activity is in the Appalachian Highland. Softwoods are less important and consist mainly of southern yellow pine taken from sections bordering the Cotton Belt. The region accounts for about one-ninth of the annual lumber cut of the United States.

REFERENCES

The Appalachian-Ozark Region is well established as a social area in *Six Rural Problem Areas* (WPA Research Monograph No. 1). Review physiography and soils in references cited in the Introduction. M. R. Campbell, *The Coal Fields of the United States* (U. S. Geological Survey, 1922), is a standard source for information concerning qualities and locations of the coals of the nation. Most of the references cited in Chapters XIV-XVI also are useful for this chapter, inasmuch as parts of the region are located within the southern states.

QUESTIONS AND PROBLEMS

1. What characteristics of the Appalachian-Ozark area make it possible to define it as an economic region? How do these characteristics differ from those used in defining the Cotton Belt? In what ways are they alike?

2. Why is the Appalachian-Ozark Region marked by extreme areal diversity in its land-use pattern?

3. How does the natural landscape of this region differ from that of the Rocky Mountains? Why do these hills hold a much larger population than mountainous areas of the western states?

4. How does the Ohio Valley section differ in natural environment and human use from the Corn Belt Region to the north? Under what conditions might this section become a part of the Corn Belt?

5. What is "general farming"? Why is it the most common type of farming in most sections of the Appalachian-Ozark Region? How does general farming differ from the self-sufficing type? Why is the latter type also common in some sections of the region?

6. What types of native vegetation prevailed in the Appalachian-Ozark Region? To what extent has this vegetation affected the economic development?

7. What natural conditions are best suited to tobacco culture? What social conditions?

CHAPTER XVIII

THE APPALACHIAN-OZARK REGION—
MINING AND CITIES

Mining

Geologists state that practically the entire Appalachian-Ozark Region shows evidence of upheaval in the distant geologic past. During this process the rocks of the region were warped and twisted and the whole area was lifted above the surrounding ancient sea. Millions of years of erosion followed these uplifts and exposed numerous deposits of minerals which the heat and pressure of the early disturbance had created. The Appalachian-Ozark Region contains practically every mineral known to man. Unfortunately, most of these are too poor in quality or too deficient in quantity to make it profitable to mine them. The actual list of mineral resources is nearly as long as the entire American list, but the group of products having national economic significance is relatively small. Coal is the dominant mineral and accounts for nearly three-fifths of the total value of mined products for the region. Petroleum and natural gas, lead and zinc, limestone and clay account for nearly all the remainder. In the aggregate, the Appalachian-Ozark Region accounts for about one-seventh of the mineral output of the United States.

Mining Districts.—Mining is of sufficient importance to dominate the economic life of four districts of the region. Largest and most important of these is (1) the Middle Appalachian Coal District of southern West Virginia and adjacent portions of southern Ohio, eastern Kentucky, eastern Tennessee, and western Virginia. This district mines more than one-third of the nation's bituminous coal and includes several counties in which mining is the dominant occupation. (2) The second-ranking mining area includes the most productive coal fields west of the Appalachian Highland. These are the coal fields of southern Illinois, western Indiana, and western Kentucky, which normally produce from 9 to 10 per cent of the nation's coal. Both the remaining mining districts are in the Ozark section. These are (3) the Tri-state zinc and lead area of Missouri, Kansas, and Oklahoma, which is the nation's leading zinc-mining area, and (4) the southeast Missouri lead district, the most important American source of lead.

Other minerals outrank lead and zinc in value, but their production is so scattered that they cannot be said to dominate any particular area. Natural gas is important in West Virginia, eastern Ohio, and western Kentucky; and petroleum is found near the northern boundary of the region in central Ohio, Indiana, and Illinois, as well as in eastern Kentucky and West Virginia. Stone is quarried in nearly every state, and is especially important in the Bedford building-stone district of southern Indiana. Lime is a valuable product in Ohio and Missouri, and south-central Tennessee produces a fifth of the nation's phosphate rock. Good deposits of pottery clay are widely distributed. Nearly all of the national production of bauxite ore comes from mines located near the margin of the Ouachita Mountains southwest of Little Rock, Arkansas. Fluorspar from mines in southern Illinois and western Kentucky accounts for 95 per cent of the national output of this valuable steel-furnace material. In the aggregate, these scattered minerals are very important, but they bring to no section the economic importance which coal, zinc, and lead give to the four major mining districts of the region.

The Middle Appalachian Coal District.—This coal district includes the central sections of the great Appalachian province which reaches from Pennsylvania to Alabama. Its great length causes this province to fall within three regions: the northern fields are in the Manufacturing Belt, the southern fields are in the Cotton Belt, and the central fields are in the Appalachian-Ozark Region. A brief description of the origin and distribution of the coal beds of the entire province is given in Chapter XXII, "The Eastern Coal Province." In that discussion the northern fields are separated from the central district on the basis of both geography and economics. Geographically there is a distinct break between the Pennsylvania and northern West Virginia fields on the north and those of southern West Virginia, eastern Kentucky, and adjacent areas on the south. (A similar break separates these central fields from the southern district. See Fig. 54.) Economically, the north Appalachian coal industry differs from that of the central district in that it sells coal primarily to near-by industries while Central Appalachian mines market their product over a broad area. The major portion of the coal of western Pennsyl-

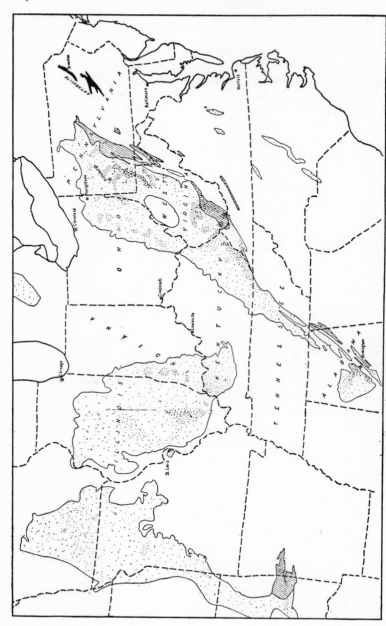

FIG. 54. Coal Fields of the Eastern United States. The most productive areas are stippled. Hatched areas contain semi-bituminous coals, and the solid black is anthracite.

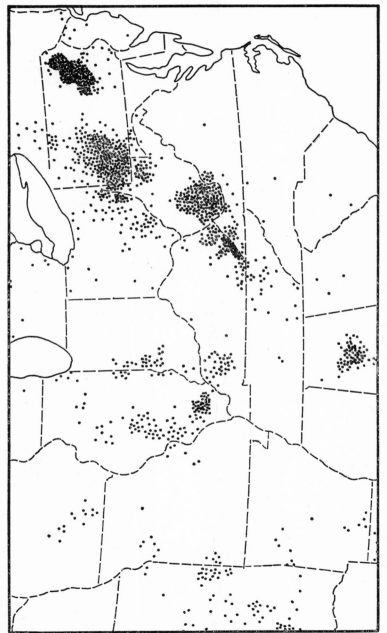

vania and northern West Virginia is burned within one hundred miles of the mines. The central Appalachians have very few industries and no large cities, and coal from these fields is sent long distances to market. A large portion goes to tidewater at Hampton Roads and Baltimore for distribution along the Atlantic seaboard. Large tonnages travel to Toledo and other Lake Erie ports to make return cargoes for iron-ore boats. Railroads haul most of the remainder westward to feed industrial furnaces in the upper Mississippi Valley and for domestic and commercial heating over that same area.[1]

The resident of Chicago, Des Moines, or St. Louis generally has a choice between Illinois coal or a higher-priced "eastern" coal. When he buys "eastern" coal, it is most likely to come from either southern West Virginia or eastern Kentucky, seldom from fields farther north. Middle Appalachian coals have acquired an excellent reputation among householders, because most of them produce much heat with little or no ash or smoke.

The distribution of coal-mining in the Middle Appalachians is indicated in the map of bituminous coal production (Fig. 55). This map shows that the heaviest tonnages come from West Virginia and eastern Kentucky. The Virginia and Tennessee production is considerably less. The district also includes the coal fields of southern Ohio. In 1936, these areas ranked as follows in percentages of the national output:

	Per Cent
Southern West Virginia	21
Eastern Kentucky	9
Southern Ohio	3
Virginia	3
Tennessee	1
District total	37

The Central Appalachian coal district has no large cities and few manufacturing industries. Its coal, like its natural gas and oil,

---

[1] In 1936, roughly two-thirds of the coal loaded at tidewater and at Lake Erie came from the Middle Appalachian District, and about two-thirds of the eastern coal moving into the Mississippi Valley came from Middle Appalachian mines. The North Appalachian District produced 39 per cent of the nation's coal, the Middle Appalachians only 37 per cent. Yet the Middle Appalachians shipped twice as much coal outside their own district as the northern fields. These figures indicate the essential economic differences between the nation's two leading coal districts.

is sent to other districts for consumption. As a consequence of this
specialization, mining is the dominant occupation over a large portion of the agricultural section previously described as the Appalachian Plateau.

**The Coal District of Illinois, Indiana, and Western Ken-
tucky.**—The third-ranking coal district of the United States occupies the southern two-thirds of the state of Illinois and smaller
adjacent portions of Indiana and western Kentucky. Like the great
Appalachian coal province, these fields belong to no particular
economic region. Coal is found under the rich prairies of the Illinois Corn Belt as well as the less fertile shale soils of western
Kentucky and southern Indiana. These fields are well located to
serve the Middle West and the western portions of the Manufacturing Belt. Their combined output averages about 17 per cent
of the national production of bituminous coal, of which approximately two-thirds comes from mines in the Appalachian-Ozark
Region. (The remainder is assignable to the Corn Belt.)

Coals of the central United States are of generally lower rank
than those of the Appalachian province: they are "softer," having
more volatile matter and moisture, and less fixed carbon. Usually,
too, they have more ash. Geologists attribute these differences to a
more quiescent geologic history. When the Appalachian Highland
was being formed, the coal seams were subjected to great pressure
because of the folding of the rocks. This pressure drove out much
of the volatile matter and water, compressed the remaining fixed
carbon, and made these coals much harder than when originally
formed. In the Upper Mississippi Basin, on the other hand, no
mountains were formed after the coal was laid down, and compression of the beds did not occur. Hence the coal is usually found
in relatively horizontal beds and when mined it shows high percentages of moisture and volatile matter.

Qualities.—Coals of southern Illinois and adjacent Indiana and
Kentucky were subject to compression by the forces which created
the Ozark Plateau. These coals are of generally higher rank than
those farther north. Fig. 56 shows the general limits of the coal
region and the number of resident coal-miners in 1930. The greatest concentration is found in (1) southern Illinois and (2) western Kentucky, whose coals are of high type, averaging from 45
to 50 per cent fixed carbon; (3) the Belleville field near St. Louis,
and (4) western Indiana, whose coals contain from 40 to 45 per

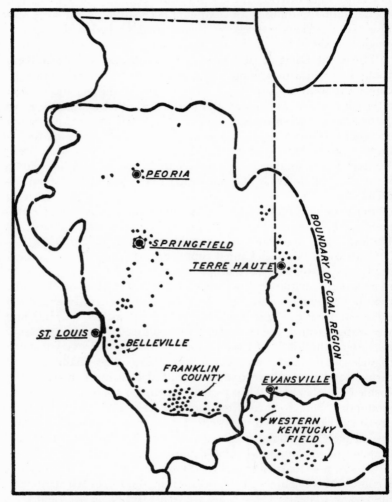

F IG. 56. The Coal-mining Area of Illinois, Indiana, and Western Kentucky. This coal area stands second only to the Appalachian coal region in the production of bituminous coal. The heavy line indicates the boundary of the coal deposits, and the dots show the relative importance of different fields. The northern portion of this coal area lies within the boundaries of the Corn Belt region.

cent fixed carbon; and (5) central and northern Illinois, whose
coals are of lower type, averaging 40 per cent or less of fixed
carbon.

Location.—It is apparent that two factors govern the distribution of mining activity in the Illinois-Indiana-western Kentucky
district. (1) The major activity occurs near the southwest margins
of the district where coals are of high rank. (2) Important mining operations are found in the somewhat lower-quality coals of
the remainder of the district. These latter coals are mined primarily because of their superior location with reference to markets. The Indiana mines, as well as those near St. Louis and in
northern Illinois, are enough nearer industrial markets to offset
the lower quality of their products.

Mining Centers.—The most famous coal mined in the Middle
West comes from Franklin County, Illinois. Here and in adjacent
Williamson County, coal-mining definitely dominates the economic life. Elsewhere in Illinois agriculture is generally more important. In western Kentucky, the leading mines are located in
Hopkins and Muhlenberg counties. Indiana coal production is concentrated in the vicinity of Terre Haute.

Markets.—Mid-westerners generally prefer southern Illinois
coal for domestic heating, and for these uses it competes directly
with higher-priced coals from the Appalachian fields. Other coals
from the district are in general use by industry and the railroads
and for commercial heating. Illinois coal for railroad use finds its
way as far west as Montana. Much Indiana coal is used by the factories of the northern part of the state. Western Kentucky coal
finds a good market in western Tennessee and Kentucky and
southern Missouri. In normal years, Illinois ranks third among the
states in coal production, with between 10 and 12 per cent of the
national output. Indiana, farther down the list, accounts for 4 per
cent of the national production.

The Tri-state Zinc and Lead District.—The sedimentary
rocks of the Ozark-Ouachita uplift are highly mineralized. Nearly
all the metallic minerals as well as coal and a number of clays are
known to be present. Not all of these exist in commercial quantities, however, and present mining operations are confined largely
to lead, zinc, coal, and bauxite. Of these the most important is zinc.

Scattered broadly over an area which stretches 150 miles west
from Springfield, Missouri, and south to the Arkansas River are

approximately one-half of the zinc reserves and nearly one-third of the lead reserves of the United States. Here in the Ozark foothills, dozens of small mines are operating on the nation's largest reserve of lead-zinc ore. The operations are often disappointing, for the ore is of low grade and a small drop in price turns profits into losses. Average Tri-state ores yield about 4 per cent zinc and 8/10 of 1 per cent lead.[2] Zinc is thus the primary product.

In the zinc industry the Tri-state district is known as a "marginal" area, whose output increases rapidly with a rise in price and tapers off with equal rapidity when prices fall. This condition is attributable both to the low grade of the ore and to the prevalence of small operators. The national position of this district thus fluctuates considerably with changes in zinc prices. The price of zinc is also an important barometer of local business conditions.

Despite these difficulties, the Tri-state district has consistently held first position in American zinc-mining for many years. In the years 1930-38, its average output was 36 per cent of the national production. Its lead output is much smaller, averaging about 10 per cent of the United States total.

Zinc recovery follows a pattern similar to that used for other non-ferrous metals. Hoisted from the mine, zinc-bearing rock is crushed, screened, and divided to yield the ore, then roasted and distilled to obtain the metal. Sulfuric acid is a by-product of the distillation process.

The earliest operations in the Tri-state district were in the vicinity of Joplin, Missouri. Deposits here were eventually worked out, and almost all present-day mining activity has shifted westward across the state line into Oklahoma and Kansas—hence the name "Tri-state" area. Recent figures show that 70 per cent of the Tri-state zinc comes from Oklahoma, 26 per cent from Kansas, and the remaining 4 per cent from Missouri. Practically the entire output is taken from five counties clustered about the junction of the boundaries of the three states (see Fig. 57). Joplin, a one-street city of 33,000 persons, is still the economic center of the district. The leading zinc markets are St. Louis and New York. Industry uses zinc for galvanizing, for mixing with copper in the making of brass, for castings, and for dozens of chemical processes.

---

[2] New York ores average 12 per cent; New Jersey ores 19 per cent; Rocky Mountain ores even higher.

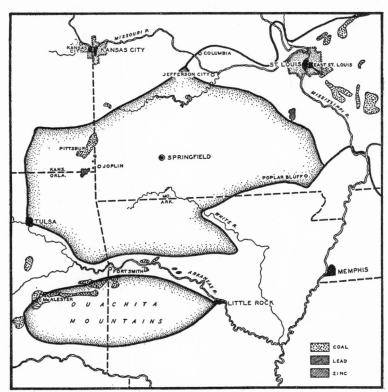

FIG. 57. Cities of the Ozark and Ouachita Sections. Agriculture in these sections is characterized by general farming, which becomes subsistence farming in the more rugged districts of southern Missouri and northern Arkansas. The Ozark section includes the nation's foremost mining centers for lead and zinc. Within the section, cities are not highly developed. Springfield commercial interests serve the western areas. The eastern Ozarks fall within the St. Louis trade territory, and the Ouachita section is served largely from Little Rock and Ft. Smith. The last three cities lie just beyond the borders of the Ozark and Ouachita sections.

The Southeast Missouri Lead District.—It is strange that so little is known about the district which for decades has been the nation's leading producer of lead. It is seldom mentioned in economic geographies and rarely appears on the so-called "economic maps," despite the fact that the southeast Missouri mines were placed in production by the French as early as 1720, and have been in nearly continuous operation ever since. Prime reason for this lack of information apparently is that production is under the substantial control of a single corporation, the St. Joseph Lead Company, a leading producer of this metal. Statistics concerning production are therefore conspicuously absent from many published reports.

The Lead Belt is a small district, not more than twelve miles long and ten miles wide, tucked away in the Ozark foothills about sixty miles south of St. Louis. The ore block really consists of a remarkably thick slab of limestone which lies at an average depth of about 260 feet below the surface. Three or 4 per cent of this limestone, which ranges from 100 to 400 feet in thickness, is an ore known as galena, which itself is a lead sulfide, 86 per cent lead. Operations consist of hoisting the galena-bearing stone to the surface where near-by smelters separate the ore from the refuse, which is known as chat. Underground workings resemble huge subterranean caverns more than ordinary mines. Operations are highly mechanized from the compressed-air drills to the large electric shovels which fill cars to be taken over some of the 125 miles of underground tracks to one of the four shafts.

The metallic content is so nearly pure lead that no attempt is made to extract the extremely small quantities of other metals. The flotation process is used for separation, and the concentrates are shipped to refineries located on the Mississippi River at near-by Herculaneum and at Alton, Illinois.

Despite the disadvantage of low-grade ore and the absence of valuable by-products, southeast Missouri lead mines have been successful. Their success is traced partially to the purity of product but more largely to their nearness to industrial markets. Lead can be shipped from these mines to Chicago or New York for six dollars per ton less than from Rocky Mountain mines.[3]

The "Lead Belt" is confined almost entirely to one Missouri county (St. Francis) and its population is not over twenty thou-

---

[3] These ores average 3½ per cent; Rocky Mountain ores average 10 per cent.

sand. Despite its small size, however, the southeast Missouri lead district has long been the leading United States producer. Its annual output averages about 30 per cent of the national production.

Other Coal Districts.—The parade of Appalachian minerals is led by coal from the Central Appalachians and southern Illinois. Additional smaller tonnages come from several fields located along the eastern margin of the Ozark and Ouachita areas, but these tonnages are less impressive than those originating in the two major districts. The most important Ozark field is south of Kansas City in the vicinity of Pittsburg, Kansas. Many of these beds lie near the surface, and strip-mining prevails. This Kansas-Missouri district mines about 1½ per cent of the nation's bituminous coal.

Summary.—No region of the United States has minerals in greater diversity than the Appalachian-Ozark Region. Production is dominated by coal, which is mined in every state in the region except North and South Carolina. After coal, the leading minerals are petroleum, gas, stone, and clay, but their production is so scattered that no mining districts have appeared. The most important metallic ores are zinc and lead. The Ozark section leads the nation in the production of both these metals.

CITIES OF THE APPALACHIAN-OZARK REGION

Our experience with urban development in the regions discussed thus far leads us to expect the economic organization of cities to reflect in considerable measure the material resources of the areas in which they are located. In regions marked by the geographic specialization of production we have found cities with highly developed facilities for exchange. In regions of more diverse economic development, on the other hand, trade and distribution are not so important. The self-sufficing farm originates few commodities for the exchange economy and has little need for trade and transportation facilities. But in a grazing section, wheat belt, or tobacco belt, little is produced for home consumption and the need for commercial services is maximized.

We have also learned that the location of commercial cities usually reflects important considerations with respect to transportation. Along the seacoasts, cities have arisen opposite good harbors which lie in the path of goods moving in international trade. In the interior, a mountain pass or river valley often serves as a transportation route and makes adjacent locations attractive for commercial development. On the western plains, railroad-building proceeded almost at random and these routes influenced very largely the location of the commercial centers which grew up in the succeeding decades.

The Appalachian-Ozark Region presents sufficient barriers to transportation to have forced railroads and highways generally to follow relatively restricted routes. The Appalachian Highland has effectively discouraged east-west transportation throughout the breadth of the region and, farther west, the Ozarks and Ouachitas have had the same effect. The region is crossed by two important natural highways, the Ohio River Valley and the Appalachian Valley. Both of these radiate in a southwesterly direction from the Middle Atlantic sector. Two north-south passages are important: the Mississippi River flood plain of the western sections and the Blue Grass-Nashville Basin-Middle Tennessee Valley break of central Kentucky and Tennessee. These breaks in the hill country have long been its most important transportation routes and have likewise given rise to some of its most important commercial centers.

An additional commercial factor lies in the fact that considerable volumes of trade move along the boundaries of the region. Adjacent sections of the Corn Belt and Atlantic coastal plain have generally smoother topography so that many railroads have skirted the Appalachian-Ozark Region. These factors have favored circum-regional locations, of which the most important are along the northern boundary (in Ohio, Indiana, and Illinois) and in the piedmont areas of Virginia and the Carolinas.

In the Appalachian-Ozark Region, attempting to determine whether transportation fosters production for exchange or productive capacity attracts transportation facilities is as futile as debating the genealogical sequence of the chicken and the egg. In general, the only important railroads penetrating the rougher areas have been attracted by prospects of a heavy traffic in bituminous coal. A small development of commercial agriculture has taken place along the railroads. The agricultural developments have been further extended in recent years by the construction of through highways. In these sections it is unlikely that the potential agricultural production ever would have appeared sufficient to warrant the construction of expensive transport facilities. In the

Loading West Virginia Coal at Toledo for Shipment on the Great Lakes.
(*Courtesy Chesapeake and Ohio Lines.*)

smoother sections, on the other hand, and along the natural transportation routes, railroad-building was easy and the productivity
of the land more promising. Finally we come to the rugged areas
which have neither coal nor productive soils. They are without
good transportation and their agriculture is of a self-sufficing type.
Such self-sufficing areas have need for few commercial facilities
and have given rise to no cities of prominence. Commercial-
farming and coal-mining areas have achieved larger urban populations, but the major developments have occurred along the
natural transportation routes which cross the region or lie adjacent
to it. In the following discussion, five chains of cities are recognized: (1) an Ohio River chain including Cincinnati, Louisville,
and Evansville; (2) a northern marginal chain which stretches
across central Ohio, Indiana, and Illinois, and ends at St. Louis;
(3) a north-south mid-regional chain which starts at Louisville
and includes Nashville and Lexington; (4) an Appalachian Valley
chain which includes Chattanooga, Knoxville, and Roanoke; and
(5) an eastern marginal chain which begins at Washington, D. C.,
and follows the piedmont south and west past Richmond to the
cigarette towns of North Carolina. These chains of cities include
nearly all the important urban centers of the region. Inasmuch
as the patterns of urban location follow the general arrangement
of agricultural sections used in the preceding chapter, these same
sections are used in the following discussion.

Population Centers.—The Appalachian-Ozark Region includes one great metropolitan center and a half-dozen lesser
metropolises, all of which have marked regional importance. Its top-
ranking metropolis is St. Louis which in 1930 had a population
of 1,294,000 in its metropolitan district. St. Louis is a city of
national importance, the largest between Chicago and the Pacific
coast. The half-dozen regional centers are Cincinnati, Nashville,
Louisville, Columbus, Dayton, and Richmond. These seven cities
carry on most of the region's wholesale and jobbing business
and are its financial centers. In 1935, they and their suburbs carried on two-thirds of the region's manufacturing.

Manufacturing.—The entire region accounts for about 10 per
cent of the national output of manufactured goods. St. Louis is
the leading center, but the most highly industrialized areas are
farther east, in southeastern Ohio. A few cities could be classified
as more industrial than commercial. This group includes Dayton,

Springfield, Mansfield, and Portsmouth in Ohio; Evansville, Indiana; Parkersburg, West Virginia; Lynchburg and Roanoke, Virginia; Winston-Salem and Durham, North Carolina, and a number of smaller cities located generally in the northern and eastern portions of the region. No section is sufficiently industrialized to warrant its inclusion within the boundaries of the American Manufacturing Belt. For the entire region, the urban pattern is definitely commercial rather than industrial. In the following pages, consideration is first given to the cities of the Ohio Valley section, including metropolitan St. Louis.

CITIES OF THE OHIO VALLEY SECTION

Metropolitan St. Louis.—St. Louis is one of the truly great metropolitan centers of the United States. Far-flung commercial interests give it a ranking of eighth among American cities in volume of wholesale trade. Diversified manufacturing industries place the St. Louis industrial area tenth in volume of manufacturing. St. Louis is the home of one of the Federal Reserve Banks, and its financial sphere embraces a large section of the Middle Mississippi and Lower Ohio valleys. In 1930, the St. Louis metropolitan district ranked eighth in size among American metropolitan centers.

The Site.—The site of St. Louis was chosen with an eye to trade. Some years before the Louisiana Purchase, a frontier trading post had been established at the present site of St. Louis. Furs and forest products were coming down the Missouri and Mississippi rivers, and St. Louis, located near the confluence of these rivers, became a thriving village. Soon it was the leading river town above New Orleans and an outfitting center for traders, prospectors, and farmers on their way west. Railroads sought St. Louis because of its influence as a trading center. The city grew with the Middle West, and its commercial interests prospered. Manufacturing industries came with the growth of population and St. Louis brand names became familiar to consumers in all parts of the country.

Manufacturing.—The array of St. Louis industrial products is imposing, but shows no specialization. The industrial area has meat-packing plants (mainly in East St. Louis, Illinois) and there is an imposing output of electrical goods. St. Louis is an important center for the manufacture of shoes, drugs, chemicals,

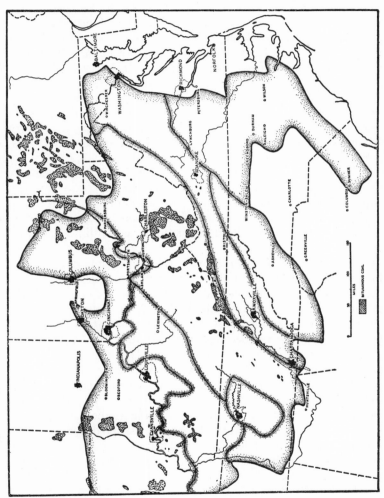

FIG. 58. Cities of the Eastern Appalachian-Ozark Region.

and beer. The largest of these lines (electrical goods) represents only about 6 per cent of the total industrial product. In 1935, the St. Louis industrial area turned out 1.8 per cent of the nation's manufactured goods. About three-quarters of the factories are in the city and its Missouri suburbs, and the remaining quarter are across the Mississippi River in Illinois. Largest of these Illinois cities are East St. Louis, Granite City, Alton, and Belleville.

Despite its importance in manufacturing, St. Louis is essentially a commercial city. As the leading mid-western railroad center outside Chicago, St. Louis is well equipped to serve its trade territory. The wholesale grocery area includes roughly the eastern half of Missouri and southwest quarter of Illinois. Territories served for other lines of goods generally are larger. Much trade comes to St. Louis from the southern Corn Belt.

Population data for the city are misleading because the city boundaries are limited by Missouri statute. In 1876, the state legislature gave St. Louis the status of a county and effectively prohibited the annexation of adjoining suburbs. In 1930, only two-thirds of the metropolitan population lived within the central city.

The Cincinnati-Dayton Area.—In the southwest corner of Ohio, in the fertile Miami Valley, lies a string of cities whose combined industrial and commercial importance exceeds that of any other industrial area of the Ohio Valley. At its southern end lies Cincinnati, frontier river port and the largest city west of the Atlantic seaboard in the decades preceding the Civil War.

Cincinnati won renown in these early days, first as a supply point for western settlers and later as the center to which they brought pork to be cured, salted, and packed in barrels for shipment down the Ohio River. Pork-packing was Cincinnati's first great industry, and the city reigned supreme as the "Porkopolis" of the West until Civil War disorders disrupted the southern market. Cincinnati then lost supremacy in meat-packing and the crown went to a rising center on the shores of Lake Michigan— Chicago. Cincinnati still packs meat, and still uses the Ohio River, but today both these institutions play minor roles in the economic life of the city. Radios, soap, playing cards, clothing, and a long list of machinery and electrical goods carry the name of Cincinnati to all parts of the country.

Cincinnati and its contiguous suburbs turn out more than 1 per cent of the national production of manufactured goods. Yet Cincinnati is truly classified as a commercial city. A great gateway to the South, it has excellent rail facilities. Its immediate trade territory includes most of the productive Kentucky Blue Grass district as well as the lower Miami Valley. Its wholesale and banking interests penetrate not only southwest Ohio but also much of Kentucky and southeast Indiana. To the visitor, the city is one of hills, conservative business, and a strong interest in race horses. To the Central Ohio Valley, it is the center for trade and finance. To the industrial world it is the source of a long list of mechanically complex products. Contiguous to Cincinnati are Norwood, Ohio, and Covington, Kentucky, whose industries resemble those of the major center except for a more pronounced specialization in heavy iron and steel products.

North of Cincinnati, on the banks of the Big Miami River, lie the cities of Hamilton, Middletown, and Dayton; and still farther north in the same valley, the city of Springfield. The entire area thus extends north and east of Cincinnati, along a single watercourse and served by a single set of transportation lines, a distance of about seventy-five miles. These cities, all smaller than Cincinnati, are both more highly industrialized and more highly specialized than the larger city. Their combined industrial output about equals that of Cincinnati, although their combined population is considerably less.

Immediately north of Cincinnati, Hamilton and Middletown are best known for heavy steel products and paper manufacture. Safes, vaults, and automobile parts are typical steel products, and coated papers are the best-known item from the paper industry.

North of Middletown, the traveler reaches Dayton, never with regret, for it is attractively built and located. Dayton was a station on the old National Road, but it impresses the tourist as being as modern as its world-famous computing machines, cash registers, and mechanical refrigerators. Dayton is an important center for the manufacture of complicated light machines, which include a number of automobile parts. The city also has rapidly growing wholesaling and banking interests. Excellent power facilities have helped Dayton's rise as an industrial center.

A leisurely hour's drive up the valley of the shallow Mad River from Dayton is the old city of Springfield. Best known as a pub-

lishing center (chiefly magazines), Springfield also has many
factories turning out auto parts and a variety of machinery.

The Cincinnati-Dayton area of southwest Ohio thus follows
a fairly familiar pattern: one older, larger, major city and a
group of smaller, more highly industrialized outlying centers.
But care must be taken against attaching Dayton and Springfield
too closely to Cincinnati. The other centers, Covington, Hamilton,
and Middletown, definitely belong in the Cincinnati metropolitan
cluster. Their industries are of the heavier types and they classify
as industrial centers with strong dependence upon Cincinnati for
many items of trade, finance, amusement, and professional service. Dayton and Springfield, on the other hand, cannot be so
classified. As stations on the National Road, they had little historical intercourse with Cincinnati, more with Columbus and
Indianapolis. Their industries are not of the heavy type, but turn
out the more highly fabricated products. Dayton, especially, has
its own highly developed trading and financial interests and is in
every sense a "complete" city. Dayton and Springfield are included in the Cincinnati area for geographic rather than economic
reasons. The entire area is a relatively compact industrial district,
whose national importance merits its recognition as such.

Other Ohio River Cities.—The Ohio River has long had
geographic significance. In pre-Civil War days it carried thousands
of emigrants to their new homes in the interior, and before the
railroad era the river was alive with steamboats plying between
Pittsburgh and Wheeling, on the east, and the newer cities to the
west and south. In that era many towns grew up along its banks.
When the railroads came they generally found the Ohio difficult
to bridge and to this day there are relatively few crossings. Pioneer
cities that were fortunate enough to obtain railroad bridges became the present-day "Ohio River Crossings" of the railroad
world. Declining river traffic was more than replaced by rising
railroad tonnages, and these cities generally continued to expand
as commercial centers. Queen city of this group is Cincinnati, but
a similar growth was experienced by Louisville and Evansville, as
well as several smaller cities up-stream from Cincinnati.

Louisville has profited (1) by having the only railroad bridge
across the Ohio River between Cincinnati and Evansville, (2) by
lying on a nearly direct route between Chicago and Atlanta, and
(3) by having a productive agricultural hinterland, including most

of the Kentucky-Tennessee Tobacco Belt. Louisville goes un-challenged as the dominant city of Kentucky both commercially and industrially. Louisville probably is best known for its tobacco market and horse racing, both prime interests in the state of Kentucky. It also is a rising center for the manufacture of cigar-ettes and other tobacco products, as well as for the distilling of bourbon whisky. Railroad shops are important employers. There is a growing output of miscellaneous machinery, but industrial interests are surpassed by trade and distribution.

Evansville occupies a strategic position because of its railroad bridge across the Ohio River to Henderson, Kentucky. Evansville's trade territory is neither so large nor so productive as the Louis-ville area, but the city serves a considerable territory from the corners of the three states which lie adjacent. Evansville manu-factures automobile bodies and parts, refrigerators, furniture, and clothing.

On the Upper Ohio River, several cities lie athwart the coal-carrying railroads which run from the Middle Appalachian coal fields to Lake Erie. Largest of these are Portsmouth, Ohio, and Huntington and Parkersburg, in West Virginia. Railroading is a leading occupation, but there also are important steel-using in-dustries which manufacture a variety of machinery and other steel products. Huntington has extensive commercial interests but the other cities are definitely industrial in nature.

Cities of the Northern Margin.—Several cities have grown up along the old National Road, long the chief competitor of the Ohio River as a route to the Middle West. Today this old high-way is the route of the National Trail (U. S. No. 40). Between its Ohio River crossing at Wheeling, West Virginia, and its Mississippi River objective at St. Louis, the National Trail is generally paralleled by the Pittsburgh-St. Louis division of the Pennsylvania Railroad. The route has given birth to a number of cities, some of which fall within the Ohio Valley section of the Appalachian-Ozark Region, while others are included in the Corn Belt or Manufacturing Belt. Five of the most important ones, St. Louis, Columbus, Terre Haute, Springfield, and Dayton, lie near the border of the Corn Belt. Of these, St. Louis, Springfield, and Dayton were considered in previous sections of this chapter. In Indiana, Indianapolis and Richmond are well within the Corn

Belt. The present discussion is therefore limited to Terre Haute and several cities in eastern Ohio.

Columbus occupies a central position in the state of Ohio, and is the commercial center for a diverse area which includes portions of the Ohio Corn Belt and the hills of eastern Ohio. The Columbus trade territory produces corn and meat animals, sheep and wool, clay products, orchard fruits, and coal. These products provide a varied economic structure, and their productivity is sufficient to give the city a ranking of sixth among wholesale centers of the Appalachian-Ozark Region.

Manufactures are highly developed, mainly along lines of metals and machinery. Columbus metal-using industries manufacture stoves, automobile parts, and a long list of miscellaneous machinery. The city also has meat-packing plants, railroad shops, and printing establishments. As capital of the state and the location of Ohio State University, Columbus has a large white-collar population.

Smaller cities of eastern Ohio include Mansfield, Zanesville, and Newark. These hill cities manufacture machinery, clay products, and glass. In the Indiana section, Terre Haute is a center for the western Indiana coal fields, an important railroad center and manufacturer of machinery and chemicals (such as alcohol and baking powder).

Cities of the Ohio Valley section generally are larger, more closely spaced, and more highly industrialized than those of other sections of the region. Industrialization is especially pronounced in eastern and southern Ohio.

CITIES OF THE OZARK SECTION

The Ozarks and Ouachitas have produced few cities. Industrialization has not extended westward into these areas, and the dominant urban interests are trade and distribution. Trade of the area is divided among St. Louis, Little Rock, Springfield, and Joplin. Little Rock was described in the chapters on the Cotton Belt as a city with interests split between cotton from the Mississippi Bottoms and minerals and forest products from the Ouachitas. St. Louis dominates many lines of trade in the entire Ozark section. Locally, Springfield is an important commercial center, the shopping city for southwest Missouri. Joplin has been described as a commercial center for the Tri-state mining district.

The vacation industry has been expanding in recent years in the

Ozarks, but thus far has produced no important centers. Missourians estimate that the section entertains a million vacation guests each summer. Two large lakes, the Lake of the Ozarks and Lake Taneycomo, add to the attraction of wooded hills, springs, caves, and a variety of other natural attractions.

CITIES OF THE KENTUCKY-TENNESSEE TOBACCO BELT

The major centers of the western tobacco section were described in connection with the agriculture of that area. Louisville and Nashville share the trade of this rich section, but both are outside its boundaries. Among local centers the largest is Lexington, economic capital of the Blue Grass district and important center for the warehousing, selling, redrying, and rehandling of tobacco. Lexington's trade territory includes the most productive part of the state of Kentucky.

NASHVILLE AND THE CITIES OF THE APPALACHIAN PLATEAU

Nashville ranks among the major cities of the South. Its location in the fertile central basin of Tennessee makes it the logical commercial center for that productive area. In addition, Nashville is located near the Tennessee Tobacco Belt and handles most of the trade of that district. Diversity of development in its hinterland is reflected in Nashville's commercial structure. The city handles tobacco, livestock, and other agricultural produce, and is also a center for Tennessee phosphate. It manufactures rayon, cellophane, shoes, and knit goods. Among Tennessee cities, Nashville is exceeded in wholesale trade only by Memphis.

Cities of the Appalachian Plateau section are interested mainly in coal. Most coal-mining cities are small but among them there usually arises an outstanding commercial center. In the Middle Appalachian coal fields, that center is Charleston, West Virginia. Charleston is the leading wholesale center of West Virginia, and its area includes the most productive coal fields of the region. Industry has come to Charleston in the form of steel, chemicals, machinery, and glass. Low-priced coal and abundant natural gas have been potent magnets to furnace-type industries.

CITIES OF THE APPALACHIAN VALLEYS

That the Appalachian Valley has long been an important highway would account for the rise of a number of important cities along its course. Additional factors contributing to the

growth of these centers have been the presence of a large variety
of mineral deposits and of excellent hardwood forests, and a
plentiful supply of labor from the neighboring hills. Appalachian
Valley cities have from the beginning been commercial centers
caring for the traffic which passes through them and acting as
distribution centers for surrounding areas. Given this initial
stimulus, manufacturing industries in wide variety soon began
to spring up. The section is rich in mineral resources, and a number of water-power sites develop cheap electricity. The valley has
abundant limestone, and the neighboring hills yield nearly every
metal known in America. None of the metals is now of national
importance, because the deposits are relatively poor; but mineral
resources have been a potent factor in attracting industrial capital
to the section. These hills, too, have long yielded good hardwood
timber for local woodworking industries as well as a number of
softwoods recently important in the manufacture of rayon and
paper. The climate is healthful, much more invigorating than in
the neighboring coastal areas, and the young people who drift in
from neighboring farms have proved themselves good workmen.
In addition, they have generally been willing to work for low
wages. In the abstract, at least, these factors would seem to point
to successful industrial development for the Appalachian valleys.

Yet these cities have not become great industrial centers. All
of them have factories which turn out a great variety of products,
but none of them have attained the high degree of industrialization which characterizes the Manufacturing Belt or even the
neighboring piedmont section of the Carolinas. The explanation
probably lies in the relatively inferior and unexploited condition of
the natural resources. Middle Appalachian mines cannot compete
with western copper and Lake Superior iron. Local fuel and power,
and even labor, have not been sufficiently cheap to attract truly
large industries.

Perhaps they are better off, these valley cities, with their great
diversity of economic interests. Certainly they escape many of
the industrial pains of the great cities of the North. Perhaps, too,
a great day is just dawning when a coordinated development of
power, transportation, and resources will attract more industrial
capital. Perhaps the great dream of an industrialized Tennessee
Valley may yet come true and stretch the American Manufacturing
Belt down the valleys from eastern Pennsylvania to the steel fur-

naces of Birmingham. A full realization of the industrial resources of the section might very well create such an effect.

But today, and for the immediately predictable future, the cities of Chattanooga, Knoxville, Roanoke, and the long list of lesser urban centers are essentially commercial in character. Their railroads, stores, wholesale houses, and similar commercial institutions invariably outshine their factories in economic importance. These are commercial cities whose industrialization is progressing but has not yet reached a position of dominance.

The Tennessee Valley Group.—The state of Tennessee has four major cities and two of these, Chattanooga and Knoxville, are in the Upper Tennessee Valley, which constitutes the southern portion of our Appalachian Valley section. These cities have extensive trading areas both in the valley and in the adjoining hills. Water transportation and hydroelectric power have been made available through the Tennessee Valley project. While the navigation feature of this huge project is of little immediate consequence, there is no denying the stimulating effect of cheap hydroelectric power, developed where two tributaries of the Tennessee River, the Clinch and the Holston, descend from the mountains. This power should prove attractive to new industries.

At the present time, Chattanooga and Knoxville rank third and fourth, respectively, among Tennessee cities in both manufacturing and wholesale trade. Knoxville manufactures knit goods, quarries and mills marble, and builds furniture. The city anticipates further industrialization as a result of cheap power from Norris Dam. The industrial development of Chattanooga resembles that of Knoxville. Knit goods are important products and there is a long list of steel-using industries whose products include boilers, plows, and miscellaneous machinery. The trade territory of Knoxville includes northeast Tennessee and adjacent portions of Virginia and Kentucky. Chattanooga wholesalers serve the southeast portion of the state and a large area in the productive cotton-growing valleys of northwest Georgia and northeast Alabama.

North of Knoxville, the leading valley city is Roanoke, major city of western Virginia, with the largest rayon mill in the world, large railway shops, and factories devoted to chemicals, furniture, and clothing. Roanoke can be classified as a semi-industrial city.

Its wholesale houses serve the central portions of the valleys of western Virginia.

In review, the cities of the Middle Appalachian valleys generally have more manufacturing than cities of the same size in other sections of the region. For the group as a whole, commercial and industrial interests are nearly in balance. In general, the Virginia valley cities are more highly industrialized than those of Tennessee. Throughout the valley, industrialization has been most pronounced along lines utilizing the section's varied mineral resources. These types of industries have been expanding in recent years.

WASHINGTON, RICHMOND, AND THE TOBACCO CITIES OF THE CAROLINA PIEDMONT

Washington, D. C.—In economics as in politics, the city of Washington belongs to no region but to the entire United States. Its location was the result not of economic advantage but legislative fiat. Its growth and importance have come about not because of a productive hinterland or strategic location, but rather because it is the operating headquarters of the greatest business institution on the face of the earth, the United States government. Washington thus holds a unique position among the large cities of the nation. Its site was chosen by legislators in search of a desirable location for carrying on governmental functions rather than by traders or business men who foresaw a profitable growth of commerce or industry. Other cities could grow large only if they offered economic advantages to the world of business, but Washington prospered to the extent that the functions of government expanded and its payrolls increased. Other cities found competition keen in the race for economic supremacy. Washington possessed a monopoly and its fate has been determined not in the competitive realm of business, but in the popular will of the American people. These historic and functional differences set Washington apart from the other large cities of the nation.

Present-day Washington greets the tourist as a city of great beauty, a well-ordered array of large government buildings, a gridiron of wide streets, a jumble of taxicabs, a welter of young government clerks arguing in the corridors at lunch hour, a city of numerous parks that are small but attractive, a procession of tourists trying desperately to see everything in a single day, a barrage of southern food from restaurants which pop out at you faster than you can choose among them, a swarm of hotels which seem to occupy every street corner, a business district that takes you back home to Dallas, or Tacoma, or Albany, a city with ambitious residential sections and squalid slums, the one large American city in which a tourist feels at home almost as soon as he has parked his car and asked the way to the Capitol building. These impressionistic observations go far to characterize the functions of the capital city. Physically, the city profits enormously by having been planned in advance. Its checkerboard streets, cut by numerous diagonal thoroughfares, minimize the traffic problem, at the same time providing many small parks at their intersections. Washington has many trees, and its buildings follow a comprehensive plan which makes for both beauty and utility.

Economically, Washington has just one important industry, the government. The government payroll is the city's largest, followed by those of the service institutions, of which restaurants and hotels are conspicuous examples. Government business brings thousands of visitors to Washington each month, and the city is a favorite attraction for tourists. It is likewise the headquarters for many organizations whose fortunes are closely connected with the operation of the government. These range from outright lobbying organizations to patriotic societies. Caring for the needs of these large groups of government employees, visitors, and representatives of private interests is the major activity of Washington business establishments. Manufacturing and shipping are developed only far enough to supply purely local needs. There is little wholesale activity. Washington is best described as a governmental city. As such, it resembles more closely the commercial center than the industrial city. But it cannot be compared successfully with any other city in the United States. Washington is a one-industry city, and in that industry it has a national monopoly.

Cities of the Virginia-Carolina Piedmont.—The piedmont area of Virginia and North and South Carolina is divided between the Cotton Belt and the Virginia-Carolina section of the Appalachian-Ozark Region. In the Carolinas, the cotton-growing piedmont is the location for nearly two-thirds of the nation's cotton-milling industry, while the tobacco piedmont turns out two-thirds of the nation's cigarettes. The agricultural boundary between cotton and tobacco is rather clearly defined, but the industrial boundary between textiles and cigarettes is less clear. An east-west line passing through the North Carolina piedmont cities of Winston-Salem, Greensboro, and Durham separates approximately the cotton and textiles on the south from the tobacco and cigarettes on the north. There is some overlapping, however, and like nearly all regional boundaries, the precise line of division must of necessity be somewhat arbitrary. In the industrial totals, the cities of Winston-Salem and Durham are included in the tobacco section, and the remainder of the North Carolina piedmont in the Cotton Belt.

Two of the three leading cigarette manufacturers have their main plants in Winston-Salem, and the third is located in Durham. These large factories dominate the economic structures of their cities and go far to make them the first and second cities, respectively, in manufacturing output in the state of North Carolina. Winston-Salem and Durham account for about two-fifths of the North Carolina output of manufactured goods. Census data justify Winston-Salem's claim of being the leading manufacturing city of the South. That position arises very largely from its preeminence in the cigarette industry. North Carolina produces two-thirds of the nation's cigarettes, and nearly all of these are turned out in the two major centers.

North of the southern boundary of Virginia there is less industrialization and the cities are farther apart. Top-ranking industrial and commercial center for the Virginia piedmont is the fall-line city of Richmond.

Richmond is more commercial than industrial, but its factory production is of greater than local importance. Cigarettes and smoking tobacco are the leading industrial products, but Richmond also has factories devoted to paper, rayon, cellophane, and locomotives.

As a commercial center, Richmond has a strategic location. North-south railroads following the coast are forced inland by the broad estuary of the James River, which is tidal up-stream to Richmond. East-west lines pass through Richmond to reach the harbors of the Virginia capes (Norfolk, Newport News, etc.). The wholesale trade territory includes a large section of central Virginia. Richmond has slightly more than one-third of both the manufacturing and wholesale trade of the state of Virginia.

Southern Virginia has several small cities, the most important of which are Danville, Lynchburg, and Petersburg. These smaller cities resemble Richmond in economic development. Lynchburg manufactures steel, textiles, and knit goods. Danville has textile mills but is better known as a tobacco market. Petersburg manufactures chemicals and tobacco products.

Cities of the upper coastal plain tobacco-cotton district of North and South Carolina are generally small and best known as tobacco markets. Largest of these are Raleigh, Rocky Mount, Wilson, and Goldsboro, all in North Carolina. They are definitely commercial, in contrast to the industrial cities of the adjacent piedmont.

SUMMARY

Cities of the Appalachian-Ozark Region generally have been products of transportation rather than of any of the other forces which lead to industrialization. Transportation is best developed around the outer edges of the region and those margins have given rise to the greatest cities. Interior cities have grown largest where intra-regional transportation facilities are best. The Middle Appalachian coal fields have not been attractive to manufacturing industries, and cities of that district are essentially mining towns (in contrast to those of the Pittsburgh area farther north). The greatest concentrations of both population and industry are in (1) metropolitan St. Louis and (2) the Cincinnati-Dayton district. St. Louis industries are generally of a local or regional character, while those of the Cincinnati-Dayton district are definitely national with a specialization along lines of electrical goods and the more complicated types of fine machinery. Several cities in eastern and southern Ohio can be classed as industrial, and the cigarette towns of the North Carolina piedmont are of the same type. With these few exceptions, practically all of the large and small cities of the Appalachian-Ozark Region are commercial in character, with major emphasis upon the collection, processing, and shipment of farm products and the in-shipment and distribution of goods to be consumed in their own trade territories.

REFERENCES

References for Chapter XVII also apply to this region. Additional information is contained in Leighton, *Five Cities,* and publications of the National Resources Committee concerning the St. Louis area. The University of Ohio studies, *Industrial and Commercial Ohio,* give good factual information concerning that state and its economic development.

1. Write a brief criticism of the text in which you contend that the Cincinnati-Dayton area should be included in the American Manufacturing Belt.
2. What sections of the Appalachian-Ozark Region are most highly industrialized? Do you expect further industrial development? Why or why not?
3. What is meant by the statement that the Tri-State zinc district is a "marginal" area in the zinc-mining industry?
4. Both Missouri and North Carolina have deposits of nearly every important mineral used by man; yet few of these deposits are worked. Why?
5. What natural factors have been important in the establishment and growth of St. Louis as a commercial city?
6. How do you account for the fact that the national center for the steel industry is in western Pennsylvania rather than in West Virginia?
7. What factors are of greatest importance in explaining the locations of the principal Ohio River cities?
8. In what respects do the areas served by the Middle Appalachian and North Appalachian coal fields differ? Why?
9. Why is part of the piedmont in the Cotton Belt and part in the Appalachian-Ozark Region? Compare the types of industrial development found in the two sections. Explain the differences and similarities which appear.
10. What natural traffic routes cross the Appalachian-Ozark Region north and south? Are there any east-west routes? Comment on the areal distribution of cities in the region.
11. Why does a portion of the Cotton Belt separate the Ozark section from central Tennessee?
12. How do those portions of the southern states which lie within the Appalachian-Ozark Region differ from adjacent portions which lie in the Cotton Belt? Consider natural resources, agriculture, manufacturing, and trade.
13. What are the objectives of the Tennessee Valley Authority? Why are they considered desirable?
14. How would you classify the cities of the Appalachian-Ozark Region according to function? How do the leading cities fall within your classification? What facts must be known concerning the natural resources of each city's tributary area in order to appreciate the nature of its economic development?

CHAPTER XIX

THE GULF-ATLANTIC COAST REGION

Location.—In a sense, the strip of seacoast which stretches south from New York Harbor to Corpus Christi Bay might be considered as the area left over after the major farm belts of the interior had taken the land best suited to their needs. The interior boundary of the region is determined throughout its length by the approximate line where cotton, tobacco, or dairying cease to become as profitable as some other type of land utilization. In a more positive sense, however, the coastal region is an area having resources of climate and soil that are different from and often superior to those of regions which form its interior border. In the north—New Jersey, Delaware, and Maryland—the sandy soils do not grow good grass but are excellent for market vegetables. The Virginia coast has good soils for tobacco and peanuts, which are also more profitable than cotton in the Georgia-Alabama section. The Florida peninsula has unquestioned resources for citrus fruits and winter vegetables. Farther west, the coast is generally too wet for cotton, but areas in Louisiana and Texas find profit in sugar cane, rice, and winter pasture for cattle. Thus defined, the region's boundaries are definitely agricultural and may be described either negatively or positively.

The Littoral.—In addition to its distinctive natural resources and agricultural development, the Gulf-Atlantic Coast Region should be distinguished from the interior regions because of its position as the littoral for nearly half the area of the United States. To the interior lie the great cotton, wheat, coal, and petroleum areas, all providing enormous tonnages for ocean shipment. Seaports of the Gulf-Atlantic Region are in the best position to handle this trade. Nearly all of the large cities of the region are seaports whose existence depends mainly upon commerce between the interior and distant parts of the world. The urban economic structure of the Gulf-Atlantic littoral is definitely commercial in nature.

NATURAL RESOURCES

Topography and Soils.—The Gulf-Atlantic Coast Region consists of the newer and lower portions of the coastal plain. (See

445

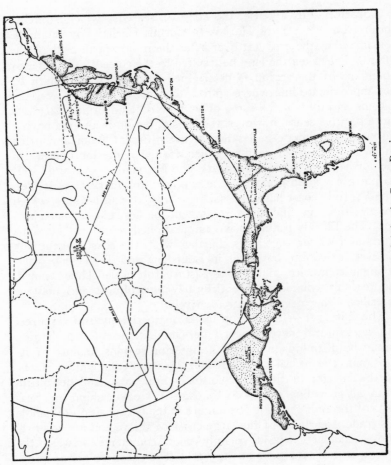

Fig. 59. The Gulf-Atlantic Coast Region.

Chap. XIV.) Its relatively recent emergence from the sea is indicated by large areas of coastal swamp and numerous old beaches whose sands have not yet been weathered into soil. The topography near the coast is monotonously flat, and becomes undulating only where the region extends some distance into the interior. Despite such generalizations, the coastal area has soils in great variety. Some of them are relatively rich and support an economically remunerative agriculture. Others are entirely barren. There is no regular pattern of soil areas. Often a few acres of good soil will be surrounded by pine barrens or deep swamps. The traveler is amazed to emerge from scrub timber into a rich truck-gardening community, only to be back in the timber a few minutes later. Some soils favor one crop, some another, and there is a large degree of community specialization. The resulting land-use map is extremely spotty and defies generalization.

The configuration of the coast has not provided natural deep-water harbors. Throughout the entire length of the region, offshore waters are relatively shallow and wave action has caused the building of bars a short distance off shore. Except for the two northern estuaries, Delaware Bay and Chesapeake Bay, there are no sheltered harbors along the entire coast that are naturally deep enough for modern ships. Everywhere a bar must be cut through, or a river straightened or deepened (usually both). Cutting through silt and sand is a relatively simple operation, however, and shallow entrances have not prevented the development of a large number of good harbors.

Climate.—Except on the Florida peninsula, climate in the coastal region differs from that of the adjacent interior only in being a few degrees warmer, summer and winter, and in having a somewhat heavier precipitation. The Florida peninsula acquires an exceptional climate because it is a peninsula, nearly surrounded by warm water, and because it is thrust far south into the subtropics. Climate, indeed, is Florida's major resource, responsible for its tourist business, citrus fruits, and winter vegetables. Without these three sources of income, Florida could support few people. All of Florida except southernmost Key West has experienced frost at some time in its history, but for practical purposes the entire peninsula is considered frost-free. Rainfall in Florida, as on the entire Gulf coast, is heavy and rather evenly distributed throughout the year. Zephyrs from the warm Gulf drift north and begin giving off rain as soon as they hit the coast. July, August, and September are the rainiest months on the Gulf coast and in Florida, and the month of minimum rainfall is November. The average annual rainfall is about fifty inches.

Florida and the Gulf coast are occasionally visited by the most destructive of storms, the tropical cyclone or hurricane. Hurricanes are large, violent, whirling storms which occasionally sweep in off the Atlantic Ocean. They develop extremely high winds, and on the seacoast usually are preceded by destructive tidal waves. Hurricanes are rare and the chance of the same place being visited more than once in a generation is very small. When one does strike, however, the destruction of vegetation and ordinary wooden buildings is almost complete. A well-developed weather-reporting service now gives coast communities ample warning of the approach of storms. Practically the entire region is subject to hurricanes, but they are most common in Florida and on the Gulf coast.

Winters along the South Atlantic and Gulf coasts are notably mild and favorable to the resort industry. In addition, the entire coastal fringe has developed a summer tourist business based on the attraction of sea breezes, bathing, boating, and fishing. January mean minimum temperatures vary from 25° F. in New Jersey to 61° F. at Miami. The summer range is less. Wilmington, Delaware, has an average July daily maximum temperature of 86° F., but no city on the Gulf or Atlantic coast is more than four degrees hotter than Wilmington in summer. Sea breezes make many beaches popular havens of retreat from the oppressive heat of the interior.

AGRICULTURE

The Gulf-Atlantic coast is a region of crop specialties. From New York Harbor south to Richmond the belt is devoted to market vegetables and poultry, and most sections are farmed intensively. Between Richmond and Albemarle Sound lies the famous Norfolk peanut district. South of Albemarle Sound there is less agriculture but vegetables are the leading source of farm income all the way to Florida. The Florida peninsula specializes in winter vegetables and citrus fruits, while southern Georgia grows peanuts. The eastern Gulf coast has little agriculture but west of New Orleans are areas dominated by sugar cane and rice. Finally, the Texas Gulf prairie is mainly in grass, the only section devoted to animal

THE NATIONAL CAPITAL FROM THE AIR. OFFICE BUILDINGS FOR MEMBERS OF THE HOUSE OF REPRESENTATIVES ARE IN THE FOREGROUND. (*Courtesy American Airlines.*)

A Large Celery Farm in New Jersey. (*Courtesy American Airlines.*)

industries. Thus the region is dominated by specialties throughout practically its entire length. Some corn is grown and, in the south, many farms grow cotton. "Piney woods cows" roam the woods of the entire region and there are a few hogs. None of these agricultural staples rise to major importance in any section of the region.

Division into Sections.—Variations in the type and intensity of agricultural land use make it desirable to divide the Gulf-Atlantic Coast Region into seven agricultural sections of varying characteristics. These are (1) the Middle Atlantic section, reaching from New York to Albemarle Sound, (2) the South Atlantic section, extending from Albemarle Sound to northern Florida, (3) the Florida peninsula, (4) the eastern Gulf coast, stretching from Tallahassee to New Orleans, (5) the Louisiana sugar district, (6) the Piney Woods of Texas and Louisiana, and (7) the Texas-Louisiana coastal prairie. Each of these sections has a distinctive type of agricultural organization.

THE MIDDLE ATLANTIC SECTION

The most highly developed agriculture of the Gulf-Atlantic coast is found on the sandy coastal-plain soils between New York and northern North Carolina. From New York to Baltimore this section lies adjacent to the Manufacturing Belt, and practically the entire agricultural activity consists of providing neighboring industrial cities with market vegetables, eggs, fruit, and dairy products. Generally these are not suburban truck-garden areas attached to a single market, but send their products to a number of cities (see Chap. XXI).

Small, specialized truck and fruit areas occupy the New Jersey district. Nearer the coast, the lands are covered with scrub pine and are known as "pine barrens." The "Del-Mar-Va" peninsula between Delaware and Chesapeake bays is occupied by a variety of agriculture, the most important products being poultry and truck. The eastern shore of Chesapeake Bay has long been famous for market vegetables and potatoes. Delaware has more poultry.

The western shore of Chesapeake Bay is highly specialized in growing tobacco for export. These are light, air-cured varieties not in general demand in the United States. The Maryland tobacco section extends from Annapolis south to the Potomac River. Production averages about 2 per cent of the national tobacco crop.

Between the Potomac and James rivers is a general-farming area, mainly forested and given over to many country estates. Commercial agriculture is not important between these rivers, but there is a growing emphasis upon truck.

South of the James River lies the Virginia-North Carolina peanut belt, whose center is west of Norfolk. This district stands second only to the Georgia-Alabama area in peanut production and produces from 30 to 40 per cent of the national crop. Production consists mainly of the larger varieties. The crop is harvested and threshed by machinery, and many peanuts are roasted locally for national markets. Peanut oil and peanut butter are important manufactured products. This same section also has numerous truck and potato farms, especially near the coast south of Norfolk.

The Middle Atlantic section ends with the Virginia-North Carolina peanut belt. In review, the section is one of marked agricultural diversification. Its soils, which vary in quality from very good to very poor, are well adapted to specialties, and the most successful of these have been market vegetables. Grain-growing sections have generally become specialized in poultry. South of Baltimore, distance from large urban markets has prompted specialization in tobacco and peanuts where soils are adequate. There is also an important production of vegetables for market. The Middle Atlantic section has been devoted to vegetable-growing for many decades. Formerly, the excess production supported an extensive canning industry, but with the growth of eastern cities these surpluses have declined, and with them the local canning industries.

THE SOUTH ATLANTIC SECTION

South of Albemarle Sound the coastal region becomes more marshy and less suited to agriculture. Most of the land is in forest and transportation facilities are not well developed. This section suffers from being too far south to compete with Middle Atlantic truck gardeners, and too far north to grow winter vegetables. Cotton has not been successful and most farms are of the self-sufficing type. The acreage in vegetables is expanding, however, and with the development of fast express service, this coastal area eventually will be able to place its garden crops in metropolitan markets two or three weeks ahead of those coming from the

Middle Atlantic section. At the present time, truck farming is most important in the South Carolina district. The North Carolina and Georgia coastal sections have less agriculture and greater dependence upon forest products and fisheries. Farms in the latter areas are generally classified as self-sufficing and part-time operations.

Back from the coast in southern Georgia and adjacent Florida is a section dominated by tobacco of the flue-cured variety. Of the same general type as the tobaccos grown in the Carolinas and Virginia, it goes mainly into the manufacture of cigarettes. Northern Florida grows small amounts of cigar tobacco. The Georgia tobacco belt also grows cotton, which generally ranks as the second crop, and considerable acreages of peanuts. This section grows from 3 to 5 per cent of the nation's tobacco.

THE FLORIDA PENINSULA

The economic development of peninsular Florida is traceable largely to climate. Without frost-free winters there would be no winter-vegetable and citrus-fruit industries, and very little agriculture. Florida soils are not very fertile and would not generally support an agriculture devoted to staple crops. In searching for clues to the success of Florida agriculture we find the sun, the rain, and the express train. Winter sun, abundant rainfall, and a little commercial fertilizer produce the crops for which Northerners will pay good prices if they are delivered promptly and in good condition. Florida leads the nation in the production of winter vegetables and stands second to California in citrus fruits. These crops, together with the winter tourist business, are the basic sources of income in the state.

Visit Florida during August and September and you will find the state nearly deserted. Oranges and grapefruit will begin to ripen in October and the gardens will be made ready for planting. Tourists begin to arrive in November, and the citrus, vegetable, and tourist businesses run full blast all winter. March brings a slackening in all lines, which continues through the summer. September is the vacation season for the people of Florida.

Agriculture on the Florida peninsula is closely related to surface features. The entire peninsula is low and large areas are in lake and swamp. In general, the fields and orchards have been sandwiched between the non-agricultural areas in a way that is

Fig. 60. Florida Specialty Areas. The agricultural geography of the Florida peninsula is complicated by the presence of numerous lakes, swamps and other non-agricultural areas. Isolated fruit and vegetable patches appear in all parts of the peninsula. In general, however, these specialty areas fall within well-defined belts. The map shows the principal fruit and vegetable belts as well as the areas in which little or no farming is done. The reader should remember that within these belts there are many small areas that are not farmed because of lakes, swamps, or other conditions prohibitive to agriculture.

Many of the areas not devoted to crop specialties and fruits have moderately good pastures which can be made to support a profitable cattle-grazing industry if the problems of disease and insects can be conquered. Notable progress has been made along these lines in recent years.

most bewildering to tourist and geographer alike. The northern two-thirds of the peninsula have a rolling topography near their center which promotes air drainage and encourages citrus culture on the hillsides. Both coasts are flat and have much swamp. The south half of the peninsula is even lower and consists essentially of a narrow rocky spur which extends down the east coast to the Florida Keys, plus the broad expanse of the Everglades and low country which make up the bulk of south Florida.

The principal Florida agricultural district occupies a belt about 125 miles wide which begins near the northeast coast and stretches diagonally south across the peninsula to the middle western coast. Within this belt lie most of the citrus groves and truck gardens.

A second belt occupies the narrow coastal strip of the southern half of the Atlantic coast. This belt, never more than twenty miles wide, extends southward past Miami and is nearly three hundred miles long. The northern portion grows citrus fruits, but the southern three-quarters are devoted mainly to winter vegetables. In addition, there are a small number of truck gardens on the north, east, and south shores of Lake Okeechobee, and a few citrus groves in the vicinity of Fort Myers. Elsewhere the great expanse of waste land gives ample evidence of the unproductive nature of the intervening country. The reader should understand that only small percentages of these "farming" districts are in farms, and that their numerous small lakes, swamps, and rivers generally occupy nearly as many acres as their agriculture.

Florida regularly produces one-third of the nation's oranges and two-thirds of its grapefruit. The fruits ripen in the fall and winter and are marketed over the eastern half of the United States. Among early vegetables, Florida is especially important in tomatoes, celery, and potatoes. There is also an important production of cucumbers (for market), strawberries, grapes, and green peas. The citrus production exceeds truck and small fruits in value. The gross farm production for the state averages between 1 and 2 per cent of the national total.

THE EASTERN GULF COAST

Tourists who travel the coastal highway from New Orleans to Tallahassee encounter much pine forest, many stray cattle, long stretches of white sand beach, but little evidence of agriculture. The few farms of the coastal fringe are generally of a subsistence type with much of the farm income deriving from forestry and fishing. Farming is more successful near the inner borders of the section and here one encounters a few fields of cotton, corn, and peanuts. There is some dairying near the cities. Most famous of these interior sections is the Louisiana strawberry district, located immediately northwest of New Orleans and Lake Pontchartrain. This small area normally produces from one-half to two-thirds of the nation's crop of early strawberries. Except for this northern fringe, the entire section is one of very little agriculture.

THE SUGAR CANE SECTION OF SOUTHERN LOUISIANA

The average American consumes a one-hundred-pound bag of sugar each year. In this bag are about thirty pounds derived from abroad (chiefly Cuba), forty pounds from American possessions, and twenty-five pounds from beets grown in the continental United States. The remaining four or five pounds are grown on the low, marshy soils of southern Louisiana, in a section known popularly as the "Sugar Bowl."

South Louisiana soils and rainfall are excellent for sugar cane. The one great drawback is the annual frost. Tropical countries can grow cane in the same field for a dozen years from a single planting. Louisiana frosts kill the plant and make annual plantings necessary. The additional cost of replanting is so great that Louisiana cane could not compete with the imported product without the benefit of a protective tariff.[1] Production has remained relatively constant in recent years, stimulated to some extent by the utilization of waste stalks for the manufacture of insulation board.

The sugar-cane area is impressive for its many lakes and bayous. Much of the land is not in farms simply because it is under water. The alluvial soils are generally productive and good yields are obtained. The sucrose content is apt to be somewhat lower than in tropical regions because of the curtailed growing season. In the tropics, new sprouts begin to grow from old plants immediately after cutting and they have at least eleven months to mature; but in Louisiana the entire time from planting to harvest is seldom as long as ten months. The sugar district continues to exist very near

---

[1] Not many years ago, the Louisiana cane industry seemed on the verge of being wiped out by the mosaic disease, but more recently this danger seems to have been averted by the introduction of Javanese varieties.

the margin of profitable agriculture, its climatic handicaps just about offset by man-made tariff barriers. The river bottom soils are better adapted to cane than to any other crop. Other sources of income are nearly insignificant. The sugar district is a cash-farming area.

THE PINEY WOODS DISTRICT OF TEXAS AND LOUISIANA

A considerable area of pine-clad hills occupies the portions of Texas and Louisiana which lie north of the coastal prairies. Here the soils are either heavy clay or are sandy and not highly productive. Less than one-quarter of the land is in farms, and forestry is nearly as important as agriculture. Here also is the timbered "Big Thicket," a nearly untouched paradise for big-game hunters. Cotton is grown in the clearings and is the principal crop. Cattle are grazed in the woods. Many farms are of the self-sufficing type. The Piney Woods section is an area of diverse economic interests which might logically be included in the Cotton Belt but for its high percentage of non-farm land, local dependence upon forestry, and relatively high degree of agricultural self-sufficiency. In these respects the area resembles many other sections of the coastal region more than the Cotton Belt.

THE TEXAS-LOUISIANA COASTAL PRAIRIE

The coastal strip which extends westward from the sugar district to Corpus Christi is a monotonously flat grassland whose horizon is broken only by occasional oil derricks and narrow belts of timber along the streams. There are few farmhouses and the landscape reminds one of the flatter stretches of the Great Plains. But the climate is much different. Heavy rainfall produces rank grasses, and there are many swamps and marshes. Toward the interior the land is a little higher and some cotton is raised. In reality, however, the coastal prairie has just two important agricultural products: rice and beef cattle.

The Texas-Louisiana Rice Belt occupies most of the coastal section between the sugar district and Galveston Bay. Here a combination of abundant water (surface and artesian) and rich muck have been utilized for rice-growing by large-scale machine methods. Low rounded dikes separate the fields and these are constructed so that planting and harvesting machines can go over them. Seeders such as are used in the wheat fields are used to plant the crop. Growing plants are flooded in the Oriental manner and water flows slowly from one field to another by gravity. When the plants reach maturity, fields are drained. The ripened grain is harvested and threshed by machinery which again resembles that in use on wheat farms. The United States produces considerably less than 1 per cent of the world's rice. Generally, however, there is a surplus for export. The Texas-Louisiana district produces about 60 per cent of the United States crop. Texas is the leading state in rice production, with about 40 per cent of the annual output.

Outside the rice district the chief dependence is upon beef cattle. The prairies are valued for winter pasture and often carry many cattle from the Great Plains through the winter. Grass was the native vegetation of the coastal prairie. Much of it is sufficiently nutritious to fatten cattle for market.

In review, the agricultural pattern of the coastal region is marked by local specialization, generally in specific crops. Recapitulation discloses local areas specialized in truck crops, poultry, tobacco, peanuts, citrus fruits, winter vegetables, strawberries, sugar cane, and rice. In their respective lines, these sections achieve national importance, but when compared with the farm output of the great interior farm belts, the entire agricultural production of the Gulf-Atlantic Region is not very impressive. There is much waste land and in most sections a considerable dependence upon incomes from forest products. Too humid for most staple crops, the Gulf-Atlantic Region is not in direct competition with the nation's major farming regions.

THE FISHING COAST

Fish are plentiful off the Gulf-Atlantic coast. The wide continental shelf extends seaward well over a hundred miles in most places, and its waters are shallow enough to support the vegetation so necessary to marine life. The number of varieties of fish caught runs well into the hundreds, but the list is headed by shellfish, most important of which are Chesapeake Bay oysters and Gulf of Mexico shrimp. Thousands of tons of inedible menhaden are seined and manufactured into oil and scrap, and there is a large catch of red snapper, "sea trout," and flounders, all famous as sea food. The Gulf-Atlantic coast has nearly one-quarter of the United States' hundred-million-dollar fishing industry.

Oysters are taken from the shallow waters of nearly every section of the Gulf-Atlantic coast, but the major oyster beds are in Chesapeake Bay and the Gulf waters off Louisiana, Mississippi, and Texas. Oysters are gathered off the bottom with long fork-like pincers. On shore, shells are opened, the oysters removed, iced, and rushed to markets over the eastern two-thirds of the country. A few are canned and cooked, but nearly all are marketed fresh. Tradition confines the eating of oysters to fall and winter months (the months with "r" in their names), but with modern refrigeration there is little reason why all of us should not follow the fishermen's practice of eating oysters the year round. Oyster shells accumulate in white piles around fishing villages. Rich in lime, the soft shells are sometimes used to surface country roads, occasionally are shipped out for agricultural or industrial uses. About half the region's oyster production comes from Chesapeake Bay, and one-fifth from the Gulf of Mexico (mainly Louisiana and Mississippi). The remainder is divided about equally between southern New Jersey and the South Atlantic coast of the Carolinas and Georgia. The entire region accounts for four-fifths of the national oyster catch.

Shrimp rank second to oysters in the Gulf-Atlantic catch and in most years their value is nearly as great. This shellfish inhabits only southern waters and about two-thirds of the catch comes from the Gulf coast, the remainder largely from eastern Florida and Georgia. Nearly two-fifths of the national catch is taken off the shores of southeast Louisiana. Eastern Florida, Georgia, Texas, and Mississippi rank next in order. Unlike oysters, the bulk of the shrimp catch is packed in cans, cooked, and sold as canned goods. Canneries are located in all the important shrimp-fishing centers.

Other shellfish consist mainly of crabs and clams. Lower Chesapeake Bay is the major center for crabs, but there is an important minor center off Louisiana. New Jersey and Virginia catch most of the clams.

Other fishery products begin with the bulky menhaden, most important off the western shore of Chesapeake Bay and the shores of middle North Carolina and southern Delaware. Menhaden fisheries require relatively elaborate handling and processing equipment on shore and for that reason there are relatively few market centers. These inedible fish have a low value but enormous tonnages are handled. Fertilizer, soap, oil, and glue are among the eventual industrial products.

The nation's sponge fisheries are concentrated off the west coast of Florida, near the city of Tarpon Springs. Divers with sharp knives separate the sponge from its moorings at the bottom of the shallow water. Industrial substitutes have depressed the market somewhat in recent years, but Florida sponges still represent about 1 per cent of the national fishery output.

Of all the swimming fish taken for food, the most important are the squeteague, or sea trout, which are found along the entire coast, the west Florida mullet, the Atlantic coast flounder, and the east Gulf red snapper. Most of these are marketed fresh, but some are smoked or frozen. Except for shrimp, the coast has very little fish-canning.

Recreational fishing is practiced along the entire coast, but attains the proportions of a major industry in some of the winter-resort towns of south Florida. The people of Florida probably derive more revenue from sport fishing than from commercial fishing, despite the fact that Florida is the leading fishery state south of Massachusetts. Gulf-Atlantic fisheries rank below agriculture, trade, mining, and forestry in economic significance, but they provide an important source of income for most of the communities along the coast.

MINERALS

The story of the Gulf-Atlantic minerals is told largely in terms of oil and gas, sulfur, pebble phosphate, and rock salt. The coastal region is practically the sole American source of native sulfur, the leading source of phosphate rock, and stands high in petroleum, natural gas, and salt. The economic structure of the Gulf coast from New Orleans to Corpus Christi is vitally affected by the mining of petroleum, gas, sulfur, and salt. Phosphate mines dominate the economic horizon of a small area east of Tampa Bay in Florida. Elsewhere, mining is unimportant, but for the region as a whole it ranks after agriculture and trade as a source of income.

The Gulf coast oil and gas fields were described in Chapter XV "Oil and Gas in the Southern Mid-Continent." Here we need only recall that oil and gas fields occupy much of the coastal belt from New Orleans to Corpus Christi and beyond. This section has been an important factor in American oil production for many years, and regularly accounts for from 10 to 14 per cent of the national output. Wells have gone deeper and deeper, until today many of the best are bringing oil from depths of more than two miles. Oil derricks are nearly always in sight on the flat grassy horizon, and seemingly boundless fields of torches burn the excess gas. Cities of the section have grown large through the handling and refining of petroleum and providing oilmen with supplies.

Sulfur and salt are found in a series of low mounds or domes which rise above the flat coastal prairie. The geological origin of these domes is not clear, but within them are found salt, sulfur, and occasionally oil and gas. Domes are found at intervals along the entire coast, but more than four-fifths of the nation's sulfur comes from a sixty-mile-square area bordering the coast southwest of Houston. Nearly all of the remainder is taken from similar formations near the Gulf coast south of New Orleans. The usual method employs hot water and steam. Drill holes reach the deposits and the water and steam are pumped in. Sulfur is soluble and readily goes into solution. When the yellow water is pumped to the surface and evaporated, good yields of dry sulfur are obtained. Sulfur has an almost endless variety of uses, but the principal buyers are the steel industries. Mines have a relatively short life and the industry is subjected to considerable local migration.

Salt was first discovered in the domes or "islands" of the south Louisiana coast during the Civil War, and the state has been an important producer ever since. The principal deposits are in five "islands" which rise about 150 feet above the north shore of Atchafalaya Bay, southwest of Baton Rouge. Largest and best known of these mounds is Jefferson's Island. Louisiana generally ranks fourth or fifth among salt-producing states, with about 10 per cent of the national tonnage. The deposits consist of thick beds of rock salt and the mines really are underground quarries. The fact that operations often go considerably below sea level without seepage emphasizes the geological uniqueness of these domes.

Phosphate rock is mined in several places near the eastern shore of central Florida, but the most important workings are about thirty miles east of Tampa Bay. Florida leads the world in phosphate production, largely because of its excellent beds of pebble phosphate. These deposits are worked in open pits by hydraulic-mining methods. Large streams of water play on the edges of the workings and carry the pebbles to the mill. Local plants concentrate the product. Its major use is for fertilizer, and large shipments go by boat to the numerous fertilizer plants along the Middle and South Atlantic coasts. Florida produces about three-quarters of the American output of phosphate rock, central Tennessee nearly all the remainder.

FORESTS

Except for the western Gulf prairie, practically all the coastal region was originally forested. Cypress grew in the swamps and pines covered the higher areas. Among the several varieties of pines, the most important has been the long-leafed yellow pine whose long straight trunk yields excellent lumber and whose sap is made into turpentine and rosin. Both lumbering and the naval-stores industries formerly were concentrated in the Cotton Belt, but as these lands were cut over, production slowly shifted toward the coast. Today the best of the South's few remaining stands of virgin timber are found in the coastal region. Lumber and naval stores are important sources of income over large areas. Here also are the beginnings of what promises to become an important southern industry: pulp and paper coupled with the growing of timber for these industrial uses.

Lumber Districts.—Lumbering is important along the entire Gulf-Atlantic coast except in those areas which were originally in grass or grassy swamp. These include the coastal prairie of Texas and Louisiana and the portion of the Florida peninsula south of Tampa Bay. Elsewhere, sawmills are rather evenly distributed.

Naval stores are produced wherever there are good stands of slash pine and long-leafed pine, but the major producing district is the eastern gulf coast. Southern Georgia and Alabama and northern Florida have more than 80 per cent of the nation's turpentine stills. Trees are tapped by "boxing," which is to cut a slit in the bark on one side of the trunk near its base. As operations continue, the exposed area is extended upward as far as a man can reach. Thus a whole side of the tree trunk is exposed and the gum oozes out. Later, the operation is repeated on the other side of the tree. Small cups are fastened to the bottom of the gash to collect the gum. A "turpentiner's" equipment consists of little more than a barrel and cart. Going from tree to tree, he collects sap, finally hauling it to the still for distillation into turpentine and rosin. Trees that have been boxed for turpentine are used for firewood or sold for pulp.

Paper and pulp mills have become more numerous in the southern states with the perfection of a satisfactory process for making paper from pine, and the depletion of northern supplies of pulpwood. Kraft paper was made from southern pines before the World War, but paper concerns showed little interest in the development until the middle 1930's. That decade saw many a new mill erected along the Gulf-Atlantic coast. Tidewater locations are preferred, not only because of access to foreign pulp (for mixing) but also because their hinterlands hold the best remaining timber lands. Most of these industries have acquired sufficient land to assure the mills a continuous supply of raw material. In the meantime a new process for manufacturing newsprint from pine has been perfected, and this industry promises to follow the kraft mills into the South. These new plants are the most tangible evidences of recognition of the South's unquestioned superiority as a place to grow timber. Pulp mills are adding momentum to the southern trend toward economic diversification.

CITIES OF THE GULF-ATLANTIC LITTORAL

The Gulf-Atlantic Coast Region includes more than half the coast line of the United States and is the natural outlet for the cotton, petroleum, winter wheat, and coal-producing districts which originate the major portion of the nation's sea-borne commerce. As a result of this movement of commerce, seaports of the region have grown into important cities, centers not only for shipping, but for distribution and finance. On the North Atlantic coast these seaports, such as New York, Philadelphia, and Baltimore, also became great industrial centers, and are included in the American Manufacturing Belt. South of Baltimore, manufacturing has been slow to develop. Cities of the Gulf-Atlantic Coast Region without exception are dominated by the interests of trade and distribution. Their harbors are busy with the shipment of raw materials. Their wholesale and financial spheres are expanded to sectional and regional importance. Their newspapers are read over broad areas, and their stores and hotels are filled with buyers and visitors from the outlying districts. Their warehouses are filled with the products of a great hinterland, and with consumer goods awaiting distribution. As commercial centers, these cities are highly developed, but their manufactures are small and almost entirely local in nature. They collect local raw materials and process them for shipment and they manufacture locally-used articles such as bakery goods. Only rarely do they have manufacturing industries of a national type.

CITIES OF THE WESTERN GULF COAST

Coastal Texas and southwest Louisiana have produced a group of cities whose economic interests are closely related to the products and occupations of their interior trading territories. These cities collect and ship cotton, wheat, petroleum, sulfur and lumber, and they import and distribute manufactured goods and supplies to the primary producers of these raw materials. Their leading industries are oil refineries, cotton compresses, and sawmills, but there is a growing list of machinery-making plants whose products go to the oil fields, mines, and farms.

Houston.—Largest and most important of the West Gulf cities is Houston, chief city, leading port, and major industrial center of the state of Texas. Houston rose in importance as a distribution center for the cotton country of south-central Texas. Long ago it became the converging point for railroads carrying cotton and wheat to Galveston harbor, and was recognized as the most important railroad center between New Orleans and Los Angeles. Later the discovery of oil and gas gave Houston a mighty boost and added important oilmen to its growing group of business leaders whose interests were in cotton, wheat, and cattle. Finally, Houston interested the federal government in making the city a seaport. A ship channel was dredged fifty miles across shallow Galveston Bay and up the small San Jacinto River to a turning basin at the eastern edge of the city. Completed in 1914, the new harbor was immediately popular, and Houston quickly took a place among the leading ports of the nation. In 1936, it ranked third among United States ports in volume of exports and second in volume of coastwise shipments.

The port of Houston is essentially a shipping port, with the volume of shipments generally ten times as great as that of receipts. Petroleum and its products dominate the list of items shipped to both foreign and domestic ports. Houston also exports

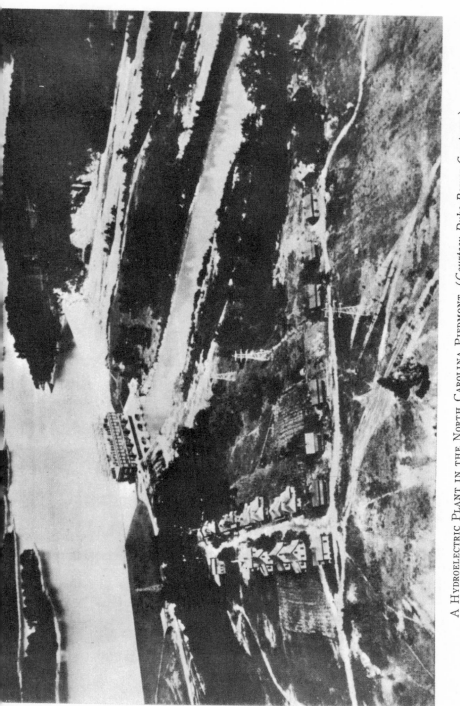

A HYDROELECTRIC PLANT IN THE NORTH CAROLINA PIEDMONT. (*Courtesy Duke Power Company.*)

cotton, and imports tropical products such as coffee and jute. When the Winter Wheat Belt has a good year, Houston handles a large percentage of its export tonnage.

Commercially, Houston serves an area in southern Texas with a population of about one million persons. In 1935, it was the fifth city of the South in volume of wholesale sales.

Oil-refining is Houston's largest manufacturing industry. Pipe lines bring oil from great distances, tapping not only the near-by Gulf coast fields but also those of central Texas. Among Gulf coast centers only the Beaumont-Port Arthur district is more important for oil-refining. In addition, Houston manufactures vegetable shortenings and cottonseed products. Its machine shops and other machinery-makers turn out a wide variety of products, especially the machinery used in oil fields.

Despite the fact that Houston has risen rapidly as an industrial center and has more manufacturing than any city south of Winston-Salem, it must be described as a commercial center. Houston is a collection-distribution center for the cotton and oil districts, a transaction center for a large and productive area in southern Texas. Its manufactures do not approach these commercial pursuits in economic significance, and arise largely out of the necessity for processing local farm and mine products for shipment to distant markets.

Galveston.—This city was the great port for the state of Texas before construction of the Houston ship channel. A superior location and better facilities have diverted much of this commerce to Houston, but Galveston has retained enough shipping to rank among the half-dozen leading ports of the Gulf coast. Galveston ships sulfur, grain, flour, and cotton and receives crude oil, sugar, and miscellaneous merchandise. Shipments exceed receipts, but there is a much better balance than at Houston.

Located on a flat island two miles off shore, Galveston has the tang of the sea. Surrounded by water, it is the favorite seaside resort of the western Gulf coast. Its famous sea wall, built to protect the city from tidal waves, is a wide boulevard lined with hotels, cabins, and seafood restaurants. Galveston has offices of railroads and steamship lines and its wholesale houses share the Gulf coast trade with those of Houston. Industrial development is small, but there are local plants manufacturing flour, rice products, and leather.

Beaumont and Port Arthur.—These two adjacent Texas cities of the Sabine River estuary are highly specialized in petroleum. Enormous quantities of crude oil from East Texas and the near-by Gulf coast fields leave this harbor each year and make it one of the nation's leading originators of sea-borne commerce. More recently, oil companies have seen profit in refining the crude at tidewater and shipping the refined products to eastern markets. Port Arthur boasts the two largest oil refineries in the world and the economic structure of Beaumont is similarly dominated by petroleum and its products. Long lines of tankers lift their decks above the flat marsh-grass to show the tourist where the Sabine River connects this port with the Gulf. Beaumont is an important commercial center, with an imposing business district and a trade territory embracing several counties in southeast Texas.

The Louisiana section of the western Gulf coast contains several small cities, most important of which is Lake Charles. Rice, oil, and lumber are taken from southwest Louisiana, and Lake Charles handles these products. The Calcasieu River provides deep water to the Gulf, over which Lake Charles exports the products of its hinterland.

NEW ORLEANS AND BATON ROUGE

Because New Orleans and Baton Rouge are the seaports of the Lower Mississippi and in a sense occupy the focal point for the commerce of the great Mississippi Basin, these cities fall in a class by themselves. If in the future the Mississippi becomes a great inland waterway, these cities are in a position to dominate its outlet. For the present they achieve prominence as the only cities of the lower river available to sea-going vessels.

Historically and geographically New Orleans is one of the great cities of the Western Hemisphere. From the days of the Spanish conquistadores to the advent of the transcontinental railroads, New Orleans held the most strategic position of any American city except New York. New Orleans was the outlet for the Upper Mississippi Basin until railroads turned that traffic eastward in the decade before the Civil War. Even since that time New Orleans has been the financial and commercial center for much of the Lower Mississippi Valley. The city has never ceased to rank high as a port since engineers first narrowed the mouths of the

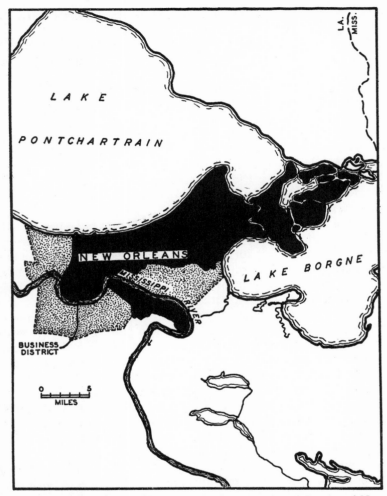

FIG. 61. New Orleans Metropolitan District. Most of the city of New Orleans lies between the east-flowing Mississippi River and an arm of the Gulf of Mexico known as Lake Pontchartrain. Ocean steamers come up the river to New Orleans to unload a variety of products (mainly from the tropics) at wharves located along the banks of the river. In recent years, a number of manufacturing industries have been located across the river from the business district, but most of the manufacturing and nearly all of the people are located north of the river. New Orleans' economic interests are essentially commercial.

Mississippi to make it deepen its own channel sufficiently to admit ocean vessels.

New Orleans is a river port, located 110 miles above the forked mouth of the Mississippi River. Its site is a five-mile-wide area between the east-flowing river and a salt-water arm of the Gulf known as Lake Pontchartrain. The site is low and was once so unhealthful that New Orleans was one of the dreaded fever-ridden ports of the world. Open canals carried drainage and sewage and provided imperfect disposition of surface waters and waste. Later the canals were covered or filled and became wide streets, the most noted of which is Canal Street, said to be the widest business thoroughfare in the world. Pumping-stations now carry the sewage far out into Lake Pontchartrain and New Orleans is a healthy city.

To the tourist, New Orleans is inevitably attractive because of its historic sites, its beautiful streets, and its old French Quarter, probably more famous for its food than any section of any American city. Its annual Mardi Gras celebration is one of the nation's favorite spectacles, and helps make New Orleans the best-known amusement center in the South.

The vacation industry is only a minor reflection of the greatness of New Orleans. To witness its economic power, you must visit its banana docks and other wharves on the Mississippi, its great banking and wholesale houses, its department stores along Canal Street, its cotton exchange, and numerous other commercial institutions. In 1935, New Orleans led all southern cities in volume of wholesale trade (but Dallas was a close second). Its wholesalers serve southern Louisiana, including the sugar district and for certain lines their territories stretch north nearly to Memphis. Her bankers serve a similarly wide territory.

At the water front, you find ships of all nations. Sugar from Cuba, bananas from Central America, bauxite ore from Surinam, and coffee from Brazil are being unloaded for distribution to the interior. Export cargoes include lumber, cotton, gasoline, and miscellaneous manufactures. In 1935, New Orleans ranked fifth in imports and sixth in exports among ports of the United States. New Orleans is the leading *importing* port south of Baltimore. It manufactures vegetable oil and clothing and refines sugar, but its manufactures are overshadowed by commercial interests.

Baton Rouge is located at the practical head of ocean navigation on the Mississippi River. New docks are capable of berthing ocean steamers. Baton Rouge receives crude oil by pipe line and inland waterway from oil fields to the north and west. Much of this oil is refined locally and large tonnages of both gasoline and crude oil move seaward down the broad Mississippi to coastwise and foreign markets. Here also are the Louisiana state capital and commercial interests serving eastern Louisiana.

CITIES OF THE EASTERN GULF COAST

No large cities have grown up between New Orleans and the Florida peninsula, but the seacoast towns of Mobile, Pensacola, Gulfport, and Biloxi have achieved considerable importance in shipping, fishing, and the winter-resort industry.

Mobile is the port for the state of Alabama and is connected by inland waterway with the Birmingham coal and iron district. Mobile Bay is formed by the drowned mouths of the Alabama and Tombigbee rivers, the basins of which cover most of the state of Alabama. These good-sized rivers made Mobile a cotton-export point many years ago. Today, narrow streets remind the visitor of the city's age, but modern office buildings show that Mobile does not live entirely in the past. The port of Mobile handles imports of bananas, fertilizer materials, and bauxite. Its exports consist mainly of lumber, cotton, iron, and steel (from Birmingham). Mobile has foundries and ship-building plants, sawmills, fertilizer factories, and paper mills. It is the third city of Alabama in wholesale trade, outranked only by Birmingham and Montgomery.

Gulfport and **Biloxi**, twin cities of the Mississippi Gulf coast, are known for lumber, fisheries, and the winter-tourist trade. The thirteen-mile strip of seacoast between these cities is lined with winter homes and hotels that attest the popularity of this section as a resort center. Gulfport ships lumber, and Biloxi is a center for the catching and canning of shrimp.

Pensacola, so far removed from other Florida cities that a legislator once referred to its representative as the "ambassador from Pensacola," likewise is best known for its harbor (Pensacola Bay), fisheries and lumber. Pensacola fishermen catch red snapper, and its harbor is a base and aviation training station for the United States Navy. Lumber from the interior passes through

Pensacola Bay to foreign and coastwise markets. The city is an important market for naval stores.

CITIES OF THE FLORIDA PENINSULA

Peninsular Florida has three major cities, all located on the seacoast. These are Tampa, on the west coast, Miami on the southeast, and Jacksonville on the northeast. All Florida cities are commercial in nature and all are more or less dependent upon the tourist business.

Tampa and its neighboring city of St. Petersburg effectively dominate the west coast of Florida. Tampa Bay is a good harbor whose principal traffic is the shipment of phosphate rock from near-by mines. Tampa also exports lumber, and imports petroleum products and fertilizer materials.

Industry is not highly developed, but Tampa is famous as the American center for the manufacture of hand-made cigars from Cuban (Havana) tobacco. There are local cement plants and fruit-packing establishments. Tampa handles a fair share of the west Florida citrus crop. The city's trade territory includes most of the west coast of Florida. Tampa ranks second to Jacksonville among Florida wholesale centers. The district is popular with tourists, especially near-by St. Petersburg.

The meteoric rise of Miami from an Indian trading post of the 1890's to a major southern city is one of the feats of American magic. Someone decided that here, where the warm Gulf Stream bathes the shore, was the best possible site for a winter resort. A real-estate boom followed in which it is said that enough lots were laid out for half the families in the United States. Land was so high-priced in downtown Miami that its only economical use was for tall buildings. Miami developed an impressive skyline which reminds many tourists of Chicago. The boom collapsed in the middle 1920's and at about the same time Miami experienced a destructive hurricane. Rebuilt and more impressive than ever, Miami wants no more land booms but does foresee a great future in the development of relations with Central and South America. Pan-American Airways make Miami the hopping-off point for air service to Latin America, and Miami probably studies Pan-American relationships more closely than any other American city. Miami hotels can accommodate more than sixty thousand guests.

Jacksonville has long been the leading city of Florida. Never seriously affected by real-estate booms, Jacksonville has continued to grow and hold its position as the business center of the state. Its wholesale territory includes the productive north portion of Florida as well as much of southern Georgia. Jacksonville has a larger wholesale trade than Tampa and Miami combined, and stands in a class with Birmingham and Charlotte of the Cotton Belt. Its harbor is the broad St. John's River, and is located 28 miles from the sea. The port ships naval stores, lumber, fruits, and vegetables, and receives petroleum products and fertilizer materials. Manufactures are concerned mainly with cigars and lumber, and are not highly developed. Jacksonville is a focal point for inland waterways. St. John's River is tidal to Palatka (55 miles) and has been improved to Sanford (90 miles). Eventually this waterway will be extended across the peninsula to the west coast. In addition, there is a continuous waterway (8 feet deep) inside the coastal bars as far north as Trenton, New Jersey, and south to Miami. At the present time these shallow waterways are little used except for the shipment of lumber on the St. John's River.

Other Florida cities include Orlando, in the midst of the citrus belt; Daytona Beach and West Palm Beach, east-coast resort centers; and Key West, the island city of the extreme southern tip of the state. Key West is interesting to the geographer because of its unique location. It is connected to the mainland by a long causeway which extends from key to key, finally terminating in the old city. Key West is the only city of the United States never to have experienced frost. Formerly it was a railroad terminus for car-ferries to Cuba, but the renowned "railroad that goes to sea" was destroyed by a hurricane and never rebuilt. Key West manufactures cigars and has a few sponge fisheries.

Nearly all of these smaller Florida cities resemble Miami in that they double their populations in the winter vacation season. In the north half of the state they handle citrus fruits and winter vegetables, as well as considerable quanties of lumber. They have few factories other than those which serve the local population.

CITIES OF THE ATLANTIC COAST

North of Jacksonville, five cities, none of them very large, handle most of the trade of the Atlantic coast sections. Savannah, Charleston, Wilmington, and Norfolk are names which have figured in American history since colonial times. All of these cities have long been important seaports, and all of them are definitely commercial today. North of Norfolk, the remaining large city of the region is Atlantic City, famed summer playground for the Middle Atlantic states.

Savannah is the major port for the cotton-lumber-naval stores district of the state of Georgia. Its harbor is the Savannah River, navigable for ocean vessels to the city 24 miles above its mouth. Savannah has an extensive and well-balanced foreign commerce, based upon imports of Chilean nitrates, German potash, and Cuban sugar, and exports of cotton, naval stores, and lumber. As in all Atlantic ports, there is a heavy in-shipment of gasoline and petroleum products from the Texas Gulf coast and California. Savannah also ships cotton goods coastwise to other American ports. It ranks second to Atlanta among Georgia cities in wholesale sales, but has relatively little manufacturing. Sawmills, turpentine stills, and a promising new paper industry are the chief industrial employers.

Charleston, South Carolina, has economic institutions similar to those of Savannah. Charleston imports fertilizer materials and exports lumber and cotton. In addition, Charleston is a coal-exporting port for the Southern Railway. Industrial Charleston manufactures fertilizers and refines petroleum. Commercial Charleston distributes consumer goods over coastal South Carolina.

Wilmington, North Carolina, resembles both Charleston and Savannah in economic development, with its river harbor handling imports of fertilizer materials and exports of cotton, and its coastal traffic dominated by receipts of California petroleum and shipments of local lumber. Wilmington also has fertilizer plants and oil refineries, but serves essentially as a commercial center for southeastern North Carolina.

Norfolk is the leading city of a small metropolitan cluster occupying the shores of Hampton Roads. This estuary is the drowned mouth of the James River and has been called "the largest good harbor on the eastern coast of the United States." Its position near the center of the Atlantic coast and near the Appalachian coal fields has given Hampton Roads a heavy tonnage of sea-borne commerce. Largely because of its coal shipments, Hampton Roads has a larger tonnage of out-going coastwise commerce than any

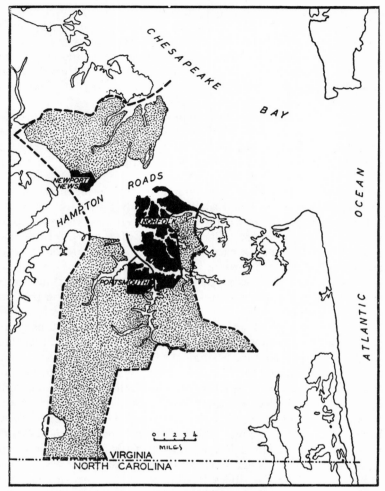

FIG. 62. Cities on Hampton Roads. The deep estuary formed by the drowned mouths of the James and smaller rivers is the largest good harbor on the Atlantic coast. The estuary is known as Hampton Roads. Upon its shores have arisen a trio of cities whose interests are closely allied with ocean shipping. Norfolk is the major city of the metropolitan cluster, an important shipping port for Middle Appalachian coal, and a jobbing center for the southern Virginia and northern North Carolina coastal areas. The United States Navy maintains an important base at Hampton Roads. Shipyards are located in all three of these cities.

other American port. There is also a large tonnage for export. Receipts are considerably smaller, but sufficient to place Hampton Roads second to New Orleans in the Gulf-Atlantic Region. Hampton Roads ports receive fertilizer materials, sugar, and pulp from foreign countries, and petroleum and manufactured goods from other ports of the United States. In addition to coal, there is a small export of tobacco.

The principal cities of the Hampton Roads district are Norfolk, Portsmouth, and Newport News. In 1930, their metropolitan population was 273,000, of whom 130,000 lived in the city of Norfolk. The location of these cities with respect to Hampton Roads is shown in Fig. 62.

The city of Norfolk is the economic center of this metropolitan cluster. The Norfolk wholesale area extends southwest almost to Raleigh and reaches down the coast nearly to Wilmington. It is the shopping center for a large portion of northeastern North Carolina, and a small area of southeastern Virginia. Norfolk is an important railroad terminus, and has a number of shipyards. Steamship lines, railroads, docks, railroad yards, and shipyards are its leading economic interests. Norfolk is eminently a product of transportation.

Portsmouth, which adjoins Norfolk on the southwest, has similar economic interests. These cities, together with several smaller suburbs really constitute a single metropolitan center, separated (but not divided) by the Elizabeth River which flows into Hampton Roads. They are the location of an immense operating base for the Atlantic fleet of the United States Navy. During the World War both the army and navy made extensive use of these harbors not only for ship-building but for sending men and supplies overseas. Hampton Roads occupies a strategic place in every plan to defend the Atlantic coast from attack.

Newport News occupies a section on the opposite (north) shore of Hampton Roads. The city takes pride in its drydocks, coal piers and one of the world's largest ship-building yards. These are the city's major industries.

The Hampton Roads cities are definite products of geography in the form of a spacious harbor, well located with reference to the Atlantic coast and the interior coal fields. Its naval base makes the government payroll one of these cities' largest. Handling the enormous tonnages which make Hampton Roads the world's greatest coal port is another leading occupation. Allied with these are the ship-building and drydock industries, likewise the product of a good location, cheap coal, and an excellent harbor. Of first importance, also, are the wholesale, retail, and banking establishments with which Norfolk serves its extensive trade territory to the south. Other manufacturing is not highly developed, but includes fertilizers and miscellaneous machinery.

Atlantic City occupies a portion of the long beach which comprises the Atlantic coast of New Jersey. As a playground for people from the cities of the Manufacturing Belt, Atlantic City is the most popular seaside resort in the United States. Fifteen million persons visit the city each year. Hotels, piers, yachts, and numerous other entertainment facilities add to the summer-vacation appeal of the famous beach. There is some commercial fishing off shore and Atlantic City wholesalers serve the adjacent coastal area. Manufacturing is not highly developed.

SUMMARY

Cities of the Gulf-Atlantic littoral show definite responses to the sea. Shipping, fishing, and recreation are leading economic interests which together with trade and distribution provide most of the income of the region. There are few factories and those which are most prominent either process local products for shipment or manufacture goods for use in their immediate trade territories. There are refineries for locally produced petroleum and sugar, and mills for processing cottonseed. For the interior, coastal cities mix fertilizer, publish newspapers, and bake bread. Some of the cities have become top-ranking seaports because of their shipments of bulky commodities such as coal, petroleum products, lumber, and cotton. Shipments generally exceed receipts, except in the case of New Orleans whose sea-borne commerce is nearly balanced. Warm waters, a cooling sea breeze, and sand beaches have lured to the Gulf coast and Florida thousands of winter tourists, and the entire length of the region is studded with summer resorts. The agriculture and mineral resources are not such as would stimulate manufacturing, and the region imports most of its manufactured products.

REFERENCES

This region also lies largely within the southern states, and the references for Chapters XIV-XVI apply. Additional information on ports and ocean shipping may be obtained from *Port Series*, Corps of Engineers, United States Army.

QUESTIONS AND PROBLEMS

1. What characteristics give the Gulf-Atlantic Coast area the properties of a region? Are these characteristics most closely related to agriculture, mining, manufacturing, or trade?

2. What is a littoral? Is a coastal area always a littoral? Name some other portions of the world which satisfy this definition.

3. What is a coastal plain? Outline the geological history of the Atlantic and Gulf coastal plains. What was Florida's geologic origin? How do these facts help explain the economic development of the region?

4. Why are beaches so often developed as pleasure resorts? Why do many southern beaches serve as both summer and winter resorts? Where do their visitors come from? Are their origins different in summer than in winter? Why or why not?

5. Why do we find specialized agriculture in each of the seven agricultural sections of the Gulf-Atlantic Coast Region?

6. Why does the Middle Atlantic section have a greater density of rural population than other sections of the Gulf-Atlantic Coast Region?

7. What is the dictionary definition of the word "truck"? How is the term applied to agriculture? Describe the appearance of a truck farm.

8. Why is only a small percentage of Florida land farmed?

9. Certain agricultural sections of Louisiana favor a protective tariff, and others oppose it. Why?

10. What types of native vegetation are found in southeastern Texas, east and north of Houston? How have these types influenced economic development?

11. Locate the most important fishery centers of the Gulf-Atlantic Coast Region and indicate the leading products of each.

12. What sections of the region are most important for minerals? What are these minerals? To what extent have they encouraged manufacturing?

13. Which of the major seaports of the Gulf-Atlantic Coast Region are located on the actual seacoast? Why are the others located differently?

14. What is the origin of the term "naval stores"? What are they? Where are they produced? For what purposes are they used?

15. Why did Houston develop into a major city? Why is it associated both historically and geographically with Galveston?

16. Why is the location of New Orleans strategic for commercial development?

17. Which city lies farthest west, Miami, Pittsburgh, or New York? Comment on Miami's position with respect to the shortest sailing routes between Europe and the Panama Canal; between Europe and Mexico.

18. To what extent is the development of the cities on Hampton Roads a reflection of physical geography?

CHAPTER XX

THE GEOGRAPHY OF AMERICAN MANUFACTURES

The Geographic Concentration of Manufacturing.—Every state in the United States has manufacturing industries of major economic importance, but in relatively few areas does manufacturing assume a position of dominance in the economic organization. In 1935, the income from manufacturing exceeded the income from agriculture in only twenty-three states, and seventeen of these states were located in the northeast portion of the country, in the area bounded by the Mississippi, Ohio, and Potomac rivers. These seventeen states normally account for about six-sevenths of the annual manufacturing output of the nation, and their factories employ about three-quarters of the nation's factory workers. Here, obviously, is the home of the American factory, and within this area we may expect to find a highly industrialized region.

A manufacturing region must conform essentially to one principle: its economic life must be characterized by manufacturing rather than agriculture, mining, trade, or any other type of economic life. It will have its quota of farmers and tradesmen, for these are necessary to provide food for its workers and to carry on the transactions and transfers of its exchange economy. It is likely also to have its miners, lumbermen, and fishermen whose living is derived from local natural resources. None of the latter occupations must be dominant, however, and where these interests exist they must be subsidiary to the major economic process, which is manufacturing. Such a region will have numerous cities with important commercial enterprises, but its major interests, its largest payrolls, its basic economic foundation, will be in the factories. In these many ways, the Manufacturing Belt will differ from all other regions. Most of its farmers, unlike those of California or the grain or cotton belts, will be producing not for a general market, but for the people of a specific city or cluster of cities. The same criteria will apply to its miners and fishermen, to its railroaders and bankers, its merchants and keepers of hot-dog stands. In a Manufacturing Belt, the factory is the central

476

economic institution, and other economic activities are subsidiary to its operation.

The Industrial City.—The function of the city in our modern exchange economy is of major importance, and a description of this function is worthy of repetition. Travelers from industrial areas often come across a sprawling town in the midst of Kansas wheat fields and naïvely but earnestly ask, "What keeps this town alive?" The horizon reveals no tall chimneys, no hulks of factory buildings, no coal tipples, no oil derricks, but blocks of stores and banks and grain elevators and dry cleaners and movies and beauty parlors and restaurants and school buildings and churches. There are a few "factories," but the eastern tourist hardly considers these bakeries, print shops, and ice plants as evidences of industrial development. Back home, such enterprises, along with the plants generating electricity, manufacturing gas, and pumping city water, are considered incidental to the city's existence. And they *are* incidental. Such institutions carry on what technically is a manufacturing business, but economically their functions are of a service nature, of the same type as the long list of retail service stores mentioned previously. The eastern tourist properly includes the manufacture of ice, newspapers, gas, and bakery goods in the same general category as the dry cleaners, laundries, garages, and retail stores, despite the fact that the statistician finds it necessary to include their operations among the lists of manufacturing industries.

This Kansas town whose reason for existence puzzles the tourist is performing the same type of service for the producers of its own trade area as does his own home city in the Manufacturing Belt. For its own wheat farmers, this town collects wheat and ships it to national or international markets in other regions or abroad. For those same producers it procures from outside sources the tools, the food, the automobiles, and other manufactured goods desired by them and utilized in their business. Unlike the eastern city it imports few raw materials, for the grain farmers' raw materials are rain, sunshine, and the atmosphere. For these workers, however, it provides medical, dental, and other professional services, banking, amusement, law and order, recreation, and education. Its physicians keep their families well, its beauticians make them attractive, its musicians keep them happy, and when the final count is ended, its morticians perform the final service.

Such cities are service stations, commercial centers for their areas of primary production, the focal point of contact between these areas and the rest of the economic world.

The industrial city has a different appearance, but its reason for existence is much the same as that of its agricultural prototype. It, too, is a service center for workers, but these workers tend machines in the factory rather than on the farm. They live in the town and therefore swell its population, but their personal needs and desires do not differ greatly from those found in rural Kansas. A major portion of the industrial city's population is also engaged in transportation: receiving shipments of raw materials and shipping out factory products to national and international markets. Another large segment is in the service occupations, catering to the personal services so important in every modern community. But the dominant occupation is manufacturing. In the factory town, the flow of income may be thought of as beginning at the factory. From the factory pay window come the pay envelopes which support the stores and movies and filling stations, as well as the outlying truck and dairy farms. From the factory bank account come the checks which support much of the transportation system, power companies, near-by coal mines and a long list of local subsidiary industries which make boxes, containers, or other parts and supplies for the major establishment; or render the industrial services supplied by machine shops, brokerage establishments, and other specialized institutions which provide both mechanical and other types of service.

Economic Specialization.—No event is better calculated to show the dependence of an industrial city upon its factory payroll than the stopping of operations in its factories. When the big plant closes down all citizens suffer, from the corner druggist to the dairy farmer at the outer margin of the milk shed. Such dependence upon a single industry is often pointed out as a great drawback to our modern exchange economy which inevitably breeds geographic specialization. In a one-industry town, closing down that industry depresses the entire city as well as those near-by farms and mines which market their products there. The shock of economic depression is often both sudden and far-reaching. The whole area tends to be either prosperous or depressed according to the national demand for its single exportable product.

From the standpoint of economic security, however, the Kansas wheat-farming center has little advantage over a manufacturing city dependent upon a single industry. Our hypothetical town in Kansas, like practically every other farm-belt city in the United States, is also a one-industry town. Its economic machine is specialized in producing just one major product and selling it to the people of a nation. In the Winter Wheat Belt of Kansas the product is wheat; but in Iowa it would be meat; in Wisconsin, butter or cheese; in California, fruits or vegetables; in Texas, cotton or oil. If the national market for this local specialty fails, if the price drops so low as to be unremunerative, the effect on the farm-belt city is just about as disastrous as the closing down of the factories in an industrial city. If wheat-farming does not show a profit, local business houses suffer. Or if there is a crop failure, the effect is of the same magnitude as if the industrial city's factories had been destroyed by fire or flood. In either case, the unquestioned economic advantages of specialization, with its great stress upon economy and efficiency, are always accompanied by the added hazard of placing all of the eggs in a single basket.

In the preceding analysis, the reader should have detected certain weaknesses resulting from over-simplification of the picture. Actually, there are comparatively few towns entirely dependent upon a single industry and few farm areas utterly devoted to a single crop. Kansas wheat districts commonly raise a few beef cattle. Industrial cities often have more than one type of manufacturing. If a particular depression is confined to a single product or type of goods, it may be alleviated locally to the extent that such diversification exists. It is still true, however, that the condition of the dominant industry profoundly affects the life of an entire community. Other primary industries may be present, but if they are small they cannot absorb the shock of failure of the major segment in the economic structure. Under such circumstances, a community progresses in much the same manner as an automobile with most of its gasoline supply shut off. It proceeds slowly and haltingly at a pace so unsatisfactory as to be actually painful to its occupants. This dependence upon certain types of economic institutions is what leads us to employ the term "economic dominance" in describing such situations.

Regional Commercial Centers.—A few of the largest cities of the manufacturing region are more important for commerce than industry. This group includes such metropolitan centers as

New York, Philadelphia, Chicago, and Boston. Their preponderance of commercial development is significant; for these cities are the great regional metropolitan centers, the commercial foci of the area. They are more commercial than industrial despite their rank as the greatest manufacturing centers in the country.

These statements are somewhat confusing. But let us take the case of New York City. New York and its cluster of surrounding cities, with about 8 per cent of the nation's population, consistently lead all industrial areas in volume of manufacturing with about 10 per cent of the national output. In commercial development, however, New York looms much larger with about 25 per cent of the national total of wholesale sales. One-tenth of the nation's manufacturing bulks large indeed, but one-quarter of the wholesale trade is considerably more impressive.

Examining New York more minutely, we obtain some insight into the true nature of a modern metropolis. Outlying cities of the Greater New York cluster invariably have some commercial development, but all of it is dwarfed by the figures for the Borough of Manhattan, which has more than 90 per cent of the wholesale trade of the metropolitan area. Looking further, we discover that this commercial development, in reality, is concentrated in the south half of Manhattan Island—an extremely small area to carry on nearly one-quarter of the wholesale transactions of the entire United States. Here also is a similar concentration of the nation's banking and financial transactions, and its ocean shipping. Shortly, we come to the notion of what many authors call the typical metropolis. The typical metropolis consists of a central business district, highly specialized in the various aspects of trade. Here are the banks, wholesale establishments, department stores, and the offices of large business firms of all kinds. This center is dominantly commercial. It is above all a center for transactions, secondarily (in most cities) a center for transfers of goods.

Industry may be found within this commercial nerve center, but factories are confined almost entirely to the production of lighter items such as clothing and various ornamental and fancy articles requiring much hand work. The heavy industries of the metropolis are beyond the central district where land is cheaper and congestion is less. Outlying districts are divided between residential and industrial developments, but neither of these land uses can afford the high rents of the central business district.

Thus the pattern of a typical metropolis appears: a commercial center with outlying industrial and residential appendages. If the metropolis is large, the appendages often extend into adjacent cities, counties, or even states. The factor of corporate boundary lines, splitting up such an economic unit into a number of small governmental units, often presents a misleading picture. We find it necessary to consolidate data for such contiguous governmental units into metropolitan districts and industrial areas in order that a unified picture of the whole economic unit may be obtained.

These metropolitan centers are as truly a part of the Manufacturing Belt economy as the industrialized areas which surround them. The extensive dependence upon exchange has brought about the concentration of many commercial functions in regional commercial centers. We must keep in mind, however, that the metropolitan districts differ markedly from their truly industrial neighbors. Their intercourse is with a much larger area. In short, they are regional (even national) centers whose existence is tied not to a mine or factory, but to thousands of communities scattered over a broad territory.

Mining Communities.—The manufacturing region includes those areas dominated by mining whose mined products are intended primarily for use in the cities of the region. Practically, this inclusion adds to our list the counties of the North Appalachian coal district and the anthracite area. The North Appalachian coal district differs from mining districts farther south principally in that it serves a somewhat more concentrated market —particularly that highly industrialized section extending from Pittsburgh eastward to the Atlantic seaboard. Inclusion of the anthracite district is less logical, but this area also conforms to the specifications of a concentrated localized market.

Agricultural Areas.—The Manufacturing Belt properly includes the agricultural areas devoted to a city-supply type of agriculture. This qualification, developed in greater detail in the next chapter, dictates the inclusion of those type-of-farming areas dominated by (1) dairying for the production of market milk, (2) poultry-raising, (3) truck gardening, and (4) the growing of certain types of fruits. The region also includes a few small agricultural districts which do not conform to all of the above requirements, but they are of small economic importance and do not alter the general regional picture. Throughout the region,

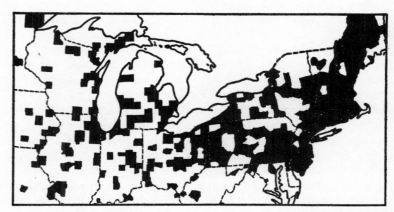

FIG. 63. Counties Having More Factory Workers than Farmers, 1930.

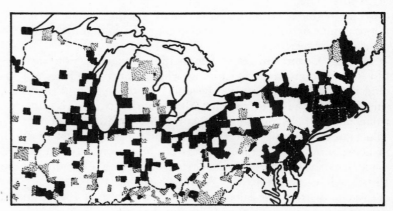

FIG. 64. Counties with *per Capita* Manufacturing Greater than the National Average, 1935. The series of charts appearing on these two pages is designed to illustrate the method used in determining the boundaries of the American Manufacturing Belt. The first step was to locate those counties which had more factory workers than farmers, as indicated by the Census of 1930. These counties are shown in black in Fig. 63. The next step was to compare each county's *per capita value added by manufacture* with the average for the nation. Census data for the year 1935 were used. Fig. 64 shows those counties which, on a *per capita* basis, had more manufacturing than the nation at large in 1935. Data are not available for the counties which are shaded.

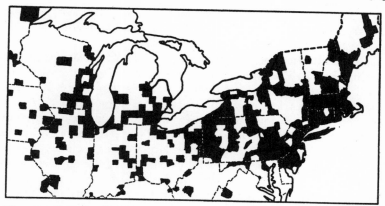

FIG. 65. Counties Having More Manufacturing than the National *per County* Average in 1935.

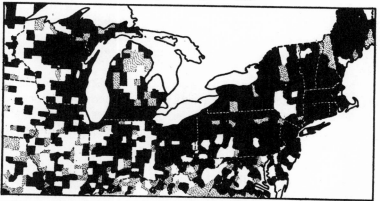

FIG. 66. Counties in Which the Ratio of Manufacturing to Wholesale Trade Exceeded the National Average in 1935. The analysis which was begun in Figs. 63 and 64 is continued in the charts on this page. In Fig. 65 only those counties appear whose value added by manufacture was greater than that of the average county in the United States in 1935. This process eliminated many counties whose total manufacturing is small. Finally, in Fig. 66, an attempt is made to eliminate those counties which are more commercial than industrial. This analysis was made by computing the ratio of manufacturing to wholesaling and including only those counties above the national average. When all four eliminations are made, we have a working basis for selecting those counties which are non-agricultural, industrialized, industrially important, and more industrial than commercial. These counties form the core of the American Manufacturing Belt, whose final delineation is explained in connection with the charts which follow.

484 GEOGRAPHY OF AMERICAN MANUFACTURES

agriculture, mining, and other economic development are subsidiary to the manufacturing industries, which constitute the basic productive activity.

Determination of Boundaries for the American Manufacturing Belt.—The American Manufacturing Belt is properly defined as that region whose economic life is dominated by manufacturing industries. It consists, first, of a large number of cities devoted predominantly to manufacturing; second, of those outlying factories and satellite urban centers which, although located beyond the corporate limits of the larger cities, actually form a part of their economic organizations; third, of the adjacent farm lands which are devoted to the production of milk and similarly perishable foodstuffs for the individual urban areas; and, fourth, of those mining districts whose mineral products are for use in these same industrial centers. It is clear that this type of economic life differs materially from that of the remainder of the United States. The difference arises partly from the dominance of manufacturing over other economic interests, but it arises also from the different place which the city holds in the regional economic organization.

Throughout the remainder of the United States, throughout the great farm belts, the city exists primarily because of the needs of the surrounding country. Cities such as Des Moines, Dallas, or Salt Lake City have grown to importance because of their services to surrounding rural agricultural areas. These services are concerned mainly with buying and processing farm products, wholesaling and retailing commodities to be consumed on the farms, providing transportation and warehousing, banking, professional services, and a long list of lesser activities, all of which we have grouped under the heading "commercial." Nearly all American cities outside the Manufacturing Belt are of this type. They exist primarily to satisfy the commercial needs of the people of their own trade territories.

An opposite relationship between cities and their surrounding areas prevails in the Manufacturing Belt. These cities exist because they have factories, and their factories generally have as their market the entire country. Surrounding farming areas, on the other hand, exist primarily to serve the individual centers, and are correspondingly dependent on them for their prosperity. In the

Manufacturing Belt, farms exist to serve their near-by cities; in other regions, cities exist to serve their near-by farms.

In general, the same statements apply to the relationships between cities and mining industries. Miners find it desirable to live near the mine just as factory workers choose homes within easy reach of the factory. The town which grows up is concerned primarily with servicing the mine and its workers rather than the people of the surrounding area. Neighboring farms are apt to be of the city-supply type. The mine is the basic economic institution of the community and holds the same central position as the factory in the industrial city.

Thus defined, the Manufacturing Belt becomes a region in which the cities, together with their surrounding perishable-food-supplying areas, are dominated by national types of manufacturing. National types of manufacturing are defined simply as those whose markets are essentially national in scope.

National industries are distinguished from local ones by the greater geographic scope of their markets. Local industries, such as bakeries, machine shops, and printing establishments, typically serve territories which are not large, generally smaller than a single state. Such industries are highly decentralized, their plants are scattered throughout the country. Every city has them, whether it is located in a farm belt, a mining district or the Manufacturing Belt. In the aggregate, however, these local types of industries never become large enough to dominate the economic life of a city.

Other non-national types of manufacturing are those which process local raw materials to reduce either their bulk or their perishability. Factories for concentrating ores may often be found near the mines; likewise, butter factories are located in the dairy belts. In both cases, a saving in transportation costs is effected if the processing is done near the point of primary production. All such local types of industries are engaging topics for the geographer, for they represent a very definite adaptation to environment. But such manufacturing industries, given little choice in their locations, are not the industries which must characterize a Manufacturing Belt. If all industries were thus decentralized over the entire populated, productive area of the United States, there would be no Manufacturing Belt. We would have no region specialized in the production of manufactured goods for national markets.

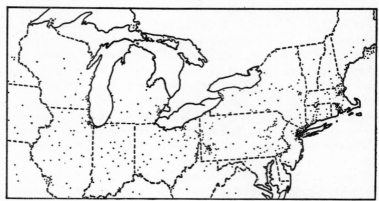

Fig. 67. Location of Cities Having Populations of Ten Thousand or
Greater, 1930.

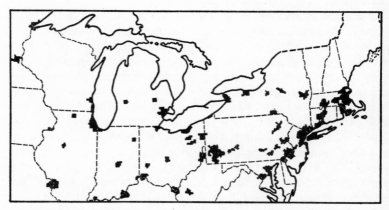

Fig. 68. Metropolitan Districts. In Figs. 63-66 certain indicators of
the extent and degree of industrialization in the northeastern United
States were charted. The composite result of those computations is a
selection of the most highly industrialized counties. Further refine-
ments can be made on the basis of the areal distribution of the city
population. Manufacturing is essentially an urban type of economic
activity and the distribution of urban population in an industrial county
gives a clue to the distribution of manufacturing. Fig. 67 shows the
location of cities having populations of ten thousand or more in 1930,
and Fig. 68 shows the location of metropolitan districts. (For a definition of metropolitan districts see Fig. 7.) Compile a list of these centers
and their metropolitan populations.

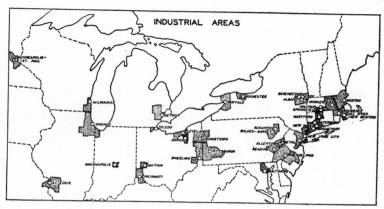

FIG. 69. Industrial Areas in the Northeastern United States.

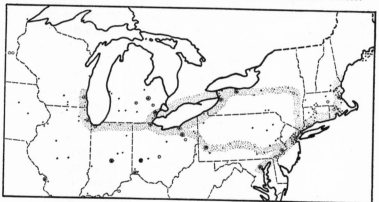

FIG. 70. Major Industrial Centers and Important Transportation Routes. Industrial areas are defined by the Bureau of the Census as consisting of a central city plus the county in which it is located and adjacent counties which are industrially important. The Bureau of the Census has established such areas (for reporting purposes) where the combined factory employment was 40,000 or greater in 1930. Detailed statistics are published for each area in the biennial Census of Manufactures. These industrial areas are the manufacturing centers of the United States. A classification of cities according to actual volume of manufacturing is used in Fig. 70. This map also shows how the leading industrial centers are grouped along the principal transportation routes. All of these indicators were considered in determining the boundaries of the American Manufacturing Belt as shown in Fig. 71.

As a matter of fact, the local industries, especially those highly decentralized ones which manufacture frequently purchased articles for a concentrated local market, are of considerable importance even in the Manufacturing Belt. Bakery goods to feed half a nation's population, newspapers, ice cream—dozens of such commodities assume considerable proportions in every city's list of manufactures. But in the Manufacturing Belt, such industries do not stand at the head of the list. Leading factory products are those which are shipped to all parts of the country. They are the manufactured products whose national production is concentrated in comparatively small areas. The Manufacturing Belt consists essentially of a consolidation of these areas.

Factors in Industrial Location

In the preceding chapters our attention has been directed to some of the factors which have been important in influencing the location of manufacturing establishments in various sections of the United States. Throughout most of these sections, manufacturing establishments were shown to be of three general types which have been designated as processing industries, local industries, and subsidiary industries. All three types are subject to powerful locational forces which go far to predetermine the locations in which plants will be established.

The Processing Industries.—In the processing industries the dominant locational force is raw materials. The major function of such factories is to make goods ready for shipment by reducing either their bulk or their perishability. Savings in transportation costs are sufficient to insure the location of such plants as near as possible to the source of raw materials. Prominent members of this processing group are a number of food-manufacturing industries such as canning, meat-packing, butter-making; and numerous mineral-reducing industries such as the smelting of metals and the refining of petroleum. Because industries of this type almost invariably seek locations near the source of their basic materials, we are inclined to associate them with the basic agricultural and extractive interests they serve. Their function is to perform the final stage in making the products of local farms and mines ready for shipment to distant markets.

Raw Materials.—The extent to which raw materials constitute an effective magnet to manufacturing industries is conditioned by

two factors, the extent of saving in transportation cost and the
expensiveness of the manufacturing process. Both factors are
fundamental. If it costs as much to ship the product as the materials from which it is made, the processing may as well be done
near the market as near the raw materials. This situation apparently exists in the cotton-textiles industries which find it about
as cheap to ship cotton in the bale as to ship the textiles into which
the cotton is made. In like manner, if a perishable material (such
as fruit) can be delivered in prime condition at no greater cost
than if it is canned, preserved, or otherwise rendered less perishable, there is small incentive to locate processing plants in the
materials-producing areas. The manufacturer compares these costs
by consulting freight rate schedules which show the rates from producing to consuming areas for each type of shipment. The results
of his arithmetic problem are a major consideration in his choice
of a factory location. But his problem of choosing the most advantageous factory site is not settled in terms of freight rates
alone.

Manufacturing Costs.—The manufacturing operation costs
money, and it is quite likely that manufacturing costs will vary
from one location to another. Perhaps the processing requires
much power (as in the reduction of aluminum ore). If power is
expensive in the materials-producing area, the manufacturer may
be forced to ship the crude materials to a location having cheaper
power despite the fact that the concentrate could be shipped more
cheaply. Much also depends upon the most economical size of
plant and the geographic concentration of the source of supplies.
It is cheaper to ship beet sugar than sugar beets, but that does
not mean that every irrigated section in the West can have a sugar
refinery. An efficient sugar refinery is a large concern which requires the product of hundreds of acres to operate at capacity.
In such industries, raw materials exert a generalized influence in
attracting plants to the areas of basic production, but technological
considerations make it unprofitable to locate plants in each producing area. In some instances, the raw materials may be so few
and widely scattered that the ideal plant location seems to bear
scant relationship to the source of supplies.

Technological Change.—It must also be recognized that technological change often exerts profound influences on the location
of processing industries. A new manufacturing process or a

change in transportation methods may render a location obsolete almost overnight. The most advantageous site for any manufacturing industry can be determined only in the light of existing technological and cultural conditions. Next week or next year the answer may be different. Thus the processing industries are defined as those types of manufacturing industries which because of savings in transportation costs are most profitably located near the source of their raw materials. The term "processing" is used because most of these industries carry on comparatively simple manufacturing operations designed to make the materials ready for shipment. The classification is not permanent because technological change often alters the relative profitableness of locations within specific industries.

Local Industries.—The other two types of manufacturing industries with which we have become familiar in other regions evidence a strong tendency to seek locations near the markets. Prominent members of these groups are the so-called local industries, which are found in nearly every population center, and a considerable number of subsidiary or satellite industries, which tend to cluster about the center for some type of basic production. The location of both local and subsidiary industries is dominated by the attraction of markets, but it is well to remember that markets are of different sorts. In general, the local industries produce consumer goods for the general consumer market of the localized areas they serve. Their products are usually perishable or bulky and their materials can be shipped more cheaply than the products into which they are manufactured. Bakeries, ice plants, and newspaper plants have been cited as good examples of local industries. In all three examples the product is perishable and the materials can be obtained cheaply. If the list of local industries were to be extended, it would also include a number whose products are essentially made-to-order or of purely local interest. Here we would find job printing, the manufacture of tents and awnings, and several other industries which grade almost imperceptibly into the service trades such as tailoring, shoe repair, dry cleaning, and laundering. Within this sphere the dividing line between manufacturing and service becomes very difficult to determine. We are inclined, in fact, to group the local industries with the service establishments in characterizing the economic development of a city. They differ from the service groups in that they turn out tangible commodities; but they locate near the consumer and their appearance in every sizable urban center is practically inevitable. They do not require elaborate plants or equipment and because they operate efficiently in small units they can be located wherever there are considerable groups of people to be served.

Subsidiary Industries.—The subsidiary industries also find greatest profit in locating near their markets, but they sell to a restricted clientele, and they handle capital goods rather than consumer goods. In other words, the typical subsidiary industry manufactures parts, supplies, or equipment which are to be used by some other industry for further production. Many producers of this type of goods find it advantageous to locate near the concerns which buy them. In previous chapters, we have found mining machinery being manufactured in mining areas, farm machinery in farming areas, and tin cans in canning districts. These are the makers of tools and other equipment. In so far as such manufacturing industries seem inevitably to be attracted to the location of some more basic type of productive activity, we are inclined to associate them with the industries they serve. We have learned to expect to find railroad shops scattered along the railroads, and foundries and machine shops in every manufacturing center.

The subsidiary industries are numerous, and in the Manufacturing Belt they become very important. But in industrialized areas there is a difference in character. In the Manufacturing Belt, they generally supply parts and equipment for other manufacturing industries, while in other regions they are more likely to serve agriculture, mining, transportation, or some other type of non-manufacturing institution.

Size of Plants.—As in the case of local industries, the plants for typical subsidiary manufacturing industries need not be large. Otherwise these industries would not ordinarily find it possible to locate plants adjacent to their markets, which in most cases are likely to be scattered. In both the local and subsidiary types of industries, a change in technology may suddenly make larger plants more efficient and bring about a rapid shift in plant locations. When such changes occur they bring about the concentration of an industry into a smaller number of larger plants and a corresponding withdrawal of the industry from many cities. Then the industry ceases to find nearness to specific markets its greatest attractive force. It no longer remains local or subsidiary, but becomes regional or national in scope, serving broad areas from a relatively small number of locations. In making this transformation the industry would have joined that group which characterizes economic development in the American Manufacturing Belt. This group finds little compulsion to seek specific sites because of either materials or markets. Its locations rather are the result of a complex of natural and cultural forces whose workings are extremely intricate.

The Importance of Competition.—In previous sections we have seen how competition tends to force certain types of manufacturing industries to seek locations near their raw materials while others find it equally advantageous to locate plants near their markets. We have found that the processing of weight-losing and perishable raw materials is generally carried on as near as possible to the areas in which such materials are produced; and we have learned that the attractiveness of raw-materials areas as sites for processing industries varies essentially with the saving in shipping costs that can be accomplished by the manufacturing process. We have also discovered that many manufacturing industries find greatest profit in locating near the consumers for their products. In many such cases, raw materials can be shipped as advantageously as finished products, or the service rendered is of such a nature that easy contact with the customer is desirable. Such industries were classed as local and subsidiary, depending upon whether they manufacture for the general consumer market (and are therefore found in every population center) or for specific types of local producers such as farmers, miners, or other manufacturers.

In all of these industries, the manufacturing processes are comparatively simple, large plants are not necessary for efficient operation, and broadly competitive conditions prevail. Products and processes have become more or less standardized and there are few monopolistic elements. The saving to be accomplished by locating in response to raw materials or markets is obvious to the managers of these industries, and competition tends to force them into these locations. Technological and institutional factors offer no serious friction to the operation of locational forces. Yet there are many manufacturing industries in which conditions of this kind do not prevail. This statement applies particularly to the industries of the Manufacturing Belt. In the manufacturing region we encounter many important industrial establishments whose locations seem to bear little relation to the presence of either raw materials or markets. Such industries apparently experience a wide choice in the selection of plant locations and most of them serve national markets from single locations. We refer to them as national industries, to distinguish them from the processing, local, and subsidiary types whose choice of location is more limited.

The Rise of National Types of Manufacturing Industries.
—Factors influencing the location of national types of manufacturing industries are well illustrated in the typical story-book histories of the growth of great American business establishments. In these industrial dramas the first character to appear is the inventor toiling away in his kitchen or attic workshop. Finally, the invention is perfected and the future industrial giant emerges from his home in search of capital with which to equip a plant. The undertaking is hazardous and money is hard to find, but eventually a small shop is set up in a spare room or abandoned building. The first products find a ready market and with the prospect of profit it becomes easier to borrow money. The plant is expanded or a new one is built and the inventor's home town eventually finds itself in possession of a thriving factory, a successfully established manufacturing industry. The story often ends at this point, with the inventor-hero comfortably established in the midst of dividend checks, happy factory workers and the acclaim of his fellow-townsmen, and we are left to assume that both he and his factory live happily ever after. But do they? We may as well add a sequel to the story.

In the first lush days of the new industry the owners were reaping the benefits of a type of monopoly. They were turning out a new product, a unique commodity. There were no competitors in those days because no one had had time to perfect an organization to turn out a rival product. In the absence of competition the firm was in a position to make good profits. But those very profits stimulated the desire of others to get into the industry. Competitive products appeared in the markets and the pioneer firm was forced to cut prices to meet competition. One day the board of directors meets and is told by the manager that earnings are declining steadily because competitors are forcing prices down. Costs must be cut or profits will dwindle and disappear.

A competitor in a distant city is underbidding in all markets and unless his prices can be met, the firm can no longer expect to sell its product. The directors ponder the situation. How can it be met? Can the factory be operated more economically? Could costs be lowered by moving the industry to another city? Or should the old line of products be abandoned and new products substituted? Each of these alternatives is examined. If internal economies will not produce the desired reduction in costs, then it appears that the plant is poorly located. The owners must then decide whether to transfer their investment to a better location, embark on a new line of products, or offer the property for sale. In any case it appears that competition has forced the relocation of the manufacture of this particular product to a more advantageous site. Thus the working of economic law reacts to the benefit of society by providing goods manufactured in the most economical locations. But the story is far too simple, too much like the story-book prelude. Actually there are a myriad of forces which arise to impede the moving of a factory from a city in which it has become thoroughly established.

In the first place, the differences in materials and marketing costs are often so slight that the advantages of one city over another are not readily detected. In the past, railroad rates could be set to favor a disadvantageous location over one more favorably situated with respect to transportation costs. In the United States the original rates bore little relationship to the cost of rendering the service, and much of this original rate structure has been retained. Certainly the local chamber of commerce would have attempted to secure a reduction in freight rates before a major industry was permitted to leave the city. This point is not particularly significant in the present problem because we have insisted throughout the discussion that location problems must be calculated in terms of freight rates rather than distance or cost, but this warning is worthy of repetition.

Nor must we overlook the point that small disadvantages in freight rates may often be offset by savings in manufacturing costs. In some industries power is of sufficient importance to make cheap power sources good industrial locations, but these differentials have been reduced appreciably with the long-distance transmission of electricity. Of much greater importance over comparatively short periods of time are differences in wage rates.

Labor normally constitutes the largest single item of expense in a factory, and savings in wages are quickly reflected in the profit account. The prospect of cheap and docile labor has attracted many industrialists to new sites. Cities in which labor is highly organized and militant in its demands for higher wages and better working conditions have often become unpopular with industrialists. Many a factory owner has withdrawn his capital from such centers to seek a location where labor is not organized, less militant, more tractable, and satisfied with lower wages. Such decisions are often short-sighted, for the simple reason that labor, like industry, is now becoming organized on a national scale. The exploitation of labor may continue in an area for a number of years, but sooner or later local workers will become organized and their demands must be reckoned with. In addition, the increasing mobility of labor is a strong force leading to wage equalization among various locations. This statement applies particularly to the semi-skilled occupations which today operate the majority of our factory machines. The only permanent differentials in wages are based upon differences in the cost of living. Over long periods of years these differences in living costs are relatively slight.

Finally, we must pay particular attention to a group of factors which make our story-book factory the exception rather than the rule in industrial location. Our factory finally fell victim to the forces of competition. In actual life, we seem more likely to encounter conditions of monopoly. Some of these conditions, such as the momentum of an early start and the perpetuation of an industry through favorable freight rates, have already been mentioned. Other monopolistic elements are worthy of consideration.

The Perpetuation of Monopoly.—We have seen how a firm manufacturing a new product may experience freedom from competition for a considerable period of time during which competitive firms are being organized and made ready for production. Under such conditions the problem of a more favorable location hardly arises since profits ordinarily are sufficient to obscure ordinary losses attributable to a slightly inferior location. In practice, many firms are able to perpetuate the advantage of an early start by bringing forth a constant stream of new products to be made in the same location. Some of these firms make a practice of abandoning existing lines as soon as they become unprofitable and substituting newer products for them. A firm that is constantly able to pioneer new and successful products is in a condition to pay little attention to the problem of seeking a more favorable location. In many industries this new-product angle is nicely taken care of by patents and trademarks which prolong the pioneering period over a series of years and reinforce the monopolistic position of the manufacturer. Others have found it possible to maintain current uniqueness in their product by bringing out new models at regular intervals. Another method is to rely upon extensive advertising campaigns to convince buyers that a particular brand excels all others and is therefore worth a higher price. Finally, there are many instances in which it is obvious that agreements against price-cutting have been reached and competition is reduced to a rivalry to give more "service," quality, or some other form of competition less effective than price-cutting. These are only a few of the ways in which certain manufacturers have been able to remove themselves at least partially from the competitive sphere. In so far as they have been able to escape the rigors of competition they have also been able very largely to escape the necessity for seeking more advantageous locations.

Investment.—The typical industrial establishment is no fly-by-night venture. Once established, it includes a large amount of specialized capital which cannot be moved or abandoned without great financial loss. There is first of all the land and buildings, immovable capital whose sale value ordinarily is very low. Much of the machinery and equipment is likely to be expensive to move. When a manufacturer decides to remove his operations to another city he is faced with the necessity of writing off a large portion of his local investment as loss. In a few industries the problem is not serious because the amount of non-mobile equipment is small; but in most instances, the prospective loss from abandonment of a location is sufficient to make industrialists very reluctant to move.

Inertia.—Finally we come to a group of migration-resisting factors which lie almost entirely outside the operation and management of a factory. Like the factors previously described, these forces tend to perpetuate industry in any city in which it has become thoroughly established. They are the factors which cause industries to become institutionalized sectors of the local social and economic structure. They represent the erection of an economic and cultural structure which functions to keep the factory in operation and at the same time makes it difficult to move into other areas in which such facilities have not been created. They are the services of highly skilled labor, finance, transportation, subsidiary industries and services, and a long list of social activities including recreation, religion, and other forms of social contact. In the established center, these facilities are highly developed. Here live the foremen and skilled artisans, few in number but essential to successful operation of the plant. These workers receive the largest salaries. They have local investments and social contacts, and it is difficult to persuade them to move. In the same manner, local banks have become accustomed to financing the operations of local industry and transportation facilities have been specialized to care for its business. A number of specialized subsidiary industries and services have grown up which perform vital functions in furnishing parts, repairs, legal advice, and numerous other services upon which the industry has come to depend. In other words, the factory has become more than a single business entity. It has been integrated into the general economic and social life of the community. All of these conditions conspire to provide a great deal of inertia for the industry that is considering migration to a more favorable location. They add a great deal of hesitancy to the selection of a new location and tend to cause such decisions to be postponed. They also add emphasis to the desire to acquire some of the monopolistic advantages mentioned in previous paragraphs.

The Complexity of Location Factors.—The foregoing analysis should provide a background for understanding the location of industries in the American Manufacturing Belt. Relatively few plant locations can be explained in terms of natural advantage. Most of the great manufacturing industries which characterize economic life in the region were not compelled to seek locations near either raw materials or markets. Power has been a significant factor in the location of very few of the leaders. Low wage rates could not have been a long-run dominant factor, because the cost of living is generally higher than in other regions. For an adequate explanation of the establishment and growth of most Manufacturing Belt industries we must look rather to the monopolistic elements which exist in so much of the region's economic development.

In American history the location of genius has been unpredictable. The most common site for an industrial genius to begin operations has been his own home town. Once established, industry tended to grow in its original location and as it grew there arose a host of economic and institutional forces whose influence was to discourage migration. Many industries were able to develop organizational advantages of a monopolistic character and the resulting monopoly profits have tended in many cases to obscure the need for migration. In the future the random nature of original locations may be altered with the concentration of research in the laboratories of large corporations. The large corporation, unlike the individual enterpriser, is in a good position to select the most promising plant location in advance of inaugurating production. In this way the element of chance in original location may be reduced. Sites can be selected upon the basis of careful locational studies and without dependence upon local finance or promotional activity. But the location of existing industries is the product of a complex of historic and geographic factors, including original sites that came into being almost by accident, the perpetuation of locations by a variety of monopolistic conditions, and the growth of local traditions, skills, and services. It is quite true that many a factory has failed in the Manufacturing Belt because it could not meet competition from other regions, but of the industries that remain—and these are the major manufacturing industries of America—the location is to be explained only by a combination of historic, economic, and geographic factors.

INDUSTRIAL GEOGRAPHY OF THE MANUFACTURING BELT

It appears that the Manufacturing Belt is a creature not so much of raw materials as of history, transportation, and economic evolution. Manufacturing industries were first important in colonial New England where local raw materials, water power, and energetic labor were assembled to create the first American factory products. Shortly thereafter, factories sprang up around New York harbor, and at Philadelphia and other tidewater cities.

This early development along the seaboard was a reflection of the young nation's economic immaturity, of a nation facing toward Europe, with its largest cities located along the North Atlantic seacoast to handle the trade with England and the Continent. There was no Manufacturing Belt in the United States before the Civil War, because during all those early decades the new nation was dominantly commercial. Its interests lay in the export of raw materials and the import of manufactured goods; and its major cities were its eastern seaports.

These eastern seaports, because of their size and maturity, were in a good position to attract the new factories which began to appear in the tariff-protected decades following the Civil War. Boston, New York, and Philadelphia had larger resources of labor and finance than the younger cities of the interior, and they were served by better railroad facilities. They became the fountain-head of the new flood of industrial development which was to spread westward almost to the Mississippi River.

Industrial development spread westward from the North Atlantic seaboard in response to the attractive forces of both raw materials and markets. East Pennsylvania iron ore was superseded by Lake Superior ore, and the Pittsburgh-Cleveland area became a good location for blast furnaces. Wheat and meat and lumber came pouring in from the West and the industrial frontier marched out across the Appalachians to meet them partway with flour mills, meat-packing plants, and woodworking mills. In addition, the westward movement of the center of population made it advantageous for many types of industries to follow this trend. Location near the consumer is a dominant feature in choosing sites for many industries, and of considerable importance in all industrial locations.

Thus the center of manufacturing followed the westward migration of farmers, miners, lumbermen, townsmen, and the rest. It followed slowly and haltingly, because manufacturing is not subject to the same locational forces as other economic activities. The processing, local, and subsidiary types of manufacturing followed the westward migration of primary production, but other types lagged behind. The geographic center of American manufacturing never got far west of the Appalachian Highland. Factories need large supplies of labor as well as raw materials. They must have power and financial assistance, and they must have well-developed transportation facilities. Manufacturing is not likely to develop extensively except in districts that are comparatively mature. It is not frontier activity. The Manufacturing Belt reached Chicago about the time the last agricultural frontiers disappeared in the western states. It has shown little tendency to extend farther west.

In its westward migration, manufacturing followed very closely the established transportation routes. Thin lines of industrial cities appeared along the major trunk-line railroads, originally built to tap the West for the Atlantic seaport cities. Pittsburgh became a great coal-mining center, then a great steel center, and the Mahoning Valley which connects Pittsburgh with Lake Erie was soon a smoky "American Ruhr," studded with blast furnaces and rolling mills. To the westward, manufacturing developed rapidly along the south shores of the Great Lakes. These positions were strategic. Railroads were forced to go around the lakes in order to reach the West. In addition, the Great Lakes provided a cheap highway over which to transport iron ore and other bulk commodities produced in the West. Buffalo, Cleveland, Toledo, Detroit, Chicago, and Milwaukee grew rapidly as industrial centers, and all of them became important in the steel and machinery industries.

In essence, the Manufacturing Belt consists of little more than long rows of cities along the best natural transportation routes of North America. One of these routes begins at New York harbor, extends up the Hudson River Valley to Albany and west to Buffalo. At Buffalo it splits, one branch running north of Lake Erie, through Canada, to Detroit and Chicago, and the other south of Lake Erie, past Cleveland and Toledo to Chicago. At Chicago, the routes fan out, but a major stem goes north to Milwaukee. This is the major natural traffic artery of the continent, and along it lie most of our great industrial cities. A second route begins at Philadelphia, and runs west across the Appalachian Highland to Pittsburgh, thence northwest to the shores of Lake Erie. This route is a location for heavy industries. The third route is the coastwise path from Baltimore northward past Philadelphia, New York, Providence, and Boston, to southern Maine. This seaboard belt, the original home of the American factory, has the obvious advantage of easy access to ocean-borne raw materials.

More than half the manufacturing of the continent is carried on within the territory immediately contiguous to these three major natural transportation routes. That industry should have chosen locations of this type is but a reflection of the extreme dependence of the American people upon transportation. The United States, as the largest land area in the world practicing the geographic

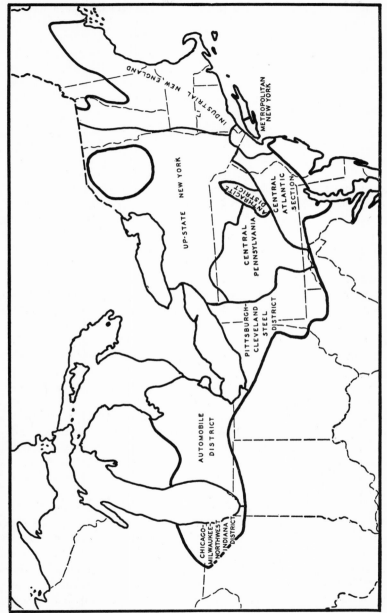

FIG. 71. The American Manufacturing Belt, showing the boundaries of industrial sections within the region.

division of labor, is more dependent upon internal transportation than any other major nation. Americans think nothing of hauling their breakfast, lunch, and dinner halfway across a continent, of hauling their iron ore as far as from Paris to Warsaw before smelting it, of manufacturing copper utensils two thousand miles from the mines. Nowhere else in the world do people haul heavy goods overland for such distances, and no other people is so completely dependent upon transportation. A European tourist remarked, "You Americans never go to get anything. You always have it brought to you. We could not afford so much transportation." Without considering the economic implications of his last sentence, we can well understand why, in American practice, the transportation routes should become the greatest centers for industry. In short, the American Manufacturing Belt is located, first on the North Atlantic seaboard, and second along the major, most strategic routes connecting the seaboard cities with the vast, productive interior, which is specialized very largely in turning out raw materials.

Factors other than transportation have influenced the location of American industries. Climate in the northeast United States is conducive to the stimulation of human energy. Man apparently accomplishes most where there are frequent changes in weather. There is sufficient rainfall to support a local supply-type agriculture and assure factory cities a supply of perishable foods such as milk and market vegetables.

The principal influence of topography has been upon transportation. Here the great topographic feature is the Appalachian Mountain system, over which transportation routes must pass. These highlands have generally discouraged transportation, and as a result there is comparatively small industrial development in the more rugged sections. The relatively few routes which cross them, however, have become sites for important industrial developments.

The Manufacturing Belt includes first of all the main stems of industrialized traffic arteries which constitute the backbone of the region; secondly, the near-by industrial cities whose economic development is of the same type as that found along the main stems; finally, the adjacent agricultural and mining areas which serve these cities directly. The extent to which the non-industrialized sections are included is indicated in the chapters which follow.

REFERENCES

Major references on industrial location are listed in the Introduction. See also Sten de Geer, *The American Manufacturing Belt,* in *Geografiska Annaler* (Stockholm), December, 1927. Information concerning industrial location is contained in a series of reports published by the Metropolitan Life Insurance Company, *Industrial Development* (1928). G. E. McLaughlin, *Growth of American Manufacturing Areas* (University of Pittsburgh, 1938), traces the industrial development of the thirty-three industrial areas of the United States, and analyzes each of them.

QUESTIONS AND PROBLEMS

1. Refer to the latest *Census of Manufactures* and compile a list of the 20 leading manufacturing states. Indicate the three leading industries of each. What figure will you use to determine industrial importance, value of product, number of workers, or value added by manufacture? Why?
2. What is meant by the term "economic dominance"? Does it imply great size? universal occurrence? political or economic control? May the sum of the recessives be of greater economic importance than the dominant? Compare this usage of the term "dominance" with its use when botanists speak of the "dominant species" of plants occupying an area.
3. How does economic specialization breed insecurity? Cite examples. Would your answer be different for the production of necessities than for luxuries? How may the people attempt to offset insecurity?
4. What are the economic functions of a metropolis? How are they reflected in differences in land use within the metropolitan area?
5. How do the relationships between cities and their trade territories differ in manufacturing areas and farming areas?
6. What is an industrial city? What does the term "industrial" mean? Is it broader or narrower than "industry"? It is correct to speak of the farming "industry," but farm workers are not ordinarily called "industrial workers." Do you agree?
7. What is the basis for including agricultural areas in the Manufacturing Region? What types of agriculture are included?
8. Review the last pages of Chapter IV, in which consequent types of manufacturing are discussed. Elaborate that discussion by indicating the major locational factors in the processing, local, and subsidiary types of manufacturing industries. Why is it generally

inaccurate to speak of a city whose industries are mainly of these types as an industrial city?

9. Why is it more difficult to understand the location of a factory under conditions of monopoly than under competition?

10. We have noted the difficulty of changing from one type of production to another in the wheat, corn, and dairy belts. Why are such shifts even more difficult in the Manufacturing Belt? What types of effort are often employed to forestall such changes?

11. Of what importance is history in understanding the location of the American Manufacturing Belt? How do natural resources and the railroads fit into this history?

CHAPTER XXI

AGRICULTURE IN THE MANUFACTURING BELT

The City-supply Type of Agriculture.—Economic life in the Manufacturing Belt is dominated by the factory. The region's principal income-producers are its factory workers, and providing perishable foodstuffs for these workers and their families is the principal function of Manufacturing Belt agriculture. Leading products of its farms are fluid milk, vegetables, fruit, and eggs, all produced primarily for sale in the near-by cities.

Localized Markets.—Agriculture in the Manufacturing Belt differs from that of all other regions primarily in that these farmers produce for a localized rather than a generalized market. An Iowa hog-raiser, a California raisin-grower, or a southern cotton farmer grows his product not for a specific city or a specific region; he may sell it almost anywhere. The New York dairy farmer or the Long Island potato-grower, on the other hand, intends his product for consumption within a comparatively small near-by area. His market is localized. Usually it is a single city. Freight rates and the perishable nature of his produce act as a protective tariff which gives him preference in these near-by cities.

In a very real sense, these dairymen and vegetable and fruit growers actually belong to the cities which they serve. They are as much a part of its economic life as its barbers, physicians, and dentists. One of the principal concerns of a large city is the maintenance of an adequate daily supply of fresh milk. Practically, its citizens have no choice but to buy from near-by dairymen. The dairymen, on the other hand, have little choice but to sell their milk in that city. A city's "milk-shed," as its milk-supply area is called, is an integral part of its pattern of existence. Its people may buy hams from Iowa or Virginia or some foreign country; may eat oranges from California or Florida; or wheat from Kansas or North Dakota; but their milk comes from local sources, from within the city's own milk-shed.

The same statement holds for market vegetables and many varieties of fruit, all of which command better prices if marketed fresh, and whose bulk discourages long shipment. In this region,

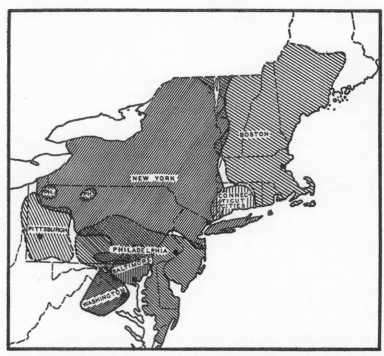

FIG. 72. Milksheds of Major Metropolitan Centers. A milkshed is the area from which a city obtains its supply of fresh milk. Seven major milksheds are shown on this map. Boundaries are drawn to include the milk dealers who send milk to a particular city. These dealers collect milk from near-by farmers. Individual dealers usually market milk in just one city, but in some areas neighboring dealers supply different cities. This situation causes some overlapping of milksheds for individual cities. The most complicated area lies north of Baltimore. Milk from that area is marketed in Baltimore, Philadelphia, and New York. The two outlying centers marked *PH* in northwestern Pennsylvania send milk to Philadelphia. All of northwestern Pennsylvania was formerly in the Philadelphia milkshed, but in recent years the city has been obtaining cream from the Middle West, and the size of its milkshed has been reduced. With a few minor exceptions, the configuration of these milksheds has not changed materially in twenty years.

we have attempted to attach to each manufacturing city all of the adjacent agricultural area devoted primarily to supplying that particular city with farm products. When consolidated, these areas become the American Manufacturing Belt.

This supply-type of agriculture—tied to a single localized market—is not confined to the Manufacturing Belt. Every city throughout the world has the same sort of supply area which begins just beyond its outskirts unless impossible agricultural conditions prevail. Schematically, we think of these as concentric circles about the urban center. First, and nearest the city, we expect to find the truck gardens which supply it with green vegetables and small fruits. Beyond the truck farms come the dairies which provide the city's daily supply of fresh milk. Historically, before modern refrigeration and rapid transportation, there were still other circles specializing in butter, root crops, meat animals, and, finally, bread grains. The development of our modern exchange economy has tended to eliminate the outer circles, leaving only those inner ones devoted to truck crops and milk. Production of other commodities has tended to gravitate toward specially favored regions such as the Wisconsin-Minnesota butter and cheese area, and the Corn and Wheat belts, whose farmers produce for a general market and not for a specific city. The truck-crop and fluid-milk areas remain, however, and although they do not always form concentric circles because of local variations in soil, topography, and accessibility, they are certain to be found just beyond the limits of every American city.

Strict accuracy and attention to the minutiae of economic geography would require the mapping of these supply areas around every American city from San Francisco to Baltimore, and they could be shown even for most of the smaller towns. There is this difference, however: Omaha's milk area is lost in a sea of corn and Wichita's is engulfed in a sea of wheat. In those areas towns are so far apart that local dairy areas may be dismissed as local variations in a general pattern of agricultural development. But in the Manufacturing Belt cities are larger and closer together. As they grew, their local supply areas extended until in many places their margins touched. In short, the city-supply type of farming eventually came to dominate the pattern of agricultural development. Intervening areas once devoted to corn, livestock, or general farming were converted into dairy districts to supply the growing cities. The Manufacturing Belt thus became, agriculturally, an area devoted mainly to dairying and the production of truck crops and fruit. It represents the consolidation of more than a thousand local city-supply areas, in each of which farmers look to their own near-by cities to consume their farm products.

Economic Implications.—Denied a wide choice of markets, Manufacturing Belt farmers experience periods of depression and prosperity which correspond closely with those of various business firms in the city they supply. If the big factory closes and lays off its men, the market for strawberries will suffer just as surely as does the demand for shoes or movie tickets or chocolate sundaes. And the orders for milk will be reduced—not so much, for milk is generally considered a necessity—but enough, possibly, to cause a break in price. Thus a city's dairy farmer, eight or ten miles from the city hall, feels the effect of its economic pulsations just as certainly as do its merchants and other business men. His eggs are in the same basket.

These farmers, on the other hand, effectively dominate their own cities' markets. Their products are both perishable and bulky. Expense involved in bringing competing products from outside areas is sufficient to keep these products out. In addition, cities have become increasingly interested in regulating their own milk supplies to the extent that outsiders, not afforded the opportunity for city inspection, usually cannot qualify for admission to its markets. Thus the natural monopoly becomes reinforced with administrative regulations and the milk-shed is firmly welded into the city's economic mechanism. It becomes practically the sole source of a city's milk. Thus protected from outside competition, the dairymen enjoy a sort of stability which tends to offset the disadvantages of being confined to a single market.

Such a system inevitably leads to a high degree of organization among the dairymen themselves. There is organization for the purpose of collective bargaining with the large dealers to whom they sell their product; for mutual regulation and cooperation; for maintaining the market and excluding milk from other areas; for arbitrating differences with city officials; for protesting price cuts and urging increases; and for other obvious purposes. Dealing with large organizations, dairymen must have large organizations intent upon protecting their interests. As a result, they are better organized than the farmers of most other sections of the country. There is also an increasing tendency toward integration, in which large milk companies have acquired land and placed the entire production-distribution system under one management.

The net result is the creation of a near-monopoly, an economic institution which has the essential characteristics of a public utility. City customers get good milk, but there is a growing recognition of the necessity to regulate price as well as quality. In its broader economic aspects the fluid-milk industry resembles the gas, light, and water industries. It furnishes a virtual necessity under conditions approximating monopoly. Such industries are classed as public utilities and are subject to regulation by public authorities.

Technology.—The prevalence of city-supply agriculture is both encouraged and threatened by technological forces. On the one hand, this type of farming has arisen and expanded solely because of the rise and development of cities. We have seen that the modern city is largely the product of technological changes in the fields of manufacturing and transportation. As the cities grew, their tributary city-supply farming areas expanded. But on the other hand, powerful technological forces have also been at work which tend to destroy the monopolistic position of the farmers. City-supply farming has become profitable because the perishable and bulky products in which it specializes cannot be shipped long distances without considerable deterioration and expense. Yet these very factors are constantly being attacked by improved methods and practices. Canning, preserving, and freezing processes are being improved constantly, and every improvement encourages competition from more remote farming areas. Improvements in refrigeration make longer shipment and storage possible. The motor truck, with its greater flexibility, economy, and speed, has expanded enormously the areas from which cities may obtain perishable products. Glass-lined tanks for use on truck and milk trains have reduced the cost of long-distance shipments of fresh milk. The city-supply type of agriculture exists in a zone of combat between rival technological forces. On the one hand are the forces of destruction which include canning, preserving, freezing, refrigeration, and rapid and flexible transportation. On the other are the city-building forces which have constantly increased the markets for perishable farm products. In the past, the city-building forces have generally been in the ascendency and city-supply agriculture has expanded with the urbanization of the nation. For the future, the war will be fought with a variety of economic and legal weapons including technological change, freight rates, and local governmental regulations. In the meantime, the city-supply farming areas remain as an important sector in the economic development of every American city.

The Milk Farm.—The fluid-milk industry is one of remarkable synchronization. Not only must the milk be handled in a sanitary manner, it must also be delivered to the right place at the right time. After milking, the milk is cooled quickly and prepared for transport to the bottling plant. Trucks whisk the big cans to the plant where it is tested, weighed, measured, filtered, clarified, and pasteurized. Then it is bottled and made ready for delivery by the well-known delivery truck. During this whole process, the milk must be handled quickly. The entire procedure is carefully timed. Milking proceeds by the clock, as do the bulk milk routes and operations at the bottling plant. As on all dairy farms, there is much work by lamplight, and the dairy herd takes no vacations. Recent extensions of electric service have done much to brighten dairy barns as well as to provide power for milking machines, coolers, separators, and other small machines which have tended to reduce the drudgery of the work. There are still no vacations, however, and work proceeds on schedule every day.

Here again, the dairyman finds his work similar to that of the worker in town. Such a farming system, with its manifold regulations and specialized services and equipment, inevitably encourages the setting up of specialized dairy farms. Years ago, city milk supplies came largely from farms of a general type, whose managers milked a few cows and considered dairying a side line. Such farms are finding it increasingly difficult to meet either the sanitary or the technical requirements for modern milk production. Dairying is today a capitalistic undertaking, increasingly concentrated on specialized dairy farms which must be organized and operated according to standards differing little from those of a modern food-products factory. Especially in the market-milk districts, this type of dairy farm has come to provide the great bulk of the supply.

In these ways the dairyman of the Manufacturing Belt faces economic problems which differ sharply from those of farmers in the other farm regions. Much closer to the city than they, both geographically and economically, he shares much of his own city's economic gyrations. In a quasi-monopolistic position because of location and local regulation, he is also subject to many influences not felt by the farmer who has a wider choice of markets. Faced with the necessity for a modern plant and a production schedule, his farm organization has become similar to that of a modern factory, specialized in a single product and with profits dependent upon the care and efficiency with which that product is produced and marketed.

Fruit, Truck, and Poultry.—To a considerable extent, the same circumstances apply to the growers of market vegetables, fruits, and poultry. In none of these lines is the regulation so extensive, but with all of them the marketing factor is very important. Eggs, small fruits, and vegetables must be fresh to command a premium in the city market. This requisite means night trucking, rapid handling, and preparation for market on a schedule. City inspectors are on hand, too, to inspect and grade all food products and to specify the manner in which they must be handled.

In these lines also, there are many long hours. Truck crops and fruit are seasonal products, but egg production goes on regularly and the hen is almost as hard a mistress as the cow. Specialized poultry farms, incorporating extensive buildings and equipment, have become increasingly common in the Manufacturing Belt in recent years.

Summary.—The Manufacturing Belt is the home of a city-supply type of agriculture, which differs from the agriculture of other areas principally in that its products are intended for a single city rather than for the general market. The farmers experience the monopolistic advantage of a favored location and the disadvantage of an inability to escape the economic fluctuations of the individual cities which they serve. The region's farms are specialized largely in the production of bulky and perishable products, most important of which are fluid milk, vegetables, small fruits, and eggs. The typical Manufacturing Belt farm belongs to one of these types. There are, of course, certain areas in which such farms do not prevail. They are not numerous, however, and do not materially alter the general agricultural pattern.

Agricultural Sections

Natural Environment.—The Manufacturing Belt does not occupy a very large percentage of the nation's best agricultural land. Historically, one of the principal causes for the first appearance of factories in New England was the negative influence of poor land. Nineteenth-century Yankees, finding they could not compete with farmers on the rich western prairies, gladly shifted their interests from their stony hills to the more remunerative manufacturing industries. Almost from the start, New England factory workers filled their lunch boxes with western meat and bread baked from western wheat flour.

As it shifted west and south, the Manufacturing Belt encroached upon better farm land. The Hudson and Mohawk valleys have rich soil, as do the southeast counties of Pennsylvania, but these areas are relatively small. The massive Appalachian Plateau lies directly to the east, and these hilly lands, although they provide much good pasture, are little better than the New England highland in matters of fertility and productivity.

Farther west, however, the plateau gives way to prairies, old lake beds, and similar areas of nearly level topography and fertile soil. Richer soils are encountered in the vicinity of Erie, Pennsylvania, and Youngstown, Ohio, and extend west and north to the boundaries of the region. Although these are timber soils, and not so fertile as the tall-grass soils of the western Corn Belt, they are above the national average in productivity, and support a remunerative type of commercial agriculture.

For convenience, the Manufacturing Belt may be divided into eastern and western portions with the axis located near the western boundary of Pennsylvania. In general, the western division has a relatively smooth topography, free from geographic barriers other than the Great Lakes. This portion has soils generally described as good (although becoming somewhat less fertile as one goes north in Lower Michigan) and of "demonstrated agricultural quality." The eastern division, on the other hand, is dominated by hills and low mountains. These rough areas have occasional fertile valleys, but most of the land is suitable only for pasture. Where general farming is attempted, it usually is of a subsistence type. Within the eastern division, however, are several areas of good, smooth land. Most notable are (1) the Mohawk Valley, (2) the Hudson Valley, (3) portions of the St. Lawrence Valley, (4) the Lake Champlain Valley, and (5) the northern Appalachian valleys and piedmont plateau of the southeastern part of Pennsylvania.

In addition, the eastern division has three areas of fairly smooth topography, but their soils are less fertile. They are (6) the New England Lowland, including the Cape Cod Lowland, (7) the lower Connecticut Valley, and (8) Long Island. An intensive agricultural development occupies all of these more productive sections of the eastern division.

The location of these major natural areas is shown in Fig. 73. Such a map is necessarily generalized to the extent of omitting many local details. In general, however, the black areas are hilly or rugged, genuine geographic barriers whose soils are infertile and whose surfaces are best utilized for pasture or the growing of timber. The white areas are undulating, in the main, and their soils are fertile. Stippled areas have a generally undulating topography, but their soils are only moderately productive in their natural state. With the application of fertilizer, however, these last-named areas can be made highly productive.

Climate.—Except for a few local variations, the climate of the Manufacturing Belt is of a distinctly continental type, characterized by hot summers, cold winters, and frequent changes in the weather. Growing seasons are long enough and rainfall is adequate for most temperate-zone crops. Corn does not mature near the northern margins, but elsewhere this staple crop matures properly if adequate soils are available. Precipitation is moderate, averaging from thirty to forty-five inches per year. Most of the moisture falls as summer thundershowers, but winter snowfall becomes increasingly heavy toward the east. The mountains of New England and New York have developed important winter-sports interests. Ski and toboggan enthusiasts seldom lack snow for their activities. The highland areas have slightly greater annual precipitation and somewhat lower annual temperatures than adjacent lowlands; but in these latitudes the Appalachian Highland is not high enough to form a significant climatic barrier.

Exceptions to this general climatic pattern occur along the east and south shores of the three Great Lakes. The areas affected are not large and the climatic effect is not great. It is sufficient, however, to account for three narrow belts along the shores, which are highly specialized in fruit-growing. They include narrow strips along the south shores of Lakes Erie and Ontario and along the west shore of Lake Michigan. Prime reason for their existence is the tempering effect of the lakes. Prevailing winds from the west

FIG. 73. Major Natural Land-use Areas in the Northeastern United States.

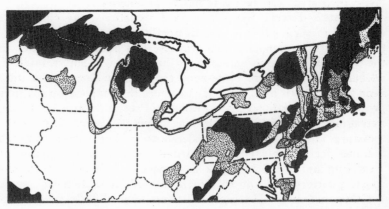

FIG. 74. Percentage of Land in Farms, 1930. The agricultural pattern of the northeastern United States has been influenced to no small degree by natural conditions. Climate is generally favorable to agriculture in all sections south of the Northern Forest and Lake Region, but there are many square miles of forbidding topography and infertile soil. The least useful farm lands are found in the Appalachian Highland and the highlands of New England. The major areas in which surface conditions are unfavorable for agriculture are shown in black in Fig. 73. The white areas are of "proven agricultural merit," and the stippled areas are moderately favorable. Fig. 74 shows variations in the percentage of land which was in farms (crops and pasture) in 1930. Less than 40 per cent of the land of the black areas was classified as farm land in 1930.

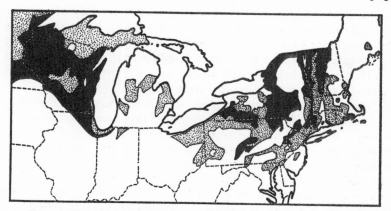

FIG. 75. Percentage of Farms Classified as Dairy Farms, 1929.

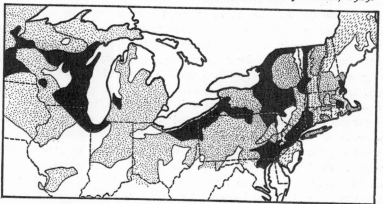

FIG. 76. Number of Milk Cows per Square Mile, 1930. The prevalence and intensity of dairy farming are shown on these two maps. In Fig. 75, a dairy farm is one on which 40 per cent or more of the farm income is derived from the sale of dairy products. The percentage of farms classified as dairy farms varies from one section to another, the greatest specialization appearing in the black areas and least in the white areas. Note the high degree of specialization in the Wisconsin butter and cheese area and in northern New York. Types of farming other than dairying are important in the areas having lighter shading. Many of these are identified as crop specialty areas in Fig. 77. In general, the most highly specialized dairy areas also have the largest number of milk cows per square mile (Fig. 76), but the correspondence is not absolute. Dairy farming often is the dominant type of agriculture in areas whose soils are too poor to support many cattle.

and northwest blow across the waters, and in early spring the prematurely warm spring zephyrs are cooled. As a result, the budding of trees is delayed from two to three weeks. That delay is important, because it prevents budding until danger of a late frost is past. Orchards and vineyards are more successful here than elsewhere in the Manufacturing Belt.

Throughout the entire region, the climate must be described as "good." It will grow a great variety of crops and there is almost never a bad year. Droughts are practically unknown. Under the year-round control of cyclonic storms, the climate has many changes: rainy days, dry days, cloudy days, bright days, all in constant procession. We have learned that such a climate is conducive to maximum human development. Certainly there is little chance for that type of mental or physical stagnation induced by unchanging weather conditions.

Adaptation to the Environment.—Both natural conditions and the presence of many cities have exerted profound influences upon the agricultural development of the Manufacturing Belt. Growing cities with their expanding demands for fresh milk, vegetables, fruits, and eggs have made it profitable to convert larger and larger local areas to the city-supply type of agriculture. Over most of the region, lands are well adapted to this sort of farm organization. Nearly two-thirds of the region consists of hills whose soil cannot support a profitable agriculture based on crops. Most of these hill districts have been converted to pasture for dairy cattle. On the lower, more tillable prairies and eastern valleys much forage and feed can be raised for dairy cows. In addition, the smoother districts have found profit in cash crops of which the most important are fruits and vegetables. Here and there general farming has lingered, usually in those sections farthest removed from the cities and least accessible to transportation. Occasionally, too, local conditions have favored crop specialties, such as tobacco in the Connecticut Valley or cranberries on Cape Cod. Such specialty areas are small and scattered, and do not alter the general picture of a city-supply type of agriculture dominated by dairying whose prime purpose is the production of market milk.

Despite the fact that it has much inferior land, the Manufacturing Belt ranks as one of the major agricultural regions of the country. The annual agricultural output, measured by gross farm income, is about one-seventh of the total for the entire United

States. This output is regularly valued at more than a billion dollars, of which about one-third is derived from crops and two-thirds from animals and their products. Dairy and poultry products account for most of this "animals and their products" group.

Dairy Farming.—The relative importance of dairying and other types of farming in the northeastern United States is indicated in Figs. 75 and 76. The Wisconsin-Minnesota Dairy Belt appears prominently on this map, but it is interesting to note that large sections of New York and Vermont show a similarly high degree of specialization. There is a difference, of course, in that the former area is devoted primarily to butter and cheese while New York and Vermont dairymen sell fluid milk almost exclusively. The only significant dairy district not thoroughly dominated by market milk is in northern New York (St. Lawrence County). This area has long been important for cheese, but its production has been declining steadily in recent years.

An indication of the intensiveness of dairying is revealed by the number of milk cows per square mile. Data for much of New England are not available, but several observations are possible despite this omission. In the first place, it appears that dairy cows are most numerous (forty or more to the square mile) in several of the "good" agricultural areas described previously under "Natural Environment." (See Fig. 73.) They are less numerous (twenty to forty to the square mile) in the poorer sections. Both situations are about what one would expect because of differences in soil capacities. There are, however, two notable exceptions to the first statement. Both in southern Michigan and in northwest New York, good lands have only a moderate number of dairy animals. It also appears that these two districts (as well as the Hudson River Valley) have generally less than 25 per cent of their farms specialized in dairying. As a matter of fact, these areas show greater diversification and less specialization in dairying than the region as a whole. Dairy products still head the list of sources of farm income, but other sources are of more than average importance.

The dominant type of agriculture of the Manufacturing Belt region is dairying with fluid milk as the major product. Yet the region contains several districts in which other farm products equal or exceed milk in economic importance. These specialty areas are worthy of special consideration.

Specialty Areas

Southern Michigan.—In addition to dairying, southern Michigan has a highly diversified farm system. Other livestock are important, especially sheep and beef cattle. But more significant are the crop specialties. Some of these are localized, but most are widely distributed. Of the local crop-specialty areas, the most important is the fruit district of the southwest corner of the state. Here, on the lee shore of Lake Michigan, have been planted orchards and vineyards whose production is sufficient to make this belt one of the nation's important sources of fruit. Apples, grapes, peaches, and cherries are the major varieties, the district producing about 2 per cent of the national output of each of these fruits. The fruit-growing development is most important in the extreme southwest county of the state, but with the construction of highways and the development of improved marketing facilities it has been extended northward into the Northern Forest and Lake Region. Fruit-raising promises soon to dominate lake-shore agriculture as far north as Grand Traverse Bay.

Other localized crop-specialty areas are the sugar-beet section south of Saginaw Bay (6 to 10 per cent of the United States crop) and two important potato-growing areas (5 to 10 per cent of the United States crop). One of the potato areas occupies the northern margin of the region between Saginaw Bay and Muskegon, and the other is in the "thumb" between Detroit and Saginaw Bay. Here are also produced more than one-quarter of the national crop of dry edible beans. Potatoes, beets, and beans, all adapted to a light soil and a short growing season, share the agricultural resources of these areas with the expanding dairy herds.

The remainder of southern Michigan consists of a roughly triangular area having its base along the southern boundary of the state and its apex near Grand Rapids. This section is warmer and has better soil than the remainder of the state. Its farms grow corn, wheat, oats, and hay, and its agriculture is a mixture of dairying and general farming.

Such diverse products give to Michigan agricultural organization the character of mixed farming. Dairying is the most important type of farm activity, but nowhere does it dominate agriculture as it does in most other sections of the Manufacturing Belt.

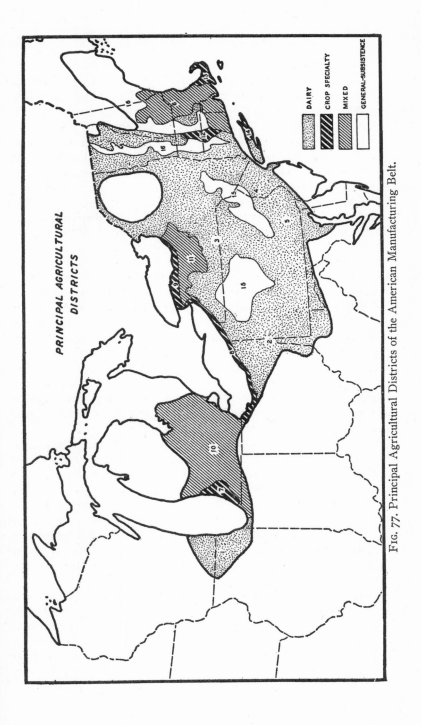

Fig. 77. Principal Agricultural Districts of the American Manufacturing Belt.

Up-state New York.—Northwest New York—from Buffalo to Syracuse—is likewise an area of general and mixed farming with dairying ascendent but not dominant. Here, along the shores of Lake Ontario, is the leading apple-growing district of the eastern United States. The state of New York regularly ranks second only to Washington in apple production, and nearly half of New York's apple trees are concentrated in this lake-shore belt. To the traveler this stretch of country appears almost as one continuous apple orchard. Grapes and pears are also important.

South of this narrow fruit belt, south of the Barge Canal and the New York Central Railroad, lie the picturesque valleys scoured to great depths in ancient glacial times and now holding the famous Finger Lakes, of which the largest are Seneca and Cayuga. These valleys, plus the valley of the Genesee River and other adjacent lowlands, are the location of general farms. Dairy cattle, small grains, hay, vegetables, meat animals, corn—all the components of a high-type, non-specialized commercial agriculture—are found in this section. Dairy products lead the list of sources of farm income, but there are also poultry products, fruit, meat animals, grains, and vegetables.

The narrow valley of the Hudson River has a mixture of dairying and general farming based largely upon fruits and market vegetables. Long an important highway, this valley proved a logical location for truck gardens once they had outgrown the areas nearer the New York metropolitan district.

The Connecticut Valley.—In New England, three areas not thoroughly dominated by dairying merit our attention. First of these is the Connecticut Valley, a narrow river plain specializing in the high-priced cigar tobaccos used for binder and wrapper. Acreages are not large, but the Connecticut Valley regularly accounts for from 10 to 15 per cent of the tobacco sales of the United States. This small area raises about half the binder tobacco and more than two-thirds of the wrapper tobacco grown in the United States. The tonnage is small, about 2 per cent of the national tobacco crop.

Southeast New England.—A broad belt of undulating country bordering the seacoast of Massachusetts, Maine, and Rhode Island is known as the "Seaboard Lowland." This district extends southward to Providence and northward to Portland. It does not have the best grade of farm land, but because it is not too hilly

and has many cities and excellent transportation, it has developed
a successful city-supply type of agriculture based primarily on cows
and hens—or, if you prefer, milk and eggs. Poultry is more important here, relatively, than in other sections of the Manufacturing Belt. Partly this is because Bostonians, possibly more than the
residents of any other seaboard city, present an extremely active
demand for "strictly fresh, newly laid" eggs. In addition, this land,
if fertilized and properly managed, yields good crops of small
grains for feed. It also produces good crops of market vegetables,
and these, together with eggs and milk, are the main sources of
income on the small hillside farms.

The Cape Cod peninsula of extreme eastern Massachusetts is
not farmed extensively because of large marsh areas and poor,
sandy soil. The marshes have proved excellent for growing cranberries. The prime requisites for successful cranberry-raising are
bogs and cheap labor for picking. Nature gave the Cape Cod
peninsula the bogs and near-by cities provide ample labor. The
Cape Cod area produces about two-thirds of the national crop.

Long Island.—The western third of Long Island is occupied
by two sprawling boroughs of the city of New York and several
small suburban cities. The remainder of the island is open country, however, and, except on numerous large estates which occupy
most of the middle portion, this is the location of an extensive
truck-garden development. Early potatoes, cabbage, and other
market vegetables are grown on the sandy flats. Small plots are
intensively farmed and the annual production is heavy.

These four sections are the only important areas in which the
better agricultural lands of the Manufacturing Belt are not dominated by dairying. It is significant that specialty areas are found
only on the better land—and not in the hills sections. It does not
follow that *all* good land is occupied by specialties, for some of
the most productive areas show a very high specialization in
dairying. Nor should we lose sight of the fact that in most of
them dairying is still the most important single source of farm
income. These areas happen to have been endowed by nature with
special gifts of climate or soil which have made the growing of
agricultural specialties relatively more attractive than elsewhere in
the region. The three lake-shore fruit belts are the products of
climate, while the other specialty areas owe their existence largely
to peculiar qualities of their soils. Southern Michigan, for ex-

ample, does not grow bumper crops of corn or wheat (although these are its leading farm crops) because its soils are not so productive as those of the grain belts. It can grow good potatoes, sugar beets, and beans, and these specialties, together with dairying, are gradually replacing the old grain and livestock type of agriculture which dominated the state's farming until recent years.

A similar transition is taking place in northwest New York. The New England coastal lowland, on the other hand, seems to have gone a step further. Eastern Massachusetts farmers, not well endowed with pasture, have increasingly turned their attention to poultry, the feed for which can be grown here with fair yields. Farming in the Connecticut Valley, and on Cape Cod and Long Island, must be considered largely as an adaptation to special soil conditions. Cape Cod bogs are nearly worthless except for growing cranberries. Connecticut Valley soils impart a special, desirable flavor to its cigar tobaccos. The sandy flats of Long Island warm up early in spring and favor the production of market vegetables. Thus an area may have turned to specialties either because its soils were too poor for staples or because they were adapted to specialty crops. Other factors are often equally important. Custom, tradition, and the presence of a marketing organization color the picture, and the availability and cost of transportation often materially affect the type of farming which will be chosen.

SUMMARY AND TREND

The geographic distribution of agriculture in the Manufacturing Belt may be outlined briefly as follows:

A. *Dairying,* with market milk as the product, is the leading type of farming throughout the region. Specialization in dairy farming is greatest in the "milk-sheds" of the largest cities, especially (1) the Chicago-Milwaukee section, (2) the Pittsburgh-Cleveland district, (3) the non-mountainous sections of New York and Vermont, (4) the hill country west of metropolitan New York, and (5) the piedmont and Appalachian Valley areas west of Philadelphia and Baltimore. All of these sections are known for either good soils for feed production, or good hill pasture. All have easy access to their own local markets.

B. *Poultry-raising,* requiring more feed and less pasture, is most important in the areas of relatively smooth topography where cultivation is practicable. Chickens are raised on nearly all farms, but the greatest egg-producing area is (6) the seaboard lowland of New England.

C. *Specialties* are important in several sections, mainly those having particularly advantageous conditions of climate or soil. Climate is the prime factor in locating the fruit districts of (7) southwest Michigan, (8) the south shore of Lake Erie and (9) the south shore of Lake Ontario, all of which specialize in orchard fruits and grapes. (10) Southern Michigan has a corn-livestock type of agriculture, mixed with dairying and the growing of potatoes, sugar beets, beans, and market vegetables. Growth of the automobile cities has speeded the trend toward a city-supply type of agriculture. (11) In northwest New York a similar trend away from general farming is observable. (12) The Connecticut Valley specializes in cigar tobacco, and (13) Cape Cod in cranberries. (14) Eastern Long Island is the location of intensive truck gardening, with primary emphasis upon potatoes.

D. *Mountain-type agriculture,* often at the subsistence level, occupies certain of the rougher and more inaccessible areas of (15) the northern Appalachian Plateau and (16) the New England Highland.

All of these farm types are increasing in importance except the last. Subsistence farming of the pioneer type is rapidly disappearing and seems to be making a last stand in the most rugged and remote areas. As more and more highways are built into these sections, farmers one by one turn to commercial farming, joining that great majority who have come to live not on the products of their soil but on the proceeds from the milk or egg check. And one by one these last rugged individualists become cogs in a great regional economic machine whose major function is to turn out two-thirds of the nation's manufactured goods.

FORESTS AND FISHERIES

Forests.—Although the Manufacturing Belt was originally forested, most of the land has been cleared and the few remaining sawmills are found mainly in the Appalachian Highland sections. Oak, maple, and hemlock are the leading types. The forest was important in establishing many an early tanning or paper industry. Paper mills are still an important feature of industrial development near the northern boundaries of the region. The mills obtain their supplies almost entirely from outside the region. Tanneries and planing mills likewise depend almost exclusively on outside supplies.

North Atlantic Fisheries.—In 1930, about one-third of one per cent of the gainful workers of the New England states and New York were employed in the fishing industry. This figure is not impressive, but it should not cause us to lose sight of the fact that North Atlantic fishermen regularly land more than one-quarter of the annual fishery catch of the United States and Alaska. In 1935, New England fishery products were valued at eighteen million dollars and those of the New York harbor area at about four million dollars.

Fish long have been plentiful in the shallow waters of the continental shelf off the North Atlantic coast. These shallows (usually less than 100 fathoms deep) are known as "banks" and are important feeding grounds because enough sunlight reaches them to grow the under-sea vegetation which supports marine life. Fisheries became an important source of income in Colonial days and the industry has added both color and income to life along the coast in succeeding years. Boston is the major market and handles nearly half the New England catch. Gloucester (Mass.) is more highly specialized in fishing than any other New England city, but it lands only about one-ninth as many fish as Boston. Portland ranks third among New England fishery ports. Metropolitan New York presents a good market for fresh fish and has its own fishing fleet which regularly lands about one-third as many fish as the fleets of New England. Fisheries south of New York harbor were considered in the chapter on the Gulf-Atlantic Coast Region.

The most important fish of North Atlantic waters both in tonnage and in value is the haddock. Cod generally ranks second, and is about half as valuable as haddock. These two species constitute nearly 60 per cent of the catch, which also includes mackerel, pollock, hake, cusk, halibut, and many others. The rapid-freezing process has made it possible to market New England fish over the eastern two-thirds of the nation, but most of the catch is still consumed in local communities.

REFERENCES

Agricultural colleges in each of the states of the Manufacturing Belt have issued a variety of bulletins concerned with all phases of agricultural development, including crops, dairying, soil problems and market problems. The Farm Credit Administration has summarized many of these studies and supplemented them with surveys of its own.

QUESTIONS AND PROBLEMS

1. What are the essential characteristics of the city-supply type of agriculture? Is it commercial or self-sufficing? general or specialized?

2. Is the Manufacturing Belt farmer more or less likely to be a member of a "community" than a Corn Belt farmer? Why? See Chapter XII.

3. In what ways does dairy-farming in the Manufacturing Belt exhibit more monopolistic elements than wheat-farming? How do these factors affect questions of individual liberty? government regulation of price?

4. As an agricultural region, the Manufacturing Belt represents the consolidation of hundreds of city-supply farming areas. Explain the meaning of this statement. What factors brought about the consolidation?

5. Name five recent inventions which have tended to decrease the importance of city-supply agriculture. What forces have tended to strengthen it?

6. Assume that technological improvements were to be introduced into all types of crop-raising which would free half the present farm population for other types of work. What would be the most likely effects upon agriculture in the Manufacturing Belt?

7. Write a brief description of the organization of the fluid milk industry, with particular reference to production, transportation, and marketing.

8. Under what conditions may farms not devoted to dairying be considered city-supply farms? What forces have tended to build up or destroy this type of agriculture?

9. What natural factors have influenced the location of the major fruit districts of the Manufacturing Belt?

10. In what ways does natural environment favor dairy-farming and discourage the growing of staple crops in the Manufacturing Belt?

11. Compile a list of the 16 agricultural districts of the Manufacturing Belt, indicating the major farm interest in each district.

12. What are the most important fishing products of the north Atlantic Coast? Where are they caught? How and where are they marketed?

13. The market-milk farm is a capitalistic venture. Why? What are the principal items of capital? How would they appear on the landscape?

CHAPTER XXII

MINERALS OF THE MANUFACTURING BELT

Minerals and Manufacturing.—Our modern industrial civilization has been made possible largely because of the availability of iron and copper to build our machines, and coal and petroleum to operate them. Students have pointed out that every great world power makes extensive use of all of these minerals; that the United States has been helped along the road to international ascendency because it is the leading producing country of all of these "key" minerals. To become great, modern nations must have machines and factories, and to have them they must have the metals to build them and the fuels to operate them. Although it would be quite possible for a nation to obtain all of these goods through international trade, the expense of shipment generally has rendered such purchases disadvantageous and has deterred such non-mineralized nations from achieving a high degree of industrialization.

In the United States, mineral-producing regions have not generally become locations for important manufacturing industries. The ores of metallic minerals (such as iron, copper, lead, zinc, and aluminum) are mined long distances from the factories which finally make them ready for use. The same statement applies generally to non-metallic minerals such as the clays, rare earths, chemical raw materials, petroleum, and natural gas. Even the number of manufacturing industries which have sought locations near the coal fields is relatively small. With the possible exception of coal, the importance of minerals in determining the concentration of industries in the Manufacturing Belt has been very slight. The significance of coal as a factor in industrial location requires greater elaboration.

The attractiveness of cheap coal varies enormously from one manufacturing industry to another. Nearly all manufacturing industries use coal, but its importance in manufacturing costs is relatively small in most types of industrial activity. In 1937, expenditures for fuel represented only 1.6 per cent of the value of the product for all manufacturing industries of the United

States. (Payment for wages and salaries was thirteen times as great.) In certain industries, however, fuel is a major item of manufacturing cost. Most prominent of these is the blast-furnace industry which in 1937 paid four times as much for fuel as for wages and salaries. In this industry 26 per cent of the value of the product was represented by fuel. At the other extreme stand industries such as clothing manufacture and printing and publishing, whose expenditures for fuel represented less than 1 per cent of the value of their products, and whose labor costs are from forty to fifty times as great as fuel costs. It is obvious that nearness to coal would be much more significant in the location of blast furnaces than in the case of clothing or printing establishments. As a matter of fact, the vast majority of American industries find fuel and power less significant than other factors in choosing plant locations. A few of the heavy coal users choose locations near the coal fields, but hundreds of others find other locations more attractive.

Transportation.—Despite the small importance of fuel in most manufacturing operations, it would be inaccurate to state that the North Appalachian coal fields have had no significance in locating the American Manufacturing Belt. The Great Lakes made it possible to bring Lake Superior iron ore to these coal fields at very low cost. Railroads tapping the coal area have established rate structures which spread the advantage of cheap coal over considerable areas. The highway and motor truck have had much the same effect. Transportation systems and rate schedules have made it unnecessary for industries to locate on the rough topography above the coal beds. The tendency has been rather for industries to grow up along the major transportation routes. Relatively few have sought locations *on the coal*. Even the blast-furnace industry has its center some distance northwest of the coal fields from which it obtains its fuel. Other industries generally have chosen sites at considerably greater distances from the coal fields. The Manufacturing Belt has coal in abundance, but the major industrial developments have appeared along the transportation routes and not in the coal fields.

Mineral Production.—The American Manufacturing Belt regularly produces about one-quarter of the mineral output of the United States. The coals, bituminous and anthracite, lead the list with about half the gross mine production of that region. These are followed in order of their value by petroleum, natural gas, and a long list of stone and clay products. Mineral production in the Manufacturing Belt is largely a story of coal as produced in the northern sections of the Eastern Coal Province, and of a long list of minor minerals, in no one of which does the region rise to national prominence. We turn first to a consideration of coal production in the entire Eastern Coal Province.

The Eastern Coal Province

The vast beds of coal which underlie the Appalachian Highland have been described as the richest and most productive in the world. In 1937, the United States produced approximately 30 per cent of the world's coal, and three-quarters of this production came from Appalachian mines. The Appalachian coal fields thus produced approximately 23 per cent of the world's coal in 1937, a figure which is fairly representative of their average importance from year to year.

Qualities of Appalachian Bituminous Coals.—Appalachian coals are described as high-grade bituminous coals. In the fuel industry, coals are ranked according to their heat value and their percentage of ash, volatile matter, fixed carbon, sulfur, moisture, and occasional other factors. Coalmen say that their fuel burns in three distinct phases, familiar to almost everyone who has fired a coal-burning furnace. (1) When coal is first heated it emits gas which is liberated from minute pockets. This gas is highly combustible and furnishes considerable heat in properly designed furnaces. (2) In the second stage the temperature has risen to the point where volatile matter ("coal tar") is released, transformed into gas, and ignited. The furnace stoker notes that at the beginning of this stage the coal appears waxy and portions of it stick to the poker. (3) Finally, the volatile matter has escaped and what remains is in reality coke, a porous mass of fixed carbon and ash which ignites when temperatures become high enough and which burns almost without smoke and with very little flame. This fixed carbon is the source of most of the heat but furnace temperatures must be high before it will burn.

Engineers use the B.T.U. (British thermal unit) as the unit for determining the heat value of coal, and in general the higher the

B.T.U. content the better the coal. But the thermal unit does not tell the whole story. Certain coals are known to have a very high thermal value but contain a high percentage of non-combustible ash. In burning these coals so much heat is used to bring the ash to incandescence so that the carbon may be ignited that very little is released for use. Fires built of such coals often burn fiercely without giving off an appreciable amount of heat. Thirty per cent is usually quoted as the maximum allowable amount of ash, but it is probable that the figure should be nearer 25 per cent. Coals with even 25 per cent ash give off very little heat. A second restriction upon the ranking of coal according to thermal content is that heat may be derived from either carbon or volatile matter. Some users prefer high-volatile coals but the trade is generally willing to pay more for low-volatile coals with high percentages of fixed carbon. The following analysis of four Appalachian coals, all of high rank, indicates the extent of these differences:

ANALYSIS OF APPALACHIAN COALS

	(1) New River, West Virginia (Low volatile semi-bituminous)	(2) Kanawha, West Virginia (High volatile bituminous)	(3) Big Sandy, Kentucky (High volatile bituminous)	(4) West Virginia (cannel)
Volatile matter....	19.2%	34.9%	38.1%	49.5%
Fixed carbon.....	74.4%	57.9%	57.2%	44.0%
Ash............	4.0%	5.7%	2.5%	5.2%
Moisture.........	2.4%	1.5%	2.2%	1.3%
B.T.U.'s (per lb.) .	14,750	14,200	14,150	14,700
Sulfur..........	.6%	.8%	.7%	.5%

These four coals were mined along the Chesapeake and Ohio Railroad within a distance of 200 miles. The New River coal (Column 1) is classed as semi-bituminous and is mined in the eastern portion of the southern West Virginia region. The term semi-bituminous is used to describe coals which rank between bituminous and anthracite. Semi-bituminous coals are higher in fixed carbon and correspondingly lower in volatile matter than true bituminous coals such as those analyzed in Column 2. Cannel coal (the name comes from candle) is very "flashy" and is often in demand for forging and open grate fires. It breaks down readily, however, and is not a "coking coal." Coke for metallurgical purposes is generally low in volatile matter, relatively high in fixed carbon and must have a high crushing strength which means comparative freedom from sulfur and numerous other impurities which produce a weak coke. Much of the Appalachian coking coal is classed as semi-bituminous. It is significant, however, that no accurate specifications for coking coal exist. Good coking coals differ markedly among themselves and there is no positive test except to place a sample in an oven and try it. Coking coal is not a grade of coal, but the best and most extensive deposits are found in the Appalachian fields.

Description of Area.—The following description of the Appalachian coal fields is taken from *The Coal Fields of the United States*, by M. R. Campbell of the United States Geological Survey.

"The Appalachian region is the greatest storehouse of high-rank coal in the United States, if not in the whole world. This nearby supply of high-grade fuel has constituted the foundation of the development of the blast furnaces, the great iron and steel mills, and the countless manufacturing enterprises of the Eastern States. The Appalachian region is a compact area of coal-bearing rocks which in general lie in a deep trough. The trough shape is well marked in its northern part, and the middle line or axis runs nearly through Pittsburgh and thence southwestward to the vicinity of Huntington, West Virginia, on the Ohio River. The lowest coal bed, if present in the deepest part of the trough, would be about 2,000 feet below the surface. The rocks in this great trough are thrown into a large number of minor wrinkles or anticlines (upfolds), especially on its southeastern side. These small folds generally bring to the surface the harder rocks just beneath the coal-bearing beds, and consequently they form ridges or mountains, as they are called in Pennsylvania and West Virginia. These die out toward the southwest, but they exert a marked effect upon the coal beds exposed at the surface as far south as the Kanawha River. In southern Virginia and Kentucky the trough flattens decidedly, and in consequence the coal beds in its middle are not so deep, but their outcrops cover a wider territory. In Tennessee the trough is scarcely apparent and the coal-bearing rocks appear to be nearly horizontal but are broken up by several small folds similar to those noted in the northern part of the region. The effect, however, is very different, for owing to the flatness of the rocks, the streams have cut away the up-bending folds, leaving great longitudinal valleys instead of anticlinal ridges, and narrow flat, intervening troughs of coal-bearing rocks. The same kind of structure, except that the troughs are more pronounced, is seen in the coal fields of Alabama, but toward the southwest the rocks gradually descend, and near Birmingham they begin to pass beneath the later rocks (Cretaceous) that were deposited on the Gulf Coastal Plain. This cover becomes deeper and deeper toward the southwest, until, in the vicinity of Tuscaloosa, the coal-bearing rocks disappear and nothing is left in sight but the soft sand and clay of the younger formations.

"Along the western margin of the Appalachian region the coal beds dip very slightly toward the east and there are no outliers of any consequence, but on the eastern margin the rocks are much more severely folded and there are many synclines (downfolds), which by the cutting back of the river valleys, have been separated from the main area and now form isolated natural fields. . . .

"The coal of the Appalachian region is generally of high rank but shows considerable variation, mainly in an east-west direction. In the reports of the Second Geological Survey of Pennsylvania it was clearly pointed out that the percentage of fixed carbon in the coals of the state increases from west to east, and also that the volatile matter decreases in the same direction. The result of this progressive change is that the coals on the eastern margin of the region are of much higher rank than are those on the western margin. . . ."[1]

Principal Districts.—It is apparent from this description that the Appalachian coal fields are not uniformly productive. Not only do qualities vary from field to field but some beds are much deeper than others and consequently more expensive to mine. Nearness to markets is also an important factor which has tended to depress the importance of southern fields and to favor coals from the northern portions of the area. Although coal is mined for local use in nearly all portions of the area, there are four major

---

[1] M. R. Campbell, "The Coal Fields of the United States," U. S. Geological Survey, *Professional Paper 100-A*, Washington, D. C., 1922, pp. 11-13.

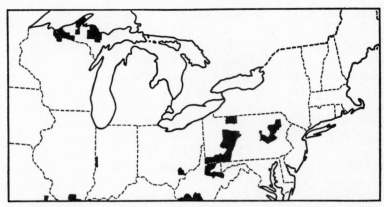

Fig. 78. Counties Having More Miners than Farmers or Factory Workers, 1930.

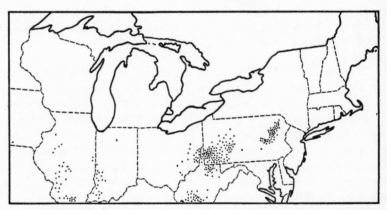

Fig. 79. Coal Production in 1935. The designation of mining districts follows a procedure similar to that developed for manufacturing districts in Figs. 63-70. Relatively few counties had more miners than factory workers or farmers in 1930, although several non-industrial counties of the Appalachian coal-mining areas stand out prominently. Compare Fig. 78 with Fig. 79, which shows coal production by counties in 1935. Extreme western Pennsylvania produces much coal but it has more factory workers than miners. Note also that a few miner-dominated counties produce no coal. These "miners" are oil workers (in northwest Pennsylvania) and iron and copper miners (in northern Michigan).

centers which dominate the industry. The location of these fields is indicated in Fig. 79, which shows coal production in 1935. First in importance are the northern bituminous fields of western Pennsylvania and adjacent portions of northern West Virginia and eastern Ohio. This area normally produces about one-third of the nation's bituminous coal. Its markets are the industries of the Manufacturing Belt, Atlantic shipping interests, and railroads and domestic consumers from New England westward.

The second bituminous area is centered in southern West Virginia and bordering portions of Kentucky and Virginia. Coals from these fields compete with northern coals in all markets. Their average production is about one-third of the national total. The third bituminous area, less important than the northern fields ($2\frac{1}{2}$ per cent of the national production), is located in the Birmingham area of northern Alabama. Here also are good deposits of iron ore and limestone, which, with the coal fields, have made Birmingham an important iron-making center. Markets for Alabama coal are confined largely to the southern states, but there is a considerable competitive area in Tennessee, North Carolina, and adjoining states. The fourth area to show a heavy concentration of mine activity is the anthracite fields of eastern Pennsylvania. Anthracite is seldom used for industrial purposes because of its high price and relatively low heat value. It is a smokeless coal, however, and is in very general use for domestic heating in New England and the Middle Atlantic states. A considerable portion of the reserves is held by the United States Navy for possible wartime use. The Navy also uses much coal from the Pocahontas field of southern West Virginia, which, although bituminous, is practically smokeless. Anthracite coal has been of decreasing importance in recent years, largely because of high production costs, numerous strikes, and the competition of other fuels such as natural gas, fuel oil, and the better grades of bituminous coal.

Transportation: The "Coal Roads."—In the United States, where relatively few manufacturing industries have sought locations near the coal fields, the transportation of coal has assumed a major importance. A number of railroads have been built into the Appalachian fields, and on most of these lines the coal traffic is so heavy that they have been designated as "coal roads" by transportation men. The coal roads connect the mining camps with the chief consuming centers and their routes indicate the flow of coal from this section—a movement which is of profound economic importance. Coal from the eastern coal fields is distributed by four major groups of transportation routes:

1. A heavy stream of coal traffic moves from the Appalachian fields eastward to the Atlantic seaboard. Most of the coal goes to feed the furnaces of industrial plants between Baltimore and Portland and is hauled the entire distance by rail. An increasing tonnage has recently been delivered to tidewater at near-by ports such as Norfolk and Baltimore from which it is distributed to the more northerly cities by coastal steamers.

2. A similar flow of coal leaves the fields westbound, the heaviest shipments going to the industrial cities of the southern Great Lakes. Most of this coal is shipped by rail but in the summer months returning ore boats carry a heavy tonnage to ports along the lakes. Pennsylvania anthracite even reaches Minneapolis by this route.

3. Anthracite coal has been important enough to attract a number of railroads whose lines radiate from these fields. On several lines, notably those leading to New England, tonnages have been sufficient to earn for them the title of "hard coal" roads.

4. The Alabama fields are served by a separate set of railroads (the "southern roads") which carry this coal to all parts of the South.

The extent of these movements varies both from year to year and from season to season. April is the low month for the coal industry, largely because of the declining demand for domestic fuel. Midsummer brings an increased demand and both production and shipments normally reach a peak near the middle of the winter (December-January).

In 1937, seven cars of coal out of every ten shipped from United States mines originated in the Appalachian fields. The remainder came chiefly from the interior fields (Illinois, Indiana, western Kentucky, etc.) and from scattered coal fields in the western states.

Production.—Figures concerning the distribution of coal are not necessarily indicative of tonnages produced. The differences lie partially in accumulated stocks at the mines but more largely in "captive" coal produced for industrial use in industry-owned mines. This coal never enters ordinary channels of commerce, but is taken directly from mines to factories, which are usually located near by. Figures for actual coal production tell a somewhat different story, as indicated in the following table:

BITUMINOUS COAL PRODUCTION, BY
STATES, 1937

(In percentages of the national total)

Pennsylvania	24.91
West Virginia	26.63
Eastern Kentucky	8.65
Virginia	3.10
Ohio	5.49
Illinois	11.58
Indiana	3.99
Western Kentucky	1.92
Other	13.73

100.00 (445,531,000 tons)

Production and Distribution of Pennsylvania Anthracite.
—Anthracite coal is a special commodity which is not in universal competition with bituminous coal. Its uses are chiefly for residential heating, and for this use it is everywhere preferred if prices are not too high and anthracite is readily obtainable. The chief markets are therefore confined very largely to (1) New England, (2) the Middle Atlantic states, and (3) those areas reached by cheap transportation on the Great Lakes. In recent years, anthracite has been experiencing increased competition from the more expensive but more convenient fuel oil and gas in domestic uses, and from the less expensive bituminous coals in the heating of larger buildings. As a result, the production of anthracite has been declining rather steadily. Production has averaged about fifty million tons, or less than one-sixth of the total tonnage of bituminous mines. From 1913 to 1929, anthracite production declined about 21 per cent, while the bituminous output increased 32 per cent. In the years following 1929, heavy tonnage losses were recorded by both fuels. In 1937, the production of anthracite was 37 per cent below the 1913 tonnage, and bituminous production was 8 per cent below the 1913 figure.

To the hundred-thousand anthracite miners and their families concentrated in a small area in the Wyoming, Lehigh, and Schuylkill valleys, and the adjacent Bernice Basin of Pennsylvania, these production trends are of more than passing interest. Anthracite fields are the most highly organized, from the standpoint of both labor and management, of all the mining areas of the country. Extreme concentration of work and the dominance of a few large companies have made this result almost inevitable. When labor troubles occur, the strikes usually are bitter and long drawn out. Consumption trends are clear, however, and these lines cast a dark shadow over that almost completely urbanized area which centers in the cities of Scranton and Wilkes-Barre, and sprawls over almost the entire northern anthracite field.

The problems of anthracite are in some measure the problems of the entire coal industry. Everywhere coal has encountered competition with other fuels and power sources—oil, gas, and hydro-electricity. The bituminous coal industry is cursed additionally with excess capacity in the face of generally declining markets. Markets for soft coal have not kept pace with our industrial expansion, partially because of the trend toward competitive fuels, but even more because of increased efficiency in coal utilization.

Railroads, generating plants, and manufacturing industries—the chief users of coal—have made remarkable progress in recent years in increasing the amount of work obtained from a pound of coal. In electric generating plants, the amount of coal required to produce one kilowatt hour has declined 85 per cent since 1901. Other industries have shown less spectacular results, but in all power uses increased efficiencies have been notable. In the face of these decreasing demands, the soft-coal industry has continued to expand. New mines have been opened until present capacities are far beyond any expected use.

For the future it appears that so long as the nation desires coal, these areas will be coal-mining centers. For they have the nation's largest reserves of high-rank coals. The market for anthracite may continue to shrink but will not disappear so long as other smokeless fuels are so much more expensive. Ultimately it appears that all bituminous coal may be reduced to a smokeless form in plants located near the mines. In the future we seem likely to have near the mine mouths electric generating plants, gas plants, coke ovens, and refineries for reducing coal to liquid form. Little coal would be sold as such, and nearly all power would be generated near the mines. Oil and gas would be piped to consumption centers, and the great pall of smoke which now hangs over our cities would disappear.

Summary.—The Eastern Coal Province readily divides into four sections: (1) the anthracite section of eastern Pennsylvania, (2) the north Appalachian section of western Pennsylvania, northern West Virginia, and adjacent Ohio and Maryland, (3) the "Middle" Appalachian section of southern West Virginia, eastern Kentucky, and adjacent areas of Virginia and Tennessee, and (4) the southern, or Alabama section of Birmingham and vicinity. The first two of these sections are included in the Manufacturing Belt. The Manufacturing Belt produces about 45 per cent of the nation's coal, including practically all of the anthracite and one-third of the bituminous output.

NORTH APPALACHIAN BITUMINOUS SECTION

The only high-rank bituminous coals to be found in or near the Manufacturing Belt are taken from this section. Here the quality is excellent, mining conditions are good and sufficient varieties are available for practically every industrial use.

Mining.—The typical North Appalachian coal mine is a "slope" or "drift," miners' names for mines which begin at an outcrop in the side of a hill or cliff and follow the seam in under the hill. Such mines are easily opened, and since little or no hoisting is required they are inexpensive to operate. In the Pittsburgh area, many of them open near an established railroad or a navigable river (especially the Monongahela). Furthermore, the coal is of good quality. It was these mines of the "Pittsburgh Bed" which early favored Pittsburgh as the "steel center of the West." Good coal, easily obtained and cheaply delivered, is a powerful stimulus to the location of heavy industry.

Fields.—The greatest concentration of coal-mining is found in (1) the Pittsburgh field which lies south and southwest of the city (7 per cent of United States production), (2) the Connellsville field, surrounding the city of that name, and famous for its coking coal (4 per cent of United States), (3) the Freeport field, east of Pittsburgh (2 per cent of United States), (4) the Westmoreland-Ligonier field, northeast of Pittsburgh (2 per cent of United States), (5) the larger and more widespread central Pennsylvania field of west-central Pennsylvania (11 per cent of United States), (6) the Fairmont field of northern West Virginia (4 per cent of United States), and (7) the Panhandle-Pittsburgh field of eastern Ohio and the Panhandle of West Virginia (4 per cent of United States).

These seven fields produce about one-third of the United States annual output of coal, and practically all the mines are located within one hundred miles of the city of Pittsburgh.

Qualities.—From these seven fields come coals adapted to almost every commercial use. Connellsville coal, low in sulfur but relatively high in volatile matter, is considered the national standard for making metallurgical coke. Coals from the eastern part of the section are generally harder, higher in fixed carbon, and in demand for domestic and commercial heating. Ohio coals are generally softer, but are extensively used for raising steam.

THE ANTHRACITE SECTION

Anthracite is seldom a direct competitor of bituminous coal. Formed under terrific geologic pressure, anthracite is nearly devoid of volatile matter. The better grades are nearly pure fixed carbon. Hence it is a smokeless fuel, very clean to handle and universally preferred for domestic heating where price differentials are not too great.

Anthracite, however, is expensive to mine, first because the formations are very irregular and second because it always contains much slate which must be removed before the coal is marketed. Huge "breakers," buildings in which the coal is broken, "picked," sorted, graded, and washed are familiar adjuncts to every anthracite mine. Much of this work must be done by hand. The marketable product is inevitably expensive even at the mining center. Add the usual freight rates to these costs, and the result is a price high enough to keep anthracite out of the markets of most sections of the United States.

Location.—The entire anthracite district embraces only 3300 square miles and the portion actually underlain with coal occupies only 480 square miles. The section is located in four adjacent valleys of eastern Pennsylvania.

The trade recognizes five fields within the anthracite area: (1) a northern, or Wyoming field (including the densely populated metropolitan areas of Scranton and Wilkes-Barre) which produces more than half the total output, (2) a western middle field (Shamokin) producing about one-quarter of the total. The remaining output is divided about equally between (3) an eastern middle field (Hazleton) and (4) a southern field. (5) The detached Sullivan County field produces less than 1 per cent of the total.

Mining.—The anthracite industry has always used much labor —for mining the coal, and for preparing it for market. The fact that it is difficult to separate slate from the coal means that great quantities of this waste must be taken from the mine only to be discarded at the breakers. Strip mining is practiced in a few places but is not generally possible. Machines of various types have been introduced into the underground workings, but despite these improvements, the output per man per day is less than three tons, only three-fifths as great as in the bituminous industry. These figures include only mining, and not the costly breaking, sorting, and washing which all anthracite must undergo. Production fluctuates chiefly with the demand for domestic heating, which in turn depends largely on the weather. It is the weather, rather than general economic conditions, that causes the major fluctuations in the anthracite industry.

Despite these handicaps, however, anthracite is still the almost universal domestic fuel over much of the northeastern United States. New England white houses unquestionably stay white longer than those in the soft-coal belts. Anthracite is smokeless and also a steady, long-burning fuel, clean and easy to handle. There is no immediate prospect that the hundred-thousand anthracite miners will quickly find themselves out of jobs because of a disappearing market.

OTHER MINERALS

Outside the coal districts the mineral industries of the Manufacturing Belt are of relatively small importance and widely scattered. These industries are of a diverse nature but they are generally concerned with six types of products: (1) oil and gas, (2) stone, (3) clay, (4) underground natural brines, (5) zinc, and (6) iron ore.

Oil and Gas.—Famous throughout the automobile world are the widely advertised Pennsylvania oils, premium-priced lubricants refined from paraffin-base crudes taken from the Pennsylvania oil fields. The Pennsylvania "field" covers parts of western Pennsylvania and adjacent New York and Ohio. In reality it is the northern portions of the Appalachian district, which extends southward into West Virginia, there to be more important for gas than petroleum. The Pennsylvania fields produce about 2 per cent of the annual national output of petroleum. Principal center of oil production is the Bradford field of northern Pennsylvania.

The North Appalachian district produces gas from the famed Oriskany sands which underlie a wide area. The total marketings are from 10 to 12 per cent of the United States total, the largest developments being in West Virginia. Most West Virginia gas is piped north into Ohio and the Pittsburgh area of Pennsylvania. Other oil and gas fields are found in central Michigan (near the north boundary of the region).

Stone.—Stone outcrops appear over most of the eastern two-thirds of the Manufacturing Belt. Most of them are of local importance only, but the aggregate production is large. Most notable of the high quality stone-producers are the granite and marble quarries of Vermont and New Hampshire. Vermont leads the nation in the production of monumental granite and marble. The principal quarries are near Rutland. In Pennsylvania, limestone and shale in the Lehigh Valley provide materials for the nation's largest concentration of cement plants. Abrasive stones are important in Ohio and New York. These include oilstones, silica, garnets, and emery.

Clays.—A wide variety of clay products is made throughout the region, but the best pottery clays are found in eastern Ohio and northern New Jersey. East Liverpool, Ohio, and Trenton, New Jersey, are the most famous pottery centers of the region.

Natural Brines of Michigan.—Wells in the vicinity of Saginaw Bay in Michigan produce natural brines which make that state the leader in several minor minerals. These brines yield magnesium, bromine, calcium, and sodium.

Similar underground waters enable Michigan to produce about one-third of the national supply of evaporated salt. Major salt-producing centers are in the Saginaw Bay and Detroit areas.

Zinc.—The Manufacturing Belt contains two important zinc-producing areas, one in northern New Jersey (Franklin Furnace) producing 15 per cent of the national output, and the other in St. Lawrence County, New York (near the Adirondacks), which produces about 5 per cent of the total.

Iron.—Pennsylvania and New York have mined iron ore for many years, but their production has been small since the ascendency of Lake Superior ore. These states still produce practically the entire national supply of magnetite. The single Pennsylvania operation, located near Lebanon, is an open-pit mine said to rank seventh in tonnage among iron mines of the United States. The New York production is near Lake Champlain.

Basic Production and Manufacturing.—A review of basic production in the northeastern states leads to the conclusion that the geographic concentration of manufacturing in the United States bears little relation to the location of basic natural resources. The single important basic industrial material produced extensively in the American Manufacturing Belt is coal. There is little doubt that the excellence of coals in the Pittsburgh district was a prime consideration in the early establishment and continued concentration of the iron and steel industries in that area. It is also true that the availability of cheap fuel is an important factor in industrial development throughout the region. But the importance of coal beds as a magnet to industry has been greatly modified by technological and artificial factors in the field of transportation. Cheap transportation in the form of low railroad and waterway rates has spread the attractive force of Appalachian coals over a broad area. Industries have not found it necessary to locate very near the mines. The major attractive force is not the mine from which the coal is taken, but the railroad line along which it is hauled. North Appalachian coal has been a significant regional force in making the Manufacturing Belt a good area in which to operate factories, but its attractive force has not been sufficiently localized to attract many industries to the specific districts in which coal is mined.

The importance of coal as a locational factor obviously varies greatly among the various types of manufacturing industries. Many processes require relatively little fuel or power and industries of these types generally find other factors more important when plant locations are to be chosen. Other industries find coal a major item of cost, and among these nearness to cheap fuel is a leading location factor. Most significant of the large fuel users are the so-called "heavy industries," whose products are manufactured principally from iron and steel.[2] In considering the various sections of the Manufacturing Belt, it seems logical to begin with the major American center for the heavy industry, the Pittsburgh-Cleveland Steel Area.

REFERENCES

References for, further reading on the coal industry were cited in Chapter XVIII. Coal-mining problems are discussed from the economic standpoint in W. G. Fritz and T. A. Veenstra, *Regional Shifts in the Bituminous Coal Industry* (University of Pittsburgh, 1935). Recent developments in coal mining are discussed in each *Minerals Yearbook*. See also the publications of state geologists for each of these states.

QUESTIONS AND PROBLEMS

1. What portions of the Appalachian Coal Province lie within the Manufacturing Belt? Why are the other portions not included?
2. Write a brief statement indicating the qualities found in various grades of coal. How do these qualities affect the desirability of coal for (a) domestic use, (b) industrial use, (c) commercial heating, and (d) railroad use?
3. Why is much Appalachian coal sold in Illinois and Missouri despite the fact that both states have coal-mining industries?
4. Every region we have studied has a coal-mining industry. When this fact is considered, how do you account for the concentration of the nation's coal industry in the Appalachian and Illinois fields?
5. Consult a recent volume of *Minerals Yearbook*. Write a brief report covering (a) uses of coal in the United States, and (b) recent improvements in the efficiency of coal utilization by various types of users.
6. Assume that each of the following industries is faced with a reduction in the demand for its products which amounts to 50 per cent of its present production: cotton-growing, coal-mining, and automobile-manufacturing. Describe the problem of readjustment

---

[2] The term "heavy industry" is not subject to precise definition. To city zoning authorities, a heavy industry is one originating smoke, noise, dust, or odor in quantities sufficient to become objectionable to adjacent residents. Cities usually set aside specific zones for heavy industries. The term is also applied to industries which handle bulky or heavy materials whose values are low in comparison with their weight or bulk. Heavy industries usually use larger amounts of power and fuel, and correspondingly smaller amounts of labor than the average for industry in general. A satisfactory statistical definition is not available, but the concept is quite useful in discussing urban land use.

in each industry, indicating how production would be reduced and the relative degree to which owners and laborers would be affected in each case.

7. Why are minerals given so much attention in the Manufacturing Belt when such small percentages of the area and population are devoted primarily to mining industries?

8. How important is coal as a factor in the location of manufacturing industries? Consider especially such industries as clothing manufacture and steel. Why are transportation facilities and freight rates important in your answer?

9. Where is the Anthracite District? Why is it one of the most densely populated areas in the United States?

10. Where are the major markets for anthracite coal? For what uses is anthracite preferred? Why has the demand for anthracite declined?

11. What is the historic and immediate importance of Pennsylvania iron ore in the location of the Manufacturing Belt?

12. Where are the Manufacturing Belt's principal deposits of zinc? What other regions furnish competition for producers in these areas?

13. Pennsylvania natural gas is worth about eight times as much per cubic foot at the wells as Texas natural gas. How do you account for this difference?

14. To what extent do the products of the Pennsylvania oil fields compete with those from Mid-Continent fields?

15. What types of agriculture are found in the North Appalachian coal fields? (See Chapter XXI.) Why?

16. Describe the qualities, sources, and uses of the coking coal used in the Manufacturing Belt.

CHAPTER XXIII

THE PITTSBURGH-CLEVELAND STEEL AREA

THE city of Pittsburgh has been the nation's iron and steel center since the early days of the nineteenth century. For nearly a century, local deposits of excellent coking coal have been combined with locally mined iron ore and limestone to produce iron and steel, first to be barged down the Ohio River, and later to be distributed over a vast network of railroads to the expanding markets of the growing nation. Pittsburgh's location was strategic. Situated at a junction of gulches where the Allegheny and Monongahela combine to form the Ohio River, at the head of navigation on that river which flows rather directly into the then-developing Middle West, Pittsburgh was a focal point for transportation routes over the mountains and a point of embarkation to the western prairies. Coal, ore, and limestone were easily barged to Pittsburgh and there was established an iron industry which soon elevated the town to first rank in iron and steel production. To this day, Pittsburgh has not lost that position of leadership, but it has witnessed a continued spread of the steel industry to other neighboring cities. This movement has taken a northwesterly direction toward the Cleveland area. First to the Mahoning Valley, then to Cleveland, the steel industry has extended, until today Ohio stands second only to Pennsylvania in steel production and its steel industry is growing much more rapidly.

The greatest factor in this northwest movement has been Lake Superior iron ore. Soon after the Civil War the vast and accessible deposits of iron ore were opened in Upper Michigan and Minnesota. With access to these cheap sources of ore, it quickly became evident that underground mining for iron in Pennsylvania would not longer be profitable on a large scale. Pittsburgh furnaces began to use Lake Superior ore which was brought very cheaply by lake barge to Cleveland and the other Lake Erie ports and transshipped by rail the remainder of the distance. With this cheap source of ore and unexcelled reserves of coking coal, the Pittsburgh steel industry expanded rapidly. Soon, however, steelmen began to show preferences for locations outside the city. In the first place, good factory sites were scarce. Pittsburgh is too hilly to provide many good ones. Furthermore, some saving in freight could be accomplished by moving nearer the Lake Erie ore-receiving ports. Still, it was not desirable to get too far from the west Pennsylvania coal fields, because freight rates on coal are nearly as important as on ore. So the shift in steel production began, but the jumps were not very long nor very frequent. In 1914, Pennsylvania still retained 48 per cent of the nation's iron and steel output and Ohio was in second position with 20 per cent. The end of the World War (1919) found Pennsylvania with 44 per cent, Ohio with 22 per cent. Decentralization continued. In 1935, Pennsylvania reported 30 per cent of the national iron and steel output and Ohio 23 per cent. Illinois and Indiana (largely the Chicago area) reported 8 per cent and 11 per cent, respectively, of the national iron and steel output.

Thus the Pittsburgh steel district expanded and became the Pittsburgh-Cleveland steel district with blast furnaces and steel mills scattered over the territory between these two centers. Pittsburgh still leads the world of iron and steel, but it in no sense dominates the industry as it did a generation ago.

The iron and steel empire of which Pittsburgh is the economic capital and Cleveland the second city, although primarily a kingdom of blast furnaces and rolling mills, is also the nation's center for the so-called "heavy industries." Thousands of tons of steel ingots and pig iron are shipped to other sections for local manufacture, but a far greater tonnage is fed to innumerable wire mills, sheet and tube plants, structural steel works, automobile parts factories and the long list of establishments manufacturing the heavy machinery which symbolizes our modern civilization.

Other industries, to be sure, have found a place in this empire of steel. The mere agglomeration of some five millions of people in the area would have caused the development of a great many local industries processing foods and other products for local consumption. In like manner, a number of parasitic industries dependent upon an abundance of woman labor invariably are found in centers for heavy industry. Thus Pittsburgh manufactures much silk, and the Cleveland area many electric light bulbs.

Another group of industries is based upon local deposits of minerals such as clay for pottery in eastern Ohio or natural gas for the glass industry of the Pittsburgh area. Finally, there is a considerable group whose location here seems entirely fortuitous. Akron continues to produce nearly two-thirds of the nation's rubber tires and tubes, and Pittsburgh and Cleveland hold high positions in the paint and varnish industries although it seems none of these cities have particularly advantageous locations for such industries beyond being near the center of national consumption of their products.

Trade and distribution are likewise important in the economic organization of the section. Both Pittsburgh and Cleveland are important centers for banking, finance, and the wholesale trade. So generally, in fact, have industries sought locations beyond the borders of these cities that they may well be thought of as commercial rather than industrial cities. In this development they have followed the general pattern so prevalent in industrial areas. As an industrial city grows, increasing pressure from commercial establishments gradually forces manufacturing plants into suburban locations. Factory sites become locations for stores, warehouses, banks, and railroad terminals. Manufacturers move their plants but retain offices near the business center. Soon the city has become a transfer and transaction center for large industrial communities beyond its boundaries, a shopping and amusement center for the millions who live in those communities. Tall factory chimneys give way to tall office buildings, and the transformation from industrial to commercial center is complete. This description is especially true in Pittsburgh where an extreme scarcity of good building sites has caused downtown real-estate prices to skyrocket to unbelievable levels; but it is also true on the flat lake plain of downtown Cleveland where trade, finance, and distribution dominate the business life.

Outside these major cities the economic pattern is definitely industrial. Lake ports are busy unloading lake-borne ore either for local furnaces or for shipment to interior points, in a vain attempt to satiate the appetites of the hundred blast furnaces which dot the landscape to Pittsburgh and beyond. Returning trains usually carry coal from Pennsylvania and West Virginia, en route to Lake Erie ports either for local use or for trans-shipment to cities of the western Great Lakes.

Furnaces fill the air with smoke and the night sky weirdly reflects their glow. In city after city the blast furnace, the rolling mill, and the coke oven are the commanding economic institutions.

Production is for the national market. Business activity here fluctuates with the prosperity or depression of the entire nation. It is, indeed, a truly industrial area in the modern sense of the word.

The Pittsburgh Area.—From its original site at the confluence of two rivers, Pittsburgh has expanded until its metropolitan area covers more than 1600 square miles. Expansion has naturally occurred along the chief transportation routes. Railroads generally follow the rivers because the narrow gulches provide the best routes across the dissected plateau country. In addition, most of the streams are navigable for coal barges and where mines are located near the streams a cheap and convenient type of transportation is available for steel mills and other factories. In consequence, Pittsburgh's expansion has taken two principal directions (see Fig. 80): (1) southward more than 50 miles up the Monongahela and Youghiogheny rivers into the heart of the coking coal area, and (2) to a lesser extent northward up the Allegheny and down the Ohio rivers. The east-west expansion has been less, but has followed the only two railroads which do not parallel the courses of the rivers. In 1930, the entire metropolitan district had a population of 1,950,000 of whom 670,000 lived in the city of Pittsburgh (which occupies about 3 per cent of the metropolitan area). Metropolitan Pittsburgh thus consists of a series of urbanized radii meeting in the central city which has perforce become its economic and social center. "All roads lead to Pittsburgh" and there is little communication between the radii except through the major center. With traffic swarming down these narrow gulches, the transportation problem has become acute. Railroads have long held nearly all available land between the bluffs and the river banks. Occasional wider spots have been occupied by factories.

The downtown business section, cramped for space and faced with high real-estate prices, has built upward in the Manhattan manner until Pittsburgh has acquired an imposing group of tall buildings. Confronted with a similar problem in regard to automobile traffic, Pittsburgh has not hesitated to build numerous bridges and to carry a portion of its traffic on double-decked streets. Residential districts, forced to the high plateau, are best reached by surface cars which attain the upper level by means of cables or racks and pinions. The University of Pittsburgh, de-

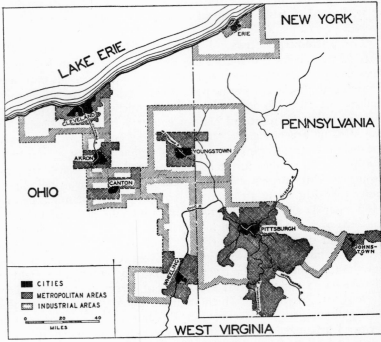

FIG. 80. The Pittsburgh-Cleveland Steel District. Of all the sections of the Manufacturing Belt, the Pittsburgh-Cleveland area shows the greatest response to raw materials and transportation. Pittsburgh started its iron-making career in competition with centers located farther east largely because of the presence of local coking coal and iron ore. But Pittsburgh did not become the dominant steel center of the nation until cheap supplies of Lake Superior ore were made available. As the steel industry grew, new plants were erected along the railroad routes between Pittsburgh and Lake Erie as well as in the Pittsburgh area and along Lake Erie. Eventually the section between Pittsburgh and Lake Erie came to be the steel center of the United States. Other manufacturing industries are found in the section, but its economic backbone is the steel and steel-products industries. Why is the ore hauled to the coal rather than the coal to the ore? Why are heavy steel products commonly manufactured near the steel centers and lighter machinery at greater distances?

siring expansion and faced with high real-estate prices, built the famed "Temple of Learning," forty stories high, the only college skyscraper in the world. In these ways Pittsburgh has found it possible to overcome the disadvantages of a poor site in order to retain the advantages of a good location.

Banking.—Excepting only Chicago and San Francisco, Pittsburgh has a larger banking business than any city west of the Atlantic seaboard. Although chiefly concerned with the steel industry, its bankers are also important in the financing of a wide variety of businesses throughout the nation.

Wholesale Trade.—Pittsburgh wholesalers reach a large and populous territory which covers the coal areas of Pennsylvania and West Virginia as well as a considerable section of southeast Ohio. Its wholesale trade is nearly two-thirds that of Philadelphia.

Manufacturing.—The Pittsburgh industrial area (see Fig. 80) normally produces from 2 to 3 per cent of the national output of manufactured goods. Approximately one-quarter of the factory production originates within the city of Pittsburgh, and the remainder is scattered among a large number of smaller communities which compose the Pittsburgh industrial area. The word Pittsburgh is almost synonymous with steel. Iron and steel constitute more than one-third of the manufacturing output of the Pittsburgh area. Miscellaneous machinery is the second product, followed by electrical goods, glass, and bakery goods. Other industries are largely local or of small relative importance.

The Pittsburgh industrial area has high national ranking in most of these industries. Nearly one-fifth of the nation's steel and one-sixth of its glass are produced here. The area produces about 6 per cent of the national output of electrical goods of all types. It is likewise a national center for the manufacture of lesser commodities such as aluminum, air brakes, refractories, and plumbing fixtures. Most of these items are of a ferro-metallurgical character and reflect Pittsburgh's leadership in iron and steel. The glass industry which extends chiefly southwest and into West Virginia and Ohio has been attracted to the area by cheap supplies of natural gas, the best fuel for firing glass furnaces.

Youngstown and the Mahoning Valley Area.—The shortest and easiest rail route between Pittsburgh and the Lake Erie ore docks runs northwestward from Pittsburgh down the Ohio River to the mouth of the Beaver River, then up the Beaver and its branch, the Mahoning, through Youngstown to Warren. North of Warren, the topography is more favorable and the railroads separate, some going to Cleveland, others to Ashtabula and the other lake ports. South of Warren all routes follow the valley and as a result the Mahoning Valley railroads carry some of the heaviest tonnages (chiefly ore and coal) in America. It was only natural that as the Pittsburgh steel industry began to expand and migrate, it should seek sites along this route. One after another, blast furnaces and steel mills began to appear in the valleys and Youngstown was soon the center of a fast-growing iron and steel area.

In 1930, the Youngstown metropolitan area had a population of 365,000 of whom 170,000 lived within the city and the remainder in a number of smaller centers, most important of which are Warren, Ohio, and Sharon, Pennsylvania. Its industrial area (see Fig. 80) includes two counties in Ohio and two in Pennsylvania with manufacturing representing slightly more than 1 per cent of the national total. About two-thirds of this manufacturing is in Ohio and the remaining third is in the Pennsylvania portion of the industrial area.

The Youngstown area is dominantly industrial, and its industry is steel. Trade and finance are developed hardly beyond local needs. Local inhabitants not connected with the steel industry are likely to be employed by the railroads which haul the ore and coal over this great artery of heavy traffic. Specialization in iron and steel is notably greater than in the Pittsburgh area. Iron and steel alone represent 55 per cent of the total factory product, and if account is taken of machinery, coke, railroad shops, and other allied industries the total rises well above 75 per cent. The principal industry outside this group is the manufacture of electrical goods, representing about 10 per cent of the combined factory output of the area. A considerable output of clay products is also reported.

Outside Youngstown, which has about one-third of the factory output of the four-county industrial area, the major centers are New Castle, Pennsylvania (population 49,000), with 7 per cent of the total, and Warren and Niles, in Ohio, with a combined output aggregating 11 per cent. Thus fully half the industry of the Youngstown area is located in smaller centers, many of them one-mill towns scattered along the major transportation lines.

The Cleveland Area.—To the New England Yankees who settled there, the site of Cleveland must have seemed almost ideal for the development of a great city. The mouth of the Cuyahoga River provided a small harbor for lake craft and certainly future lines of land transportation must follow closely the south shore of Lake Erie as the most desirable route from New England and New York to the West. Nor has history decreased the virtue of their choice, for Cleveland stands today in one of the best commercial locations in America. Railroads have come and skirted the lake, placing Cleveland on the busiest transportation route in the country. Lake Superior ores were discovered and Cleveland has become the operating center for three-quarters of all Great Lakes shipping. With ore and coal shipments passing through her harbor, Cleveland has become a strategic crossroads for American commerce. And where such crossroads develop there also grow important commercial cities.

The Cleveland metropolitan district had a population of 1,-200,000 in 1930, of whom 900,000 lived within the city and the remainder in a ring of small municipalities which adjoin it. The city itself covers a relatively large area (711 square miles) and thus includes not only the central business-financial-shopping nerve center but a large percentage of the outlying factory districts as well. A considerable industrial development has spread to the westward, however, and the Cleveland industrial area includes an additional county (Lorain) in that direction.

Because of its interests in lake shipping, Cleveland's sphere of wholesale activity is far flung. The city serves a considerable area of northern Ohio rather intensively, but one is apt to find Cleveland merchandise on the shelves of many an establishment along the Upper Great Lakes.

In banking as in wholesale trade Cleveland falls somewhat behind Pittsburgh, but Cleveland's financial importance is comparable with that of St. Louis, Detroit, Kansas City, or Los Angeles. Home of one of the regional Federal Reserve Banks, Cleveland is generally recognized as one of the major financial centers of the United States.

Manufacturing.—Although manufacturing in the Cleveland industrial area has shown a definite specialization in iron and steel, that specialization is much less than in the Pittsburgh and Youngstown areas. Iron and steel represent approximately one-ninth of factory production in the Cleveland area. Specialization has been along lines of iron and steel products rather than basic materials. Prominent in the list of manufactures are bolts, nuts, washers, screws, forgings, machine tools and accessories, motor vehicles, stamped and enameled ware, structural steel, and wire. If cognizance is taken of such products, considerably more than half the industrial output may be allotted to the ferro-metallurgical industries. Cleveland thus falls easily in the list of iron and steel centers, but it must be recognized as essentially a producer not of the basic materials but of the more highly manufactured products. In short, Cleveland is a steel *products* center.

Other industries have also grown to importance. Cleveland has come to rival Pittsburgh as a center for the manufacture of electrical goods, with a production four-fifths as large as that of the Pittsburgh area. Clothing for both men and women is also a product of growing importance. In these ways the Cleveland industrial output shows greater diversity than that of Pittsburgh. There are fewer furnaces but about as many machine products and a longer list of important industries not related to iron and steel. The total factory output of the Cleveland area is about seven-eighths as great as that of the Pittsburgh district, or about 2 per cent of the national total.

Canton.—The economic development of the Canton area is decidedly similar to that of Youngstown. The steel industry is preeminent. Blast furnaces and rolling mills account for half the industrial output and much of the remainder consists of roller bearings, stainless steels, alloy steels, and suction sweepers, in all of which Canton has a high national ranking. There is also a large production of paving brick in the area.

Akron.—The reader need hardly be reminded that Akron rubber factories consume nearly 40 per cent of the world's raw rubber or that Akron manufactures more than 70 per cent of the nation's automobile tires. Akron tire factories produce 150,000 tires daily in seasons of brisk demand.

It might be truthfully said, however, that although Akron means almost everything to the rubber-tire industry, the tire industry likewise means almost everything to Akron. It is difficult to find a city more highly specialized in the manufacture of a single type of product. Rubber tires and tubes regularly represent two-thirds of the factory output in the Akron industrial area. The rapid rise of Akron and the tire industry is paralleled only by the rise of the Michigan automobile cities. In 1937, the city of Akron held third place in manufacturing among the cities of Ohio, and its manufacturing represented three-quarters of one per cent of the national total. Just now Akron is attempting to attract other industries in the hope of diversifying its industrial structure and perhaps rendering its economic life more nearly "depression proof."

Erie.—The city of Erie has a site comparable to that of Cleveland. Located on the south shore of Lake Erie it has splendid transportation facilities and handles much ore and coal. Without the rich hinterland or the direct route to Pittsburgh coal, it has grown much less than Cleveland, but its industrial development has been similar. The Erie district manufactures about three-tenths of one per cent of the national factory output, and about two-thirds of this production comes from the city of Erie. Iron, steel, and machinery are the major industrial products, but Erie also holds high rank as a manufacturer of electrical goods, household utensils, and paper. Prominent among the steel products are boilers, tanks, and engines. Industrial activity in the Erie area is diversified, despite the fact that steel products dominate the field. Its industrial development has thus been strikingly similar to that of Cleveland.

The Wheeling Area.—The city of Wheeling was among the very first "western" towns to arise in the westward migration which followed the Revolutionary War. The old Cumberland Road crossed the Ohio River at Wheeling and for many years the town was its effective western terminus. There the pioneers unloaded their wagons, placed their equipment on barges and embarked down the Ohio to find new homes. Wheeling's first interests were commercial and those interests have remained paramount to this day. Industries have located in Wheeling but larger developments have occurred in the numerous smaller river towns which line both banks of the Ohio River, especially to the north.

In 1930, metropolitan Wheeling had a population of 191,000, of whom 62,000 lived in the city, 52,000 in neighboring West Virginia suburbs, and 77,000 across the river in the state of Ohio. The industrial area (which is much larger; see Fig. 80) likewise occupies portions of both states. Approximately one-sixth of the factory production of the industrial area originates in the city of Wheeling. An additional one-third comes from the "panhandle" counties to the north and the remaining half from Ohio communities on the opposite bank of the river. The combined factory output of the area is about one-half of one per cent of the national total. The type of industrial development is similar to that of the neighboring Pittsburgh area. Iron, steel, and their products comprise more than 60 per cent of the output. The Wheeling area has blast furnaces, rolling mills, and machinery plants. Tin plate is a product of particular importance. Pottery and glass rank next with about 14 per cent of the total output. Large local deposits of potters' clay, coupled with good supplies of natural gas make East Liverpool, Ohio, a leading center for porcelain, tableware, and other clay products, and the same industries are important in several other cities of the area. Other industries are generally of local importance only.

Johnstown.—The eastern extremity of the Pittsburgh-Cleveland district includes the city of Johnstown whose interests are definitely allied with iron and steel. Johnstown occupies a strategic location on the main transportation route between Pittsburgh and the Atlantic coast. It has important railroad interests, but the dominant local industry is steel. Johnstown has both blast furnaces and steel mills. Steel plates, bars, and wire are the principal products. Easy access to excellent coal has been important in the city's growth as a railroad and industrial center.

Other Areas.—The cities and industrial areas just described include practically the entire Pittsburgh-Cleveland Steel District. Outside these industrial areas, manufacturing is not highly developed and where factories are found their products are similar to those in the major centers. Iron, steel, and their products everywhere dominate the industrial scene, with scattered clay, glass, and electrical goods industries usually occupying second position.

Summary.—The Pittsburgh-Cleveland steel area is one of the major industrial sections of the United States, with an output aggregating nearly one-tenth of the national production of manufactured goods. Fully half the nation's iron and steel industry is concentrated here and from this district comes most of the nation's heavy machinery. Ferro-metallurgical industries dominate the industrial structure of seven of the eight industrial centers included within the district. The eighth, Akron, is the world center for the rubber goods industries. Of the steel centers, Youngstown and the Mahoning Valley are definitely earmarked as specialized producers of the heavy, basic materials—iron and steel. In Pittsburgh, Wheeling, Johnstown, and Canton, these industries still predominate, but there is a greater diversity of products. Cleveland and Erie show still greater diversification, although both are primarily producers of machinery and other iron and steel products. Other industries exist alongside these leaders, the most important being electrical goods, pottery, and glass. Cheap woman labor has been important in attracting the first of these, and local supplies of natural gas for their furnaces has proved attractive to the other two.

The area has developed as the nation's steel center chiefly because of (1) access to lake-borne iron ore from the Superior mines, (2) an abundance of good coking coal and limestone, and (3) a location near the center of the national market for iron and steel products. In recent decades the steel industry has shown a slight tendency toward decentralization, with a small but apparent movement westward, especially to the Chicago area, and a similar movement to the eastern seaboard in order to have access to imported ores. The westward movement is observable within the area, the Cleveland section having shown more rapid growth in recent years than the Pittsburgh area. In the future, this decentralization may doubtless be expected to continue, but inasmuch as no other area seems capable of offering such excellent locational advantages, preeminence of the Pittsburgh-Cleveland area in steel industries seems destined to continue.

THE GEOGRAPHY OF IRON AND STEEL

The story of the American steel industry is told largely in terms of Lake Superior ore, Great Lakes shipping, and Appalachian coking coal. From the great mines at the head of Lake Superior the ore is sent by boat to the lake ports along the lower lakes. Coking coal is mined principally in the Connellsville field of southwest Pennsylvania and in southern West Virginia. Leaving the mines it meets the ore somewhere between mine and lake shore. Coke ovens may be erected either near the mines or near the blast-furnace centers. Limestone, the third essential ingredient for the blast furnace, is generally available in this same territory. A typical charge for a blast furnace consists of a thorough mixture of ten parts ore, eight parts coke, and two parts limestone.

FIG. 81. Distribution of the Capacity for Pig Iron, 1935.

FIG. 82. Distribution of the Capacity for Steel Ingots, 1935.

FIG. 83. Distribution of the Capacity for Hot-rolled Steel, 1935.

The geographic distribution of the principal phases of the iron and steel industry is shown in Figs. 81, 82 and 83. Historically, the three phases of steel-making were independent units, but in recent years there has been a pronounced tendency to locate blast furnaces, steel furnaces, and rolling mills at the same sites. Thus we find considerable similarity in the maps showing the geographic distribution of capacities for pig iron, steel ingots, and rolling-mill products.

Location Factors.—The concentration of all three phases of the iron and steel industry in the same centers reflects the workings of complex locational factors. In the first place, the manufacture of pig iron is essentially a processing industry utilizing two major raw materials extracted in widely separated areas. In 1937, American blast furnaces used about 1 1/3 pounds of coal (in the form of coke) and 1¾ pounds of iron ore (plus smaller amounts of stone and scrap) to produce one pound of pig iron. The ore came largely from Minnesota and the coking coal from Pennsylvania. Inasmuch as ore is the heavier commodity (but not *much* heavier) we might expect coal to be hauled to the ore rather than ore to the coal. Transportation rates by way of the Great Lakes are about the same for each commodity. Why was the heavier ore hauled to the lighter coal? Differences in labor costs would not be significant because the process is highly mechanized. The answer lies in the availability of markets and is closely tied up with manufacturing economies in the industry.

Practically, the pig-iron industry has just one market for its products and that market is the steel industry. Since the steel plants are located south of the Great Lakes, there is no profit in manufacturing pig iron in Minnesota if it must be shipped all the way to Pennsylvania to find a buyer. But why is the steel industry in Pennsylvania? Would it follow the blast furnaces to Minnesota to obtain cheaper pig iron?

Such a shift is not likely. The steel industry uses materials other than pig iron. One of these is scrap. In recent years steel furnaces have been fed more scrap than pig iron. About half the scrap accumulates around the mills and the remainder is purchased. Prime source of purchased scrap is the populous states, among which Pennsylvania and Ohio are heavy contributors. A Minnesota steel mill would be far from sources of purchased scrap, which is at least half as important as pig iron as a raw material for steel.

Furthermore, the tail cannot be expected to wag the dog. The steel industry is many times as large as the pig-iron industry. In 1937 steel employed twenty times as many workers as iron, and its value added by manufacture was twelve times as great. From the locational point of view, the steel industry differs materially from the iron industry. Out of every dollar's worth of pig iron turned out in 1937, eighty-one cents was spent for materials (including twenty-six cents for fuel) and six cents for labor. But in the steel industry a dollar's worth of product represented only fifty-five cents worth of materials (including only four and one-half cents for fuel) and twenty-seven cents for labor. These proportions are significant. They place blast furnaces in the same category as other processing industries such as petroleum-refining and meat-packing; but they place steel-making much nearer the average of American industries in the proportionate cost of materials and labor. Fuel costs in steel-making are not high enough to make coal a dominant locational factor. Left to its own devices the steel industry would not necessarily choose the same locations as the blast-furnace industry. As a matter of fact, it is not left to its own devices, because the two industries are so closely interlocked both economically and managerially that they have in most cases become a single industry.

In the United States the iron and steel industry has been subject to integration. It is a field for large corporations which typically own blast furnaces, steel works, and rolling mills. Many of them operate iron mines, railroads, coke ovens, ore boats, and coal properties. A variety of motives prompted integration, but among the obvious economies was the consolidation of iron with steel. A central feature of recent improvements in steel technology has been the saving of fuel through preserving the "heat" from one process to another. Older mills cast their iron into pigs, reheated the pigs in a steel furnace whose product was cast into ingots, and again reheated the ingots before running them through the rolling mill. The modern mill uses a continuous process, and the metal is never allowed to cool from the time it leaves the blast furnace until it emerges from the rolling mill as sheets, bars, tubes, or rails. Thus, in effect, the blast furnace has become an important source of fuel for the steel mill because it now delivers "hot metal" instead of cold "pigs." To effect this economy, it must be located near by; and the steel furnace must also be located near the rolling mill to which it delivers its product. Continuity requires contiguity, and the three processes are compactly grouped at the same site. (Similar considerations prompt the location of coke ovens near the iron and steel furnaces in order that the gas may be used as fuel.)

Thus the iron industry and the steel industry have for the most part been combined into the iron and steel industry, so closely integrated that only the accountants and statisticians can tell where one leaves off and the other begins. For locational purposes they must be considered together; and since steel is so much more important than iron, its locational problems generally are given greater weight.

Steel needs low-priced raw materials (especially pig iron and scrap), but it also needs to be near the market, because the product is heavy and distribution costs are high. The problem is further complicated by the fact that iron and steel plants must be large to be efficient. A relatively small number of plants can serve the entire nation. The United States has need for few steel centers. Sparsely populated regions cannot support a steel works that is large enough to be efficient.

In this manner, the iron and steel industry has chosen its locations. A slight saving in raw-material costs that might have been effected by locating near the ore beds was more than offset by savings in distribution costs accomplished by locating nearer the national markets. In a choice between ore and fuel, the fuel area was favored because it was nearer the center of steel consumption. Yet the industry did not go all the way to the coal fields because adjacent locations offered smoother topography and better transportation facilities. The necessity for large plants has retarded decentralization, so that the center of production has remained near the center of steel consumption. At the same time, the industry has not found it profitable to stray very far from the source of its three major raw materials, coal, ore, and scrap. The major steel center remains in the Pittsburgh-Cleveland district and the most important minor centers are located along the southern Great Lakes which provide cheap transportation for all three types of raw materials.

Steel-using Industries.—These basic industries are only the beginning, industrially, of the long process of transportation and fabrication which brings steel and its products to the final consumer. From the Pittsburgh-Cleveland district, railroads and trucks distribute bars, sheets, and shapes to foundries and machine shops scattered across the Manufacturing Belt. In this district, however, the iron is born, and here definitely is the genesis of the greatest industrial undertaking of modern civilization—the metals and machinery industries.

The Pittsburgh-Cleveland industrial area is a center for heavy industry, a smoky section of heavy materials, heavy traffic, and heavy products. It is the home of giant industrial plants devoted mainly to the creation of capital goods for use in further production in other areas. The district is relatively young when measured by the span of American economic history. In the realm of economics, its star has been rising steadily throughout recent decades. The Pittsburgh-Cleveland district exhibits the major characteristics of recent economic evolution in the United States—large corporations, large plants, and elaborate use of power and machinery.

From this section we turn to Industrial New England. Between the two sections there is little room for comparisons, much material for contrast. The American industrial revolution began in New England and here are located some of the nation's oldest industrial institutions. New England has no coal and few heavy industries. Its major products have long been consumer goods, meant to be worn, or eaten, or otherwise used directly by individual consumers. New England has little smoke and few large factories. Its white houses will provide a marked contrast with the smoke-stained houses of the steel workers. But New England is unhappy because many of its manufacturing industries are finding other locations more attractive, and adjustment to their loss has been difficult. In recent years, New England's industrial star has been descending. Here we shall want to pay more attention to the importance of economic history and the effect of evolution upon industrial location.

REFERENCES

The steel industry is given a thorough treatment in C. R. Dougherty, M. G. de Chazeau, and S. S. Stratton, *The Economics of the Iron and Steel Industry* (University of Pittsburgh, 1937). Zimmermann, *World Resources and Industries,* devotes four chapters to the steel industries, and gives a good discussion of location. Good descriptive material is available from the Iron and Steel Institute. Refer also to the business research publications of the University of Pittsburgh and Ohio State University. A series of articles on various steel corporations and other heavy industries appears in *Fortune.*

QUESTIONS AND PROBLEMS

1. Outline the history of the location of the American iron and steel industry, giving particular emphasis to the importance of fuel, ore, and markets in the choice of sites for iron and steel plants.

2. Consult an encyclopedia and write a brief explanation of the difference between iron and steel.

3. How do you account for the fact that the national center for the steel industry is not in West Virginia or Minnesota?

4. Why has the steel industry grown to importance in Ohio, a state without important deposits of iron ore or coking coal?

5. During occasional labor difficulties there has been talk of the rubber tire industry decentralizing its production by establishing plants in various sections of the country. What factors should be considered in attempting to reach a conclusion on the soundness of such a program?

6. Why are blast furnaces, steel furnaces, and rolling mills commonly owned by the same companies and located at the same sites?

7. In 1938, the California iron and steel industry used seven times as much scrap as pig iron, while that of Ohio and Pennsylvania used about equal quantities of scrap and pig iron. Alabama used 50 per cent more pig iron than scrap. How do you account for these differences?

8. What is a "continuous" steel mill? What are its advantages over other types?

9. How does the Youngstown industrial development differ from that of Cleveland?

10. In what way has topography both aided and hampered the growth of the city of Pittsburgh?

11. The built-up area of Cleveland is nearly semicircular while that of Pittsburgh is somewhat star-shaped. Account for this difference.

12. Why has the manufacture of articles such as lamp bulbs and silk textiles often become important in heavy-industry centers?

13. Review Chapters XXI and XXII, and describe the surface features, agriculture, and mining of the Pittsburgh-Cleveland district.

14. Why is the iron and steel industry of the Pittsburgh-Cleveland district largely a product of transportation?

15. How would you expect business conditions in Youngstown or the Wheeling area to be affected by a world war? a depression in the automobile industry? Would your conclusions apply to Pittsburgh, Cleveland, and Akron? Why and why not?

CHAPTER XXIV

INDUSTRIAL NEW ENGLAND

A map showing the locations of American manufacturing industries reveals heavy concentrations in the New England states of Massachusetts, Connecticut, and Rhode Island, and a small portion of New Hampshire and Maine. Here, in a small district which aggregates less than one-half of one per cent of the land area of the United States, are concentrated more than 5 per cent of the nation's population and nearly 10 per cent of its manufacturing. To distinguish it from the remaining rural and non-industrial portions of New England, the section has become known in the literature of industrial geography as Industrial New England.

Historically, Industrial New England is the genesis of the American Manufacturing Belt. In pre-Revolutionary War days these colonies bore the first buds of what was to blossom as the American factory system. Following the Revolution, textile manufacturing, first of the genuine "factory" industries, was introduced in these states. In Civil War days, New England manufacturers, firmly established by this time, largely armed and clothed the Union armies. With the opening of the West, Yankee farmers of the area, finding a day's labor in the factory more remunerative than on the stony soil, very generally gave up grain and livestock farming and became factory workers. Since that time southern New England has been dominantly industrial—and today Massachusetts, Rhode Island, and Connecticut are the most highly urbanized and industrialized states in the Union.

Not that the economic development of New England has been marked by continuous progress and prosperity. In retrospect, it seems that no section of America has been beset with more serious problems or greater economic disappointments. Disappointment came early from the poverty of the soil which was not sufficiently productive for profitable competition with fertile western prairies. Next the Yankees tried fishing and found it profitable. Fishing led to a very successful era of ocean shipping and world commerce. In the 1830's and 1840's New England's fishery-

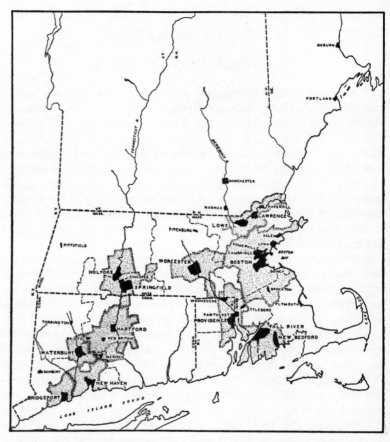

Fig. 84. Industrial New England. The map shows most of northern
(agricultural) New England as well as southern (industrial) New
England. There is comparatively little industrial development north
and west of a line drawn from Portland to Springfield, but these areas
are important sources of milk for the industrial cities of the section.
In 1937, New England Industrial Areas ranked as follows in percentages of national manufacturing: Boston (2.7%), Bridgeport-New
Haven (1.6%), Providence-Fall River-New Bedford (1.2%), Hartford (0.8%), Worcester (0.8%), Springfield-Holyoke (0.5%). Note
the differences in boundaries between industrial areas and metropolitan
districts.

trained sailors and ships built of local white pine were ranked with the world's best. Then came, all too quickly, an era of foreign competition and the introduction of iron ships. Yankee fortunes were withdrawn from the sea to build railroads, open the West, and finally to build factories to supply this new country. Cotton mills, woolen mills, iron foundries, and hardware and machinery plants grew more numerous as Boston and New England poured money and manufactures into the expanding western states. Nearly every power site on nearly every southern New England stream—and there are hundreds of them—became a factory location. New England manufacturing soon became specialized along definite lines—cotton goods, wool goods, leather products, and metal manufactures. Since Civil War days the economic situation of New England has been very largely a reflection of prosperity or depression in these lines of manufacturing industry. Agriculture, fishing, shipping, and forestry have become distinctly secondary to manufacturing as sources of employment and income. No section of America is more thoroughly dominated by manufacturing than the section here described as Industrial New England.

New England today, which is essentially Industrial New England, is again experiencing an era of economic disappointment. Many of its larger industries are moving factories to other sections of the country which seem to offer greater profit. The nature and extent of these problems will be considered in the following pages. Many of them are serious; but in the background is New England's long and successful history. Yankee ingenuity and skill have conquered such problems before and New Englanders confidently expect them to do so again. Here, in fact, is the great economic asset of this section throughout its history —the skill and inventiveness of its labor.

Historic and Geographic Factors.—History and geography are so thoroughly intermixed in New England industrial development that it is often impossible to distinguish primary from secondary causes. Much of New England's industry is definitely mature. Many industries have occupied the same sites for more than one hundred years. The geography—the coast line, the hills, the streams—has, of course, changed hardly at all in a hundred years; but the importance of these physical features has changed enormously. Boston harbor, for example, was a leading factor in making that site a great seaport and a great city—but there are murmurings that it is too small and too shallow for modern liners. Lack of coal was not serious a century ago when most of the power was taken from streams, but today New England's lack of steam coal is considered a serious shortcoming by many industrial leaders. It is true, also, that if today New England industry were to be started anew, many factories would be located differently, and many cities would not be built. Other sites would be more advantageous. These divergent historical and geographic factors are well illustrated in the rise and development of the cotton-textile industry.

THE COTTON-GOODS INDUSTRY

History credits Samuel Slater with operating the first successful American cotton mill. This mill was established in Providence, Rhode Island, in 1790. It was not until 1813, however, that a mill was erected which provided for both spinning and weaving. It was located at Waltham, Massachusetts, where water power was taken from the Charles River. The venture was so successful that the Charles River could not provide sufficient power, and new sites were selected. The town of Lowell was established for cotton manufacturing in 1823 and here the industry was so prosperous that Lowell grew to be the second city of Massachusetts by 1860. Manchester and a dozen other river-falls towns sprang up in neighboring New Hampshire and Maine. A similar and simultaneous development occurred in western Massachusetts on the Connecticut River. Holyoke, now noted for paper, was planned as a cotton manufacturing town. To the south of Boston a similar development was taking place in the Blackstone Valley between Worcester and Providence.

Thus the early cotton-goods industry experienced rapid and thorough decentralization. Cotton mills sprang up in all parts of southern New England because they must be erected at water-power sites, and such sites were scattered along the dozens of small streams which drop down from the highlands. These small streams were excellent for power. Their flow was relatively steady, their water was clear (for bleaching and dyeing) and they were small enough to make damming relatively easy. Other states had larger streams and more power, but many of these were not usable, partly because of the difficulty of building dams, but mainly because power could not be transported more than a hundred feet. A single dam could serve only the two or three mills that could be crowded about it. Thus in the early 1800's, interior New England was a nearly ideal location for cotton manufacture.

The situation changed with the coming of steam power. About 1850, southern New England was faced with an alarming scarcity of mill sites. Before this situation became acute, however, the steam engine was perfected to a point of becoming usable, and by 1850 many mills had begun to use steam power in seasons of slack water. Once steam proved practicable, new locations became possible and the New England textile map began to be altered. Coal, in those days, was cheapest at tidewater, and because of that advantage tidewater mills were soon erected. The Fall River and Lowell developments, as well as the mills around Narragansett Bay and at Newburyport, Salem, and Portsmouth date from this period. These two types of southern New England locations describe the American cotton-goods industry of about the year 1880. The boundaries of Industrial New England had already appeared. It was marked on the north and west by a group of towns located at falls in the rivers and on the east and south by mill towns located at tidewater. *Power* was the dominant factor in both types of locations. There were very few American cotton mills outside this small area.

After 1880, two factors became increasingly important. First was the increased use of electricity, which made possible the transmission of hydro power and the utilization of power sites on larger rivers. Second was the rapid rise of the southern piedmont area in cotton-goods manufacture. The South had good power, cheap labor, and was nearer the raw material. By 1914, it was apparent that New England could not compete with southern mills in the coarser cotton textiles. This trend was forgotten during the next seven years when World War demands kept all plants running at capacity, but in the post-war period the trend was resumed.

New England still leads the nation in the production of a few of the finer grades of cotton textiles, but the southern piedmont is far ahead in the total output of cotton goods. In 1937, only 21 per cent of the nation's cotton goods was manufactured in New England. The whole industry, meanwhile, has been confronted with a declining consumption of cotton clothing, coupled with a decline in "staples" and a correspondingly increased emphasis upon specialty and style goods.

In New England, these changes have affected most adversely those plants in the north and west portions of the area. Mills in those sections were from the beginning large institutions, Boston-financed, and devoted largely to the production of staples. Mills in the south and east generally are smaller, locally financed, and better adapted to changes in demand. Located largely in the Providence-Fall River-New Bedford district, they specialize in the finer grades of cotton textiles, and hence constitute the bulk of the present-day New England cotton-goods industry.

Organization.—Meanwhile, the cotton-goods industry in New England as elsewhere follows technical and business procedures which have not altered materially in recent decades. The mills receive cotton in the bale which is cleaned, twisted, and spun into yarn. The yarn itself is woven into cloth, most of which is "gray goods," unbleached, unpatterned, and uncolored. Mills usually sell gray goods to "converters," merchants who contract for the dyeing, bleaching, and finishing of the cloth, and who place it on the market. Chief purchasers are the "cutting-up" trade (clothing) and industrial users (shoes, other manufactures). Somewhat less than half the output goes into wholesale and retail channels. Most of the product is marketed in the city of New York, which is the great American market for cotton goods. Mills usually sell their output through selling agents and commission houses. Relatively few mills maintain sales organizations or market their products direct to retailers.

The cotton-goods industry thus consists of several types of specialized establishments each of which typically operates independently of the rest. The manufacture of staples is divided into two distinct phases—first the production of gray goods, and second the dyeing, bleaching, and finishing operations. Relatively few mills carry on both of these stages. Cotton specialties, such as sewing thread, ribbons, lace, and other small wares, are usually produced in independent plants, most of which are fairly small. It is the latter type of plant which produces most of the silk-rayon-cotton mixtures.

Location.—The center for the smaller mills which produce most of the finer types of cotton textiles is the Providence-New

Bedford-Fall River area. Of these neighboring cities, New Bedford and Fall River are the most highly specialized in cotton-goods production. New Bedford, with a national reputation for fine cotton fabrics, is the leading New England city in cotton-goods production. Most of the mills in the Providence section are located in the outskirts of the city, especially in Pawtucket and the neighboring cities of the Blackstone Valley. This area produces about 10 per cent of the national total of cotton goods.

Outside the major center the industry is rather thoroughly decentralized, with important mills scattered along the seaboard lowland from the Androscoggin Valley in Maine to the Connecticut Valley in Connecticut. These scattered mills produce about the same quantity of cotton goods as those of the Providence-Fall River-New Bedford area.

WOOL MANUFACTURES

Before one can discuss the wool-manufacturing industries he must understand the differences between the two major products, woolens and worsteds. Practically all mills specialize in one or the other of these products, and very few manufacture both. Important technical and economic differences distinguish the two manufacturing processes so sharply that they are generally considered as separate industries. Woolens in general are those wool fabrics, such as flannels, which are loosely woven and have a soft, brushed surface. Worsteds, on the other hand, have a tighter weave and harder finish. Nearly all the heavier suitings are worsteds. Soft wools such as those from the Merino sheep are preferred for woolens, but the harder-finished worsteds are best made from the coarser wool of dual-purpose sheep.

In the manufacturing process, wool is first scoured and washed to remove the natural grease. This process demands much clear water, a strong feature in New England locations. After scouring, the wool is made ready for weaving by a process which separates the long fibers, or "tops," from the shorter ones which are known as "noils." The "tops" go largely into worsteds while the "noils" are used mainly for woolens. After this separation the fibers are combed or carded to straighten them. Once straightened, the fibers are spun into yarn, usually by a machine known as a mule spinner. The yarn then goes to the looms where it is woven into cloth. Dyeing takes place either "in the wool," the yarn, or the cloth stage of manufacture. Solid colors may be dyed in the cloth stage; but where different colored patterns are desired, the dyeing must be done in one of the earlier stages, usually in the wool before it is carded or combed. Very little wool cloth is ever printed.

The finishing process consists essentially of shrinking, brushing, and pressing the goods. The chief economic difference between woolen and worsted mills is in size of plants. The average worsted mill is a large institution using much machinery and a high percentage of woman labor, as is typical in the cotton-goods industry. These plants carry on the complete fabrication process from wool to cloth, may utilize brands and trade-marks, and even engage in national advertising. The average woolen mill, on the other hand, is a relatively small institution, having perhaps a hundred workers, most of whom are men. Unlike cotton mills, the typical woolen or worsted mill is a complete factory whose processes begin with raw wool and end with the finished product ready for market. Sales usually are made through selling agents, located principally in New York and other clothing centers.

Historically, wool manufacturers chose New England locations primarily because of the availability of water power, clear water, and near-by wool. The first two factors have been and still are important in maintaining New England's supremacy in wool textiles. The third factor, nearness to wool, soon disappeared when New England mills grew faster than New England flocks of sheep. But this loss was in no small way counterbalanced by the development in Boston of an excellent wool market.

The Boston wool market is the largest in the United States and second only to London in world importance. It is no mere pit in which wool is bought and sold. For when one speaks of the Boston wool market, one thinks of huge warehouses, sufficient in size to store an entire year's clip of wool in the United States, of dealers and brokers, and of Boston bankers who finance most of the wool manufacturers of the United States. Wool is purchased in the Boston market primarily from dealers whose stocks are in local warehouses. A typical transaction allows the mill sixty days and the transaction is financed by Boston banks. At the end of sixty days the cloth is ready for market and the loan repaid. Such transactions are excellent for commercial banks because of their "liquidity" or early date at which they will be paid. This liquidity of investments has done much to assure the continued soundness of Boston banks.

Location.—The principal New England centers for worsteds are Lawrence and Providence, with the greatest activity in Providence and neighboring Woonsocket. The production of woolens is more scattered, the greater number of plants being in the northern part of the industrial area. Both New Hampshire and Maine have a large output of woolens. A number of smaller towns north and west of Boston are also important. The city of Boston manufactures both woolens and worsteds.

Competition.—Although New England has lost its leadership in the manufacture of many types of cotton goods, there has been little if any migration of the wool-manufacturing industries. New England manufactures about two-thirds of the national output of suitings, dress goods, overcoatings, and coatings and has long held that premier position. In the wool-manufacturing industries, New England is considered a center for style goods. Its share of the output of yarns and staple wool goods (such as blankets) is smaller; but for the entire industry New England is the undisputed leader. Outside these states, the principal wool manufacturing centers are in Pennsylvania and northern New Jersey.

OTHER APPAREL INDUSTRIES

New England textile manufactures have long used both silk and rayon, but these textiles are of greater importance in the Middle Atlantic textile area of Pennsylvania, New Jersey, and New York. Approximately one-sixth of the nation's silk-textile production is in New England, and in this section Connecticut is the leading state. Most of the Connecticut mills are in the New London-Providence area of the eastern third of the state.

Connecticut also has in Danbury the nation's leading center for the manufacture of felt hats, made largely from imported rabbit fur. Similar textile specialty centers are to be found in many sections. Woonsocket, for example, is famous for handkerchiefs, while Bridgeport, New Haven, and Worcester manufacture corsets. A journey through industrial New England brings the traveler to dozens of such textile specialty centers.

Leather and Rubber Products.—The tanning of leather in New England began shortly after colonization and became firmly established as a national industry based on local supplies of hides and tanbark. Bark was the dominant location factor in the early days and hides were taken to the small tanneries located at the edge of the timber. Later, the introduction of chemical tanning made possible the erection of more permanent and larger plants, and these generally were located nearer the seacoast where both labor and transportation facilities were more plentiful. The New England tanning industry is concentrated in a small section northeast of Boston, practically all of it lying within forty miles of the city. Peabody, Danvers, and Woburn are the leading tannery centers, but there are also plants in several adjacent cities. Massachusetts stands second only to Pennsylvania in tannery output.

The tanning industry is dwarfed by the boot and shoe industry which uses 85 per cent of all the leather produced. Tanneries and shoe factories grew up simultaneously in New England, but it is safe to say that one of the great factors keeping the tanning industry in these states is the presence of a large boot and shoe industry. Tannery operators find it advantageous to be near their market.

New England produces about one-third of the United States output of boots and shoes, and Massachusetts has always been the leading producing state. The major portion of New England shoe production comes from a narrow coastal area which runs northward from Brockton and Boston to southern Maine. Brockton, Haverhill, and Lynn are highly specialized in shoe production, but there are also important factories in Salem, in Manchester and Nashua, New Hampshire, and in Auburn and Lewiston, Maine.

In New England, the rubber and leather industries are closely allied because both are concerned chiefly with the manufacture of footwear. These two types of products are not manufactured in the same factories, however, or even in the same area. The rubber-footwear industry is concentrated in the cities which lie to the west of Boston and within a radius of forty miles. Cambridge, Somerville, and Woburn have important rubber factories, devoted mainly to the production of rubber footwear.

METALS AND MACHINERY

The metal-using industries employ about one-quarter of all New England factory labor and stand second only to the textiles group whose payrolls include about one-third of the factory workers. The metals and machinery industries are an extremely diverse group, utilizing all the metals from iron to silver and gold, and turning out products which range from the heaviest machinery to silverware and jewelry.

Raw Materials.—In general, New England metal-using industries purchase their materials from outside sources in metallic form. There is little primary reduction of ores, mainly because New England has neither the ores nor the fuel with which to reduce them. A tidewater blast furnace at Everett (near Boston), which uses Maine limestone and foreign iron ore, is the single important exception to this statement. Factory materials for New England metal industries come by rail or water in the form of blooms, billets, slabs, bars, wire, plates, sheets, and other finished and semi-finished forms. Because of distance from raw materials, fuel, and markets, most of the national metal-using industries are devoted to the production of the more highly finished and complicated products. Local supplies of skilled labor have been paramount in the location of this type of industry.

The origin of New England metal-products industries is perhaps best traced to the early development of the brass industry in central Connecticut. Here, in Colonial days, Yankee craftsmen perfected methods of alloying copper, zinc, and tin to produce brass and bronze products which were marketed by the historically famous Yankee peddlers. Trade secrets were carefully guarded and held in single families for several generations with the result that brass and bronze products from the Naugatuck and Connecticut valleys long excelled those from other areas. The list of products from these forges soon expanded enormously. Clocks, silverware, and cutlery appeared on the list together with many types of hardware and small machine tools. The metal-using industries extended northward into western Massachusetts and eventually electrical appliances and machinery were added to the list.

In the meantime, a very considerable local demand for factory equipment was arising from the expanding textile and shoe industries. New England still manufactures about two-thirds of the nation's textile machinery and a similar portion of the shoe machinery.

Location.—The major concentration of New England metals and machinery manufacture is in Connecticut and western Massachusetts, with important local centers in the Boston and Providence metropolitan areas. Most of the heavy industry of the latter cities is classed as local and consists of foundries, machine shops, and other establishments which serve primarily the local markets. The Boston area has an important output of electrical goods, mainly attributable to the large General Electric plant at Lynn. There are also extensive shipyards at Quincy and Charlestown.

Providence, together with the neighboring towns of North Attleboro and Attleboro (in Massachusetts), produces about one-third of the national output of jewelry. The city of Providence also produces a wide variety of files, screws, and similar types of tools and hardware.

The major production of hardware and tools is found in middle and southern Connecticut. The names of Bridgeport, New Haven, and Waterbury are nationally famous for hardware, tools, and small machinery. Paralleling this development is a similar concentration of brass and bronze industries as well as the production of silverware and silver plate. Of the cities in this territory, Bridgeport is most famous for office machines, household appliances, and similar types of light, complicated machinery. New Haven's products are somewhat heavier, including firearms, wire, and railroad equipment. Waterbury is specialized in brass production, with clocks and watches in second position. Meriden is best known for its silver plate, while Ansonia is a center for brass manufactures. New Britain and Stamford are the best-known centers for hardware.

Farther up the Connecticut Valley, the city of Hartford is nationally famous as an insurance center but it also has an impressive production of typewriters (Underwood, Royal), brushes (Fuller), and precision instruments. Two-thirds of the nation's typewriters are manufactured in Connecticut. Near-by Bristol manufactures ball bearings and springs.

The Massachusetts portion of the Connecticut Valley continues this emphasis upon metals and machinery. Springfield and Chicopee manufacture radios, refrigerators, and other electrical goods as well as heavier articles of machinery. Neighboring Holyoke is nationally famous for its fine writing paper.

Between the Connecticut Valley and Boston lies Worcester, second-ranking industrial city of Massachusetts. Worcester manufactures are definitely allied with steel, the major products being machinery for textile mills and similar uses.

Extreme western Massachusetts has an industrial development

similar to that of Springfield. The Pittsfield plant of General Electric is the outstanding industrial institution of that area.

The Geographic Distribution of Manufacturing in New England

By this time the reader will have concluded that the industrial structure of New England is highly complicated and difficult to remember. He should have noted, however, a number of definite characteristics which distinguish this development. These may be summarized briefly:

1. *Decentralization of Manufacturing.*—New England manufacturing is carried on in a large number of small and medium-sized cities, and not concentrated in the major metropolitan centers. The reasons for this decentralization are largely historic, centering around the availability of water power.

2. *Concentration of Commercial Development.*—The only truly commercial city of New England is Boston, which has comparatively little manufacturing but enormous commercial interests. Boston is the economic capital of New England, and the only city which even faintly challenges its position is Providence, Rhode Island.

3. *Specialization.*—The typical New England factory town is definitely specialized along certain lines of industrial production. Nearly all of them are "one-industry" towns if the term "industry" is used in a broad sense. In the textile districts they are known as "mill towns." Despite this specialization, however, there are comparatively few "company towns" which are dominated by a single establishment. Each town usually has two or more competitive plants producing the same lines of manufactured goods.

4. *Agglomeration of Industrial Types.*—This specialization by cities has tended to overflow and become specialization by areas. Not only individual cities but whole communities of them have become specialized along certain lines. Geographic specialization is apparent for textiles, shoes, and machinery, the major manufacturing interests of New England. By observing which industries are dominant it is possible to divide Industrial New England into two distinct areas, one

of which is occupied largely by textiles and shoes and the other by metals and machinery. A few exceptional cities appear in each area which do not properly fall within the classifications used. These exceptions are rare, however, and do not materially affect the validity of the entire analysis.

NEW ENGLAND INDUSTRIAL CENTERS

The geography of Industrial New England readily divides itself into four major sub-sections, each more or less separated from the rest and having a distinctive type of industrial development. The sub-sections are (1) the Connecticut Valley of central Connecticut and western Massachusetts, and the associated neighboring valleys of the Housatonic and the Naugatuck in western Connecticut, a metals-machinery area with about 3 per cent of the nation's manufacturing; (2) the Narragansett Bay-Blackstone Valley group, which includes Providence, Fall River, New Bedford, and Worcester, and is specialized in cotton and wool textiles with important admixtures of metals and machinery industries. This sub-section accounts for slightly more than 2 per cent of the nation's manufacturing; (3) Greater Boston, coextensive with the Boston metropolitan district, which manufactures nearly 3 per cent of the nation's factory goods with a notable specialization in wool textiles, shoes, and electrical goods; (4) the Merrimack Valley of northeast Massachusetts and southeast New Hampshire, conveniently grouped with the near-by valleys of the Kennebec and Salmon Falls rivers, in Maine and New Hampshire. This area is best known for its shoes and wool textiles, but also has several important cotton mills. It has nearly 1 per cent of the nation's manufacturing, with two-thirds of its output concentrated in the Merrimack Valley. These four sub-sections account for about 90 per cent of the manufacturing of New England, or roughly 9 per cent of the total for the nation.

The Connecticut Valley Area.—The development of the brass industry of Connecticut and its expansion into a long list of metal-using industries were described in a previous section. Today, the metals and machinery industries are the most important economic institutions in Bridgeport, Hartford, Springfield, Waterbury, New Haven, and New Britain. Brass and its products, hardware, and electrical goods are the leading products of the area. In addition, Holyoke is noted for paper, Danbury for hats.

The Narragansett Bay-Blackstone Valley Area.—As the second city of New England, Providence has important commercial interests as well as manufacturing pursuits. Providence is dwarfed commercially by Boston, however, and its economic foundation lies in its manufacturing establishments, the most important of which are textile mills specializing in the lighter and more highly finished products. Fall River and New Bedford are cotton-textile cities. Worcester has a relatively diverse industrial development rather evenly balanced between machinery and the textiles-clothing group.

Greater Boston.—Many decades have passed since Boston, taking its cue from the railroads which radiate from the city, began calling itself "The Hub" of New England. Throughout those years, however, Boston has continued to maintain its position as the focal point for commerce and finance in this six-state area.

Located on a good harbor, colonial Boston early asserted its supremacy over other cities of the North Atlantic coast. In the years following 1776, Boston ships circled the globe in the heyday of the famed Yankee clipper ship. When American capital retired from the sea before the onslaughts of British-built iron ships, Boston fortunes went into textile mills, shoe factories, and railroads. The names of Boston banks became synonymous with conservative large-scale finance and Boston became the recognized center for education and the arts, its position challenged only by Philadelphia, which was performing a similar function in the Middle Atlantic section of the Atlantic seaboard.

It is fair to record that with the advent of the present century Boston had begun to show signs of losing its ascendency. The city of New York took the lead, first in shipping, later in trade, finance, and manufacturing. The southern piedmont was developing as a cotton-milling district and shoe factories were springing up in the outlands. Boston and New England were not growing so fast economically as the rest of the country. During the later decades, migrations continued. For New England, adjustment to these trends has meant an emphasis upon new industries, greater industrial diversification. This same change in emphasis is apparent in Boston. Its bankers, formerly willing to finance only certain types of industries, now seek more diversified portfolios. The Port of Boston, long congested, has been improved and enlarged. Boston and New England are preparing for a future of greater industrial diversification.

Metropolitan Boston, as defined by the Bureau of the Census, had a population in 1930 of 2,307,897, which gave it a ranking of fourth among the metropolitan districts of the nation. The metropolitan district consists of a number of contiguous independent cities of which the largest are Boston, Cambridge, Somerville, and Lynn. The built-up area is nearly circular with a radius of twenty-five miles. The center of the circle is the small peninsula which was the site of the original settlement, adjacent to the drowned mouths of a half-dozen small streams which form Boston harbor.

The Port of Boston consists of inner and outer harbors with a total area of about forty-seven square miles. The approaches are rocky and formerly were shallow, but channels are now maintained to a depth of forty feet. In contrast to other Atlantic ports, Boston receives much more water-borne commerce than it ships. During the period 1925-1934, Boston's foreign trade tonnage was 90 per cent imports and only 10 per cent exports, and about the same ratio applied to its domestic water-borne commerce. Ships enter Boston harbor loaded with coal from the Middle Atlantic ports, petroleum from the Gulf ports, and sugar from Cuba; but most of them are unable to secure return cargoes. Prime reason for the lack of goods for shipment is the fact that New England itself produces no excess of bulky materials. In addition, Boston is placed at a disadvantage over Middle Atlantic ports because of higher freight rates from the interior. Boston handles comparatively little of the nation's wheat export. Its tributary territory for exports is distinctly local and not productive of large tonnages. Boston ranks seventeenth among the ports of the world in volume of ocean shipping, and fifth among the ports of the United States. Its commerce is about one-fourth as great as that of the Port of New York.

The central business district of Boston is housed on the nose of the mile-wide peninsula which was the site of the original settlement. On the east half of this peninsula are found the department stores, banks, and offices of commercial Boston. There are few tall buildings because the foundation material is soft. To the tourist, the narrow, crooked streets of the old town present the most bewildering traffic problems imaginable.

The central business district has some light industry, but the main manufacturing areas are across Fort Point Channel in South Boston, and across the Charles River in East Boston, Charlestown, Chelsea, Everett, and Somerville. The first three of these districts are part of the city of Boston, but the others are independent municipalities—a part of the metropolitan cluster. Boston's industry has been described as allied with leather, shoes, electrical goods, and textiles. In addition, one finds large printing establishments, oil refineries, and numerous bakeries and similar industries designed to serve the local metropolitan market.

The wholesale and banking interests of Boston are about on a par with those of Philadelphia. Only New York and Chicago have larger commercial and financial enterprises than these cities. Boston wholesale territories cover nearly all of New England and her banks serve this same territory. No New England city has arisen to challenge Boston's historic position as economic capital of the New England states.

The Northern Section of industrial New England is dominated industrially by wool textiles and shoes. Lawrence is the leading wool center, but there are many small mills farther north. The shoe district begins in Brockton, south of Boston, and extends northward through Lowell, Haverhill, Nashua, and Manchester to Lewiston, Auburn, and the north boundary of the district. Cotton textiles are also important in this area. Portland, Maine, is essentially a commercial city, located on one of the many good harbors of the Maine coast. Portland ships some grain, but its harbor is mainly devoted to receiving coal, petroleum, wood pulp, and pulp wood. Paper manufactures are important in the Portland area.

THE SIGNIFICANCE OF INDUSTRIAL CHANGE

The industrial transformation which has been taking place in New England emphasizes many of the features of industrial change which have taken place on a national scale in recent decades. By the time of the World War, the New England states had reached a stage of comparative economic maturity. Fortunes made in a century of fishing, shipping, and manufacturing were securely invested at home and abroad. Second- and third-generation New England capitalists were living well on the incomes from investments which were chosen for a minimum of risk and a maximum of security. Ownership was rather thoroughly divorced from management by an investment device known as the Massachusetts trust. Under this arrangement, an estate was placed in a trust fund for the benefit of the heirs, but under the management of a trustee. Only the income from the trust passed to the heirs, not the ownership of the securities. The trustee managed the estate in such a way as to secure a steady flow of income to the beneficiaries. He invested in those securities which promised certainty of income, and was in no position to take chances in new enterprises. For the smaller investor, the New England savings bank functioned in much the same manner, investing depositors' funds in high-grade bonds and carefully avoiding speculative investments. Such a system effectively separates ownership from control and at the same time places the control of enterprises in the hands of persons who are unable to take speculative chances. Place the ownership of an industry in the hands of persons who have no voice in its management, and turn the management over to persons whose first duty is to assure the owners a steady flow of income, and you have gone far to discourage chance-taking in that industry. Place the bulk of an area's investment capital in these same hands, and you have done much to discourage the introduction of new industries into that area. Many students believe that this lack of speculative capital had done much to impede New England industrial progress as early as 1915. Many of the same students pointed to a similar lack of speculative desire as a cause for the failure of the nation to recover quickly after the depression of the 1930's. In the case of New England, there is little doubt that the separation of management from ownership imparted a very conservative tone to both finance and industry. The extent to which this conservatism held down industrial progress is difficult to estimate.

In any event, New England failed to keep up with the parade of national industrial progress. In the years 1914-1921, the New England states had about 13 per cent of the manufacturing of the United States. After 1921, New England's share of the nation's manufacturing declined steadily. In 1925, it was 11 per cent; by 1937, it had fallen below 10 per cent. Greatest losses were in the cotton-textile industries. New England had more than half the national cotton-goods industry in 1914, but only about one-fifth of it in 1937. This loss was serious, because cotton textiles had been New England's leading manufacturing industry. Other leaders, such as wool manufactures and shoes, have shown a lesser tendency to migrate, but even in these lines most of the new plants have been built outside New England. Losses in the textiles and shoe industries have been the major feature in the failure of New England industrial production to expand as rapidly as that of the nation at large since 1914.

Can these industrial losses be offset? Will the large numbers of unemployed workers find employment in other industries, or must they migrate to sections offering better opportunities for work? Of course, there is no ready answer. There is no indication that the industries that have departed will return. Cotton-mill operators say they prefer piedmont locations because the labor is more tractable, wages are lower, power is plentiful, and products can be delivered to national markets just as cheaply as from New England. Boot and shoe manufacturers sought locations farther south and west mainly to be nearer the markets.

New England was able to resist these trends for many years largely because of acquired prestige. This section was noted for the high quality of its manufactured goods, its fine woolens and cotton goods, its high-grade shoes. Behind this reputation was the skill of its workers who excelled those of other sections in operations involving hand work and careful manipulation. New England's first important industrial losses occurred in items such as the coarser textiles and work shoes. But the machine was fast making the skilled worker less essential in factory production. Inventors perfected spinners and looms that were "almost human" in their capacities to turn out high-quality textiles without the services of skilled operatives. Simplified machinery invaded the shoe industry. Chemists discovered the secrets of the Connecticut brass-workers and taught them to Detroit mechanics. Through all of these technological advances New England lost heavily, because its major industries were old and well established. Capitalists did not hesitate to exploit their markets by building plants in locations which promised lower manufacturing costs. Improved machinery made it possible to exploit the low-wage labor of other areas, just as it has made it possible for Japanese textiles to drive English textiles from many markets in the Orient.

How extensively can New England compensate these losses? Apparently, it can offer industries just about the same inducements it has been able to offer before. In the past, there has been just one long-run inducement—alert and easily trained labor. For the short run, there is the inducement of empty factory buildings that can be secured very cheaply and the added promise of excellent cooperation from local governmental and business groups. But the latter considerations will not prove attractive unless there is promise of continued profit. New England has few industrial raw materials and no coal. It is not located strategically with respect to national markets. If new industries can be found, industries in which automatic machinery has not yet replaced skilled labor, and capital can be persuaded to invest in them, New England can recoup its industrial losses. In the highly mechanized industries whose products do not reflect the skill of the worker, New England's future does not seem very bright.

To a considerable extent, this type of industrial transformation seems already to have gained considerable headway in New England. New industries are coming in and many of them are making new industrial products. Expansion in the production of small electrical devices and complicated machines has been particularly noticeable. New England capital is extending a welcome hand to promising inventors who desire to manufacture a new product. An offer of a rent-free factory building and a little capital is an excellent inducement to industrial fledglings who wish to test their wings. The extent to which these types of manufacturing will be able to offset past and prospective losses is difficult to predict, but the course seems to be the most rational one left open to an area whose principal industrial resources lie in the ability and aggressiveness of its laborers and business men.

References

The Industrial Structure of New England (U. S. Department of Commerce, 1930) provides good background reading and statistical information up to 1927. For later information see reports of the New England Council and various state planning boards. There has been a wide range of magazine articles on the industrial problems of New England. Consult some index such as *Industrial Arts Index* for recent articles.

Questions and Problems

1. New England has been described as an "area in industrial transition." What is meant? Consult recent magazine articles for more complete information on this problem.

A Portion of the Boston Fishing Fleet. (*Courtesy American Airlines.*)

2. Why should the author devote so much attention to economic history in explaining the present economic development of New England?

3. Prepare a brief statement analyzing the food supply of the city of Boston. Use milk, flour, meat, and market vegetables as pertinent examples.

4. What is the Boston metropolitan district? How does it differ from the city of Boston in area, population, and industrial development?

5. What steps are being taken in New England to compensate for the loss of many cotton-textile plants? For what types of industrial development is New England best suited? Why?

6. Why is industrial development in New England more highly decentralized than in the Pittsburgh-Cleveland area?

7. One of the most striking features of the New England urban landscape is its comparative freedom from smoke. Why?

8. Why have the wool-textile industries not followed the example set by cotton textiles in seeking locations outside New England?

9. How do you account for New England's leadership in many metal-products industries such as those which manufacture typewriters, silverware, and builders' hardware?

10. Why does the port of Boston have a much larger tonnage of incoming than outgoing shipments? What commodities constitute the bulk of this trade?

11. What factors account for the rise of cities in the Connecticut River Valley? What types of industries are most important in these cities?

12. Why is the paper industry important in the northern portions of New England?

13. In what ways does the industrial structure of New England cotton-textile centers differ from that of textile centers in the southern states?

14. Why do fewer than 5 per cent of the people of Massachusetts live in the open country?

CHAPTER XXV

METROPOLITAN NEW YORK

In the realm of economics, New York is the city of superlatives. For here at the mouth of the Hudson River has arisen the greatest concentration of economic power that the world has yet seen. Regardless of what criteria are chosen to measure a city's greatness, New York invariably takes position as the economic capital of the United States—the commercial and industrial center for the nation as well as the continent of North America.

The city of New York is but one of those large American cities which early outgrew its corporate boundaries. A whim of history made the Hudson River a state boundary line between New Jersey and New York, and decreed that the great metropolis which grew up at its mouth should lie partly within the jurisdiction of both states. Contiguous municipalities have grown up and these form a cluster, the pattern which is so common in metropolitan developments. On the New York side almost the entire development has been in the five boroughs of the city of New York; but the New Jersey portion has a large number of independent cities, largest of which are Newark and Jersey City. Urbanization has spread eastward along the north shore of Long Island Sound until several communities in near-by Connecticut are logically included within the metropolis. From its aegis, the little Dutch seaport at the south tip of Manhattan Island, New York has expanded until today its metropolitan area would be nearly circular were not the southeast quarter of the pie occupied by the sea. Within that area live nearly one-eleventh of the people of the United States. Of these, slightly less than one-third live in New Jersey and two-thirds in New York. The Connecticut portion has only about 1 per cent of the metropolitan population.

Despite this multiplicity of local governmental units, the New York metropolitan district forms a single economic unit. Workers, shoppers, and merchandise cross city and state lines almost indiscriminately and the entire cluster is marked by economic interdependence. Metropolitan New York, as defined by the Port of New York Authority, includes 369 separate municipalities, of which 251 are in New Jersey, 111 in New York, and 7 in Connecticut. These municipalities, ranging in population from a few hundred to more than two million, are the individual stones in the great edifice which is the economic capital of the United States.

What are the reasons for this great concentration of population and economic power? Why should this tiny Dutch settlement have expanded until it has one-eleventh of the population, one-ninth of the manufacturing, one-quarter of the wholesale trade, and one-half of the banking of the United States? The answer is found partly in the excellent harbor, well situated to handle the trade with Europe, partly in the Hudson-Mohawk depression, which offers the easiest route across the Appalachian Highland to the interior, and partly in the foresight of local citizens who saw the great potentialities of these two resources as aids to transportation and trade. A young nation, purchasing many manufactured goods and paying for them with the products of the farm, mines, and forests, was bound to develop an enormous trade with Europe. All seaboard cities yearned to handle this trade and most of them built roads, canals, and railroads into the interior in an effort to capture it. In this competition New York had the advantage of the "water-level" route to Buffalo and the interior prairies. That resource was first made to pay dividends with the completion of the old Erie Canal in 1825, later by the paralleling railroad which became the New York Central. After 1825, New York outdistanced its rivals and by the beginning of the Civil War had established itself as the leading American commercial city. Since that time, New York has experienced no serious rivalry from other cities for the transatlantic trade. The Erie Canal fell into near-disuse in the later railroad era, but the rising eastern railway systems eagerly extended their lines to New York. Competition among the railroads gave New York an early advantage in railroad rates. The harbor, spacious, deep, and almost completely landlocked, has proved adequate to care for the great concentration of shipping.

In the meantime, of course, the United States began to mature economically, and the importance and character of its foreign commerce changed. By the time of the World War, the United States was exporting fewer raw materials and importing fewer manufactures. The nation had become more nearly self-sufficing, especially in manufactured goods which were now being exported

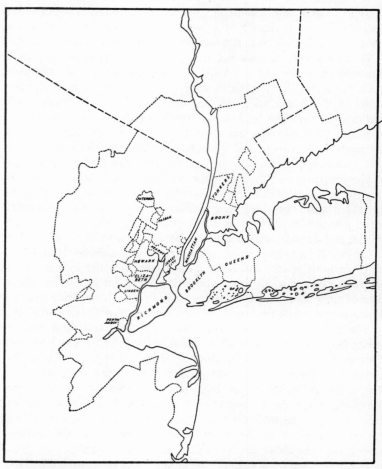

FIG. 85. Metropolitan New York. The most important municipalities in the New York metropolitan cluster are named on this map. Locate the five boroughs of the city of New York. In New Jersey, the principal cities are Newark and Jersey City, but there are dozens of smaller ones, some of which are highly industrialized, others almost purely residential. It is interesting to note that the metropolitan district is almost circular in shape, except that one-quarter of the pie is in the Atlantic Ocean.

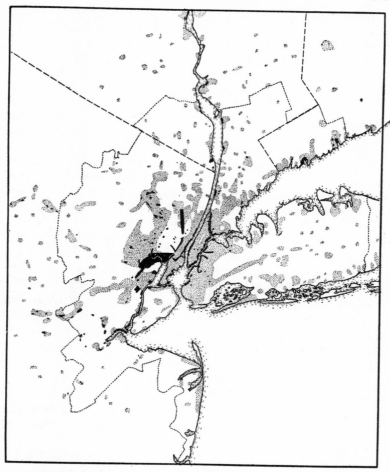

FIG. 86. Major Land Uses in the New York Metropolitan District. The map classifies land uses as industrial (black) and residential-commercial (stippled). The white areas are largely unoccupied by urban development. Some of them are parks, others are naturally unsuited to city building. The development of three north-south urbanized belts is evident. On the west, the Newark-Paterson group is separated from the Jersey City-Bayonne-Richmond group by the Meadows. On the east, the Brooklyn-Manhattan-Bronx group is separated from the Jersey City group by the Hudson (North) River. Bridges, tunnels and ferries have lessened the potency of these barriers in recent years.

in considerable quantities. In those days certain New Yorkers were asking whether, if the nation continued to become more nearly self-contained, New York might continue its leadership. A nation substantially without foreign trade has little use for great seaports. Optimistic Chicagoans, looking at the future through the other end of the telescope, predicted a great inward migration of business and industry that would make their city the future business center of the nation. Chicago was to have gained what New York lost, because it was a correspondingly great center for internal transportation and trade.

That this shift in the economic center of gravity has not occurred is now a matter of history. First came the World War which caused foreign trade to skyrocket, and choked New York harbor with shipping for the first and only time in history. The World War also opened new vistas of foreign trade and international finance. New York became the (temporary) financial center of the world while London was concentrating on financing the war, and post-war years brought a remarkable intrusion of American dollars and American goods into the markets of the world. Emphatically, America did not forget about foreign trade, but achieved a new interest in it. For this new scheme of pushing American capital and manufactured goods into the four corners of the world, New York was well equipped.

It had the physical equipment and financial resources, and it was the accepted center for foreign trade and finance. The World War inaugurated New York as a *world* center of trade and finance, with interests paralleling those of London. In this new role, it has continued to expand and to remain the undisputed leader in American trade.

New York started and grew as a commercial center and it has retained that characteristic throughout its history. The greatness of New York is to be found not so much in its factories as among the great rail-end piers at Jersey City, the ocean liner berths on lower Manhattan, the crowded skyscrapers of Wall Street banking houses, and the great stores, theaters, and newspapers of the mid-town district. These are the earmarks of a great commercial center—a focal point for transfers and transactions. Essentially, these are the foundations upon which metropolitan New York stands. Among these evidences of commercial pre-eminence, we are inclined to turn first to the area's greatest commercial magnet—the harbor.

THE PORT OF NEW YORK

"New York is the most important seaport of the United States, and ranks among the foremost of the world. This pre-eminence is primarily due to its unexcelled harbor, which makes it a center of convergence for maritime commerce. It has a water front of about 770 miles with a developed frontage measured around piers and slips of nearly 550 miles. Of the total water-borne commerce of the United States about 50 per cent by value is handled at its piers and about 75 per cent is financed by its banking institutions."[1] Thus succinctly does the Corps of Engineers, United States Army, describe the importance of those various river mouths and arms of the ocean upon whose shores has arisen the greatest metropolis of the Western Hemisphere. Among the great natural assets of metropolitan New York, the greatest is this fine harbor, spacious, well located for the trade with Europe, seldom closed by fog, and never choked with ice.

Facilities.—When the early Dutch explorers sailed into the labyrinth of waters around the mouth of the Hudson River, they recognized the excellence of the harbor and the desirability of the island at the mouth of the river as a site for a port to carry on trade with the mother-country. Their tiny settlement which soon sprang up on the toe of Manhattan Island looked out upon the best natural harbor on the east coast of the continent, the almost completely landlocked Upper Bay, with an area of about seventeen square miles. Upper New York Bay is simply the drowned mouth of the Hudson River, itself nearly a mile wide for many miles upstream and deep enough for large ocean vessels even in the present day. But these were not the extent of the harbor facilities. To the east, Upper Bay is connected with Long Island Sound by the half-mile wide strait known as East River; and to the north is the shallow Harlem River, really a minor mouth of the Hudson, which makes Manhattan an island. Large additional harbor areas are found to the west in Newark Bay, an estuary of the Passaic and Hackensack rivers. Newark Bay has two outlets, one to the south known as Arthur Kill, which empties into Raritan Bay, and

---

[1] "The Port of New York," Part I, Port Series No. 20, Corps of Engineers, United States Army, Government Printing Office, Washington, 1932, p. 1.

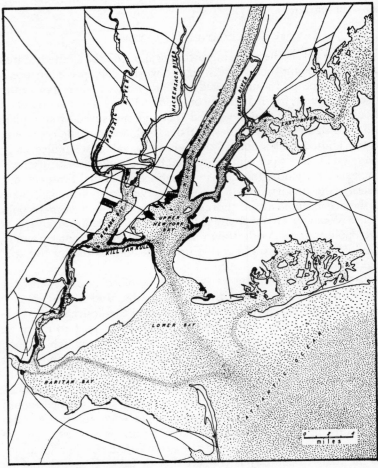

FIG. 87. The Port of New York. The manifold waters of the bays and rivers which serve the Port of New York cover large areas. The map shows (in solid black) the location of the principal port developments and the major railroads which serve them. The depth of the various channels is indicated by the density of the shading. Note how channels have been dredged to connect the outer harbor with various sections of the inner harbor. Specialization of different sections of the port to handle various types of shipments is explained in the text.

an east-flowing branch, Kill Van Kull, which empties into Upper Bay. The Dutch found this western (New Jersey) group to be much shallower than Upper Bay, but a modern generation has made it navigable by dredging. All of these landlocked waters— Upper Bay, the Hudson, Harlem, and East rivers, Newark Bay, the Passaic and Hackensack rivers, Arthur Kill and Kill Van Kull —constitute what is known today as the Inner Harbor of the Port of New York.

Seaward of the Inner Harbor, less protected from storms but still adequate anchorages in nearly all weather, are the waters which constitute the Outer Harbor. This Outer Harbor consists essentially of Lower Bay, Raritan Bay, and Jamaica Bay. It is landlocked except for about six miles of open sea between Sandy Hook and Rockaway Beach. This stretch is marked by a broad sandy bar across which five entrances have been cut.

Development of these harbors has naturally been greatest in the sections having greatest depth of water and easiest access from the land. Docks and wharves are most numerous along (1) the Lower Hudson River, lining the lower half of the Manhattan shore as well as the opposite bank in Jersey City and Hoboken, (2) the northwest shore of Upper Bay (Jersey City and Bayonne), (3) the east shore of Upper Bay (Brooklyn), (4) both sides of the adjacent East River, (5) the south end of Arthur Kill (Perth Amboy, etc.), and (6) Kill Van Kull (Bayonne). New port works are under construction on (7) Jamaica Bay and (8) Newark Bay which seem destined to make these areas important sectors in the sea-going trade. In general, the waters of the Outer Harbor and Newark Bay are undeveloped except as noted above. Newark Bay is very shallow except for a single channel near its east shore, and much dredging will be necessary before it can be made navigable for ocean ships.

Commerce.—The Port of New York handles nearly half the American foreign trade if the figure is based on the *value* of goods handled. Tonnage figures are less impressive, because water-borne traffic passing through this port is above the average in value. The Port of New York regularly handles about one-quarter of the tonnage of United States foreign trade.

In addition to this heavy volume of foreign trade, the port handles an enormous coastwise traffic with other United States ports. The volume of coastwise traffic is nearly twice as great as the volume of foreign commerce. Finally, when a complete analysis is attempted, one finds a very heavy traffic within the port, from one section to another, which is definitely local but adds to the economic use made of these waters. For the period 1926-1930, the commerce of the Port of New York was distributed as follows:

	Percentage of Total Tonnage
Foreign:	
Imports	13.3
Exports	9.0
Domestic:	
Coastwise receipts	22.5
Coastwise shipments	8.5
Internal	6.5
Intra-port	33.6
Local	6.6
Total	100.0 (129,669,053 tons)

This table shows the water-borne commerce to be 22.3 per cent foreign, 31 per cent coastwise (with other U. S. ports), and 46.7 per cent internal, intra-port and local. The latter terms need some explanation. Internal traffic (6.5 per cent) is that carried over inland waterways, mainly crushed stone, sand, and gravel brought down the Hudson River. Intra-port traffic (33.6 per cent) moves from one part of the port to another and consists largely of goods hauled by car ferries and lighters. Car ferries operate mainly from the various railroad terminals in Jersey City and this type of shipment is in greater use here than in any other part of the world. Local traffic (6.6 per cent) moves within the confines of a single section of the port and is analogous to switch-track movements on a railroad—a sort of local-delivery arrangement which has grown up because waterways are less crowded than rails and streets. This combined movement makes the port the busiest in the world. The volume of shipping (net register) entering the Port of New York is more than twice as great as that entering London, the second-ranking port of the world.

Organization.—If this breakdown of the types of traffic using the Port of New York were compared with those of other world ports, the comparison would reveal an exceptionally high percentage of commerce having origin and destination within the port. In most ports of the world this type of traffic is vehicular, carried by railroads and trucks. It is a switch-track, transfer, delivery-service type of operation which ordinarily is not carried on by boat because of the expense of trans-shipment. That two-fifths of the commerce of the Port of New York is of this type reflects both the peculiar geographic setting and unplanned historic growth of the port.

Historic Aspects.—The Port of New York was spawned in an era of water-borne commerce, grew to importance in the pre-railroad era, and inherited the difficulty of having been divided between two separate states. Railroads did not get into Manhattan until the island was rather thoroughly built up, and then found rights-of-way obtainable on only one central street (Park Avenue) and along a portion of the Hudson River shore. Even today, only two railroads have facilities for bringing freight trains to Manhattan and their switching and warehouse facilities fall far short of meeting the needs even of local merchants, not to mention rail-ship transfers of goods to and from the interior. In addition, only two lines extend into Brooklyn. The remaining railroad companies, through sheer lack of space for tracks and warehouses, were forced to build their terminal facilities elsewhere—mainly on the New Jersey shore. The Hudson River was long considered too wide to bridge and too expensive to tunnel. Finally, when bridges of this length became practicable, the river had so much shipping that bridges would have had to be built high above the water. Railroad bridges of this height would require so much land for approaches that the cost would be prohibitive. Even a highway bridge, whose approaches can be considerably steeper and more circuitous than those for a railway, is considered impracticable south of the middle of the island. (The George Washington Bridge is far north, nearly ten miles from the main traffic center of Manhattan.)

In time, New York grew large, sprawling eastward on railroad-poor Long Island and westward across the marshes of New Jersey. The port became the great gateway for the foreign commerce of the United States, and tidewater locations were in demand by industries and railroads alike. In addition to this vast foreign trade, extremely large tonnages of freight accrued from the heavy concentration of population and industry.

Geography.—In the beginning, possibly it could have been foreseen that a difficult transportation problem would arise. But mankind has seldom produced such far-seeing minds and seldom paid attention to those it has produced. Like Topsy, the Port of New York "just growed."

It might possibly have been foreseen that three islands, Manhattan, Long Island, and Staten Island, would be difficult to reach by rail once navigation had preempted the waters which separate them from the mainland. The long peninsula which constitutes the New Jersey shore of the Hudson River is nearly as inaccessible because of the great marsh which lies behind it (the Meadows). Newark Bay, the only large harbor directly accessible from the mainland, was choked with mud. Here indeed was a great natural harbor, ideally situated to become a great world port. But by the time New Yorkers came to recognize the fact, the Port of New York found adequate development difficult. The situation was further complicated by lack of coordination between the efforts of the states of New York and New Jersey.

In simple terms the problem boils down to the statement that everyone wants to reach Upper Bay at Manhattan Island, and there simply is not room for such a concentration of business. Skyscrapers have provided the thousands of offices which business wanted at this center, but there is no such device for taking care of ships and trains and goods. In practice, a considerable specialization of various sections of the port has developed. Rail-end piers on the New Jersey shores place cars on ferries for Manhattan and Brooklyn or load ships directly for the sea-going trade. These car-float barges, of which there are more than one hundred thousand, make the Hudson River between Jersey City and Manhattan the most congested section of the port. Here also in lower Manhattan are docked the great transatlantic liners as well as many barges from up the Hudson. Miscellaneous merchandise of great variety is handled by this section of the port.

A similar sort of commerce is found along the East River, except that here are smaller vessels, notably those bringing foodstuffs from Central and South America. East River wharves along Lower Manhattan are filled with the pungent odors of coffee, tea, bananas, spices, and similar tropical products. The opposite (Brooklyn) shore receives much sugar for local refineries.

The heaviest traffic outside these waters is handled in the "New York and New Jersey Channels" between Staten Island and the mainland. These channels receive much heavy freight—

petroleum for Bayonne refineries, gypsum, coal, copper ore, and pottery clay; and they carry much bunker coal with which to supply ships using the port. Tonnages are enormous but aggregate values are low.

The Brooklyn shore of Upper Bay likewise handles many heavy materials such as iron and copper, rubber, lumber, coal, and coke. Here also are the properties of the port's two great terminal companies. With a combined frontage which includes nearly two-thirds of the Brooklyn shore of Upper Bay, these huge enterprises offer almost every conceivable shipping facility. They can handle any type of freight from light package goods to the heaviest articles. Their water-front properties include complete facilities for light manufacturing, which are leased to industrial firms. Recent trends toward smaller orders have lessened the demand for warehouse space but these concerns still handle much merchandise. Newark Bay receives a great deal of coal from the coastwise trade; and improvements now nearing completion will enable it to relieve the Hudson of some of the general merchandise traffic.

The Port of New York still suffers from lack of adequate facilities for bringing freight to the central transfer center in Lower Manhattan and for loading directly from rail to ship; there is much expensive ferrying of cars in car-floats. (It costs as much to deliver a car of merchandise to Manhattan from rail-end in New Jersey as to haul it from Albany to Jersey City.) There is inevitable loss of time in loading, unloading, and reloading, and there is undue storage in railroad cars and on car-floats because of the lack of properly placed warehouses. Nevertheless, New York is the favored port among shippers. It costs somewhat more to use it, but here are many ships, frequent sailings, a vast local market, competent financial agencies, and other advantages which outweigh the additional expense incident to congestion. The Port of New York is equipped to handle a greater variety of shipping than any other American port. Shippers say that New York gives better and more complete service on cargoes of miscellaneous merchandise than any other port on the Atlantic seaboard. Furthermore, the port is awake to its problems and responsibilities as the gateway for American foreign trade. In 1921, the states of New York and New Jersey perfected a compact—a treaty establishing a board known as the Port of New York Authority, whose business is to plan the future development of the entire port. Not only has this board drawn plans. It has also built vehicular bridges connecting all five boroughs with New Jersey, and has tied Manhattan with New Jersey by both a bridge and vehicular tunnels under the Hudson. In the future it will do more to carry out its excellent plan to increase the capacity of the Port of New York to carry on American foreign trade cheaply, quickly, and efficiently.

THE SITE

The shores of good harbors are not often ideal sites for building great cities, because the very indentations which make good harbors often make access to the interior difficult. New York is no exception to this statement. The site is fragmented both naturally and politically. He who attempts to build a city on three islands and two peninsulas, all separated by waters devoted to ocean shipping, is certain to encounter difficulties. These barriers are never insurmountable, but surmounting them with bridges and tunnels is very expensive, occasionally financially impossible. In metropolitan New York, until comparatively recent times, such barriers remained very generally unconquered. More recently, a system of tunnels and bridges has been projected which promises soon to link together all of the detached fragments for purposes of land transportation.

First of the barriers to be bridged was the Harlem River. This was not a major feat, because the river is a narrow one. Manhattan was tied to the mainland early in its history. Later came the Brooklyn Bridge, engineering marvel of its day, which was soon followed by other bridges making Brooklyn easily accessible from Manhattan. The Hudson River was more difficult, likewise the Meadows, the great swamp at the head of Newark Bay.

By 1910, the usable portions of the growing metropolitan area were seen to consist of three roughly parallel strips, separated by two formidable barriers. On the east was the Bronx-Manhattan-Brooklyn strip, connected by bridges. Across the Hudson lay the peninsula which holds Jersey City, Bayonne, Hoboken, and their hilly up-river neighbors. This peninsula was rather effectively isolated on the west by shallow Newark Bay and the marshy Hackensack Meadows. Railroads had crossed it but there were no adequate highways. The eastern strip included a long string of cities extending from Perth Amboy through Elizabeth and Newark and far up the Passaic River past Paterson and Passaic. These three strips still appear prominently in the map of urban development. Barriers which separate them, however, are rapidly disappearing.

In 1910, the Pennsylvania Railroad drove a tunnel under the Hudson and erected a passenger station in mid-town Manhattan. Other tunnels followed, the latest ones being for motor vehicles. Vehicular bridges now connect Staten Island (Richmond) with Bayonne, Upper Manhattan with the New Jersey shore, the Bronx with Manhattan and Queens. A final link in the circle will be a vehicular tunnel under the Narrows to connect Brooklyn with Staten Island. Finally, a long viaduct connects Newark with Jersey City. Thus barriers have been overcome for purposes of the all-important motor-vehicle transportation. Railroads have done less well, but eventually belt lines will be constructed to relieve the harbor of much of its congestion. Barriers remain to the extent that they cannot be crossed at random. But they have lost much of their potency, and man apparently has provided a sufficient number of overflow outlets to permit Manhattan's pent-up economic life to seek less congested sites in near-by areas.

MANUFACTURING

It was nearly inevitable that America's greatest commercial center should also become its most important manufacturing center. New York became preeminent among American cities largely because of its resources for commercial development; but New York also had definite resources for manufacturing which fostered expansion along certain lines.

Probably the greatest reason for the development of manufacturing in the New York area is the great concentration of population. Local industries sufficient to supply a population of eleven millions would bulk large in themselves. A commercial metropolis inevitably has a large number of printing plants, bakeries, and similar establishments catering to local needs.

A second factor of nearly equal importance is the presence in New York of a large labor supply, much of which historically has been derived from immigration. As the principal port of entry for immigrants from Europe, New York for decades has had access to a large pool from which it could obtain workers at relatively low wages. This factor of large supplies of immigrant labor is often cited as the prime reason for the development of New York's greatest manufacturing industry, the manufacture of clothing.

A third factor in New York's industrial development is associated with the prestige value of locations in the accepted center of the nation's social and economic life. As the nation's style center, New York has become a favorite location for firms manufacturing women's apparel, cosmetics, and many lesser items which must reflect late style changes. The same prestige value apparently applies to the publishing business, for a majority of the nation's large publishers maintain headquarters in New York. A portion of this prestige harks back to the days when Americans imported many types of high-quality manufactured goods from Europe. As the major import center, New York became a national source for these goods. When American industrialists started to manufacture them, New York was a logical site for their factories.

Finally, we come to a fourth factor in the industrial attraction of locations along a great and well-managed water front. The Port of New York offers good sites for a variety of industries whose raw materials are obtained from sea-borne commerce. In like manner, it has proved a good location for many industries whose goods are manufactured for export. These four factors—a concentrated market, abundant labor, prestige, and access to ocean shipping—have been basic in the industrial development of the New York metropolitan area. They account very largely for its evolution as the major manufacturing center of the United States.

Local Industries.—More than half the goods manufactured in metropolitan New York are consumed directly by the people who live in the area. These products are generally of the same types as those manufactured in every city in the United States: bakery products, confectionery, newspapers, ice cream, manufactured gas, and a long list of other goods, generally designed for immediate consumption and best manufactured near the market. Local industries comprise a major fraction of the metropolitan industrial structure.

National Industries.—The services which New York performs for the nation relate to finance, shipping, wholesaling and a short list of important manufactured products. The outstanding product of New York factories which is destined for national markets is clothing, especially a wide variety of women's apparel including dresses, coats, suits, fur goods, and millinery. The metropolitan area is also the nation's leading center for printing books and music and for the manufacture of paints, soap, and several lesser commodities whose raw materials are derived largely from foreign trade. All of these types of industries occupy well-defined areas.

The Clothing Industries.—More than half the national clothing industry is housed in a 200-acre area on the lower west side of Manhattan Island. Its factories are the unpretentious upper floors of buildings whose street floors house the bulk of the nation's wholesale garment business. The garment industry is a giant in terms of volume or number of workers, but its factories are small, and there are hundreds of them. Most garment-makers work on a small-order basis. A few dozen dresses of a particular design and material are turned out to meet a particular order, to be followed by another small order that is entirely different. There is no standardization, for New York garments are style goods, and style implies a certain amount of uniqueness.

The garment-making industry was one of the last to accept straight-line production methods. Garment-making originated very largely as contract tailoring for men's clothing. Individual workers (mainly immigrants) would contract with wholesale clothiers and the garments were made up in the home. Later certain economies were discovered in cutting the cloth in a central location and sending a bundle of pieces out to be worked up in the home. Home work was often carried on under extremely poor conditions and at very low wages. The system was fought by health authorities, factory inspectors, and organized labor. Many garment-makers tried the factory system and found it more economical. Today, home work has nearly disappeared from the New York garment industry, and most of the products are made in factories.

When the clothing worker was first brought from his home into a factory, there was little change in the work system. The cutter still cut stacks of cloth and the pieces for a garment were collected in bundles and turned over to individual workers. More recently, assembly-line techniques have come into general use. By this system, workers become specialized in a particular operation (such as collars or buttonholes). More specialized machinery has been introduced, and the worker output has been increased. Manufacturers have found that this system gives improved performance even when individual orders are small.

The New York garment industry is little more than a glorified made-to-order industry. Its greatest strength lies in that feature. New York garment factories produce style goods. More highly standardized articles such as shirts, house dresses, hosiery, underwear, and work clothing are more likely to be manufactured in other parts of the country. The permanence of the New York garment industry depends very largely upon the city's ability to maintain its position as the national style center and buying headquarters for the nation's retail clothiers.

Heavy Industries.—Metropolitan New York is not a national center for the metals and machinery industries, but it is important in several other types of heavy industry. In general, these industries are dependent upon water-borne commerce. Most of them are located along the New Jersey shores in the western portions of the port area. Chemicals, electrical machinery, soap, petroleum products, and paints are important products of these tidewater plants. All of them rely greatly on ocean shipping for raw materials or distribution of their products. Crude oil from South America, soap oils from the Orient, and drying oils from South America and Asia feed the huge refineries and soap and paint factories. Here also one finds foreign copper being refined and electrical goods and farm machinery being turned out for foreign markets. All of these industries have sought the New Jersey water front.

The major center for heavy industry is the Newark-Kearney-Harrison district, whose most important product is electrical goods. Farther south, Bayonne is dominated by oil refineries, and the New Jersey shore of Kill Van Kull is lined with plants devoted to copper, clay products, chemicals, oil, and similar products whose materials come in chiefly by water. This strip also includes large plants for the manufacture of soap, paint, and farm machinery. He who follows the water front from Perth Amboy northward past Linden, Elizabeth, Newark, Harrison, and Kearny generally has a smoky journey. Smoke and fumes from a variety of furnaces fill the air throughout the area. Here is the leading center for heavy industry of the New York metropolitan district.

Other Heavy-industry Zones.—Back along the water front, there are numerous heavy industries in both Jersey City and

Brooklyn. Shipyards are located in Brooklyn and on the north shore of Staten Island (Richmond). Jersey City manufacturing is dominated by the activity of its many railroad shops. The last-named activities differ materially from those of the Newark group. Ship-building and railroad shops are there because of commerce. The heavy industries of the Newark strip have been established there because of accessibility to water-borne materials. Jersey City and Hoboken, like the Borough of Richmond, must be classified as commercial areas. The boroughs of Brooklyn, Queens, and the Bronx are definitely residential, as are most of the small cities such as Mount Vernon and New Rochelle which join the Bronx on the north.

Textiles.—North of the Newark heavy-industries area lie the textile towns of the Passaic Valley, notably Paterson, Passaic, and Clifton. Paterson became a leading American silk-textile center in the days when such plants were established to utilize woman labor from families whose menfolk worked in near-by iron works. More recently, the silk industry of Paterson has declined with the decreasing popularity of silk woven goods. Cotton textiles are produced in Passaic and Clifton but these towns are better known for dyeing and finishing than for spinning and weaving. The textile area also reaches the Hudson River and crosses it into Westchester County, New York. Yonkers makes carpets and rugs, and adjacent towns have numerous small textile mills.

Trade and Finance

Manhattan.—With these industrial, commercial, and residential areas as a background, we return to Manhattan, nerve center of the metropolitan district. More specifically, we can return to the lower half of Manhattan, for the north half is largely residential. Here we find, south of Fifty-ninth Street, the major plexus of the economic life of the metropolis. Here is at once the oldest and newest in New York. Here, literally, are the people who give the orders that run this metropolitan machine and much of the entire nation.

Sociologically it is significant to think of the lower half of Manhattan in terms of "East Side-West Side," but economically it is more fruitful to speak in terms of the two prominent nests of sky-scrapers—Downtown and Midtown. Downtown New York is the citadel of finance which is epitomized in Wall Street. Here the stock markets, commodity exchanges, banks, and other financial institutions have crowded together until the great canyon which is Wall Street is the neck-straining mecca of all tourists. Not far away (nearer the Battery) are the offices of foreign shipping firms and the financial offices of many a major American corporation. Manhattan's financial district really occupies a relatively small area in the south extremity of the island, its institutions lining the narrow, crooked streets of old New Amsterdam. The entire area occupies less than one square mile of land, but on these acres are housed the leading markets of a continent. Most famous is the "money market," centering in the New York Stock Exchange, whose traders occupy the skyscraper offices of Wall Street. Economically, the function of this financial market is to bring together prospective lenders and borrowers of loanable funds. Its traders deal in securities, evidences of debt and ownership, and they represent buyers and sellers scattered from one end of the world to the other. For this important commodity, capital, Wall Street is the national market place. Here also are the banks which finance foreign trade, and the offices of steamship lines which carry it. That portion of Downtown Manhattan which lies west of Broadway is occupied very largely by the offices of steamship lines and other shipping agencies.

Less spectacular, but of comparable importance in our exchange economy, are the commodity exchanges, all of which are concentrated in this small sector of Manhattan. In these exchanges, traders buy, sell, and set the daily price of America's cotton, coffee, and numerous other types of produce.

The southernmost square mile of Manhattan Island is thus preeminently a transaction center, a place where exchanges are made on paper. Relatively few goods are transferred here. Exchange rather takes the form of interchanges of orders, checks, drafts, stocks, bonds, and similar negotiable instruments which direct the flow of capital and goods in the modern economic order.

The Midtown section is newer. Its skyscrapers are more scattered and it is by all odds more glamorous. Perhaps its most significant (but not most imposing) structures are the Grand Central Terminal and the Pennsylvania Station, which bring the hordes of visitors to the city. Midtown has the great mercantile establishments. Here is the most impressive section of Fifth Avenue, famous for fashions; and Times Square, heart of the theater district; and most of the great hotels; and the business offices of hundreds of great American corporations. Midtown is definitely commercial—it sells goods. And it has the trappings which accompany salesmanship—theaters, night clubs, hotels, railroad stations, and a thousand other attractions aimed primarily to cater to the out-of-town buyer. Its skyscrapers—Empire State, Chrysler, Radio City—are known throughout the world. Its theaters, its opera, and its art are topics of conversation in the tiniest American hamlet. Its radio programs amuse the nation. New Yorkers say it is not New York, but a brilliant section of the city set aside for outsiders. Students would say it is not New York—that the real economic power of New York certainly lies nearer Wall Street. The Midtown section is in fact a specialized area of a great city, but a very significant indicator of the primary reason for that city's existence—a focal point for commerce brought about by a fine harbor and easy access to a vast productive hinterland.

Areal Specialization.—Metropolitan New York is a complex study in urban economic geography. From one point of view, the district represents the apex of the structure which constitutes the national exchange economy. Viewed in this way, the development of the metropolis is strictly a consequence of the development of the nation. Without the growth of a great commercial nation there would have been scant need for the skyscrapers, exchanges, docks, and factories which have brought to this area the largest concentration of urban population in the Western Hemisphere. This type of inquiry leads to an analysis of the parts played by New York in the functioning of the national economy. It brings forth an amazing list of commercial and industrial functions which clearly mark the area as the economic capital of the nation.

Another line of inquiry is concerned with major land uses within the metropolitan district. With so many functions to perform, it is not surprising to find that the area has developed a marked degree of geographic specialization. Much of this specialization can be related to the manner in which the physical characteristics of the site have affected the historical development of the area. Heading the list of natural advantages is New York's excellent harbor, valued as a transfer point for sea-borne commerce moving to and from the interior, as an accessible source of sea-borne factory materials, and as a good place to manufacture certain products for sale in foreign countries. Today the shores of the manifold channels of New York harbor are occupied largely by docks and factories dependent upon water-borne commerce. A second natural advantage lies in the well-traveled Hudson-Mohawk depression, which hastened New York's development into the nation's leading port by providing the easiest route across the Appalachian Highland to the interior plains. Man-made railroads and canals made New York harbor easily accessible to the nation's commerce and favored the city's rise as its foremost commercial center. Growing commercial interests generally sought locations in what soon became the heart of the metropolitan area, the lower half of Manhattan Island.

Other factors must be considered in any appraisal of the rise of the New York area. Important among them is the steady supply of cheap labor which New York derived from abroad. This supply of immigrant labor was renewed annually, almost without interruption, until the flow was halted by a change in the national immigration policy about the time of the World War. Immigrants came to New York because most of the ships docked there. Seeking employment, they were quickly attracted to the growing manufacturing industries of the area. They and their children almost exclusively have manned the large clothing industry which in the principal manufacturing enterprise of the district. During all these decades, a plentiful supply of immigrant labor gave New York a definite advantage as a location for many types of manufacturing industries.

Another group of favorable factors is more difficult to define because its components are largely institutional. Here we find such undeniably important elements as style, custom, prestige, and the momentum of an early start. New York early assumed a position as the nation's style center (lately contested by Hollywood) and New York-made clothes thereafter assumed a certain prestige not based on price. In addition, the availability of local finance and certain types of specialized markets undoubtedly influenced the establishment of a number of manufacturing plants. It is even asserted that a well-known manufacturer finally chose a New York location because his wife wanted to associate in New York society! We should also mention the fact that local organizations, both governmental and private, have done much to encourage industrialization. No one of these factors compares in importance with the commercial attractiveness of the site or the

THE MIDTOWN SECTION, NEW YORK. (*Courtesy American Airlines.*)

The Harbor at Baltimore. A Sugar Refinery Is in the Foreground.

presence of a large supply of labor. But each of them has had a share in building up the large commercial and industrial establishments which are now so thoroughly incorporated into the economic structure of the district.

The location of industries not attracted by tidewater locations shows a definite pattern. Manhattan is the center for the apparel industries, and numerous textile plants are found in the New Jersey sections which lie away from the harbors.

Beyond the industrial and commercial zones the land-use pattern is residential. Many Manhattan workers commute from the four outlying boroughs or from the almost purely residential areas which occupy the north and east portions of the metropolitan district. Most of the New Jersey cities are more nearly self-contained, with industrial, commercial, and residential districts in close proximity.

In these ways the various types of economic activity which have found metropolitan New York a desirable location have tended to choose the sites best suited to their use. Heavy industry and shipping have sought tidewater locations. Light industry remains near the best sources of factory labor. Trade and finance have preempted two important areas on Manhattan Island as well as hundreds of smaller local-use districts in all portions of the metropolitan district. The remaining sections are available for residential purposes. These types of geographic specialization mark the area which serves as the economic capital of the United States.

REFERENCES

The most satisfactory analysis of New York City to appear in recent years is in the issue of *Fortune* for July, 1939. The entire issue is devoted to the various aspects of life in New York. Much of the material in this chapter is taken from *Regional Plan of New York and Its Environs*, a series of studies by the Regional Plan Association. The material for the port is taken very largely from the *Port Series*. Numerous guidebooks are available for those who desire a more intimate knowledge of the city's geography.

QUESTIONS AND PROBLEMS

1. Why has the city of New York surpassed all other American cities in population and economic importance?
2. Contrast the industrial development of Manhattan Island with

that of Metropolitan New Jersey. Why have these differences appeared?

3. New York stands first in the manufacture of many commodities. Of what general types are they?

4. "New York resembles Washington, D. C., in that it belongs to no region but to the entire United States." For what lines of economic activity is this statement true?

5. How is the function of the city of New York revealed by the skyscrapers of the downtown and mid-town sections? by the lower west side?

6. Why has the transportation problem been so serious in the New York metropolitan area?

7. What types of manufacturing industries are found along the New York waterfront? In what sectors are they located? Why have they chosen these locations?

8. Write a brief description of relief features in the New York metropolitan area.

9. Consult a recent volume of the *World Almanac*, and write a brief statement describing the principal bridges, tunnels, and subways serving Manhattan.

10. What natural advantages favor New York harbor over other Atlantic harbors? What man-made advantages favor it?

11. Describe the general pattern of population distribution in the New York metropolitan area. How do you account for this pattern?

12. Why has the population of Manhattan been declining in recent years? Do you consider this trend favorable or unfavorable? Why?

13. Compile a list of the services New York is likely to render an Illinois farmer, a West Virginia coal-miner, or a Wyoming rancher during the course of a year. Can you classify these services?

14. Why are the nation's foremost financial markets located in New York? In what area are they concentrated? Why?

15. Why does New York rank high in the manufacture of certain types of wearing apparel and not in others? What are these types? What areas are in the best position to challenge New York's supremacy? In what ways might technological change threaten the New York apparel industries?

16. Why is Metropolitan New York a good place to manufacture soap? to refine gasoline? to refine sugar? Where are these factories found? Why?

17. How does the economic development of Jersey City differ from that of Newark? Why?

CHAPTER XXVI

UP-STATE NEW YORK

THE industrial development of the part of the state of New York which lies outside the boundaries of the New York Metropolitan District is explained largely in terms of railroad geography which in turn is mainly a reflection of topography. In order to connect the city of New York with the productive interior prairies, railroad-builders were confronted with the necessity of crossing the Appalachian Highland. This highland is too low to constitute an effective barrier to land transportation, but it is difficult enough so that railroads have found it desirable to take advantage of the most acceptable routes across it. Engineers have often dreamed of building a railroad straight across these hills and valleys but the enormous cost of such an undertaking has prevented its enactment. Railroads have continued to use their relatively circuitous routes through the valleys and gorges which penetrate the highland.

Railroads tapping the West for the city of New York have taken four general routes: (1) southwest through Trenton and Philadelphia, and thence westward to the interior plain (principally the Pennsylvania Railroad; Reading; and Baltimore and Ohio); (2) westward, through Allentown and the anthracite district (Delaware, Lackawanna and Western; Lehigh Valley; Central of New Jersey); (3) northwest, through the valleys of the headwaters of the Delaware River (Erie; New York, Ontario and Western); and (4) northward, up the low narrow valley of the Hudson River to Albany, thence west along the equally favorable valley of the Mohawk River to the lake plain south of Lake Ontario (New York Central Lines). Each of these routes has its own important advantages, but the easiest and most economical is the route through the Hudson-Mohawk depression.

The Hudson-Mohawk Traffic Artery.—Years before the railroad was more than an experimenter's toy, the state of New York planned and built a barge canal to connect Buffalo with the navigable portions of the Hudson-Mohawk River. The Erie Canal was relatively easy to build because it followed what once was an outlet for much of the Great Lakes watershed back in glacial times when the mouth of the St. Lawrence River was choked by a glacier. The depression shows signs of having carried an enormous volume of water in that era, and by this method the stream reduced its valley almost to the level of the Lake Ontario plain. Drainage was later established through the St. Lawrence River, but the era left the state of New York with the lowest route across the Appalachian Highland between the St. Lawrence River and Atlanta. The Erie Canal was opened in 1825, and became an important factor in the rapid rise of the city of New York in the decades which followed. It was not long, however, before a series of short railroads paralleled the river and canal the entire distance from New York to Buffalo. These short lines were soon consolidated end-to-end into the first long, interregional railroad line in America, the New York Central. Barges gave way to boxcars, but the Hudson-Mohawk depression continues to this day to be one of the major traffic arteries of the continent.

Rise of Cities.—Urban development followed the growth of commerce. Albany, at the great bend in the route, became an important transportation center. Factories sprang up all along the line, for here were the obvious advantages of access to rail-borne materials and to rail-reached markets. Rochester was considered a good location because of power from the falls of the Genesee River. Syracuse had excellent deposits of salt. Buffalo, at the eastern terminus of Great Lakes shipping, boomed as a transfer center, and soon the power of Niagara Falls was harnessed to increase the attraction of the Buffalo-Niagara Falls area as a location for industrial concerns. From a path for commerce, the Hudson-Mohawk depression developed into a location for commerce and industry.

This concentration of urban development was further advanced by the presence in west-central New York of a series of important geographic barriers—the so-called Finger Lakes. These long, narrow, and surprisingly deep lakes effectively thwart east-west transportation over a belt some forty miles wide south of Syracuse and Rochester. Farther east, the rough topography of the Catskill Mountains is a similarly effective barrier. The Erie Railroad skirts the south edge of both barriers, traversing a relatively rough area across the southern part of the state to reach Lake Erie by a direct but relatively difficult route which utilizes the valleys

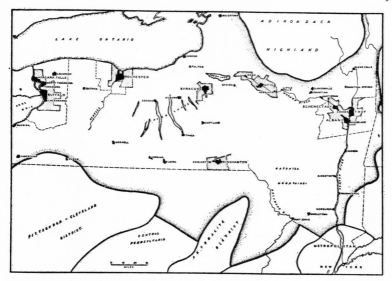

FIG. 88. Up-state New York. Urban development in this section has occurred principally along the major transportation routes. Oldest and most important of these routes is the valley followed by the Hudson and Mohawk rivers which provides a nearly level route between Lake Erie and the Metropolitan New York section. The western end of this route is occupied by the Buffalo-Niagara Falls metropolitan district. East of Buffalo the cities are closely spaced in a chain which reaches the Hudson River in the Albany-Schenectady-Troy metropolitan district. Most important of the intervening cities are Rochester, Syracuse and Utica, but there are many smaller centers of greater than local economic importance.

A second string of cities occupies sites along another important east-west transportation route which crosses southern New York. These cities are smaller in both population and economic developments than those of the Buffalo-Albany chain. Binghamton is the leading member of this group.

Important barriers to transportation are found in the state of New York. Most important of these is the Adirondack Highland which is part of the Northern Forest and Lake Region. South of the Adirondacks a second mountain barrier, the Catskill Mountains, has served to divert commerce into the low Mohawk depression which separates these two highland areas. A third natural barrier occurs in the Finger Lakes of central New York. These lakes have been barriers to east-west transportation and have helped concentrate the cities of up-state New York into the two chains which appear so prominently on the map.

of the headwaters of the Delaware and Susquehanna rivers. Along this route has arisen a string of cities, smaller than those of the Hudson-Mohawk route, but with a similar economic development. Binghamton and Elmira are the largest cities of this string. Physiographic factors have been largely responsible for aligning the cities of up-state New York into two distinct groups: (1) a Hudson-Mohawk group, which occupies the valley and spreads out toward the west onto the lake plain of Lake Ontario, and (2) a southern hill group, lying generally near the southern boundary of the state in a series of valleys of the headwaters of south-flowing rivers. The latter group was joined, historically, by the main line of the Erie Railroad. There are marked similarities in the industrial development of these two groups of cities, but the discussion is simplified by considering each group separately and by further dividing the northern group into an eastern and western portion.

Northwest New York

The cities of northwest New York differ in both their setting and their economic development from those of the remainder of the up-state New York section. Other cities are generally locked in relatively narrow valleys, but these occupy nearly level sites on the lake plains of Lake Ontario and Lake Erie. Industrially, the northwest cities are generally devoted to producers' goods—metals and machinery—while their eastern neighbors manufacture mainly consumers' goods in the textile-clothing group. Nearness to the Pittsburgh-Cleveland steel center and access to lake transportation are important factors in the emphasis upon the heavier industries in the western portion of the Hudson-Mohawk traffic artery.

Buffalo and Niagara Falls.—Buffalo was well equipped by nature to become both a commercial and an industrial center. Its location above Niagara Falls made it the natural eastern terminal for lake-borne commerce; and its position opposite the Mohawk depression made it a logical point of trans-shipment for lake-borne traffic destined for New York or Boston. Commercial cities nearly always arise at points of trans-shipment, of loading and unloading, of changes in the type of transportation. In Erie Canal days, Buffalo unloaded east-bound lake traffic from lake boats onto canal barges and performed the reverse function for west-bound commerce coming in over the canal. In the railroad era which followed, Buffalo continued to be an important point of trans-shipment, especially for such heavy commodities as wheat and ore.

With such excellent facilities for receiving materials and marketing goods, Buffalo early began to attract manufacturing industries. Here apparently was a good place to mill Dakota wheat which could be brought in very cheaply by boat from Duluth; and to manufacture steel from lake-borne cargoes of ore and coal; and, in a later period, to manufacture and assemble automobiles, parts for which could be brought in cheaply from Detroit, Toledo, and Cleveland. Buffalo commercial interests continued large, but its economic structure soon came to include many industries based on lake-borne raw materials.

In addition to its superiority as a transportation center, the Buffalo area early developed the great power resources of Niagara Falls. Niagara was the first major hydroelectric development on the American continent and the cheap electricity from its turbines has attracted a very special group of industries classified as electrochemical and electrometallurgical. These are the electric-furnace industries whose products run the gamut from carborundum and heavy chemicals to cellophane and shredded wheat. In such industries power is a major manufacturing expense, and these firms generally seek locations where electricity is both plentiful and cheap. Most of the plants are located in the city of Niagara Falls, but they are also found in Buffalo and the smaller cities of the area.

The steel industry of the Buffalo area has its most important development south of the city. There along the lake front are found blast furnaces, steel works, and rolling mills. Buffalo is equipped to supply practically any product regularly turned out by the iron and steel industry. In 1935, Buffalo stood sixth in blast-furnace capacity and fifth in steel-ingot capacity among the iron and steel centers of the United States. In 1937, steel was the leading industrial product of the Buffalo industrial area, but in years of lesser activity in the heavy industries, steel yields first position to chemicals.

Buffalo's third manufacturing industry is motor vehicles. The city has branch plants of the leading automobile makers and the main plants of one or two well-known smaller concerns. Flour-milling ranks fourth in the list. Buffalo frequently ranks ahead of Minneapolis as the nation's leading flour-milling center. Below these in the list are the local industries such as bakeries and printing establishments, and a long list of miscellaneous industries in which various items of machinery are conspicuous. Outside Buffalo and Niagara Falls, the most important suburban centers are Lackawanna, noted for steel; Lockport, which makes automobile parts, saws and wallboard; and North Tonawanda, whose factories turn out fiber materials, machinery, and office equipment.

Paced by the metals-machinery group, the industries of the Niagara Falls-Buffalo district turned out 1.7 per cent of the national production of manufactured goods in 1937, and ranked tenth among industrial districts of the United States.

While these industries place Buffalo definitely in the list of industrial cities, its commercial development is important. Of the 821,000 persons inhabiting its metropolitan area in 1930, a sizable percentage was engaged in commercial activity. Buffalo wholesale houses serve a rich trade territory in northwest New York and adjacent Canada. Her extensive railroad yards are busy with the transfer business inherited by Buffalo from Erie Canal days. The Port of Buffalo regularly ranks with Duluth-Superior, Chicago, and Detroit as one of the major freight-receiving ports on the Great Lakes. Buffalo's industrial importance is traceable largely to those same factors which made it a booming commercial town more than a century ago.

Rochester.—The name of the city of Rochester has long been before the American public as the national center for the manufacture of cameras, optical goods, scientific instruments and certain types of electrical equipment, and as an important source of men's clothing and women's shoes. Through the national advertising of Eastman, Michaels-Stern, Fashion Park, and numerous other Rochester firms, the city is probably better known for products demanding highly skilled labor than any city in the nation.

Skilled labor of a highly technical type undoubtedly is Rochester's greatest present-day industrial asset. In the past, however, Rochester was first important because of power generated by the falls of the Genesee River, and because of splendid east-west transportation facilities provided by canal and railroad headed eastward toward the Mohawk depression.

As the third city of New York State and economic center for much of the Finger Lakes district, Rochester has developed important commercial interests centered in the jobbing and shopping trade of that area. In 1930, the Rochester metropolitan district held a population of 399,000. Its industrial area (Monroe County) produced eight-tenths of one per cent of the nation's manufactured goods in the year 1935. Rochester has no large suburbs. Its industries, nearly all of the lighter types, are located within the city. Its harbor on Lake Ontario has recently been improved to make the city accessible to Great Lakes shipping.

Syracuse.—Located about seventy-five miles east of Rochester and almost exactly halfway between Albany and Buffalo, the city of Syracuse commands the central portion of the urbanized belt along the old Erie Canal. When the site for the city of Syracuse was released by the Indians, the treaty provided that the former owners might always have access to the salt deposits which lay within it. The same salt deposits still provide a foundation for a considerable segment of the Syracuse industrial structure. Soda ash, not salt, is the major product, burned from local salt in plants located west of the city. Chemicals, however, are not the chief industrial products of the Syracuse area. Essentially, Syracuse is a foundry center, and its largest industrial employers are the makers of tool steel, automobile gears, and bearings.

Metropolitan Syracuse had a population of 245,000 in 1930, of whom 209,000 lived within the city. Syracuse is connected to Lake Ontario by a branch of the New York Barge Canal, the canalized Oswego River. Oswego is the lake terminus, and Fulton is the largest city along the route. Hydroelectric power is developed in two large plants. Oswego and Fulton have extensive interests in pulp and paper as well as in silk, wool, and cotton textiles. Oswego has a large match factory. The canal gives easy access to Canadian pulp, and Oswego trans-ships much coal brought in by rail from Pennsylvania mines and bound for Canadian lake ports.

Rome is included by the Bureau of the Census in the Utica metropolitan district, but there are two reasons for making it the eastern outpost of the northwest New York section, thus separating it from Utica which logically belongs in the northeast section. In the first place, Rome is located on the Lake Ontario plain, in the Lake Oneida Valley, and thus belongs to a different physiographic province from its blood-brother, Utica, which is just within the plateau province. In the second (and more important) place, Rome's industrial development is along lines of metals and machinery, while Utica's major industrial interests are in textiles and clothing. By reason of physiographic setting and economic development, Rome is properly included with the cities of northwest New York. More specifically, it is a center for the manufacture of steel wire, cables and tubes, and of copper and brass products, especially household utensils.

Other Cities of Northwestern New York.—Smaller cities of the section show an industrial development similar to that of the larger ones. Batavia manufactures farm machinery, brass, and aluminum castings. Geneva and Auburn, located at the north ends of two of the Finger Lakes, manufacture stoves, boilers, and other machinery. Auburn is especially noted for the manufacture of Diesel engines for locomotives, and for its rope and carpets. At the south end of the lake district, Ithaca and Cortland manufacture a variety of machinery and steel products. Farther east, Oneida is famous for its silver plate.

Summary.—Northwest New York accounts for about 3 per cent of the nation's manufacturing. About half this manufacturing is found in the Buffalo district, one-quarter in Rochester, one-eighth in Syracuse, and the remainder in relatively small cities scattered over the section. Metals and machinery dominate the lists of industrial products throughout the section, although there are certain local exceptions, notably in Rochester which produces a wide variety of manufactured goods notable for their use of technically skilled labor. Physiographic factors have made the Syracuse-Rochester-Buffalo belt a great traffic artery and thus have given it its greatest industrial asset.

NORTHEASTERN NEW YORK

A few miles east of Rome the tiny Mohawk River flows down out of the Adirondack Mountains and turns eastward toward Albany through the narrow trough which separates the northern Appalachian Plateau from the Adirondacks. This trough, now traversed by the main line of the New York Central Railroad and the New York State Barge Canal, is the location for a compact group of cities which make the valley almost completely urbanized from Utica to Albany. In contrast to the western portion of this traffic artery (northwest New York), cities of the Mohawk Depression are closely spaced, squeezed together in a valley which is eighty miles long and generally less than ten miles wide.

In this valley, transportation has attracted industry. In 1937, the section turned out about 1 per cent of the nation's manufactured goods. Production was divided among a score of cities, most important of which were Schenectady, Albany, Troy, and Utica. The first three of these lie sufficiently adjacent to form a single metropolitan district.

The Albany-Schenectady-Troy Metropolitan District.— Albany, near the head of navigation on the Hudson River, was chosen by the Dutch as the capital for their interior settlements along the Upper Hudson. Later, its strategic location made it the successful candidate for selection as the capital for the state of New York. Albany's position makes it a crossroads for internal commerce. Natural, low-level routes extend west to Buffalo, south to the city of New York and north to Montreal by way of Lake Champlain. It is furthermore on the direct route from Buffalo to Boston, early improved by Boston capital by the building of two railroads, the Boston and Albany and the Boston and Maine, the latter of which uses the Hoosac Tunnel under the main southern arm of the Green Mountains.

Albany began as a commercial city and always has remained one. Great railroad yards occupy many of the outskirts of the city. In these yards, freight trains are broken up, classified, and remade to go to their various destinations. Albany's largest payrolls are those of its wholesale and retail stores, but second to these are the payrolls of its railroads. In recent years, Albany has also blossomed as a seaport. A twenty-seven foot channel is maintained from the Port of Albany to the mouth of the Hudson River, 143 miles south. The head of tidewater on the river is at Troy, six miles north, which is the terminal for the barge canals from Buffalo and Lake Champlain. Albany trans-ships much wheat and soda ash which are barged in from Buffalo and Syracuse. It receives and distributes gasoline from down-river refineries; logs, lumber, and wood pulp from Puget Sound, Portland, Sweden, and Canada; wheat from Portland and Seattle; barley from San Francisco; rye from Poland. The volume of ocean commerce is not great, but the rapid acceptance of the port by foreign shipping interests after its opening in 1932 would seem to point toward future growth. Manufacturing is not highly developed. Albany factories are concerned mainly with supplying local markets or with servicing the railroads. The major industrial development is to be found in the two other cities which share this metropolitan district: Schenectady and Troy.

Troy is located just above Albany on the opposite bank of the Hudson. Half a century ago Troy was the national center for a great collar and cuff industry whose genesis is traced to the inventive genius of a Troy housewife who perfected the "four-piece shirt" to keep down laundry bills. Changing styles have more recently weakened the demand for Troy's major product, and Troy factories have gradually shifted emphasis to shirts, handkerchiefs, and other accessories of male attire. Troy, however, still makes 90 per cent of America's collars and cuffs. Cohoes and Rensselaer have manufacturing industries similar to those of Albany and Troy. Foundry products, textiles, and clothing are important in these suburban cities.

Schenectady is located about fifteen miles northwest of Albany on the relatively smooth delta of the Mohawk River. The city is best known as the home of two large industrial corporations, General Electric and American Locomotive. Schenectady has the home office and main plant of the General Electric Company, and that corporation is the major factor in the town's economic existence.

The Albany-Schenectady-Troy district is marked by economic specialization, but along a variety of lines. Albany, the commercial city, manufactures for local needs and the railroads. Schenectady is the home of heavy industries, led by electrical machinery and locomotives. Troy is highly specialized in textiles and clothing. Combined, these cities present a remarkably diverse and well-balanced economic development. North of Troy, in the valley of the Upper Hudson River, the cities of Glens Falls and Saratoga Springs handle much of the retail and shopping trade of that area. Glens Falls generates power and has developed into an important shirt-manufacturing center. Saratoga Springs is best known as a resort city with well-developed mineral springs, resorts, horse-racing, and other recreational and entertainment facilities.

Amsterdam, Johnstown, and Gloversville.—West of Schenectady, we encounter a trio of cities definitely specialized in the manufacture of textiles and clothing. Amsterdam claims distinction as the second city in the world in the manufacture of wool carpets and rugs. It also has a large production of brooms and knit goods. Johnstown and Gloversville for more than a century have been the twin centers of the American leather glove and mitten industry. In most years these cities manufacture 40 per cent of the entire national output of gloves and mittens. Leather tanneries and a nationally famous gelatine factory are also located here.

Farther west, Herkimer, Little Falls, and adjacent cities manufacture typewriters, desks, office furniture, paper and knit goods.

Utica, at the western end of the northeast New York section, is best known for knitwear and cotton goods. The Utica metropolitan district, which includes the city of Rome (outside this section) reported a population of 191,000 in 1930, of whom 102,000 lived in the central city. Utica is an important distribution center and has extensive railroad interests.

The northeast New York section is marked by industrial specialization, mostly along lines of textiles and clothing. Schenectady, the great exception to this statement, is a center of heavy industry. Elsewhere in the section, the marked specialization in textiles, rugs, gloves, knit goods, and clothing designates this area as primarily a manufacturer of consumer goods. Long-established industries, with great pride in their products and an imposing array of specialized skills among their laborers, mark the industrial development of the many cities of the section.

Southern New York

The line of cities most readily identified as those lying along the main line of the Erie Railroad shows economic characteristics similar to those served by the more northerly "water-level" route of the New York Central Lines. There is a western group devoted mainly to metals and machinery and an eastern group dominated by textiles and clothing. These southern cities of the state of New York have not grown so large as those of the northern string. Nor would we expect it. Their hilly hinterlands are less productive and have provided less material for commercial development; and their transportation facilities have not been so good.

Southwestern New York has a half-dozen small cities whose combined industrial production is about four-tenths of one per cent of the national total. Most important of these is Jamestown, division point on the Erie railroad, and manufacturer of office furniture, textiles, and lumber products. Jamestown is a center for the Chautauqua County resort area. Dunkirk, located on the shore of Lake Erie, is a machinery center.

Olean is located in the oil fields and divides its attention between oil-well supplies and railroad shops. Hornell is mainly a railroad town with additional interests in silk and furniture. Corning is the home of a famous glass works, attracted to this area by good natural gas and glass sand. Elmira manufactures tools and machinery and is a leading producer of fire engines.

The industrial development of southwest New York is closely related to local natural resources. Jamestown based a furniture industry on local supplies of hardwoods and later shifted to metal furniture made from steel produced in near-by plants. Olean and Corning took advantage of their location on oil and gas fields. Elmira, with easy access to Pennsylvania coal and iron, specialized in machinery. The general development in this section has been along heavy-industry lines.

Binghamton and the Southeast New York Section.—Located just north of the Pennsylvania state line, in the narrow valley of the Upper Susquehanna River, the city of Binghamton has developed an important center for the manufacture of shoes. The principal shoe factories are located in the western suburbs, Endicott and Johnson City, each taking its name from that of the major firm. Other shoe factories, a camera factory, and machine shops nearly complete the list of Binghamton industries.

In addition to its factories, Binghamton has important commercial interests. As the largest city of the New York-Pennsylvania border, Binghamton serves the jobbing and shopping interests of a large territory. In 1930, the Binghamton metropolitan district had a population of 130,000 of whom 77,000 lived in the central city, the remainder largely in the two industrial suburbs of Endicott and Johnson City.

Railroad Towns.—Southeastern New York contains a half-dozen cities best described as railroad towns. All of them grew to importance as railroad junctions and none of them have developed extensively along other lines. Reasons for their development are largely physiographic.

The reader will recall that the great structural fold known as the Appalachian Valley extends northeast from the Allentown-Bethlehem district of Pennsylvania, and continues across the northern tip of New Jersey, finally joining with and becoming the Hudson River Valley about fifty miles above Manhattan Island. This same valley continues northward, becoming the Lake Champlain Valley and finally merging with the valley of the St. Lawrence River in Canada. The particular service rendered by this valley in southeast New York was to provide a route for the shipment of anthracite coal from Pennsylvania to New England. Two railroads (Lehigh and Hudson River, and Lehigh and New England) were built up the valley almost exclusively for this traffic. These "bridge lines" secured other valuable traffic from the Franklin Furnace (New Jersey) zinc district, and much non-anthracite business from Pennsylvania, and were later joined by branch lines from other roads. In addition, these roads crossed the main lines of the Erie, New York Central and several smaller companies. An important development of interchange traffic resulted, and at these interchange points, cities grew up. Unable to compete with the superior industrial advantages of tidewater locations, they developed little manufacturing. Hence, to this day, they are best classified as "railroad towns."

Most important of these railroad towns are Newburgh, Middletown, Port Jervis, Beacon, Kingston, and Poughkeepsie. In addition to their major railroad interests, these towns have factories which turn out textiles and clothing. The largest factory production is found in the city of Poughkeepsie. Industrially, these cities belong in the textiles-clothing group. None of them, however, are highly industrialized.

NORTHERN NEW YORK

North of the Hudson-Mohawk traffic artery, the unproductive bulk of the Adirondack Mountains effectively discourages the development of transportation and cities. It is significant, however, that the mountains are bounded on all sides by low valleys which have become the location for railroads and cities. On the south is the Mohawk depression, previously described as a major traffic artery. On the west and north are the lake plains of Lake Erie and river plains of the St. Lawrence. The eastern boundary of the Adirondacks is formed by the low trough of the Lake Champlain Valley, topographic extension of the great Appalachian Valley which extends the length of that mountain system and is occupied in southeast New York by the Hudson River. The Champlain Canal crosses the divide between the headwaters of the Hudson River and Lake Champlain at an elevation of 149 feet above sea level. Important railroad lines follow these lowlands and form a ring around the Adirondack barrier.

Except in the previously described Mohawk depression, the cities along the railroads which encircle the Adirondacks are not highly industrialized. Leading manufactures generally consist of paper and wood products. Railroads are important and commercial interests generally exceed industrial interests in economic importance. Watertown has paper mills, machine shops, and garment factories. Ogdensburg, on the St. Lawrence River, is a railroad terminus with a similar economic development. Massena has a large aluminum refinery. Ogdensburg and Massena serve the zinc-mining area at the edge of the adjacent Adirondacks.

On the shores of Lake Champlain, Burlington, Vermont, and Plattsburg, New York are commercial centers serving the Champlain Valley dairy area. Burlington has textile mills, while Plattsburg's major industrial interest is paper. Plattsburg is an important gateway to the famous Saranac Lakes area of the Adirondacks.

In general, the industrial development of that portion of the Adirondack ring which lies north of the Mohawk depression is a mixture of the older wood and paper industries, whose raw materials come from the neighboring mountains, and the somewhat newer textile-clothing group. The textiles and clothing industries have been more or less parasitic on the heavier industries, and represent an overflow from the adjacent textile-clothing districts of New England and northeast New York.

SUMMARY

The location of urban economic development in New York State is best considered in connection with the major transportation routes which cross the state. Foremost of these routes is the east-west Mohawk depression which has become the location for a string of industrially important cities extending from Buffalo to Albany. Across the southern portion of the state, a lesser string of cities is found along the old main line of the Erie Railroad. These two urbanized chains include most of the industrial development of up-state New York. Each chain can be divided near the middle into a western segment, whose leading industries are concerned with metals and machinery, and an eastern segment, whose principal factory products are textiles and clothing. Outside these districts most of the cities are small and industry is not highly developed. In northern New York, paper and wood products are important, and in southeastern New York the main factory products are textiles and clothing.

REFERENCES

Reports of the New York State Planning Board are of value in understanding this area. Several chambers of commerce and power companies have provided information on the industrial resources of the area.

QUESTIONS AND PROBLEMS

1. Describe the agricultural development of the state of New York (see Chapter XXI) and show how the location of various agricultural districts is related to urban development in the state.

2. In accounting for urban development in the area between Albany and Buffalo, how much emphasis should be given to (a) topography, (b) the old Erie Canal, and (c) the New York Central railroad?

3. Why are the cities of Buffalo and Albany said to occupy strategic locations?

4. What general differences in industrial development are noted between western New York and eastern New York? What important exceptions to these generalizations should be mentioned? What reasons for these areal differences in types of industrial development might be cited?

5. What types of cities are found in the "Adirondack ring"? What minerals are important here? (See Chapter XXII.)

6. Why do rural conditions prevail over most of southern New York state?

7. What importance should be attached to water power as a factor in the location of manufacturing industries in New York state?

8. What are electro-chemical and electro-metallurgical industries? Why are they found in Niagara Falls? Are they decreasing or increasing in national importance?

9. The author finds it difficult to describe the industrial development of Rochester without mentioning brand names and the names of firms. Why?

10. What items in the natural environment help explain the development of the "railroad towns" of southeast New York?

11. Why did Johnstown, Gloversville, and Troy become important in the manufacture of certain types of wearing apparel? What are these types?

12. Does the Albany-Schenectady-Troy area constitute a true metropolis? Why or why not?

13. Binghamton is the major commercial center of southern New York. What types of primary production are found in that section of the state?

14. What differences are noted in the industrial development of Syracuse, Rome and Utica? To what extent can you account for these differences?

15. Why did cities appear at the north and south ends of the Finger Lakes and not along their sides?

16. What are the major minerals of southwest New York? To what extent have they influenced the industrial development of that area?

CHAPTER XXVII

THE CENTRAL ATLANTIC INDUSTRIAL SECTION

EASTERN Pennsylvania and that portion of the coastal area which extends southward from metropolitan New York to Baltimore constitute a distinctive section of the Manufacturing Belt. Here we find an industrial development almost as old as that of New England and in some ways comparable with it. Here also are good harbors and large industrialized seaports. Here are old and stable financial institutions and nationally renowned mercantile and manufacturing establishments. And here are some of the best farm lands and richest mineral deposits of the United States. Yet the diversity of these resources is such that economic development is dictated by none of them. The Central Atlantic section's great mineral is anthracite coal, but the mines have produced no great furnaces, no steel industry as in the Pittsburgh area. Their harbors shelter the ships of all nations and their wholesalers serve many states; but none of these seaports has extended its commercial interests to become a great national center such as New York. Yet the Central Atlantic section is one of the major commercial and industrial areas of North America. Its factories, which turn out nearly one-tenth of the nation's manufactured goods, are noted for the diversity of their products. The Central Atlantic section is a leading producer of textiles, clothing, steel, and machinery.

Districts.—For convenience in discussion, cities of the Central Atlantic section are grouped into four districts, the boundaries of which are closely related to the natural resources of the area:

1. First and most important are the "fall-line" cities, including Philadelphia, Trenton, Wilmington, and Baltimore. This string of cities grew to importance because of advantageous locations at the heads of navigation of the rivers which emerge here from the piedmont and start their journeys across the flat coastal plain. All of these cities are seaports and all of them occupy once-important water-power sites. Although somewhat removed from the actual seacoast, these fall-line locations constitute the economic seaboard of the Middle Atlantic coast of the United States. For

623

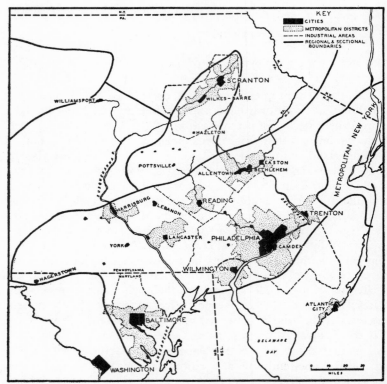

FIG. 89. The Central Atlantic Industrial Section. Industrialization and urban development in the Central Atlantic section have followed a definite areal pattern. On the east, the coastal plain has few cities. Its development is mainly agricultural and the area was therefore included in the Gulf-Atlantic Coast Region. The Manufacturing Belt begins on the east with the fall-line cities of Trenton, Philadelphia, Wilmington and Baltimore. All of these cities were established as seaports and both Philadelphia and Baltimore handle large tonnages of ocean shipping today. These two cities carry on most of the manufacturing of the section. West of the fall line, another chain of cities occupies sites in the Appalachian Valley. Bethlehem, Allentown, and Reading are important members of this group. Transportation was a leading factor in the establishment and growth of both the tidewater and valley chains of cities. The map also includes the Anthracite District and a portion of the Central Pennsylvania section.

along this line land and water transport meet. The fall line was particularly important in the establishment and early growth of these cities.

2. A second group of cities occupies the valleys of southeastern Pennsylvania. These valleys are the Pennsylvania portion of the Appalachian Valleys, described in previous chapters. In Pennsylvania, the valleys run northeasterly across the southeast quarter of the state. They are separated from the fall line by a narrow belt of low piedmont hills. They have long had good transportation and their cities have developed both industrially and commercially.

3. Central Pennsylvania is a rugged area, generally hostile to both agriculture and transportation. Its western portions are dominated by mining and include the non-industrial portions of the North Appalachian coal fields. Its eastern portions, on the other hand, have few minerals and little urban development.

4. The anthracite district occupies a rugged ridge and valley area of central eastern Pennsylvania. It is highly urbanized and its economic structure is dominated by anthracite coal. These districts, with their varying resources, constitute the Central Atlantic section of the American Manufacturing Belt.

The Fall Line.—European colonists arriving on the shores of North America saw the advantages of a number of fall-line locations south of New York. Physiographer and geographer alike draw a nearly straight line from the mouth of the Hudson River southwest through the present cities of Trenton, Philadelphia, Wilmington, Baltimore, Washington, and on southward past Richmond, Virginia. This line marks the boundary between the undulating clay hills of the piedmont and the flat, sandy coastal plain. Crossing it, one experiences a change in topography, soil, and agricultural development. The line is known as the fall line because rivers coming out of the piedmont generally have falls or rapids near the place where they enter the coastal plain. The falls or rapids are important for two reasons: first because they mark the head of navigation, and second because they present possibilities for the development of water power. Hence the fall line was early considered a good place to build cities, especially if a particular river were large enough to be used by seagoing vessels.

On the Middle Atlantic coast the best combinations of power and navigation were offered by the Delaware River, which skirts the fall line for more than fifty miles (between Trenton and Wilmington), and by some of the streams entering Chesapeake Bay (especially at Washington on the Potomac and Baltimore on the Patapsco). All of these cities save Washington were founded in early Colonial days.

To the fall-line cities, the ocean served first as an outlet for raw materials to be marketed abroad, and later, as the nation matured, as a source of imported raw materials for local factories. Water-power developments helped the factories, but in the long run they were aided more by easy access to Pennsylvania coal. Through the decades of industrial expansion all of the cities except Washington became the location for important manufacturing industries. Railroads tapped the interior and brought them coal, ores, and foodstuffs, and provided channels for the distribution of their manufactured products. Their harbors gave them similar access to the materials and markets of foreign countries. Philadelphia and Baltimore became industrial cities of the first magnitude.

The Piedmont.—Industrialization was not confined to the fall line but extended westward along the railroads and canals which crossed the piedmont. This migration was inaugurated by the iron and steel industries which early saw a saving in moving nearer the fuel, but it was followed by the whole family of machinery industries, and finally by the labor-consuming textiles-clothing group. The migration continued across the entire piedmont area of southeast Pennsylvania and brought this district within the Manufacturing Belt. Today it is an important center for both the metals-machinery and textile-clothing groups of industries. The entire Central Atlantic section regularly produces between 8 and 9 per cent of the nation's manufactured goods. Philadelphia and Baltimore dominate this development, but about one-third of the section's industrial production is derived from plants not located on tidewater.

THE FALL-LINE CITIES

METROPOLITAN PHILADELPHIA

History and Site.—When William Penn sent his commissioners to America to establish the colony which was to bear his name, he directed them first to select a site for his pre-planned Great Towne. Penn had directed them to select "a spot that was most navigable, most dry and healthy, and where boats might load and unload without lighterage." In compliance with his instructions, the founders selected a gently sloping, wooded peninsula at the confluence of the Schuylkill and Delaware rivers, some eighty-eight navigable miles above the mouth of the latter river.

William Penn had definite ideas as to the manner in which Philadelphia should be laid out. His plan contemplated two square miles of territory divided into rectangular blocks, with streets forty and fifty feet wide. In the center was to be a square of ten acres to house public buildings, and near the corners of the rectangle were to be four squares of eight acres each. True to their instructions, Penn's commissioners platted what is today the central business district of the city. City Hall Square is still the economic center of the city, and most of Philadelphia's business is done within the rectangle made by the four outlying squares (Logan, Rittenhouse, Franklin, and Washington). The gridiron street pattern remains intact save for the recently cut diagonal parkway which leads northwest from the City Hall. Penn's streets have proved embarrassingly narrow for motor traffic, so that most of them are one-way thoroughfares with parking permitted on only one side. The relatively large original blocks have been cut by numerous alleys, but the checkerboard pattern remains. The two major axes, north-south Broad Street and east-west Market Street, are still the major streets of the city, and their intersecton at City Hall is the busiest place in Philadelphia. But we are neglecting the history, a history and tradition which probably have a greater influence upon the present economic life of Philadelphia than on that of any other major American city.

From its very inception Pennsylvania was the most successful colony in attracting Europeans and their money. In the "City of Brotherly Love," Penn offered much in the way of religious freedom and democracy, not to mention free land on some of the fattest acres of the Atlantic seaboard. Philadelphia grew rapidly, with its English Quakers, Germans, Scotch-Irish, and Welsh finding a ready living handling the produce of a rich soil and mild climate. By 1760, Philadelphia had passed Boston in population and was the largest city of the New World. Philadelphia was the logical location for the national capital and retained the seat of government until 1800. At about this time, however, potent competition for the title of first American city appeared in the rapidly rising city of New York. New York passed Philadelphia in population after 1800, but its race was not really won until the Erie Canal began to bring it the products of the western prairies. After 1825, New York forged ahead rapidly.

Philadelphia saw the importance of western markets; but, lacking a practicable canal route through the Appalachian Highland, local capital early projected and built the "Main Line," nucleus of the present-day Pennsylvania Railroad. The "Main Line" gave Philadelphia access to the prairies and their markets. Philadelphia capital invested heavily not only in the railroad but also in the anthracite properties to the north and in the coal lands of the Pittsburgh Bed to the west. Early Philadelphia industries grew and prospered. Its harbor proved adequate for shipping, and its merchants and bankers were successful. In traditionally conservative manner, Philadelphia expanded and held its position as the second-ranking city of the Atlantic coast, exceeded in importance in the entire Western Hemisphere only by New York and Chicago.

From the vista of two and one-half centuries, it appears that Penn's commissioners chose well. Philadelphia has remained a good port, a healthy city, an excellent focal point for commerce. Its important fortunes, established wealth, and respect for the arts all attest to its maturity as a great city.

Expansion and Growth.—It was not many years before Philadelphia outgrew its original site. Expansion occurred in all directions, westward across the Schuylkill, northwest along the "Main Line," and north and east along the Delaware. Across the Delaware, meanwhile, the city of Camden, New Jersey, and its suburbs were assuming importance as a sector of the metropolitan area. In 1930, the population of the Philadelphia metropolitan district was 2,847,000, of whom about 68 per cent lived in Philadelphia (the county and the city are coextensive), 4 per cent in Camden, 20 per cent in the Pennsylvania suburbs adjacent to Philadelphia, and 8 per cent in the New Jersey suburbs outside Camden.

In recent years this expansion has been marked by a pronounced migration of the wealthy and upper middle classes to the rolling country west of the city. There they have built some of the most beautiful residential suburbs to be found in the United States. This migration outside the limits of the city and county has rendered many sections of the old city somewhat shabby and unattractive. It has contributed to a long-standing unsavory political situation, dominated by political bosses controlling the votes of local residents who generally were not the real owners of the city.

Commerce and Finance.—Downtown Philadelphia has remained essentially commercial, with important firms in wholesale and retail lines as well as in banking, finance, and shipping. The principal shopping center is the area along Market Street near the City Hall, led by the nationally famous Wanamaker firm. Philadelphia banks, not so powerful as those of New York and Boston, still keep the city among the three or four leaders in American finance. There is no clearly defined financial district, but the major banks are near the shopping center.

Philadelphia's trade territory includes the rich agricultural, manufacturing, and mining districts of the eastern half of Pennsylvania and the southern half of New Jersey. Three major railroads serve the city and gridiron its trading area.

The Port of Philadelphia, located on the Delaware and Schuylkill rivers, is a major one, currently ranking eleventh in the list of world ports, and third (below New York and Baltimore) in North America. The traffic is of a very diverse nature and includes an extensive foreign commerce with nearly all nations. Petroleum and its products head the list of items, accounting for about three-quarters of the coastwise trade. Crude oil from Venezuela, raw sugar from Cuba, and miscellaneous cargoes from Europe are the principal imports, while gasoline and miscellaneous merchandise are exported to all parts of the world. About one-third of the port's tonnage (chiefly oil) is handled along the Schuylkill, the remaining two-thirds along the Delaware.

Manufacturing.—Philadelphia factories, like those of New York and Boston, are devoted principally to the production of consumer goods rather than capital goods. Most Philadelphia factory products are worn or eaten or used in the home. As befits a great commercial center, it has large printing and publishing interests in both the newspaper and magazine fields. There are probably more Philadelphia-made radios in American homes and automobiles than are made in any other city. A Camden soup manufacturer outsells all competitors. But none of these industries is dominant. The chief characteristic of Philadelphia industry is its remarkable diversity and the large number of relatively small plants. Largest Philadelphia factory payrolls are in the textiles and clothing industries. Knit goods, silk hose, men's clothing, carpets and rugs, and wool manufactures are the products of dozens of factories scattered among the residential-commercial sections north of Market Street.

Beyond this list of consumer goods is a group of the heavier industries, attracted to this location by the advantage of a good harbor and access to good coal. Lying near the harbors are oil refineries, a locomotive works, shipyards, linoleum factories, sugar refineries, and similar establishments, many of whose materials are derived from foreign trade. While there is no well-defined center for heavy industries, nearly all these plants are located in the south portions of the metropolitan district. The Philadelphia area, in fact, leads in the production of many lines of manufactured goods, varying from silk hosiery to radios and locomotives. Despite this leadership, despite the fact that its industrial area has 4 per cent of all American manufacturing, despite its nationally known brands and products, industrial Philadelphia cannot be associated with any single line of manufacturing. The Philadelphia industrial development is peculiarly diverse, more so than that of any other large American city. The city manufactures nearly everything imaginable, leads the nation in a few of these, but is dominated by none. It has been indicated that most of its industries are of the lighter type, dependent more upon local labor skills and good market organizations than upon a location strategic from the standpoint of raw materials. Further generalization is hardly possible.

In summary, Philadelphia, like New York and Boston, is essentially a commercial city. Its railroads tap a rich market area, and its harbor shelters the ships of all nations. Philadelphia factories, even as its banks and stores and clubs, are conservative institutions more jealous of quality than ambitious for quantity. In all of these we find the city's greatest asset—careful, hard-working laborers. Philadelphia is not spectacular in industry, finance, or trade, but we have the feeling it is built solidly and will endure.

Outlying Industrial Cities.—Other industrial centers of the Philadelphia-Camden industrial area are found principally (1) southwest of the city along the Pennsylvania bank of the Delaware River, and (2) northwest, in the railroad-lined valley of the Schuylkill. The southwest area is dominated by those same heavy industries which occupy the south part of the city. Good harbor facilities have attracted petroleum refineries, locomotive works, ship-building plants and paper mills, most of which occupy water-front sites. Chester is the largest city of this group. The Schuyl-kill Valley section is also noted for its steel and machinery plants. Norristown, Pottstown, and a number of smaller cities have factories devoted to these heavy industries.

Outside these two industrialized belts there is less manufacturing. Northeast of Camden, Burlington (New Jersey) shares the heavy-industry development of the cities farther down the Delaware River. Outlying cities of the Pennsylvania section are either dominantly commercial or devoted to industry of the lighter types. Factories north and northeast of Philadelphia manufacture much clothing, knit goods, and textiles.

Summary.—The eight counties which constitute the Philadelphia industrial area produce about 4 per cent of the nation's manufactured goods. Of this total, about 65 per cent is produced in the city of Philadelphia, 23 per cent in the outlying Pennsylvania counties, 8 per cent in Camden and 4 per cent in outlying New Jersey cities. Philadelphia manufactures both producers' and consumers' goods but its industrial output is dominated by the latter. In general, the heavier producers'-goods plants have sought sites along the water front in the south part of the city, and this same type of development extends southward to the boundary of the area at the Delaware state line. Heavy industries also dominate the Schuylkill Valley from Philadelphia northwest to the boundary of the area, and occupy certain water-front locations in Camden.

The lighter, consumer-goods industries are found mainly in the northern half of the city. The products include clothing, textiles, knit goods, wool manufactures, carpets and rugs, foodstuffs, radios, and cigars. Camden is noted chiefly for its production of radios, soups, and cork products, and thus falls in the same consumer-goods category. The textiles-clothing belt also extends northward out of Philadelphia.

TRENTON

The city of Trenton is located at the fall line at the point where the Delaware River emerges from the piedmont. At that same place the Delaware turns abruptly from southeast to southwest and follows the fall line past Philadelphia and Wilmington. Such a location gives Trenton the double advantage of a navigable river and a site on the direct land route between Philadelphia and New York. Today the Delaware River is little used save by sand and coal barges, but the land route is a rumbling artery of trains and trucks.

Trenton has profited from its location on a major traffic artery. The location has encouraged the growth of numerous industries which manufacture steel and its products, including many types of machinery. In addition, Trenton is favored with good local supplies of pottery clay and claims distinction as the leading pottery city of the United States. (It is worth noting, however, that the pottery industry is more important in the state of Ohio than in the state of New Jersey.) There are also extensive factories which produce miscellaneous rubber products. Metropolitan Trenton had a population of 190,000 in 1930, and its output of manufactured goods regularly aggregates about one-fourth of one per cent of the total for the United States.

WILMINGTON

The city of Wilmington, Delaware, is probably best known as the location for the home office of the giant Du Pont chemical interests. Economic capital and chief city of Delaware, Wilmington is the distribution center not only for that state but for much of the eastern shore of Chesapeake Bay. These factors have given Wilmington the character of a commercial city, essentially a distribution center for a productive agricultural area which includes most of the Chesapeake peninsula. (Wilmington calls the peninsula Del-mar-va, derived from the names of the three states sharing it.) The Pennsylvania Railroad's network of lines on the peninsula converges on Wilmington and there is a significant super-highway extending southward from the city to tap the area.

Industrially, Wilmington's interests are diverse. The Du Ponts have large factories here but their main interests are elsewhere. Wilmington has tanneries, paper mills, railroad shops, and textile mills. It is especially noted for its production of glazed kid, hard fiber, and rubber hose. Its marine terminal on the Delaware River gives Wilmington access to the shipping lanes of the world.

BALTIMORE

Baltimore grew to importance first as a shipper of bituminous coal, later as a center for the canning of oysters and excess fruits and vegetables from coastal plain farms, then as a manufacturer of minor textiles and clothing, and finally as a major center for heavy industry. Today one thinks of Baltimore first in terms of a few giant industries, all relatively new and all depending heavily upon water-borne raw materials. Baltimore is still one of a half-dozen leading cities in the manufacture of men's and women's clothing, but the major economic contribution is made by those heavy industries down at the water front—steel, fertilizer, copper, and machinery.

The site of the city of Baltimore is at a point where the piedmont hills meet a three-armed inlet from Chesapeake Bay which is the drowned mouth of the Patapsco River. This estuary provides an excellent harbor which brought the site to the attention of the early explorers and prompted its selection as the seat of the proprietary colony of Maryland. There is a comparatively level business district, but the residential areas have pushed more and more into the surrounding hills. Like Philadelphia, Baltimore calls itself a "city of homes" and possesses many a charming residential suburb.

The harbor has always been Baltimore's greatest economic magnet. Nearer the interior than New York and Boston, Baltimore has lower rail freight rates. This differential is sufficient to offset a somewhat longer ocean route to the ports of the world, and has favored Baltimore as an export point for such bulky commodities as coal and wheat. Baltimore ranks second to New York among North American ports in tonnage handled. This ranking arises largely from a heavy export and import trade in bulky low-grade commodities.

In most years, approximately two-fifths of Baltimore's export trade is coal, and one-third is grain. Imports show similar characteristics, being about one-third iron ore and one-quarter crude oil. Sugar, manganese ore, and fertilizer materials make up most of the balance of the imports. In the coastwise trade, Baltimore ships coal, iron, and steel and receives petroleum, fertilizer materials, and lumber.

This description of water-borne traffic gives a good clue to the industrial development of the city. Down at the water front is the nation's largest tidewater steel mill, its largest copper refinery, numerous fertilizer plants, a sugar refinery, a large electrical-goods plant, shipyards, and some of the nation's largest grain elevators and coal piers. A few great industries, specialized in heavy commodities and tied to foreign trade, are the dominant accents in the Baltimore industrial landscape. To their private wharves come iron ore from Chile, Cuba, Norway, and Sweden; oil from Venezuela, Colombia, Mexico, Texas, and California; sugar from Cuba; manganese ore from Russia; potash from Germany; nitrates from Chile; and phosphate from Florida. Over the great commercial docks go coal for South American countries and Europe, and steel and machinery for the seaports of America.

The lighter industries have remained and still contribute an important portion of the factory output. Men's and women's clothing and men's shirts are the major items. In 1930, the clothing industries were the city's leading industrial employers, but the volume of manufacturing for the heavier industries was far greater.

Commercially, Baltimore serves a large area in Maryland, Virginia, and the South Atlantic states. As the farthest south of all American cities with populations of a half-million or over, Baltimore has achieved considerable prestige as a shopping center. In 1930, its metropolitan district reported a population of 949,000 of whom 805,000 lived in the central city.

With its recent rapid increase in heavy industry, Baltimore must be classified as an industrial city—farthest south of the great industrial cities of America, and the southern extremity of the American Manufacturing Belt. The Baltimore industrial district manufactures from 1 to 1 1/2 per cent of the nation's factory products. Its major plants are the heavy industries located along the waterfront of Baltimore's excellent harbor.

SOUTHEASTERN PENNSYLVANIA

Even the casual map-reader is impressed with the fact that the major cities of southeastern Pennsylvania are arranged in three roughly parallel lines having a northeast-southwest direction. On the east are the fall-line cities of the Delaware River, including Philadelphia, Trenton, and Wilmington, located in three states but occupying contiguous metropolitan districts. Some forty miles west lies a second row, marked by York, Lancaster, Reading, Allentown, Bethlehem, and Easton. Still farther west is a third, less prominent row which includes Harrisburg and Lebanon. If these cities are located on a relief map the reason for their arrangement becomes plain. Low, roughly parallel belts of hills cut across the fertile areas, and have influenced the location of main transportation routes. A belt of low hills separates the Philadelphia group from the broad structural valley on which Lancaster, Reading, and Allentown were built. These hills were never serious barriers to transportation but they offered no very good industrial sites (except where crossed by the Schuylkill River). The interior valley has long been a great highway with good transport facilities. It is divided, however, for most of its length by a ridge which effectively separates the Harrisburg-Lebanon string from neighboring cities to the east. Within these two western valleys have sprung up a variety of important industries whose combined factory output is about 2 per cent of the national total.

The Allentown-Bethlehem-Easton District.—The northern end of the Lehigh Valley is occupied by three adjacent cities which, together with their suburbs, comprise a metropolitan district with a population of 332,000 persons (1930). The Allentown-Bethlehem-Easton district is definitely industrial and contributes about one-half of one per cent of the nation's annual output of manufactured goods.

Allentown and Bethlehem are twin cities astride the Lehigh River. Easton is located about twelve miles east where the Lehigh empties into the Delaware River. Phillipsburg, New Jersey, just across the Delaware River from Easton, is the fourth city of the district. Prime reasons for the industrial growth of this area are (1) good local deposits of iron ore, limestone, and slate, and (2) good transportation facilities along the main southern outlet from the anthracite mines to the north. The Lehigh River was early canalized for use by anthracite barges and its valley was later followed by railroads which soon came to handle most of the traffic. Local iron ore deposits and good fluxing limestone attracted the steel industry. These ores are little used today, but the Bethlehem Steel Company works at Bethlehem is still one of the leading steel plants of the nation and the major industrial establishment of the district. Limestone was responsible for bringing to the Lehigh Valley the nation's greatest concentration of cement plants. The American cement industry is highly decentralized, but because of its nearness to seaboard metropolitan centers the Lehigh Valley has long been the leading producing area. Allentown has the home offices of the nation's largest cement companies, many of whose plants are located just north of these three cities. The major steel industry also spawned numerous plants devoted to the production of heavy machinery. Such factories are found in all of these cities. Motor trucks, pneumatic machinery, furnaces, and numerous other foundry products are representative. Steel, machinery, and cement identify the district as a center of heavy industry.

It has been observed that heavy-industry centers often develop numerous lighter industries adapted to the use of woman labor. In the Allentown-Bethlehem-Easton district the lighter industries are dominated by silk and rayon textiles and knit goods. In 1935, about one-third of the manufacturing of the area consisted of clothing and textiles, which were nearly as important as the heavy-industry group.

Reading and its industrial area report a factory output aggregating about one-third of one per cent of the national total. Like the Lehigh Valley cities, Reading's first industrial development was mainly along lines of steel and machinery, with growing parasitic industries devoted to textiles and clothing. In Reading, however, the parasitic industry outgrew the host, and today the major industrial payrolls are in the hosiery industry. Reading has many knitting mills producing hosiery, undergarments, and many other articles of clothing knit from silk, rayon, and cotton. In 1937, approximately half the factory workers of this area were employed in the knit-goods industries. Other allied products make Reading dominantly a textile-clothing city.

Lancaster is smaller than Reading but just as highly industrialized. Lancaster County regularly produces one-fourth of one per cent of the nation's manufactured goods. The industrial pattern is similar to that of Reading and the Allentown-Bethlehem group except that there is a greater diversity of products. Steel and machinery are important but the larger payrolls are in the silk, rayon, and other textile industries. Lancaster is especially famous for its linoleum and watches. Silk is important in Lancaster, but silk mills are also found in many of the smaller towns of the county.

As the trading center for Lancaster County, often cited as the richest agricultural county in the United States, Lancaster has well-developed commercial interests. Here are the rich farms of the envied "Pennsylvania Dutch" whose commercial production of tobacco, potatoes, and dairy products is handled largely by Lancaster business houses.

York usually is associated with Lancaster geographically and industrially. Like Lancaster, York serves a productive agricultural county, but industrially it differs from its eastern neighbor. York County factories turn out about the same volume of production as those of Lancaster, but the emphasis is more definitely on capital goods. Ice machines, refrigerating equipment, bank safes and vaults stand high in the list of manufactured products. In addition, York factories turn out tire chains, wall paper, and food products. The textile-clothing group is not highly developed.

Harrisburg occupies a strategic location where the Susquehanna River crosses the Appalachian Valley. Both routes have long been important highways and the location at their intersection is the natural commercial focus for a large area. Here in an early day, coal met iron and a steel industry grew up. Steel and machinery still dominate the industrial output, but railroad shops and food-processing industries also have large payrolls. State capital of Pennsylvania, important railroad and distribution center, and the home of thriving heavy industries, Harrisburg is proud of the diversity which marks its economic development.

Lebanon is situated in a section of the Appalachian Valley known as the Lebanon Valley. Its industrial development is similar to that of Harrisburg, with steel, machinery, and silk the principal products.

Other Appalachian Valley cities are smaller but their industrial development follows much the same pattern. Steel products, machinery, and textiles are the major products.

Central Pennsylvania

Economic development in the central Pennsylvania section is a combination of mining, agriculture, and manufacturing, with manufacturing generally in a secondary position. The eastern district of the section is underlain with coal and includes some of the most important mining districts of the North Appalachian coal area. Here coal is king, coal mines are the major employers, and agriculture and manufacturing are secondary interests.

The northwest portion of the central Pennsylvania section is also dominated by minerals, but here the products are oil and gas. Refining the famed Pennsylvania motor oil is a leading manufacturing industry, and there are also glass and pottery plants utilizing local gas to fire furnaces and kilns burning local sand and clay. In this district oil and gas lead the economic parade, followed by refining and the clay and glass industries, all trailed by agriculture.

The remainder of the section has little in the way of minerals and must be classed as agricultural. It is crossed by numerous railroads, however, and along their lines have sprung up a number of factories devoted to a variety of products. Most important in the industrial development of this district are the two "gateway" cities which occupy the most strategic locations with reference to railroad transportation. Both lie adjacent to the coal district, at the margin where the dissected plateau of the coal country gives way to the ridges and valleys farther east. These cities are Altoona and Williamsport, both important railroad centers and both having a variety of manufacturing industries. The central Pennsylvania section has about six-tenths of one per cent of the nation's manufacturing, of which about one-quarter is in these two cities, the remainder divided among half a hundred smaller ones.

Altoona occupies a strategic location opposite a gap in the ridge which separates the plateau from the ridges and valleys. The gap is used by the main line of the Pennsylvania Railroad and Altoona has become an important division point on that line. Railroad shops employ the majority of its industrial workers. Machinery, truck bodies, and silk are produced in its factories. In 1930, the Altoona metropolitan district had a population of 114,-000 and extended westward almost to the boundary of the metropolitan district of Johnstown. Johnstown's greater dependence on steel dictates its inclusion in the Pittsburgh-Cleveland section, but Altoona, with its gateway position and important railroad interests, truly belongs to the central Pennsylvania section.

Williamsport shows an economic development similar to that of Altoona. Its railroad interests are less highly developed, but it is a division point of major importance. Its industries are of the steel-using types. Williamsport is well known for its automobile motors, boilers, valves, and steel rails.

Outside these cities, the industrial development follows a fairly uniform pattern. Most common are the plants devoted to steel products and machinery; but there are many glass works and clay-products plants utilizing local sand and clay and burning local gas and coal. Here and there one finds a woodworking plant, reminiscent of the days when Appalachian lumber was more plentiful. In general, the glass and clay works are most important in the northwest portion of the section—that area underlain with natural gas. The eastern portion, which lies adjacent to both the anthracite district and southeast Pennsylvania, has a number of small textiles and clothing factories. The southern margin has some lumbering. In these ways, central Pennsylvania partakes economically of the development of its more highly industrialized neighboring sections: glass and machinery on the west and north, and textiles and machinery on the east and southeast. On the south the section merges into the lumber and subsistence farming economy of the Middle Appalachian Highland.

CITIES OF THE ANTHRACITE DISTRICT

The geographic concentration of the anthracite beds and the large amount of labor required for extracting the coal and preparing it for shipment have caused this area to develop one of the major metropolitan districts of the United States. Extending for nearly sixty miles along the upper Susquehanna and Lackawanna rivers, the Scranton-Wilkes-Barre metropolitan district in 1930 had a population of 652,000 persons, of whom 143,000 lived in Scranton, 87,000 in Wilkes-Barre, and the remainder in half a hundred smaller cities and boroughs. The Scranton-Wilkes-Barre district ranks seventeenth in population among metropolitan districts of the United States.

Despite a fairly impressive development of manufacturing and trade, the anthracite district is essentially a mining area. The great majority of its male workers are on the payrolls of mining corporations and the prosperity of the district can be measured very accurately in terms of the demand for anthracite coal. A cold wave in Boston, New York, or Philadelphia is front-page news for local newspapers for it means a likely increase in mining activity to supply domestic needs in those seaboard cities.

It was inevitable that a permanent mining industry employing male labor should attract parasitic industries. Years ago silk mills were erected in Scranton and Wilkes-Barre to take advantage of the supply of woman labor. This same situation attracted makers of men's shirts and women's clothing. More than half the manufacturing of the Scranton-Wilkes-Barre area is devoted to textiles and clothing. The remainder is essentially local: bakeries, printing establishments, railroad shops, and similar industries which serve the local population. The total industrial output is about three-tenths of one per cent of the national total. The Scranton-Wilkes-Barre area is less highly industrialized than the other major population centers of eastern Pennsylvania.

South of the Scranton-Wilkes-Barre district lies a cluster of smaller cities whose interests likewise revolve about anthracite coal. These cities—Hazleton, Pottsville, Shenandoah, Shamokin, and several others—serve the southern portion of the anthracite district in the same way that Scranton and Wilkes-Barre serve the more productive northern portion. Their interests are first of all the mining, preparation, and shipment of anthracite. Nearly all have railroad shops and many build and recondition railroad cars and other equipment. There are also small steel and machinery industries. Lighter industries manufacturing silk textiles, knit goods, and men's shirts are found throughout the area.

In summary, the economic development of the anthracite district follows a definite pattern. First comes the basic income-producer, anthracite coal, the mining and preparation of which requires much labor. Second in line are the railroads, which radiate from the district in all directions. Manning the railroads and keeping them supplied and equipped occupies a large segment of the population. A third group includes the lighter industries, rather unjustly called parasitic because they utilize the woman labor from families whose menfolk work in the mines and collieries and on the railroads. These factories make the anthracite district an important source of silk textiles, men's shirts, knit goods, and other small garments. Finally, the economic structure includes a large number of local and subsidiary industries devoted either to supplying parts and repairs for the basic industries, or to providing bakery goods, printing, and similar locally used articles for the million persons who live in the district. At the base of the entire structure, however, is the district's great natural resource —anthracite coal.

SUMMARY

The urban pattern of the Central Atlantic section shows definite effects of the geographic environment. Deep embayment of the coast has encouraged the growth of cities not along the actual seacoast but at the head of navigation of those bays and rivers which indent it. This same fall line which stops navigation is the seaward margin of a belt of piedmont hills. The piedmont itself has spawned few cities; but at its interior margin lie the Appalachian valleys. The Appalachian valleys of southeast Pennsylvania have long been important transportation routes to the South and Southwest. Along these routes, interior cities have grown up and become centers for a variety of industries. Elsewhere in central and eastern Pennsylvania there is less manufacturing. The section includes important bituminous coal mines in central Pennsylvania and northern West Virginia, as well as the highly urbanized Pennsylvania anthracite district. In neither of these areas, however, is manufacturing highly developed. Both have a rough topography which has discouraged transportation.

Manufacturing in the Central Atlantic section is marked by diversity of products. Baltimore and Bethlehem are important centers for steel and heavy machinery, but Philadelphia and many adjacent cities of southwest Pennsylvania are best known for textiles and clothing. The anthracite district is dominated by mining, but has important silk textiles industries. Central Pennsylvania has few factories. Nearly every type of manufactured product is made in the Central Atlantic section of the Manufacturing Belt.

The long economic history of the Central Atlantic section is perpetuated in many of its industrial institutions. This history accounts very largely for the growth of cities at the fall line and along the major transportation routes. The effect of recent economic change is also in evidence in many districts. The anthracite area is faced with a general decline in demand for its major product, and declines in mining have not been compensated thus far by a rise in manufacturing or other economic interests. The historic position of southeast Pennsylvania as the center of the American iron industry has been perpetuated in a large output of iron and steel and their products. But the center of American steel-making has long since moved westward to Pittsburgh, and some of the newest steel mills have been built at tidewater locations (such as Baltimore) which have good access to foreign ores. The most significant industrial change during recent decades has been the rapid growth of textile mills for silk and rayon, knit goods, hosiery, and other highly standardized items of wearing apparel.

Consumer goods have gradually replaced the iron and steel products as the leading industrial products of both Philadelphia and southeastern Pennsylvania. In Baltimore, on the other hand, heavy industries have recently come to dominate industrial production.

REFERENCES

The usual references on industrial location should be consulted. A good article on Philadelphia appeared in *Fortune* for June, 1936. A series of Works Progress Administration studies is concerned with employment trends in the city, as well as in Lancaster, Pennsylvania. Consult *Minerals Yearbook* for recent trends in anthracite.

QUESTIONS AND PROBLEMS

1. What natural features have significance in explaining the areal distribution of cities in the Central Atlantic section? Are these features of greatest significance in explaining the original locations, growth and development, or present importance of these cities?

2. Why are there so few cities on the actual seacoast south of New York harbor?

3. The author makes little effort to explain the lack of industrial development in the Anthracite district. How would you account for this situation? (Relief and railroad maps will help with your answer—also a glance at the local economic history.)

4. Compare the industrial development of metropolitan Philadelphia with that of Metropolitan New York, with particular reference to (a) national importance, (b) types of industries, and (c) types of locations.

5. In what respects does the physical geography of Metropolitan Philadelphia resemble that of Metropolitan New York? Are there further resemblances in the areal distribution of business and manufacturing?

6. Of what significance is the piedmont in accounting for the areal distribution of cities in the Central Atlantic section? Has the Appalachian Valley developed many cities? Why or why not?

7. What types of manufacturing are found in Lancaster and York? Describe the economic development of the trade territories served by these cities.

8. The Allentown-Bethlehem-Easton district is described as a center for heavy industries. What are these industries? Why are they found here?

9. Write a brief description of economic development in central

Pennsylvania, emphasizing agriculture, mining, and cities. Relate these developments to the natural resources of the area.

10. Important changes in the industrial structure of Baltimore have occurred in recent decades. What are these changes? How do you account for them? Do they reflect mainly (a) new trends in the use of local natural resources, or (b) broader economic and technological changes that are regional or national in scope?

11. What forces caused Trenton to become an important city? Which of these forces are most important today?

12. Why do we find a considerable development of the iron and steel industries in southeast Pennsylvania? Is the industrial pattern of this area changing? Cite evidence to support your answer.

13. How do the apparel industries of the Central Atlantic section differ from those of Metropolitan New York? How do you account for these differences?

14. What are the commercial and industrial advantages of the city of Wilmington?

CHAPTER XXVIII

DETROIT AND THE AUTOMOBILE DISTRICT

It was little more than an accident that Detroit became the center of the American automobile industry. In the 1890's Michigan timber was running out and grain-farming was becoming increasingly unprofitable. Only an incurable optimist would have predicted a brilliant future for the little city on the Detroit River. Detroit, in fact, had comparatively few advantages to offer as a location for industry. The main transportation routes lay well to the south, skirting Lake Erie and swelling the commercial importance of such cities as Toledo and Cleveland. Detroit was off the beaten path, farther from Appalachian coal and the center of population than these southern neighbors; and now that the lumber was gone, Detroit and southern Michigan had no significant industrial raw materials to offer.

Yet Detroit did have a number of optimists among its leaders and it boasted several sizable fortunes among its lumber barons. It also had, most fortunately, the organizing genius of a young mechanic who insisted that the horseless carriage would some day be a universal institution. Henry Ford and these alert local capitalists symbolize the rise of Detroit. Here, as in a few other cities, mechanical genius has been encouraged and organizing ability rewarded. The automobile stands unquestionably as one of the greatest social forces in the history of mankind. The origin and development of the machine must be credited to these pioneers of the city of Detroit. Independent to a very large degree of outside capital and outside management, they have erected the greatest manufacturing industry of the present day.

The automobile industry is not, of course, a single industry, but a large and complex group of manufacturing enterprises. The automobile, after all, is a machine and as such embodies a wide variety of parts and materials. Primarily, like nearly all machines, it is a thing of steel, and the steel furnace mothers most of its hundreds of parts. But beyond that point the routes are divergent. Nearly every part is made from special steel prepared according to a special formula. Axles and frames must be tough and shock-

644

resistant; spring steel must be prepared differently, likewise steel for the motor block. Very hard steels, often electrically refined, go into the bearings. Then, of course, there are the huge sheets which feed the presses that stamp out fenders, bodies, and hoods. Every one of these and dozens of others must be prepared with different alloys and by different rolling and finishing methods.

But with all of these steel parts, the car is far from complete. Other metals, brass, aluminum, copper, tin, zinc—nearly all the members of the metals family—go into electrical devices, trimmings, pistons, and other vital parts. Glass is used by the acre, and upholstery fabrics by the mile. Tires come in from Akron by the trainload, and these in turn involve a chain of subsidiary industries. Detroit automobile plants are the nation's leading purchasers of a long list of factory products ranging from steel and glass to rubber products and fine varnishes.

The automobile is thus an assembled product, drawing parts from many other industries and raw materials from all sections of the continent. In the past the great dream of motor manufacturers, especially Ford, General Motors, and Chrysler, was the integration of these plants and processes under a single ownership. Automobile makers bought ore lands in Minnesota, hardwood forests in Upper Michigan, coal mines in the Appalachians, and invested liberally in plants to manufacture all of the parts and accessories used in their respective models. Many of these new plants were set up in Detroit. Before many years, however, integration was seen to bring many disadvantages, and of late years relatively little expansion by motor firms has been along these lines.

Perhaps the greatest drawback to extreme integration is the inflexibility of manufacturing processes. Changing models, with all the attendant retooling, is difficult even in the small plant, but when it involves redesigning processes and products all the way from mine to assembly line, model-changing becomes a major operation. Not many years ago the automobile industry decided on relatively radical changes for ensuing models. One large manufacturer, the most highly integrated, found necessary changes so difficult and time-consuming that the model was delayed several months and the loss ran into millions of dollars. Smaller concerns, on the other hand, simply prepared specifications and let contracts accordingly. If a new wheel is to be used, let the wheel manufacturer retool for it; and the same policy goes for many other parts. The standard practice today is to let most of these contracts to independent concerns, which in general seem better able to shift their processes to meet changed demands.

The practice of contracting parts is by no means uniform, however, and generalization is difficult. Most makers manufacture their own motors in the home plants. Wheels, axles, and bearings are commonly purchased on contract. Frames and bodies are both made and purchased. All large motor makers have body factories and all of them manufacture frames, but all of them likewise buy many of these items on contract from independent firms. Headlamps, bumpers, and hardware come in the same category, as do bolts and nuts. Glass, on the other hand, is usually purchased in the market; and automobile makers manufacture few tires.

All of this diversity means that the motor industry has long since passed the stage of being purely a Detroit industry. Nearly every state has factories manufacturing some type of automobile parts. It is logical, however, that most of these plants should be near the major center from which most of the assembled cars are shipped. Thus it has come about that the automobile industry has moved into nearly every city in Michigan and has made extensive inroads into the neighboring states of Ohio, Indiana, and Wisconsin. In dozens of cities of these states the largest payrolls go to persons employed in manufacturing something for use in an automobile: wheels, bodies, bearings, lamps, springs, bumpers, and the whole long list. In southern Michigan the automobile-parts industries so thoroughly dominate the industrial structure that this area has been included with Detroit as a separate section of the Manufacturing Belt. The section as delineated includes all of southern Michigan, the adjacent city of Toledo in Ohio, and a small area in northern Indiana. We shall refer to it as the Automobile Section of the American Manufacturing Belt. Other products, some of them of national consequence, are manufactured within this section, but the major industries of the area are devoted to the production of motor vehicles.

Cities.—The Detroit metropolitan district with a 1930 population of 2,100,000 ranks sixth among American population centers. The circumstances attending the rise of Detroit as a great industrial center are familiar to the reader. Credit must be given to local business men. It must not be inferred, however, that Detroit lacks industrial advantage. For Detroit has most of the locational advantages of which other cities of the Great Lakes boast. It has, above all, ready access to lake-borne ore and coal; and it is not far removed from the center of population of the United States and Canada (combined). It lies adjacent to the most populous region of Canada and occupies one of the two most important crossings of the Great Lakes waterway. Detroit lies on a direct line between Chicago and Buffalo. Commercially, it is well located to serve the lower peninsula of Michigan. Thus it seems probable that Detroit might have become an important city even without the automotive industries; but it is highly improbable that it would have achieved its present greatness for at least several more decades.

Like all great metropolitan centers, the Detroit area is a cluster of municipalities grouped around a major center. Approximately three-quarters of the people of Greater Detroit live in the city. Outside Detroit, the major cities are Pontiac, Dearborn, Highland Park, and Hamtramck, the last two completely surrounded by the city of Detroit.

Heavy industries are definitely concentrated along the Detroit River south of the city. In this section lie River Rouge and Wyandotte, prominent steel centers serving the automobile industries. The Great Lakes Steel Company plant at Wyandotte is said to be the largest in the world. Here also are plants devoted to heavy chemicals. Neighboring Dearborn and River Rouge hold important divisions of the Ford Motor Company. Highland Park and Hamtramck are more definitely residential, the latter city being inhabited largely by Polish-speaking people.

Outside the Detroit metropolitan area lies a ring of lesser cities, all within an hour's drive of the major center. Largest and industrially most important of these is Pontiac, whose residents reach Detroit over the famous 204-foot super-highway which connects the two cities. Most of Pontiac's 65,000 persons are connected with the automobile industry, dominated locally by three important divisions of General Motors (Pontiac, Fisher, G. M. Truck). An hour's drive west of Detroit's center lie Ypsilanti and Ann Arbor, and the city of Mt. Clemens is located about the same distance to the north. A like distance to the south lies Monroe on the shore of Lake Erie. All these cities have automobile-parts factories, mixed with miscellaneous machinery industries. Ann Arbor is

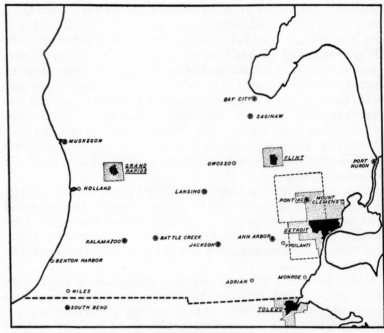

FIG. 90. Cities of the Automobile Section. Detroit is the national center of the automobile industry and the major industrial center of the state of Michigan. Neighboring cities also produce many automobile bodies and parts, so that the industry has become the leading economic interest of southern Michigan and small portions of adjacent Indiana and Ohio. Toledo, second city of the section, has a diversity of economic interests ranging from the shipment of lake-cargo coal to the manufacture of automotive equipment and small machinery. The automotive industries usually provide Toledo's largest industrial payrolls, but its interests are more diverse than those of any other city in the section. In Michigan, Grand Rapids is famous for furniture and Battle Creek for breakfast foods. Flint, Pontiac, and Lansing are identified with the automobile industry, as is South Bend in Indiana.

The text describes the location of important cities in this section in terms of an "inner ring" and an "outer ring" around the city of Detroit. Locate these two groups of cities on the map. How do these cities function in the economic organization of the Automobile Section?

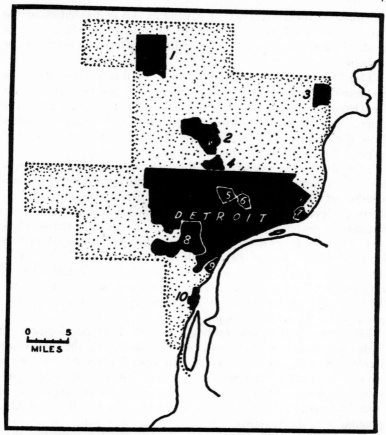

FIG. 91. The Detroit Metropolitan District. The rapid rise of the automobile industry is a story of American industrial magic. Most of this magic was worked in the city of Detroit, which grew from a moderate-sized city to the fifth largest in the United States within three decades. Detroit's area increased with its population and the city expanded north, west, and south. A huge industrial center grew up at the south edge of the city. Other automotive plants appeared in outlying centers such as Pontiac and in various sections of the city of Detroit. Today, Metropolitan Detroit consists of the older city plus its greatly expanded additions to the north and west. It also includes several independent cities indicated by numbers on the map: (1) Pontiac, (2) Royal Oak, (3) Mt. Clemens, (4) Ferndale, (5) Highland Park, (6) Hamtramck, (7) Grosse Pointe Park, (8) Dearborn, (9) River Rouge, and (10) Wyandotte.

the home of the University of Michigan. These five cities of the "inner ring" send many laborers to Detroit during rush seasons in the motor factories, thereby adding to Detroit's acute traffic problem.

The "Outer Ring."—Beyond these semi-suburban cities, we encounter a group of larger cities which form an outer ring about the Detroit metropolitan center. The "outer ring" includes seven cities, all located at distances between sixty and eighty-five miles from the center. In all of them the automotive industries are the largest element in the industrial development.

The city of Toledo, Ohio, is the largest of the industrial centers which happen to fall within this "outer ring." Toledo is not a satellite of Detroit, but there are similarities in the two cities' industrial developments. Historically, Toledo was an important automobile center almost as early as Detroit, but its recent development has been more diverse. Yet the leading employers of factory labor in Toledo are its automobile factories, most of which produce bodies and parts. Toledo also manufactures many types of machinery as well as glass products. It has important oil refineries. The Toledo industrial output averages about two-thirds of one per cent of the national total.

Diversification is not confined to industrial development in Toledo. Located at the west end of Lake Erie, the city is an important port for the receipt and distribution of lake-borne commerce. It lies adjacent to the main east-west transportation routes between Chicago and the eastern seaboard. Indicative of Toledo's maturity and taste is its excellent art gallery, notably popular with its citizens.

The Michigan members of the "outer ring" are smaller than Toledo and generally more highly specialized in the automobile industries. Flint and Lansing are the largest of these automobile cities, both contributing heavily to that industry. The city of Flint is thoroughly dominated by automobiles, being the home of several divisions of General Motors. Lansing, with about half the industrial output of Flint, is dominated similarly by the motor industries.

Other cities of the "outer ring"—Adrian, Jackson, Owosso, and Port Huron—likewise contribute bodies and parts to the dominant industry of the section. Here the specialization is less pronounced and one finds numerous smaller plants producing a variety of steel products and machinery. Throughout the entire Detroit-Toledo-southeast Michigan area, however, the automotive industries set the pace of industrial development.

This area, consisting of Detroit and its two "rings" of outlying cities, really contains the heart of the American automobile industry. The complex industry consists of more than a heart, however, and we find the same plants heading the lists of leading industries in most of the remaining cities of the section.

Saginaw and Bay City.—Old lumber towns in the Saginaw Bay area, these neighboring cities have lately seen the introduction of important divisions of the automobile industry. Both cities have long produced a wide variety of machinery and tools. Many of the experienced metal-workers in these plants now turn their skills toward fulfilling auto-makers' contracts for parts.

Southwest Michigan.—Almost directly opposite Milwaukee on Lake Michigan, the city of Muskegon has long had much lake commerce. Factories followed commercial development and specialized in foundry products and electrical goods. Electrical and other equipment for automobiles are important products.

Inland from Muskegon, the city of Grand Rapids is best known as the national center for the furniture industry. Proximity to timber supplies apparently figured in the early development of this industry in Grand Rapids. In recent decades, however, the furniture industries have become more and more decentralized, with the greatest developments occurring in the large cities. Grand Rapids retains its position as style center, with the designing and managing offices of several large producers. Furniture still heads the list of Grand Rapids factory products, but it no longer dominates industrial development. Automobile body factories now utilize the skills released by the waning furniture industry and Grand Rapids seems destined to join the procession of Michigan cities ruled by the automobile. Many of the furniture factories of near-by Muskegon and Holland have undergone the same change. Holland is also widely known as a center for the manufacture of furnaces.

The stove and furnace industries are also important in Kalamazoo and Battle Creek. Kalamazoo has important factories producing paper and pharmaceuticals, and Battle Creek is known universally as the national center for the production of breakfast foods. Benton Harbor and Niles, in the extreme southwest corner of the state, have diverse industrial developments partially based on the large production of fruit in that area.

Northern Indiana.—The Manufacturing Belt includes in northern Indiana a group of five cities which logically belong in the automobile section of the region. South Bend, principal city in the group, is best known as the home of the Studebaker Corporation, which has been making automobiles since the days when that machine was a horseless carriage. Other machinery products are also important here as well as in near-by Mishawaka, Elkhart, La Porte, and Michigan City. Elkhart is noted as the national center for the manufacture of band instruments. These north Indiana cities have received a portion of the "overflow" of the automobile industry from the Detroit area. The reader will recall that many bodies and parts are also produced in the central Indiana section of the Corn Belt region which lies adjacent to this section.

Summary.—The automobile district accounts for from 7 to 10 per cent of the United States output of manufactured goods of all kinds. Production is concentrated in the city of Detroit, which normally accounts for between 3 and 4 per cent of the nation's factory output. Industries of the district are devoted primarily to the production of the wide variety of parts which make up an automobile. The district accounts for more than two-thirds of the entire automobile industry of the United States, and a considerably larger percentage of the finished machines. Detroit, its metropolis, is the center for the management and most of the assembly of finished cars. Outlying factories are generally devoted to bodies and parts. Practically two-thirds of the industry of Detroit is directly associated with the production of automobiles. This section is the center for the newest member of the family of giant American industries.

LOCATION FACTORS IN THE AUTOMOBILE INDUSTRY

With the factual background of the automobile district before us, it becomes possible to examine in greater detail the factors which have influenced the location of this top-ranking American industry. We have already concluded that the location of automobile plants is not to be explained with any degree of adequacy in terms of raw materials or markets. The more potent locational factors apparently lie in the realm of corporation economics. These factors are well illustrated in the history and organization of the

three major corporations which dominate the automobile field—
General Motors, Ford, and Chrysler.

The automobile industry is largely owned and operated by three big corporations. General Motors, Ford, and Chrysler normally turn out nearly nine-tenths of the nation's automobiles and rank among the leading industrial corporations in size, earnings, and organizational complexity. Largest and most complex of these automobile concerns is General Motors, maker of two-fifths of the nation's automobiles and a leader in many other lines of industrial products. The far-flung holdings of General Motors make the corporation almost an industrial empire in itself. The rise and development of this organization provides a fruitful case study in the location of American manufacturing industries.

General Motors: *Organization.*—Back in 1908, a Michigan promoter who had accumulated a fortune in the carriage industry foresaw a brilliant future for the automobile and an excellent profit for the company that could control the major processes in manufacturing a complete line of cars. The industry already counted fifty competing makes of automobiles and was ripe for consolidation. General Motors was organized as a holding company whose sole function was to secure control of operating companies by purchasing their capital stock. Later, the majority of these companies were liquidated, but their organizations were continued as separate divisions of General Motors.

Consolidation and Growth.—The first act of General Motors was to acquire control of a half-dozen of the better-known automobile concerns (including Buick, Oldsmobile, and Cadillac) and about a dozen parts manufacturers. The corporation made money in the years of industrial expansion which followed, and the plan of consolidation was continued. Other well-known firms (notably Chevrolet) were acquired and the list of subsidiaries manufacturing parts and accessories grew longer. General Motors outgrew Michigan and acquired plants in nearly all of the northeastern United States. It outgrew the United States and set up warehouses and factories abroad. It also outgrew the automobile industry, as we shall see presently. In all of this expansion, about the only field shunned by General Motors was basic materials. The corporation did not acquire iron or coal mines or railroads, as has its major competitor, the Ford Motor Company. The Fisher Body Division did own large timber holdings in northern Michigan, but this was a minor variation in the general policy. General Motors still owns no mines, weaves no upholstery fabric, and makes no tires or glass, but its subsidiaries can manufacture just about all of the thirty thousand parts that go into a modern automobile.

Non-automotive Lines.—The quest for control of the production of these parts has led into some of the strangest alleys ever entered by a major industrial corporation. In acquiring control of a business, General Motors often found itself producing lines of goods not even remotely related to automobiles. The electrical field is a good example. In acquiring the Delco interests in Dayton, General Motors was looking for starters, generators, and other automotive electrical devices. These it secured, but with them came an extensive line of non-automotive electrical devices and, what is more important, one of the most alert research staffs in the country. With scarcely a moment's hesitation, the management elected to continue not only the non-automotive lines it had acquired but also the researches to develop new products in these fields. Thus General Motors came to manufacture electric refrigerators, heating systems, aircraft, Diesel engines, railroad locomotives, and a bewildering array of lesser items in no way connected with the automobile industry.

Non-automotive lines contribute perhaps as much as one-sixth of the total sales volume of the corporation. In recent years these lines have been growing rapidly, but they have not grown large enough to obscure the major business of the corporation, which is the manufacture of automobiles.

Management.—Expose a man to the immensity of General Motors with its hundred scattered factories, its thousands of separate products, and its sales volume which exceeds that of all other American corporations. Show him the list of products, which includes two out of every five automobiles on the road, many of the thousands of parts which go into them, and runs on and on through household appliances and motors that range in size from the midget that operates your electric razor to the Diesels that pull trains and drive ships. Tell him of the huge sales organization and the subsidiary that finances customers' partial payments. If you can keep him quiet that long, pause briefly and he will inquire, "How do they manage such a business?" It is hardly an exaggeration to state that General Motors does not manage its various divisions. The philosophy always has been to operate each division more or less independently of the rest. We find General Motors dealers competing as strenuously with one another as with Ford or Chrysler. Some of their cars even compete with each other in the same price range. General Motors automobile plants may use parts made by one of the subsidiaries or by an independent manufacturer. Competing automobile makers frequently use parts manufactured by General Motors. Thus a sort of competition is maintained, not a competition based on price, but a competition to produce a car that will sell best for the price that the American customer is most likely to pay. Motor makers do not cut prices. There is no competition in the sense that wheat farmers compete with one another. The pricing system involves the determination of the approximate price at which a firm can sell enough automobiles to operate the plant at a given capacity. Having determined this "break-even" price, the makers then proceed to design a car that in their opinion will sell best within the desired cost range. Under this system, with or without collusion, it is inevitable that competing cars will be offered at approximately the same price. If, by fortunate designing, a maker sells more than his estimate, he can make a profit. Or, in years of prosperity, many makers may exceed their sales estimates. In these years Detroit and the automobile district experience good times, and their prosperity is further reflected in the parts factories of many cities outside this area.

Location.—What factors have influenced the location of the automobile industry? Even if we confine our question to the General Motors omelet, the unscrambling process is virtually impossible. Why is General Motors activity centered in Michigan? Is it because William Durant, its early promoter, happened to begin his consolidation with plants located in Flint and Detroit? Would the corporation's history be the same if Durant had started with the equally promising plants then operating in Cleveland, Toledo, or Chicago? Has Michigan any inherent natural advantages for making automobiles? Could it have retained leadership throughout the years if the industry had become highly competitive? It is safe to say that no person has the answers to all of these questions. General Motors and Ford certainly made Michigan the automobile center of the world. Probably they could have done as well elsewhere. In a young and dynamic industry, there are many monopolistic elements which obscure the minor losses incident to slightly inferior locations. General Motors started in Michigan almost by accident. Three decades of expanding markets and a continuous procession of new products have not brought about the competitive conditions which might necessitate relocation. When General Motors acquired its subsidiaries, it was concerned primarily with excellence of product rather than cost. Its assembly plants use motors and frames produced in Detroit, Flint, Pontiac, Lansing, and Saginaw. Their electrical units may come from Dayton, Ohio, or from Anderson, Indiana. Headlamps come from Anderson and Muncie, bearings from Bristol and Meriden, in Connecticut, from Harrison, New Jersey, and from Dayton, Ohio. Radiators are made in Lockport, New York, and the grilles for them come from Detroit. All of these plants belong to the General Motors family, but their scattered locations indicate that the automobile is an assembled product whose parts come from widely scattered sources. The final assembly is carried on by plants nearer the market. General Motors assembles cars on the Pacific coast and in Kansas City, St. Louis, Atlanta, Baltimore, Buffalo, Tarrytown, and other cities scattered across the nation. Decentralized assembly permits a saving in freight costs, but the decentralization policy has been confined entirely to the final manufacturing process. The individual units are made in plants located largely in the same cities as held these plants when General Motors acquired ownership of them.

The Ford Motor Company.—Business men will tell you that there is a world of difference between the Ford Motor Company and General Motors. They will point out that Ford is essentially a family concern with very few outside stockholders, whereas General Motors has one of the longest stockholder lists in American business. They will indicate that new plants were added by the Ford Motor Company almost entirely through the reinvestment of profits, whereas most General Motors lines were acquired by floating additional stock. Such financial considerations lend important background to the divergent history and development of the two leading producers of American automobiles. They go far to explain the differences in organization and location which distinguish these huge agglomerations of industrial capital.

The story of Henry Ford is the crowning epic of the favorite American cycle whose theme is "from rags to riches by dint of hard work, courage, economy, and thrift." It begins with a brilliant inventor in his tiny workshop and brings him through discouraging years of hardship and perseverance to the very pinnacle of fame and fortune as the man who has served best and profited most in the industrial era. It shows him as the successful pioneer in assembly-line production, the supreme achievement of the principle of bringing the work to the worker rather than requiring the worker to move from one task to another. It shows him as a great exponent of mass production, of the integration of various stages of manufacture under a single ownership, of the necessity of paying careful attention to producing the type of commodity that people want and can pay for. In many ways, the rise of the Ford Motor Company, which is practically synonymous with the business life of Henry Ford, symbolizes American industrial achievement. It also shows the enactment of the industrial philosophy of a single individual.

The physical development of the Ford Motor Company revolves about six significant principles, most of which differ from those followed by General Motors. (1) The manufacturer should control the basic processes underlying his production. For Ford, this principle has led to the construction of blast furnaces, steel mills, ore boats, mines, rubber plantations in Brazil, ocean freighters, and numerous other institutions which originate basic materials or bring them to the automobile factory. (2) Control of production of the more highly standardized parts is desirable, even if these parts are also the product of well-organized existing industries. Ford manufactures both glass and tires as well as the motors, chassis, and other parts commonly made by automobile manufacturers. In both these respects, Ford policy differs from that of General Motors, which buys its steel, glass, tires, and numerous other standardized materials and parts from other industries. (3) The manufacturer should control the production of non-standardized parts in so far as they cannot be obtained more cheaply or in adequate quantities or qualities from dependable parts manufacturers. Here the policy of Ford does not differ greatly from that of General Motors. Both concerns buy parts extensively from outside sources, but they also manufacture many of them in their own plants. (4) When a new manufacturing activity is undertaken, it is generally more desirable to build a new plant rather than buy out existing interests. In this respect, Ford differs radically from General Motors. Nearly all Ford plants are Ford-built, but most General Motors plants were acquired through the purchase of existing concerns. General Motors divisions have expanded their plants, but most of this expansion has occurred at the site of the original acquisition. These differences account largely for the greater decentralization of General Motors and the greater concentration of Ford operations in Detroit. They bear a definite relation to another Ford principle, (5) that centralization of manufacturing operations is desirable. Ford manufacturing operations are highly concentrated in the two square miles of the famous Rouge plant at Dearborn. This bewildering array of coke ovens, blast furnaces, steel mills, foundries, machine shops and assembly lines employs far more men than ever were on the General Motors payroll in Detroit. The Ford Motor Company is essentially a Detroit industry in so far as manufacturing is concerned, whereas the largest General Motors plants are in outlying centers such as Flint and Pontiac. (6) Finally, the Ford plan embodies decentralized assembly plants to which go trainloads and boatloads of bodies, fenders, motor assemblies and other parts in more or less pre-assembled form. Decentralized assembly permits savings in freight and provides a readily accessible supply of parts for all sections of the country. General Motors follows this same policy, but Ford has the larger number of assembly plants outside the automobile district. Perhaps these six principles were never spread on the minutes of that small group which constitutes the Board of Directors of the Ford Motor Company, but they are evident to any student of the history of the automobile industry. They go far to explain the differences between Ford and General Motors, the most important of which are concerned with control over basic processes and the acquisition of additional facilities. They help explain why the Ford interests are highly concentrated in metropolitan Detroit while those of General Motors are more far flung and more diverse.

The Chrysler Corporation.—The third member of the "Big Three" among automobile manufacturers is younger and smaller than either General Motors or Ford, but it is far larger than any of the remaining competitors. The Chrysler Corporation was formed to acquire existing companies much in the manner of General Motors. Its automobiles—Plymouth, Dodge, DeSoto and Chrysler—are directly competitive with those of both General Motors and Ford. Like General Motors, Chrysler owns several separate automobile factories. The Chrysler Corporation also owns a number of bodies and parts plants, some of which are outside the Detroit area. Its products include several non-automotive lines, most notable of which are marine motors and air-conditioning equipment, but they are of minor importance to the corporation. Unlike General Motors, Chrysler has concentrated most of its activities in metropolitan Detroit. Detroit was the home of the major corporations which were consolidated to form the Chrysler Corporation, and Detroit has remained the dominant center for its operations.

Location Factors.—In review, it is apparent that Detroit became the center of the automobile industry largely through the pioneering effort of Henry Ford, whose famous Model T led the industry for two decades and finally sold more than 25 million units. Ford started his manufacturing career in Detroit and has remained a leading automobile maker to this day. Among the competitors, consolidation first appeared under the name of General Motors which now owns plants in Detroit, but has its major operations in outlying cities. The Chrysler Corporation was formed as a consolidation of firms whose main plants were in Detroit. In a rough way we may say that Detroit's supremacy in automobiles is traced first to Ford, second to Chrysler, third to General Motors, and fourth to the hundreds of independent parts and accessories plants which operate there. Outside Detroit, in the remainder of the automobile district as well as in other sections, the leading concern is General Motors with parts and accessories plants and other allied interests scattered over the entire northeastern United States. The location of these diverse segments of the automobile industry can be understood only in the light of its history and economic position. The industry has grown rapidly and there has never been an extended period of competition severe enough to prompt the conclusion that the matter of scientific plant location was ever a paramount consideration. We conclude, with the man on the street, that there are no good reasons why the industry should be concentrated in this section, but on the other hand there are no good reasons why it should not be.

REFERENCES

An excellent series on the General Motors Corporation appeared in *Fortune* during 1938-39. See also Zimmermann, *World Resources and Industries*. Consult Introduction for references regarding pricing under conditions of monopolistic competition.

Questions and Problems

1. What factors must be considered in accounting for the concentration of the automobile industry in the Detroit area?

2. Explain how differing philosophies of industrial organization have affected the location of the automobile industry.

3. How did the automobile industries happen to become important in outlying locations such as Toledo, South Bend, Flint, and the Indianapolis area? Do these developments represent either migration or decentralization from the Detroit center? How did the typical automobile-parts plant outside Detroit get its start?

4. What commercial and industrial advantages exist at the site of the city of Toledo?

5. What are the principal economic interests of Saginaw and Bay City? What industries first brought these cities to prominence?

6. Like certain other sections, southern Michigan has witnessed marked changes in economic development in recent decades. This statement applies to Detroit and to many smaller centers such as Muskegon, Grand Rapids, and South Bend. What are the "older" and "newer" industries of these cities?

7. What manufacturing industries other than those concerned with automobiles are important in the Automobile Belt? Where are these industries most important?

8. The history of the automotive industries is marked by periods of centralization and other periods of decentralization. What forces activated these trends? To what extent have they influenced the present location of the industries?

9. What types of agricultural development are found in southern Michigan? What minerals are important? What effect have these economic activities had upon the economic functions of cities in the area?

10. What sections other than southern Michigan must be given consideration in any analysis of the automotive industries? What types of products do they turn out?

CHAPTER XXIX

THE CHICAGO-MILWAUKEE-NORTHWEST INDIANA SECTION

Location.—Few locations in the world are better suited to the development of great commercial and industrial cities than the southwest shores of Lake Michigan. Here the Great Lakes system, the world's greatest inland waterway, penetrates farthest into the rich mid-western prairies and provides an excellent low-cost highway for sending out farm produce and bringing in the heavy materials of industry. And here also have arisen good facilities for land transportation, for Lake Michigan is not only an excellent highway for water transportation; it is likewise a potent barrier for transportation by land. In reaching the western farm belts, railroads were compelled to run their lines around the south end of the lake. Their principal converging point became the city of Chicago.

Transportation.—When railroads first penetrated the vast Mississippi Basin, Chicago was their most logical goal; and when the trans-Mississippi country was opened up, Chicago was the favored eastern starting point for the western railroads. Small wonder that Chicago soon became the railroad center of the country: a western terminus for the eastern trunk lines, and an eastern terminus for the so-called "transcontinental" roads which stretch westward to the Pacific coast. Chicago today has more railroads than any other city, but not a single railroad goes through it—all of them terminate there. Freight cars and Pullmans are switched from one road to another to continue their journey; day-coach passengers must change trains. In the transportation field, Chicago is truly the city "where the West begins."

Commerce.—It has long been observed that where transportation lines converge and transfers are made, cities develop. With half a continent, including the world's greatest commercial farming regions, served by its railroads, Chicago has become the leading market for farm produce in the entire nation. As the nation's market place for livestock, wheat, and other grains, Chicago inevitably developed extensive financial interests. It stands today

Fig. 92. The Chicago-Milwaukee-Northwest Indiana Section. Chicago and Milwaukee were founded opposite shallow harbors for small lake boats. Both cities grew large with the coming of railroads and the opening of the West. Chicago proved an attractive location for the iron and steel industry, whose greatest present-day activity is in the south part of the city and across the state line in northwestern Indiana. Milwaukee became a national center for the manufacture of heavy machinery. The intervening cities of Racine and Kenosha became noted for automobiles, while, to the interior, important steel-products industries grew up along the "Outer Belt" and at Rockford, Beloit, and Janesville.

as the dominant mid-western center for banking and wholesaling. Inevitably also it serves this same vast area as a center for recreation and culture. Chicago mail-order stores, calling themselves the nation's foremost merchandisers, handle 70 per cent of the nation's mail-order business. Chicago markets set the prices of hogs, cattle, wheat, butter, and other farm products from which the people of the great interior farm belts derive their living. Like New York, Chicago belongs to no single region, but to a major segment of the entire United States.

Chicago thus took its place as economic nerve center for the great mid-continent agricultural areas. First as a transfer center, then as a transaction center, it has come to assume a position second only to New York in the fields of business and finance. The Federal Reserve Bank of the Seventh District, with headquarters in Chicago, is second largest in the system. Chicago stock and bond markets are exceeded in importance only by those of New York. In many lines, of course, Chicago is first. As a wheat and livestock market and in many other types of business allied with farming, Chicago leads the nation.

It was inevitable that such an agglomeration of commercial interests should have brought the establishment of manufacturing plants. Meat animals must be butchered and their products made ready for shipment. Farm markets must be supplied with vast quantities of items which are best manufactured in the farm areas. The mere presence of three million persons in this metropolitan area would have given rise to thousands of factories built to supply local needs for manufactured products.

Iron and Steel.—But Chicago has not been forced to rely upon these local and regional types of industry for its development as a manufacturing center. Today the Chicago area is second only to the Pittsburgh-Cleveland district as a center for the iron and steel industry. Iron and steel, basic materials of the heavy industries group, are advantageously manufactured near the market because of the great cost of shipping the finished products. But there must also be available cheap iron ore, coking coal, and limestone. Denied the attractiveness of local deposits of ore and fuel, the steel industry will locate near the market only if cheap transportation is available for these items. In the Chicago area this transportation advantage is provided by the Great Lakes. With the Lake Superior mines at one end of the system and the Appalachian coal fields near the other, the Great Lakes offer unsurpassed facilities for cheap assembly of the major materials of the steel industry. Anywhere along these shores, coking coal and ore can be combined with near-by limestone, blast furnaces charged, and rolling mills operated with a minimum of transportation cost. Thus, so far as the assembly of materials is concerned, one lake shore site is about as good as another. The deciding point, therefore, is nearness to the market.

The steel industry, however, is not subject to marked decentralization. Greatest economies are obtained from very large plants. For maximum efficiency, blast furnaces must be so large that not more than a few hundred are needed to supply the whole country. In 1935, a total of 258 were operated in the United States, of which fewer than one hundred were in blast at any one time. The steel mill itself is likewise best operated in very large units. In addition, certain definite economies result from having a compact plant. These take the form of saving the "heat" in pig iron by passing it directly to the steel converter in a molten state; of utilizing the "producer gas" from blast furnaces as fuel in steel furnaces, and of similar savings in manufacturing costs. In the present state of our technology, it is not likely that the country will ever have a large number of steel centers. Despite the desirability of locating near markets, cost of shipment definitely ties the industry to sites having cheap transportation of raw materials; and the necessity for large plants keeps the number of actual plant locations down to a minimum.

"Big Steel" Builds Gary.—In 1906, the southern tip of Lake Michigan seemed to officials of the United States Steel Corporation a good place to erect a new steel plant to serve the expanding markets of the Middle West. The big corporation was then in control of the major steel plants of the country, but most of its capacity was in the Pittsburgh area. Western markets were growing rapidly and "Big Steel" foresaw profit in serving them from a plant on the western Great Lakes. Here in the sandy dune country of the northwest corner of Indiana they laid out the town of Gary and built what was then the largest steel mill in the world. The Steel Corporation was not the first to erect blast furnaces in the Chicago area, nor has it been the last. Its coming did serve, however, to place this section in line to become the second-ranking steel area of the country. In recent years, the

Chicago-Milwaukee-Northwest Indiana area has produced annually from one-fifth to one-fourth of the nation's iron and steel. In 1937, about two-thirds of the output came from northwest Indiana and the remainder largely from the Chicago area. In Indiana, the great center is Gary. Chicago mills are situated at the south edge of the city. Wisconsin has one or two mills, but their production is much smaller.

The major mid-western steel center is thus definitely located at the south end of Lake Michigan. Steel's kingdom runs from Gary westward across the Illinois boundary and includes the Calumet district of south Chicago. Lake steamers tie up at lake-shore docks or penetrate short lake-water canals to unload their ore and coal beside the giant blast furnaces. From the blast furnaces, near-by steel mills receive the still-hot pig iron and refine it into steel. Not far away, the rolling mills receive the steel, and roll and reroll it into a thousand varieties of the heavier steel products: structural steel, railroad rails, thin sheets for automobile bodies, and thinner sheets for tin cans. Here coal is made into coke and the liberated gas used to fire steel-mill furnaces. Near by also is a cement mill which converts blast-furnace slag into a salable product. But here, essentially, are the heaviest of the heavy industries: the blast furnaces, converters, and rolling mills which turn out the largest and heaviest of the long list of products made from iron and steel.

Heavy Industry.—Machinery, we have noted, is apt to be manufactured near the steel center; and this statement holds in the Chicago area. Chicago is the national center for the manufacture of railroad equipment, telephone supplies and many other types of electrical equipment, as well as of numerous other kinds of machinery more or less dependent upon iron and steel. Most of these metal-products plants are located north and west of the steel center. Many of the largest are at the western edge of the city. Machinery also is the leading factory output in Joliet, Aurora, and Elgin, the chief cities of the "outer belt." Excavating machinery, agricultural implements, and garden tools are prominent in these outer reaches of the Chicago area. Milwaukee is also an important center for the same types of products.

The automobile industry, long the leading user of steel, has made of this area a production center second only to the Detroit district. More than 10 per cent of the nation's motor vehicle production originates in the Chicago area, but this production comes largely from the Wisconsin and Indiana districts. Most important is the cluster of auto factories which one finds in Milwaukee, Racine, and Kenosha. Here are the several plants of Nash Motors, and here are a number of well-known parts factories including the famous A. O. Smith plant, the first completely automatic automobile frame factory. In this plant all lifting, moving, and conveying is done by machinery, the only labor used being technical and non-manual. Approximately 5 per cent of the nation's automobiles, including bodies and parts, are manufactured in the Wisconsin portion of this area. Most of the parts come from Milwaukee, the finished cars from Racine and Kenosha as well as Milwaukee.

Farther west, the cities of Janesville and Beloit in Wisconsin turn out farm machinery, boilers, wire, and numerous other metal products. Rockford, Illinois, located in the same vicinity, produces machine tools, hardware, and farm equipment. An old-time furniture industry, long important in these three cities, has spawned many younger lines of activity, such as electric refrigerators and hardware.

Like the remainder of the western Manufacturing Belt, the Chicago area is dominantly a land of steel and its products. The pattern, too, is much the same as in the more easterly sections. Its center—its basis and fountainhead—is the great primary steel center at the south end of Lake Michigan. Machinery and other steel-using plants fan out from this center in all directions but chiefly toward the west and northwest, for in these directions lie the markets for the products. In general, the type of product varies noticeably with the distance from the center : heavy and relatively simple products such as steel rails and girders are manufactured near by, while the lighter and more complicated articles are manufactured in the more distant plants. The Chicago area thus stands as the western outpost of the great steel-using industries which are so fundamentally a characteristic of our industrial age. Primarily these western plants serve the mid-western market for machinery and steel products of all kinds. Their list of products is not so long nor is the quantity so great as in the Pittsburgh-Cleveland area, and the industries are neither so old nor so well established as in the Cincinnati-Dayton district. Production has expanded greatly in the past quarter-century, however, and the Chicago-Milwaukee-Northwest Indiana territory is well established as the second-ranking steel and machinery center of the nation.

Processing Industries.—There are, of course, many manufacturing industries not dependent upon steel or any of its products. Many of them are older than steel and most of them are closely related to the natural resources of the Middle West. Chicago, for example, is the leading meat-packer and producer of corn starch. The Milwaukee district tans much leather and produces much cheese. It should be noted that the non-steel group of industries is dependent here as elsewhere primarily upon the products of the farm and forest—corn, meat animals, dairying, wood for paper and furniture, and (historically) bark for tanning. Both Chicago and Milwaukee owe much of their industrial importance to their great west-stretching hinterlands, where productive dairy, wheat, and livestock farms not only produce industrial raw materials, but also give rise to rich local markets.

Local Industries.—Then, of course, there are the ubiquitous local industries, necessarily large in an area of more than five million people. Chicago and Milwaukee are so well served by railroads and highways that the local industries supply areas larger than might be anticipated. It is interesting to note that with a half-dozen exceptions there is hardly an important city in Indiana, Illinois, or Wisconsin within seventy-five miles of the shores of Lake Michigan. The country is so level and transportation facilities are so accessible that no better than average locations exist. Chicago and Milwaukee bakers and publishers and all the other local-type manufacturers actually monopolize exceptionally broad belts of rather densely populated rural territory.[1]

---

[1] The necessity for brevity dictates the omission of a long list of less important industries, many of which have national prominence: (1) The Hammond-Whiting territory refines much gasoline from mid-continent crude. This development goes back to the day when Indiana was a leading oil-producing state. Oilmen say mid-western gasoline prices are still based on the price in Whiting, plus the freight to individual cities—a basing-point price similar to "Pittsburgh-plus" in the older days of steel. (2) Chicago is an important clothing center, a pioneer producer of factory-made men's clothing. The principal firm is Hart, Schaffner and Marx. (3) Like other great cities, Chicago makes much furniture, and outranks all other American cities except New York in this product. It must be remembered, however, that the furniture industry is highly decentralized. (4) At one time and another, Chicago has been a leader in the hectic business of radio manufacture. (5) Chicago is a national center for the manufacture of musical instruments. Elkhart, Indiana, is the nation's band-instrument center. (6) South Bend is the home of the Singer Sewing Machine. (7) Elgin is nationally famous for its watches and is an important butter market. The reader may extend this list by referring to any standard trade survey.

Commerce v. Industry.—Chicago, indeed, is essentially a commercial city, just as is the city of New York. It is true that Chicago is the second-ranking industrial center, just as New York is first. But the economic importance of Chicago is above all centered on State Street and La Salle Street, in the Board of Trade, the "Loop" hotels, the railroad stations, and other temples of trade and finance rather than in the furnaces of south-shore steel mills or the conveyor-belts of great meat-packing houses. Statistics substantiate this conclusion: in 1929, Cook County (Chicago) had 6.4 per cent of the nation's manufacturing, but accounted for 8.5 per cent of its wholesale trade. Its population was 5.7 per cent of the urban population of the United States.

Chicago's dominant economic interests are concentrated in the "Loop," a five-by-seven-block area containing less than one-quarter square mile which was circumscribed decades ago when the elevated railroad first constructed a loop around which to run its trains in order to get them turned around and headed back toward their respective termini in the residential districts. Within the Loop or adjacent to it on Michigan Avenue are the shops, hotels, and theaters with which Chicago serves and entertains its midwestern visitors; here is the Grain Exchange, largest in the nation; a stock market and financial district (on La Salle Street) second only to New York's own Wall Street. Consider also the nature of the city's most famous large buildings, all adjacent to the Loop: the Opera Building, Tribune Tower, the Daily News, the Merchandise Mart, the Furniture Mart—all symbolic of the city's dominant interests. Factories and mills and works are of commanding importance; but Chicago remains a commercial city, economic capital and nerve center of a vast, productive agricultural empire in the middle of the North American continent.

Land Use.—Metropolitan Chicago offers interesting opportunities for the study of urban development on a site substantially free from geographic barriers. Lake Michigan, to be sure, constitutes an undeniable barrier on the east, but in other directions the land is substantially flat and there are no watercourses or other natural features capable of impeding urban development or focusing it into restricted channels. The original village grew up on the shore of the lake around a frontier fort located at the mouth of the shallow Chicago River. The river itself offered no inducements to navigation and was narrow enough to be easily bridged.

From its original site, Chicago had an opportunity to expand north, west, and south, almost without limit.

Actually, the main directions of growth have been north and south. Geographers generally attribute Chicago's elongated slope to the influence of railroad transportation, coupled, to some extent, with the tempering effect of the lake on summer temperatures. From the very early days, Chicago's central business district has been in the Loop, located just south of the mouth of the Chicago River. Preferred residential areas have been along the north shore, north of the Loop and within a mile of the lake. Such locations are occasionally bathed by cooling breezes off the lake during the hot mid-continental summer. Industries generally chose sites south of the Loop. There the transportation facilities are better because the main lines of railroads from the east and south skirt the south shore of the lake and come into downtown Chicago almost side by side. In addition, south-shore areas originally had numerous lakes and swamps and were not considered desirable for residential use. These two migrations carried the Chicago metropolitan area north along the lake to Evanston and beyond, and southward past South Chicago, Hammond, and Whiting to Gary. Modern rapid transit carries south-shore commuters to the Loop with trains that occasionally follow mile-a-minute schedules. Transportation facilities are also excellent from the north shore, many of whose trains follow main-line routes leading to Milwaukee.

Expansion to the westward has been much slower and less pronounced. The western suburbs of Chicago are composed of a group of industrial and residential cities, all of which are nearer the Loop than either South Chicago or Evanston. Lack of expansion to the west is related to the lack of strategic locations. Railroads leaving Chicago for the west originally struck out across the flat prairies, each in its own direction, no two following the same course. It was many years before Chicago capital provided a rim for all of these spokes by building a half-circle belt-line railroad around the city from Winnetka on the north to Gary on the south. This belt line lies about thirty miles from the Loop. Several cities have arisen at its junctions with the major western railroads. In the Chicago area, railroad junctions became strategic locations.

The Two Chicagos.—Present-day Chicago shows the effect of these evolutionary processes. If you were to draw a line west from the Loop, you would cut the city into nearly equal portions. On the north side you would have mainly residential areas, inhabited largely by local service groups and white-collar workers from the Loop. There are a few light industries, but the land-use pattern is definitely residential. This is the commercial Chicago, business center of the Middle West.

Industrial Chicago extends southward from your east-west line. Here in the western suburbs are large electrical plants and the makers of many types of light machinery. The southern section contains the stockyards, national center for the meat-packing industry, and many scattered industrial plants. Farther south, the industrial horizon becomes smokier and the industries are heavier, culminating in the steel mills and petroleum refineries of the southeast portion of the metropolitan district. There are thousands of blocks of residential areas, occupied mainly by workers in the near-by industrial plants. This is the industrial Chicago of the Manufacturing Belt, an area of very different function and appearance from the Chicago which lies north of the Loop.

Milwaukee.—The city of Milwaukee, noted among business men for its aggressiveness in business, has in a sense duplicated the economic development of Chicago. Its commercial growth, however, has not been so marked. With 1 per cent of the nation's urban population in 1929, Milwaukee had 1.4 per cent of the manufacturing and eight-tenths of one per cent of the wholesale trade. It must be classified as an industrial city. Its wholesale and financial spheres of influence should not, however, be overlooked. Milwaukee wholesalers serve most of the state of Wisconsin. The rich lake counties to the north patronize Milwaukee almost exclusively, and its wholesalers also reach into the upper peninsula of Michigan. Milwaukee will be remembered primarily, however, for diversified industry, ranging from automobiles and farm machinery through leather and beer to shoes and silk hose. This city, in fact, is a national center for all of these types of factory products.

Unlike Chicago, Milwaukee grew up as two separate municipalities on opposite banks of a shallow river. These were united long ago but the old north-south division still applies to much of Milwaukee's economic development. Here, as in Chicago, the major industrial districts have grown up south of the business center, extending southward with few interruptions to include the lake

STEEL MILLS, GARY, INDIANA. (*Courtesy American Airlines.*)

DOWNTOWN DETROIT AND THE DETROIT RIVER. (*Courtesy American Airlines.*)

cities of Racine and Kenosha. Milwaukee's western suburbs are also important industrially. Automobiles, bodies and parts, farm and other machinery are manufactured in these areas. Residential districts occupy most of the northern portions of the city.

Summary.—The Chicago-Milwaukee-Northwest Indiana industrial district can best be remembered in terms of transportation, steel, and trade. With one-tenth of the nation's factory output it is an important sector in the industrial life of the nation—an important section of the American Manufacturing Belt. But alongside the factory worker are the clerk and office worker who maintain in this section a great mid-continental business and financial center. Fundamental to this concentration of industry and trade is a single geographic factor—Lake Michigan. Without this member of the Great Lakes, on a vast plain without barriers to transportation, there would have been no concentration of railroads, probably no great commercial center. Without the lake there would be no cheap iron and coal, no national center for steel and machinery. Lake Michigan takes its place along with our mountain systems as one of the dominant geographic features influencing American economic development.

The Industrial Frontier.—Our consideration of the American Manufacturing Belt ends with the Chicago-Milwaukee-Northwest Indiana section. It ends with what many people consider the industrial frontier of the nation, the present westward limit of an area of industrialization that has spread westward since the nation was founded. Yet we know that many fallacies are involved in such a statement. The Chicago section does represent an industrial frontier, and it has nearly all the characteristics we would expect to find in a frontier zone. But it would be inaccurate to say that it is *the* frontier, because the industrial region has extended southward as well as westward, and in recent years industrialization has proceeded more rapidly in the South than in the Middle West. Furthermore, certain inaccuracies are implied in speaking of the areal expansion of American manufacturing as a "movement" or in referring to the outer limits of the manufacturing region as a "frontier." The geographic expansion of American manufacturing has been marked not so much by continuous extension of the outer margins of a region as by a series of "jumps" from one area to another and the later industrialization of intervening areas.

History, Technology, and the Natural Environment.—We have found that the location of relatively few manufacturing industries is to be explained solely in terms of the natural environment. Much depends upon man's ability to use the forces and stores of nature. Human productive capacity varies from one decade to another with changes in technology. The demand for various types of goods and services varies with social change.

In early American history the most significant industrial enterprises were concerned with processing the products of the land for home use or shipment to Europe. Industrial processes were simple, plants were small, and there were few "factories" in the modern sense of the term. The railroad came and during the middle decades of the nineteenth century the geographic scope of exchange was increased enormously. Trade with Europe grew and the cities of the Atlantic seaboard became rich from handling it. Processing plants were set up at tidewater to make the goods ready for shipment. Still there was little modern "manufacturing." At the beginning of the Civil War the vast majority of industrial establishments were of the processing types. They added little to the value of the materials they consumed. The more highly fabricated articles were imported from Europe, and the consumption of such articles was very small. In pre-Civil War days the average American consumed relatively few factory-made products, and these were largely imported from Europe. Seaboard merchants grew wealthy handling this exchange of outgoing raw materials and semi-manufactures for incoming manufactured goods.

The Civil War brought a mighty stimulus to American industrial development which is attributed variously to the rapid growth of the country, increased war demands, and the enactment of high protective tariffs against imported manufactured goods. Many new factories were built. After the war the national population continued to expand and the protective tariffs were continued.

It was logical to set up most of these new factories in the North Atlantic cities. Seaboard cities were already established as sources of manufactured goods from abroad. They had the largest supplies of labor (from immigration) and the largest bank accounts and credit ratings. When eastern importers turned manufacturers they built their factories near by. New England became a center for textiles and shoes, New York for clothing, and southeastern Pennsylvania for iron and steel. These same tidewater fortunes went into the railroads and until the end of the nineteenth century effectively controlled freight rates to the advantage of seaboard manufacturing and real-estate interests.

In the meantime, the processing industries followed the westward march of basic production. Cincinnati and Chicago became meat-packing centers, and Minneapolis a flour-milling center. But the more complicated manufacturing processes were conducted very largely in seaboard factories.

The first important movement of industry from the Atlantic slope came with the introduction of Lake Superior iron ore in the years following the Civil War. This ore could be delivered so much more cheaply on the western edge of the Appalachian coal fields than ore could be mined in eastern Pennsylvania that the steel industry hurdled the Appalachian Highland and made Pittsburgh the national steel center. Later the industry found profit in locations between Pittsburgh and Lake Erie, and the Pittsburgh-Cleveland steel district came into existence. The steel industry again hurdled a broad area when it jumped across a large slice of farming country to set up a new center in the Chicago area. It performed similarly in opening up new plants at Birmingham and Baltimore.

We recall that these shifts in the location of the steel industry generally have represented industrial growth and not true migration. Nearly all the older areas have continued to produce steel. The newer locations represent increases in industrial capacity reflecting the increased national demand for steel and its products. But many of the older steel areas are now dominated by other types of manufacturing.

While the seaboard cities were losing ascendency in steel and machinery, they were gaining very rapidly in the manufacture of textiles and clothing. New England had become specialized in the manufacture of these types of consumer goods even before the Civil War, but later decades brought the almost complete industrialization of the area along these lines. New York saw the clothing industries rise to first position and the same lines of manufacturing rose to first importance in Philadelphia, Baltimore, and southeastern Pennsylvania. By the time of the World War, textiles and clothing well-nigh dominated the industrial development of the Atlantic seaboard from southern Maine to Chesapeake Bay. Steel-products industries had followed the blast furnaces west of the Appalachians—to the Pittsburgh-Cleveland area, the Chicago-Milwaukee area, and the Cincinnati-Dayton area. The processing industries had moved into the farming, mining, and forest regions. But the North Atlantic coastal strip remained the home of most other types of manufacturing.

Since the World War, three significant industrial changes have altered the character of the Manufacturing Belt. All of them began in earlier years, but their most pronounced effects have been experienced since 1920.

The most significant industrial change of the twentieth century has been the rise of the automobile industry. Growth of the automobile industry has brought about the rapid industrialization of Detroit and southern Michigan and the addition of that section to the Manufacturing Belt. A second change of major importance lies in the migration of the cotton-textiles industry from New England to the southern piedmont. This migration has caused a drastic realignment of the New England industrial structure. In accomplishing the shift, the industry hurdled the Middle Atlantic states and established a new center hundreds of miles from the old one. There is reason to believe that textile-using industries may follow the spinners and looms in sufficient numbers to cause the eventual addition of the entire piedmont area to the American Manufacturing Belt. A third type of change has occurred with the increasing interests of certain types of industries in water-borne commerce. Accessibility to sea-borne raw materials was largely responsible for the blossoming of Baltimore as a heavy-industries center and for the location of factories for soap, paint, linoleum, and numerous other products in the New York and Philadelphia areas. Other plants manufacturing bulky products (such as farm machinery) for foreign trade have also sought tidewater locations. All the important Central Atlantic ports from New York to Baltimore have seen the rise of these types of industries in recent years.

Thus the boundaries of the American Manufacturing Belt have been achieved. It is a history of industrial growth and relocation, but it cannot be interpreted as a continuous outward movement from an original center. The movement is better described as a series of "jumps" by basic manufacturing industries from one area to another. In any one period, the map of industrialized areas has appeared as one major area with a number of outlying industrial "islands" beyond its borders. Those industrial islands appear on the map today—in the southern piedmont, the Cincinnati-Dayton area, the Indianapolis-Fort Wayne area, and in eastern Wisconsin and northeastern Illinois. Some students believe that these areas will continue to grow industrially and that the gaps which separate them from the Manufacturing Belt will soon be occupied by additional industries and a city-supply type of agriculture. Such an evolution would extend the boundaries of the region to include the outlying areas. At the same time there is evidence of the evolution of another industrial area which promises to remain permanently disconnected from the Manufacturing Belt. This is the Los Angeles district of southern California. The extent to which these changes will occur depends upon a multitude of factors, not the least of which are changes in demand and technological development. The boundaries of the American Manufacturing Belt are not permanent. Like every other economic region, the area dominated by manufacturing will change with future changes in the culture of the American people.

<h3>REFERENCES</h3>

The University of Chicago has issued a number of excellent studies giving results of ecological investigations in the city of Chicago. The meat-packing industry is described in R. A. Clemen, *The American Livestock and Meat Industry* (Ronald, 1923). Many brochures have been issued. Among the best is *Chicago* (American Publishers Corporation, 1929).

<h3>QUESTIONS AND PROBLEMS</h3>

1. Why has Lake Michigan been an important factor in the economic geography of the United States?
2. What is meant by the statement that Chicago has a "dual personality"? How is this dual role reflected in the areal distribution of economic life in the Chicago metropolitan district?
3. How do you account for the elongated shape of the city of Chicago? Is this elongation an advantage or a disadvantage?
4. In what ways does the economic development of Milwaukee resemble that of Chicago? What are the major differences? Can you give reasons for them?
5. What is the Chicago "Loop"? Why did it become the center of Chicago business life?
6. Describe the urban transportation system of the city of Chicago.
7. In what ways does the industrial structure of the cities of the

Chicago-Milwaukee area show the effect of nearness to the great farm regions of the central United States?

8. Why is the Chicago-Gary area a good place to manufacture steel? Why is it not more important?

9. What two types of economic development are most important in the cities of the "Outer Belt"?

10. What reasons can you give for the development of the automotive industries in the Milwaukee-Racine-Kenosha area?

11. Obtain a copy of a railway guide and map the area reached by overnight passenger and mail service from the city of Chicago. Include all trains leaving Chicago after 11 P.M. and all cities reached by 7 A.M. How does this area compare with the area served by a metropolitan newspaper such as the *Chicago Tribune?* Is it larger or smaller than the Chicago wholesale grocery territory? Why?

12. Have the railroads of the Chicago and Milwaukee areas been a centralizing or decentralizing influence? Why? Give examples. Has Lake Michigan had a similar influence? Why?

13. What is the principal economic function of the city of Whiting? Why did this development occur?

14. Little attention is given in the text to lake traffic passing through the ports of the Chicago-Milwaukee-Northwest Indiana district. Which would you expect to be greater, receipts or shipments? Why? What commodities would likely be most important? Where would they originate? What would be their destinations?

15. What types of economic activity occupy the cities of the extreme western portion of the Manufacturing Belt? How do you account for these developments?

CHAPTER XXX

GEOGRAPHY AND ECONOMIC CHANGE

Characteristics of Economic Regions.—Previous chapters have considered the geographic basis of economic life in the United States. For purposes of analysis the nation was divided into ten regions distinguished by different types of economic development. Economic life in nine of these regions is characterized by the production of foods, industrial raw materials, and semi-manufactures for national markets. The tenth region is devoted essentially to manufacturing and likewise has the entire nation for its market. In the manufacturing region, agriculture and other types of economic development are generally subsidiary to industrial development and are essentially local in character. In the other regions the reverse relationship is noted. Manufacturing is generally subsidiary to the more basic types of economic activity and is generally local in scope. There is marked interdependence among the various regions and a relatively high degree of specialization in specific types of economic activity in each of them.

The American economic system is an extremely complicated mechanism, nearly impossible of human comprehension in its detailed aspects. In order to simplify the analysis a functional approach has been used throughout the preceding chapters. In every section of the United States an attempt was made to discover the basic economic interests, the types of production which provide the foundation for local economic life. Some basic forms were found in agriculture, others in mining, lumbering, fishing, and national types of manufacturing. In every case those enterprises were selected which provide the best clue to the complete economic development of individual communities. Of necessity, these key activities were stressed throughout the discussion. Subsidiary activities, which form a fairly uniform pattern wherever the basic enterprises exist, were largely thrust into the background. It is hoped that the reader will not permit this emphasis upon key enterprises to obscure the fact that in most communities they do not produce even a majority of the income. Our emphasis upon the farmer who grows the wheat, the miner who mines the coal, and the machinist who runs a lathe should not obliterate the railroader who hauls the products, or the merchants, bankers, lawyers, physicians, bootblacks, teachers, and other workers who provide only services and not goods. We should remember, however, that the location of farming, mining, and other types of basic production is of prime importance in determining the location of the remaining types of economic activity.

A similar warning should be repeated against underestimating the importance of intra-regional trade. Throughout the discussion, major emphasis has been placed upon regional specialization and the exchange of commodities among the various regions. As a distinguishing feature of the national economy, inter-regional trade is extremely significant. Yet we know from our daily lives that exchange among local producers for local consumption frequently employs more persons and has greater economic significance than trade with other regions. Because it follows a fairly uniform pattern from one community to another, the existence and importance of intra-regional trade have not been reiterated in the discussion of each area. The reader should not permit this lack of repetition to obscure the fact that large volumes of trade are carried on entirely within the boundaries of each region.

Business Activity.—If you were to ask a farmer in western Montana about local business conditions, he would likely begin talking about the price of copper. A railroad man in Kansas answers the same question in terms of the wheat crop. A restaurant proprietor in Tulsa is worried about the price of oil. A filling-station attendant in Paterson tells you that business is dull because women are wearing less silk this summer, and a hotel proprietor in Hibbing fears that the automobile strike will close the iron mines earlier than usual because of reduced demands for steel. "How's business?" is a favorite question in every section of the United States, but it is very likely to be answered in terms of the key activities of the community rather than of the immediate affairs of the solicited individual. Every community is likely to have an economic main spring which, although small in itself, largely governs the pace of local economic activity. To understand the economic life of an area we must first know the nature of its key enterprises.

A similar problem in applied economic geography also arises in connection with variations in national business activity. All of us know that the activity of various lines of business fluctuates constantly. We also know that the intensity of prosperity and depression varies greatly from one type of business to another. Most of us have seen the maps of business conditions, with their areas marked "good," "fair," and "poor," which business magazines publish from time to time. Those maps show the local manifestations of fluctuations in various lines of national business. A drought places a black spot over South Dakota and declining steel outputs make Youngstown a poor place to sell goods. In recent years, the greatest fluctuations in activity have been experienced by those industries which manufacture capital goods. The markets for consumer goods generally have been more stable. Steel and machinery areas have been more subject to economic chills and fever than textiles and clothing areas. In other words, the western portions of the Manufacturing Belt generally have experienced greater fluctuations in business activity than the eastern sections. Farm areas have been affected by changes in general business activity as well as fluctuations in the prices for particular products. Periods of general prosperity or depression are likely to affect all types of business activity and will be felt in all communities, but the more frequent changes in individual lines of business generally affect only restricted areas. The geographic incidence of fluctuations in business activity is of prime importance to the sales managers of national business concerns.

Economic Change.—These relatively short-lived oscillations in business activity are not to be confused with the long-run trends of economic change. Fluctuations in business activity that are felt to be temporary do not ordinarily alter the areal distribution of economic life. Local people feel the restriction of a current recession and impatiently await the return of normal conditions; but so long as they feel that the interruption is only temporary, they do not move to other areas or enter other occupations. In some instances, however, the temporary situation becomes permanent. Months and years go by and the key industry fails to reopen. Gradually the community dwindles or takes on new characteristics. These transformations of an area from one type of economic occupancy to another generally reflect the workings of long-run economic forces.

We have witnessed the operation of economic change in all regions. On the boundary between the Corn and Wheat belts we saw farmers shifting from one grain to another with changes in the prospective profit. We also noted that such changes have become more difficult and costly with the introduction of specialized equipment which can be used for one crop but not the other. On the boundaries of the Dairy Belt we found these shifts occurring still more slowly because of the necessity for large investments in specialized capital necessary for dairy farming. This type of inertia reaches a maximum in the Manufacturing Belt, where million-dollar factories and institutionalized community organizations are extremely expensive to abandon. In the Manufacturing Belt we also observed many attempts to perpetuate industries in established locations by a variety of monopolistic practices. Changes in the economic structure of individual areas occur most rapidly in those sections occupied by highly competitive enterprises whose operations involve small amounts of specialized capital. They occur most slowly in sections whose enterprises require much non-mobile specialized capital and operate under largely monopolistic conditions.

In any event we must not lose sight of the fact that business is run for profit. Once an area has demonstrated its undesirability as a location for a particular type of production, the forces of migration are set in motion. Many steps may be taken to delay the actual exodus. Wages may be cut, taxes lowered, or lower freight rates secured. Much will be done to postpone the day when the loss on plant and equipment must be recognized. But if the ultimate profit appears greater in some other location, we know that sooner or later the step will be taken—and the economic character of the area will be changed, either through abandonment or through the introduction of other types of enterprise.

So long as the economic life of the American people is subject to fundamental change, the boundaries of economic regions will not remain fixed. The years bring changes in the demand for particular commodities and this is reflected in expansion and contraction of the producing areas. New machines and processes upset old cost relationships and make new locations desirable. A government passes new laws or a commission renders new decisions which alter old cost differentials and make new types of economic development appear more profitable than the old ones in certain areas. The entire mechanism of change works within the limits imposed by the natural environment. Alterations in the economic structure can be made only to the extent that natural resources are available. The natural environment sets the stage within whose limits the economic drama must be enacted; but the action of the drama is dictated very largely by the players themselves and the stage properties with which they are equipped.

REFERENCES

The reader should consult recent books on economic history for the concept of change in economic life. The literature is very extensive. Both the National Resources Planning Board and the Works Progress Administration have made good studies of recent technological changes and unemployment.

QUESTIONS AND PROBLEMS

1. The United States has been likened to an empire with a small, densely populated "center" devoted to business, finance, and manufacturing, and large outlying areas devoted to the production of raw materials and serving as markets for manufactured goods. Elaborate this scheme by indicating which areas are devoted to the production of foods and industrial raw materials. Indicate the types of manufacturing and commercial institutions found in those regions. Which regions are most highly specialized and which ones are most nearly self-sufficing? What is the role of the American Manufacturing Belt? Present any available evidence which might indicate that centralization and regional specialization along these lines are breaking down.

2. Construct an outline for an economic analysis of productive activity in some neighborhood with which you are familiar. Show the basis of income-producing activity within the area. Indicate whether various types of production are for local, regional, or national markets. In what ways may the development of this local economic structure be related to natural resources? to historical evolution? What part does the area play in the regional and national economy? What types of capital and consumers' goods are used in the area? What are the sources of these goods?

3. A friend wishes to make a two-thousand-mile automobile trip and asks you to plan a route that would enable him to see as many types of productive activity as possible. Lay out the route and indicate approximately what he should expect to see on such a trip.

4. Procure a copy of the latest decennial census of the United States. Turn to the tables showing usual occupations for the nation, the state, and the county or city in which you live. Write a brief statement of the differences in occupational distribution in these three areas, explaining the reasons for these differences and their significance in accounting for the local economic structure.

GLOSSARY

Agricultural specialties—farm products other than staples. The term implies that the product either is not standardized or is not widely produced.

Alluvial—earth material washed from one place and deposited in another by moving water.

Area—a plane surface having bounds.

Areal—pertaining to area.

Commercial agriculture—agriculture in which the products are grown for sale rather than for family use; *opposed* to self-sufficing agriculture.

Consumers' goods—articles in a finished state which are used to satisfy human wants directly.

Culture—the aggregate of human experience created by man in the process of living.

Cyclone—a meteorological term describing a large area of low pressure and its associated winds, currents and other meteorological features; not to be confused with the tornado, a small, violent, whirling storm common in the middle United States.

Distribution—disposition of goods from a center, such as a city; in economics, the division of the product among producers, or among the factors of production.

Diversification—variation; applied generally to a situation in which income is derived from several sources.

Division of labor—the separation of a productive process into phases or tasks, each of which supplements the others, and none of which is complete in itself. The division of labor contemplates specialization by tasks or areas.

Economic institutions—any sort of organized arrangement under which groups of people conduct the economic process.

Economic process—the operation involving any portion of a system of production, exchange, distribution or consumption; more commonly, the operation of a system of production and exchange. The work performed by the sum total of economic institutions.

Economic specialization—a consequence of the division of labor. Individual producers devote their labors to repetitive performance of the same tasks. Individuals or areas engage in single types of production, and exchange their surpluses for the other goods and services needed by them.

Economic system—the collection of rules, principles and institutions

683

by means of which a people carries on production, exchange, distribution and consumption; the *rules of the game* in economics. The American economic system has been characterized by private property, individual initiative, free competition and private profit. Other systems may utilize different principles.

Entrepreneur—one who undertakes the organization, management and risk-bearing of a business enterprise. One who coordinates the use of land, labor and capital.

Erosion—the wearing down of earth features by wind, water or ice.

Escarpment—steep slope at the edge of a high area.

Exchange economy—an economic system characterized by production for sale (or barter) in the market rather than for use by the producer.

Farm organization—the methods and techniques used in operating and managing a farm.

Glaciation—erosion or deposition by moving ice.

Integration—the organization of a productive process in such a manner that the various stages or phases are under the control and management of a single economic enterprise; in manufacturing, the unification under a single management of the various stages of production, as from raw material to finished product.

Intensive farming—the intensiveness of farming varies directly with the amount of energy applied to each acre. The term intensive farming implies liberal applications of labor and capital in order to attain maximum productivity from each acre of land.

Littoral—strip of land along the seacoast.

Location—position, or site; the process of establishing something on a particular site.

Loess—soil deposited by air currents or wind as wind-blown dust.

Margin—border; edge; areal limit. *See also* marginal producer.

Marginal producer—in economics, the producer whose income and costs are approximately the same; the first to abandon production if prices fall.

Market—a place where buyers and sellers meet, and exchanges take place; the mechanism of exchange; the conditions of supply, demand and price which attend the sale of a commodity or service.

Mineral reserve—minerals known to exist but not yet mined.

Monopoly—control over supply sufficient to affect prices received.

Optimum—most favorable condition or degree.

Ore—metal-bearing rock.

Parasitic industry—a term commonly used to designate an industry which is attracted to heavy-industry centers by the supply of low-priced female (or child) labor.

Physiography—history and description of the present surface of the earth; geomorphology.

Piedmont—foothills; generally formed by the erosion of adjoining mountains.

Plateau—a broad, elevated tract of land which overlooks adjacent areas in at least one place, and has considerable areas at or near its summit level. Plateau surfaces vary from rugged to nearly level.

Primary production—the first stage in a productive process; generally confined to processes involving the use of native materials.

Production—economists recognize two types of production: (1) the creation of utility in wealth, and (2) the performance, by free persons, of services which satisfy human wants directly.

Real wage—worker income expressed in terms of purchasing power; worker income expressed *not* in money terms but in terms of the quantity of goods and services which can be purchased with it.

Resources—those features of the environment which appear useful in the consideration of the present state of our culture.

Supply economy—an economic system characterized by production for use rather than production for the market.

Technology—methods whereby science is applied to the productive process.

Truck farm—a farm devoted to the growing of garden vegetables for market.

Utility—the capacity to satisfy human wants; usefulness; the quality which makes goods or services desirable.

INDEX